Emma Goldman

EMMA GOLDMAN

A DOCUMENTARY HISTORY OF
THE AMERICAN YEARS

Candace Falk, EDITOR

Barry Pateman, ASSOCIATE EDITOR

Jessica M. Moran, ASSISTANT EDITOR

Susan Wengraf, ILLUSTRATIONS EDITOR

Robert Cohen, CONSULTING EDITOR

1. *Made for America, 1890–1901*
2. *Making Speech Free, 1902–1909*

Emma Goldman

A DOCUMENTARY HISTORY OF THE AMERICAN YEARS

VOLUME ONE

Made for America, 1890–1901

CANDACE FALK · EDITOR

BARRY PATEMAN · ASSOCIATE EDITOR

JESSICA M. MORAN · ASSISTANT EDITOR

SUSAN WENGRAF · ILLUSTRATIONS EDITOR

ROBERT COHEN · CONSULTING EDITOR

UNIVERSITY OF CALIFORNIA PRESS

Berkeley   Los Angeles   London

The publisher gratefully acknowledges the generous contribution to this book
provided by the General Endowment of the University of California Press Associates,
and by the National Historical Publications and Records Commission.

FRONTISPIECE

The young Emma Goldman just after her arrival in the United States from Russia
in 1885. Fermin Rocker remembers his father, the eminent German anarchist
activist and historian Rudolf Rocker, commenting wryly that his friend and
comrade Emma Goldman was "made in America." (Emma Goldman Papers)

University of California Press
Berkeley and Los Angeles, California

University of California Press, Ltd.
London, England

© 2003 by The Emma Goldman Papers

Library of Congress Cataloging-in-Publication Data

Emma Goldman : a documentary history of the American years / Candace
Falk, editor ; Barry Pateman, associate editor ; Jessica M. Moran, assistant
editor.
p.   cm.
Includes bibliographical references and index.
ISBN 0-520-08670-8 (v. 1 : alk. paper).
1. Goldman, Emma, 1869–1940.   2. Anarchists—United States—
Biography.   3. Anarchism—United States—History—Sources.
4. Freedom of speech—United States—History—Sources.   I. Title:
Documentary history of the American years.   II. Goldman, Emma,
1869–1940.   III. Falk, Candace, 1947–   IV. Pateman, Barry, 1952–
V. Moran, Jessica M., 1977–
HX843.7.G65   E427   2003
335'.83'092—dc21
[B]   2002028943

Manufactured in the United States of America

10   09   08   07   06   05   04   03
10   9   8   7   6   5   4   3   2   1

The paper used in this publication meets the minimum requirements of
ANSI/NISO Z39.48–1992 (R 1997) (*Permanence of Paper*). ⊗

We dedicate our work to all
who champion liberty and strive for
social and economic justice.

SPONSORS

The Emma Goldman Papers thanks all of our supporters, including these sustaining sponsors for the volumes, for helping to keep history alive through their generous contributions.

National Historical Publications and Records Commission

University of California, Berkeley, Office of the Vice Chancellor for Research

Lois Blum Feinblatt, Irving and Lois Blum Foundation

Cora Weiss, Samuel Rubin Foundation

Judith Taylor, The Murray and Grace Nissman Foundation

Stephen M. Silberstein

National Endowment for the Humanities

Furthermore: A Project of the J. M. Kaplan Fund

the late Art and Libera Bortolotti

Ben and Ida Capes family:
David Capes, Judith Capes,
Bonnie Capes Tabatznik, Susan Chasson,
and Albert Chasson

Mecca Reitman Carpenter

the late Marcus and the late Harryette Cohn

Eric Alan Isaacson and Susan Kay Weaver

Carolyn Patty Blum
Mariam Chamberlain
Patrick Coughlin
Barbara Dobkin, Ma'yan, The Jewish Women's Project
E. L. and Helen Doctorow
Marilyn French
The Funding Exchange
Peter Glassgold and Susan Thibodeau
the late Alice Hamburg (Agape Foundation)
Louis and Sadie Harlan
Nancy Hewitt and Stephen Lawson
Ronald Hill
Ronald Hogeland
Bill Jersey and Shirley Kessler, Catticus Corporation
Deborah Kaufman and Alan Snitow
Hannah Kranzberg
Maya Miller
Joan K. Peters and Peter Passell
Robert Segal and Nancy Bissel Segal
Michelle Shocked and Bart Bull
Judith Smith and family
Shirley Van Bourg

The list of donors to the Emma Goldman Papers Project as well as donations in remembrance of and in honor of others continues with Emma's List, beginning on p. 591.

CONTENTS

THE DOCUMENTS

ILLUSTRATIONS

Lunching in Paris with Emma Goldman, Theodore Dreiser pleaded with her, "You must write the story of your life, E.G.; it is the richest of any woman's of our century." It had not been the first time a friend had suggested that she chronicle her life. With the assistance of her comrades, she heeded the advice, collected the necessary funds, and began to write her remarkable autobiography, *Living My Life*. Goldman wanted very much to share her life, thoughts, and struggles with the people she had sought to influence and change, and she hoped the publisher, Alfred A. Knopf, would charge a minimal sum for the book. "I am anxious to reach the mass of the American reading public," she wrote a friend, "not so much because of the royalties, but because I have always worked for the mass."

Emma Goldman succeeded in a variety of ways in reaching "the mass," both a reading and listening audience. *Living My Life* went through several editions, her life has been portrayed on film and in song as well as on stage, and numerous biographies have been written. None of these, however, is as critical as the publication of the four volumes of selected letters, speeches, government documents, and commentaries from the Emma Goldman Papers Project, making that vast and invaluable resource available to scholars, students, and a reading public throughout the world.

This is a truly remarkable achievement, the culmination of several decades of collaborative work, including an international search for documents, the identification of correspondents, and the preparation of biographical, historical, and bibliographical guides. To appreciate the magnitude of this task is to know that Goldman's papers were as scattered as her scores of correspondents, in private collections and archives here and abroad, even in places like the Department of Justice, whose agents had seized a portion of her papers before ordering her deportation. Only the commitment of many friends and comrades over many decades, and the untiring efforts of librarians, scholars, and archivists, have made these volumes possible.

In closing her autobiography, Emma Goldman reflected over her tumultuous years on this earth: "My life—I had lived in its heights and its depths, in bitter sorrow and ecstatic joy, in black despair and fervent hope. I had drunk the cup to the last drop. I had lived my life. Would I had the gift to paint the life I had lived!" It will now be left to scores of scholars, students, artists, and dramatists to use this extensive collection to enrich their accounts of an extraordinary career. This is more, however, than material for future biographers; it is an indispensable collection for studying the history of American social movements. That is clear from the moment one scans the list of Goldman correspondents and finds the names of some of the leading cultural and political figures of her time, alongside the names of less known but no less important men and women who shared—and did not share—her commitments.

Emma Goldman came out of a unique and expressive subculture that flourished in America in the late nineteenth and early twentieth centuries. The participants included some of the nation's most creative and iconoclastic artists, writers, and intellectuals, most of them libertarians, some of them revolutionaries. What drew them together was their rejection of the inequities of capitalism and the absurdities of bourgeois culture and politics. That led them to embrace such causes as the labor movement, sexual and reproductive freedom, feminism, atheism, anarchism, and socialism. They represented everything that was irreverent and blasphemous in American culture. In their lives and in their work, they dedicated themselves to the vision of a free society of liberated individuals. They were too undisciplined, too free-spirited to adapt to any system or bureaucratic structure that rested on the suppression of free thought, whether in Woodrow Wilson's United States or in Vladimir Lenin's Soviet Russia. "All I want is freedom," Emma Goldman declared, "perfect, unrestricted liberty for myself and others."

The economic depression of the 1890s introduced Americans to scenes that contradicted the dominant success creed—unemployment, poverty, labor violence, urban ghettos, and, in 1894, an army of the unemployed marching on the nation's capital. In that spirit, Emma Goldman engaged herself in these struggles, employing her oratorical powers to stir audiences and awaken them to the perils of capitalism and the violence of poverty. According to newspaper accounts of her address in 1893 to a crowd of unemployed workers in New York City's Union Square, Goldman implored them, "Demonstrate before the palaces of the rich, demand work. If they do not give you work, demand bread. If they deny you both, take bread. It is your sacred right." That statement was Goldman at her oratorical best, and it did not go unnoticed. For her exhortation she was arrested, convicted, and sentenced to a year's imprisonment. It would be only one of many arrests, whether for lecturing on anarchism, circulating birth control information, advocating workers' and women's rights, or opposing war and the military draft.

The life of Emma Goldman is a forcible reminder that the right to free expression in America has always been precarious. Intellectual inquiry and dissent have been perceived—often for good reason—as subversive activities, and they have, in fact, been known to topple institutions and discredit beliefs of long standing. To be identified as public enemies, to be hounded as disturbers of the peace, was the price Goldman and her comrades paid for their intellectual curiosity, expression, and agitation. During her lifetime, Emma Goldman was denounced for godlessness, debauchery, free thinking, subversion, and for exposing people within the sound of her voice to radical and unconventional ideas. Her life provides a unique perspective on the varieties of anarchist and feminist thought, radical and socialist movements in the late nineteenth and early twentieth centuries and the causes championed, the position of women in American society (and within radical organizations), and the political repression that followed the outbreak of World War I and the imprisonment and political exile of dissenters. In 1919, Goldman was deported to Soviet Russia, where she found something less than a revolutionary utopia. Her stay in Moscow provides an intimate glimpse of both the promise of the Russian Revolution to American radicals and their subsequent disillusionment with its betrayal. Her exile continued in Germany, France, Britain, and Canada, bringing her finally into the Spanish Civil War and still another chapter in the turbulent history of radicalism in the twentieth century.

Since the birth of the United States, Americans have struggled to define the meaning of freedom. That has often been a difficult and perilous struggle. For Emma Goldman, freedom required individuals to shake off the "shackles and restraints of government." The price of freedom, she came to recognize, was eternal vigilance, a wariness of those who in the name of protecting freedom would diminish freedom, and resistance to rules, codes, regulations, and censorship (no matter how well intended) that would mock free expression by restricting or penalizing it. Free speech meant not only the right to dissent but more importantly the active exercise of that right in the face of attempts to suppress it. And, perhaps most important of all, it insisted on the right of others to speak out on behalf of what the majority believed to be wrong, freedom for the most offensive and disturbing speech. That was the true test of freedom of speech. "Free speech," Goldman declared, "means either the unlimited right of expression, or nothing at all. The moment any man or set of men can limit speech, it is no longer free."

What Emma Goldman said provoked controversy, both within and outside the radical movement, and not all radicals were enamored with her political positions. Margaret Anderson, a radical editor and literary modernist, appreciated Goldman's sheer presence more than her ideological commitments: "Emma Goldman's genius is not so much that she is a great thinker as that she is a great woman." But whatever one might think of Emma Goldman's political views, actions, blind spots, and vision, few individuals in American society so exemplify the tradition of dissent and nonconformity. Few brought more passion, intensity, exuberance, perseverance, and self-sacrifice to the causes she espoused. Even when she failed to convert people to her positions, she compelled many of them to reexamine their assumptions and to question the accepted wisdom and elected leadership.

For much of her life in America, Emma Goldman defined the limits of political dissent. True loyalty to a nation, she believed, often demanded disloyalty to its pretenses and policies and a willingness to unmask its leaders. To Goldman, liberty was more than an ideology, it was a passion, to be lived and breathed each day. "Liberty was always her theme," said Harry Weinberger, her lawyer and close friend: "liberty was always her dream; liberty was always her goal . . . liberty was more important than life itself." And, as he went on to suggest, free expression has always led a precarious existence. "She spoke out in this country against war and conscription, and went to jail. She spoke out for political prisoners, and was deported. She spoke out in Russia against the despotism of Communism, and again became a fugitive on the face of the earth. She spoke out against Nazism and the combination of Nazism and Communism and there was hardly a place where she could live."

It must be said, however, that Goldman did not speak out with equal fervor about the most repressive and violent denial of human rights in her lifetime. She identified with the struggles of oppressed workers, and the New Declaration of Independence she issued in 1909 proclaimed that "all human beings, irrespective of race, color, or sex, are born with the equal right to share at the table of life." But in a time of racist terror and severe racial subjugation (political, social, and economic), far more severe than any of the violations of civil liberties she so courageously deplored and fought, Emma Goldman avoided the South and mostly ignored the struggle for black rights and racial equality, a struggle that involved not only black Americans but a coterie of progressive white allies. Perhaps she was trying to appease the racism pervading the labor and socialist movements. More likely, she was unconscious of this contradiction in her life's commitment to "the wretched of the earth." Whatever her personal feelings about these matters, they would occupy little space in her writings or speeches, and hence are mostly absent from these volumes.

The Emma Goldman Papers Project at the University of California at Berkeley, in selecting, editing, and annotating the documents for this valuable series under the direction of Candace Falk, has brought into our historical consciousness a most extraordinary woman, whose passion, spiritual qualities, and commitments illuminate a certain time in our history, even as the lesson she taught remains timeless: that social and economic inequities are neither unintentional nor inevitable but reflect the assumptions, beliefs, and policies of certain people who command enormous power over lives. Her life forces us to think more deeply and more reflectively about those individuals in our history— from the abolitionists of the 1830s to the labor organizers of the 1890s and 1930s to the civil rights activists of the 1960s—who, individually and collectively, tried to flesh out and give meaning to abstract notions of liberty, independence, and freedom, and for whom a personal commitment to social justice became a moral imperative. No better epitaph might be written for Emma Goldman than the one composed in 1917 by A. S. Embree, an organizer for the Industrial Workers of the World imprisoned in Tombstone, Arizona: "The end in view is well worth striving for, but in the struggle itself lies the happiness of the fighter."

LEON LITWACK,
MORRISON PROFESSOR
OF AMERICAN HISTORY,
BERKELEY, CALIFORNIA

History is the evocation of an authentic past, built through innuendo and inference—a pursuit both palpable and elusive. A small detail illuminates history's subtleties, performs its alchemy, as a photographic image holds time luxuriously still—creating a sacred space for reflection and the illusion of comprehending the intricacies of a world long past. *Emma Goldman: A Documentary History of the American Years* is comprised of selected documents—rare glimpses of a valiant life dedicated to the creation of a radically new social order: "freedom, the right to self expression, everybody's right to beautiful radiant things."[1]

As in a photographic album, where the spaces between the images—the unrecorded intervals—create an imagined narrative, portraying a single life in constant interplay with others, so do the documents in this selected edition, chronological but not linear, form a montage of the unfolding of Goldman's public life. Personal correspondence, newspaper reportage, government surveillance reports trailing her in Europe, court transcripts showcasing the drama of her arguments before judges and jurors, lecture notes and manuscripts, and previously unpublished documents reflecting the international reach of the anarchist movement all tell a story not only about Goldman, but about a time and place when the price of freedom was inordinately high.

In every age, there are individuals who assume the role of public guardians of freedom. Emma Goldman, complex and often paradoxical, merits a place among such transcendent spirits. Her words live on as a reminder—and as a warning.

FRAMING THE DOCUMENTARY HISTORY

The format for the presentation of historical material in this multi-volume documentary history of Emma Goldman is consistent with her core role as a champion of independent thought. Each document is anchored by annotations that explicate the historical context, deepen and invite interpretation, and illuminate a vast and relatively unknown world. Searching for sources on the complex political history of anarchism took years of collaborative and global detective work. Unearthing significant papers and unraveling the un-

---

1. Emma Goldman, *Living My Life* (New York: Knopf, 1931), p. 56; abbreviated as *LML* hereafter.

derlying stories of the people and events have required—and inspired—the scholarly devotion, intellectual balance, and careful preservation of authenticity upon which these volumes rest. While the selected documents cannot capture the whole of Goldman's life nor describe all the people and events surrounding her, this multi-volume edition does serve as a road map to the past and a route into a rich and not yet fully explored terrain of history—especially of the history of anarchism.

Even though in the late nineteenth and early twentieth centuries anarchism's challenge was feared and shunned by historians, who purged this marked political history from U.S. tomes, because there was a strong written and oral tradition among anarchists, the continuity of their culture and lore was assured. Served by a collective memory, the survival instinct of anarchists was anchored in the heroics of their movement. Pamphlets and newspapers expressing a variety of ideas were the anarchists' epicenter— they read, republished, and honored political tracts from their past. Anarchists retold the inspiring stories of their courageous predecessors, building on their own history to create a more glorious vision of the future for all. With tremendous fanfare, they celebrated anniversaries—honoring the defeat and loss of life in the uprising of the Paris Commune of 1871,[2] and the death and hallowed last words of the Haymarket anarchists in 1887. They modeled themselves, their lives, their cooperative efforts, and their political strategies in relation to those who preceded them. Ritual remembrances allowed for the renewal of a vow not to forget those whose sacrifices and challenges might otherwise have been obliterated by the conservators of traditional history. What anarchism might signify in the United States at the beginning of the twentieth century was in flux and took shape through varied forms of collective meditation on the relationship between political theory and practice. The young Emma Goldman would play a significant role in the anarchists'—and the nation's—ongoing discussion about the concept of, and possibilities for, freedom.

It is in the spirit of the tradition of remembrance and respect that we present this documentary history of Emma Goldman's American years, along with a chronology of her life and the anarchist movement as well as biographical appendices of prominent individuals, periodicals, and organizations. Pieced together, these texts fix a moment in time, add clarity and nuance to Goldman's work, to the surrounding culture, and to the ideas and activities of the anarchists. Offering a critical engagement with the past, the array of original sources presented in these volumes promote accuracy and fairness. The documents display the anarchist movement at its best and its worst—in its reach for egalitarian cooperation and in the depth of its sectarian controversies, in its articulation of a "beautiful ideal" and in its engagement with the prevailing undercurrent of political violence in a violent era. Each volume in this documentary edition provides the backgrounding data from which those who yearn for social equality and freedom will find much to admire about Goldman—and also a fount of new material from which to raise important, and possibly disconcerting, questions about her life and times.

---

2. See Letter to Max Metzkow, 25 March 1897, esp. note 2, for elaboration on the remarkable spectacles and performances staged to honor the Paris Commune.

The historical documents in this selected edition, especially those in vol. 1, *Made for America, 1890–1901,* that chronicle the initial decade of Emma Goldman's political life, may surprise those whose image of Goldman has been colored by the softening filter of her autobiography, *Living My Life* (1931). A lighthearted portrait of Goldman as a cultural rebel, the woman who dances in the revolution has been evoked on t-shirts and etched into the public consciousness for more than thirty years since the reprint of her auto- biography in 1970.[3] Although not completely inaccurate, this image ignores the darker shadows of her political militancy.

In her autobiography, Goldman couches her militant political engagement in a nov- elistic and stylized optimism and obscures her intermittent despair. She tilts her para- doxical and all-encompassing political stance, one that mirrored the poles of her own per- sonality, to emphasize her seemingly boundless empathy, while still brandishing her piercingly sharp-tongued severity. Casually embedded in the recounting of her life and passionate loves in the autobiography is a casting of herself as a modern-day counter- part to Judith, the biblical heroine of bloody justice who cut off the head of Holofernes to avenge the wrongs of her people.

Goldman used her autobiography as an opportunity to reveal and finally unburden herself of years of secrets about her clandestine involvement with her closest friend and comrade—Alexander Berkman—in his attempt to assassinate the steel magnate who had ordered the use of violence to quell a strike. She conceptualized her autobiography as adding her voice to Berkman's prison memoirs, foregrounding Berkman as "the pivot around which my story was written," and asserted that "my connection with Berkman's act and our relationship is the leitmotif of my 40 years of life."[4] Goldman in her mem- oir revealed her belief that her shadowy engagement with the violent edge of the revolu- tionary anarchist movement was in complete harmony with her less fearsome role as a luminary of women's freedom and free expression, thus distinguishing herself from her mainstream and liberal contemporaries, who struggled to reconcile the cloak-and-dagger impression of her political work. Shrewdly, however, as she composed her dazzling au- tobiography and epic entry into the historical record, she chose not to brandish these out- wardly contradictory traits.

In one of the most remarkable memoirs of the twentieth century, and among the very few written so eloquently about a woman's experience by an American immigrant steeped in the political realm, Goldman documents the passionate intensity of a life lived in the service of an ideal and creates a narrative coherence through her portrayal of the tireless pursuit of a singular vision. A major literary accomplishment, the autobiography was intended to sweep the reader into history, rather than to expose and explicate its precise detail.

3. *Living My Life* (reprint, New York: Dover Publications, 1970). Pagination of 1970 edition replicates 1931 edition.
4. EG to Arthur Leonard Ross, 13 January 1929, *EGP,* reel 20.

Goldman was profoundly aware of the difference between the act of reporting history as it happens and of writing from hindsight and remembrance. She recounted her refusal, when asked while still young to write the story of her life: "I have barely begun to live."[5] Only in her twenties, Goldman was too busy witnessing and participating in her era to step back and to record the amazing events; she explained that "When one is standing right in the middle of the battlefield surrounded by enemy fire . . . one can not judge things objectively" (see Letter to Max Nettlau, 24 November 1901).

But by 1927, she had the "leisure" of exile and almost four years to write her autobiography. Deported from the United States during the Red Scare of 1919 after opposing conscription during the First World War, she had made an attempt to serve the revolution in Russia but fled to Europe for refuge from disappointment, settling briefly in France, the place where she would ponder and write about her life. At the age of 58, she was a battle-scarred warrior, far away from the intensity of political activism of her youth and from the United States, the country where she felt most at home. She was possessed with a longing to return and a determination not to be forgotten and anxious to record her life and times. Her American friends even hoped that her book would attract a popular readership that might sway the U. S. government to allow her reentry.

Outwardly shunning the fantasy that the book would facilitate her return, she drew the broad canvas of her life without excluding elements that still might seem threatening to the government authorities that had expelled her only a decade before. Not surprisingly, however, as an exiled anarchist, she underplays the extent of her clandestine entanglements. The silent omissions from her narrative create a more uniformly positive rhetorical effect, protect aging, militant comrades from the censure of public exposure and prosecution, and perhaps shield her from the embarrassment and dangers of full personal and political exposure. Instead, she chose to foreground her inner drama and to embed the specifics of her varied political activity with the forces of history around her, "in bitter sorrow and ecstatic joy, in black despair and in fervent hope."[6]

Remarkably exacting in its presentation of the character of Goldman's emotional life, the autobiography fills in the story of Goldman's family, childhood,[7] and personal development, her sense of adventure, and her love and appreciation for those in, and close to, the anarchist movement around her, and also delineates her major life shifts. Yet, *Living My Life*, like most memoirs, while a treasure trove of information, ideas, and emotion, still never offers the reader the full story of her personal life, nor could it have presented a completely accurate historical record. Writing mostly from memory rather than written records, and prey to lapses, Goldman understandably conflated past events. Especially in light of repeated government confiscations of her personal papers, she rarely could confirm dates and places. She gathered only relatively few of her letters from

5. *LML*, p. v.
6. *LML*, p. 993.
7. For more on Goldman's recollections of her harsh early life, especially in Russia and Germany, see *LML*, esp. pp. 58–60 and 66–69.

friends who had saved and cherished them over the years. She complained throughout the writing process that she had no access to articles from early periodicals to refresh her memory. Among the more poignant and benign examples of her conflations of history was her account of coming to the United States in 1885 with her sister Helena, "eyes filled with tears" as they "stood pressed to each other, enraptured by the sight of . . . the Statue of Liberty suddenly emerging from the mist . . . the symbol of hope, of freedom, of opportunity! She held her torch high to light the way to the free country, the asylum for the oppressed of all lands."[8] In fact, she imagined herself approaching the statue, which was still in process, not yet fully assembled nor on its pedestal.

Although the autobiography remains a compelling narrative of Goldman's personal and political evolution, it now has an apt complement in this documentary edition of Goldman's papers. Selected essays and travel letters, personal correspondence, interviews, newspaper accounts of her speeches, and government surveillance reports extended beyond a narrow interest in Emma Goldman the individual. These volumes display her impressive engagement with the complexity and depth of the fin de siècle world she inhabited and the broad spectrum of people, events, and ideas brought together by her expansive and inclusive philosophy of anarchism.

A NOTE TO OUR READERS

Documents from Goldman's early life, now pieced together for the first time in this debut volume, create a dramatic representation of little-known aspects of her personality, thoughts, and activities. Mentored by the most powerful and talented anarchist speakers and many of the most challenging radical thinkers of her time, Goldman incorporated their voices and created a unique harmony of ideas and sentiments, at once identifiable with a particular time and place in history, and profoundly universal. Marked by a politics born of youth, the lure of freedom remained her vital center.

These early documents also reveal Goldman's prescient and unusual belief that it was not only possible, but in fact preferable, to frame the seemingly contradictory forces of destruction and construction, of chaos and harmony, within one's self and one's vision. We offer our work as a primary source for assessing the work of the young Emma Goldman in all her complexity, a woman who had the courage to look straight into the fires of despair and violence raging around her—and as an illuminating exposé of her quest to "contain multitudes."[9]

THE YOUNG EMMA GOLDMAN STEPS ONTO THE POLITICAL STAGE

Made for America, 1890–1901, vol. 1 of this documentary history of Emma Goldman's American years, opens with a brief newspaper report of an 1890 lecture by "an eloquent

8. *LML*, p. 11.
9. A paraphrasing of "(Do I contradict myself? . . . I am large, I contain multitudes)" from Walt Whitman's "Song of Myself," number 51, *Leaves of Grass*. Whitman's free and open spirit was admired by anarchists and his poetry praised for its celebration of life in all its contradictions.

woman." It was uncommon in the 1890s to see a woman on the lecture circuit, especially one in her early twenties. Goldman later would attribute her success as a lecturer in part to being a woman, claiming that the novelty of a female speaker always guaranteed an inquisitive audience. After more than a decade on the road, she mused that in the end, however, the real challenge was "to hold them. . . . not talk to them as a woman, but as a comrade." She often remarked that her desire was not to "topple men off their pedestal in order to take it" but rather "to share it" (see "Talk with Emma Goldman," Interview in the *New York Sun*, 6 January 1901). One newspaper reporter of the time observed: "No care of the prettiness of manner or speech can stay her. Her voice may break, her knowledge of English may fail her: but she is more effective than art could possibly make her, more eloquent than the completest elegance of speech could give. She snarls, she sneers, she thunders at her audience, and she is as indifferent to their rage as to their approval" (see "A Character Study of Emma Goldman," Interview in the *Philadelphia North American*, 11 April 1901). In 1890, when Goldman stepped onto the political stage at the age of twenty-one, eager to hold and inform her audience, the seeds of her uncompromising vision, emotional intelligence, and razor-sharp analyses of an array of political and cultural issues had already taken root.

She had immigrated to a country of rebels, a destination of choice for those who fled oppression. Born in Kovno, Lithuania, in 1869, she left Russia and her father's stern patriarchal hold when she was sixteen, settling in Rochester, New York, at the end of December 1885 with a married sister. After three years, she fled a brief, and for her, distasteful marriage.[10]

Under the strict scrutiny of German Jewish bosses, she had worked in an austere garment factory with other Eastern European Jewish girls. Cringing at the squalid working conditions of her adopted home and the injustice that seemed reminiscent of a world she thought she had left behind, she dreamt first of the liberating force of love, and then, of revolution.

INSPIRED BY THE HAYMARKET ANARCHISTS

Goldman came of age in an era permeated by labor agitation and violence. She marked her political transformation, her "spiritual birth,"[11] to the chilling moment when she became aware of the horror and significance of the death of the Haymarket anarchists. Newspapers across the world reported about the violent events at a 4 May 1886 rally in Chicago called to protest the killing of four striking McCormick Harvester plant workers; over a hundred policemen marched up to stop the demonstration when a bomb exploded at Haymarket Square. Casualties, most from police bullets not bomb fragments, totaled close to seventy, including seven dead policemen. Although the identity of the bomb thrower was never established, official blame fell upon the anarchists of Chi-

---

10. For a detailed account of Goldman's early marriage and young adulthood in Rochester, see *LML*, pp. 15–25.

11. *LML*, pp. 7–10.

cago.[12] A traumatized public, hungry for revenge, and anxious to tame a burgeoning labor movement, looked to the courts to quell the insurgency.

According to the accused anarchist Albert Parsons, the Illinois state attorney indicted him and his comrades "because they were leaders . . . no more guilty than the thousands who follow them." In the closing argument at the Haymarket trial, he made no attempt to veil his intent: "Gentlemen of the jury; convict these men, make examples of them; hang them and you will save our institutions, our society."[13] Many radicals of Goldman's generation[14] traced their political awakening to that solemn day—11 November 1887—when Parsons and his fellow Chicago anarchists George Engel, Adolph Fischer, and August Spies were executed. On the day of his execution, Spies argued that history would absolve the Haymarket anarchists and predicted that a day would come when the silence of their deaths would reverberate as a revolutionary call to action that could never be suppressed. His eloquent prediction deeply moved the seventeen-year-old Emma Goldman, who was haunted by the image of the four who were hung. Louis Lingg, who had ingested dynamite rather than allow the State to execute him, "stood out as the sublime hero of the eight [and] became the beacon of our lives."[15]

Her despair turned to inspiration after she heard the German socialist Johanna Greie Cramer speak during the trial on the fate of the accused Haymarket anarchists.[16] Convinced of their innocence, Goldman resolved to avenge their deaths. Within two years, she extricated herself from a life of unhappy domesticity and factory work and dedicated herself to the vision of justice she believed the Haymarket anarchists represented.

THE EXCITEMENT OF NEW YORK CITY

In August 1889, at the age of twenty, Goldman left Rochester with "a great ideal, a burning faith" and arrived alone in New York City.[17] Leaving behind the disappointments and provincialism of her first immigrant years, she opened herself to the thrill of a world unconfined by the strictures of traditional social norms, determined to find a means of economic support that served rather than hindered her ideals and a family of choice and openness. Having entered the movement with the perspective of youth, Goldman would remain acutely attuned to the expression of freedom and autonomy. The preeminent New World metropolis represented hope and possibility, even in adversity. New York City's immigrant community on the Lower East Side was a vibrant polyglot culture, with a café or

---

12. For more information on the Haymarket case, see Paul Avrich, *The Haymarket Tragedy* (Princeton: Princeton University Press, 1984) and David Roediger and Franklin Rosemont, eds. *Haymarket Scrapbook* (Chicago: Charles H. Kerr Publishing, 1986).

13. For Albert Parson's paraphrasing of State Attorney Julius Grinnell's statement to the jury, see Robert Justin Goldstein, *Political Repression in Modern America—From 1870 to the Present* (Cambridge: Schenkman Publishing, 1978), p. 40 n. 84.

14. Among those in Goldman's circle inspired by the Haymarket anarchists were Alexander Berkman, Voltairine de Cleyre, and "Big Bill" Haywood.

15. *LML*, p. 42.

16. For Goldman's account of the event, see *LML*, pp. 7–10.

17. *LML*, p. 10.

saloon for almost every political persuasion and for every immigrant's country or town of origin.[18] Goldman felt especially at home among German- and Yiddish-speaking anarchists and appreciated those who both shared her roots and had cast off confining Russian Jewish religious orthodoxy. She immersed herself in heated political discussions, mostly in her German mother tongue. These gathering places offered a colorful respite from long hours working in sweatshops and living in squalid tenement housing; the saloons provided a refuge for forgetting the horror of sickness and poverty that permeated daily life and a locus for empowerment born of camaraderie. Mainstream journalists, intrigued by Goldman's exotic life, waxed poetic about some of Goldman's German associates, who, accustomed to bursting into song and especially uninhibited after hours of talking and drinking beer, enlivened the atmosphere of the cafés and saloons she had begun to frequent. Impromptu political discussions, engaged in by many who had recently been imprisoned in Europe, stretched into the wee hours of the morning. These safe havens provided an open forum for debate and for lashing out against economic and social exploitation and served as a hotbed for organizing public demonstrations intended to ignite the righteous indignation of others.

REVELING IN A SWIRL OF IDEAS

Anarchist politics and culture, with a central focus on the concept and practice of freedom, was a seamless match for the young Goldman's temperament and desires. The most open of all political philosophies, anarchism sparked her imagination. She found the anarchist movement both politically and intellectually engaging, and gradually created a blend of ideas of her own.

Goldman believed that everything that challenged the mind and encouraged individual freedom would advance the movement. A voracious reader, she integrated a host of radical ideas with the themes of classic works of literature and political theory to form her vision of anarchism. She strove less for originality than for synthesis and, in so doing, wove her own distinct pattern of thinking. This quality of incorporating and transforming the work of others into her own may have contributed to doubts among traditional political theorists about the merits of her intellectual contribution. She believed in the interconnections between the old and the new, between past and present ideas. In her anarchist lexicon, pretensions of even the possibility of complete originality conjured up images of self-inflation—and a short-sighted dismissal of the evolution of the social, political, and historical context of individual thought. Creativity, like everything else she valued, was a patchwork. Goldman's personal development as a complex political thinker was grounded in her openness to a rich variety of ideas, within and beyond anarchist theory.

A PATCHWORK OF ANARCHIST THEORY

Goldman began by familiarizing herself with anarchist literature and sifted through the movement's internal debates on competing premises for economic and political change.

---

18. For a vivid account of Lower East Side life, see Morris Hillquit, *Loose Leaves from a Busy Life* (New York: Macmillan, 1934).

She admired and honored great thinkers, picking and choosing from their works, changing her emphasis over the years. From the works of Michael Bakunin she took the spirit of revolt, a strong atheist streak, and ideas of anarchist collectivism with its focus on distributing resources according to the individual effort rather than need. In this early period, however, she was persuaded to distance herself from Bakunin's economic theories in favor of Peter Kropotkin's vision of anarchist communism with its emphasis on the right of individuals to the resources necessary to meet their basic needs—giving what one could but taking only what one needed from the shared accumulation of wealth.[19] Kropotkin's ideas were popularized by, among others, Joseph Peukert in his newspaper, *Die Autonomie*. She incorporated ideas on insurrectionism from Errico Malatesta, and from Johann Most, among others, the recognition that *attentats*—individual acts of political violence—were an inevitable response to the State's use of violence to maintain its power. Goldman's first interest in syndicalism and its espousal of the power of the general strike as a tactic for the emancipation of the working class was piqued when she was in Paris and met French anarcho-syndicalists associated with the barred 1900 anarchist congress.[20] Goldman's faith in the inexorable progression of history toward freedom was reinforced by her reading and discussion of Kropotkin[21] and theories adopted from Karl Marx, both of whom believed that people would inevitably act on their natural desire for freedom.

She was drawn to anarchist individualists in the United States who emphasized social relationships and lifestyle and who focused first on individual liberty—especially the activities of Moses Harmon and the *Lucifer* group, whose early work for free speech she particularly admired. Members of the *Lucifer* publishing group had defied obscenity laws enacted under the 1873 and 1876 Comstock Acts and willingly gone to jail for challenging the marriage code and for daring to discuss in print its blunting sexual and emotional impact—free-speech activities that were broadly defined, along with radical literature, as "obscene."[22]

Friedrich Engels's book *The Origin of the Family, Private Property, and the State* was widely read among anarchists, and no doubt contributed to Goldman's belief that marriage was at root an economic arrangement and the primary foundation for the concept and practice of private property—an idea upon which she would elaborate in lectures on the subject throughout her life. Goldman incorporated many of these ideas into her conception of anarchist communism in America, the political philosophy she found most

19. See Kropotkin's arguments in "Anarchist Communism: Its Basis and Principles," in George Woodcock, ed., *Peter Kropotkin: Fugitive Writings* (Montreal: Black Rose Books, 1993) and also Kropotkin's *The Conquest of Bread* (Cambridge: Cambridge University Press, 1995). For Bakunin's ideas, see Sam Dolgoff, ed., *Bakunin on Anarchism* (Montreal: Black Rose Books, 1980).

20. For introductions to syndicalism, see Rudolph Rocker, *Anarcho-Syndicalism* (London: Pluto Press, 1989) and Linder and Wayne Thrope, eds., *Revolutionary Syndicalism* (Aldershot: Scholar Press, 1990).

21. Peter Kropotkin, "The Spirit of Revolt" among other works by Kropotkin.

22. For more on Moses Harmon and the periodical *Lucifer*, see Hal D. Sears, *The Sex Radicals: Free Love in High Victorian America* (Lawrence: Regents Press of Kansas, 1977) and Martin Henry Blatt, *Free Love and Anarchism: The Biography of Ezra Heywood* (Urbana: University of Illinois Press, 1989).

compelling. Not yet fully formulated, its tenets were being worked out in the journals *Firebrand* and *Free Society*, which she read from cover to cover.

INDIVIDUALIST TRADITION

Goldman astutely drew on the most liberal doctrines of the founding fathers of her adopted country, especially Thomas Jefferson's and Thomas Paine's belief in individual freedom and in the tyranny of too much government. She incorporated the fervor for civil disobedience from Henry David Thoreau and the celebration of the unharnessed spirit from Walt Whitman. She found kindred militant rebels in Wendell Phillips and John Brown. Her homage to this radical tradition was an important signal of Goldman's Americanization and of her remarkable ability to combine old and new world thinkers into her hybrid notion of anarchism.

She was introduced to the ideas of Friedrich Nietzsche in Vienna in 1895 and especially appreciated his theories about the centrality of individual will outside of conventional morality. Goldman had read the German philosopher Max Stirner before 1892, when she claimed to be motivated by self-interest; broadly defined in the Stirnerite sense, an egoist's self-interest was the realization of the full freedom of the individual to follow his or her own sensibilities.[23] She also recognized that strategic use of the label "egoist" sometimes served as an ideological disguise to protect others from implication in collective acts of political violence.

While Goldman identified with elements of individualist anarchism, she simultaneously distinguished herself from it. Benjamin Tucker, editor of the philosophical magazine *Liberty: Not the Daughter, But the Mother of Order* (a subtitle borrowed from Pierre-Joseph Proudhon), was the most prominent American individual anarchist.[24] Beginning in 1886, *Liberty* featured articles debating the issue of whether egoism or natural rights was the basis for individualist theory. While the sovereignty of the individual was always paramount to the creation of a voluntary society, anarchist communists and anarchist collectivists differed from individualist anarchists in their insistence on economic cooperation, mutualism, and the rejection of private property. Some individualists, influenced by reading and discussions of Max Stirner's work, took the idea to its logical extreme, rejecting even the notion of natural rights, or the will of any group, and accepted only individual desire as the criterion for action. Many American adherents of this strain had been influenced by early translated segments of Max Stirner's book, *The Ego and Its Own*. The

---

23. For more on Max Stirner, see his *The Ego and Its Own* (London: Rebel Press, 1993) and James J. Martin, *Men Against the State* (DeKalb, Ill.: Adrian Allen Associates, 1953). Also see Letter from Alexander Berkman, 20 August 1892, esp. note 2, and Letter to *Free Society*, 17 February 1901, esp. note 4, for a fuller account of the use of the term "egoist."

24. For more on Benjamin Tucker and the periodical *Liberty*, see Paul Avrich, *Anarchist Portraits* (Princeton: Princeton University Press, 1988); James J. Martin, *Men Against the State* (Colorado Springs: Ralph Myles, 1970); Michael Coughlin and M. Sullivan, eds., *Benjamin Tucker and the Champions of Liberty: A Centenary Anthology* (St. Paul, by the editors, 1986); and Martin Blatt, *Free Love and Anarchism: The Biography of Ezra Heywood* (Urbana: University of Illinois Press, 1989).

variety of political expression sanctioned by individualist anarchists in Europe, many of whom were Stirnerites, included direct action and propaganda by the deed, guided by free will and accountable only to one's self. American individualists discussed the issue, even imagined a confederation of individualists, but rarely identified with political violence. Among the elements of American individualist ideology to which Goldman was attracted, sexual radicalism and free love were paramount. She agreed with and promoted their view against any form of either intervention or sanction by the State of the social and sexual relationships between women and men but differed on the issue of private property.

Also drawn to the modernists of her time, Goldman digested their ideas into her anarchist body politic—and thus her life and work became an intellectual template for the most forward and far-reaching possibilities of the era.

SEXUALITY AND GENDER: THE IDEAS OF SIGMUND FREUD

Goldman's signature integration of gender interests into her political vision developed gradually. Her early models of political thought and action were primarily European male anarchists and American individualist anarchists, who were steeped in the theory of vehement rejection and distrust of the State. Although her message during the early 1890s was equally militant, Goldman infused that message with an interest in sexuality that would later expand both the scope of her concerns and the composition of her audience.

She was more psychologically oriented than her anarchist communist comrades— many of whom were economic or political determinists, marked by the influence of Karl Marx, Michael Bakunin, and Peter Kropotkin. For her the scales were even—inner and outer freedoms were necessary elements for meaningful social and political transformation, and no formulaic change in social conditions was a guarantee against subjugation to one's inner tyrants. She pondered these issues, not only in relation to her own childhood (remembering her harsh and sometimes violent father, whose abuse she witnessed and endured), but also with respect to the psychology of political violence.

Goldman was especially taken with the ideas of Sigmund Freud,[25] whose lectures she attended in Vienna in 1895, and later at Clark University in Worcester, Massachusetts, in 1909 (the city in which she had had an ice-cream parlor years before). Freud's work confirmed her belief in the formative influences of childhood and her instinctual sense that sexuality was a critical social force, inextricable from the political advocacy of free expression. This early period of Goldman's intellectual and emotional development coincided with the period of Freud's career when he had begun to connect hysteria with a theory about women's frustrated, repressed sexuality, and to expose the prevalence of incest. Goldman was riveted by Freud's discussion of topics others considered taboo. She used his psychoanalytic theories to broaden her own thinking, especially about the forces

---

25. *LML*, p. 173. See also Freud's "Aetiology of Hysteria," published in 1896 after being presented to the Viennese Society for Psychiatry and Neurology earlier the same year; trans. James Strachey, in *The Standard Edition of the Complete Psychological Works of Sigmund Freud*, vol. 3, pp. 189–221 (London: Hogarth Press, 1962).

that stunt women's emotional development and how secrecy can mask the horrible underside of family life. These ideas added texture and depth to her discussion of free love.

Goldman also appropriated Freud's focus on sexuality as a driving force but transformed it to suit her own belief in the power of love and sexual desire as crucial cohesive elements of social harmony. Her autobiography is a testimony to Freud's influence (and as well to Frank Harris's, who lived in Nice, close to her writer's cottage in Saint-Tropez, and who had published a four-volume memoir laced with his sexual experiences).[26] Goldman framed her self-portrait to include vivid descriptions of her sexual encounters (ranging from the horror and shame of being raped in her teenage years to the ecstasy and romances of her adult life).

Exposed to cutting-edge ideas about the fundamental importance of sexuality and committed to the anarchist tradition of free love, Goldman combined two streams of contemporary theory to buttress her own sensual nature and unconventional life choices. The young Emma Goldman reveled in the sensuality of engagement. She raised her many concurrent love affairs to a matter of political principle. She fixed her lifetime self-image in this erotic phase as a sexual free spirit and began to link the concept of "love" to her anarchist vision—believing that the desire for harmonious relations between the sexes was universal, and that it was the most potent of all metaphors for social and political unity.

BRIDGING SEPARATED TERRAINS

Goldman's ideas about love and sexuality placed her at the center of a perennial debate among anarchists about the relative political importance of such personal issues. In the United States but especially in Europe, the anarchists' agenda was generally one of all-inclusive engagement with labor issues, confrontations with state power, and theorizing about anarchist communism, collectivism, individualism, and syndicalism.

At a meeting in 1897 in Chicago called to support the jailed *Firebrand* editors (who dared to publish, among other things, Walt Whitman's "A Woman Waits for Me"), Lucy Parsons, wife of Haymarket anarchist Albert Parsons, scoffed at their emphasis on sexuality and maintained that the risks involved in discussing free love were wasteful to the anarchist movement and distasteful when other more serious and pressing problems demanded attention.[27] Lucy Parsons's ideas resonated with a large, mostly male constituency, who tipped their hats to the importance of sexual freedom in the transformative vision of anarchism but wished it away from their lofty place of pure political discourse.[28] Then at the secret session of the banned Paris congress of 1900, some of the French delegates objected to Goldman's reading of Missouri anarchist Kate Austin's paper "The

---

26. The four volumes of Frank Harris's *My Life and Loves* were first published by the author in Paris, 1922–1927.

27. For a fuller account of the meeting, see "Letters from a Tour," Series in *Sturmvogel*, 15 December 1897, esp. note 34.

28. The Pittsburgh Manifesto of 1883 includes the appeal for "equal rights without distinction of sex or race."

Question of the Sexes: A Report on the History of the Free Love Movement in the U.S."—insisting that it would only serve to increase misconceptions of anarchism.

In their theories, anarchists were ahead of their time. They believed in equal rights for all, without distinction of sex or race. There was considerable support for "free lovers," and of the men and women who, like the *Lucifer* Group, lived out, and were sometimes arrested for, their anarchist ideals of personal freedom.[29] Yet, even within their own ranks, there were always anarchists who either shared the biases of the mainstream culture in deeming sexuality a predominately personal matter, or for whom even the most compelling issues of private life remained secondary both to their concerns about the public good and for the safety of their comrades.

Often the storm center of controversy on other issues, Goldman assumed the role of bridging these separate terrains.

ROOTED IN THE RUSSIAN REVOLUTIONARY TRADITION

To Goldman, anarchist ideals had an inspirational quality reminiscent of those of the Russian revolutionaries whose presence had swirled around her in St. Petersburg in her teenage years just before she came to the United States.[30] She linked anarchism to the soulful novels she read as a girl. She was especially drawn to the provocative and often suppressed fictionalized story of a political commune, N. G. Chernyshevsky's *What Is to Be Done?* which she had read when she was fifteen. Chernyshevsky's 1863 work had inspired a generation of radical intelligentsia in Russia to political action.[31] Goldman adapted its model of a Russian radical cooperative, its worldview about the centrality of free women who worked together with men in the service of the people and abided by a strict code of ethics within the context of violence, its idea that individual contentment can never be disconnected from the contentment of others, and its belief in the nonexclusivity of intimacy and love. She integrated these tenets of Chernyshevsky with the more directly political writings of Kropotkin, Bakunin, Malatesta, among others, into the theory and practice of anarchism as she imagined it would evolve in the United States.

Though dominated by a German contingent of exiles, adherents to anarchism who had immigrated to America knew no geographical boundaries. As immigrants, they brought with them the experience and excitement of the practice of anarchism from England,

29. See "The Right of Free Speech in America," Essay in *Die Brandfackel*, 13 September 1893, note 1, and "Marriage," Essay in the *Firebrand*, 18 July 1897, note 1, for details on the free-marriage trials and the Comstock laws.

30. For more on the Russian revolutionary tradition, see Franco Venturi, *Roots of Revolution* (New York: Universal Library, 1966).

31. V. I. Lenin titled his famous essay "What is to be done?" (1902)—in which he argues for a coherent and tightly controlled democratic centralist party of revolutionaries to carry out the social revolution —after Chernyshevsky's novel, having read it just after his brother was executed and recognizing its power to influence and inspire the lives of emergent revolutionaries. *Sobranie materialov*, p. 182; cited in Chernyshevsky's sixteen-volume collection, *Polnoe sobranie sochinenii*, 11: 706. From Irina Paperno, *Chernyshevsky and the Age of Realism: A Study in the Semiotics of Behavior* (Stanford: Stanford University Press, 1988).

Italy, France, Spain, and Russia. In Goldman's youth, Jews, driven by persecution, spread across the globe but were united by a common tradition and a religious text that was read and debated, week after week, year after year; the transition to anarchism, bound by ideas rather than the state, was almost seamless for many secular political Jews. By no means monolithic in their beliefs, anarchists in America and those in Europe argued passionately with each other about the fine points of theory and practice—whether their emphasis should be on production or consumption, whether noble ends justify repugnant means, and when and how to react to the issues of the day. Not the least of these current issues was when, and whether, the use of political violence was philosophically or strategically appropriate.

PROPAGANDA BY THE DEED

Goldman was influenced by European anarchists, socialists, and militant workers who were part of a tradition of agitation, both planned and spontaneous, and who employed tactics ranging from strikes and sabotage to political assassination.[32] These tactics made sense especially in places like Germany, which had become a stronghold of socialism but, with the enactment of repressive laws, had barred propaganda efforts and imposed lengthy jail sentences for labor agitation. In Russia too, a revolution was brewing; Tsar Alexander II had been assassinated, radicals were subject to exile, and Jews to pogroms. It was even speculated that the failed attempt taken against him in 1866 mimicked Rahkmetov's similar attempt in Chernyshevsky's popular novel.[33] The small group of Russian radicals known as Narodnaya Volya (People's Will), who were predominantly from the gentry elite and who succeeded in killing Alexander II in 1881, had employed terrorist tactics with a large measure of success and considerable tacit approval from an international community for whom despotism had come to be equated with tsarism.[34] The air was thick with discussions of political violence. Anarchist congresses in London in 1881 (attended by many prominent thinkers and activists in exile) and in Pittsburgh in 1883, overwhelmingly favored "propaganda by the deed"—*attentats*—the use of violence against violence. In spite of the intense political repression and waves of reaction spurred by such acts, there was optimism among anarchists about the possibility for revolutionary change. *Les Temps Nouveaux* (New Times), a French anarchist communist paper, published a somber international *attentat* balance sheet in its 24–30 September 1898 issue, tallying the relatively small number of leaders lost—four heads of State killed and twelve wounded—in comparison to what it estimated as three million acts of violence committed against the people, including wars. Most often, the conservative and reac-

---

32. For further discussion of propaganda by the deed, see Paul Avrich, *The Haymarket Tragedy* (Princeton: Princeton University Press, 1984) and Caroline Cahm, *Kropotkin and the Rise of Revolutionary Anarchism 1872–1886* (New York: Cambridge University Press, 1989).

33. Cited in Iu. Steklov, *M. N. G Chernyshevskii: Ego zhizn' i deiatel' nost', 1828–1889*, 2nd ed., 2 vols. (Moscow-Leningrad, 1928), p. 132; see Paperno, *Chernyshevsky and the Age of Realism*, p. 30.

34. For a brief definition and history of nihilism, see note 1, "Berkman's Career Here," Article in the *New York World*, 25 July 1892.

tionary individual use of the same tactics were omitted from anarchist discussions of the heroics of political violence. A formidable cluster of immigrant radicals, especially those who had recently arrived from Germany and Russia and shared this frame of mind, while longing for the promise of freedom in their new country, also presumed that selective use of force might be an effective and necessary means for fundamental change —and, if necessary, retaliation.

In its early use, the phrase "propaganda by the deed" was intended simply to distinguish between theorizing about revolutionary change and taking "direct action" to advance those ideas. Bakunin's 1870 "Letters to a Frenchman on the Present Crisis" encouraged anarchists to "spread our principles not with words but with deeds, for this is the most popular, the most potent, and the most irresistible form of propaganda." This call to action was not immediately interpreted as an incentive for violence, nor to incite the symbolic targeting of those individuals perceived as collaborators in, or perpetrators of, the brutal injustice around them. Spanish and Italian anarchists took Bakunin's words as a call for small-scale uprisings and spontaneous strikes—collective seizures of power intended to set an example, and a pattern for others to follow.

Not until the 1878 attempts on the life of the German emperor Wilhelm I on two separate occasions by the socialists Max Hodel and Carl Eduard Nobiling, did anarchists begin to equate "propaganda by the deed" with individual or small-group *attentats* (or assassinations). The March 1881 assassination of the Russian tsar Alexander II by the radical Russian group Narodnaya Volya—intended as a bold call for revolutionary change—really did influence the direction of history thereafter, and anarchists adopted propaganda by the deed as their strategy of choice. Reflecting this shift, the July 1881 London International Social Revolutionary Congress attended by, among others, Peter Kropotkin, Errico Malatesta, and Louise Michel, adopted a resolution endorsing "propaganda by deed" and urging the study of "chemistry" in preparation for the use of explosives. Thus the phrase became synonymous with individual and group acts of targeted assassination as well as of general terror, not only for anarchists but for the public at large. The same policy was adopted among anarchists in the United States, with the Pittsburgh Manifesto of 1883 widening the parameters of the phrase by calling for "destruction of the existing class rule, by all means, i.e., by energetic, relentless, revolutionary and international action!" Of the eight Haymarket anarchists, especially the anarchist communists Louis Lingg, George Engel, and Adolph Fischer supported armed insurrection and individual acts of propaganda by the deed. The anarchist periodicals Goldman would have read in her formative political years between 1889 and 1892, *Die Autonomie* and *Freiheit*, were permeated with violent rhetoric. They not only supported the use of violence and praised those who carried it out, but Johann Most, the editor of *Freiheit*, who was one of Goldman's earliest mentors, even authored the 1885 *Revolutionary War Science* as a working manual for the *attentater*.

In 1894, residual doubts about the efficacy of the tactic of propaganda by the deed began to surface among anarchists, and was best articulated by Kropotkin's assessment in *La Révolte:* "a structure based on centuries of history cannot be destroyed with a few kilos of explosives." His words tacitly encouraged the need for education, and reinforced the complexity and extended timeframe needed to create popular support for truly revolutionary changes. Although Kropotkin never repudiated the *attentat* as a right of revenge and even praised the heroism of such acts, his emphasis had shifted from a wholehearted belief in the success of such tactics, to an appreciation of the act's symbolic intent, focusing instead on addressing public misconceptions about anarchism, and organizing loosely structured federations—leagues, trade unions, schools, discussion groups —that would work on many levels to create the basis for a grand transformation. The anarchist communist strand within the movement in the United States attempted to hold the tension between destruction and construction, without abandoning either pole.

Goldman's position on the issue of propaganda by the deed bore the important influences of Kropotkin and of the anarchist communists in the United States and Europe. By 1901, when the issue touched her life most immediately—with the assassination attempt on the President of the United States by an anarchist who had attended a Goldman lecture that glorified the heroism of those who engaged in targeted acts of violence —her essay, "The Tragedy at Buffalo," reflected her shift away from the belief that such an act could spark a workers' revolt; she had acted on this belief nine years earlier when, in 1892, she and Alexander Berkman conspired to kill Carnegie Steel Company manager Henry Clay Frick after Pinkerton gunmen shot and killed striking workers, and she never abandoned her assertion of the right of the individual to "act" against organized violence of the state. No longer focused on the effectiveness of such tactics, Goldman shifted her manner of addressing the issue of political violence to educating the public about the forces that drive an assassin to his act, hoping to elicit sympathy for the vulnerable psychological state and heightened sensitivity of those who choose to risk themselves as martyrs in an act of revenge intended as a harrowing cry against the injustice and cruelty surrounding them.

BROTHERS WAR

Shortly after the execution of the Haymarket anarchists, the American anarchist movement consisted primarily of Jewish anarchists. Pionire der Frayhayt (Pioneers of Liberty), a rank-and-file Jewish workers group, came together to defend the Haymarket anarchists on 9 October 1886, the day of their sentencing. The group was soon joined by anarchist writers and organizers—Saul Yanovsky, Hillel Solotaroff, David Edelstadt, and Roman Lewis, among others—and concentrated in the eastern cities of the United States, coalesced in 1890 around the publication *Freie Arbeiter Stimme* (Free Voice of Labor). The paper galvanized the Yiddish anarchist community and articulated its strong links to the militant International Working People's Association.

The IWPA's 1883 Pittsburgh Manifesto had been authored primarily by Johann Most and reflected his contempt for palliatives of reform; instead, he called for the destruction of privilege based on social class and for the establishment of a free society based on the cooperative organization of production, a formulation identified as economic collectivism by Michael Bakunin. Most's German-language paper *Freiheit* had a run of thirty years (from 1879 to 1910) and a tremendous following among both German and Jewish anarchists, who were drawn to its violent political rhetoric in this period of history when violence against labor was rampant, and many anarchists and socialists imagined that revolution was imminent.

Like other political movements engaged in formulating a general vision of the future, differences emerged, not only in theory but also in personality and preference. Rallying around Joseph Peukert and his paper, *Die Autonomie* (published from 1889 to 1895), German anarchist communists distinguished themselves from anarchist collectivists (who used ability as a criterion in the distribution of goods and services) by their enunciation of the criterion of distribution according to need. Threatened and angry, Johann Most, who was accustomed to dominating the movement, became embroiled in a heated clash of egos, in part under the guise of a political debate about conflicting philosophical positions on anarchism. Sweeping the European German anarchist community during the 1880s, this vicious split, in which Most and Peukert each accused each other of treachery, became known as the Bruderkrieg (the "Brothers War") and continued to reverberate throughout the movement in the 1890s.[35] Also festering in anarchists' collective memory was the fate of the militant anarchist hero Johann Neve, who was arrested in Belgium in 1887 after smuggling dynamite across the border to be used by the German movement. Rumor had it that Peukert had either deliberately or inadvertently identified Neve to a police agent, a betrayal believed to have resulted in Neve's death in prison. The high drama around Neve, who was seen as a man of great integrity and a martyr for the cause, transcended factionalism and occupied the storm center of European anarchism. Goldman and Berkman identified with elements of both theoretical standpoints and maintained alliances with many followers of both Most and Peukert. By 1890 Goldman and Berkman favored Peukert's position over Most's; later she asserted in *Living My Life* that *Die Autonomie* "seemed to express anarchism in a clearer and more convincing manner" and that his tenets "were much closer to what anarchism had come to mean . . . than those of *Freiheit*."[36] Berkman even recommended to a conference of Jewish anarchists in New York City in 1890 that they embark on a full investigation of the spy charges against Peukert before assuming his guilt.

Immigrant radicals, still in thrall to political developments in Europe, tended to emulate the splits and tensions between the various factions of the issues between the anarchist and socialist movements abroad, allowing them to overshadow their own emergent identity as an indigenous movement. Although the philosophical template for Goldman's political ideas had been set, events and personalities in the anarchist movement

35. For further discussion on the Brothers War, see Heiner Becker, "Johann Neve," *The Raven* 1 (May 1987) and Andrew Carlson, *Anarchism in Germany* (Metuchen, N.J.: Scarecrow Press, 1972). Also see note 3, "Berkman's Career Here," Article in the *New York World*, 25 July 1892, for details of this most divisive feud in anarchist history.

36. *LML*, p. 74.

were ever changing. Given the intrigue within the ranks, Goldman's transcendent ability to incorporate new ideas kept her remarkably modern and continuously identified as an open and forward thinker.

MUTUAL ATTRACTION

When the young, bright, attractive Emma Goldman entered the New York anarchist political arena, militant European men dominated it. Burning with a desire to serve humanity, to be active in the cause of freedom, she welcomed mentors and comrades, and the stimulation of their new ideas. Mutual attraction marked this moment in her young life. The reciprocal sizzle of sexuality and politics was a fitting tonic for her spirit and often expressed itself in intimate crossing of ethnic and national boundaries, though still within a mostly non-English-speaking immigrant world. The clandestine dangers, woven so tightly into the fabric of anarchist culture, intensified her excitement and underscored the importance of building trust among comrades whose secrets had far-reaching consequences. Captivating intimate relationships emerged from and fed her enthusiasm for her new political engagement. Foremost among her early mentors and lovers were Alexander Berkman and Johann Most.

Alexander Berkman, known by the Russian diminutive Sasha, was an immigrant close to Goldman's own age, and first caught her eye at Sachs's café on Suffolk Street, the unofficial headquarters of young Yiddish-speaking anarchists in New York City's Lower East Side neighborhood. Eastern European Jews, especially from Russia, had fled anti-Semitism and the pervasive oppressiveness of tsarist rule in the 1880s. To cushion the harsh anonymity of their arrival, new immigrants clustered into small enclaves bound together by a common language and culture. The mutual attraction between Emma and Sasha was intensified by their shared revolutionary and Russian heritage. Their love and friendship would become the emotional center of both their lives.

Berkman modeled himself after his uncle, the Russian revolutionary Mark Andreyevich Natanson, Sasha's personal ideal of a "noble and great man."[37] Sasha immigrated to the United States in 1888 and joined the militant New York City organization Pionire der Frayhayt (Pioneers of Liberty) the same year; the group launched the country's first Yiddish-language anarchist paper, *Varhayt* (Truth), the predecessor of *Freie Arbeiter Stimme* (Free Voice of Labor). The *Varhayt* editorial collective combined rank-and-file labor militants with highly educated writers and lecturers. Berkman was also an active member of the anarchist periodical *Freiheit* (Freedom), whose driving force was Johann Most.

Graced with tremendous oratorical talent, Most was respected for the many prison sentences he had endured in the service of the cause, and for his willingness to voice in-

---

37. Natanson was a founder of the Chaikovsky Circle of Russian revolutionaries and of the group Zemya i Volya (Land and Liberty) and later, of its militant faction Narodnaya Volya (People's Will), the radical group that practiced the use of terror. See "Talk with Emma Goldman," Interview in the *New York Sun*, 6 January 1901, note 10, for more on the impact and legacy of the Narodnaya Volya group.

cendiary ideas in a manner more dramatic and convincing than any speaker Goldman had ever heard. His prolific vitriolic writings, especially *Die Gottespest* (The God Pestilence; 1888) and *The Beast of Property* (1890), were staples of the movement as well as his powerful defenses of the political rationale for *die Propaganda der That*—"propaganda by the deed." *Revolutionary War Science* (1885), Most's weapons manual, which Berkman used, was especially provocative.

Many years her senior, Most took Goldman under his wing. He recognized her potential as both political protégé and lover. Goldman was honored to have attracted the attention and friendship of a man who was such a force in the movement. She was a quick study, and it was not long before Most sent her on the road, in 1890, to Rochester, Buffalo, Cleveland, and Baltimore to deliver her first public lectures on the contradictions inherent in the movement for an eight-hour workday. Goldman seized the opportunity to challenge the overriding system of power and exploitation, echoing many of the sentiments of the groundbreaking 1883 Pittsburgh Manifesto, a document drafted by Most, among others, that had reflected the views of many of the Chicago Haymarket anarchists. The manifesto established the parameters of anarchist discourse—"the destruction of existing class rule by all means" and "the establishment of a free society based upon cooperative organization of production" and "equal rights for all without distinction of sex or race."

Goldman found the experience of lecturing intoxicating—especially when she departed from Most's ideas and followed her own inspiration. The crowds welcomed this bold newcomer who spoke on such topical issues as "The Right to Be Lazy" (a title she borrowed from the book by Paul Lafargue),[38] hurling insults at a system of privilege that left so many people either impoverished or literally worked to death. Goldman delivered her message at first only in her German mother tongue, a language easily understood by both Yiddish and German audiences, and especially appealing to newly arrived immigrants. Many among them, who had participated in militant groups abroad, were intent on continuing their fight for social and economic justice in a country that held more grandiose promise than it actually delivered. Goldman railed against factory owners who felt threatened by organized labor and against the political system that made immigrants targets, vulnerable to exploitation and indiscriminate violent attack should they dare to strike for greater economic rights.

LABOR VIOLENCE

In this extremely volatile time, it was actually quite difficult to assess, even metaphorically, who threw the first stone. Statistics show that in the United States between 1881 and 1905, there were 37,000 strikes, independent of those called for by a central union. Between 1877 and 1903, 500 such confrontations escalated into interventions by state

---

38. Paul Lafargue, *Das Recht ouf Faulheit* (Zurich: Verlag der Volksbuchhandlung, 1887).

and federal troops on behalf of the owners against the strikers, with untold numbers of fatalities.[39] Records were poorly kept and inaccurate because many of those killed were "foreign" workers, not yet "citizens" of the United States, whose deaths were not considered worthy of official tally.[40] New immigrants, who could work but generally could not vote, had little hope for any official recourse to counter the extreme exploitation to which they were subjected, although a significant few forged links to New York City's Tammany Hall political machine. Often the disenchanted among them gravitated however toward direct-action tactics—strikes and sabotage. The fact that the State did not adequately represent the interests of the oppressed rendered the anarchist perspective all the more enticing to this militant sector of exploited workers.

Whether the union movement could have sustained the militancy of its beginnings is unclear. The extraordinary use of armed force to squelch militant union tactics and to halt even the discussion of reorganization of the workplace allowed for only the most reformist unions to thrive. Thus, it is not surprising that in this battle to gain influence and respectability in the United States, the bombs and assassinations associated with the violent edge of the anarchist spectrum became a source of tension for the moderate sector of the labor movement.

When Goldman entered the political arena, between 1890 and 1900, there were significantly more incidents of labor unrest than during the previous decade—over 16,000 strikes and lockouts with over four million employees engaged in the attempt to redefine the conditions of their work.[41] Although most anarchists viewed the eight-hour movement as an inadequate palliative to an inherently unjust economic system, the labor movement was a natural point of entry for someone eager to make a difference in the lives of working people. At the end of the nineteenth century, however, the price of striking for higher wages and sometimes for reduced hours (with victory won only half of the time) was all too often one's life.

ANARCHISM BRIEFLY DEFINED

Goldman voiced the political intent of the anarchists and would later extend their principle of freedom to the pressing social and cultural issues of her time: "We seek the establishment of Anarchy, or, in other words, a freedom from government of any kind; a community of interests based upon common production of equal and necessary character; we seek a perfect liberty for each individual to enjoy the grand and glorious products of nature; we seek for each an equal liberty to cultivate the talents and abilities as well the

39. See "Advised Strenuous Measures," Article in the *Boston Daily Globe*, 13 September 1897, notes 1, 2, for details on the Hazleton massacre; see "Letter from a Tour," Series in *Sturmvogel*, 15 December 1897, note 29, for details on the United Mine Workers' strike; and see "The Effect of War on the Workers," Transcript of Address in *Freedom*, 20 February 1900, note 6, for details on the Coeur d'Alene strike.

40. Alan Trachtenberg, *The Incorporation of America: Culture and Society in the Gilded Age* (New York: Hill and Wang, 1982), pp. 90–91.

41. Thomas Sewell Adams and Helen L. Sumner, eds., *Labor Problems* (New York: Macmillan, 1907), p. xx; data from the *Sixteenth Annual Report of the U.S. Commissioner of Labor*.

attainments of the highest knowledge" (see "The Law's Limit," Article in the *New York World,* 17 October 1893).

SPREADING THE WORD

As a traveling lecturer, Goldman served the important role of spreading horrific information about, and the perspective of those who fell victim to, labor violence—events often suppressed from mainstream newspapers. The barring of radical journals from the mails under a broadly interpreted law against "obscenity" meant that Goldman's lectures might be the only source of sympathetic information about labor troubles.

Over time, Goldman became especially adept at rallying solidarity and raising funds for labor organizing across the nation. In these early years, she solicited funds for the striking women garment workers and for the languishing anarchist newspapers *Free Society* and the *Firebrand,* among other worthy causes.

Her speaking career was launched among the immigrant left—a community that remained her loyal audience and refuge, as her public gradually widened to include English-speaking Americans. When she stepped onto the political stage at age twenty-one, she embarked on what was to become a continuous lecture trail. Her tours served the multiple purpose of providing a forum for her political message and an incentive for her youthful exploration of the expansive cultural and geographic terrain of the United States, molding her unique pattern of Americanization—and contributing to her growing ability to reach, understand, and learn from the varieties of culture and history of her vast adopted country. Such forays into the country's interior were rare for immigrant working girls clustered in New York City, and fed Goldman's yearning to break away from conventional expectations.

LIVING COMMUNALLY

When Goldman returned to New York City from her first month-long lecture tour, she was inspired to extend her political vision to her daily living arrangements. An informal commune began to take shape, organized in part by readers and supporters of Most's newspaper *Freiheit.* She had dreamed of finding a cooperative based on free association in work, in love, in political vision—to match the one depicted in her beloved novel, Chernyshevsky's *What Is to Be Done?* Closely approximating her desires, her household consisted of Sasha and his cousin Modest Stein, known as Fedya, along with her young friends Anna and Helene Minkin. Goldman imagined herself to be Vera Pavlovna (whose many lovers lived together or frequented the same quarters without hiding their affections, fully within each other's gaze). She linked Fedya to the novel's portrayal of Vera's brother, and Berkman to Rahkmetov (a role he too ascribed to himself), Chernyshevsky's pure revolutionary. The group lived together first in New York City and later in New Haven, Connecticut, where they loosely organized themselves around an attempt to establish a women's sewing cooperative. Jealousies cropped up as the group's personal entanglements thickened. Johann Most would later become intimately involved with Helene Minkin, and Sasha with her sister, Anna Minkin. The tension of their informal summer commune in New Haven eventually became unbearable, prompting their return to New York City. Emma, Sasha, and Fedya—by this time, a loose *ménage à trois*—broke away from the larger collective living group.

Still attached to the idea of creating a life outside of the city, Emma left the drudgery of piecework sewing behind and migrated to the town of Springfield, Massachusetts, in the spring of 1892. There she joined Fedya, who had arranged a job for her with his employer—a busy photographer who was sympathetic to their cause. In this underdocumented period of Goldman's life, only scantily reported in her autobiography, one may surmise that there was much to hide—both personal and political. She did write about her next move, to nearby Worcester, where with Sasha and Fedya she started and faced the failure of their own photography studio. Then, stirred by accounts of the tsar's latest atrocities, they came upon the all-American idea of opening an ice-cream parlor to fund their return to Russia. But even double scoops could not secure a steady flow of cash, off-season in a hot-weather business, thus dashing their hopes of joining the international supporters of the brewing revolution in their mother country.

ATTENTAT—AND THE DELUGE

At the same time, industrial violence racked the United States, with the governors of five states calling for the National Guard to quell labor unrest—against miners in East Tennessee and in Coeur d'Alene, Idaho, against switchmen in Buffalo, and to counter general strikes in New Orleans, Louisiana, and Homestead, Pennsylvania.[42]

On 6 July 1892, Goldman burst into the small room in back of the flat she shared with Sasha and Fedya frantically waving a half-open newspaper. Berkman described her agitation as "the cry of a wounded animal . . . the bitterness of helpless agony." Barely able to speak she blurted out—"Homestead. Strikers shot. Pinkertons have killed women and children."[43]

The Pinkerton gunmen, ostensibly there to protect strikebreakers, shot at striking workers at the Homestead steel mill in Pennsylvania. An ambiguous order from industrial magnate Henry Clay Frick ended in a bloody conflict between striking workers, detectives, strikebreakers, and armed guards. Even before Homestead, Emma, Sasha, and Fedya felt compelled to respond to the plight of workers in their adopted home and sealed their commitment to die for the cause of anarchism.[44] Together they plotted to retaliate against Frick, the manager at the Carnegie steel company's mill.

For justice to triumph over adversity, Goldman and her circle presumed that such extraordinary forces of repression necessitated counterviolence. Sasha would carry out their plan. Emma attempted to prostitute herself to get money for the gun. Fedya worked

---

42. See "Berkman's Career Here," Article in the *New York World*, 25 July 1892, note 13, for a detailed account of the events at Homestead.
43. Alexander Berkman, *Prison Memoirs of an Anarchist* (New York: Mother Earth Publishing Association, 1912), p. 1.
44. *LML,* p. 62.

out the logistics and vowed to follow through on the act, should anything go wrong. They helped write and distribute a workers' manifesto, anticipating that their *attentat* would spur the workers to rise up in righteous indignation. The night he arrived in Pittsburgh, Sasha signed into a hotel under the name of his literary revolutionary archetype, "Rakhmetov." But the tactics of their Russian counterparts failed them in America. Sasha injured Frick but failed to kill him. An associate of Frick's helped restrain rather than defend Sasha, who was later attacked by a carpenter who tried to hit him with a hammer as he faced arrest. Berkman was sentenced to twenty-two years in prison. Fedya, who went to Pittsburgh after the arrest to finish where Sasha had left off, was foiled by an informer.

Impetuously and with a sense of outrage, the twenty-three-year-old Goldman, the twenty-two-year-old Berkman, and a small group of their friends had planned the retaliatory *attentat* against Frick, holding him responsible for the indiscriminate deaths of the strikers. Berkman would spend the next fourteen years in prison. Only when he was behind bars did he gradually begin to comprehend the insularity of his act and why the very workers he intended to defend had not come to his defense, although he had no regrets about alienating the ever-growing moderate contingent of the labor movement. Sasha's most severe punishment, however, was the hurtful condemnation of the prominent anarchist Johann Most—the most vociferous challenger of Berkman's political judgment.[45] Anarchists by no means gave unilateral support to acts of political violence and argued bitterly among themselves on the issue. Yet, whether ends justify means was less an issue for the anarchists than whether oppressors would retreat in fear or workers would rise in victory after having destroyed the old order to create the new.[46]

Although too-sparse evidence protected Goldman from the punishing hand of the law, she could not escape the censure of a suspicious public. Her private acknowledgment of shared guilt and her sustained belief in the symbolic significance of Berkman's act fueled a legal and political campaign on his behalf that punctuated every aspect of her life until his release in 1906.

Equally important was Goldman's personal support from afar; she acted as Berkman's emotional anchor as he cycled in and out of the abyss of depression—especially in prison. Haunted by the dire consequences of their joint actions, Goldman's identity would be forever entwined with his, her freedom tainted by his confinement, her development as a thinker and as a woman never far from his imagined gaze.

Paradoxically, a relatively short prison sentence of her own provided Goldman a respite from survivor's guilt. Goldman was arrested and, in October 1893, convicted of incitement to riot for uttering sentiments that might encourage the poor to demand,

45. See Letter to *Der Anarchist*, 30 July 1892, note 1, which provides the first English translation of Most's position paper against Berkman's act.
46. See Letter from Alexander Berkman, 19 October 1892, note 3, for an exposition published in *Prison Blossoms* of the reasoning behind Berkman's attempt to kill Frick; see also Letter to Augustin Hamon, 25 June 1897, note 7, for a statement of organized labor's distaste and disapproval of Berkman's attack on Frick.

then take, bread "as their sacred right." During the first year of Berkman's imprisonment, Goldman had been free to follow her own inclinations and interests. In her own ten months behind bars, lonely encounters with society's imprisoned outcasts would become their poignant commonality.

AN ANCHOR IN THE STORM

Even the horrors of a prison cell could not squelch Goldman's hunger for engagement with political and intellectual life, nor hamper her development as a young woman who reveled in both the turbulence and excitement of her times. Anarchists affirmed freedom of the individual, espoused free love, fought against possessiveness, welcomed variety. Goldman's intimate life was never eclipsed by Berkman's incarceration. Even while they were together, before his imprisonment, Sasha had been involved with their roommate Anna Minkin and Emma with his cousin Fedya. At a December 1892 meeting organized to support the commutation of Berkman's prison sentence, Goldman found herself attracted to Ed Brady, an erudite Austrian anarchist, seventeen years her senior, recently released after serving eight of a twelve-year sentence to hard labor in Vienna for distributing anarchist literature.

Although no extant letters between them have been located, Goldman wrote about Brady extensively in her autobiography, and her comrade Harry Kelly eulogized him in 1903 in the London monthly *Freedom,* as "one of the kindest hearts that ever beat . . . the movement has lost a tower of strength in his death." Goldman lived with Brady from 1893, then after her release from Blackwell's Island prison in 1894, to early 1899, casting him off because of his intermittent possessiveness, both of her activities and of her other involvements. She resumed their friendship in 1901 when she needed his companionship. Brady proved to be among the most influential of her lover-mentors, fostering her political and cultural education as well as her sexual maturation. Among the many gifts their relationship bequeathed to her was an introduction to, and lifelong love of, literature. Goldman found him "the most scholarly person I had ever met" and praised him as "a born teacher [whose] patience was boundless"; he was also a masterful cook.[47] Her six years with Brady, from ages twenty-four to thirty, provided the steadfast, though stormy, environment for her young womanhood.[48]

Brady's office supply business, which she helped promote during the spare moments she snatched away during her lecture tours, often provided a material cushion for their political work. In spite of his personal longing for convenient domesticity, their shared political vision—especially Brady's commitment to the efforts to free Berkman and to act as Goldman's comfort and support when she too was in jail or on the road lecturing—provided a critical and sustaining frame for the early period of her political engagement.

The young Emma Goldman's decade-long initiation into political activism was one of

---

47. *LML,* pp. 115–116, 118.
48. See *LML,* p. 151. Other intimacies and flirtations cushioned this time of Goldman's life. Their stories are interwoven in her autobiography, veiled with suggestive inferences to love and true passion.

complete immersion—sometimes harsh, sometimes dazzling, a dramatic rite of passage into an uncertain world. She responded with all her energy and passion to a call to battle in a terrain of seemingly infinite possibility.

HISTORICAL CONTEXT AND NARRATIVE GUIDE TO THE DOCUMENTS

A noisy 1892 labor demonstration sets the action for the first volume, *Made for America, 1890–1901.* The loud cacophony of immigrants shouting in German, Yiddish, Russian, and English greet Emma Goldman, already reputed for her eloquence, as she mounts a cart to shout her message, only to have her platform hitched to a horse by an opposing faction. Socialists, determined not to let anarchists speak that day, pull her out of earshot. Almost comically, the newspaper account mocks Goldman for continuing her tirade in vain, fading into the distance.

The sharp focus on Goldman does, in fact, recede as the front-page coverage of Alexander Berkman's failed assassination attempt on Carnegie steel plant manager Henry Clay Frick unfolds. Unfortunately, a police seizure and purging of personal papers that chronicled the years preceding Berkman's act also interrupts the documentary trail of Goldman's debut into a life of political engagement. Thus, the first volume of the selected edition of Goldman's papers has a later-than-desired point of entry.

AFTERMATH OF THE *ATTENTAT*

While the mainstream press cranks out details of Berkman's *attentat,* an internal feud breaks out among anarchists in what became the U.S. movement's most sensational and hotly debated political stories of the era. Did Berkman's act weaken the movement and leave it more vulnerable to suppression? Did the intent of Berkman's act succeed in delivering a blow to the system of wage slavery even though it was a tactical failure? Was it a pivotal case in point of the complex distinction between the concept and reality of the anarchist tactic of "propaganda by the deed"? Was Berkman out of step with American labor and the hold of American economic and political forces? Or was Berkman a hero, a martyr for the cause of labor—the "Brutus of the 19th century" (see "Emma Goldman in London," Article in *Liberty,* October 1895), a man who had the courage to depose a tyrant and willingly risked his life to avenge the deaths of striking workers? Was he the victim of slanderous attack by Johann Most, a man whose dominance as a strategist for the international anarchist movement had been eclipsed temporarily by Berkman's individual act of violence? Did personal animosity or political difference obscure the subtlety of Most's critique—his praise of Berkman and simultaneous condemnation of his act? Intermingled with reports and opinion pieces in the German anarchist press is Most's position statement, "Attentats-Reflexionen," a portion of which is published here for the first time in English translation (see note 1, Letter to *Der Anarchist,* 30 July 1892). Goldman, though later known for her compassion, makes Most, her former lover, the target of her unmitigated fury. She attacks Most's arguments as the pathetic ravings of a jealous old man, a "miserable coward, a liar, a dissimulator, and above all a weakling." She counsels against cultivating "such demagogues, who through us and our pennies become 'great men'" and warns that because of such personages, "the movement will be hampered and the ruling class will triumph" (see Letter to *Der Anarchist,* 30 July 1892).

Goldman's relentless campaign to win support for Berkman—her determined attempts to shorten his prison sentence, ease his load, and educate the public about what she contended was the heroic dimension of his act—dominates her life during this early period. Her distinctive voice and her potential contribution to the theoretical debates raging around her were muted by her concrete engagement with Berkman's plight. Letters from Berkman, often sent *sub rosa* to avoid prison censors, were cherished items from which Berkman later wrote *Prison Memoir of an Anarchist* and testaments to the sustaining power of their friendship as well as chronicles of their struggle to melt the cold iron bars of his cell with their love. He wrote of her "affectionate letters" to him as "the only break in the terrible sameness. . . . With closed eyes I sense its weight, like the warm pressure of your own dear hand, the touch reaching softly to my heart, till I feel myself lifted across the chasm into your presence. The bars fade, the walls disappear" (see Letter from Alexander Berkman, 18 November 1892). Berkman, who identified with political martyrs and with the heroes and heroines of Russian novels, wondered "What will become of me, I don't know. I hardly care. We are revolutionists, dear: whatever sacrifices the Cause demands, though the individual perish, humanity will profit in the end. In that consciousness we must find our solace" (see Letter from Alexander Berkman, 18 November 1892). The dark side of such confident declarations was his inner "terror," the reckoning with the possibility that it might be all for naught—"reality seized me and I was swept by a paroxysm of anguish" (see Letter from Alexander Berkman, 30 November 1892).

Goldman tried (as did the anarchist Voltairine de Cleyre), often to no avail, to counteract Berkman's bouts of depression—a condition born of both circumstance and temperament. Just when he seemed to be sinking beyond rescue, the companionship of his co-conspirators and fellow prisoners, Carl Nold and Henry Bauer, assuaged his pain. Nold and Bauer, German activists in Pittsburgh's eight-hour workday movement, had been sentenced to five years in the same prison as Berkman for distributing an incendiary manifesto to the Carnegie steel plant workers at Homestead. Together, this trio created a secret magazine, *Prison Blossoms*—excerpts of which have been translated from German and published in English in this volume for the first time. The three anarchists differentiated themselves from other inmates by describing themselves as those who "suffer for an ideal" and coined the term "political prisoner" (see Letter from Alexander Berkman, 4 March 1893). Years later, in 1918, Goldman and Berkman would launch the League for Amnesty for Political Prisoners, a contentious campaign to persuade prison officials to deliver mail to them addressed as "political prisoners" even though the government claimed that there were no political prisoners in the United States.

Goldman built on the broad appeal of this concept as a strategy for strengthening support for Berkman in Pittsburgh, the site of his trial and the seat of government officials with the power to grant a pardon or shorten his sentence. Berkman's eloquent and heartrending letters chronicling the experiences of his first incarceration and the couple's attempts to see each other punctuate the narrative of the first volume of this documentary history. Berkman writes to Goldman as his "Immutable," "Sister Sonya," his "beloved sailor Girl," and "Musick" and she to him as her Russian "Tolsogub," her man with sensual thick lips. His prison letters are remarkable documents—poignant examples of the contrast between censored and uncensored, messages coded and encoded, modulations of tone calibrated to a multiplicity of potential readers—and are a tribute to the continuity of intimacy in the face of the enforced separation of prison. Berkman's letters to her indicate that in hers to him (which sadly were lost or confiscated by prison authorities), Goldman had repeatedly sent assurances that his isolation would not drag on and tried to distract him with tales of her engagement in the events on the outside, especially in correspondence that eluded the pen of prison censors. Yet, "the injustice of the law" and the prison system which "breeds rottenness" (as her own experience would prove) cast an ominous shadow on this daunting period of Goldman's life (see "My Year in Stripes," Article in the *New York World,* 18 August 1894).

GLARING POVERTY: ARRESTED FOR URGING THE POOR TO DEMAND BREAD

Goldman's letters to others during this early period provide glimpses of her daily routine, working twelve hours a day at a sewing machine as the country sank into the depression of 1893. Massive unemployment and a bankrupt U.S treasury made the possibility of the government's collapse not so distant a threat. She noted that funds for anarchist propaganda were drying up; for example, *Der Anarchist* (which had moved from St. Louis to New York) closed its presses (see Letter to Max Metzkow, 27 June 1893).

Glaring poverty, the sight of the throngs of unemployed, and the ostentatious few who held the bulk of the nation's wealth catalyzed Goldman to gradually begin speaking out against injustice—to take the risk of standing again on the speaker's platform and reclaiming her nascent political voice, shedding the fears of public censure raised by her association with Berkman. The mood of the country was changing, and the forces of labor activism strengthened in this time of desperation. The dedication on 25 June 1893 of a monument erected on the gravesite of the anarchists of the Haymarket affair drew a crowd of 8,000—even attracting many foreign delegates attending the world fair in Chicago. The decision, on the day after the commemoration, by Illinois governor John Peter Altgeld to unconditionally pardon the remaining Haymarket anarchists and to condemn their legal proceedings as a case of judicial murder, signaled a crack in the system and broke the hold of what otherwise had seemed like a monolithic enemy.

Labor took this as a message of hope, but conservators of order feared that the government was becoming too lenient. Massive demonstrations by the unemployed were raucous gatherings of men and women predominantly under the age of twenty-five and primed to take to the streets and demand work and food. In August 1893 in New York City, in this charged atmosphere, Goldman addressed a crowd of over 5,000 and urged them to demonstrate before the palaces of the rich and demand bread, directing them to take it, as their "sacred right," if it was denied.

Each newspaper account of her speech reflected the bias of the beholder.[49] The reporters of the *New-Yorker Staats-Zeitung*, describing the crowd as "professional agitators, fanatics, utopians and demagogues," misleadingly presented the portion of Goldman's talk in which she linked anarchism to the American liberal tradition as if it were a transcription: "'This is the land of Thos. Jefferson, John Brown, Abe Lincoln,' shouted the loudmouth in bad English, 'and in it hundreds of thousands are crying out for bread. If those men could witness this meeting, they would blush in shame. The rich live splendidly and in their pleasures and their women have everything that the heart desires, but the wage slaves are worse off than the colored people in the time of slavery. These bad times are not due to the silver crisis, they have other roots. You demand bread, and if you cannot acquire it through peaceful means, you will get it by force. Unite and take it by force, if you cannot get it peacefully'" (see "Badly Advised," Article in *New-Yorker Staats-Zeitung*, 22 August 1893). Her words, and those of the others who spoke that day, were considered grounds for arrest. Police stopped her in Philadelphia as she was about to address a rally of the unemployed, extradited her, and forced her to face her accusers in New York. The characteristically extreme language of nineteenth-century law displayed in the police affidavit offers a glimpse into the government's demonized projections: "one Emma Goldman being an evil disposed and pernicious person and of turbulent disposition, together with divers other evil disposed and pernicious persons to the number of fifty and upwards, unlawfully, wickedly and maliciously intending and contriving to disturb the public peace, and to excite the citizens of this State to hatred and contempt of its government and laws, and to raise and make riots, routs and unlawful assemblies within this State . . . with force and arms . . . did threaten to take steal and carry away the goods, chattels and personal property of the good citizens of the State of New York, and did make other wicked, malicious unlawful threats" (see Police Affidavit, 25 August 1893).

She responded in German, in the New York City–based anarchist communist newspaper *Die Brandfackel*, with vituperative invectives to match the pitch of her accusers. Angry at "the fact that the ruling class in America has been committing the most despicable acts and most shameless assaults upon the working people using the so-called liberal institutions of a republic as a cover," she warned that she would find "other ways and means to open the eyes of the people and speak to them so that the hearts of the capitalist Caesars of America will tremble; I will yet rip the mask of lies from the faces of this cowardly band" (see "The Right of Free Speech in America," Essay in *Die Brandfackel*, 13 September 1893). Outraged at being arrested for attempting to organize the unemployed in a time of extraordinary hunger, Goldman compared the wretched state of free expression in the United States to the despotism of Russia—a theme that would echo throughout her life in her many commentaries on the subject. In fact, all of Goldman's early pleas for free speech were tied to a virulent critique not only of police repression,

49. See "Badly Advised," Article in the *New-Yorker Staats-Zeitung*, 22 August 1893, note 7, for a slightly different account of the *New York World*'s Goldman's speech delivered in German.

but of capitalism itself. She believed that challenging ideas were kept away from the laboring masses, ignorant of their plight. Only later did Goldman intermittently de-emphasize this in order to solidify free speech as a right in the interest of the middle class—as well as for the poor.

NEWSPAPER'S RISING STAR EXPOUNDS ON GOLDMAN'S VIEWS

The dark side of government harassment was countered by the bright prospect of trans-forming negative attention into an opportunity to communicate ideas to the general pub-lic. Interest in her trial grew in tandem with remarkable publicity. Goldman had become a celebrity, a fate sealed by the publication of Nellie Bly's exclusive front-page interview in the *New York World*. Goldman's published remarks roused a growing movement of women drawn to but often not completely satisfied with suffrage solutions; later news-paper coverage indicates that Goldman eventually attracted the lively edge of the liberal reform mainstream who flirted with radicalism and bohemianism and often were dis-couraged by the many compromises inherent in their own programs for gradual change. Among the many facets of Bly's article was a psycho-political explanation of the roots of Goldman's identity as a revolutionist, going back to her childhood in Russia. Goldman told the journalist that self-interest rather than altruism was her motivating force: "I am an Anarchist because I am an egotist. . . . I never hurt a man in my life, and I don't think I could . . . what others suffer makes me suffer." Addressing the issue of greed and big business—often commenting on what she called "commercial theft," Goldman made the astute assessment that stock exchange boards were merely a format for "respectable" commercial gambling.

She also answered the questions most frequently asked of anarchists—where they stood on issues of God ("I believe in nature, nothing else"); work ("No one is lazy. They grow hopeless from the misery of their present existence. . . . [If] every man would do the work he liked, and would have as much as his neighbor, so [he] could not be unhappy and discouraged"); crime ("We do not grant there is anything to steal, for everything should be free"); marriage, love, and childrearing ("Let there be nothing but voluntary af-fection and there ceases to exist the prostitute wife and the prostitute street woman. . . . Mothers who would rather do something else than care for their children could put them in the schools, where they would be cared for by women who preferred taking care of children to any other work"); and violence ("I don't believe that through murder we shall gain, but by war, labor against capital, masses against classes, which will not come in twenty or twenty-five years . . . until then I am satisfied to agitate to teach, and I only ask justice and freedom of speech").

Impressed by Goldman's articulate, searing responses (and her linking of wage slav-ery to domestic slavery), Bly altered her portrayal from the initial description of Goldman as just a young "little bit of a girl" to the closing description as a "modern Joan of Arc" whose imprisonment would undoubtedly be less for Goldman's "offense" than for her beliefs in anarchism. Bly also softened the usual image of Goldman with such details as a woman who loves her bath, likes her dresses "plain and quiet," but above all loves books and surrounds herself with them (see "Nellie Bly Again," Interview in the *New York World,* 17 September 1893).

EARLY BATTLES ON THE CONTESTED TERRAIN OF FREE SPEECH

The lengthy transcript of Goldman's 1893 trial for unlawful assembly and incitement to riot, with its focus on the intent and exact wording, in English and in German, of Goldman's speech at the demonstration of the unemployed, is a remarkable document—among the most telling cultural and political remnant in the collection. Framed by urban industrialization, it is a window through which to view class tensions in the United States. The transcript conveys the tone of the era—of labor and politics, of the creative mix of mostly non-English-speaking immigrant cultures, of the omnipresent undercurrents of violence at labor demonstrations where both angry revolutionaries and club-wielding police exchanged blows. In the urban milieu of New York City, Goldman could simultaneously address a huge crowd and still try to hide her revolutionary words from the skulking presence of government stenographers by speaking in her native German tongue. The varied statements of the witnesses demonstrate the phenomena of conflicting perceptions of those who attended the same event, whether on the side of the police or of the anarchists. Each person's testimony is a cultural artifact of its own. In telling his story, the first detective made sure to emphasize the negative impact of Goldman's speech—urging the hungry to demand bread—as witnessed by the excitement of the crowd: "hats were waved in the air" ("People vs. Emma Goldman," Excerpt from Trial Transcript, 4 October 1893). Even the repetitions in the proceedings, with defendants each giving their own version of the same Goldman speech as well as their perceptions of the responses of the crowd, and the cross-examinations of each witness, form the basis of an interesting meditation on history, memory, and perception—and on what constitutes truth in the context of unjust law. The perceived threat of an anarchist using the metaphor of the hungry demanding bread to represent the idea of taking action against depravity was reminiscent of the French anarchist Louise Michel's incendiary speech of 1883, and of the book, *The Conquest of Bread,* by Peter Kropotkin, that had just been published in 1892.

Goldman's testimony, and those of her close associates Ed Brady and Claus Timmermann (Timmermann received a six-month sentence stemming from the same event), deepens the picture, not only of the event, but also of her life—as does the hectoring voice of her prosecutor. Goldman testified "in her own behalf, that she lived in this country eight years. She had delivered many public speeches in this country. She was in the habit of preparing her speeches and committing them to memory. She had written out the German speech that she delivered on the night of the 21st of August, 1893, and she had memorized it. She had made notes of the English speech that she delivered on that night, before she went to the meeting. There was not very much difference between the English speech and the German speech. She had been requested by several of the unemployed to speak at that meeting. She saw Detective Jacobs at the meeting. She had heard the testimony of Detective Jacobs, on the stand; she denied everything that he said, it was not true" ("People vs. Emma Goldman," Excerpt from Trial Transcript, 4 October 1893).

The feverish pitch on both sides of the political spectrum mirrored the mood of outrage and defensiveness in a country permeated by disparities of wealth during the 1893 depression and the false premonition among some contemporary anarchists that another revolution, of the same historic proportions that swept France and America in the late eighteenth century, was imminent. Goldman astutely surmised that until that day (which she earnestly estimated would come to pass by 1915), she would focus the attention of her public work on education—for which free speech was critical. In her concluding testimony, speaking in her own defense, Goldman championed freedom—and free speech—as a basic human desire. "The striving for freedom is not the creature of my brain, nor that of any other being; it lies rooted in the people, and the contentions of the past, the struggles between the people and their oppressors, show but too plainly that the people are desirous of being freed from their burdens." Her testimony was as much directed to journalists whose reports might sway the public as it was to the jurors already prejudiced against her. She pleaded that "The press misrepresented anarchists, by trying to represent them as murderers, thieves and robbers, and as if they were only desirous of taking all the money of the capitalists and putting it in their own pockets" (see "People vs. Emma Goldman," Excerpt from Trial Transcript, 4 October 1893). Goldman believed that she spoke for working people who were ignorant of the causes of their plight but whose applause marked their approval of her ideas (see "The Law's Limit," Article in the *New York World,* 17 October 1893).

As he pronounced the guilty verdict, the judge underscored his pride in American institutions, acknowledged Goldman as "a woman beyond the average in intelligence," and expressed his relief that "only a few, compared with the great number of our citizens . . . believe in your doctrines." In a speech Goldman had prepared but did not deliver in court, Goldman reflected bitterly on her eight years of fighting for justice in America and on her guilty sentencing for making "the ruling masses uncomfortable" for showing the workingman "the real reason of their misfortune"; she spoke out against the "state of 'order'" achieved by "the Winchester rifle and Gatling gun" pointed at laborers who dare to devise a "means to remedy their need." In a parting invective hurled at the court, she ended her prepared statement by echoing the words spoken by Louis Lingg upon his sentencing at the conclusion of the Haymarket trial: "I tell you, the day of reckoning is not far—a time when no concessions will be granted to the tyrants and despots. . . . You have convicted me, you may pass sentence of imprisonment upon me, but I tell you that I hate your laws [and] your 'order,' for I know but one 'order'—it is the highest potency of order—Anarchy" (see "The Law's Limit," Article in the *New York World,* 17 October 1893).

In this early period, before the groundswell of political pressure forced the government to provide federal protection of the right of free speech, the definition of the right was pliant and arbitrary. In this volatile atmosphere, it was no surprise that Goldman was found guilty. Unraveling the legal doctrine behind Goldman's verdict—the myriad definitions of unlawful assembly, of liberty and license, of what constitutes inciting a riot—is a fascinating point of entry into the dramatic battles fought, before and after Goldman's case, in courtrooms and in the streets. The right to organize labor was the most hotly contested setting for the fight for free expression; threatened capitalists and industrialists both resisted, relying on the heavy hand of government authority to enforce their own interests instead of protecting workers' rights. A plethora of free speech fights rippled from the contested ground of labor unrest—and uncontrolled masses of the unemployed had already begun to riot. Goldman, among others, stood in the battlefield between labor and capital, both as provocateur and as an upholder of the inalienable right of free expression. The struggle to secure that right extended to the fight for sexual freedom, resulting in a successful alliance between liberals and radicals. It did not, however, attract the masses to the anarchist cause. Ultimately these battles succeeded in laying the foundation for meaningful guarantees across a wide political continuum for the right of free speech (see vols. 2 and 3), temporarily rescinded when the nation entered the First World War.

A controversy also swirled around the issue of printed speech. Just after her trial, the *New York World*'s coverage subverted local government censors by publishing the speech Goldman had intended to deliver at the end of her trial. Though newspapers played an important role in advancing the right to written speech when the spoken word was in danger of suppression, reporters often made a point of distinguishing their own political sympathies from the content of the anarchist speeches they helped disseminate by tagging on an undercutting comment. In her barred speech, Goldman made sure not to limit her commentary to the importance of free expression; she also mounted a direct attack on private property, the State, and the Church. The reporter noted that not long ago such invectives resulted in the martyrdom of the Haymarket anarchists, or burning at the stake, "the reward of numberless men [and women] of advanced thought," and mused, with some surprise, that the desire for freedom should still prevail. A mixed message emanated from the scandal-mongering press analogous to the judge's explicit respect for Goldman's intelligence even as he punished her for challenging the institutions that signify stability. For example, after extensive coverage of Goldman's trial, one journalist ended his article with the quote of the attorney who had withdrawn from her case: "She is like all fanatics . . . a little bit gone" (see "The Law's Limit," Article in the *New York World,* 17 October 1893).

INTERPRETER OF SOCIAL MALADIES

A counterbalance to the documents chronicling Goldman as mainstream media star, interpreter of social maladies, and the voice of conscience in America is provided by the unmediated texts of her communication with other anarchists. Her public persona differed as she moved from one political universe to another. Especially before 1893, Goldman's written language of choice was German and her most eager following were German- and Yiddish-speaking comrades. The German-language documents in *Made for America* reveal that even as Goldman adapted to the United States, she remained deeply identified with Europe and expressed herself more vociferously to the formidable immigrant non-English-speaking subculture of which she was a part. For the anarchist press, where she usually wrote in German, she was far more militant. There she could focus on political violence with a seasoned audience who appreciated the fine points of debate on bombings in Europe or strikes in the United States. She could comment about the American legal system with more vehemence. She underplayed issues of party politics, which were of concern to liberals and to the general radical left, while continuing to stress the importance of the liberal doctrine of free speech to anarchists. The many German-language articles ferreted out of short-lived anarchist journals, retrieved and translated for this edition, complement impressions of Goldman's oratorical power gleaned only from her English lectures and writings and constitute a distinct and significant fragment of the story of her public life.

PRISON MISSIVES

Among the most revealing Goldman letters written during her ten months in prison are those smuggled out away from the gaze of prison guards—sometimes torn and later reassembled or secreted out under the jackets of sympathetic prison staff or visitors to other inmates. Many of Goldman's letters were written for and published in anarchist periodicals—allowing her to remain a presence in the movement even while she was incarcerated. In these communiqués, she pointedly described the system of "class justice" to which she had fallen victim. She mocked her judge as a "hyena standing in the service of the capitalist class" and noted that he had more power to sentence people arbitrarily than would have been permissible in Russia or in Europe, places known for their intolerance of political dissent (see "American Justice," Essay in *Die Brandfackel*, November 1893). German anarchists, especially, followed Goldman's case closely and interpreted her prison sentence as an ominous signal that American legislatures had begun to mimic the draconian anti-anarchist laws of Europe.

Like many prisoners, Goldman used the time to educate herself—not only about prison conditions, but also to read political and literary masterpieces, solidify her social critique, and become more fluent in written and spoken English—gradually shedding the tell-tale trilling roll of her "r's"—and hoping to shed the greenness of the unschooled immigrant. Her friends brought her books to read; Justus Schwab sent through Ed Brady Voltaire's *Candide* and works by the American writers Walt Whitman, Ralph Waldo Emerson, Henry David Thoreau, Nathaniel Hawthorne and the English philosophers Herbert Spencer and John Stuart Mill. Even the prison library and its flirtatious librarian offered classics by women whose gender was disguised by pen names—George Eliot, George Sand, and Ouida.

Goldman was determined to extend the reach of anarchist ideas across America. Upon her emergence from New York City's Blackwell's Island prison in 1894 and mindful of the many anarchist comrades behind bars across the globe, she was intent on using the public attention directed at her release as an opportunity to educate the American public about the harshness of prison life. She hoped that by spreading stories of prison atrocities, coupled with her old refrain on the absurdity of the current state of the law on issues of free speech, she could add a new element to what seemed like an endless struggle against an escalating tide of repression. She also vowed to redouble her efforts on Berkman's behalf. In the compelling first-person narrative she sold to the *New York World*, Goldman told the story of her arrest and her life in prison—women's treatment, the inmates, the warden, the food, the work, and the chastening experience of the injustice of the law as it reinforced her faith in anarchism. She lamented that during her time in prison "I met no convicts that were at all well to do. All were poor, miserable, broken-down remnants of humanity. Reared in the streets of New York, surrounded from earliest infancy by the vilest associations, none of them is educated. All are aged long before their time by privations and poverty." She described the "female wing" with its "large mess hall, with sixty-seven cells, a large room for the chapel and a ward for the sick. The cells are short and narrow, dark and damp. A piece of canvas stretched across two irons represents the bed, two blankets, a straw pillow and a pail completed the outfit. . . . Supper consisted of a pan of greasy black liquid called 'coffee' . . . made by pouring boiling water over burnt bread. The 'ladies' of the 'hotel' seemed very hungry; they ate their portions in silence . . . not due to improvement, but to the rules, which forbid talking at meals. This was one of the hardest rules for new female boarders to obey." Describing the humiliation inherent in the system, she vowed to "defy prison and prosecution." At the same time, she acknowledged that as a high-profile inmate, Goldman was given relatively lenient treatment; she was released from backbreaking work as a seamstress, trained as a nurse, and never experienced the worst of it—although she reported that "what I had witnessed in that hospital made my blood run cold and filled me with indignation and horror" (see "My Year in Stripes," Article in the *New York World*, 18 August 1894). Compounding the physical constraints and vileness of her time, she remarked on the sadistic psychological torment inflicted on the prisoners. Her long, descriptive letter, published exclusively by the *New York World*, helped to exorcise some of the haunting feelings she so needed to shake in order to successfully reenter the world outside her prison cell and was also an immediate vehicle with which to spark public outrage at what she believed was an otherwise hidden institutional hell. Goldman used the newspaper's payment as a nest egg with which to set up an apartment with her lover Ed Brady. Disseminating information about her time in prison also served as a corrective to the mainstream newspaper's dismissive articles about the "little anarchist" published at the beginning of her imprisonment.

TALKING THE TALK, DRESSING FOR THE WALK

Goldman's descriptive account, published the day after her release from prison, hooked the public on daily news of her whereabouts and paved the way for in-depth reporting of public celebration of her release. In a *New York World* article entitled "Hailed Emma Goldman," her New York City well-wishers were characterized as a "polyglot assemblage." The newspaper reported that Goldman, in fine rhetorical form, proclaimed to a cheering crowd whose "din and racket was worse than that on the baseball field when the home nine wins out on a tied score in the last inning": "I have come back to you after having served ten months in prison for talking. If the representatives of your Government intend to prosecute women for talking, they will have to begin with their mothers, wives, sisters and sweethearts, for they will never stop women from talking" (see "Hailed Emma Goldman," Article in the *New York World,* 20 August 1894).

The press, reflecting their readers' curiosity and fear as well as a heightened interest in protest and strikers in a year when federal troops broke up the Pullman railway car strike, now was more fascinated with Goldman than ever. Newspapers were filled with blatant sensationalism, replete with vicious mockery and shameless prejudice against radicals, immigrants, and people of color, and permeated with graphic gender bias. Goldman—a woman in the spotlight, an anarchist, a Jew, and a political activist who was both eloquently appealing and terrifyingly challenging to the public—was favored more and more by journalists of all stripes as a lively subject for big-spread feature articles.

Obsessed with the details of her outward appearance, the press tried to make sense of, and find links between, Goldman's exotic personality and her provocative ideas. The newspapers produced artful line drawings, every bit as expressive as their written descriptions of Goldman and, in a parallel manner, presented caricatures of her physical traits ranging from grotesque to alluring. Always measured against the conventional scale of femininity, Goldman was even the subject of the phrenological interest of the time, with its underlying ethnic and class bias. Observations about her appearance often opened with the comment that Goldman only "professes to be a Russian Jewess," and preceded to illustrate how her particular physiognomy was characteristic of those who have an "ineradicable instinct to hold an opinion" (see "Character in Unconventional People," Article in *Phrenological Journal and Science of Health,* February 1895). The expression of surprise at her "good looks"—with reference to her light brown hair and blue-gray eyes—was as unwelcome as the invocation of negative stereotypes projected onto voluptuous Jewish women. Goldman embraced a more cosmopolitan identity but could not control the narrow public perception of her ethnicity.

The combined effect of endless ethnic insults and the public's constant judgments about her looks left her feeling vulnerable and tapped into her particular mix of insecurity and vanity. The Stockton, California, *Daily Record,* for example, noted in a 22 July 1899 article (which called her the "Queen of Anarchy") that Goldman's "appearance would indicate that in her the seeds of anarchism had been generously nurtured and developed." She met the harassment of the press's jaundiced gaze with the protective shield of stylish clothing, which she considered completely consistent with her politics, an outward signifier of creativity and daring. Journalists fetishized Goldman's sense of fashion with long descriptions such as "The modest blue serge Eton suit, with a blue muslin shirtwaist and scarf, had no suggestion of bloomers, and the light brown hair, not banged but falling loosely over the forehead and gathered in a little knot behind, was very pretty and girlish" (see "Nellie Bly Again," Article in the *New York World,* 17 September 1893)—

professing surprise that Goldman shared concerns common to other women. Newspaper articles sometimes documented her wardrobe more thoroughly than the content of her lectures. The 8 September 1897 Providence, Rhode Island, *Evening Bulletin*, for example, noted with some irony that "she's looking trim and neat in a blue dress and jaunty alpine hat as she sat in the cell" without an equal embellishment of the political issues that landed her in jail. Later, her cultivated manner of dress allowed her to "pass" among her middle-class supporters, but not without raising suspicion among the more working-class members of her audience—many of whom dressed well, but never with such extravagance.

EMBRACING THE WORKING CLASS IN ALL ITS COMPLEXITY

Goldman was an ardent champion of the working class, never wavering in her loyalty and identification, especially with the plight of immigrant labor, even as she expanded her reach to English-speaking audiences, many of whom were from the middle class and some of whom came to hear her more out of curiosity than of conscious necessity. Yet, as an anarchist, she had a complex relationship to organized labor. A firm supporter of the right to a living wage and, later, to a shorter workday, she diverged from many union activists in her basic distrust of capitalism, and of all leaders, whether labor or management, and disdained their quest for government reform and tacit acceptance of capitalism: she believed that neither the wage system, nor hierarchical management, nor the corrupting influences of power could ever be reformed.

Instead, as an anarchist with syndicalist leanings, Goldman advocated a more cooperative vision of the organization of labor, supporting the more extreme tactic of the general strike to end wage slavery and bring about a new social and economic order. Moreover, as she developed in her role as a ubiquitous gadfly, she often spoke at union halls to open forums of members receptive to a good debate. While some trade unions admired her courage and bold critique of the system, and included among their members those whose politics were completely aligned with hers, others deemed the anarchists unrealistic and too extreme, with union officials especially sensitive to the anarchist rejection of any hint of the necessity for a hierarchical structure of power. Although many labor officials differed with the anarchists on the issue of political violence, their support or repudiation was complex and surprisingly did not always coincide with a proscribed radical or conservative political trajectory. Some labor organizations preferred to distance themselves from the all-encompassing anarchist critique of capitalism, fearing that a connection with anarchism might diminish what little negotiating power the unions managed to win. In 1895, the *New York World* reported that the unexpected presence of a single anarchist in the room of a meeting of striking tailors stirred up significant discomfort. Goldman disavowed the paper's misleading reports about her engagement in the forthcoming strike and used her letter to send a message to the union tailors: "My sympathy is fully with the strikers, and I sincerely hope they will succeed in their efforts to better their condition, but they will do well not to put too much faith in their leaders or they will fail, as others have" (see "Emma Goldman's Attitude," Letter to the *New York World,* 2 August 1895).

Goldman's aversion to bosses—whether union or management—also extended to a wariness of the undifferentiated power of the masses. Goldman trusted only the free association of individuals in an environment that supported critical thinking, as she was later to write in her lectures on the drawbacks of majority rule, her critique of liberal democracy. Although she was disparaging of the inherent paradoxes of the union strategy of the American Federation of Labor—its language of economic determinism and glorification of the working class, while still advocating an elitism of skilled craft unionism and the cultivation of leadership, which she abhorred—her heart was with their struggle, and she recognized the significance of their growing strength and allied herself with the alleviation of poverty and the improvement of the quality of daily life for all working people. She found points of resonance primarily among immigrant trade unionists—especially Jewish and Italian workers. Goldman was a welcome speaker at meetings of the United Mine Workers, especially at its Italian anarchist branch in Springfield, Illinois. Between 1891 and 1901, among the many unions she spoke before was the American Labor Union in Newark, New Jersey; the Glass Blowers' Union in Monaca, Pennsylvania; the Brewers' and Malters' Union, the Painters and Decorators Union, and the Scandinavian Painters Union in Chicago, Illinois; and the United Labor League in Philadelphia, Pennsylvania. In spite of ideological differences and sporadic tensions, she marched in the 1891 May Day parade with the Working Women's Society of the United Hebrew Trade Organization, a radical confederation in which Morris Hillquit was an organizer, that had close ties to the Socialist Labor Party. She was grateful for their later loyal support of Berkman. The thriving American Federation of Labor, a moderate union of predominantly skilled workers, however, kept their distance from Goldman and the anarchists, who in turn were especially reproachful of the AFL president, Samuel Gompers, characterizing him as the epitome of conciliatory leadership. The Central Labor Unions, local councils made up of several trade unions, were varied in their radicalism; those with a considerable anarchist membership opened their doors to Goldman, especially in Boston, Massachusetts, and in Detroit, Michigan. The most prominent anarchist labor group was the International Working Men's Association (IWMA)—a federation of groups that was especially strong from 1883 to 1892. The IWMA served as a base for organizing and integrating the sometimes conflicting tendencies of the two movements—trade-unionism and anarchism—as well as providing a destination and ready audience for Goldman's many lecture tours.

The international labor movement was potentially the most powerful base of public support for Alexander Berkman's release. A new generation of workers, untainted by the controversy of the past among anarchists and union organizers about Berkman's tactics, gladly joined the campaign to mount public pressure for the reduction of his sentence—and cast him as the avenger of violence against striking workers. Many unions responded generously, including those whose gradualist tactics were unambiguously nonviolent, by offering money and influence to help Berkman's cause. Employing a strategy common to the movement, Goldman almost single handedly escalated the pressure to free Berkman by internationalizing the protest—extending her plea in person to labor groups across the Atlantic. In the summer of 1895, she set sail for Europe.

KINDRED SPIRITS AMONG EUROPEAN ANARCHISTS

Upon her arrival in London, Goldman was met with heavy surveillance. In an era when propaganda by the deed was an international phenomenon especially widespread in Europe, police spies from various countries cooperated in the hope of foiling potential aggressors. A would-be assassin often gathered ammunition in one country, attacked an identified tyrant in another country, and then fled for safety to a third country. The government made no distinction between Goldman and others they considered to be overtly violent interlopers. An official circular from the German government announced the intention of a Russian "about 26–28 years old" with "a mastery of the German language" to travel from New York to London, then possibly to Germany, cautioning against this "exceedingly dangerous person," and requesting notification of her arrival (see Official Circular of the German Government, 25 September 1895). Which nation she happened to visit mattered little to the surveillance agents in the United States, Germany, France, and Russia, who trailed her. All found her guilty by her associations with those considered the most important and dangerous anarchists of her time.

Apart from the constant shadowing, her arrival in London was full of respect and excitement, interesting meetings, and lots of intense discussion. She cast herself as an emissary of the working class in an address to a public meeting at South Place Institute (see "Emma Goldman in London," Article in *Liberty,* October 1895). Goldman reported on and analyzed the condition of workers in the United States and underscored the limits imposed by American cultural values, or lack thereof, as well as the country's unemployment statistics and history of racial and ethnic oppression. In part because she still identified strongly as a European, she exhibited keen insight into the issues of international concern. She spoke eloquently on labor to British audiences, who were impressed with her knowledge about their own struggles. Goldman articulated a vision of a working class unified across national boundaries, presaging European syndicalism just around the corner.

To solicit support from the international anarchist movement for Berkman's release, the young Goldman introduced herself to its movers and shakers—to prominent intellectuals, theorists, and activists. Among the luminaries she met were Peter Kropotkin, Errico Malatesta, James Tochatti, Augustin Hamon, and Louise Michel. Russian revolutionary exiles gathered to meet her in the apartment of Marie Goldsmith, a Russian anarchist and scientist living in Paris. In her autobiography she recounted that she even managed to fit in a nursing course on midwifery and children's diseases in the exciting cosmopolitan city of Vienna, where she attended Wagner's operas and Freud's lectures and read voraciously—especially the works of Friedrich Nietzsche, whom she dubbed in 1915 "the intellectual storm center of Europe." She quickly familiarized herself with European propaganda work and took it upon herself to report back to the American anarchist press about what she had learned (see "Eastern and European Propaganda," Letter to the *Firebrand*, 24 May 1896). Informally, she had begun to assume the role of an anarchist emissary. She and her American comrade Harry Kelly, who was sometimes based in London and traveled back and forth to the United States, invited European anarchists to visit the United States and encouraged an informal pan-national exchange.

Among the most important Europeans who would later visit her in America were the Russian anarchist Peter Kropotkin and his close associate, the English anarchist John Turner. Kropotkin's visits in 1897 and in 1901 opened new doors. His novel inclusion of ethical arguments added an important dimension to the existing economic and social theories of anarchism. Quickly adopted in the United States, Kropotkin's ideas also refined Goldman's sense of anarchism as a moral force. Interest in his lectures and curiosity about this geographer and Russian-prince-turned-anarchist, especially on college campuses in 1901, brought new money to the anarchist movement that would become the foundation of support for several groups and periodicals. Turner's 1896 tour too proved mutually beneficial; he was an eloquent spokesperson for the necessity of linking organized labor to anarchism and for the importance of a militant workers' movement. Following through on her offer to arrange Turner's lecture tour, Goldman forged new links to English-speaking American groups and began to perfect the art of managing a successful political speaking tour, with its important advance work, all skills that would serve her own long lecturing career well.

Goldman, honored to share the platform with Turner at his final New York talk, was startled but not vanquished when her nemesis Johann Most jumped out of the audience and tried to stop her from speaking. This surprise retaliation—for the incident years before when Goldman had mounted the stage to strike Most with a toy horsewhip while he articulated his disapproval of Berkman's act—was a dramatic display of Most's intention to continue to challenge Goldman's portrayal of Berkman as the avenger of labor; it was also a reminder that respect for the free expression of opposing ideas was often difficult, even among anarchists. Of the many problems Goldman faced in organizing Turner's U.S. tour, in retrospect, by far the most profound centered on the issue of free speech. The frequent difficulty in getting access to speaking venues foreshadowed the overwhelming obstacles Turner would face upon his return in 1903 in the wake of a harsh series of anti-anarchist laws; the close ties Goldman developed with him during these early years set the stage for the legal challenge of the 1904 Turner case (see vol. 2).

The survival of the anarchist press was especially important following the anarchist expulsion by the socialists from the London congress of the socialist Second International in July 1896; it was a critical time for consolidating the movement's strength.[50] With the sharp break, strategic differences especially on issues of political action and electoral re-

---

50. See Letter to Augustin Hamon, 28 April 1896, note 2, for details on expulsion of anarchists from the Second International; also see "Observations and Suggestions," Letter to *Free Society*, 22 April 1900, note 12, for a history of the many previous congresses and political splits.

form reinforced the divisions between anarchists and socialists. It was incumbent upon Goldman and other anarchists to develop a distinct synthesis of their own. She rode the tide of active participation and cooperation in the development of theories of anarchism —in print through journals and books, and in discussions at meetings, lectures, and international congresses—and joined the attempt to foster the solidarity necessary for the anarchist movement to thrive.

CAUGHT IN THE CROSS FIRE OF THE ANARCHIST PRESS

Goldman supported an array of anarchist journals, not only by contributing occasional articles and reports of her speaking tours, as well as of tours made by others, but also as a distributor and solicitor of funds. She hoped to increase the journals' circulation whenever possible, thereby expanding their loyal but relatively small readership and extending their ever-endangered shelf-life. She relied on the printed word to spread the news about Berkman's case and was grateful for the willingness of the international anarchist press to keep news about him current. Her interests were not confined solely to Berkman's defense fund. Goldman continued to take part in debates about the theory and practice of anarchism. Because she believed that unity strengthened and internal fragmentation weakened the movement, she welcomed every occasion to keep lines of communication open—a position she found easier to support in theory than in practice.

No emissary of the anarchist movement could avoid criticism from their comrades. Sparring seemed like the necessary evil of political activism; government and press detractors often seemed more tolerable than dissension within the movement. Lively debates among anarchists were an integral part of the movement's celebration of the free will and free expression of each individual. Perhaps because Goldman was willing to go the extra mile for her comrades, and believed that her honor and sense of ethics were above reproach, Goldman experienced any attack or criticism of her work very personally. Although she welcomed debate about her ideas, she was livid when *Firebrand* impugned her character by publishing a letter accusing her of misappropriating Berkman defense fund money for her personal use—she would face similar accusations throughout her political life. She wrote to the paper: "According to my understanding of Anarchist principles, those who have *never* subscribed a cent, *never cared* for Berkmann's release, have no right to ask any accounts of whomsoever, and to poke noses into other people's affairs" (see "The Berkman Fund Again," Letter to the *Firebrand*, 5 August 1896). A series of communications shot back and forth in which Goldman firmly expressed her belief that the editors should have defended her. The editors argued that since they routinely published appeals for funds, they also had an obligation to publish objections, never intending anything "personal"—claiming that they merely intended to put into practice their belief in the unlimited right to free expression. Frustrated by what seemed to Goldman as the *Firebrand* editors' intransigence under the guise of airing differing opinions (and unaware of her own contradictions on the matter), as well as her failed attempt to galvanize her supporters to write to the paper about the absurdity of such a claim, Goldman vowed that should she ever have her own journal, she would never stoop to personal attacks against other anarchists in print—a promise to which she could not completely adhere. Believing it to be counterproductive and vulgar, she closed her 5 August 1896 letter to the *Firebrand* with the prediction that if they continued in this manner "they will only put nails to their own coffin."

Yet, many anarchists dismissed Goldman's personal concerns because they too disapproved of censorship of any kind; they defended the publication of such missives as a matter of free expression, even when personal squabbles were exposed. Goldman only a few years before had sunk to similar depths in her attack on Most as Berkman's betrayer (although she still believed his transgression more profound than the petty misdeeds ascribed to her); now intolerant of such calumny, she believed that the dignity of the anarchist vision was diminished, and its champions, for whom integrity needed to be a core value, were personally insulted by bitter fighting within the anarchist ranks. Accepting criticism was never Goldman's strong point; it proved to be an unavoidable sore point that plagued her to the end.

STIRRING THE PUBLIC CONSCIENCE

In spite of this temporary setback in the pages of *Firebrand,* by 1896 Goldman had begun to hit her stride on the speaker's platform. Her 21 November 1896 lecture in Pittsburgh delivered in German to 250 "free to starve" laboring people, was proof of her growing confidence, her intellectual and political range, and her biting eloquence. In her role as public intellectual, she strove to educate and inspire. Her speeches dazzled audiences with the artistry with which she integrated ideas and events—creating a coherent picture on a political canvas of otherwise disparate elements.

The *Pittsburg Leader* reported on two wide-ranging lectures in which Goldman addressed the differences between anarchists and socialists, exposed the dynamic of class as it permeated prison walls, compared the persecution of the Jews in Russia and the United States, and critiqued electoral politics; her talk included topical jabs at President McKinley, remarking that "McKinley is also a good man, but his past record as governor is against him." She then went on to compare the threatened state of civil liberties in the United States with the tyranny of tsarist Russia. She incorporated references to Jean-Jacques Rousseau, Thomas Paine, and Thomas Jefferson, and linked their ideals to those who, like the Haymarket anarchists, "dared to advocate the rights of humanity." She noted that November was the month of commemoration for the death of the Haymarket anarchists and how the memory of the horror of their hangings seemed unbearably close. Goldman echoed the sentiment of August Spies as he addressed the jury, as she analogized their deaths to other forward thinkers who faced a similar fate: "Jesus was crucified, Huss was burned, Bruno was killed" (see "Goldman's Cry Against Society," Article in the *Pittsburg Post,* 27 November 1896). She taunted her audience, reminding them that it was less than a decade since the Haymarket hangings, and that they were only one generation away from the memory of civil war, threatening the possibility of slipping back thirty or forty years to the restoration of slavery. In this same speech in which she embraced many of the attributes of American liberal democracy, she exposed its chilling underside—its lynching, hangings, and almost medieval prison conditions (also referred to later in "The Effect of War on the Workers," Transcript of Address in *Freedom*, 20 February 1900).

In her second speech of the week, she spoke more militantly and even directly advocated the bomb thrower's "holy" act, which she believed was calculated to redress the crimes that plagued the people. Immigrant anarchists began turning to her by 1893, even before Most's death in 1906, as their spokesperson of choice. Their active participation in Berkman's defense was proof that Most's critique had not squelched her efforts.

THEORIZING THROUGH THE BARS

Goldman made every effort to keep Berkman informed about the groundswell of interest in his case, trying to lift his spirits, to offer him hope. Berkman lived vicariously through Goldman's experiences; his letters to her offer his regular comments on events on the outside. Her life, no matter how free, was never free from the haunting, harrowing images of his life in prison. Her joys and sorrows were his, and even the smallest moments of contentment cutting through his pervasive misery were also hers. He experienced the days of communication with her as "momentous [bringing] a glow into the prisoner's heart to feel that he is remembered, actively, with that intimate interest . . . your letters are so vital, so palpitating with the throb of our common cause" (see Letter from Alexander Berkman, 4 December 1896).

Prison censors intermittently denied Berkman the right to stay engaged with anarchist news by barring the delivery of anarchist papers like *Solidarity,* one among a growing number of English-language newspapers that played a critical role in reinforcing the growing anarchist communist tendency in the movement in the United States. As Goldman and Berkman refined their ideas about the theories and practices of anarchism, they also dreamed of creating a publication of their own.

WHAT IS THERE IN ANARCHY FOR WOMAN?

In 1897, Goldman published an essay on marriage in *Firebrand.* The essay reflected the ideas of the champions of sexual freedom, Ezra and Angela Heywood, editors of *The Word,* and Moses Harmon, editor of *Lucifer, the Lightbearer.* Both Harmon and the Heywoods had been persecuted and imprisoned under the 1873 and 1876 Comstock laws for advocating free love and contraception. Goldman's essay advocated sexual freedom, but as a purist she went on to label freethinkers and liberals, radicals and socialists, as hypocrites for ascribing to conventional practices in the realm of marriage and the family, no matter how radical their political ideas. She transposed the ideas of Bakunin's *God and the State* by noting the analogy of how common it was to dispel religion without relinquishing the authority of God and government, to the common practice of marriage, an institution difficult to shake, even for anarchists, who rejected sexual dominance and strove for equality in intimate as well as political life.

Goldman also analyzed love as an experience tempered by class and integrated a discussion of prostitution into her analysis of the more exalted myths about marriage, by identifying marriage as economic prostitution. In her attempt "to break the chains of mental and physical slavery," she echoed ideas from Friedrich Engels's *Marriage, the Family, and the State* when she noted that marriage relations "are the foundation of private property" and give "the man the right and power over his wife, not only over her body, but also over her actions." Declining to address "the few exceptional cases of marriage which are based on love, esteem and respect . . . [as] exceptions that only verify the rule," she boldly asserted that "conditions cannot be changed until this infernal system is abolished. . . . I demand the independence of woman; her right to support herself; to live for herself; to love whomever she pleases, or as many as she pleases. I demand freedom for both sexes, freedom of action, freedom in love and freedom in motherhood." Goldman concluded her essay with the declaration that "Marriage, the curse of so many centuries, the cause of jealousy, suicide and crime, must be abolished if we wish the young generation to grow to healthy, strong and free men and women" (see "Marriage," Essay in the *Firebrand*, 18 July 1897).

This essay, which drew on debates among anarchists in *Liberty*, was delivered also as a rousing lecture and became the kernel of many more over the years that similarly stressed the importance of consistency between public and private life. Goldman linked forward-thinking ideas brewing in radical political circles with those of the burgeoning women's movement, reminding all to beware of hypocrisy—especially as it was infused in personal relationships. Her first travel report, published in installments in the German anarchist communist paper *Sturmvogel* (Storm Bird, the title of Maksim Gorky's poem to the storm petrel—whose presence signified impending turbulence) in December 1897, detailed the persistence of local officials' attempts to suppress her talks on this taboo subject. Free love, she decreed, was freedom against slavery in the realm of the affections.

Goldman's lecture on the "new woman" has a distinctly modern sensibility. It was not only a celebration of what the new woman could and should be, with the promise of a life of freedom, but it was also a declaration of her conviction that such freedom could never be accomplished without the "new man." She counseled that the new woman movement "demands an equal advancement by the modern man" (see "The New Woman," Transcript of Lecture in *Free Society*, 13 February 1898).

She disdained the moralism of the women in the temperance movement and asserted that you couldn't make men abstain from drink by smashing saloons. She couldn't stand the self-righteousness of the suffragists, who believed that a woman in power would be superior to men and not subject to the same forces of greed and concession that go hand in hand with party politics. Countering what she considered to be the hypocrisy of protective legislation and the glorification of motherhood, as well as the misguided emulation of the male, Goldman insisted that women without equality were destined to be slaves to society (see "What Is There in Anarchy for Woman?" Interview in the *St. Louis Post-Dispatch Sunday Magazine,* 24 October 1897, and "The New Woman," Transcript of Lecture in *Free Society,* 13 February 1898). Such inequality was intensified within the institution of marriage. Few among even the most progressive circles escaped Goldman's searing critique. She challenged both the separatist and the essentialist vision—disclaiming the special status and condition of women—and proclaimed that true freedom for woman could only come through the mutual friendship of man.

On 24 October 1897, the Sunday magazine of the *St. Louis Post-Dispatch* interviewed Goldman for a front-page article entitled "What Is There in Anarchy for Woman?" This issue attracted readers across the political spectrum. Leading the story was her answer, that anarchy held out "More to woman than to anyone else—everything which she has not—freedom and equality." In an example of the gender-polarizing bias of the public gaze, Goldman was described in the same article as "in every sense a womanly looking woman, with masculine mind and courage." The twenty-eight-year-old Goldman, at the prime age for raising a family, was given free range to critique the current state of marriage and the family. She described the married woman as "the servant, the mistress, and the slave" of her husband and children, a person who not only loses her individuality but even her name. She urged women to take their place in the business world beside men, to insist on equal wages, and to demand communal care of children. Goldman articulated the importance of freedom and equality in relationships and the over-arching concept of love as a force for creating harmony in the world and at home. Although she lacked sophistication when addressing the care of children, unaware of the importance of consistency and continuity of childcare (in part because she had never raised a child), she astutely focused her attention on spreading responsibility away from the beleaguered parents to the community at large. These ideas were consistent with the many communal experiments with new variations on parenting and childcare taking place in small enclaves across the nation. She also asserted that no marriage court could control affections. And, in what must have been a response to the reporter's question on whether anarchy could get rid of heartaches, she capriciously remarked, "the human race will always have heartaches as long as the heart beats in the breast"—a sentiment echoed by Errico Malatesta in 1900.[51]

Goldman joked about the public's perceptions of the hidden dangers in her message, about being blamed randomly for bombs, and about the number of policemen who stalked her lectures, claiming to have counted up to fifty in the hall just the week before. This "priestess of anarchy" knew how to charm and inspire her readers as well as her live audiences, not to mention many of the journalists who began to feature Goldman more

---

51. Errico Malatesta, the anarchist theorist, in his essay "The Jealousy."

regularly in the columns of their newspapers as an emergent star, on a par with mainstream celebrities of the era.

FAR-FLUNG TRAVELS OF A WANDERING JEW

The "hard news" about Goldman's early tours across the country and the details of her political commentary were reported most fully in the anarchist press. Goldman's first extensive travel diary was published in the aptly and poetically named German-language periodical *Sturmvogel*. It was published in five installments from December 1897 to February 1898, stretching the customary emotional range of the paper's field reports (see "Letters from a Tour," Series in *Sturmvogel*, 15 December 1897). Her travel letters were not only full of detail about attempts by the police to suppress her talks, her many arrests along the way, entertaining commentary on her quips with boisterous audiences full of local color, but also replete with poignant descriptions of her feelings as a woman alone on the road traveling without the protection of a mate or money. Included were insider information on the various anarchists who eased her way, vignettes about Samuel Gompers, the Social Democracy of America (just formed in July 1897 with a significant number of anarchists in tow), and Eugene Debs's urging the labor conference in St. Louis to refrain from their attempt to unseat Gompers. She commented on the complacency of some coal miners, about moral zealots and pervasive Comstockery, the similarity between the plight of the farmer and the industrial worker. She added her insights into the tensions among German anarchists and expressed her desire for a more unified movement that would not only attract younger activists but also mirror modern sensibilities and popular concerns.

In her series of travel letters in *Sturmvogel*, Goldman reflects on her belief in the direct link between deeds and emotions, her struggle with the burden of the responsibility of communicating what she had witnessed as she toured the country, and her recognition of the inadequacy of words to express the world of emotions or experience. Goldman's travel writings are fascinating artifacts of a woman on the road, a "wandering Jew" with a restless, unsettled spirit, who enjoyed intermingling with new faces, habits, and was exhilarated by the raw experience of her own strengths and weaknesses, unfettered by the monotony of ordinary everyday life.

Goldman's experiences on tour serve to document the prejudices against women traveling alone. Turned away from all the local inns, she once took refuge with a respectable family, but their violent domestic squabbling impelled her to run out into the rain in the middle of the night in search of a hotel willing to house "hussies" (see letter no. 2, "Letters from a Tour," Series in *Sturmvogel*, 15 December 1897). Vivid descriptions of her experience of frequenting bars and being accosted by the gaze of sexual predators, who assumed she was there for only one reason, fueled her critique—but also played a role in creating her lifelong self-image as a woman who attracted the erotic desire of men. Her writings from the road convey a sense of playfulness, as well as outrage, at the sexual politics triggered by the spectacle of her presence.

There are many cadences to Goldman's voice in this volume. Evidence of Goldman's capacity to be both insider and outsider permeates the documents. Goldman can be observed as an outsider to the dominant culture, writing in her native German for an already militant immigrant audience—caustic and sarcastic, hurling invectives. This audience, also the readership for many foreign-language anarchist periodicals, was often a mix of Germans and Jews, drawn to the vituperative style of her German and the lyrical literary influences of her Russian roots. Some were more patient than others about her minimal facility with Yiddish, a language she considered somewhat vulgar and less eloquent than her native German, in spite of the great Yiddish literary figures who later caught her attention, especially Sholem Asch, David Pinski, and Jacob Gordin.

Especially among new immigrants, vacillation between loyalty to and ambivalence about their country and culture of origin was common. Goldman hoped to leave behind the elements of her past she identified with narrowness and conventionality. She gravitated toward German high culture with its masterpieces of literature and philosophy, as well as toward American idealism with its seeming freedom from timebound tradition, and she remained a shining star in Yiddish radical circles, the group with a familial feel that eased her way into public life in the United States. Rejecting Jewish religious orthodoxy, she nonetheless embraced the messianic fervor of her roots, the desire to correct the world, and the devotion to learning and to questioning authority engrained in the talmudic tradition of weekly scholarly and philosophical commentary and interpretation of Old Testament text and Jewish law. Most of all, she adapted the contemporary Jewish sense of the power of a people bound together by a shared vision without reliance on the formal, unifying structure of a nation state as completely consistent with her definition of anarchism. Goldman adapted a Jewish cultural norm as she extended her hammock of support beyond her biological family ties and lived out the commonly held belief that a strong community was integral to the survival of her people; she welcomed the opportunity to meet new comrades as she created circles of lasting friendship everywhere she went.

Her tours often were hosted by Jewish and German anarchists who busily performed the advance work for her lectures. Without a trace of ethnic exclusivity, they opened their homes to her and shared the kinship of a common culture and a commitment to freedom for all. Her travel writings can be read for their record of immigrant anarchist perceptions of the American interior—and as Goldman's way of providing an introduction to those who otherwise might not have the opportunity or the means to travel through the vast mysterious expanses of their chosen country.

Reporters covering her tours offered their readers colorful descriptions of town squares with "packing box" lecturers in every corner, and told of how Goldman attracted audiences away from gospel wagons and once, in Providence, Rhode Island in 1897, even from ventriloquists (see "Anarchy," Article in the *Providence Evening Bulletin,* 4 September 1897). Her own descriptions of the sparkling energy and surprising militancy of small farm-town anarchists like Kate Austin were combined with vivid evocations of the ominous tension of the cities, where in one confrontation with the police, she labeled a particularly behemoth representative of law and order as a "lard-dripping monster" (see letter no. 2, "Letters from a Tour," Series in *Sturmvogel*, 15 December 1897).

In an era when newspapers exhibited a blatant bias against the left, traveling lecturers like Goldman often served a critical role of spreading the word about the radical perspective. She spoke about issues the mainstream papers ignored, including such atrocities against labor as the Hazleton massacre where Slavic coal miners were shot from behind during a peaceful march. She portrayed the devaluation of immigrant workers and the vulnerability of strikers to violence. Skilled at illuminating international events that had an impact on the United States, she analyzed the war with Spain, various *attentats* against European rulers, and the arbitrary harshness of the Dreyfus case in France, which she believed to be reminiscent of the heavy hand of the law in the trial of the Haymarket anarchists.

Goldman, who had an extraordinary talent for creating a sense of familiarity and connection with her listeners, revealed in her travel diary her technique for personalizing an audience. She would scan the crowd for "one real, honorable and great person [like] hidden gems, who live and suffer anonymously yet give out so much light that they make a person forget for a moment the vale of tears around us" (see letter no. 1, "Letters from a Tour," Series in *Sturmvogel,* 15 December 1897). Her ability to speak so intimately to a large group called forth her disarming emotional intelligence and definitely eased the public's reception to the political bite of her message. And yet, almost in equal proportion to her success as a lecturer, Goldman experienced a profound sense of the shortcomings of relying on the spoken word to alleviate the suffering of those who faced extreme violence, who risked their lives for freedom.

IMPATIENT WITH GRADUALISM

Goldman was often as impatient with herself as she was with liberal, even socialist, strategists of reform. She cried out "like a wounded animal" in complaint about her métier for being all too gradual to tackle the enormous social, economic, and political problems at hand. She documented the mixed experience of attempting to address labor and reform groups at a conference during a major United Mine Workers' strike. By the time of this conference, the strike was nearly over, and Samuel Gompers, the president of the American Federation of Labor, had discouraged workers from attending. In Eugene Debs's presence, Goldman was prevented from speaking by the socialists.[52] When Debs, the president of the American Railway Union and chief organizer of Social Democracy of America, who had promised her the floor, did not come to her defense, she accused him of cowardice—remembering that he had confided to her in private that he identified with anarchism and had called himself her "comrade."[53] Disappointed, Goldman wrote disparagingly about Debs, positing that his political position as the leader of

---

52. T. P. Quinn, "Reflections of E. V. Debs," *Free Society*, 3 July 1898, pp. 6–7.
53. *LML*, p. 220.

Social Democracy in America evolved through tactical compromise, claiming that he "collapses like a fly in the slightest gust of wind" (see letter no. 4, "Letters from a Tour," *Sturmvogel,* 15 December 1897). At this point in his career Debs was enthusiastic about strategies for the socialist colonization of targeted areas across the country, but he quickly bent to an electoral strategy and chose to bow out of many critical conflicts within his own party. Only much later, in 1918, in the contested era of agitation against conscription law when they were both in jail, was Goldman and Debs's profound respect for each other solidified.

Even those closer to Goldman's ideology were subject to her public censure. Since 1894, when she had turned to lecturing in English to a wider audience, she realized how profoundly isolated immigrant anarchists were from the American cultural landscape. Goldman began her work as a forger of links between these disparate worlds and earnestly believed that she could help to alleviate the vulnerabilities of her "foreign" comrades. She even found herself genuinely attracted to the openness of the American dream. She lambasted German anarchists for their dogmatism, their "club" fanaticism, for withdrawing into "choral societies" and lodges of raucous drinking, for railing against and alienating the youth from the German left. Their flamboyant insularity fueled her belief that for anarchist ideas to spread in America, immigrant anarchists had to make the effort to speak and organize in English, to extend their reach beyond the radical circles bound to their country of origin.

She applauded the efforts of the anarchist communist journal *Firebrand,* whose publication she announced at the Paris congress as marking the growth of that tendency in the United States, and praised the journals *Free Society* and *Solidarity* as critical tools for the Americanization of anarchism. Gradual assimilation among immigrant anarchists, who were now more proficient in English, coupled with the demise of *Sturmvogel* (in 1899), *Die Brandfackel* (in 1895), and *Der Anarchist* (also in 1895), which left Most's *Freiheit* as the only U.S.-produced, German-language anarchist publication still in circulation, reinforced the need for a pivotal figure like Goldman to bridge the old world with the new.

In an economy of scarcity, when it was difficult to keep a publication funded and distributed, Goldman's physical presence, her face-to-face contact with a variety of audiences, and her remarkable energy and persistence created personal and political alliances that transcended the limitation of the printed word. Eventually she would cover the map of the United States, speaking in every town, especially budding urban metropolises, where an anarchist or labor group was willing and interested in hosting her. A report in *Solidarity* on 15 July 1898 estimated that from February to June of 1898, she visited 18 cities in 16 weeks. She kept up this pace over the next 22 months, holding over 66 meetings.[54] Her admirers across the country formed the fabric of support that eased

54. See Chronology for listing of cities EG visited between January 1898 and October 1899, when she returned to New York to prepare for her departure for London in early November.

her way, providing the local housing, food, and the organizational detail that were crucial to the success of her meetings.

Goldman experienced each encounter as a confrontation with the new, a welcome challenge, and the confirmation of a new openness to anarchist ideas across the nation. She was proud to perform this labor of love gratis—she would take money for expenses, even a hotel room, but vowed never to take money to propagate her vision; she later surmised that "the work of a true propagandist cannot be paid. . . . I claim that one can only give the best of one's self when actuated by love to the thing one gives, out of one's innermost desire to be useful, to oppose that which one considers wrong, and such a product of one's thoughts, nerves, blood, and the whole make-up, is above any remuneration" (see "Some More Observations," Letter to *Free Society,* 29 April 1900).

She had wedged her way into an almost exclusively male (and mostly paid) lecture circuit, crossing language barriers and extending beyond the immigrant community; she took pleasure from her role as an informal anarchist ambassador and was showered with accolades for her oratorical talents even from many who did not share her political perspectives. But, while playing to the audience and enjoying their adoration, Goldman was never naïve enough to rest on her laurels. She would later share with a reporter her ominously prophetic intuition: "I looked at the crowd that followed hurrahing for me the other night, and I said in my mind to them, 'You cheer for me, you follow me, but you'd hang me if your mood changed'" (see "A Character Study of Emma Goldman," Interview in *Philadelphia North American,* 11 April 1901). She recognized that while many were lured to her talks by their interest in, or support of, her political perspective, others were drawn primarily to the entertaining spectacle of an orator who was in vogue. Although anarchism had always been the domain of a small minority, Goldman ascertained that receptivity to anarchist ideas was as much a product of the times as it was of her own efforts.

A pointed example of her vulnerability to the shifts in the political climate came with Spain's declaration of war on the United States in April 1898, which revived the nation's patriotic front and threatened to set back its relatively new air of openness. Over the next twenty years, her consistent left critique of war as a quest for spoils by capitalists compounded with her boldness on the issue of militarism when the United States entered the First World War ultimately set the stage for Goldman's deportation. Her classic anarchist analysis on the subject was first laid before the public during the U.S. conflict with Spain and its colonies. War and adversity provided an intrepid political propagandist like Goldman with fertile ground for raising provocative and potentially unpopular ideas about the faces of the enemy: "Truth is a dangerous weapon in the hands of working men and women. Your enemy is not in Spain, but in Washington; not in Madrid, but here in San Francisco, in New York, in Chicago. I believe in holding up a looking glass before you, so that you can see and know yourselves. When you are educated, when you realize your power, you'll need no bombs, and no dynamite or militia will hold you" (see "Emma Goldman, Anarchist," Interview in the *San Francisco Call,* 27 April 1898).

REVOLUTIONARY POTENTIAL OF THE MIDDLE CLASS

Although Goldman remained loyal to the downtrodden and exploited, especially in her early years as a political activist, she would set herself apart from the traditional left in the United States by her willingness to depart from a dogmatic beholdenness to all things working class, even risking the appearance of seeming positively bourgeois in her quest for personal refinement.

Her feeling of entitlement to creature comforts, ascribing the code of deprivation to the churches, raised some eyebrows among purists in the radical anarchist ranks. In her autobiography she would celebrate her espousal of "everybody's right to beautiful, radiant things."[55] Goldman selectively incorporated an aesthetic sensibility as a life-enhancing quality best cultivated by all. She scoffed at the ascetic left's ambivalent conflation of the love of beauty with ruling-class indulgence. Drawn to the many accoutrements of leisure and privilege, Goldman appreciated refinement wherever she found it. Given this affinity, it was no surprise that eventually she would choose to introduce anarchist ideas to the middle class, and middle-class culture to the working masses.

She offered her ideas to the middle class, couching them in the language of the educated, and addressed concerns based less on money than on one's internal experience of deprivation. The ease of her reach across class lines came in part out of deference to the rise of Russian revolutionaries among the elite—the class from which she believed radicals in America would also emerge—and in part because of a desire, common among immigrants, to retrieve the respectability they had taken for granted in their country of origin. She assessed and compared her audiences—the diversity of their class, gender, and ethnic makeup, and the spectrum of their political beliefs. She was aware of the many impoverished coal miners, whose daily struggle to survive was harsh enough to prove that economic conditions alone do not foment revolutions. Goldman proclaimed that "it is useless to appeal to the overfed, but still of less use to appeal to the underfed. To be successful, we must reach the class whose brains have not yet been destroyed by starvation" (see "A Short Account of My Late Tour," Letter to *Solidarity*, 15 July 1898). She urged her comrades to disregard those who enter the movement purely to better material conditions as "a menace to the cause"—reminding them of the importance of moral, intellectual, and spiritual development that "no amount of turning social conditions topsy turvy will better" (see "Talk with Emma Goldman," Interview in the *New York Sun*, 6 January 1901). Her ideas about the positive role of modest material comfort in support of one's serving a social cause set her apart from some economic determinists and purely philosophical anarchists, and from communists who appealed almost exclusively to the working class. She, like Bakunin, saw the revolutionary potential of intellectuals and disaffected students—all those who didn't fit easily into the conventional social fabric. Goldman drew many people graced with the advantage of education and money to her lectures who otherwise might have been dismissed by some anarchists as too bourgeois to be open to radical ideas.

55. *LML*, p. 56.

Believing in the revolutionary potential of those who had been born to privilege was not a new idea for someone who had come of age in Russia, inspired by the nihilists and by the circle of gentry who joined together to kill Alexander II. Goldman's heroine, Sophia Perovskaya, who was integral to the plot against the tsar, was the daughter of the governor-general of St. Petersburg. The nihilists created a culture that strove for the unity of the intelligentsia and the laborer in the factory and field against the tyranny of tsarist oppression. Their pivotal literary heroes and heroines (who appear in Chernyshevsky's *What Is to Be Done?*) included doctors and others from an educated elite, who join together to begin a cooperative sewing shop, thus shifting their proclivity from the professional content to the form of work and privileging instead the value of communal production. Yet even as they devote themselves to the contentment of others, Chernyshevsky's characters also believe in the fulfillment of life's pleasures, especially the political and personal value of free love—the catalyst for much of the controversy around his book.

It was common for revolutionaries to cast off their association with their privileged beginnings in the service of the underclass. Peter Kropotkin was perhaps the most emblematic of this tradition, as one who had abandoned his princely title in the service of the people. Goldman admired Kropotkin's revolutionary spirit but also his refinement, and described him as "the heir of a brilliant career, with but one ideal, one purpose in life—the liberation of the human race from serfdom, from all physical as well as spiritual serfdom."[56] Goldman extracted from Kropotkin's writings a devotion to ethical as well as economic liberation that fortified her attraction to anarchism, and she placed a nobility of the spirit as among the highest value for anarchists.

Goldman matched her appreciation for nobility of the spirit with her fear and distaste for "vulgarity" (her catch-all expression for the coarse and unrefined)—a term she never associated with "obscenity" (the government's catch-all expression for the condemnation of free love and sexual deviance), which made her challenging ideas, especially about sexuality, more palpable to the middle class. Goldman reveled in the joys of sexual pleasure, in the personal courage of its expression in a world bound by oppressive convention— especially for women. Her experience as a woman shaped her perceptions and allowed her to articulate an aspect of freedom otherwise on the distant borders of acceptability not only to the general public but among the doctrinaire male anarchists as well, whose political attunement was more completely focused on the plight of the working and unemployed poor.

The *San Francisco Call* commented on Goldman's success—especially in the arena of reform relating to free speech and women's freedom. They marveled at the rapidity with which an immigrant woman not yet thirty years old, "five feet of feminine anarchy," had made an impact on the vast and varied political culture of her adopted country, while hastening to note that in past centuries such outspokenness might have resulted in being

56. EG's tribute to Peter Kropotkin on his seventieth birthday was published in *Mother Earth* (December 1912); the essay appears in vol. 3.

"boiled in oil" or "beheaded" (see "Emma Goldman, Anarchist," Interview in the *San Francisco Call*, 27 April 1898).

Freethinkers, who generally challenged God but not the State, and who, up until then, with few exceptions, also thought of anarchists as a dangerous fringe to be treated "like lunatics"[57] for their extreme anti-statism, began to offer Goldman venues for her lectures. Even conservative clubs and unions vied for her bookings—drawn to her magnetic personality and to the overlaps between her anarchist critique and the reform issues of the day. The *San Francisco Call*'s 27 April 1898 interview highlighted what they considered Goldman's more sensational observations, especially on the issue of racism when she raised the question "who does the lynching in the South, white or black?"— going a step beyond the liberal press that condemned the horrific brutality of the method of punishment but often stopped short of imagining the innocence of the victims of the lynching mob. Although anarchists clearly espoused racial equality, Goldman herself was guilty of adopting a political style that mirrored the custom of separate racial spheres of her time. Yet, in spite of this common failing, even among radicals, the barbarism of race hatred firmly set in the texture of turn-of-the-century life in the United States fueled Goldman and her circle's fury against a system that would tolerate such transparent injustice.

Fortunate to have the ear of the nation, with all the heightened press attention to her ideas, she still scoffed at any attempt to place her on a pedestal. Goldman rebuffed questions that expected her to foretell the particulars of the future, asserting that it was not her place to design a blueprint for an anarchist society: "I may be a fool [but] I am not a prophet."

CAUTIONING AGAINST THE SEDUCTION OF LIBERAL REFORM

In the seedtime of one of the most fervent eras of progressivism in the history of the United States, the moral purity of the anarchists, while serving as an admirable and indispensable antidote to what Goldman considered the duplicity and compromise inherent in the electoral process, left them isolated from the majority of Americans, who staked their hopes on progressive reform. Acting as a gadfly of conscience, Goldman was quick to note how business favors won votes, how much more the rich had to gain than the working poor from the system as it was, and how power intoxicated and corrupted the nation's leaders. Preaching strongly that "unless we bring our acts in conformity with our ideas, we will never progress, never change conditions" (see "'Ideas and Men,'" Letter to *Free Society*, 10 July 1898), Goldman continued with an assertion that no anarchist could be a "rascal"—a term she considered synonymous with "politician." And yet everywhere, including in her own ranks, she found examples of hypocrisy. The inclination to play both ends of the political continuum, the temptation to engage in electoral politics to which even anarchists were vulnerable, was, by Goldman's standards, a heinous crime, and justified the dropping of her resolve against stooping to personal attacks.

57. Robert Ingersoll publicly labeled Goldman "insane" (see Letter to *Solidarity*, 15 March 1898).

Though he denied the accusation, there raged a heated debate about the participation in the political party process by the co-founder of the anarchist papers *Freedom* and *Firebrand*, Henry Addis. The discussion reverberated through the anarchist press for six months and remained part of an ongoing debate about anarchist morality under capitalism. It raised thorny strategic issues that further splintered the movement. In an era of "reform," the lines between the various strains of the left were often blurred by good intentions, by the shared desire for a more equitable and just world—and sometimes by political opportunism. Surprising political alliances held the potential for alleviating oppressive conditions but tainted the over-arching anarchist position that "political action is a folly . . . it corrupts the people and will never set them free."

Goldman added complexity to the ongoing argument about anarchist engagement in party politics by noting that in January 1897 anarchist Saverio Merlino's declaration in *Il Messaggero,* Rome's bourgeois daily, urged electoral support of socialist and republican candidates both as a means to combat the threat to liberty represented by Italy's reactionary government and as a necessary step in deposing the reactionary regime of Prime Minister Francesco Crispi.[58] While Goldman never claimed to support Merlino's tactics, she distinguished his "good" strategic reasoning from the monetary gain Addis ostensibly received for participating in electoral politics, which, in her view, lacked any semblance of principle. Ironically, Addis claimed to have used the money from his one-time work for a politician to pay the costs of booking Goldman's speaking venue, a fact which made the debate ever more complicated—and from which Goldman recoiled.

When Goldman addressed the issue of participation in party politics to her many Jewish audiences, she likened the anarchist who advises others to vote to the Jew who employs a Christian to perform tasks that religious convention forbids on the Sabbath, sanctified as a day of rest; she argued that both are implicated in the act. This metaphor from her own culture became a common signifier of hypocrisy in her lectures and writings, although she made sure to excuse those in thrall to the "prejudice and superstition" which "knows no logic," differentiating them from anarchists who she claimed ought to know better than to mix worlds (see " 'Ideas and Men,' " in *Free Society,* 10 July 1898).

The Church too, and the distinction some Catholic priests made between deeds and words, between the innocence of thinking malicious thoughts and the guilt when acting upon them, was easy game for analogies for Goldman's notion of well-intentioned duplicity in electoral politics. During this period, Goldman began to develop her thinking on religion and hypocrisy for what would in 1913 be expanded into a formal essay entitled "The Failure of Christianity."[59] She directed many of her comments to her earlier lecture hosts at Liberal Clubs, havens for discussion of freethought, whose organizing premise was distinctly anti-religious. In a fascinating aside, Goldman refers to Christ as a re-

58. See " 'Ideas and Men,' " Letter to *Free Society,* 10 July 1898, notes 1, 4, and 5, for contextual detail on Merlino's involvement in the election in Italy.
59. Her essay, plus a second one on the topic of hypocrisy, were published together as a pamphlet entitled *Victims of Morality and the Failure of Christianity, Two Lectures* (New York: Mother Earth Publishing Association, 1913).

former with advanced ideas based on sentiment and not reason; this comment won the praise of the prominent liberal letter writer F. B. Livesey, although she later clarified her preference for modern reformers whose philosophy is based on both sentiment and reason, and leaves "no room for gods, devils or their emissaries" (See Letter to the *Detroit Sentinel,* 25 July 1898). Thus, the notion of intelligent consistency took precedence in Goldman's lexicon of respect, confirming the influence on her understanding of anarchism as a product of the Enlightenment, with its belief in progress born of reason.

This pursuit of the rational was not synonymous with an endorsement of the system of compulsory education. From Goldman's perspective, schools were the training ground for the docility necessary to become a cog in the wheel of industrial capitalism. Furthermore, public education's general program and standards left too little time to accommodate "the individual abilities and inclinations of . . . pupils." She insisted that the concept of compulsion and learning were antithetical, and that the goal should be the nurturance of "thinking and reasoning young men and women," not the creation of "automatic machines" (see Letter to the *Detroit Sentinel,* 25 July 1898). These ideas formed the kernels of her later work for the Modern School movement and of her emergent critique of conventional notions of higher education, a popular critical trend in the United States and in Europe.

In the 1890s, militant anarchists dominated New York City's urban radical landscape but could never gain a mass footing across the nation. As the Socialist party gradually gained momentum, tapping into the desire for a more moderate electoral approach to social change, the anarchists' rejection of gradual reform as well as their acceptance of the inevitability of violence relegated them to the fringes of the radical movement. The tactics of militancy and violence that had been central to much early labor union activism were steadily displaced. Although Goldman and many anarchists often used the term "socialist" interchangeably with "anarchist," she was especially disparaging about the emergent Socialist party in the United States. Goldman castigated its leadership for excluding her in fear that she might dissuade its members from taking the electoral route or spur challenges to their labor negotiation policies. She often repeated her disappointment at Debs's failure to stand up to the socialists on her behalf at an early stage of his political career as emblematic of the compromise his position entailed as the emerging leader of Social Democracy of America, even for a man of vision and integrity.[60] Such personal schisms, which only time and shared political hardship could dispel, and the many internal battles within the left, influenced the evolution of radicalism in the United States.

The value Goldman placed on critical thinking extended to the political organizations of her time, which, like many socialist-dominated union groups, often shunned any as-

---

60. See "A Short Account of My Late Tour," Article in *Solidarity,* 15 July 1898, note 2, for a history of the formation of the Social Democracy of America; also see "Gives Her Side," Letter to *Free Society,* 31 July 1898, note 1, for the detail on Debs's reneging on a promise.

sociation with anarchist ideas and allowed only for discussion of their own political perspective. Goldman, who had come to anarchism from a European context (before the 1896 expulsion of anarchists from the International), at a time when the boundaries between anarchists and socialists had been more permeable, ironically, witnessed its most intense period of differentiation and fragmentation. In the 1890s, a debate between an anarchist and a socialist was often as entertaining as it was edifying. Outsiders, for whom the identities of the two groups merged, were incredulous to witness the level of ire and insult each hurled upon the other.

As Goldman became a more seasoned lecturer, she refined her amazing ability to judge character and to quickly size up the personality of the cities and towns along her route. The observations interspersed in her political travel reports make marvelous additions to the study of local history in America. She calibrated her talks accordingly. The discovery of pockets of openness infused her with the hope that the essence of anarchist ideas could act as a tonic against narrowness within and outside the movement. In 1898, her source of optimism came from the West Coast, where audiences seemed much less dogmatically sectarian and "not so much in the grip of politicians, bigots and hypocrites as the East. Sunday laws, moral laws, laws prohibiting speech in the open air, etc., are little known in the far West, and I hardly think ever will be. This alone makes life pleasanter on the Pacific than here, where every [policeman in a] bluecoat exercises the power of a Czar" (see " A Short Account of My Later Tour," Essay in *Solidarity,* 15 July 1898).

A WAVE OF ASSASSINATIONS, A SEA OF POLITICAL REPRESSION

By the fall of 1898, acts of political violence by anarchists returned with a vengeance. The world was abuzz with news of assassinations—which in the last several years included the shooting of the Spanish prime minister Antonio Cánovas del Castillo by the young composer Michele Angiolillo, the killing of the French president Marie François-Sadi Carnot by Sante Caserio, and the murder of the Austrian empress Elizabeth by Luigi Luccheni. Goldman was in the hot seat once again, called to unravel the complex philosophical strands that tied anarchism to individual acts of terror. Her support of such acts was predicated on the concept of retaliation. She repudiated the attack on the Austrian empress, a woman she considered "harmless, unhappy and not unkind" who had never been directly responsible for any atrocities and was the victim of a misdirected young man, himself "a product of present economic, political and social injustices" "who . . . did not know father or mother." Somewhat callously, Goldman refused to accept any presumption that such acts committed by "social outcasts" could mar the grandeur of the philosophy of anarchism any more than "the moon can dim its splendor at the barking of a dog" (see "New York Anarchist Leaders Denounce the Murder of Austria's Empress," Letter to *New York World,* 18 September 1898). Like a mantra, she repeated her position, always asserting that political repression breeds its own violent antagonists. In a 25 July 1898 letter to the *Detroit Sentinel,* she warned that the chilling effect of Comstockery (the suppression from the mails of anarchist literature under Post Office official Anthony

Comstock's definition of "obscenity") on free speech and a free press, by diminishing a common belief in the use of the pen as "anarchy's best weapon," might create the desperation that breeds acts of violence. Yes, anarchism stood for "peace, safety and liberty, and does not recognize the right of one to rule, injure or coerce the others," but she also believed that in an era of violent injustice, counterviolence was inevitable. She articulated her belief, which she shared with Kropotkin, that revolutionary violence was part of the natural process of change: "We might as well fight against cyclones, earthquakes, tornadoes, lightning and other phenomena, as to fight against individual acts of violence. They have been and will be as long as we retain the causes which produce them; and I look upon such occurrences as warnings of the coming danger to the tyrants of the world" (see Letter to the *Detroit Sentinel,* 25 July 1898).

As the nineteenth century drew to a close, Goldman found an opportunity for reaching a wider audience primed to think about history. Goldman's letter to the *Detroit Sentinel* includes this warning about the future: "every anarchist is also a student of history, and as such he or she must recognize that the ruling classes have never granted privileges to the oppressed until forced to do so by the latter . . . the struggling masses of the present century can expect nothing from their masters, and if they want to change their conditions and bring about a state of society in which no one shall enjoy the toil of his fellow man they will only succeed through social revolution, never through peaceful methods" (see Letter to the *Detroit Sentinel,* 25 July 1898). Goldman's assumption that positive change for the working people would be predicated on bloodshed underestimated both the co-optive power of modern capitalism in the United States, the force of organized labor, and the persistant circumvention of repressive law.

EFFORTS TO FREE BERKMAN

Goldman learned to navigate the legal system to find a ruling that might lessen Berkman's prison sentence, but she refused to supplicate on his behalf. Documents issued by the Berkman Defense Association illustrate the persistence of the group's attempts to move "heaven and earth" to have him pardoned, even devising a way to contact Andrew Carnegie himself through Benjamin Tucker, the editor of *Liberty.* The Berkman committee refused Tucker's draft letter of repentant supplication, recoiling at his characterization of Berkman's *attentat* as "a foolish act of barbarism," rejecting his twists of phrase, most notably "they come here to-day in an attitude of sincere repentance, no longer as reformers, but as reformed, and asking for liberty as a reward of their reformation." This insiders' exchange documents the fault lines and fissures that ran through American anarchism, the premium on saving political face, maintaining loyalty to the significance of an act of violence in spite of its dire consequences, and on the value of personal integrity within the movement, even as it attempted to "work the system" it opposed, on Berkman's behalf (see "An Undelivered Speech," Exchange of Letters in *Liberty,* January 1899). This strategy proved to be the last effort to free Berkman legally—the next action of the defense committee would be the gathering of clandestine support for his breakout attempt from prison.

A VOICE FOR ANARCHISM

By the end of the 1890s, Goldman was probably the most proficient spokesperson in the United States to the general public for the core values of the vast and misunderstood spectrum of anarchist ideas, as well as a fount of intellectual engagement with her own comrades. Among Goldman's most popular lectures was "Authority vs. Liberty," in which she anticipated and answered common questions as well as defined pivotal terminology about anarchism. Ironically, after delivering three other lectures on anarchism in Barre, Vermont, in January 1899, she was barred from giving her fourth talk, on the topic of suppression of liberty by authority. Circumventing the ban by utilizing the right to free written speech, a transcript of her talk was circulated in Barre, and Abe Isaak took the liberty to publish the full text of her lecture in his 5 March 1899 issue of *Free Society*. In the lecture, Goldman declared: "Everything good and noble, grand and beautiful, wise and useful, has been done by the spirit of liberty, from the love of freedom, in spite of and in the teeth of government and authority. When man will have recovered from the effects of authority, when he will understand that freedom is the most precious thing, when he will be free to live, to work, to act, to develop, to enter into social relations with whom he is in sympathy, then warfare, conquests, robbery, theft, corruption, poverty and all the ornaments of the State, all the burden of authority will be looked upon as relics of barbarism." She defined the concept of authority with complexity and not entirely negatively, affirming the positive authority of ideas in science, art, and literature that command respect—an idea that already had been posed by Bakunin in *God and the State*. What she objected to was authority in its manifestation as forceful suppressor of her speeches: "behind your chief of police are the clubs and pistols of your policemen; and it is this brutal force that makes authority a curse to humanity." She blamed the government for instilling hatred for anarchism and anarchists, for spreading the impression that anarchism was antithetical to the best interests of the people. With Berkman in mind, she predicted that one day her audience would realize that it was the anarchists "who at the risk of their own lives and comforts try to free you from the clutches of your masters" and that the anarchists' philosophy was "based on that stern, undisputable logic that liberty is just as necessary for man as air, light and food" (see "Authority vs. Liberty," Transcript of Lecture in *Free Society*, 5 March 1899).

Goldman ultimately believed that anarchism embodied the highest form of personal and political evolution. To a reporter from the *Detroit Evening News*, Goldman even made a characteristically provocative link between class privilege and educational attunement to affinity for anarchist ideas. She defined an anarchist as "a person of higher independence—not the commonly mistaken enemy of law and order." She posited that "the higher the education of a class, the more anarchists it contains. Doctors, lawyers, professors, newspapermen, many of these are anarchists, but they dare not, perhaps, declare themselves. Even the freest man is tied to his surroundings. We are dependent upon one another, therefore we must make concessions. Yes, personally, I believe we should all have the courage of our convictions, but I would not condemn as cowards those who do not have that courage" (see "An Interrupted Interview," Interview in the *Detroit Evening News,* 14 March 1899).

The press, especially liberal journalists who may have secretly identified with elements of Goldman's political philosophy, either romanticized the exotic aspects of the life of the bohemian left or sometimes indulged in tongue-in-cheek disparaging descriptions. A *Detroit Evening News* interview characterized Goldman as "a strange little woman who was born out of the social conditions of the period" and described her surroundings in novelistic detail: "in a rear room of the Hotel Randolph late last night [a] few choice spirits had gathered to celebrate the visit of their guest of honor—their doctrinal saint—Emma Goldman. The incense of cigarettes were burned before her shrine. Long-necked, dark bottles gave forth pale Rhine wine, and white-aproned waiters carried in flagons of foaming beer. These people were Bohemians in all the sense conveys. Their simple, unrestrained enjoyment shamed the artificial apings of their American cousins. They lived in the land of Lotus, where carping care is left on the border, and all within is sunshine and happiness." A chorus of German anarchists interrupted Goldman's interview intermittently, singing verses such as "Where there are happy songs, settle down calmly / Wicked people have no songs" (see "An Interrupted Interview," Interview in the *Detroit Evening News,* 14 March 1899), thus demonstrating once more that anarchists lured new recruits not only for their high ideals but also for the fun and sense of abandon that was so much a part of the culture of freedom.

The 15 July 1899 edition of the *Oakland Enquirer* heralded the arrival of Emma Goldman as "a real live anarchist . . . who might be taken for a college student or an exponent of suffrage. She is of medium height, with hair tending toward the Titian, with strong features and wears eyeglasses. She speaks with a considerable vehemence and a foreign German accent." According to the article, the topic of her speech—"Aim of Humanity"—was typical of her large, all-encompassing themes.

The newspaper account described Goldman's speech as countering religious ideas of fate and destiny with human will. She explored definitions of individual contentment and posited that most people strive "to reach the highest amount of happiness or satisfaction . . . with the least expense of time and energy is the common end of human life." She noted, with some irony, that the country's forefathers associated religious freedom with happiness and asserted that "the church practically controls the education, the morals and the ethics of the country, and while persons who may differ from accepted beliefs are not subjected to the rack and thumbscrew they are often subjected to ostracism." She complained repeatedly about how restrictive news coverage made it difficult to educate oneself about world social and economic conditions. The newspapers, permeated with sensational news, rarely reported "the proceedings of labor meetings or

[the] speeches of those who are trying to better the conditions of the working classes. They are simply jumping jacks in the hands of capitalists who own them." Convinced that "there can be no real equality without equality of opportunity," she pointed an accusatory finger at the class system of education in the United States with universities serving as "show places of the sons of aristocrats" instead of being "filled with the sons of the working class" and contrasted this inequality to the situation in Germany, where from 1848 to 1880, university students were the leaders of radical thought. She concluded her talk about the meaning of life, urging her audience to "give what we have of ability and talent to educate and to help others. It is only through this that we will realize the true aim of life." By positing human interdependence at the core of her belief system (a concept similar to Kropotkin's "mutual aid"),[61] Goldman's talk almost took on the veneer of a religious sermon—except, of course, for her avowed belief that submission to God and to the State and its laws was antithetical to true freedom and human happiness (see "An Anarchist Propagandist," Article in the *Oakland Inquirer,* 15 July 1899).

CHANGING COURSE IN EUROPE

In 1899, taking her own advice to heart, Goldman went one step further and began to explore the idea of becoming a doctor as a more effective means than nursing to contribute to the health and well-being of the people. Wealthy admirers, who believed in her potential over—and perhaps in spite of—her politics, offered to foot the bill.[62] Advanced schooling in medicine was more readily available to women in Europe than in the United States. Goldman, who had just turned thirty, felt more confident and more firmly set in her identity than when she had studied nursing and midwifery in Vienna in 1895. She was also eager to play a role in the International Revolutionary Congress of the Working People scheduled to take place in September 1900, in conjunction with the Exposition Universelle, the world fair, both being held in Paris that year.[63] The prospect of lecturing in England, Scotland, and France for a year before undertaking medical studies in Switzerland was equally appealing.

Perhaps the most salient subtext of her trip, especially after the recent decision to stop pursuing Berkman's pardon, was the secret escape plan to tunnel him out of his prison. Well under way, the plan was funded under the guise of support for legal action and advertised in *Freie Arbeiter Stimme* (by Saul Yanovsky) and in other papers as a new appeal for Berkman; it held the promise of freedom far from the clutches of the American prison system and of a grand reunion in Europe for the two long-separated comrades. It is likely that their anticipated dramatic meeting was the center around which the other

---

61. Ideas for Peter Kropotkin's essay "Mutual Aid" (1902) evolved from a series of articles published intermittently in *The Nineteenth Century* between September 1890 and June 1896—some of which he may have discussed with Goldman during her 1895 London visit.

62. See "The Red Queen Is Here," Interview in the *Pittsburg Leader,* 24 September 1899, note 2, on EG sponsors Herman Miller and Carl Stone.

63. See ibid., note 3, for a brief history of anarchist congresses from 1881 to 1900.

elements of her trip were planned—with schooling, meetings, lectures merely a cover for her decision to leave the United States. All participants were careful not to leave a paper trail, lest their plan be discovered and their efforts thwarted. Later, however, both Goldman (in *Living My Life*) and Berkman (in *Prison Memoirs of an Anarchist*) revealed much of the detail of these illegal attempts to free him from prison, albeit with false names for the participants in the plan.

Included in the first volume are letters written by Goldman in German to Max Metzkow, her anarchist friend and contact in Pittsburgh, which contain the most explicit references to this escape plan, along with Berkman's letters carefully coded to communicate covertly past his prison censors. Just a month before Goldman was about to set sail, it was rumored that a prison skirmish erupted, and a shot was fired, possibly wounding Berkman and precipitating his further confinement in a solitary cell. In fact, in December 1899, the prison brawl had been spurred by a fellow inmate's fatal attack on Berkman's pet bird. Relieved that it was not her comrade who was hurt, she interpreted the incident as just a temporary setback, and went on to complete her Midwest tour, anticipating their rendezvous in Europe, as planned.

Goldman joked about giving America a rest, having in the last eight months "delivered 210 lectures on economic, sociological, ethical and sexual subjects" (see Letter to Augustin Hamon, 27 September 1899). During her last tour through the country in 1899, the *Pittsburg Leader* reported that Goldman was said to have baptized babies in beer, a rumor she denied: "for in the first place we do not believe in baptism at all." Actually, the coincidence of nineteen recent births to anarchist families in Spring Valley, Illinois, was only a pretext for calling a meeting of mothers and children. An offhand comment about how she might prefer beer or wine to the water in which Christian children were baptized led to the misunderstanding, one that Goldman, who was already known as the "high priestess of anarchy" (a titular honor that sometimes included requests for officiating not only over commemorative celebrations, but over funerals as well), found comical. Goldman likened the reaction of the town's mayor upon spotting her carrying a red flag at a town procession to a bull impelled to charge.

Spring Valley, Illinois, was a center of Italian anarchism and the home base of Guiseppi Ciancabilla, editor of *L'Aurora*. Threatened by this anarchist stronghold, the town's mayor made a desperate attempt to rescind the permission he had afforded the sacrilegious Goldman. According to a Pittsburgh newspaper, which professed amusement at alarmist stories about Goldman's visits to small towns on the outskirts of their city, it was time for this "Anarchist of international notoriety [who was dressed] in a neat fitting black suit with tailor-made jacket and a small toque" to head toward more cosmopolitan territory (see "The Red Queen Is Here," Interview in the *Pittsburg Leader*, 24 September 1899).

By February 1900, Goldman was dazzling British audiences with her lecture entitled "The Effect of War on the Workers," in which she addressed issues posed by the recent Boer War in the context of English history. Her speech was phenomenally brave, given the popular support for the war in England, with British workers among the most patriotic. Cleverly quoting the English political philosopher Thomas Carlyle's piercing articulation of the pathos of war and militarism, she told a cautionary tale of the American experience during the Spanish-American War and the violent repercussions the war set in motion against striking miners, including lynching of African Americans in the American South. In her talk, intended to redress the wrongs of the war on the working class and its accompanying racial atrocities, Goldman counseled the British workers not to do the bidding of others. She warned, "all class and racial hatred is but the result of your ignorance, and . . . while you willfully choose this ignorance you become the easy tools of your Governors, who are too cowardly to go out and fight themselves" (see "The Effect of War on Workers," Transcript of Address in *Freedom*, 20 February 1900). Paradoxically, but like many of her contemporaries, Goldman lacked a deeper understanding of race in her idealization of the foes of British imperialism—a sentiment among radicals fueled by the deaths of over 28,000 Boer civilians in British concentration camps[64] that ignored the racism of the Boers, which would eventually lead to institutional segregation in the form of apartheid. She championed the Boers over the British, ignoring the South African blacks caught between two imperial powers of European heritage. Recollections in her autobiography almost thirty years later of her lecture to English workingmen (a decidedly different account from comments she had written at the actual time of her visit) touted her celebration of the English as "a people whose history is surcharged with the spirit of rebellion and whose genius in every field is a shining star upon the firmament of the world"—harkening to "the immortal works of Shakespeare, Milton, Byron, Shelley, and Keats, to mention only the greatest in the galaxy of poets and dreamers of your country . . . the most precious heritage of a truly cultivated people."[65]

Goldman strove to be respectful of the culture and class of the audience she addressed; always a quick study, she directed her talk to the current problems facing the British worker, especially in light of the Boer War, and illustrated her ideas with examples from their own history and from her experience in the United States.[66] Through this synthesis, she said, she hoped to bring them a step forward in the battle against ignorance, passivity, and injustice, which crossed all national bounds. Later, in the 22 April 1900 issue of *Free Society*, the subtext of her reference to "ignorance" became clear. She surmised that free speech in England was a hollow shell because "this sacred right is not suppressed by the government, like in our 'blessed land,' but by the people themselves. By the 'people' I do not only mean the ignorant, whisky-saturated, patriotism-maddened workers, but also the mental wage slaves: clerks, bookkeepers, cashiers, typewriters, commercial travelers, and other flunkies to money and titles. . . . In England, where patriotism in the present war is based upon nothing but commercialism, the brutality of the people is simply beyond any comprehension and rather discouraging" (see "Observations and Suggestions," Letter to *Free Society*, 22 April 1900). Suppression by the

---

64. Thomas Pakenham, *The Boer War* (New York: Random House, 1979), pp. xxi–xxii.
65. *LML*, p. 256.
66. In her autobiography, Goldman recounts a very different lecture delivered at this time than the contemporary accounts suggest, creating a different emphasis many years later (*LML*, pp. 255–257).

people themselves seemed much harsher to Goldman than a hall lined with policemen dressed in blue uniforms and brandishing clubs.

To offset her frequent encounters with audiences lacking insight into social and political forces of oppression, Goldman engaged in strategic and philosophical discussions with anarchist peers. In the spring of 1900, Goldman traveled from London to Paris with Hippolyte Havel, a Czech anarchist communist, journalist, and editor she had met in London—an intriguing but moody comrade, "a veritable encyclopedia" of the movement, exactly her age, who with notable synchronicity actually had been in jail in Vienna in 1893, at the same time she was in jail in New York City. They intended to participate in the International Revolutionary Congress of the Working People—known colloquially as the "Paris congress"—scheduled to take place in September.

Goldman's European trip was not only an opportunity to confirm her place in the international movement but also a chance to reestablish and make new friendships. She enjoyed the camaraderie of anarchist historian Max Nettlau and continued to learn from and integrate the ideas of the anarchist theorist Peter Kropotkin. Within her first months in London, based at the home of her old friend Harry Kelly, she was lecturing with anarchists Louise Michel, Peter Kropotkin, Varlaam Cherkesov, Tom Mann, and Tarrida del Marmol on behalf of victims of Italian political repression; and she attended a Russian New Year's party along with other Russian revolutionary exiles. She went on tour in Scotland, met Tom Bell, the militant Scottish anarchist, and gravitated back to London as a center for anarchist activity and friends. Paris, the site of the planned international anarchist conference and of the world fair, promised to be a perfect convening point for many of her friends, including "Artists musicians, journalists & other bohamians" (see Letter to Augustin Hamon, 27 September 1899).

Her experience in Paris seemed like a crazy quilt of the old and the new—a familiar European culture reminiscent of her past, a shared sense of the weightiness of political concern; even the food and the coffee were more to her liking. And yet, she had become accustomed to the casual style of the Americans, the more fluid identity among immigrants as they put down roots in a country that was home for many cultures, and the relative openness to strong women—like herself. In spite of the overall ecstasy of her trip to Paris, one can imagine how she bristled, especially in Europe, when the constructs of her chosen cosmopolitan identity were toppled by subtle asides and seemingly inescapable ethnic stereotyping—and was particularly alarmed at the rumor that her friend Augustin Hamon, the French anarchist and editor of *L' Humanite nouvelle* then working at the New University in Brussels, was "infected by the disease of Anti-Semitism" [67]—a prejudice most anarchists consciously attempted to eradicate. She delivered a few lectures but never truly hit her stride in Paris, nor was she completely successful in crossing the barriers of cultural and gender bias.

The experience of displacement is not uncommon to those who, like Goldman, choose to pursue their studies outside their country of origin, or to tourists of any age or

---

67. EG to Augustin Hamon (13 November 1899), *EGP,* reel 1.

gender. This feeling of dislocation was accentuated by the fluctuating enthusiasm of the handful of anarchists hosting her along the way. The unpredictability of her experience was tempered also by the varying levels of professional competence of those who did the advance work for her few formal talks—a problem she would encounter again and again over her next twenty years as an itinerant lecturer. After her warm welcome in London, she was stunned by her treatment in Paris, by what she considered her comrades' lack of sensitivity, hospitality, and solidarity. Gradually, more positive encounters eclipsed her rocky beginnings, and looking back years later, she wrote: "The inspiring atmosphere of our movement in Paris and my own delightful experiences in the city made me wish to prolong my stay." [68] It was during these trips back to Europe that Goldman began to realize that she had become more an American than a European and felt a calling to act as a liaison. She was propelled by the open pluralism of the American identity and its inclusiveness that allowed her to never have to choose to leave her culture of origin completely behind. Established European theorists viewed the young Goldman, a rising star of the anarchist movement, as an immigrant harbinger of the freshness of America, an intriguing national hybrid, and the object of intellectual curiosity and of sexual desire.

Goldman's interest often extended beyond her anarchist circles as she gravitated toward the cutting edge of the culture. In Paris, she was drawn to the excitement of the new, to the greater convergence of politics and art, and to a distinctly modern sensibility. After visiting the Palais des Beaux Arts but steering clear of the old masterpieces, she summed up the poles of her aversion and attraction in a letter to the historian Max Nettlau: "I have little interest in things of the past. I want life, the real, and not what once was" (see Letter to Max Nettlau, 31 June 1900).

In fact, Goldman was so entranced with the bohemian lifestyle that medical school began to take a back seat to the stimulation around her. She predicted that the pastoral environment of Berne, Switzerland, would depress her, and although her fluency in German allowed for a full understanding of the lectures, she worried that most formal programs for physicians included Latin, a requirement far too demanding for her desired combination of political and cultural activity. Having set the bar perhaps too high, she dropped her plan of studying medicine when she realized she lacked the qualifications for the rigorous program. Goldman eventually lost the financial support of the men funding her trip, who rescinded her living expenses once she decided not to attend medical school. She salvaged her plans with a practical compromise and learned the new Viennese electric techniques of scalp and facial massage. She was thrown back on Ed Brady, among others, to fund her stay, and she resumed her familiar reliance on comrades to host her speaking tours. She plunged into a less conventionally studious life of learning in Europe, more carefree but no less intense.

Goldman's primary preoccupation during this time, however, continued to be with Alexander Berkman and whether his escape plan would succeed. She hoped to meet him in Munich. From there, they hoped to travel together to London to Max Nettlau's house

68. *LML*, p. 280.

in mid-July 1900, then continue on to celebrate his resurrection as a free man in Paris at the anarchist congress in September. Meanwhile, in Pittsburgh, led by a German anarchist (whose code-name was "Tony"),[69] Eric B. Morton (a Norwegian-born anarchist code-named "Ibsen") along with an assistant (code-named "Yankee") were busy digging the tunnel; as they dug, Chicago anarchist Vella Kinsella sang and played the piano in a house situated above the action, to drown out the noise of the shovels. But, on 26 July 1900 prison officials discovered the tunnel; not knowing for whom it was dug, they immediately ordered Berkman and others into solitary confinement. Morton quickly fled to France to join Goldman and to avoid being tracked by prison authorities in the United States. Crestfallen, and with all hopes for Berkman's escape dashed and no rendezvous imminent, Goldman drowned her sorrows by throwing herself even more intensely into the preparations for the Paris congress.

The surveillance arm of the police in each country Goldman visited was put on official alert based upon the reputation that preceded her. Often in close contact, should they need to cooperate in their attempts to keep track of her whereabouts, they responded to the pervasive fear that their country's rulers would be the next in line for assassination. The collection of primary sources in these volumes includes many interesting government surveillance documents, offering an inside view of governments in their demeanor as threatened and punishing pursuers of dissenters. A communiqué from the German Royal Prussian Police to the French Interior Ministry illustrates a potentially comic incompetence. Fearing that there may have been a "dangerous purpose" for Goldman's trip to Paris, the German police sent a warning that Goldman and a companion intended to leave London, though, at the time of the report, their spies seemed to have lost Goldman's trail, leaving the Germans begging to be kept "informed of their actions and movements, should you manage to find them" (see Communiqué from Royal Prussian Police to French Interior Ministry, 12 March 1900). A French surveillance document reported on anarchist meetings Goldman addressed; it also asserted that she "has relations with the named Havel," intimating that they may have been lovers as well as political comrades. The French police chief observed that Goldman was "very intelligent" and "dangerous as far as theoretical propaganda is concerned" (see French Intelligence Report, 22 May 1900). On his recommendation, the French government would issue an expulsion order—more than four months after Goldman had left the country (see Extradition Order from the French Government, 26 March 1901).

In Paris, the closely watched Goldman addressed the organizational committee for the upcoming anarchist congress on the state of the American movement, and attended a series of related meetings building up to the September meeting, including the women's congress in June. She planned to make a brief appearance at an early August meeting of the International Conference of Neo-Malthusians, a group that interested her for its advocacy of the political and evolutionary importance of birth control to maintain the abun-

69. According to the anarchist scholar Paul Avrich, in consultation with the Emma Goldman Papers.

dance of resources necessary to sustain life, rather than the regrettable belief of some in the race and class survival of the fittest.

Her talk on the state of the American movement to her European comrades, reprinted in the 8 April 1900 issue of *Free Society,* is a marvelous documentary summary of her assessment of its progress. She emphasized the plethora of journals, the success of her recent lectures (reaching almost 60,000 people in an eight-month span), and the expansion of the audience to "American people, not the foreigners," as further proof of the importance to international anarchism of tending to this new and fertile terrain. While relatively few among her audiences ever joined the anarchist ranks, Goldman boasted that "the American trades unions, social and literary clubs, ethical and philosophical societies, no longer look upon us as bomb-throwers, wild beasts, drunkards, or uncombed and unwashed tramps, (this idea having been manufactured by our enemies, and . . . the daily press), but meet us friendly, invite our lecturers and listen with interest to the exposition of the philosophy of Anarchist-Communism" (see "The Propaganda and the Congress," Transcript of Address in *Free Society,* 8 April 1900).

Regrettably most American anarchists did not have the means to send more delegates, a situation that generated some dissension in the movement on issues of representation and fairness, especially from the anarchists who clustered around *Freiheit,* who raised questions about the whole endeavor. Kropotkin countered the disparagement with a call to all anarchists, urging that they participate, if only by essay, if they could not attend. Representatives from the various tendencies in the movement vied to speak at the congress, and Goldman added her recommendations to the list. She suggested Voltairine de Cleyre, a woman of integrity known as an anarchist "without a tag," and her dear friend Harry Kelly, temporarily based in Europe. Everywhere money was being raised for representatives to attend the anarchist congress, and the excitement mounted.

The Paris congress was intended to be a strategic reunion to build bridges of support, engage in serious self-criticism, plan for the future, and refute those who proclaimed that "Anarchy is dead." A major show of force was sure to be noticed, in part because the eyes of the world were focused on the world fair then going on in Paris. Goldman posited that if anarchism could be established as a major movement, perhaps more would join the ranks, especially those in the middle class who lacked the courage to be identified as anarchists. She expected the importance of the congress to be on a par with the First International in 1872, when the mutualists (anarchists who supported Proudhon's ideas about mutual barter exchanges) gathered around Bakunin, split off from Marx, and met at Saint-Imier to establish their own organization, the Anti-Authoritarian International. She hoped the 1900 congress also could erase the memory of the Second International in London in 1896, where the anarchists were expelled—an event that permanently added the "narrowness, discipline and intolerance of parliamentarian Socialists" to the anarchists' list of manifestations of "invasion and despotism" to be battled (see "Observations and Suggestions," Letter to *Free Society,* 22 April 1900). An earlier meeting of anarchists planned for Paris in 1898 was faced with threats of suppression by French authorities and, of necessity, had been convened in secret. In spite of this ominous history, the anarchists thought that this time, especially with the international draw of the Paris Exposition Universelle on display, they could hold their meetings in the light of day.

However, the likelihood of holding the congress was threatened by a new wave of repression that rippled throughout the world. On 29 July 1900, anarchist Gaetano Bresci assassinated King Umberto of Italy. In the final hours before the anarchist congress was scheduled to begin on 19 September, the French council of ministers barred all social and political gatherings associated with the meetings and then forcefully squelched the slated participants' efforts to launch a massive protest on the evening of 18 September. To prohibit all anarchist activity, they invoked the 1894 *lois scélérates* ruling, which had been issued in response to an earlier rash of political violence. Accustomed to sudden acts of suppression, the anarchists quickly scaled down and secretly convened a few meetings. Protest posters, hung throughout the city, berated the government's disallowing of public speeches and anarchist gatherings. In spite of the suppression during this time, the French anarchists actually gained ground and reinforced their ties to the labor movement, sympathetic to their plight. But, looking back later, Goldman came to think that the fact that the anarchist congress was called at all had been naïve. She concluded that its planning represented a "child-like belief that some governments are better than others; that if our gatherings are suppressed in Germany, Italy, Spain, and Russia, they surely must be permitted in France . . . in Paris, the city of revolution, the history of which has been written with the blood of its people, the sons and daughters of which have stood on the barricades, days, nights, weeks, fighting and dying for Liberty . . . the only city that is ruled by a 'radical' government and Socialistic minister" (see "The Paris Congress," Letter to *Free Society*, 25 September 1900).

The clandestine proceedings, the intended presentations, reports, and manifestos, the record of debates and discussions, all were printed as a supplement to *Les Temps Nouveaux* and distributed internationally. Out of the meetings, a Bureau of International Correspondence was organized. The committee would share information about the economic, political, and ethical state of the movement in each country, to build solidarity and cooperation and a network of support for traveling anarchists, and most immediately, issue and circulate among labor unions a protest against the suppression of the Paris meeting of the International Revolutionary Congress of the Working People.

In her desire to be closer to Berkman, Goldman planned to leave Europe shortly after the September meetings. She did attend the Neo-Malthusian congress from August 4 to 6 as planned, just days before the pre-meeting sessions of the anarchist congress. The proceedings reported in the journal of the Malthusian League mentioned, "Goldman informed the conference on the illegal status of birth control dissemination in the United States."[70] Moving from one meeting to another, Goldman began stocking up on birth control literature and contraceptives for her trip back to the United States.

Though they lost track of her whereabouts, the French police reported Goldman's de-

70. *The Malthusian* (September 1900), p. 68.

parture in November from Paris to Boulogne in the company of Hippolyte Havel and Eric B. Morton (though the police knew Morton only by the alias John Leroy, a name he adopted to avoid arrest after the discovery of the escape tunnel). Goldman's time abroad ended early in December as her ship entered New York harbor. Her identity was more than ever entwined with America. Having left her adopted country for almost a year, she began to recognize and accept the intensity with which it had become her home.

BRIDGING THE CONTINENTS: THE LECTURER RETURNS

Even from Paris, Goldman had kept one foot in each world, and remained in constant contact with propaganda work in the United States. She had counseled her American comrades to resist the temptation to rely on European anarchist lecturers, and instead to look to the many talented speakers already in their own midst. And although American anarchists had benefited from the previous tour of the eloquent English anarchist, John Turner, she reminded them that the laboring people of his own country also sorely needed him.

As she began to turn her attention more fully back to the speaker's trail in the United States, she wrote about her mixed feelings about political lecturing—the contradictions, the balancing act of financial support, reliance on one's comrades for hospitality and railway fares, her insistence on the purity of intent. Given that Goldman eventually devoted most of her life to lecturing, these early ruminations are particularly important touchstones, the ethical moorings from which her life's work evolved. In a reflective mode, she wrote to *Free Society* in April 1900: "I for one would never consent to make a business of lecturing. It seems to me that the work of a true propagandist cannot be paid; that the very thought of being paid for what one says, must rob one of the enthusiasm and devotion for our cause. I claim that one can only give the best of one's self when actuated by love to the thing one gives, out of one's innermost desire to be useful, to oppose that which one considers wrong, . . . I am aware that a propagandist cannot live on ideals, yet if the comrades would only extend more . . . *hospitality* and *solidarity* . . . one could easily tour from five to six months in the year, . . . more than any one ought to do, if he really is desirous to serve the cause" (see "Some More Observations," Letter to *Free Society,* 29 April 1900).

Goldman also abhorred the notion of an anarchist lecturer becoming a wage slave to her comrades and was determined that it was a role that could be better supported by other means. She sometimes scraped by with income gleaned from publishing opinion pieces in mainstream papers. When she was in Paris, disappointed by a Parisian newspaper's policy of excluding articles written by foreigners, Goldman tutored French students in English, briefly attempted a business as a tour guide, and occasionally catered dinners for her friends. Given her dire circumstances there, she was appalled by what she considered to be the insensitivity of anarchists who were so accustomed to material comfort that they could not even recognize need when they saw it, and became convinced that the Church or farmers were more generous than her own comrades (see Letter to Max Nettlau, 15 May 1900).

She had envied her friend Max Nettlau, whose inheritance allowed him to follow his political inclinations without financial worry. She marveled at his ability to travel and collect material for his biography of Michael Bakunin, whom she considered among the few worthy people "who have led such a rich life and have contributed so unendingly to the general good in such a unique, individual manner." She coveted Nettlau's luxury of time, but doubted whether she herself would have had the endurance necessary to research and write a biography, a task she considered mammoth—"that requires a level of perseverance and tenacity of which I unfortunately cannot boast." Considering herself "too much of a gypsy to carry out anything that requires patience," Goldman also envied the permanence of the written word, believing that Nettlau had "certainly accomplished a great deal" through his literary works toward social and political transformation, in many ways more effectively than her "fourteen years of agitating." Written when she had been in Europe without much of an audience and little of her own writing in process, Goldman described herself to Nettlau as "completely miserable"—wondering about her chosen work, ruminating on the depressing thought that perhaps "not one person has become an Anarchist or revolutionary through lectures" (see Letter to Max Nettlau, 31 June 1900).

By 1900, Goldman had developed a distinctive style of lecturing—a quick humorous quip about the police, or current politics, or even about the person who introduced her, followed by a sweeping talk linked to contemporary issues that displayed her signature political and cultural critique of hypocrisy. Her intention was always to reach a varied audience through reason and emotion, always ending her talks with a rousing articulation of a vision of hope for a better world within reach. Goldman transcended her immigrant identity; even with traces of a strong Russian accent, her erudition obscured her lack of formal education, and enabled her to continue to widen her circles, and her influence. Energetic and easily able to create a rapport with her listeners, she became a performance artist in the service of the cause of anarchism—attracting many to the spectacle of her inimitable form of political theater. Her lecture style was more colorful, her repertoire of subjects broader, and her radius of travel in the United States wider than most others in her circles. After her formal lecture, during the question period, her biting wit often left the audience in stitches. She joined the ranks of several prominent women anarchist lecturers, but stood as the lone immigrant in the group. In the 1890s, those who knew her best were immigrants who appreciated her early lecture style that matched the intensity of their labor struggles. By 1900, she had expanded her range of topics, and matched the pitch of her lectures to the variety of audiences she was grateful to address.

The resumption of her public lectures in the United States had an ominous beginning. As Goldman entered a hall in New York City its proprietor threatened "to turn out the lights should the meeting develop into one of Anarchistic tendencies." In response to his harsh proclamation, Goldman callously praised the assassin of King Umberto of Italy for taking a stand against the tyranny of a despot and recklessly declared that, given the current mood of the masses, she would hate to be "in the shoes of a monarch or of President McKinley" (see "Rented by Emma Goldman," Article in the *New York Times*, 12 December 1900). Within the next year, the American president would be dead and the newspapers would allege that his assassin, after attending her lecture in Cleveland on 5 May 1901, had been inspired by Emma Goldman to commit his fatal act.

Paradoxically, during the nine months before the McKinley assassination, Goldman had reestablished herself in America more effectively than before. A broader audience, curious about her experiences in and perceptions of Europe, attended her lectures and avariciously read newspaper reports of Goldman's ideas and whereabouts. The phenomenon of public demand for her opinions in turn increased the scope and force of her convictions. As she reacquainted herself with the state of the movement in America, her new lecture series reflected an awareness of the increased strength of labor. She was impressed with the groundswell of radicalism demonstrated by the recent and relatively large outpouring of votes for the Socialist Party presidential ticket of Eugene Debs and Job Harriman, and treated their popularity as a political advance, without dropping her general critique of party politics. She lectured throughout the Northeast and Midwest, challenging labor to go one step beyond trade unionism; her topics included "Anarchism and Trade Unionism," "What Will Lessen Vice," "Cooperation a Factor in the Industrial Struggle," "Modern Phases of Anarchism," and "On the Failure of the Free Unions."

She even helped arrange Kropotkin's 1901 tour, his second in the United States. Following through on the program set forth by the Paris congress to strengthen and encourage cooperation across national boundaries, Goldman and Kropotkin cemented their friendship even further. The overwhelming reception to his visit, with colleges vying for bookings, was an indication of his continued draw. He had come first in 1897 as a delegate to the British Association for the Advancement of Science, addressing the National Geographic Society as an eminent scientist and geographer, as well as a prominent anarchist. His appeal increased by 1901, with his impressive range of interests and professional credentials adding credibility and "respectability" to anarchism (in spite of Kropotkin's support for the principle and practice of propaganda of the deed, of *attentats*). In this window of openness to provocative political ideas, Goldman was front-page news, a gadfly for ideas and opinions, and a personality who sparked the public's imagination, interest, respect, and sometimes, justified fear that her verbal prowess could topple what little stability existed in the social order around her.

A long interview in the 6 January 1901 *New York Sun* probed for biographical insight about Goldman's intellectual and political development and showcased her prediction that, in the new century, women would lead the way. Saturated with novelistic detail, the account described Goldman as a fascinating woman with "the mouth of a worker and the eyes of an enthusiast" and with the unmemorable face of "girl students of Russia. Intelligent, desperately earnest, lighted from within by an ideal and a purpose, yet calm as a mask, save for the eyes"—[she is] "a forceful woman with brains and experience, under the influence of a great enthusiasm." The article documented Goldman's recollections of Russia, where "one breathes in revolutionary thought with the air, without being at all definitely interested in anarchy one learns its principles." Nostalgically, she described the social and intellectual freedom of Russian women, their camaraderie with "thinking men," underscoring her belief that the "feminine mind needs rubbing against masculine mind" in a relationship of serious study and mutual respect. Because they think, she concluded, women and men become anarchists.

Her own path had been more circuitous. Born to relative privilege, she recounted that she "hadn't come in actual contact with the want and suffering of the world until [she] joined the wage earners." As she recalled the story of her political transformation in New York City and her involvement with striking laborers, Goldman articulated clearly why she did not consider herself a political leader: "A leader must be a diplomat . . . make concessions to his party, for the sake of holding his power . . . give way to his followers in order to be sure they will sustain him. I can't do that. I am an Anarchist because I love individual freedom, and I will not surrender that freedom. A leader must sooner or later be the victim of the masses he thinks he controls." Although she described her initial attraction to anarchism as an emotional response to human suffering, she emphasized the importance, once again, of the rational foundation for political belief, her pledge to study and think, to "make passion bow to wisdom," to avoid the tendency to be "carried away from the truth by sentiment" (see "Talk with Emma Goldman," Interview in the *New York Sun*, 6 January 1901).

HALF-TRUTHS

As always, she was forced to prove that all anarchists don't "carry bombs in our coat pockets" and to assert that individual acts of violence were provoked responses born of oppressive social and economic conditions. She underscored her respect for the person "willing to lay down his life for the cause of humanity" as a "noble" act, even if it was "mistaken." The *New York Sun* nevertheless reported that Goldman was unpopular with the large sector of militant anarchists for "her disbelief in bloody streets as a pathway to the millennium."

Some anarchists took issue with the particulars of this interview, in part because they depended upon her to articulate for the public a consistent position on violence as a viable tactic. Goldman too was painfully aware that her position was more complex than reported and was often misunderstood by the mainstream press. To counteract the preponderance of misinformation, she relied on the anarchist papers to print her objections, clarifications, and a more nuanced, carefully crafted expression of her position. In the anarchist press, she could record the changes in her emphasis, not only about violence but also about workers, and correct the misinformation created by rumors circulating about her in the movement. In fact, Goldman's attitude about the efficacy of violence was inconsistent. Her firm support of the *attentater*, however, ultimately cast a shadow over her public veneration. In response to the critique of the *New York Sun* interview, she adopted a principled refusal to judge an act by its result. By asserting that above all she believed in the lessons gleaned by the act's intent and in an "innate sense of justice and a rebellious spirit" (see "An Open Letter," Letter to *Free Society*, 17 February 1901), Goldman contradicted an earlier pronouncement that violent acts were only as effective as the change in thinking they provoked. Yet to understand what may have appeared as vacillation, Goldman's answers to the usual questions asked of anarchists by the mainstream press required the studied ability to read between the lines. Goldman sometimes uttered half-truths to unsuspecting journalists in order to redirect the discussion of violence.

The dark residue of the association of anarchism with political violence marked Goldman's life—forcing her to grapple, in varying degrees of clarity, with issues that she found profoundly troubling. She was willing to withstand the controversy within the movement, the mixed emotions elicited by newspaper reporters privileging one person's position above all others, because she believed in the importance of extrapolating the social significance of such difficult problems for a wider audience. Goldman took her success to be a signifier of renewed openness to anarchist ideas. Given her mission, the inevitable inaccuracies and distortions in the *New York Sun* article seemed a small price to pay.

PRIVILEGED WOMEN AND SOCIAL TRANSFORMATION

Predictably her interviews almost always turned to the topic of women. She used these occasions to encourage more participation both within and outside the anarchist movement—applauding the efforts of the Kansas farm–based activism of Kate Austin and the urban focus of Voltairine de Cleyre in Philadelphia. In spite of her biting criticism of the ignorance and frivolous preoccupation of most American women, Goldman presaged the importance of the American woman to the cause of freedom, predicting that "The movement will come from the middle class, but it will spread." She compared the American woman favorably to her French, German, and English counterparts. "It is a matter of course for the American woman to be free . . . [she has] liberty—home, public, social, educational, religious. She is bound to forward our cause." Counseling her sisters not to "rave against man and exalt woman" as the suffragist did, but to meet them "on logical ground," she asserted that "the question of sex has no place in a great movement toward truth" (see "Talk with Emma Goldman," Interview in the *New York Sun*, 6 January 1901). Nonetheless, outrage against gender injustice was integral to Goldman's vision and strategy for change; this sensibility and sensitivity to the importance of women's freedom laced through all her political work—whether or not she ranked such issues as the most vital to her cause.

Goldman began to work through her controversial interest in and appeal to the middle class. Still caustic in her condemnation of the insensitivity and indulgence of class privilege and "respectability," with its coerced conformity, she also was frustrated with the movement's singular focus on the working class, the ways in which labor unions assuaged workers' suffering but dulled their impetus to fight for a larger vision of the transformation of the relationship of work and production. She complained that the worker "boasts of his right to choose his master, not knowing that he thereby forfeits his right to be his own master." Freedom, she believed, was like "a delicate plant [that requires] proper care and attention, or it fades away." She longed for the advent of "the intelligent worker of the world [who] stands up for his rights, and works with those whose aim in life is the establishment of equal liberty in all phases of life."

In 1901, she continued her ruminations about the ways in which social and economic class background intersected with anarchist propaganda. She enjoyed discussing such issues with "Prince" Kropotkin, who by his very being confirmed her ideas about extending the anarchists' message to the privileged. Berkman's initial resistance to these ideas frustrated her. Her frequent disagreements with him on the issue convinced her that his confinement with the desolate poor in prison obscured his ability to assess a shift in the political potential of different strata. Goldman continued to circulate her lecture cards to the rich and the poor, spoke to as many audiences as would have her, while she herself worked, sometimes twelve hours a day, saving up to support her tour. On the perennial lookout for noble spirits, for those who strove for consistency in thought and action, Goldman found more and more comrades in every stratum as the years went on—many of whom she considered anarchists even if they were themselves unaware of the fitting label for their beliefs.

A HARBINGER OF CHANGE

Among the more dramatic events signifying Goldman's renewed popularity in the United States was her bold free-speech fight in Philadelphia, the home of anarchist Voltairine de Cleyre. Goldman vowed to defy the mayor's prohibition of her talks, and was fortunate to have been interviewed by an admiring writer, Miriam Michelson, for the 11 April 1901 issue of the *Philadelphia North American* as a signifier of a broader trend in the nation. Goldman seized the opportunity to compare the suppression of free speech in Philadelphia to despotism in Russia: "The methods of Russia are of the tenth century; the intellectual development of America is of the twentieth. They don't go very well, do they?"

Her retort to Michelson's doubts about the imminence or practicality of anarchism was disarming, and represented a significant change in her perception of the timing and inevitability of revolution: "It is my nature to be what I am. . . . As long as I live I must be a crusader. What I think, what I feel, I must speak. Not for a hundred, not for five hundred years, perhaps, will the principles of anarchy triumph. But what has that to do with it? 'Is it right?' not 'Is it hopeless?' is the touchstone of courage and principle." Entranced with this "stout . . . broad hipped . . . sturdy-looking, quick-moving, intense woman," Michelson gave Goldman full range to express her beliefs—from her accusation that the shady mayor suppressed her speeches only to appear more moral than he was, that the infringement on the right of free speech was inevitably dangerous to the free press, that she was opposed to prisons on the contention that "no human being, however degraded, is irredeemable," a principle she would apply even to corrupt mayors and police lieutenants.

Goldman reiterated her hopes for the middle class: "It is the middle class and the professional people that are being educated to whom theories of life like mine appeal." But she did not view winning them over, or any class, as essential. "Just so long as there remain in the world men and women ready to die for principle, there will be hope for mankind. It is from the minority that the strength to uplift the world has always come"—a kernel of the lecture on minorities and majorities she would deliver in later years.

Michelson's assumptions were challenged by her awe at Goldman and raised questions for her about gender and identity. She marveled at Goldman's lack of conventional female constraint: "There is no 'no thoroughfare' for her mind. She dares to follow wherever conviction leads." Yet the reporter seemed surprised at Goldman's evident love of the "feminine . . . flowers and pretty things," some too expensive for her means, including stylish clothing and "pretty things in the shop windows." Michelson found it refreshing to hear her complaints about her physical portrayal in the press, which Goldman attributed not to vanity but to revulsion for vulgarity. Applauding this new sensibility, Michelson expressed her own strong opinion that Goldman should be allowed to speak so that all might "learn something [about] the difference between tenth and twentieth century methods of governing" (see "A Character Study of Emma Goldman, " Interview in the *Philadelphia North American*, 11 April 1901).

Goldman did succeed in speaking many times that month in Philadelphia, repeating her ominous refrain ("free speech does not exist in America unless it suits the government") once to over two thousand people, once dramatically on the steps of the City Hall, and a few times surreptitiously tagged onto another event or union meeting. When she appeared under the auspices of the Single Tax Society of Philadelphia, the hall was filled to capacity and "her every utterance was greeted with unanimous applause" (see "Tyranny of Police Publicly Denounced," Article in the *Philadelphia North American*, 12 April 1901). Building momentum, she looped her way to the Midwest—to Pittsburgh, Cleveland, Chicago, and back through Buffalo, then on to Rochester, reuniting with her family in July before her intended return to New York City.

AN ASSASSIN IN HER MIDST

In the audience of one of Goldman's lectures in Cleveland in early May 1901, a meeting monitored by two uniformed police and one undercover agent, was Leon Czolgosz, the future assassin of President McKinley. Whether it was really Goldman's talk, "The Modern Phase of Anarchy," at the Liberty Association of the Franklin Liberal Club that led Czolgosz to his act is a matter of historical conjecture. Although all public figures are subject to a modicum of projection from their beholders, this particular Goldman talk was definitely incendiary and emotionally rousing—and did glorify the *attentater* as a martyr for a higher cause.

Several months later, when Goldman saw Czolgosz's picture in the paper following the assassination, she recognized him as the young man who had approached her during intermission at this Cleveland lecture, asking for suggestions from her for something to read. From a list of anarchist writings available and advertised then in *Free Society*, it is likely that she had recommended Kropotkin's *Appeal to the Young*. Thinking back, she remembered that in her lecture she had scowled at the police, hurled invectives at the detectives in the hall as "the meanest and most despicable creature in the universe," crying out against "the galling yoke of government, ecclesiasticism and the bonds of custom and prejudice." She had asserted that "anarchism [had] nothing to do with future governments or economic arrangements" and spoke approvingly of the motives in all the recent acts of violence carried out by men "unable to stand idly by and see the wrongs that were being endured by their fellow mortals" (see "Defends Acts of Bomb Throwers," Article in *Cleveland Plain Dealer,* 6 May 1901).

Shortly after the Cleveland talk, Gaetano Bresci, the assassin of King Umberto of Italy, allegedly was murdered in prison. Goldman wrote a dramatic eulogy for the 2 June 1901 issue of *Free Society.* Her piece was circulated widely and probably read by Czolgosz, who had visited the Chicago office of the magazine in July on the same day Goldman departed for Buffalo and Rochester. In the office, Czolgosz evidently spouted references to violence and raised fears among the editorial group that he might be a provocateur. Goldman remembered seeing him among the group that accompanied her to the Chicago train station to bid her farewell, but dared not reveal it to the press or the police. Her article read: "Each age has had its John Browns, its Perovskayas, its Parsons, Spies, Angiolillos, and its Brescis, who were misunderstood, persecuted, mobbed, tortured, and killed, by those who could not reach the sublime heights attained by these men. Yet they have not lived in vain, for it is to them that we owe all that is good and noble, grand and useful in the world . . . and the world will have to learn that while one Bresci is killed, hundreds are born ready to lay down their lives to free mankind from tyranny, power, ignorance, and poverty" (see "Gaetano Bresci," Essay in *Free Society,* 2 June 1901).

Such poetics about the martyrs of "the deed"—which certainly could inspire future acts—were no doubt fueled by Goldman's profound attachment to Alexander Berkman. At the time, Berkman was just emerging from a long period of solitary confinement, having been barred temporarily from letter writing, prohibited from any visitation, emotionally brutalized by his prison experience, and on the verge of suicide. Goldman was stricken with grief as she read his letters that recounted the raw experience of the horrors of prison life. Every generalized public reference she made to the daring resolve of those who committed individual acts of violence also served as an incantation to Berkman and his courage as he endured the harsh consequences of his act.

Between 19 and 24 August 1901, Goldman at long last was granted visitation rights as Berkman's "sister," for the first time in nine years. The mood of the country suddenly seemed more open. A new law would hold the possibility of commuting his sentence. She had some money to travel, released from her long nights as a nurse with supplementary income from promoting Ed Brady's stationery and office supply business. Goldman's "restless spirit" seemed contained for an instant.

In Buffalo, on 6 September 1901, Leon Czolgosz, who had been stalking President McKinley during his visit to the Pan American Exposition, shot and fatally wounded him. After Czolgosz's arrest, the newspapers across the world reported the claim that "Emma Goldman's Words Drove Him to Murder" (see "Assassin's Trail of Crime from Chicago to the Pacific Coast," Article in *San Francisco Chronicle*, 8 September 1901)—a headline distortion of his confession, in which he stated that the last person he heard speaking was Emma Goldman but that she did not tell him to kill the president. It is unclear whether or not the San Francisco Hearst newspaper—hungry to counter its previous harsh coverage of McKinley—fabricated the seemingly verbatim interview with Czolgosz, but it succeeded in setting off waves of incrimination against Goldman. He was reported to have said that "Her doctrine that all rulers should be exterminated was what set me to thinking so that my head nearly split with the pain. Miss Goldman's words went right through me, and when I left the lecture I had made up my mind that I would have to do something heroic for the cause I loved." When he ended the story of his obsession and pursuit, he restated his motive, with no regrets: "I am an anarchist. I am a disciple of Emma Goldman. Her words set me on fire."

In an era when free speech was still very much a contested terrain, the fear of violence following the McKinley assassination precipitously tipped the balance away from the anarchists, whose utterances, once again, became synonymous with terrorism. The conflation of incendiary words and violent action intensified. It had been only fourteen years since the execution of the Haymarket anarchists in Chicago, and Goldman, now demonized, feared for her life. Suddenly the eyes of the world were searching for her. The nation was in shock, the public's fascination with her turned to disdain. She was terrified at the level of hatred hurled at her. The 8 September 1901 *Chicago Tribune* caricatured Goldman as a devil surrounded in flames, a "wrinkled, ugly, Russian woman, who owns no god, has no religion, would kill all rulers, overthrow all laws, and who inspired McKinley's assassination" (see illustration on p. 461).

Goldman was lecturing in St. Louis when she read about the assassination of the president. Her first response was to lie low and stay out of sight. Then, upon reading about the arrest of her *Free Society* comrades in Chicago, she bravely and voluntarily rushed to be near them—in the city that only fourteen years earlier had seen the Haymarket anarchists hanged. She even arranged an exclusive interview with a Chicago newspaper at a fee high enough to provide her friends with the necessary bail for their release. As she waited in a friend's apartment, posing as a Swedish maid, the police barged in and found her. Insisting that it was just a matter of time before she would have given herself up, Goldman grabbed her sailor hat, her toiletries, and a book, and followed the detectives onto a streetcar to the police headquarters, glad that she had something to read along the way.

After her arrest and interrogation she begged them to allow her to send a telegram to her sister—a quick way to assure her that Goldman was safe and to urge her to "comfort mother." She told the police that she had found out about her alleged involvement in the assassination through the newspaper—like most other people. She explained her presence in Chicago as a desire to be close to her friends from *Free Society* now under arrest, and recounted how she had taken the train from St. Louis.

Cleverly, she had avoided detectives, spending several days around town, even shopping at Marshall Field's department store. But alone in a cell, even if it was "the best room in the annex," her playfulness was gone and she burst into tears at the thought of a facing a ten-year prison sentence and $5,000 fine for an act in which she perceived herself as having had no part, carried out by a person she barely knew (see "Story of the Arrest of Anarchist Queen," Interview in the *New York World*, 11 September 1901).

Goldman was relieved when no legal grounds could be found to prosecute her for the McKinley assassination, and was convinced that her luck may have been attributable to "official rivalry and jealousy, and [her] absence from New York [at the time of the assassination], to which [she owed her] release" (see Letter from Alexander Berkman, 20 December 1901). Czolgosz's actual statement to the police on the night of the assassination absolved Goldman and confirmed that, although she was the last one he had heard talk against the government, "She didn't tell me to do it."[71] He exhibited a canny resistance to leading questions, and consistently denied any direct involvement with her; he purported to have seen her only once as part of a large crowd at her Cleveland lecture and covered up the fact that he had accompanied her, along with members of the militant *Free Society* group, to the railway station in Chicago. But, even in the absence of any formal establishment of guilt by association or official punishment, her life would forever be entwined with Czolgosz's act; the outside world, which may not have known her name before, would now associate Goldman with acts of terror.

In the weeks before Czolgosz's electrocution, Goldman, true to her pattern of affirming the valor of the intent of a person who engages in individual acts of violence in the name of freedom, came to his support. The movement was divided, though it is also possible that a modicum of posturing in their public protests may have served also to shield other anarchists from any suspected engagement in the act. Still, some considered Czolgosz "a lunatic,"[72] McKinley an inappropriate target, and the act a catalyst for a terrible wave of repression. Even Berkman voiced his opposition against it. He believed that his own *attentat* against Frick, who was the actual perpetrator of bloodshed against labor, was more effective than the targeting of McKinley, a relatively benign symbol of national wealth and power. Ironically, he argued that the McKinley assassination was an act sure to be misunderstood by the masses (a position similar to Most's critique of Berkman's act only nine years before). Goldman held fast, identifying Czolgosz as an outsider, psychically susceptible to the suffering of the world surrounding him—perhaps not even an anarchist, but " a soul in pain [who] could find no abode in this cruel world . . . lacking in caution . . . but daring just the same . . . I cannot help but bow in reverenced silence before the power of such a soul, that has broken the narrow walls of its prison, and has taken a daring leap into the unknown."

As to violence, Goldman predicted that it would "die a natural death when man will

71. *People vs. Leon F. Czolgosz*, 6 September 1901, in Courthouse Archives, Erie County, Buffalo, N.Y.
72. In Letter from an Unknown Correspondent to *Lucifer*, vol. 5, no. 41 (31 October 1901), p. 2, with Goldman's reply in *Lucifer*, vol. 5, no. 43 (21 November 1901).

learn to understand that each unit has its place in the universe, and while being closely linked together, it must remain free to grow and expand." As to the dissension among the anarchists (which in her pain and panic loomed larger than life even though many anarchists, including Kate Austin, Harry Kelly, Voltairine de Cleyre, and those who clustered around *L'Aurora,* actually agreed with her), she counseled them to value both the inner and outer human condition: "Anarchy is the philosophy [which includes] every branch of human knowledge pertaining to life. . . . Anarchists ought to be students of psychology and honestly endeavor to explain certain phenomena, not only from a politico-economic but also from a psychological standpoint" (see "The Tragedy at Buffalo," Essay in *Free Society,* 6 October 1901, and "Emma Goldman Defines Her Position," Letter to *Lucifer, the Lightbearer,* 11 November 1901).

She found herself defending the subtleties of her position to the readers of *Lucifer;* the journal reported her as saying to the press that "as an Anarchist, she was opposed to violence. She deplored the assassination of McKinley, and said that if the people want to do away with assassins they must do away with the conditions which produce murderers."[73] Goldman corrected their impressions, asserting that she had not the occasion to "deplore or applaud the assassination." Shortly after Czolgosz's execution, Goldman, unnerved and grieving, tried to correct the misrepresentation of her statement to her comrades in a letter to *Lucifer* written on the day of the solemn commemoration of the fourteenth anniversary of the death of the Haymarket anarchists; she romanticized Czolgosz as "a man with the beautiful soul of a child and the energy of a giant." In the letter, she may have merged her own feelings of isolation in the face of rampant demonization by the mainstream press and genuine fears for her own life, with her projection of Czolgosz's "pitiful loneliness"—embittered by the fact that a few anarchists actually joined conservatives in questioning his sanity. Yet, even as she underscored the need to comprehend the complex psychological makeup of an *attentater,* she allowed for only simple one-dimensional positive perceptions: the portrayal of a sensitive soul colliding with a cruel world.

Goldman probably did have a more textured understanding of psychological deviancy than her political comrades, not only because of her fascination with Sigmund Freud, but also through her work as a nurse. Her letter to Max Nettlau, for example, was written during a brief lull in her fourteen-hour workday as a nurse, while "taking care of a neurotic, so you can imagine that I am in frightfully great demand" (see Letter to Max Nettlau, 24 November 1901). And yet, the distinguishing characteristic that always elevated any person in Goldman's eyes, no matter how troubled internally, was a commitment to the cause of freedom. Thus, she could tolerate with great patience, and even reverence, the "strange behavior" of Berkman in prison upon emerging from solitary confinement. He had apologized to Goldman for his silence during their late summer prison visit and for his obsessive playing with "the shiny little trinket that was dangling

---

73. Referring to a meeting at the Manhattan Liberal Club of 8 October 1901, *Lucifer* (October 1901).

from your watch chain" as if it represented "all of my dreams of freedom, the whole world of the living" (see Letter from Alexander Berkman, 20 December 1901). She honored Berkman and Czolgosz as sensitive souls and martyrs for the cause of justice, disregarding the negative effects of the trauma that Czolgosz may have inflicted on a country reeling from the shock of his actions.

And yet privately Goldman recounted in her autobiography that "the most terrible thing I had yet experienced"[74] was the psychological impact of Berkman's denunciation of Czolgosz's act, remembering that he doubted "whether it was educational, because the social necessity for its performance was not manifest . . . therefore the value of the act was to a great extent nullified." He had contrasted it to similar acts in a despotic regime like Russia where its intent would be understood immediately. Berkman counseled Goldman: "The real despotism of republican institutions is far deeper, more insidious, because it rests on the popular delusion of self-government and independence. That is the subtle source of democratic tyranny, and as such, it cannot be reached with a bullet." Continuing on this vein, Berkman's own sense of superiority stuck like bones in Goldman's throat: "In modern capitalism, exploitation rather than oppression is the real enemy of the people. Oppression is but its handmaid. Hence the battle is to be waged in the economic rather than the political field. It is therefore that I regard my own act as far more significant and educational than Leon's. It was directed against a tangible, real oppressor, visualized as such by the people" (see Letter from Alexander Berkman, 20 December 1901, and *Prison Memoirs of an Anarchist*, pp. 412–17).

While Goldman grasped the elements of truth in Berkman's argument, she was still grieving over the horror of the recent electrocution of Czolgosz and the public's gawking, vengeful fascination with the gory mechanics of his execution, and also feeling under fire from all sides herself; she had mustered her courage in the face of her false implication in Czolgosz's act and voiced support for his intent. Given these circumstances, she found the timing of Berkman's remarks especially callous—especially since Berkman had escaped Czolgosz's fate by sheer circumstance rather than by design. Goldman was tangled in a dangerous and complex web and caught by strong contradictory emotions that elicited a deep well of loneliness during what proved to be, and was remembered in her autobiography as, one of the most difficult phases of her life. It seemed positively shocking for her to face the storms of reaction around her without the tacit and unqualified support of her closest comrade. Reluctantly she drew upon her own reserves, and by necessity differentiated herself and her evolving political identity further from Berkman— a painful but ultimately important step in Goldman's political and personal development.

Perhaps the cataclysmic impact of the McKinley assassination on her own life was the basis for the hyperbole in her 6 October 1901 article in *Free Society* "The Tragedy at Buffalo." It opens with an exhortation: "Never before in the history of governments has the

---

74. EG to AB, 23 November 1928, IISH and *EGP*, reel 20.

sound of a pistol shot so startled, terrorized, and horrified the self-satisfied, indifferent, contented, and indolent public, as has the one fired by Leon Czolgosz when he struck down William McKinley, president of the money kings and trust magnates of this country." While acknowledging that "this modern Caesar was [not] the first to die at the hands of a Brutus," Goldman completely ignored the history of the United States before her arrival. She neglected to mention the shock waves set in motion by the relatively recent assassination of President Abraham Lincoln in 1865 in the post–Civil War era when an embattled nation struggled to maintain some semblance of unity. Nor did she acknowledge the confusion set in motion by the seemingly random assassination of President James Garfield in 1881, who like President William McKinley, on the surface, appeared to be a rather benign symbol of the consolidation of industrial capitalism.

Surprisingly, the tally of deposed leaders in the United States in the period just preceding Goldman's emigration was higher than it had been in Europe and Russia where the aura of assassinations appeared to be omnipresent. The assassination of the president destabilized the apparent confidence that was building at a time when the United States was in transition from an agricultural to an industrial economy; when alliances between capitalists and government were strengthening; when labor militancy escalated the demand for an equitable share in the value of their work; when women began to work outside of the home and to challenge usual categories of domestic power; and when freed slaves struggled to find a place in a culture in which they had been disempowered and disenfranchised.

In the wake of the McKinley assassination, a desire for revenge unified the fragmented and wounded nation. More than ever, anarchism was equated with terrorism in the collective mind of the mainstream public; the hunt for the logic behind what might otherwise may have seemed like a random act of violence was on, with newspapers busy telegraphing warning sirens across the world, searching hungrily for the blueprint of conspiracy. Everyone in Goldman's circle was suspect. Loose affiliations across the borders between liberalism and radicalism receded. Although some anarchists were amazingly vocal in their support of Czolgosz, many anarchists laid low. They cautiously reached out to one another, as they too feared random acts of violence—especially from an angry vigilante mob. Many labor unions, including those with a record of militancy, publicly condemned the act, distancing themselves from the anarchists, in the quest to keep what little progress they had won for workers intact. In this heated environment, it took tremendous courage to claim even the slightest identification with anarchism. Acutely aware of the need to shift this correlation, Goldman rose to the challenge.

Still recognized by the fuming press as a prophet of anarchism, Goldman persisted in her unwavering mission to impart a more complex awareness to the public of the issues, and by necessity, took the long view. Goldman focused on the need for education about anarchism and urged her comrades to distribute the proceedings from the anarchist congress to the broadest possible constituency. She even briefly entertained the idea of publishing a book about her life's work up to this point, or an anthology of essays on anarchism. In an environment of suppression by intimidation in the shadow of newly drafted but not yet enacted anti-anarchist laws, Goldman also dared to open a Social Science Club in New York City for a series of lectures intended to counter the rampant misinformation about anarchism and to keep the lines of communication among her comrades open. She claimed that most people "who on other occasions have had a good word for us, have drawn back in a cowardly fashion, and what of our own people? . . . I am telling you if we need one-half century to bring clarity to our own ranks, how much longer to lift the cloud which hangs over the spirit of the masses" (see Letter to Max Nettlau, 24 November 1901).

A variant on the heavy hand of repression Goldman had witnessed in Europe began to build in the United States. Goldman was all too aware of the fact that the Haymarket anarchists had been hung only fourteen years before on flimsier evidence than that which had been hurled at her after Czolgosz's arrest. Within days of the McKinley assassination, the National Association of Merchants and Travelers adopted resolutions calling upon the U.S. government to bar anarchists from entering the country. An anti-anarchist immigration law was proposed. The police commissioner in New York ordered a careful census of all anarchists in the city to "make conditions disagreeable for those named." A general wave of reaction rippled through the nation, and mention of even the word "anarchist" was grounds for suspicion. Anarchist presses were ransacked. In Spring Valley, Illinois, the militant Italian anarchist paper *L'Aurora* was shut down and its editors run out of town. In New York City, the musical comedy *The New Yorkers,* which contained three anarchist characters, had to be rewritten to eliminate them from the show. An angry crowd attacked the offices of the Yiddish anarchist paper *Freie Arbeiter Stimme.* Johann Most was arrested for publishing in the German-language anarchist paper *Freiheit* a reprint of an article on political violence, written several years earlier and included merely as a space-filler, to his misfortune, just days before the assassination. At the Western Penitentiary in Allegheny City in Pennsylvania, Berkman, tainted by the assumption of guilt by association, was sent back into solitary confinement.

Under the pseudonym E. G. Smith, Goldman pieced together a life of partial hiding. She remained deeply involved with her political comrades, continuing to participate in meetings, but with a slightly lower profile. Her attempt to build support for anarchism among liberal free-speech advocates and middle-class women was temporarily suspended; the climate of the nation had been too shaken by the death of its president to tolerate or herald anarchist speech. The anti-anarchist mood of the country made caution advisable until the furor over the McKinley assassination had passed. The veil of physical safety customarily afforded to women had fallen in proportion to the public's desire for revenge. In her autobiography, Goldman recounted being beaten by a policeman as she was being transferred from one jail to another, who "landed his fist upon my jaw, knocking out a tooth, and covering my face with blood. Then he pulled me up, shoved me into the seat and yelled, 'Another word from you, you damned anarchist and I'll break every bone in your body!'"[75] Such frightening experiences were unavoidable in the path she had chosen. In 1901, during what was perhaps the most terrifying period of her life, Goldman countered her profound despair with hope and accepted her fate without resentment or sentimentality. She weathered the storms of political transformation with remarkable resilience—a quality she would need to call upon in the turbulence ahead.

LOOKING BACK

When they were in their early twenties, Goldman and her comrades Alexander Berkman and Modest Stein sealed their *ménage à trois* with a youthful "pact to dedicate their lives to the cause in some supreme deed, to die together if necessary, or to continue to live and work for the ideal for which one of us might have to give his life."[76] Goldman and Berkman especially were bound in body and soul by their public complicity in the attempt to avenge the deaths of striking workers—and lived out the elation and sacrifice implied by the drama of their gesture. *Made for America, 1890–1901,* documents their story as it began to unfold—when Goldman entered the political stage and Berkman was behind bars—each a constant presence in the others' life. Their voices are the bookends that unite this volume.

In an age in which speech itself was a heavily contested right, Goldman challenged social and economic norms and, in so doing, articulated rarely voiced but commonly held yearnings. The first volume of this documentary history tracks the beginnings of Emma Goldman's political emergence as an immigrant radical, whose battle with America elicited the country's best and worst—its most visionary edge and its most repressive arsenal. Goldman, a Russian Jewish immigrant, had forged a place in the vast and varied political terrain of the United States. She embodied the paradox of her times: her "beautiful ideal" of anarchism—an attitude of life, a theory, and a practice of complete freedom—seemed to fit the open spirit of the American dream. Yet her belief in the inevitability of political violence—the destruction of the system of injustice that would allow for the construction of a new social order—left her vulnerable to the forces of reaction and placed her firmly in the margins of the culture.

Goldman, who asserted that she never courted violence, also questioned the appeal of the purely pacifist position. She labeled pacifism as a signifier of privilege and obliviousness to the brutality of government and corporate safeguards of political power—especially against the demands of labor. Yet the issue of political violence was equally problematical for anarchists—victimized by the public's misapprehension of the intent of the few among them who engaged in such acts and torn apart by their own awareness of the deadening repression that often followed their attempts at retaliation against injustice.

For her compassion for the perpetrators, Goldman would be marginalized and forever entwined with their fate. She, like the anarchist theorist Peter Kropotkin, never

---

75. *LML*, p. 307.
76. *LML*, p. 62.

wavered in her empathy for those "sensitive souls" who commit political violence—even when she considered their acts tactically unwise. Nor did she express regret when these events set in motion waves of severe reaction and repression, remarking that they often did more to bring anarchism into public attention than any book or pamphlet. Paradoxically, Goldman rarely commiserated with the common person who experienced ripples of terror and revulsion in the wake of such acts—those whose fears allowed for no tolerance for the distinction among anarchists between targeted *attentats* and generalized acts of terror. In response to public rancor and the pervasive resistance to pursuing a compassionate investigation of the conditions that propelled political violence, she remained indignant to the end.

Her primary commitment to anarchism and her lifelong association with Alexander Berkman, who was by far the more militant of the two and the one who carried out "the act" and directly supported others similarly engaged—kept the shadowy edges of violence close by. Her relationship to Berkman and his act predisposed her to avoid condemning other anarchists who resorted to violence, no matter how far her method of political practice had shifted from theirs. Although she had colluded in planning the *attentat* on Frick, even confessing to it in her memoir, Goldman's most powerful weapon was not physical violence but the spoken and written word. Her own writings and the published reports of her lectures bear witness to the uncanny power of her eloquence to leave her audience—across class, cultural, and, in some cases, even political, divides— spellbound. Her words inspired others to action—and flamed their desire to transform the world. Her persuasive oratorical powers, however, were less feared because of the association of anarchism with violence than because of the public's even greater dread of the anarchist challenge to social and cultural norms, especially on the issue of sexuality—the most powerful metaphor for freedom in all aspects of life. Goldman enlivened the battle for the right to free expression; her persistent resolve sparked a gathering force to win what she considered "the greatest and only safety in a sane society." [77]

Goldman engaged with every facet of the movement, with every fiber of her being. For a young woman in her twenties, she had a remarkably forceful vision—both for herself and for the world she hoped to transform. The selected documents in *Made for America* reveal Goldman's early empathy for the impoverished masses and the beginnings of her desire to engage the privileged in the long battle to change a world in which the gaps between the rich and poor were staggering. They reveal as well the acuity of her cultural critique, her quest for consistency, and the high value she placed on personal integrity— all elements of the largesse for which she would be celebrated later on. The documents also display the palpably unavoidable pettiness and sectarianism within the anarchist movement, the personal jealousies, and often misguided grandiosity. This documentary history of Goldman's American years also allows the reader to explore the reasons for the

---

77. "Statement to the Inspector of Immigration," *New York Times,* 28 October 1919.

anarchists' use of violence in reaction to what was perceived by Goldman and her circle as the appallingly brutal government and industrial repression and exploitation of the laboring masses.

The strength of her character dwarfed her frailties — of intermittent self-righteousness, aggrandizement of her cause over all others, biting sectarianism against other, less purist factions of the radical movement. Her characteristic conflations of personal loyalty with political principle, and her surreptitious internal battle between the sometimes diametrical pulls of emotion and reason, account, in part, for the apparent inconsistencies in her political arguments. Friendship and emotional intimacy were critical factors for developing the trust and cooperation necessary for building a movement and a social structure consistent with anarchist ideals. Her ideas on the subject of violence, by necessity veiled, are ultimately difficult to unravel, and are permeated with duplicity in the name of protecting the guilty. Paradoxically, what detractors might consider to be Goldman's delusions of grandeur, actually served her well. Her heightened sense of responsibility and self-confidence, among other aspects of her psychological makeup, allowed her, even at an early age, to believe that she had the power to take on the world; and, she did. As she emerged from the polyglot of her immigrant culture into the vast and rocky political landscape of the United States, she matured into a courageous, romantic, empathic, eloquent, and integrative thinker. Above all, Goldman strove to be a person of principle and consistency. She faced her own demons and those around her, and evolved into one of the most extraordinary figures of her time—in a world that was harsh and, in many ways, still remains mysterious and impenetrable.

The first volume closes in 1901 when the two anarchists and comrades reflect upon the ways in which they had changed in the years since Berkman's *attentat*. Independently, both Goldman and Berkman had developed a new compassion for their adversaries, suddenly recognizing their shared humanity. In a particularly open and honest letter (smuggled out to avert the gaze of the prison censors), Berkman articulated the essence of both his and her deepening transformation (see Letter from Alexander Berkman, 20 December 1901): "I was especially moved by your remark that you would faithfully nurse the wounded man, if he required your services, but that the poor boy, condemned and deserted by all, needed and deserved your sympathy and aid more than the president. More strikingly than your letters, that remark discovered to me the great change wrought in us by the ripening years. Yes, in us, in both, for my heart echoed your beautiful sentiment. How impossible such a thought would have been to us in the days of a decade ago! We should have considered it treason to the spirit of revolution; it would have outraged all our traditions even to admit the humanity of an official representative of capitalism. Is it not very significant that we two—you living in the very heart of Anarchist thought and activity, and I in the atmosphere of absolute suppression and solitude— should have arrived at the same evolutionary point after a decade of divergent paths?"

Berkman countered Goldman's attribution for this change as the "ennobling and broadening influence of sorrow" by reminding her that others who endured the horror to which they had been subjected might have grown more embittered. He reflected on the softening of the heart as part of the progression of their maturation: "The love of the people, the hatred of oppression of our younger days, vital as these sentiments were with us, were mental rather than emotional. . . . Only aspirations that spontaneously leap from the depth of our soul persist in the face of antagonistic forces. At 30 one is not so reckless, not so fanatical and one-sided as at 20. With maturity we become more universal; but life is a Shylock that cannot be cheated of his due. For every lesson it teaches us, we have a wound or a scar to show. We grow broader; but too often the heart contracts as the mind expands, and the fires are burning down while we are learning. At such moments my mind would revert to the days when the momentarily expected approach of the Social Revolution absorbed our exclusive interest. . . . Humanity was divided into two warring camps: the noble People, the producers, who yearned for the light of the new gospel, and the hated oppressors, the exploiters, who craftily strove to obscure the rising day that was to give back to man his heritage. . . . The splendid naivety of the days that resented as a personal reflection the least misgiving of the future; the enthusiasm that discounted the power of inherent prejudice and predilection! . . . But maturity has clarified the way, and the stupendous task of human regeneration will be accomplished only by the purified vision of hearts that grow not cold" (see Letter from Alexander Berkman, 20 December 1901).

Whether compassion, in fact, could be a force of healing in their troubled world is a question whose answer was yet to unfold.

CANDACE FALK, JUNE 2002
CHAMAKOME RANCH, CAZADERO
& THE EMMA GOLDMAN PAPERS,
UNIVERSITY OF CALIFORNIA, BERKELEY

SELECTION

The documents in this volume are selected from the comprehensive microfilm edition of the *Emma Goldman Papers,* published 1991–1993. In addition, this volume contains documents discovered after, and in some cases as a result of, the publication of the microfilm collection. In selecting documents for this volume, which covers the earliest part of EG's career, the editors have tried to select the most representative (and in some cases the only) documents to illustrate EG's life and career between 1890 and 1901. Because so little of EG's correspondence from this period has survived, the reader will notice a large percentage of the documents have been drawn from EG's published writings in the anarchist press, as well as from accounts of EG in mainstream newspapers. Close to 80 percent of the extant correspondence from the early years of her career has been selected for this volume, some of it written in German and translated here for the first time. We include a number of letters from Alexander Berkman to EG, although unfortunately no correspondence from EG to Berkman from this period has survived.

Documents fall into three general categories: personal correspondence, published writings (including newspaper accounts of EG's lectures as well as interviews with her), and government reports.

The majority of the documents in vol. 1 are drawn from the radical and popular press. The published documents are selected to reflect EG's activity within the anarchist community and include her early articles on anarchism, free speech, marriage, and violence, as well as correspondence and travelogues, all published in the anarchist press. The documents selected illustrate her entrance into and evolution within the political anarchist movement in the United States and Europe. Also included are a number of reporters' accounts of her lectures and early interviews with her, selected as representative of mainstream media interest in EG as well as offering another perspective on EG's political ideas and actions. The New York City dailies, and especially the sensation-seeking *New York World,* made a point of covering the lives and culture of the recent immigrants on Manhattan's Lower East Side.

The government documents illustrate the fragile and adversarial relationship EG had with state agencies and officials both in America and Europe. While the number of government documents will increase in later years as EG's notoriety and her perceived influence increases, it is apparent that, from 1895, EG was recognized as a central figure in a movement that threatened the stability of the state, and hence was regarded as a person warranting surveillance. The government documents reveal the interplay between revolutionary activity and the opposing structures of state power.

FOREIGN-LANGUAGE DOCUMENTS

English was not Goldman's first language. As a seventeen-year-old immigrant, her primary languages were German and Russian though she possessed some command of Yiddish. Later she would also gain some competence in French and Italian. Her English spelling and syntax, especially in these early American years, was sometimes faulty and idiosyncratic. We have left it as it is. In the interest of documentary purity, we have provided, where space allowed, the original German text, followed by English translation, of pertinent correspondence as well as several of Goldman's philosophical essays and her travel reports from lecture tours.

ARRANGEMENT

The documents are arranged chronologically, according to date of authorship or publication of text. Documents dated only by month and year are placed at the beginning of the month. Documents dated only by year are placed at the beginning of the year. Where possible, a place of authorship is also provided and added to the date line at the beginning of a document. For documents of the same date, EG's correspondence is placed first.

TEXT

Documents are presented in their entirety, except for several newspaper articles that cover a broad range of topics; in such cases, we have excerpted only the section focusing specifically on EG. Also, EG's 1893 trial transcript has been excerpted for reasons of length and to keep undue repetition to a minimum. A summary of any text that has been excised is provided at the end of the truncated document. These documents may also be consulted in their entirety in the microfilm edition.

FORMAT

Some features of all the documents have been standardized for this volume. All documents include a title line identifying them as correspondence, essays, articles, interviews, or government documents. Styles of dates and place names have also been standardized; the date and place line immediately follows the document title. For correspondence, salutation and signature lines have been placed consistently. In the body of the documents, paragraphs have been indented consistently, and empty lines between paragraphs have been closed up. Immediately following the text of the document is a location line describing the origin or physical location of the document as well as the repository, archive, or institution where the original document may be found. The location line may be expanded as a short paragraph identifying and describing any textual irregularities not reproduced in the document, information about any excised portions of text, alternate versions, publication history of the document, or accompanying matter such as photographs or illustrations.

TRANSCRIPTIONS

EG was largely an autodidact and an inveterately bad speller. Her correspondence most dramatically reflects her rapid progress both intellectually and linguistically in the first decade and a half of her career. With Goldman's correspondence we have rendered the transcriptions of the originals in a very literal form. All misspellings and grammatical errors are preserved. Words and characters struck out in the original, indicating an abandoned thought or construction, are transcribed when legible with a strike-out bar through them.

Spacing between words has been made regular. A single space is used between sentences. Minor punctuation errors have been silently corrected by the editors. Often EG would demarcate the end of a sentence with a large space but no period, followed by a capital letter to mark the beginning of the next sentence. Periods have been silently added by the editors to standardize the text and increase readability. Apostrophes have been silently inserted in place of the thin spaces that EG often used to denote contractions or possessive constructions.

Two informal shorthand markings in particular have not been preserved: EG's placement of a bar over the letter "u" to distinguish it from an "n" and over a consonant to indicate that it should be doubled. Both practices were common in German script at the end of the nineteenth century and appear mainly in EG's letters written in German, though she occasionally carried them over into her letters in English as well. Instead, the bar over a "u" has been ignored, while barred consonants have been rendered as double consonants. (In one instance a footnote signals the alteration in the transcription, where the barred consonant occurred in EG's signature and her intention might be of interest to the reader.)

Interlineations and superscripts are brought down to the line. Long dashes at the end of a line or paragraph are rendered with a dash of standard length. Hyphens at the end of a line in an original document are not preserved unless they are normally part of the word.

In printed texts a less literal transcription policy is used than for EG's own manuscript texts. Obvious typos are silently corrected, as are misspellings. Older or otherwise legitimate alternate spellings are preserved, such as the older spelling of "Pittsburg" in a number of cases. This same practice applies to third-party government documents. Editorial insertions are rendered in italics and enclosed in square brackets, for example [*reminds*]. Conjectured words are also set in italics, followed by a question mark, for example [*comrade?*]; and illegible text is indicated by [*illegible*].

Readability, the convenience of the researcher, and a desire to prevent unnecessary confusion have informed the transcription policy. Certain elements in EG's correspondence that are less likely to be of interest to the student or historian have therefore been standardized.

ANNOTATION

Footnotes provide brief elucidation of specific persons, radical newspapers and organizations, and events mentioned or alluded to in the body of a document. Annotation is provided at the first substantive mention of the person, event, or periodical. Fuller contextual information is provided in the appendixes: the Chronology as well as in the three alphabetical directories of personal biographies, periodicals, and organizations. In addition to clarifying names, dates, and events and providing minimal cross-references to documents mentioned or cited in a given text, the footnotes alert the reader to vagaries in the original document not reproduced in this edition. Footnotes also briefly identify important themes and ideas that informed the intellectual and philosophical development of EG.

Annotation also provides missing voices in a particular discussion or debate, or refers the reader to other sources in the microfilm edition or elsewhere that are directly related to a particular document. This has been done as thoroughly and consistently as possible, but the reader must be aware that the amount of material relevant in certain cases, even with respect to material contained in the microfilm edition, remains too vast to account for absolutely.

CHRONOLOGY

The Chronology provides both a broad overview of important events during the period from 1869 to 1901 as well as a day-by-day record of EG's activities and movements (in as much detail as is possible to document from the historical record). The Chronology also traces EG's introduction to platform speaking, identifying where possible the date, location, and topic of her lectures.

DIRECTORIES

In addition to the annotations and the Chronology, the three directories help to contextualize the radical history of the period—the labor strikes, political events, social movements, and organizations and political figures, whether well known or obscure—that were integral to EG's world. Each volume is intended to stand alone, although the reader should be aware that the directories are time-bound primarily by the years covered in the volume, and thus may not cover the entire history of a person's life or an organization's trajectory.

INDIVIDUALS

The personal biographies in the Directory of Individuals add further detail to the short identifying footnotes accompanying the documents. Each directory entry gives the individual's dates, nationality, and a short history of his or her political and social activities especially during the period of this volume. Where applicable, the entry also identifies the person's oeuvre, including periodicals contributed to as well as books and pamphlets published.

PERIODICALS

The Directory of Periodicals identifies the important radical, anarchist, and socialist newspapers and magazines that were part of the political world in which EG operated. All periodicals in which EG's writings were published, as well as other contemporary periodicals that informed the political world in which EG lived, are listed. Each entry identifies publication dates and locations as well as editors and principal contributors. The periodical's political orientation is identified and, where possible, EG's participation in the life of the periodical or the view the periodical took toward EG's political career is described.

ORGANIZATIONS

The Directory of Organizations adds further documentation to the complex political world of which EG was a part. Entries identify important organizations mentioned or alluded to in the documents, giving contextual history to the period that helped to define the anarchist and radical movement in America.

ABBREVIATIONS

DOCUMENT DESCRIPTIONS
FORM

A	autograph
P	printed
T	typed

TYPE

D	document (trial transcript, printed leaflet, etc.)
L	letter
Pc	postal card
W	wire or telegram

SEAL

f	fragment
I	initialed
S	signed
Sr	signed with signature representation
U	unsigned

EXAMPLES OF DOCUMENT DESCRIPTIONS

ALS	autograph letter signed
ALSf	fragment of a signed autograph letter
API	autograph postcard initialed
PLSr	printed letter with signature representation
TDS	typed document signed
TDSr	typed document with signature representation
TLI	typed letter initialed
TLS	typed letter signed
TLSr	typed letter with signature representation
TLU	typed letter unsigned
TWSr	typed wire with signature representation

REPOSITORIES, ARCHIVES, AND INSTITUTIONS

CLU	University of California, Los Angeles Institutional Location: Department of Special Collections, Research Library
CSmH	Huntington Library, San Marino, Calif.
CtY-B	Beinecke Rare Book and Manuscript Library, Yale University, New Haven, Conn.
CtY-S	Sterling Memorial Library, Yale University, New Haven, Conn.
DLC	Library of Congress, Washington, D.C.
DNA	National Archives, Washington, D.C.
GA RF	Gosudarstvennyi arkhiv Rossiiskoi Federatsii (State Archive of the Russian Federation; formerly TsGAOR, the Central State Archive of the October Revolution), Moscow
IEN	Northwestern University Library, Special Collections Department
IISH	International Institute of Social History, Amsterdam
IU-U	University of Illinois, Chicago, Library
MBU-ab	Boston University Libraries, Special Collections. Institutional Location: Anna Baron Papers
MBU-EGP	Boston University Libraries, Special Collections. Institutional Location: Emma Goldman Papers
MCR	Schlesinger Library, Radcliffe College, Cambridge, Mass.
MH-H	Houghton Library, Harvard University, Cambridge, Mass.
MHi	Massachusetts Historical Society, Boston
MiU	Labadie Collection, Department of Rare Books and Special Collections, University of Michigan Library, Ann Arbor
MnHi	Minnesota Historical Society
NN	Rare Books and Manuscripts Division, The New York Public Library, Astor, Lenox and Tilden Foundations
NNC	Butler Library, Columbia University, New York
NNMA	New York City Municipal Archives
NNU	New York University, New York
NSyU	Syracuse University

OTHER ABBREVIATIONS

PERSONS

AB	Alexander Berkman
EG	Emma Goldman

PUBLICATIONS

EGP	Candace Falk et al., eds., *The Emma Goldman Papers: A Microfilm Edition.* Alexandria, Va.: Chadwyck-Healey, 1991–1993; reference is by reel number.
LML	Emma Goldman, *Living My Life.* New York: Alfred A. Knopf, 1931; reprint, New York: Dover Publications, 1970.

Article in the _BALTIMORE CRITIC_

Baltimore, 25 October 1890

An Eloquent Woman Talks to the Foreigners in German of Their Condition and How to Remedy It.

Miss Emma Goldman, of New York, delivered two addresses to workingmen in this city on Sunday last. The first one was at Industrial Hall, where she spoke to the International Workingmen in the afternoon, and at night spoke before the Workingmen's Educational Society at Canmakers' Hall.

Miss Goldman is a young woman of perhaps twenty three years of age, and is a fine speaker. She was born in Germany, but at an early age left her native country to go with her parents to Russia, where she began to notice the oppression of the poor, and, like many others, she immediately set to work to study out some means to alleviate their condition. At the Canmakers' Hall meeting she said, among other things, that when she came to this country and saw the magnificent buildings, and then saw the wretched squalor of the tenement houses, she wondered and cried "Oh! How did it come to pass that such grand and Magnificent things can exist so close to such wretched misery." And she was of the opinion that conditions in this country were almost as bad as in Europe.

She said that wages were comparatively less in this country than in Russia, since in the latter country everything is so much cheaper. Another thing was that in Russia they knew that there exists a tyrant, but in America all were supposed to be free; yet men are hanged for free speech,[1] while others were sent to Blackwell's Island.[2] Yet there are people to teach you how to throw off the yoke. The same general conditions exist in all countries, and the authorities and those whom we are accustomed to look for advice appear to be in league against us. Michael Cohn[3] and William Harvey also made addresses.

Baltimore Critic, 25 October 1890.

1. A reference to the execution of four anarchists in November 1887 for their alleged part in the Haymarket riot the previous year.
2. Most likely a reference to the prominent anarchist Johann Most, who was fighting a year's prison sentence to Blackwell's Island for a speech he gave 12 November 1887, the day after the execution of the Haymarket anarchists. He eventually served the sentence, from June 1891 to April 1892, for incitement to riot.
3. Anarchist Michael Cohn was a physician and also a financial supporter of EG throughout her life.

> **Article in the _NEW YORK WORLD_**
>
> _New York, 3 May 1892_

Anarchists in Charge.

Herr Most's Friends Captured the Union Square Meeting.

They Hooted Secretary Lloyd and He Left in Disgust.

Half the Speakers Declined to Address the Meeting—A Rabid Female Agitator
Delivered a Fiery Appeal Until She Was Carted Away—The Demonstration
Was an Inglorious Fizzle—Police on the Scene.

Probably the angriest people in the city this morning are the members of the Central Labor Union, for their May-Day celebration last night in Union Square, on which they had based such great expectations, was captured by the Anarchists, and it looked at one time as if the whole thing would end in a riot.

As the plaza began to fill up at 8 o'clock it was noticed that the biggest crowd was congregating around the truck on the east side of the square from which Anarchist John Most had announced he would speak.[1]

B. Witkowski was the Chairman, and when the signal to start was given he came forward and had just said "Workingmen," when cries of "Most! Most! We want John Most!" began to ring through the air.

"Mr. Most is not here," Witkowski replied. "You can't hear him, and I hope you will keep quiet." This only incensed Most's friends, and they shouted louder than ever.

George K. Lloyd, Secretary of the Central Labor Union, came forward.[2] He has a strong voice and thought he would be able to manage them, but he only added fuel to the flame. "John Most is not here," he screamed, "and if he was he would not speak, for, let me tell you, we're not Anarchists."[3] Then they started yelling and hissing.

"It's no use trying to speak," said Lloyd. "I'll leave you in disgust," and with that he

---

1. The announcement of Johann Most's intention to speak at the rally appeared in _Freiheit_, as well as in handbills distributed by Jewish anarchists. In various papers on the Sunday preceding the demonstration, the Central Labor Union (CLU), organizers of the event, in an effort to spurn any connection to the anarchists, formally announced their intention to deny Most permission to speak. See _Freiheit_, 30 April 1892, p. 1; _Arbeiter-Zeitung_, 6 May 1892, p. 2; _Der Anarchist_, 7 May 1892, p. 4.
2. George K. Lloyd served as the recording secretary to the New York City Central Labor Union during 1891–1892.
3. Conflict in the crowd's reaction may have been indicative of the political divisions within the organization. Some other CLU locals were more open to anarchist membership. For instance, Charles Mow-

jumped from the wagon. There was an instant rush towards him by Most's friends, and trouble seemed imminent.

Inspector McAvoy and Capt. McLaughlin had 100 policemen drawn up in line behind the cottage,[4] and when the row started the Captain took along a dozen men and made for the truck. He got there just as Lloyd escaped, but he looked as if he would like to charge the crowd.

"All right, Captain," shouted Witkowski, "we'll quiet them."

They sent to the cottage for Henry Weismann, editor of the *Bakers' Journal,* and who is supposed to be a friend of Most.[5] When he commenced to speak they all cheered. His speech was very mild, and he strongly urged them to look to the trades unions for their emancipation and to let politics alone.

After that the Anarchists had it all their own way. A Mrs. Goldmann, a disciple of Most, clambered on the truck and started off on a harangue in German. She is a little woman, with spectacles and a squeaky voice, which sounded as if some one were crying in distress. How to get rid of the crowd puzzled the Central Labor Union officials, until some suggested hitching the horse to the wagon. The idea was acted on, and just as the female agitator gave one tremendous wail the horse was whipped up and started off, but this did not discourage the speaker, for she kept up her screaming until she was out of hearing distance from the crowd. Then she dropped from the tail end into the street.[6]

Johann Most, internationally renowned German anarchist and early mentor to Emma Goldman. (Labadie Collection, University of Michigan)

---

bray and Harry Kelly were both influential in the Boston Central Labor Union, which sponsored John Turner's lecture in that city on 4 May 1896, after Turner attended a regular session meeting of the CLU on 3 May 1896. See also Letter to Max Metzkow, 2 December 1896, below, for examples of CLU support for Alexander Berkman.

4. The cottage, a wooden chalet in front of which ran a colonnade, was located on the north side of the square. Speakers used its porch as a rostrum from which to address crowds gathered on the wide plaza facing it.

5. Henry Weismann (1863–1935), a prominent German anarchist and trade unionist, was editor of *Bakers' Journal.*

6. EG's address was reported sympathetically and in great detail the following day in the Yiddish-language anarchist periodical *Freie Arbeiter Stimme.* A critical account appeared in the 6 May 1892 *New York Arbeiter-Zeitung,* a Yiddish Socialist Labor Party weekly: "while the glasses of the 'well-known' Mrs. Goldman blazed and her voice squealed, the horse got the propaganda of the whip and the anarchist speaker made progress far away with horse power in Hotzeplotz. They were left with long noses. Mrs. Emma Goldman nevertheless courageously continued her shrieking, as long as her voice could still be heard. And then she even more courageously jumped down from the wagon onto our poor earth which must bear the burden of so many fools."

Meanwhile the people on the piazza of the cottage had not been having an easy time, for when three of the speakers, A. Jablonowski,[7] Charles F. Wilson[8] and Charles Sotheran,[9] were called on to speak, they flatly refused unless Henry Weismann, J. H. Edelmann, W. C. Owen and R. Lewis, who were also announced as speakers, were sent away.[10]

Chairman Lapine was in a terrible way. He implored them not to create any confusion but to speak for the good of the cause, but they wouldn't appear on the same platform with those four. Jablonowski and his friends are members of the Central Labor Union and the Socialist Labor party. Henry Weismann is the man who split the Central Labor Federation and formed the New York Federation of Labor because of the presence of the Socialists.[11]

The other three were members of the Socialist Labor party and afterwards separated from them and formed the Socialist League.[12] This was the cause of all the jealousy.

7. Possibly Ludwig Jablinowski (b. 1856), a cigar maker and member of the Socialist Labor Party (SLP) and the New York City CLU, for which he served as financial secretary from 1884 to 1886. Active in Henry George's mayoral campaign in 1886, Jablinowski was a founder in 1889 of the New York Central Labor Federation (CLF), an organization opposed to the CLU. Jablinowski lectured on labor issues in the New York area around 1892 and in San Francisco in 1893. He was a reporter, and later editor, for the SLP's propaganda organ, the *People,* and a reporter for the *New Yorker Volkszeitung.* Jablinowski was part of the SLP faction that opposed the newly formed and anarchist-influenced Socialist League, which split from the SLP in 1892.

8. Charles F. Wilson was a rock driller by trade and member of the New York City CLU and the SLP (in the faction that opposed the Socialist League). Wilson ran for office in both New York City and state elections on the SLP ticket several times between 1891 and 1893. In 1893 he served on a committee of the SLP designated as a liaison with a delegation of French socialist workers.

9. Charles Sotheran (1847–1902) was a journalist and socialist who helped launch the SLP. He wrote for various New York newspapers, including the *World* and the *Sun.* He ran for Congress in the tenth ward of New York City—the Lower East Side neighborhood—in the 1894 election on the People's Party (or Populist Party) ticket. Sotheran was expelled from the SLP by Daniel De Leon supporters in the 1890s, and subsequently supported the Socialist Party. His works include *Horace Greeley and Other Pioneers of American Socialism* (New York: Humboldt Publishing, [1892?]) and *Percy Bysshe Shelley as a Philosopher and Reformer* (New York: C. P. Somerby, 1876).

10. John Edelmann and William C. Owen were both anarchists and members of the Socialist League; Roman Lewis was a member of the anarchist group Pionire der Frayhayt (Pioneers of Liberty).

11. In 1889 the socialist trade unions and the SLP organized the New York Central Labor Federation (CLF) after ties were broken with the New York Central Labor Union, which was affiliated with the American Federation of Labor (AFL). The CLF then applied for affiliation with the AFL, which Samuel Gompers and the Executive Council of the AFL granted. Later that year, the CLF reunited with the CLU. However, a quarrel between the organizations led to another split, which was eventually reconciled, with the aid of Gompers. However, when the CLF reapplied for its charter from the AFL, Gompers rejected its application, noting that the SLP was among the organizations it represented and arguing that the AFL as a trade union could not represent a political party. This led to a bitter dispute between the SLP and the AFL with Daniel De Leon, editor of the SLP paper *Daily People,* calling for socialists to leave the AFL. In August 1891 several New York City unions led by Henry Weismann organized the New York Federation of Labor in the hope of unifying labor activists independent of party politics.

12. The Socialist League was a New York anarchist organization founded in 1892 by John C. Kenworthy, William C. Owen, and John H. Edelmann, among others. It was modeled on the Socialist League of

About twenty organizations marched to the Square, and when the meeting started nearly three thousand people were present. When they found how things were going many left in disgust. The speakers from the cottage were Jacob Latzer, Henry E. Hicks,[13] W. C. Owen, Hugh Greenan,[14] R. Blissert,[15] Andrew Murray, J. Mayers and S. H. Jacobsen.

The hottest speech was made by Hugh Greenan, of D. A. 49,[16] who wanted the working people to make "city officials and policemen understand that they're our servants and we're their masters."

Resolutions were passed urging the toilers to sink petty differences and band together for the reduction of the hours of labor.[17] It was said that Anarchist Most was seen on the outskirts of the crowd, but this could not be verified.[18]

New York World, 3 May 1892, p. 1.

England, which had been established in 1884. The New York group argued that "the social question has to be served not by any special clique but by the people at large" (*Solidarity,* 13 August 1892).

13. Henry E. Hicks was a member of the SLP who was active in the New York area around 1892, mostly as a speaker on labor issues and workers' rights. In 1892 Hicks ran for election as mayor of New York City as the People's Party (or Populist Party) candidate and was defeated by Thomas F. Gilroy, a Democrat.

14. Hugh Greenan was a member of District 49, the New York branch of the Knights of Labor, which was later absorbed into the Socialist Trades and Labor Alliance, a Socialist Labor Party organization. Greenan emerged as a speaker for the American Federation of Labor in 1892, amidst the controversy surrounding the New York Federation of Labor's split from the AFL.

15. Robert Blissert (1843–1899) was a tailor, Irish nationalist, and labor activist. After being blacklisted by employers for participating in the 1867 London tailors' strike, Blissert immigrated to New York City. He was active in the Tenth Ward Council of the International Working Men's Association, the Amalgamated Trades, and the Labor Union of New York. In 1872 Blissert attended the annual congress of the International Working Men's Association as the proxy delegate from San Francisco, was elected president of the convention, and spoke in opposition to employing Chinese labor in the United States. By 1882 Blissert had become a leader in the New York branch of the Knights of Labor, and helped found the Central Labor Union. He also was among those who organized the 1882 parade in New York, often referred to as the first recorded celebration of Labor Day. He was a member of the American Free Soil Judicial Commission (1894), which had grown out of the single-tax movement. When the Knights of Labor began to lose power to the AFL in the 1890s, Blissert relinquished his labor leadership position to open his own tailor shop in Manhattan.

16. District Assembly 49 of the Knights of Labor was organized in July 1882 and encompassed most of the New York City and Brooklyn locals. With the decline of the Knights in the 1890s, District Assembly 49 joined with other local labor organizations to create the Socialist Trade and Labor Alliance, the first socialist labor federation in the United States.

17. For the text of the resolutions, see *Bakers' Journal,* 7 May 1892, p. 1.

18. According to the 6 May 1892 issue of the *Arbeiter-Zeitung,* Johann Most "remained calmly standing not far away in the square, like a general observing a battle from afar."

Article in the *NEW YORK WORLD*

New York, 25 July 1892

Berkman's Career Here.

Noted as an Autonomist and a Believer in Peukert's Ultra Doctrines.

Detectives Hanley and Wade, who, as told in the *Sunday World*, were assigned by Inspector Steers to look up any confederates that Alexander Berkman may have had in this city, did not report yesterday. Inspector Steers refused to allow the detectives to be interviewed. The Inspector's theory, it is said, is that Berkman has Nihilist[1] accomplices in New York. These Nihilists, it is believed, were back of Berkman in his infamous plot, and are ready, in case of any failures to commit individual crimes, to sacrifice themselves in turn to carry out their murderous schemes.

No information as to the progress Hanley and Wade are making in their search for Nihilists, or as to whether they are shadowing the right people, could be obtained from the Central Department officers.

It was learned from one source last night that not only Detectives Hanley and Wade, of Inspector Steers's staff, but in fact the majority of the sixty men from the Central Department, were scouring the city in search of accomplices who may have plotted with Berkman. Inspector Steers is also working to obtain as complete a record as possible of Berkman's career in New York.

THE ASSASSIN AN AUTONOMIST.

Berkman belongs to the wildest school of Anarchists. They maintain the right of individuals to seek vengeance for private or public wrongs without any responsibility resulting to their society for the criminal acts of each individual member of it. Every member

---

1. From the Latin *nihil* ("nothing"), the term was often used derogatorily by opponents to identify radicals who purportedly believed in nothing and rejected all positive social values. The expression became popular in Russia in the mid-nineteenth century and was used to describe intellectuals who, influenced by Western ideas, advocated revolutionary change. Its literary archetype was Bazarov, a central character of Turgenev's novel *Fathers and Sons* (1862). Though commonly and erroneously applied to anarchists by outsiders, anarchists occasionally used the term to position themselves within a specific Russian radical tradition. AB himself explained the use of the term in a 1907 letter to Bolton Hall: "It was Turgenev who originated the term nihilist . . . prior to the introduction of terroristic tactics in Russia. The term was intended to characterize the 'sons,' who had emancipated themselves from the ideas and ideals of their 'fathers,' and who consequently denied all existing institutions and beliefs. . . . In Russia, nihilism was the social and political equivalent of universal atheism, so to speak" (AB to Bolton Hall, 16 April 1907, Alexander Berkman Archive, IISH). The letter was reprinted in *Mother Earth* 2, no. 3 (May 1907).

Alexander Berkman ("Sasha") in 1890. Goldman's young lover and later, lifelong comrade and friend. (Labadie Collection, University of Michigan)

is supposed to be a self-constituted judge, jury and executioner all rolled into one. They call themselves Autonomists, and take their name from a paper called *Die Autonomie,* published at one time in Vienna by the originator of the organization, one Joseph Peukert,[2] an Austrian. Peukert's teachings were so criminally rabid he was twice sentenced to imprisonment for treasonable utterances. He was finally banished from his native country in 1884.

Then he went to London. He afterwards traveled all over the world, leaving in his track little knots of hare-brained enthusiasts with a smattering of learning. Berkman was one of Peukert's pupils. He read Peukert's writings about what the Autonomists call the "glorious gospel of humanitarianism." Peukert paid a visit to this country in 1890 and organized a band of Autonomists. Berkman was one of the first to join.

In Anarchistic circles it is said that John Most was jealous of Peukert and circulated rumors to the effect that the Austrian was a spy.[3] This led to a rumpus between the Reds

2. Joseph Peukert was editor of several anarchist publications in Europe and the United States, including *Die Autonomie,* which never was published in Vienna.
3. Beginning in the 1880s, much of the German anarchist movement split roughly into two camps: one led by Joseph Peukert and the other by Johann Most and Victor Dave. Although the split was, in large part, the result of a personal conflict between Peukert and Most, it was also political: Peukert opposed

and the Ultra Reds and is said to have had something to do with Berkman leaving Most's employment.[4]

A DISCIPLE OF PEUKERT.

It was on June 15, 1890, that Joseph Peukert came here to talk Anarchy to the Radicale Arbeiter Bund.[5] The meeting was held in Clarendon Hall. Berkman was at the meeting. Peukert denounced Most, and was surprised to find the lights go out and hear half the members shout for Most.

Berkman claimed to be the organizer of the "Pioneers of Liberty, Group of New York."[6] The members claimed to be men of the most advanced school of theorists and do not disclaim their Anarchistic principles. It will be remembered that on the Day of Atonement the Pioneers of Liberty hired the Labor Lyceum, in Brooklyn, to make a burlesque of the religious exercises.[7] As this is one of the most sacred holidays of the Jewish religion the police were asked to suppress it. Most was to have spoken at the meeting, but he refrained from doing so when he was threatened with arrest.

---

the theoretical and tactical tenets of Most's Bakuninist anarchist collectivism, a system of collective economic organization where goods are distributed based on work done by the individual or group. Instead, Peukert promoted Kropotkin's conception of communist anarchism, a system of collective economic organization where goods are distributed according to individual or group need. However, there are nuances and contradictions. The rivalry was also fueled by Peukert's critique of Most's publication *Freiheit* (distributed in Europe by Dave), for its autocratic censorship, and by Most's response to the founding of a new competing anarchist publication, *Der Rebell* (edited by Peukert in collaboration with Otto Rinke), which threatened the financial and ideological supremacy of *Freiheit*. The rift was deepened when Dave and his followers expelled Peukert and his followers from the Whitfield Street Club in London, the First Section of the Kommunistischer Arbeiterbildungsverein (Communist Workers' Education Association). In February 1886, Peukert and his followers formed Gruppe Autonomie (Autonomy Group) and, in November, began publishing *Die Autonomie*. The split was irrevocably solidified in February 1887 with the arrest of Johann Neve, who was smuggling explosives and propaganda into Germany. Neve was a charismatic figure highly respected by all for his personal bravery and his ability to work within the anarchist movement across lines of political difference. Arrested in Belgium, Neve was almost immediately handed over to the German police. Peukert was implicated by many anarchists as complicit in the arrest because of his association with Karl Theodor Reuss, who eventually was exposed as a member of the Berlin Political Police and the person apparently responsible for Neve's capture. Although other anarchists characterized Peukert's involvement with Reuss as careless rather than malicious, Peukert's reputation was destroyed by allegations that he was a police spy. This bitter split in the German anarchist movement would never heal, and its remnants carried over to the movement in the United States.

4. EG recalled in *Living My Life* that AB worked as a compositor on *Freiheit* around 1890. At a national conference of Yiddish anarchist organizations in New York on 25 December 1890, AB proposed that the charges between Most and Peukert be investigated. AB's suggestion enraged Most, which prompted AB and EG to break ties with Most and *Freiheit*.

5. Radikaler Arbeiter-Bund (Radical Workers' League), a German-language New York City anarchist autonomous group, published *Der Anarchist*.

6. The Pioneers of Liberty was a Jewish anarchist group in New York City, founded on 9 October 1886 — the day the sentences on the Haymarket anarchists were announced. AB was a member.

7. Provocative anti-religious Yom Kippur "balls" were held in this period by secular Jewish anarchists and socialists — and especially by the Pioneers of Liberty — the festivities featured dancing, dining, "atheist entertainment," and, intermittently, more direct attacks on Orthodox Jews.

Peukert is a firm believer in bombs and firearms. He is a tall man, with black mustache and goatee.

WHAT THE ASSASSIN'S ACQUAINTANCES SAY.

Berkman had very little money while in this city, yet he appears to have devoted the greater part of his time to promulgating his pessimistic ideas, and devoted time that he might have occupied in bettering his material fortunes to frequenting Anarchistic and Socialistic gatherings and their headquarters and proclaiming his opposition to existing social conditions. Well educated, philosophic, cool, deliberate in his methods, temperate in his habits of life, bold in his plans, cool in executing them, and wholly unscrupulous, he was possessed of those characteristics which go to make up the Anarchistic assassin.

There may be and doubtless are among the Anarchistic element in New York some men who approve of what Berkman has done, but from Herr Most down to his humblest follower none would openly approve the tragic method of "removing" the chief of the Carnegie works. Most was ready to admit that he felt no regret that Frick had been shot, and many Socialists and Anarchists expressed similar views, but not one was found who was willing to proclaim himself a so sufficiently advanced Autonomist as to declare in favor of attempting to redress wrongs by the bullet or the knife of the assassin.

Several German printers, some of whom worked on Most's Anarchistic organ, the *Freiheit*, who were seen yesterday were willing to recall what they knew about Berkman, but declined to allow the use of their names in connection with the publication of what they had to say.

"He was a constant frequenter at Anarchistic headquarters, at No. 85 East Fourth street," said one man yesterday, "and never missed one of the weekly meetings.[8] At closed meetings of the Anarchists he did not hesitate to express his radical views of the individual right to redress the wrongs of the working classes, and he usually spoke with force and feeling. It was evident that his heart was in the work, and his cool, calm manner indicated that he had the pluck and nerve to carry out any scheme he might plan."

"I knew Berkman very well," said another German printer. "He impressed me as possessing a great deal of personal force and strong character. He made no attempt to disguise his social views, and he was a pronounced though not a loud-mouthed Nihilist. He had very little money, and was, through necessity, very economical, but this did not appear to bother him. His habits were very simple, and he spent no money in drink. Although it was apparent that he had seen better days, as far as money went, he made no complaints and asked no favors, and always managed to pay for what he got. Berkman was seen in this city only a few days ago, and if he had no money at his command it is surprising how he managed to support himself and pay his fare to Homestead. It is my belief that he was supplied with money from some outside source, but by whom I am unable to say."

8. Paul Wilzig's saloon was the meeting place of the International Club Freiheit.

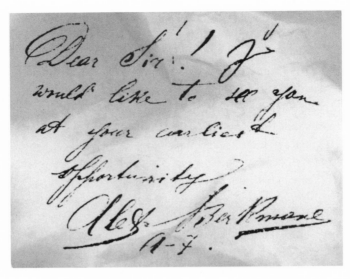

(top, facing page) Mug shot of Alexander Berkman taken by the Pittsburgh police shortly after his arrest on 23 July 1892 for the attempted murder of Carnegie Steel Company manager Henry Clay Frick, shot and wounded by Berkman in an attempt to avenge the deaths of striking workers shot by Pinkerton guards under Frick's orders. (IISH) (top, this page) This handwritten note was presented to Frick's secretary by Berkman moments before his assassination attempt. The note reads "Dear Sir! I would like to see you at your earliest opportunity, Alex Berkman." The annotation "A7" below Berkman's signature matches the police catalogue number on his mug shot. (IISH) (above) Sketch from the *New York World* of 26 July 1892, purporting to show Berkman's assassination attempt on Frick.

Nicholas Alenikoff,[9] President of the Revolutionist Society of Nihilists, has his place of business at No. 205 East Broadway. There was a sign on the front door yesterday, labeled, "gone for the day." Similar notices appeared on the doors of other Anarchists who did not wish to talk about the case.

"All I know about Berkman's movements while in this city," said a man who knew him at Anarchist headquarters, "was that he was employed for some time in the shirt factory of Mr. Zimmerman, No. 718 East Eleventh street. He went there after he left the Jersey factory on Greene street, where he formerly worked. All his spare time he devoted to agitation methods. I recollect that several months ago he went to Worcester, Mass., and other New England towns, with the intention of forming Anarchistic societies and strengthening those already in existence among Russians there. He was engaged in this work for some time."

WHERE IS THIS YOUNG RUSSIAN?

Some people say that Berkman was accompanied to this country by a young Russian named Aronstam,[10] who studied in the same college with him at Kovno, Russia. An uncle

---

9. Nicholas Aleinikoff (ca. 1861–1921), Russian-born Jewish American socialist, lawyer, and intellectual of the Am Olam (Eternal People) colonization movement. Following the pogroms of the early 1880s, he immigrated to the United States where he organized the Am Olam radical communal Jewish colonies, became a leading spokesman for the Jewish community of New York, and founded or was involved with a number of working-class Jewish organizations, including the Propaganda Association for the Dissemination of Socialist Ideas Among the Immigrant Jews (known as the Propaganda Association); the Russian Working Men's Union; the Russian Working Men's Party (which became the Russian-Jewish Working Men's Association, and later the Jewish Working Men's Association); the Russian Progressive Association; and the Russian-American National League. By 1892 Aleinikoff was fully engaged in practicing law in New York City and remained a staunch socialist despite his relationships with anarchists. In an interview with the *New York Times*, which appeared on 26 July 1892, he denied knowing AB and declared himself "the first among any body of men to deprecate violent and high-handed notions by Anarchists or any one."

10. Modest Aronstam, AB's cousin, immigrated from Russia in 1888 and changed his name to Modest Stein sometime after 1900.

of this young man Aronstam, Elias A. Aronstam, is in business as a druggist at No. 1904 Third avenue, this city. Mr. Aronstam said yesterday that his nephew, Modest Aronstam, came to America about five years ago.

"Whether he was accompanied by any person," said Mr. Aronstam, "I am not in a position to say. I do know that Modest gave trouble to his parents by refusing to finish his course at college. He did not do well when he came to this country.

"He got under certain influences which were not for his good. The last I heard of Modest was two years ago, when he came to me for money to take him home again to Russia. I am inclined to think he returned to Russia, but I am not sure."

What the pernicious influences were that his nephew suffered from Mr. Aronstam did not say. He said that he had never seen Berkman, and that he had never heard of him until he read the account of the shooting of Mr. Frick in Saturday's *Evening World.*

AN ANARCHIST PAPER'S REVIEW OF THE HOMESTEAD TROUBLE.

Der Anarchist, a weekly Anarchist paper published by Carl Masur,[11] of No. 315 East Forty-fourth street, has a two-column article from the pen of Bergmann[12] in this week's issue of the paper. It is headed, "The Tragedy at Homestead." It reads:

"What happened at Homestead[13] between the working classes and capitalists during the past two weeks is the birth of a new era on the American labor question. The major-

---

11. Carl Masur edited and managed *Der Anarchist.* Other editors included Claus Timmermann, Joseph Peukert, and Otto Rinke. The *World* reporter quoted Masur in the excised portion of this article: "I knew Berkman when he was in New York, but did not know him intimately. I only know by reputation of his anarchistic views, but there was no doubt that he was a pronounced Anarchist. As to his relations with Miss Goldman I can say nothing. I know very little about the woman. She attended some meetings of Anarchists, and was in sympathy with them, I believe. I have not heard from her for some time and have no idea where she is at present." The 30 July 1892 issue of *Der Anarchist* included an article by EG on AB's act.

12. Referring to AB, whose legal name was Alexander Schmidt Bergmann.

13. On 29 June 1892, workers at the Carnegie Steel Company in Homestead, Pennsylvania, and members of the Amalgamated Association of Iron and Steel Workers went on strike to protest a proposed wage cut. Three years earlier, in 1889, the union had won a strike against the company and negotiated a three-year contract, which was set to expire on 30 June 1892. Henry Clay Frick, the company's general manager known for his anti-union policies, had ordered a solid board and barbed wire fence built surrounding the steel works while negotiations between the union and the company for the renewal of the contract were still taking place. On 28 June the company began a lockout of the workers and stopped negotiations. By 30 June the entire work force was locked out. On 5 July, Frick issued his final orders to the Pinkerton National Detective Agency for the 300 strike-breaking detectives that he had commissioned before the strike (and, allegedly, the wage negotiations) began. Early in the morning of 6 July workers spotted the approaching army of Pinkertons and tore through the company fence in an effort to stop the Pinkertons from entering the factory. A gun battle ensued between the Pinkerton force and workers that lasted until the evening. Three detectives and seven workers died during the battle or from wounds suffered, and many more were wounded, including women and children. Six days later National Guard troops ordered by the governor of Pennsylvania arrived in Homestead to restore order. Anarchists in the area, including Henry Bauer, Carl Nold, and Max Metzkow, had gone to Homestead to agitate among the workers. Nold and another anarchist printed a leaflet in English urging the workers to reorganize the steel

ity of the American working class are blind to the socialistic side of the question. They believe in the old story of self-made men, that is, that every man has the key to the method of becoming a millionaire.

"Those who do not believe this must believe that they are born as a beast of burden, that is to work continually. In no other part of the world do the capitalists trample on the workingmen with such brutality as they do in this country against all laws and morals. The public offices and institutions in city and State are used for squeezing money out of the people. The American people can see this every day. The working class believe firmly that they have the law with them, and that the rich and poor are alike as far as the law is concerned, but when the iron fist of the tyrant crushes them it is about time to give up this sentiment. The drama which was played at Homestead illustrates this plainly. After the workingmen sent back the hired assassins who were employed by the capitalists, the capitalists then sent the State machine going. In the name of the law the people bow to capitalism. But what position did the working class take to this outrage? They believed they were entitled to the same rights as millionaires. Such things as cannons, Winchester rifles, swords and other implements of war were not made for capitalists alone. They have nothing to do with settling the wage question. The workingmen are just as good citizens as their employers. The workingmen went so far in their blind obedience to the law that they took the militia, banquetted them, made much of them in every respect, and would have treated them as friends, had not the commanding officers given the workingmen the well-earned kick. This was the first stream of cold water and it did its work well. The General, with real American brutality, made the strikers understand that they did not come there for their benefit, but they came there in the interest of the robber system of capitalists. This was not sufficient to the workingmen, who wanted to see what Frick & Co. would do in the works, with scab labor under guard of cannon and bayonets.

"Finally the capitalists caused warrants to be issued for the arrest of the most intelligent and energetic of their leaders in the name of the law.

"This was not enough to open the eyes of the workingmen.

"They still believe in the law and think they have an impartial Judge, from whom they will get their rights. They believe they have the same right to prosecute the millionaire as they are being prosecuted.

"What irony! You would not think it possible that people who have gone through so much would stand it very long. But it is so. The workingmen are thick-headed and it will

---

mill in accordance with revolutionary anarchist principles. On 8 July Bauer and two other anarchists traveled from Pittsburgh (six miles away) to Homestead to distribute both the leaflet and anarchist periodicals in English, German, French, Bohemian, and Italian. AB, who arrived in Pittsburgh late on 13 July, met Nold the following day and stayed with him for the next eight days, where he also met Bauer. (Nold's home was also the location of the printing press used to publish Nold and Bauer's leaflet.) On 23 July AB entered Frick's office, shot and stabbed him, but did not succeed in killing him. AB was arrested immediately. Two days later, on 25 July, Nold was arrested on conspiracy charges and the next day Bauer was also arrested on suspicion of conspiring with AB.

take a good many hard knocks to put sense into them. The blows, however, must fall so heavy that they must be made to understand it. Frick & Co. seemed to be well pleased with the idea that they will get along with scab labor.

"The second act has only begun. The thick-headed American workingmen should at last see that the laws are all against them and in favor of the great robbers. In the latter end they will ascertain that the working organizations as they are to-day will not be strong enough to work against the robber system. They must learn that non-union men who are driven to work in their places through hunger and starvation are their friends, and to us Anarchists it is left to sow the seed on good ground, so that Anarchism should thrive.

"And this trouble at Homestead must be the beginning of the crusade."

A SOCIALIST PAPER SAYS FRICK HAS HIS OWN MEDICINE.

The *Volks-Zeitung,* the socialistic daily paper published at 184 William street, came out Sunday with the following headlines of the Homestead tragedy. First, in German, were the words "Bullets for Frick." Next came the word "Nemesis." Then, in English type, were the words "A Dose of His Own Medicine."

At the office of the *Volks-Zeitung* it was said that Berkman had been a subscriber to the paper and that it was sent to him regularly in New Haven, where he worked as printer up to five months ago. Then he came to this city and purchased the paper from the stand.

BERKMAN AND MISS GOLDMAN.

Although Assassin Berkman while in this city appears to have had very little leisure, and, if the statements of his associates are to be credited, very little money, yet he found opportunity to indulge in at least one romantic adventure. The woman who figures in the case was Miss Emma Goldman. She is described as being a Russian or German, about twenty-seven years of age, of medium height, inclined to plumpness of figure, and of comely face. She is a blonde and wears glasses.

Like Berkman, she is a Nihilist, or Anarchist, and was a regular attendant at the weekly meetings of the International Workingmen's Association,[14] at No. 85 East Fourth street, of which body both she and Berkman were active members.

She made herself conspicuous at the May Day demonstration of the Central Labor Union at Union Square on the evening of May 2 last, at the time the meeting was captured by the adherents of Herr Most.[15]

As the crowd began to assemble about 8 o'clock it was noticed that the greater number of people was congregating on the east side of the square, from which Most had announced his intention of speaking. When Chairman Witkowski called the crowd to order there were cries for "Most!" "Most!"

14. This is a reference to the International Working People's Association (IWPA), sometimes known as the Black International.
15. See "Anarchists in Charge," Article in the *New York World,* 3 May 1892, above.

Secretary Lloyd,[16] of the Central Labor Union, came forward and said:

"John Most is not here, and if he was he couldn't speak, as we are not Anarchists."

Lloyd sprang from the wagon, and at the same moment friends of Most rushed forward in a threatening manner. Capt. McLaughlin, with 100 policemen, restored order, but after that time the Anarchists ran things to suit themselves.

Then it was that Miss Goldman, the sweetheart of Berkman, made herself conspicuous by climbing on top of the truck. The Central Labor Union men were puzzled to know how to get rid of the crowd, when some one suggested hitching a horse to the truck. This was done, and just as Miss Goldman began to harangue the crowd the horse was whipped up and the truck was driven away. The agitator in skirts was not, however, wholly suppressed by this device, and she continued to appeal to the crowd and proclaimed her Anarchistic ideas as long as her voice could be heard.

HER SPEECH AFTER THE SHOOTING.

Miss Goldman has a strong face, with intelligent, animated expression, and the use of spectacles gives to her a studious, intellectual appearance. She speaks German, English and Russian. At a secret meeting of Anarchists, at No. 85 East Fourth street, Saturday night, she was present and made a forcible address.[17] She alluded to the shooting of Frick by Berkman and appeared to be well satisfied with what Berkman had done. She said she knew that he was sincere and earnest in the cause of Anarchism and that his deed in Pittsburg showed what he would risk for the sake of the cause he had espoused. Miss Goldman spoke in an excited manner, and many of the listeners were surprised at her radical notions. After her speech she talked about Berkman. She admitted he was a friend of hers, but declined to say whether he was her lover. She said that Berkman's parents were not living and that she did not believe he had any relatives in this country.

Whatever the precise relations between Berkman and Miss Goldman were, it is known that he was an ardent admirer of the young woman and there is reason for believing that she reciprocated his attachment. The attentions Berkman bestowed upon the young woman necessarily compelled an expenditure of money in escorting her to places of amusement and entertaining her in other ways. This leads many who knew Berkman to speculate as to where the money came from if he was so poor as represented by other persons to be. It seems to be conceded by a good many of Berkman's old associates that while he made no display of money, yet he had some mysterious source from which he drew supplies, as a great part of the time he was idle and at others his earnings would barely support him in the most economical fashion.

16. The wording of George K. Lloyd's statement here varies slightly with his disclaimer as quoted in the 3 May *New York World* article.
17. The meeting was not secret; *Freiheit* had announced that Most was scheduled to lecture that night before a meeting of the IWPA.

ONCE WORKED IN NEW HAVEN.

A dispatch from New Haven says that Berkman appeared in that city five years ago with a woman whose name is given as Emma Goldbaum. This is possibly the Emma Goldman with whom Berkman, or Bergman, was seen here. The woman gave several lectures in New Haven in small German halls and lived with Berkman at No. 25 Silver street. Whether they were ever married does not appear, but the inference is they were not. After living together some time they separated, and Berkman went to work for Paul Gephardt, who publishes a German paper called the Connecticut *Volks Blatt*. He was six months with Gephardt, and there gained a little knowledge of typesetting.

He was a very quiet fellow while in New Haven, belonged to none of the anarchistic or socialistic societies, and was known to only half a dozen people in the town. After a six months' stay in New Haven Berkman disappeared. [. . .]

New York World, 25 July 1892, p. 3. The excised remainder of this article reprints resolutions passed at an 11 July meeting of the Socialist Labor Party urging the abolition of capitalism and the uniting of labor into one political party and demanding "that the thugs, who took part in the midnight assault on the Homestead workingmen, and their employers, H. G. Frick and William and Robert Pinkerton, be tried and executed as murderers." The article spuriously places AB at the meeting and suggests he may have been driven to his act by the proclamations made there.

Interview in the *NEW YORK WORLD*

New York, 28 July 1892

Anarchy's Den.

Emma Goldman, Its Queen, Rules with a Nod the Savage Reds.

Peukert, the Silent Autonomist, the Power Behind Her.

Berkman, the Assassin, the Tool of These Leaders.

Their Headquarters in a Cheap Flat on Fifth Street.

[. . .]AND HERE WAS EMMA GOLDMAN.

In the far right-hand corner of the second room, near a dusty, cobwebbed window, sat a woman. Alone in that gathering of hard-faced, half clad men, enveloped in a dense atmosphere of choking smoke, she reclined placidly in a barroom chair, reading. She seemed rather pretty. The back of her chair was tilted against the rear wall, and her left foot rested on the rung of a chair in front of her. A white straw hat, with a blue band streaked with dotted white, lay on the table at her elbow.

Chestnut-brown hair that had been parted on the side fluffed over her forehead, leaving only a trace of the part. At the back the short hair was as negligently arranged. She has a shapely head; a long, low, white forehead; light bluish-gray eyes, shielded by glasses; a small, finely chiselled nose, rather too wide at the nostrils for symmetry; a colorless complexion; cheeks that once had been full, but now are slightly sunken, giving a moderately pinched appearance to a face that loses its beauty of form in the rapid decline to the chin. The mouth in repose is hard and sensual, the curves gross, the lips full and bloodless.

A neck that once was rounded was still well poised, but as she turned her head the tendons bulged out into scrawniness, and blotches here and there added to the sharp disappointment one met with after leaving the upper part of the face. A trim figure, five feet four or five inches tall, well moulded with hard flesh, clothed in a white blouse, a tan-colored belt and a gown of blue sateen striped with white, and tan shoes.

That was Emma Goldman as she sat in the Anarchist drinking den[1] at 5 o'clock yesterday afternoon.

---

1. Zum Großen Michel, the saloon at 209 Fifth Street and the regular meeting place of the Gruppe Autonomie (Autonomy Group) as well as the address of *Die Brandfackel* and of Claus Niedermann, who

A sketch of Goldman at Justus Schwab's saloon in New York City's Lower East Side, an anarchist meeting place. The sketch appeared with an article in the 28 July 1892 *New York World.*

"You are Miss Emma Goldman?"

"I am."

The reporter passed some pleasantry and she smiled. Her lips wreathed into lines that were uglier than when her face was in repose. The two front teeth were set wide apart, and on either side there were dental hollows, making the interior of the mouth look black, or rather that dull opaque hue characteristic of the mouths of some snakes. She spoke English well, with a positive tone, but there was a noticeable accent.

edited *Die Brandfackel* while its editor and founder Claus Timmermann was imprisoned on Blackwell's Island in 1893. The reporter later noted that "the walls were hung with advertisements of Anarchistic papers and on a rack were bound files of *La R[é]volt[é], [Die] Autonomie* and other periodicals evidently of Anarchistic views."

PROUD OF BEING AN ANARCHIST.

"Yes, I know Berkman. He is a splendid man—a man of brains and courage. Am I an Anarchist? I am, and I am proud of it. They have arrested Mollock, I see. Well, I am sure that Mollock had nothing to do with that little affair in Pittsburg."[2]

"But Mollock and Berkman were friends?"

"Oh, yes, they were friends, and I suppose Mollock owed Berkman some money. In fact, I know he did, and that is why he sent it to him."

"When did you last see Berkman?"

"Oh, some time ago; a week, maybe, or ten days. I don't remember exactly."

"Did he tell you where he was going and what he was going to do?"

"No, he does not make confidences with people in that way about such matters!"

"But you are his wife?"

"Ha! ha! yes, I am his wife, but in the anarchistic way, you don't know what that is! The anarchists don't believe in marriages by law. We want no law and when we agree to marry, why ha! ha! there you are."

"The anarchist wife then does not expect the confidences of her husband?"

"Why should we? But that is a matter I don't propose to discuss."

"You lived with Mrs. Mollock?"[3]

"Yes."

"The name under the bell is Pollak, is that her real name?"

"I suppose so. She is Mollock's wife, as I am Berkman's. She couldn't live with her first husband and went with Mollock."

"But Mollock signs his name to his letters to her as Pollak?"

"Is that so?"

Miss Goldman tried to be arch. It was a dismal failure she did not repeat.

"THE POLICE MAKE ME TIRED."

"Mollock met his wife in Buffalo, and when they came here Berkman assisted them and we all lived together in Chrystie street. No, I don't know where his wife is now, but I believe she has gone to Long Branch to see her husband. The papers made a big fuss about me, but I have not been concealing myself. I have been around town all the time."

"Were you called upon last night by Chief O'Mara, of the Pittsburg police?"[4]

---

2. Police in Long Branch, New Jersey, acting on a request from Pittsburgh police, arrested Frank Mollock on the basis of his having sent six dollars to AB in Pittsburgh on or around 23 July. Mollock admitted sending the money but denied any part in AB's attempted assassination of Henry C. Frick, the "little affair" EG refers to in this interview. AB recounted in prison how he had tried to collect money owed him by various comrades immediately after arriving in New York on 10 July.

3. Josephine Mollock, whom EG and AB had lived with, apparently locked EG out of the apartment under pressure from the landlord after AB's *attentat*.

4. Pittsburgh police chief O'Mara had recently claimed that AB's attempt on Henry C. Frick's life was part of an anarchist conspiracy to murder seventy millionaires whose names appeared on a list discovered in the desk drawer of Pittsburgh anarchist, and suspected accomplice, Henry Bauer.

"No, I was not. The police make me tired. They are mostly fools. They go about mysteriously and do nothing. All they ever did was to put that old fool, Most,[5] in jail."

"You are a friend of Most's?"

"A friend! The old fraud! I only wish that when I had a chance to do it, I had made him give me some of his money. He is a coward, and an Anarchist for revenue only."

"Were you not his Anarchistic wife before he took up with Lena Fischer[6] and you met Berkman?"

"Ha, ha, ha!"

Again that hard, unmusical laugh. This time it had a ring of insincerity in it that belied her words. "I was not," she said decisively.[7]

"When was it that you had a chance to make him give you money?"

"You reporters are too impertinent. I hate reporters."

"Why?"

"Because I hate all inquisitors. I have travelled all over this country, lecturing to the groups, and I have spoken here when that paltroon Most was afraid of the police. Yes, I am a Russian, but from what part of Russia I don't propose to tell. But above all I am an Anarchist."

"You are proud then of your lover's achievement?"

"Indeed I am; we all are."

"You received several telegrams last Saturday; were they from Berkman?"

"Now, I don't propose to say any more. I have told you enough, and I suppose you will write a lot of lies. You all do, because your people must pander to the capitalists who give you bread, and the capitalists like to read the lies about us Anarchists."

"Won't you tell me when you last heard from Berkman?"

"That is no concern of the public. Now, sir, I will say no more. If you were to ask questions all night I would not answer."

THE OTHER ANARCHISTS AROUSED.

One by one the swarthy, half-clad and grimy Anarchists in the front room had been coming near to where their queen sat. Some one of them probably gave her a sign to say no more. A dozen stalwart black and redbearded Anarchists stood a few feet back of the reporter. Another reporter approached and asked Emma Goldman a question. With her

---

5. Johann Most had recently been released from prison where he had served a sentence (June 1891 to April 1892) for his alleged "incendiary" speech on 12 November 1887, the day after the Haymarket anarchists were executed.

6. Lena Fischer was the sister of Haymarket anarchist Adolph Fischer, although the reporter may have confused her with Helene Minkin, a young anarchist who had lived with EG and AB, and later married Johann Most.

7. In fact, EG had been drawn to Most as a lover and mentor soon after she first moved permanently to New York. He encouraged and helped organize her first lectures, sparking the beginning of her public speaking career.

eyes glancing with a significant look at the group of her friends, she said in a voice far louder than was necessary, so loud that it could have been heard in the front room:

"I have nothing to say. Will you not let me alone?"

As if her words were a signal, half a dozen Anarchists closed about the reporter, waving their fists in the air and hurling oaths and objurgations in German and Russian at the reporters. One man stood near a table with an ice-pick in his hand.

"ALL REPORTERS SHOULD BE KILLED."

The group grew larger. Emma Goldman rose to her feet. One burly Anarchist, broader chested than Sullivan,[8] clinched his fists and, with face aflame with beer, heat and anger, exclaimed in German that all reporters should be killed.

"Yes, he can understand German!" he howled. "You——!"

"No," replied the woman in German, "he is an American." She smiled that hollow cavernous smile, her eyes shone behind her glasses. A glad and proud look was on her face, and while she made a faint display of quieting her slaves her pale face took on some color and she stood there wreathed in smiles amid smoke and beer fumes. [. . .]

New York World, 28 July 1892, p. 2; includes sketch of EG. Excised from this article are brief interviews with Claus Timmermann and Fritz Oerter, both of whom protected themselves from police investigation with vague and evasive responses to the reporter's queries. The headline refers to Joseph Peukert, anarchist communist and a leader of the Gruppe Autonomie (Autonomy Group).

8. A reference to the first American world heavyweight bare-knuckle boxing champion, John L. Sullivan, who held the title from 1882 to 1892.

Eingesandt.

Lange Jahre hat es ein Mann fertig gebracht, sich als Held und Märtyrer hinzustellen, die größten Schurkereien zu verüben und zu verläumden und so die besten Kräfte zu untergraben.

Und dies alles unter dem Deckmantel des Anarchismus, ohne daß auch nur eine Hand sich erhoben hätte, die Maske von dem Gesicht dieses Mannes herab zu reißen.

Der Mann von dem ich hier spreche ist John Most der "Anarchistenführer", der Mann, der es wagt, sich an die Seite eines Krapotkin, einer Perowskaya und anderer Helden unserer Bewegung zu stellen.

Genossen und Freunde, wenn ich jetzt die Feder ergreife, um Euch diesen Most in das richtige Licht zu stellen, so ist es wahrlich nicht persönlicher Haß, (ich bin gerade im Interesse der Bewegung noch nicht gegen Most aufgetreten), sondern die Empörung über die Haltung dieses Schuften, unserem Genossen Berkmann gegenüber. Ja, die Empörung die einen jeden ehrlichen Arbeiter ergreifen muß, über dieses verläumderische Treiben, über dieses Denunziantenthum dieser Demagogen.

Die Genossen werden das Interview, das M. mit einem Reporter hatte, an anderer Stelle übersetzt finden.

Was, frage ich, kann einen Menschen veranlassen, so gemein, so niederträchtig zu handeln?

Einfach der schmutzige persönliche Haß, der Neid und die Furcht ist es, was diesen Menschen treibt so zu sprechen. Most ist feig, feig bis zum Äußersten, daß ist jeden bekannt, der ihn nur ein bischen genau kennt.

Ich, die ich ihn leider gut kennen gelernt habe, die jeden Charakterzug zur Genüge studirte, ich behaupte, daß Most ein ganz erbärmlicher Feigling, ein Lügner, Schauspieler und zugleich ein Waschlappen ist.

Alle seine sogenannten heroistischen Thaten sind nicht der Liebe zur Sache, der Ergebenheit zum Prinzip entsprungen. Oh nein! Es war Berechnung, es war ganz schmutziger Ehrgeiz, der ihn zwang "sein" Prinzip (?) zu vertreten. Was hat denn Most bisher Großes geleistet? Ein paar Jahre hat er im Gefängniß, wo es ihm nebenbei bemerkt, sehr gut erging, zugebracht, das ist alles. Die Arbeiter haben ihren letzten Cent hingegeben, um es diesen Parasiten an nichts fehlen zu lassen.

Wo es aber galt, irgend eine That zu vollbringen oder andere zu unterstützen, da hat er sich stets feige und erbärmlich gezeigt.

Ich führe nur aus letzter Zeit einige Beispiele an, die Versammlung auf Union Square

Der Anarchist.

ANARCHISTISCH-COMMUNISTISCHES ORGAN.

Herausgegeben von den autonomen Gruppen Amerika's.

Entered as second class matter at the New York Post Office.

Erscheint wöchentlich.

Abonnementspreis: Ganzjährlich $1.60, viertel-jährlich 40c.	Alle Briefe und Gelder sind zu adressiren: CARL MASUR, 432 E. 14. STR., NEW YORK.	Agentur für Europa: R. Gundersen, 98 Wardour Street, Soho London W. England.
Jahrgang V. — Nr. 23.	New York, 15. Juli 1893.	Preis 3 Cents.

Masthead from *Der Anarchist,* German-language anarchist communist paper edited by Joseph Peukert, in which prison correspondence between Alexander Berkman and Emma Goldman was published. (Labadie Collection, University of Michigan)

am 1. Mai, wo er aus Furcht nicht hinkam, troztdem er Wochen zuvor aufforderte die Genossen möchten sich an der Maidemonstration betheiligen—Weiter die Versammlung in Philadelphia, die er deshalb sich nicht zu adressiren getraute, weil kurz zuvor Genosse Hoffmann verhaftet wurde.

Und die größte und gemeinste Feigheit die jetzigen Handlung Most's. Aus Angst und persönlichem Haß erzählt er allerlei Lügen über Genossen Berkmann. Anstatt diese That propagandisch auszunützen, versucht er sie in den Koth hinab zu ziehen. Nichts ist ihm zu schlecht, um es gegen B. anzuwenden. Er erzählte unter anderem dem Reporter, daß B. ein sehr ungeschickter Arbeiter sei, troztdem er mir und anderen gegenüber hundertemal betheuerte, daß B. ein sehr geschickter und fleißiger Arbeiter sei.

Aber weil B. frei und offen M. die Meinung in's Gesicht sagte, weil er gesagt hat, daß er alles andere eher sei, als ein Anarchist, weil B. die Corruption und den Schmutz in der "Freiheit" aufgedeckt, wurde er Mitte Juli entlassen, mit dem Versprechen bald wieder eingestellt zu werden.

Genossen! wenn in Euch noch ein Funken Selbstachtung vorhanden ist, wenn Ihr nicht theilnehmen wollt an den Schurkereien dieses Charlatan, dann bedenkt diese Worte.

Ihr seid es, die ihn ernähret, die ihn Mittel schafft, um ein feines Leben zu führen. Durch Euren Schweiß und Euer Blut, hat er sich einen Namen erworben. Hat er doch so oft gesagt, er sei lieber Carl Schurz als John Most.

Genug der Worte, denn man müßte ein Buch schreiben, um all die elenden Handlungen zu behandeln.

"Die Polizei will ihn verhaften." Eine größere Dummheit, eine größere Schande könnte der That B.'s nicht gemacht werden. B. würde Most niemals etwas anvertrauen, einfach weil er diesen Schwätzer kennt. Most hat schon manche That eines Genossen hintertrieben, so manche Tapfern abgehalten etwas zu thun. Das fanatische russische Volk hat die Niedertracht eines Alexander III. erkannt, hoffentlich werden auch die aufgeklärten deutschen Genossen endlich die elenden Handlungen eines Most erkennen.

Denn solange wir solche Demagogen groß ziehen, welche durch uns und unsere Groschen "Größen" werden, wird die Bewegung gehemmt sein und die herrschende Klasse triumphieren.

Worte helfen bei solchen Menschen nichts; eine Tracht Hiebe würde diesen Menschen wohl nicht ändern, aber ihm das Maul stopfen.

EMMA GOLDMANN.

Submitted.

For many years one man has succeeded in portraying himself as a hero and martyr, perpetuating the greatest roguery, slandering, and thus undermining the best forces.

And all this under the veil of Anarchism, so that not even one hand would ever be raised to rip the mask from the face of this man.

The man about whom I am speaking is John Most, the "Anarchist Leader,"[1] the man who dares to place himself alongside Kropotkin, Perowskaya and other heroes of the movement.

---

1. EG was responding to an interview with Most that appeared in the *New York World* on 27 July. Most's position on AB's act is also articulated in the article "Attentats-Reflexionen," which he composed on 31 July and in which he questioned the efficacy of propaganda by the deed under present conditions in the United States. Most submitted his article to anarchist press committees in New York and Allegheny. Both unanimously approved the piece, but the former thought it best to withhold publication until tempers cooled while the latter argued for its immediate publication. Most's article finally appeared in *Freiheit* on 27 August. The following excerpts from *Freiheit* (27 August 1892, p. 1; translated from German) display both Most's argument against the tactical efficacy of AB's act and his attempt to acknowledge the personal courage of AB's intent.

The other set of people in this country only needed to hear *who* the would-be assassin was, to forget about all the resentment they may previously have held against the cad and assassin Frick and to make a hullabaloo about the former, joining in the hysteria of the nativist press. A Russian Jew—a man without regular employment—an enfant perdu—that was enough to stir up all the prejudices of Americans against the would-be assassin, as in a dust cloud made by buffaloes stampeding through a wildfire. The fact that this man is also an Anarchist—all the more terrible. Americans have never heard anything good about the Anarchists—now suddenly all the nonsense was revived which their press had been funneling into their indecently long ears—especially since 1886. Should *such* a mood signify propaganda in *our* sense? If so, then go on! Let's keep shooting the next best monopolists. One cannot really call that dangerous because the panderers of Americanism want to fricassee us anyway.

But we have a *different* opinion, have had it since time immemorial and have always said it—: in a country where we are so poorly represented and so little understood as in America, we simply cannot afford the luxury of assassination. Where on every main square in the country one has barely a few active forces, there it is more than frivolous, there it is *suicidal*, to hand them over to the clutches of the overpowering enemy provoked through the *attentat*, without drawing even one person into the movement [*ohne daß im Übrigen auch nur ein Hund vor den Ofen gelockt wird;* literally, "without enticing even one dog to leave his warm and cozy little corner behind the oven"]. [. . .]

If some *stranger* had said to us that he wanted to shoot Frick, we probably would have said to him that that was his business. And in our hearts would have stirred something like *joy*, for haters of tyrants such as we can surely have no sympathy for a monstrous bloodsucker such as Frick. A *Berkmann* would surely have been the last person whom *we* would have instructed to commit such a deed, for he has, as has been implied above, no less than *all* of the characteristics which would stimulate the most idiotic prejudices of idiotic Americans and thereby awaken a general antipathy for the act and make easier the inevitable campaign against Anarchists.

So that we are not misunderstood, we want to express our opinion somewhat more clearly about the assailant *himself*.

We were always somewhat uneasy about Berkmann because we considered him to be eccentric; we became thoroughly his enemy when he joined the New York Autonomist clique whose entire doings consisted already for years in rolling obstacles in the way of a reasonable and systematic anarchistic agitation, in ripping apart that which we had built up etc., and when he behaved among those people in a particularly fanatical and poisonous manner toward us.

All that, however, cannot and must not stop us from saying here openly: Berkmann demonstrated great heroism

Comrades and friends, if I now seize the pen to put Most in the proper light for you, it is truly not out of personal hatred (in the interest of the movement, I have not yet spoken out against Most), but out of indignation over this scoundrel's behavior toward our comrade Berkmann. Yes, the indignation that must grip every honest worker, indignation over the malicious conduct and denunciatory practices of this demagogue.

The comrades will find the interview that M. had with a reporter translated in another place.[2]

What, I ask, can induce a person to act in such a petty and base manner?

It is simply ugly personal hatred, envy, and fear that drove this man to speak in such a way. That Most is rotten, rotten to the core, is apparent to everyone who knows him at all.

I, who unfortunately came to know him well and have sufficiently studied his every characteristic, maintain that Most is a wholly miserable coward, a liar, a dissimulator, and above all a weakling.

All his so-called heroic accomplishments did not arise from devotion to the cause or dedication to principles. Oh no! It was calculation, wholly disgusting ambition that compelled him to advocate "his" principles(?). What great things has Most accomplished up to now? He spent a couple of years in prison, where, by the way, he had quite an easy time of it, and that is all.[3] The workers have given up their last cent so that this parasite would not want for anything.

But wherever he was counted on to complete an action or support others, he showed himself to be cowardly and miserable.

I will cite a few recent examples. The gathering in Union Square on May 1 where, out of fear, he did not appear, although weeks before he called upon comrades to participate in the May Day demonstration[4]—also the gathering in Philadelphia that he did not dare to address because Comrade Hoffmann had just been arrested.[5]

---

with the *attentat*, just as since then he has behaved quite bravely in jail. In this regard one owes him all respect and one can only regret—completely apart from the fact that in spite of everything else the *attentat* was a complete failure and also that the most serious consequences will in all probability result from it for our party—, that this energy was not saved up for a *bigger* and *more suitable* deed.

2. Most's interview first appeared in rough translation on 27 July 1892 in the *New York World* and was reprinted in the 30 July issue of *Der Anarchist*.

3. Most, in fact, served a number of prison sentences. In 1869 he spent a month in prison in Vienna for an incendiary speech. In 1870 he was sentenced to five years in prison for high treason for his participation in a free speech demonstration, although he was released after serving a few months. After being expelled from Austria he was summoned to court forty-three times while editor of the *Chemnitzer Freie Presse*, again serving prison time in February 1873. In 1874 he was sentenced to two years in prison for giving a speech on the Paris Commune in Berlin. In March 1881 he was sentenced to sixteen months in prison in England for applauding the assassination of Alexander II in *Freiheit*. In the United States, Most served a prison term from June 1891 to April 1892, for an allegedly "incendiary" speech he gave on 12 November 1887, the day after the Haymarket anarchists were executed.

4. A reference to the May Day demonstration at Union Square orchestrated by the New York City Central Labor Union. Most, who was scheduled to speak at the event, was not present (although some reports alleged his presence). See "Anarchists in Charge," Article in the *New York World*, 3 May 1892, above.

5. Possibly Dr. Julius Hoffmann, who in 1893 paid EG's $5,000 bail bond after her arrest for incitement to riot.

And the greatest and most vile cowardice comes in Most's current behavior. Out of fear and personal hatred he tells all kinds of lies about Comrade Berkmann. Instead of using this act for propaganda purposes, he is trying to bring it down to the level of filth. For him nothing is so bad that it cannot be used against B. Among other things he told a reporter that B. was an inept worker, although he swore to me and others a hundred times that B. is a very skillful and diligent worker.

But because B. told M his honest opinion to his face, because he said that he was anything but an Anarchist, because B. uncovered the corruption and filth in *Freiheit,* he was let go in the middle of July with the promise that he would be brought on again soon.

Comrades! If you still possess a spark of self-respect, if you do not want to take part in the mean tricks of this charlatan, then consider these words.

It is you who nourish him, who create the means for him to lead a fine life. Through your sweat and your blood he has acquired his name. How often he has said that he would rather be Carl Schurz[6] than John Most.

But enough words. One would have to write a book to deal with all his miserable deeds.

"The police want to arrest him." A greater idiocy, a greater disgrace could not be made out of B.'s deed. B. would never entrust something to Most simply because he knows this gossipmonger. Most has already frustrated several of his comrades' acts, and thus has kept several courageous people from doing anything. The fanatical Russian people have recognized the vileness of Alexander III,[7] hopefully the enlightened German comrades will finally recognize Most's wretched behavior.

For as long as we cultivate such demagogues, who through us and our pennies become "great men," the movement will be hampered and the ruling class will triumph.

Words do not help with such a person; a good thrashing would probably not change such a person, but it might shut his mouth.[8]

Emma Goldmann

Der Anarchist, 30 July 1892, p. 4. Translated from German.

6. Carl Schurz (1829–1906) was a German immigrant and participant in the 1848 revolution. In America he befriended Abraham Lincoln and took part in the Civil War. He was a Missouri senator, radical Republican, lawyer, and journalist. After the Civil War, Schurz advocated civil service reform and the formation of the Liberal Republican party. He served as secretary of the interior from 1877 to 1881.
7. Alexander III (1845–1894), tsar of Russia from 1881, reversed many of the liberalizing trends of his father, Alexander II, who had emancipated the serfs, instituted a system of limited local self-government, and relaxed censorship and control over education. After his father's death at the hands of radicals, Alexander III reinstated control over the peasantry. He subjected minorities to Russification, increased police power, limited the power of the local assemblies, and tightened censorship and control over education.
8. Later, on 18 December 1892, EG would confront Most and strike him in the face with a toy horsewhip at a meeting at 98 Forsyth Street in New York City.

Aufruf!

Genossen und Freunde!

Der heldenmüthige Versuch des Genossen Berkmann, die menschliche Gesellschaft von einer Bestie zu befreien, hat in allen hoch- und edelfühlenden Menschen ein sympathisches Echo gefunden, und gewiß sind viele, wenn nicht alle, bereit, diese ihre Sympathie dadurch auszudrücken, für die Erleichterung des in den Klauen kapitalistischen Schergenthumes befindlichen Opfers ihr Scherflein beizutragen.

Genosse Berkmann ist ebenso wie wir gesonnen, die bodenlosen Säckel der herrschenden Gerechtigkeitshuren und ihren Zuhältern nicht mit sauer verdien-Arbeitergroschen zu füllen. Aber Berkmann ist gänzlich mittellos im Kerker und daher außer Stande, die nothwendigsten Lebensbedürfnisse—außer mit ungenießbarer Gefängniskost—zu befriedigen. Eine Anzahl Genossen hat es daher übernommen, den Genossen Berkmann durch Collecten mit Mitteln zu versehen, sich mit menschliche Nahrung versehen zu können. Zu diesem Zwecke sind Sammellisten angefertigt worden, welche allen Genossen zur Verfügung stehen, die Gelder zu sammeln bereit sind.

Die Eingänge und Verwendung der Gelder wird im "Anarchist" quittirt.

Gelder und Nachfragen nach Sammellisten sind einstweilen an die Adresse des "Anarchist" zu richten.

FÜR DIE UNTERSTÜTZUNGS-GRUPPE
E. GOLDMANN.

Attention!

Comrades and Friends!

The heroically brave attempt of Comrade Berkmann to liberate human society from a beast has found a sympathetic echo in all high- and noble-minded people, and certainly many, if not all, are ready to express their sympathy by contributing their bit to the relief of the victim caught in the clutches of capitalistic myrmidons.

Comrade Berkmann is as intent as we are on not filling the bottomless purses of the reigning whores of justice and their pimps with the hard-earned pennies of workers. But Berkmann is in jail entirely without means and therefore unable to satisfy—except with inedible prison food—the most essential needs of life. A number of comrades have therefore taken it upon themselves to provide Comrade Berkmann through a collection with the means to supply himself with human food. Collection lists have been prepared for this purpose and are available to all comrades who are willing to collect monies.

Receipt and use of the monies will be acknowledged in the *Anarchist*.

For the time being, monies and inquiries about collection lists are to be directed to the address of the *Anarchist*.

FOR THE SUPPORT GROUP
E. GOLDMANN.

Der Anarchist, 13 August 1892, p. 1. Translated from German.

Liebe Freundin!

Deinen Brief vom 15. d. M. habe ich erst heute erhalten und sage ich Dir tausend Dank für denselben. Gewiß hast Du Recht, daß die Genossen nicht prinzipiell handeln, wenn sie Geld zu einem Vertheidiger sammeln. Zwei Pittsburger Vertheidiger haben sich erboten, mich unentgeltlich zu vertheidigen. Als Anarchist, der das Gesetz voll und ganz verwirft, die heute bestehenden bekämpft und sie als Klassengesetze nicht anerkennt, brauche ich keine Vertheidiger, die vom Gesetz für mich ein Almosen erbetteln. Ich erkenne über mich keine Gesetze als meinen Willen.

Als überzeugter Egoist, als Anarchist, als Revolutionär habe ich meine That vollbracht. Ich werde meine That vor Gericht nicht zu beschönigen suchen, sondern ich werde frank und frei erklären, daß ich von den Richtern keine Gerechtigkeit erwarte, daß ich mir bewußt war, als ich die That beging, daß ich die ganze Strenge einer Gesetzgebung fühlen werde, die nur für die Besitzenden und gegen die Armen gemacht ist.

Ich werde mich selbst vertheidigen, d. h. ich werde meine Gründe, warum ich Frick tödten wollte, auseinandersetzen, ich werde sagen, was wir Anarchisten wollen, und wie wir zu handeln haben. Ich fühle mich glücklich, daß ich den Feinden Anklagen ins Gesicht schleudern kann, denn ich fühle mich als Ankläger, nicht als Angeklagter.

Ich habe keine Gerechtigkeit zu erwarten von Leuten, die uns knechten und zu Thieren herabwürdigen. In einer Gesellschaft, in der die einen prassen, die anderen hungern, wo jede natürliche Regung unterdrückt wird, wo der größte Barbarismus herrscht, giebt es keine Gerechtigkeit. Ich hätte noch viel zu sagen, aber es nähme zu viel Platz ein. Ich werde alles beim Prozeß sagen, was dann ja bekannt wird.

Den Anarchisten aber, die stets das Gesetz bekämpfen und doch Tausende von Dollars für Vertheidiger ausgeben, diesen erkläre ich, daß sie kein Recht haben, sich Anarchisten zu nennen, denn dieses Geld wird viel besser zur revolutionären Propaganda (wo es sehr nothwendig ist) verwendet.

Die jüdischen Genossen ersuche ich, kein Geld zu einem Vertheidiger zu sammeln, mögen sie es zu einer Propaganda, wie die Meinige verwenden.

Meinen näheren Genossen und Freunden danke ich für alles, was sie für mich gethan haben. Ich befinde mich wohl, und mögen mich unsere Feinde auch auf lange Zeit einkerkern, ich werde stets derselbe bleiben. Allen Genossen ein Lebewohl. Hoch die Anarchie!

Alexander Berkmann

Dear Friend!

I have only today received your letter of May 15th, and I extend to you a thousand thanks for it. You are certainly right that the comrades are not acting in a principled way if they are collecting money for a defense attorney. Two Pittsburgh defense attorneys have offered to defend me without pay.[1] As an Anarchist who completely and totally rejects the law, who stands against it in its present form and, it being class law, does not recognize it, I need no defense attorney who begs for alms from the law for me. I recognize no law over me except my own will.

I carried out my deed as a dedicated egoist,[2] as an Anarchist, as a revolutionary. I will not seek to whitewash my deed before the court, rather I will frankly and openly explain that I expect no justice from the judges, that I knew when I committed the deed that I would feel the full severity of legislation that is made only for the possessors and against the poor.

I will defend myself; thus I will explain my reasons for wanting to kill Frick, and in explaining this I will say what we Anarchists want and how we have to act. I am happy that I can fling accusations in the face of the enemies, for I feel like the accuser, not the accused.

I do not expect any justice from people who enslave us and reduce us to the level of animals. In a society in which some feast while the others starve, where every natural instinct is repressed, where the greatest barbarism rules, there is no justice. I would say more, but it would take too much space. I will say everything during the trial, and then all will be known.

To the Anarchists, however, who constantly fight the law and nevertheless spend thousands of dollars for defense attorneys, to them I declare that they have no right to call themselves Anarchists, for this money would be much better used for revolutionary propaganda (where it is badly needed).

I ask of my Jewish comrades not to collect any money for a defense attorney; they should use it for propaganda like mine.

1. Carl Nold's and Henry Bauer's attorneys, E. D. Moore and Joseph Friedman, offered to represent AB.
2. The term "egoist" (or, alternately, "egotist") was understood to be associated with the individualist branch of anarchism, often considered incompatible with anarchist communism. Grounded in the writings of Max Stirner, the philosophy of egoism claimed that enlightened self-interest was the only realistic basis for human conduct; the state and communism were rejected because they sought to chain the individual to the general will. AB identified himself as an egoist again in a letter to *Solidarity*. See *Solidarity* (New York), 9 February 1893, p. 1. EG also used the term in an 1893 interview. See "Nellie Bly Again," Interview in the *New York World,* 17 September 1893, below.

As for my intimate comrades and friends I thank them for everything that they have done for me. I am well and should our enemies choose to imprison me for a long time, I will remain the same always. To all comrades a farewell. All hail Anarchy!

ALEXANDER BERKMANN.

Der Anarchist, 27 August 1892, p. 4. *Der Anarchist* printed AB's 20 August 1892 letter with this introduction: "Comrade Goldmann received the following letter from Comrade Berkman." Reprinted in *Die Autonomie,* 10 September 1892, p. 4. Translated from German.

THEUERE FREUNDIN!

Du wirst gewiß geglaubt haben, daß ich Dich und alle lieben Freunde vergessen habe, weil ich so lange nicht schrieb. Ich habe Dir einige Briefe geschrieben, da ich jedoch auf keinen derselben eine Antwort erhielt, so kam ich zu der Gewißheit, daß man dieselben gar nicht abschickte. Den letzten Brief erhielt ich am 25.8.

Ich war mir bewußt, daß ich als Proletarier und dazu als verhaßter Anarchist von den Richtern keine Gerechtigkeit zu erwarten hatte, daß man aber mit soviel Gemeinheit, mit solchem Raffinement bei meinem Prozeß vorgehen würde, hätte ich doch nicht gedacht. Ich wurde ähnlich den russischen politischen Gefangenen auf administrativem Wege fortgeschafft.

Die ganze Komödie dauerte kaum 2 Stunden. In größter Eile verurtheilte mich der Richter zu 22 Jahren Zuchthaus. Natürlich gab man mir keine Zeit zum Sprechen und da ich noch dazu nicht fließend genug englisch spreche, so konnte ich nicht viel sagen. Ein paar Stunden später brachte man mich in mein neues "Heim". Die herrschende Klasse ist sehr konsequent in ihren Handlungen; wir Anarchisten sind ihnen im Wege, bekämpfen sie; mit einem Wort, sind ihre gefährlichsten Feinde. Kriegen sie darum einen von den unseren in ihre Hände, dann machen sie kurzen Prozeß. Die Bourgeoisie hat die Macht und sie versteht sie der Gerechtigkeit zum Hohne anzuwenden. Würden wir Anarchisten ebenso in unserm Handeln sein, würden wir mit eiserner Rücksichtslosigkeit vorgehen, würden wir mit jedem Tyrannen und Ausbeuter ebenfalls kurzen Prozeß machen, die Macht der herrschenden Klasse würde platzen wie eine Seifenblase. Denn ein Nichts ist ihre Macht, ohne die Unterstützung der Proletarier. Leider sehen die Arbeiter nicht ein, daß sie es sind, die ein Recht auf alle Genüsse der Erde haben und daß alle Herrscher, vom kleinsten Ausbeuter bis zum Zaren, überflüssig sind. Aber Ihr Überzeugten, Ihr die Ihr wißt, wer unsere Feinde sind, laßt Euch durch meine Verurtheilung nicht abhalten, weiter zu agitiren, die Lehren des Anarchismus zu verbreiten, bis alle Menschen frei sind. Glaubt mir liebe Freunde, daß ich mich nicht im Geringsten unglücklich fühle. Ich habe das Bewußtsein: recht gehandelt zu haben und das ist das höchste Glück, die höchste Befriedigung für einen Revolutionär. Auch weiß ich, daß es noch viele Frauen und Männer gibt, die trotz Kerker und Schaffot weiter arbeiten zum Stürze der heutigen Gesellschaft. Mit diesem Brief nehme ich Abschied von allen Freunden und Genossen und sage allen Lebet wohl. Ich werde nur einmal im Monat schreiben können und auch da nur sehr wenig. Besuchen kann man mich einmal in drei Monaten. Man hat mir noch keine Arbeit gegeben. Zum Lesen bekomme ich die täglichen Zeitungen und Bücher aus der Bibliothek. Schreibe oft, ich darf Briefe erhalten, ebenso sende mir Geld. Lebe wohl, bleibe muthig und stark.

Mit revolutionärem Gruß, Dein Freund!
Alex. Berkmann

DEAR FRIEND!

You must think that I have forgotten you and all my dear friends as I haven't written in so long. I wrote you a few letters, but because I never received an answer to them, I came to the conclusion that they were never sent. I received the last letter on August 25.

I understood that as a proletarian and as a hated Anarchist I could expect no justice from the judges, but I would not have thought that my trial would be conducted with so much cruelty and with such cunning. Like the Russian political prisoners, I was dispatched by administrative means.

The entire comedy lasted barely two hours. In great haste, the judge sentenced me to 22 years in the penitentiary. Naturally I was given no time to speak, and since I also can't speak fluent enough English I could not say much. A few hours later I was brought to my new "home." The ruling class is very resolute in its actions; we Anarchists are in their way fighting them; in a word, we are their most dangerous enemies. When they get one of us in their hands, they make short work of it. The bourgeoisie has the power, and, scorning justice, understands how to use it. If Anarchists acted that way, proceeding with brutal disregard and summarily dispatching every tyrant and exploiter, the power of the ruling class would burst like a bubble. Its power is nothing without the support of the proletariat. Unfortunately the workers don't realize that they are the ones who have a right to all the pleasures of the earth and that all rulers, from the smallest exploiter to the tsar, are superfluous. But you Believers, you who know who our enemies are, don't let yourselves be hindered by my sentence from continuing to agitate and spread the teachings of Anarchism until all people are free. Believe me, dear friends, I don't feel the least bit unhappy. I have the peace of mind of having done right, and that is the greatest happiness, the greatest satisfaction for a revolutionary. I also know that there are still many women and men who, despite jail and the scaffold, work toward the overthrow of today's society. With this letter I take leave of all friends and comrades and say farewell. I will only be able to write once a month, and even then only very little. I can have visitors once every three months. I still have not been given any work. I receive the daily papers and books out of the library to read. Write often, I may receive letters; likewise send me money. Farewell, stay courageous and strong.

WITH REVOLUTIONARY GREETINGS, YOUR FRIEND!
ALEX. BERKMANN.

Die Autonomie, 29 October 1892, p. 4. Translated from German.

To MAX METZKOW

New York, 8 October 1892

DEAR COMRADE!

Received your letter already days ago, but I couldn't answer you because I expected a letter from B.[1] I can hardly consider your suggestion because I don't intend to stay in America for that long. Should my hope to leave America in the beginning of November not come true I will certainly accept your proposal. But it is very possible that I will be in P[2] by the end of next week. This is the case for the following reason. I have already told you that no one can see B for another 3 months, in other words on December 20. I have also written to B that I won't be able to see him anymore in that case, as I won't stay in America until then.[3] He asked the prison inspector if it would be possible to make an exception as I, his girl friend, would be leaving and would not be able to see him, and whether I could be allowed to visit him now. The inspector granted B's request and because of it has sent me a visitor's card issued in my name (naturally not G.) that is only given in exceptional cases.[4] B insists that I should now come to P as he has to see and speak to me once more. However I would have to go there no later than next week. But what to do now? I have not one cent and in such a short time can raise very little. If I calculate only from here to P, I will need at least 12 D. Maybe I will be able to raise 6 D. Could you help me out a little? I expect some money to be sent from Detroit next Saturday, but that will already be too late. I will have to leave on Thursday at the latest. If you could spend 6–7 D, I would pay it back to you in P because I would write to D[5] that the money should be sent to P. I urge you to respond immediately. I gave the 2 D to Masur.[6] You write that I should not correspond with anybody regarding my arrival and yet you yourself have spoken to Nold[7] about it as he wrote to me. I don't write to anybody except N every now and then. I didn't write to him about my arrival. By the way, I consider him an honest

1. EG refers to Alexander Berkman by his last initial only.
2. Pittsburgh.
3. This is the only extant suggestion that EG was planning to leave the United States at this time.
4. EG obtained a pass to see AB under the name Niedermann, adopting the surname of Claus Niedermann, who had assumed the editorship of *Die Brandfackel* in 1893 while Timmermann was in prison; she described herself as AB's married sister traveling to the United States from Russia. Given the distance his sister had supposedly come to see him, AB was to be granted two visits, but the second was rescinded when EG's real identity was discovered.
5. Detroit.
6. Carl Masur.
7. Carl Nold; EG refers to Nold in the following sentence by his last initial only.

comrade who just cannot tear himself away from the fanaticism for M.[8] Again I ask you to answer me immediately even if you can't send any money. Naturally I hope that you will try hard.

ALf, Joseph Ishill Collection, MH-H. Translated from German. Reprinted by permission of the Houghton Library, Harvard University.

8. Johann Most.

DEAR SISTER:[1]

It is just a month, a month to-day, since my coming here. I keep wondering, can such a world of misery and torture be compressed into one short month? . . . How I have longed for this opportunity! You will understand: a month's stay is required before we are permitted to write. But many, many long letters I have written to you—in my mind, dear Sonya. Where shall I begin now? My space is very limited, and I have so much to say to you and to the Twin.[2]—I received your letters. You need not wait till you hear from me: keep on writing. I am allowed to receive all mail sent, "of moral contents," in the phraseology of the rules. And I shall write whenever I may.

Dear Sonya, I sense bitterness and disappointment in your letter. Why do you speak of failure? You, at least, you and Fedya, should not have your judgment obscured by the mere accident of physical results. Your lines pained and grieved me beyond words. Not because you should write thus; but that you, even you, should *think* thus. Need I enlarge? True morality deals with motives, not consequences. I cannot believe that we differ on this point.[3]

1. Because a letter to EG was likely to be read more closely by prison censors and possibly even intercepted, AB did not address her by name, nor express the full range of his thoughts and feelings unless he was fortunate enough to smuggle them out *sub rosa*. He clarified the coded terms of endearment with which he addressed EG in his own annotation to this letter as printed in his 1912 *Prison Memoirs of an Anarchist:* "The Girl; also referred to as Sonya, Musick, and Sailor" (p. 136).
2. AB refers here to his cousin, Modest Stein, as "the Twin" and later in this letter by the Russian diminutive "Fedya" (for Fyodor, or Theodore in English). AB and Fedya were so inseparable that friends often called them "the Twins." AB, EG, and Fedya lived together just before AB's imprisonment. AB in *Prison Memoirs of an Anarchist* and EG in *LML* used the code name Fedya so as not to implicate Modest Stein in their illegal activities.
3. In the handwritten prisoners' publication *Prison Blossoms*, AB articulated his motives for the attack on Frick: "For several days succeeding my arrest I remained in ignorance concerning the physical condition of Mr. Frick. But when it transpired that Mr. Frick would recover, it seemed to me that this circumstance, purely accidental as it was, would not tend to produce any minimizing effect on the signification and importance of my act; for a deed, such as mine, that is its meaning does in no way depend upon the physical consequences (to the parties concerned) incidental to that act, but must have for its criterion the purpose underlying the deed and should be estimated according to the moral effect—called propaganda—produced by such an act. As far as my purpose and aims were concerned, it mattered very little whether my shots were fatal or not; indeed viewed from the true anarchistic standpoint, it did not matter the slightest difference what the outcome, the physical results of my attempt were. I had, as already stated, no private axes to grind, no personal wrongs to avenge, no private feelings to satisfy. Whether Frick was among the living or the dead was a matter comparatively indifferent to me. It might popularly be supposed that the object of my attempt was to remove an obnoxious person. Yet nothing could be further from my real purpose. It was my aim, first and last, to express, by my deed, my sentiments toward the existing system of legal oppression and industrial des-

I fully understand what a terrible blow the apostasy of Wurst[4] must have been to you. But however it may minimize the effect, it cannot possibly alter the fact, or its character. This you seem to have lost sight of. In spite of Wurst, a great deal could have been accomplished. I don't know whether it has been done: your letter is very meagre on this point. Yet it is of supreme interest to me. But I know, Sonya,—of this one thing, at least, I am sure—you will do all that is in your power. Perhaps it is not much—but the Twin and part of Orchard Street[5] will be with you.

Why that note of disappointment, almost of resentment, as to Tolstogub's relation to the Darwinian theory?[6] You must consider that the layman cannot judge of the intricacies of scientific hypotheses. The scientist would justly object to such presumption.

I embrace you both. The future is dark; but, then, who knows? . . . Write often. Tell me about the movement, yourself and friends. It will help to keep me in touch with the outside world, which daily seems to recede further. I clutch desperately at the thread that still binds me to the living—it seems to unravel in my hands, the thin skeins are breaking, one by one. My hold is slackening. But the Sonya thread, I know, will remain taut and strong. I have always called you the Immutable.

ALEX.

Berkman, *Prison Memoirs of an Anarchist,* pp. 136–37.

---

potism; to attack the institution of wage-slavery in the person of one of its most prominent representatives, to give it a blow—rather morally than physically—this was the real purpose and signification of my act" (*Prison Blossoms,* ca. 1893–1894, not paginated). Carl Nold later published a very similar piece reflecting on AB's understanding of his *attentat*. See Nold, "A Reminiscence of Alexander Berkman," *Firebrand,* 25 July 1897, p. 4.

4. Annotated by AB in *Prison Memoirs* as "John Most." AB and EG had been in the habit of referring to Most as Hans Wurst ("John Sausage"), a common phrase meaning "clown," or someone not to be taken seriously. According to Most's biographer Rudolf Rocker (himself an anarchist), AB later denied any such derogatory intention, insisting that this was a code name to protect Most from being implicated in the *attentat*.

5. Annotated by AB in *Prison Memoirs* as "54 Orchard Street—the hall in which the first Jewish Anarchist gatherings were held in New York. An allusion to the aid of the Jewish comrades." The office of the Pioneers of Liberty was located at this address.

6. AB's annotation reads: "Tolstogub—the author's Russian nickname. The expression signifies the continued survival of the writer." The Russian word means "fat lip" and was used to describe AB, who was known for his full lips.

MY DEAR SONYA:

It seems an age since I wrote to you, yet it is only a month. But the monotony of my life weights down the heels of time,—the only break in the terrible sameness is afforded me by your dear, affectionate letters, and those of Fedya.[1] When I return to the cell for the noon meal, my step is quickened by the eager expectation of finding mail from you. About eleven in the morning, the Chaplain makes his rounds; his practiced hand shoots the letter between the bars, toward the bed or on to the little table in the corner. But if the missive is light, it will flutter to the floor. As I reach the cell, the position of the little white object at once apprises me whether the letter is long or short. With closed eyes I sense its weight, like the warm pressure of your own dear hand, the touch reaching softly to my heart, till I feel myself lifted across the chasm into your presence. The bars fade, the walls disappear, and the air grows sweet with the aroma of fresh air and flowers,—I am again with you, walking in the bright July moonlight. . . . The touch of the *velikorussian*[2] in your eyes and hair conjures up the Volga, our beautiful *bogatir*,[3] and the strains of the *dubinushka*,[4] trembling with suffering and yearning, float about me. . . . The meal remains untouched. I dream over your letter, and again I read it, slowly, slowly, lest I reach the end too quickly. The afternoon hours are hallowed by your touch and your presence, and I am conscious only of the longing for my cell,—in the quiet of the evening, freed from the nightmare of the immediate, I walk in the garden of our dreams.

And the following morning, at work in the shop, I pass in anxious wonder whether some cheering word from my own, my real world, is awaiting me in the cell. With a glow of emotion I think of the Chaplain: perhaps at the very moment your letter is in his hands. He is opening it, reading. Why should strange eyes . . . but the Chaplain seems kind and discreet. Now he is passing along the galleries, distributing the mail. The bundle grows meagre as the postman reaches the ground floor. Oh! if he does not come to my cell quickly, he may have no letters left. But the next moment I smile at the childish thought,—if there is a letter for me, no other prisoner will get it. Yet some error might happen. . . . No, it is impossible—my name and prison number, and the cell number marked by the Chaplain across the envelope, all insure the mail against any mistake in delivery. Now the dinner whistle blows. Eagerly I hasten to the cell. There is nothing on

1. "Fedya" is AB's code name for his cousin Modest Stein.
2. The term *velikorussian* means "Great Russian," or the essential Russian.
3. Annotated by AB: "Brave knight—affectionately applied to the great river." A *bogatyr'* is a hero in Russian folklore.
4. Annotated by AB: "Folk-song."

the floor! Perhaps on the bed, on the table. . . . I grow feverish with the dread of disappointment. Possibly the letter fell under the bed, or in that dark corner. No, none there,—but it can't be that there is no mail for me to-day! I must look again—it may have dropped among the blankets. . . . No, there is no letter!

Thus pass my days, dear friend. In thought I am ever with you and Fedya, in our old haunts and surroundings. I shall never get used to this life, nor find an interest in the reality of the moment. What will become of me, I don't know. I hardly care. We are revolutionists, dear: whatever sacrifices the Cause demands, though the individual perish, humanity will profit in the end. In that consciousness we must find our solace.

ALEX.

Berkman, *Prison Memoirs of an Anarchist,* pp. 148 – 49.

> **From ALEXANDER BERKMAN**
>
> *Western Penitentiary, Allegheny City, Pa., 30 November 1892 — Sub rosa*

BELOVED GIRL:

I thought I would not survive the agony of our meeting, but human capacity for suffering seems boundless. All my thoughts, all my yearnings, were centered in the one desire
to see you, to look into your eyes, and there read the beautiful promise that has filled my
days with strength and hope. . . .[1] An embrace, a lingering kiss, and the gift of Lingg[2]
would have been mine. To grasp your hand, to look down for a mute, immortal instant
into your soul, and then die at your hands, Beloved, with the warm breath of your caress
wafting me into peaceful eternity — oh, it were bliss supreme, the realization of our day
dreams, when, in transports of ecstasy, we kissed the image of the Social Revolution. Do
you remember that glorious face, so strong and tender, on the wall of our little Houston
Street hallroom? How far, far in the past are those inspired moments! But they have filled
my hours with hallowed thoughts, with exulting expectations. And then you came. A
glance at your face, and I knew my doom to terrible life. I read it in the evil look of the
guard. It was the Deputy himself. Perhaps you had been searched! He followed our every
moment, like a famished cat that feigns indifference, yet is alert with every nerve to
spring upon the victim. Oh, I know the calculated viciousness beneath that meek exte-
rior. The accelerated movement of his drumming fingers, as he deliberately seated himself between us, warned me of the beast, hungry for prey. . . . The halo was dissipated.
The words froze within me, and I could meet you only with a vapid smile, and on the instant it was mirrored in my soul as a leer, and I was filled with anger and resentment at
everything about us — myself, the Deputy (I could have throttled him to death), and — at
you, dear. Yes, Sonya, even at you: the quick come to bury the dead. . . . But the next moment, the unworthy throb of my agonized soul was stilled by the passionate pressure of
my lips upon your hand. How it trembled! I held it between my own, and then, as I lifted
my face to yours, the expression I beheld seemed to bereave me of my own self: it was
you who were I! The drawn face, the look of horror, your whole being the cry of torture —
were *you* not the real prisoner? Or was it my visioned suffering that cemented the spiritual bond, annihilating all misunderstanding, all resentment, and lifting us above time
and place in the afflatus of martyrdom?

    Mutely I held your hand. There was no need for words. Only the prying eyes of the
catlike presence disturbed the sacred moment. Then we spoke — mechanically, triviali-

---

1. Note the relative openness of AB's letters smuggled out of prison *sub rosa,* avoiding the censoring eye
of the prison authorities.
2. AB's annotation reads: "Louis Lingg, one of the Chicago martyrs, who committed suicide with a dynamite cartridge in a cigar given him by a friend."

ties. . . . What though the cadaverous Deputy with brutal gaze timed the seconds, and forbade the sound of our dear Russian,—nor heaven nor earth could violate the sacrament sealed with our pain.

The echo accompanied my step as I passed through the rotunda on my way to the cell. All was quiet in the block. No whir of loom reached me from the shops. Thanksgiving Day: all activities were suspended. I felt at peace in the silence. But when the door was locked, and I found myself alone, all alone within the walls of the tomb, the full significance of your departure suddenly dawned on me. The quick had left the dead. . . . Terror of the reality seized me and I was swept by a paroxysm of anguish—

I must close. The friend who promised to have this letter mailed *sub rosa* is at the door. He is a kind unfortunate who has befriended me. May this letter reach you safely. In token of which, send me postal of indifferent contents, casually mentioning the arrival of news from my brother in Moscow. Remember to sign "Sister."

WITH A PASSIONATE EMBRACE,
YOUR SASHA.

Berkman, *Prison Memoirs of an Anarchist,* pp. 150–51.

GIRL AND TWIN:[1]

I am writing with despair in my heart. I was taken to Pittsburgh as a witness in the trial of Nold and Bauer.[2] I had hoped for an opportunity—you understand, friends. It was a slender thread, but I clung to it desperately, prepared to stake everything on it. It proved a broken straw. Now I am back, and I may never leave this place alive.

I was bitterly disappointed not to find you in the courtroom. I yearned for the sight of your faces. But you were not there, nor any one else of our New York comrades. I knew what it meant: you are having a hard struggle to exist. Otherwise perhaps something could be done to establish friendly relations between Rakhmetov and Mr. Gebop.[3] It would require an outlay beyond the resources of our own circle; others cannot be approached in this matter. Nothing remains but the "inside" developments,—a terribly slow process.

This is all the hope I can hold out to you, dear friends. You will think it quite negligible; yet it is the sole ray that has again and again kindled life in moments of utmost darkness . . . . I did not realize the physical effects of my stay here (it is five months now) till my return from court. I suppose the excitement of being on the outside galvanized me for the nonce . . . . My head was awhirl; I could not collect my thoughts. The wild hope possessed me,—*pobeg!* The click of the steel, as I was handcuffed to the Deputy, struck my deathknell . . . . The unaccustomed noise of the streets, the people and loud voices in the courtroom, the scenes of the trial, all absorbed me in the moment. It seemed to me as if I were a spectator, interested, but personally unconcerned, in the surroundings; and these, too, were far away, of a strange world in which I had no part. Only when I found myself alone in the cell, the full significance of the lost occasion was borne in upon me with crushing force.

1. AB is referring to EG and his cousin and close friend Modest Stein.
2. On 9 February 1893 Carl Nold and Henry Bauer were both sentenced to five years in Western Penitentiary on two charges: incitement to riot (stemming from their distribution of a handbill addressed to the striking Homestead workers on 8 July 1892) and conspiracy (with AB) to commit murder. Bauer was also charged a fine of $50 and sentenced to sixty days in county jail for contempt of court when he refused to name the other men involved in distributing the leaflet. For Bauer's discussion of the leaflet and its effect, see "A Fateful Leaflet," *Free Society*, 17 April 1898.
3. AB's annotation for "Mr. Gebop" reads: "Reading backward, *pobeg*; Russian for 'escape.'" (AB uses the Russian word *pobeg* again, in the next paragraph.) Rakhmetov is the model revolutionist of N. G. Chernyshevsky's novel *What Is to Be Done?* (1863). AB used the name here as a pseudonym for himself, as he had at the hotel in Pittsburgh the night he arrived there on his mission to kill Frick.

But why sadden you? There is perhaps a cheerier side, now that Nold and Bauer are here. I have not seen them yet, but their very presence, the circumstance that somewhere within these walls there are *comrades*, men who, like myself, suffer for an ideal—the thought holds a deep satisfaction for me. It brings me closer, in a measure, to the environment of political prisoners in Europe. Whatever the misery and torture of their daily existence, the politicals—even in Siberia—breathe the atmosphere of solidarity, of appreciation.[4] What courage and strength there must be for them in the inspiration radiated by a common cause! Conditions here are entirely different. Both inmates and officers are at loss to "class" me. They have never known political prisoners. That one should sacrifice or risk his life with no apparent personal motives, is beyond their comprehension, almost beyond their belief. It is a desert of sordidness that constantly threatens to engulf one. I would gladly exchange places with our comrades in Siberia.

Carl Nold, arrested for incitement to riot and conspiracy to murder Henry Clay Frick (with Alexander Berkman and Henry Bauer). Nold met Berkman in 1892, worked with him in prison on the journal *Prison Blossoms,* and later worked on the Berkman Defense Association. (Labadie Collection, University of Michigan)

The former *podpoilnaya*[5] was suspended, because of the great misfortune that befell my friend Wingie, of whom I wrote to you before. This dove will be flown by Mr. Tiuremshchick,[6] an old soldier who really sympathizes with Wingie. I believe they served in the same regiment. He is a kindly man, who hates his despicable work. But there is a family at home, a sick wife—you know the old, weak-kneed tale. I had a hint from him the other day: he is being spied upon; it is dangerous for him to be seen at my cell, and so forth. It is all quite true; but what he means is, that a little money would be welcome. You know how to manage the matter. Leave no traces.

I hear the felt-soled step. It's the soldier. I bid my birdie a hasty good-bye.

SASHA.

Berkman, *Prison Memoirs of an Anarchist,* pp. 174–75.

4. In Russia, unlike in the United States, the state recognized the concept of political prisoners and exiled many to Siberia, including AB's uncle and inspiration, Mark Natanson, in 1872 for his revolutionary activities.
5. AB's annotation reads: "*Sub rosa* route"; *podpoilnaya* is Russian for "secret" or "underground."
6. AB's annotation reads: "Russian for 'guard.'"

DEAR COMRADE METZKOW.

Owing to illness I find myself in this city, not far from NY.[1] Why is it that you have not even responded with one line to my last letter, which I wrote close to 6 weeks ago? What crime have I committed? Or were you so busy that nothing could be heard from you? As I said before, it looks sad in NY. The A[2] is in the process of closing down and hasn't been published in 3 weeks. These Anarchists have given up. I think I will stay here until the end of July. Please write about how things look in Pittsburg, and how you are doing.

WITH REV GREETINGS
YOUR EG.

My address E Hochstein 188 St Joseph st R NY

APcl, Joseph Ishill Collection, MH-H. Translated from German. Reprinted by permission of the Houghton Library, Harvard University.

1. EG fell ill in the spring of 1893 while organizing for the commutation of AB's sentence and working ten to twelve hours a day at a sewing machine to support herself. She recuperated for two months in Rochester, where her sister Helena Hochstein rented a private room and found her a lung specialist who diagnosed EG with early stages of tuberculosis. Though EG improved under her sister's care, she left for New York in July before she had recovered completely to take part in the political activities surrounding the nation's severe unemployment crisis (see *LML*, pp. 120–21).
2. The initial *A* refers to the journal *Der Anarchist.*

Schlecht Beraten

In's Fahrwasser des Anarchismus gerathen die Arbeitslosen.

Die gestrige Demonstration auf Union Square.—In Brandreden wird radikaler Unsinn verzapft und denen, die nach Brod schreien, wird ein Stein gegeben.

Professionelle Hetzer, Volksverführer, Utopisten und Demagogen machen sich die mißliche Lage, in welche infolge der allgemeinen Geschäfts-Depression ein großer Theil der Arbeiter gerathen ist, weidlich zu Nutze und tragen durch die maßlose Aufreizung der niederen Klassen das ihrige dazu bei, daß die Situation sich, wenn dies möglich ist, noch verschlechtert. Beweis hierfür ist die Demonstration, welche gestern Abend stattfand.

Mit einer zweiten großen Massenversammlung auf dem Union Square, noch größer als die am Samstag stattgehabte, schloß der gestrige Tag für die Arbeitslosen.

Etwa fünf tausend Menschen hatten sich auf dem großen Platze, der so manche Volks-Demonstration gesehen, eingefunden und besonders unter ihnen auffallend war die Zahl der jungen Leute unter 25 Jahren. Der Demonstration auf dem Square ging ein Umzug der Arbeitslosen heran, welcher um 7 Uhr Covenant Hall, No. 56 Orchard Str., verließ und etwa 2500 Mann stark die Orchard Str. hinauf ging, die Houston Str., Ave. A, 2. Str., 2. Ave., 13. Str. passirte und um 7^1/$_2$ Uhr auf dem Square eintraf.

Der Umzug war ein sehr ruhiger und der einzige zu erwähnende Vorfall war, daß Kapitän Devery in der Orchard Str., zwischen der Rivington und Delancey Str., einem der Männer eine schwarze Flagge wegnahm und sie konfiscirte.

Auf der Terrace vor der Cottage am Square präsidirte David Levy, während zwei Lastwagen zu beiden Seiten der Cottage als Rednertribünen verhielten. Dr. Theodore Kinzel, der erste Redner, erklärte, daß er ein Anarchist sei, worauf er die bestehende Gesellschaftsordnung kritisirte, die "sociale Revolution" ankündigte und den Anwesenden rieth, sich für dieselbe vorzubereiten.

Unter den anderen Rednern war es besonders der Schneider John Timmermann, welcher durch seine aufreizende maßlose Redeweise die Anwesenden packte. "Wir müssen Brod haben", rief er; "wenn die Kapitalisten Euch ohne Brod lassen, so sind sie Mörder und wenn sie uns kein Brod geben, so müssen wir es nehmen. Wir sind keine Politiker und haben nichts mit der Politik zu thun." Nachdem er von der französischen Revolution gesprochen, erklärte er, daß auch hier Straßenkämpfe stattfinden würden.

"Bereitet Euch auf die sociale Revolution vor. Gewalt gegen Gewalt! Ich sage Euch, die Zeiten werden noch schlechter werden, wie sie jetzt bereits sind, und man wird uns auf den Straßen tödten. Ihr habt die Paläste gebaut, Ihr habt alles geschaffen, aber Ihr selbst habt nichts. Fordert Brod! Es ist Euer Recht, dasselbe zu verlangen, und könnt Ihr es nicht bekommen, so könnt Ihr es ja nehmen." Er schloß mit den Worten; "Hoch lebe die Anarchie!"

Nach ihm sprachen Arthur Morton, F. Herschdorfer und Barnet Brave. Letzterer erklärte, daß man sie Anarchisten nenne, weil sie Brod verlangten, und man rufe dann die Polizei herbei, sie zu verhaften. "Wenn sie einen verhaften, sollen sie alle mitnehmen, alle unsere Familien. Man hat mir mitgetheilt, daß ich verhaftet werden soll. Sie sollen es nur thun. Ich kann im Gefängnis nicht schlimmer daran sein, als ich es jetzt bin, denn morgen soll ich ermittirt werden. Giebt man uns kein Brod, so werden wir es nehmen."

Emma Goldmann sprach dann zu der Menschenmenge, welche begierig den Wortschwall der Petroleuse verschlang und denselben stürmisch applaudirte.

"Das ist das Land eines Thos. Jefferson, eines John Brown, eines Abe Lincoln," geiserte die Maulheldin in schlechtem Englisch, "und in ihm schreien Hunderttausende nach Brod. Könnten jene dieser Versammlung beiwohnen, so würden sie vor Scham erröthen. Die Reichen wohnen herrlich und in Freuden und ihre Frauen haben alles, was das Herz begehrt, aber die Lohnsklaven sind schlimmer daran, wie die Farbigen in der Sklavenzeit. Die schlechte Zeit kommt nicht von der Silberkrise her, sie hat andere Ursachen. Ihr verlangt Brod und wenn Ihr es nicht auf friedlichem Wege bekommen könnt, so werdet Ihr es Euch mit Gewalt holen. Vereinigt Euch und nehmt es mit Gewalt, wenn Ihr es nicht friedlich bekommen könnt. Man hat in den Zeitungen berichtet, daß Arbeiter nach Albany gehen wollen, um dort Forderungen zu stellen; was werden sie erhalten? Nichts. An solche Geschichten glaube ich nicht mehr. Verlaßt Euch auf Eure eigene Kraft, da die Kapitalistenklasse die Polizei bewaffnet hat. Nochmals, könnt Ihr kein Brot bekommen, so nehmt es mit Gewalt. Geht hinaus in die sociale Revolution!"

Der Wortlaut der Brandrede ist nur deshalb bemerkenswerth, weil sich voraussichtlich die Polizei mit der Urheberin derselben befassen wird.

Nur wenige Redner sprachen nach Emma Goldmann. Es hatte sich inzwischen das Gerücht verbreitet, daß die Polizei beschlossen habe, Timmermann und Emma Goldmann wegen ihrer Reden zu verhaften und dies sah um so wahrscheinlicher aus, als sich wohl ein Dutzend Detektives auf der Platform befand.

Plötzlich verschwand Timmermann, und man konnte nicht in Erfahrung bringen, ob er verhaftet worden sei oder ob ihn seine Freunde fortgeschmuggelt hätten. Nachdem Emma Goldmann geendet, entfernte sie sich langsam in Begleitung einiger Freunde. Mehrere Reporter folgten, sowie ein kleiner Menschenhaufen. Durch den Park ziehend, schwoll der Zug im Nu um Hunderte an und als er um die Cottage gehend die Ecke der 17. Str. und 4. Ave. erreicht hatte, befanden sich nahezu tausend Leute in Emma's Gefolgschaft.

Immer größer wurde das Gedränge. Es ging die 4. Ave. hinunter bis zu 14. Str. und als man dieselbe erreichte, waren wenigstens 2000 Personen in dem Zuge. Plötzlich kam der Haufen zum Stillstehen. Emma hatte eine in westlicher Richtung fahrende Car bestiegen und mehrere Leute waren nach ihr hinaufgesprungen. Die Car entfernte sich und langsam ging die Menge auseinander. Es hieß, daß sie noch später verhaftet werden würde.

Im Laufe des Tages fanden zwei sehr ruhige Massenversammlungen der Arbeitslosen statt, eine in Covenant Hall, No. 56 Orchard Str., und die andere in Pythagoras Hall in der Canal Str. nahe der Bowery. In letzter sprachen A. Jablinowski, Jos. Lederer, M. Hillkowitz und Jac. Milch, welche die Anwesenden ermahnten, keine Ruhestörungen zu begehen. In der ersteren sprach Emma Goldmann, welche die entgegengesetzte Maßnahme empfahl. [. . .]

Badly Advised.

The Unemployed Step onto Anarchist Ground.

Yesterday's Demonstration in Union Square.—Radical Nonsense Pronounced in Fiery Speeches and those Screaming for Bread are Given a Stone.

Professional agitators, fanatics, utopians and demagogues are heartily taking advantage of the critical situation in which a large number of the workers have fallen into as a result of the general economic depression, and are contributing through the extreme provocation of the lower classes to making the situation, if such a thing is possible, even worse. Proof of this is the demonstration that took place yesterday evening.

Yesterday ended for the unemployed with a second large mass demonstration in Union Square, even larger than the one that occurred on Saturday.[1]

About five thousand people showed up in the large square which has had its share of peoples' demonstrations, especially noticeable among them were the number of young people under 25 years old. Also joining the demonstration in the square was a procession of the unemployed which had set out from Covenant Hall, No. 56 Orchard St., at 7 o'clock, and, some 2500 men strong, went up Orchard St., crossed Houston St., Ave. A, 2nd St., 2nd Ave., 13th St., and arrived in the square at 7:30.

The procession was calm and the only incident worth mentioning was that Captain Devery[2] seized a black flag[3] from one of the men on Orchard St., between Rivington and Delancey St., and confiscated it.

1. On Saturday, 19 August, EG attended an afternoon meeting of the unemployed at Golden Rule Hall. In the early evening (about 6 o'clock) she and Adolph Ury led a march of about a thousand anarchists, according to the *New York Times*, from the hall to Union Square. The meeting was hampered by a heavy police presence and a steady rain. One of many to address the crowd at Union Square, she spoke on "the grinding heel of the monopolies" and the "capitalist press" (*New York Times*, 20 August 1893, p. 1).
2. Captain William S. Devery was head of the 11th precinct of the New York police during the series of unemployment demonstrations by anarchists in August of 1893, repeatedly breaking up meetings and closing meeting halls. He later served as chief of police from 30 June 1898 to 21 February 1901.
3. Black, as the color symbolic of anarchism, first appeared in 1883 in France at a demonstration of the unemployed headed by Louise Michel and Émile Pouget. They carried a black banner to honor the martyrs of the Paris Commune. The same year an anarchist paper in Lyons adopted the title *Le Drapeau Noir* (The Black Banner). Lyons had a long tradition of using black banners in "bread and work" demonstrations. On 27 November 1884 the black flag was flown at a rally addressed by Albert Parsons in Chicago, and in 1905 a Russian anarchist terrorist group called itself Chernoe Znomia (The Black Banner). In this period, however, red generally dominated as the color symbolic of anar-

David Levy presided on the terrace in front of the cottage in the square while two trucks on either side of the cottage served as speakers' podiums. Dr. Theodore Kinzel, the first speaker, declared that he was an Anarchist, upon which he criticized the existing societal order, proclaimed the "social revolution," and advised the audience to prepare themselves for it.

Among the other speakers it was the tailor John Timmermann[4] in particular who thrilled the audience with his provocative, intense speaking style. "We must have bread," he cried; "if the capitalists leave you without bread, then they are murderers and if they don't give us any bread, then we must take it. We are not politicians and have nothing to do with politics." After he spoke about the French Revolution, he declared that street fighting would also take place here. "Prepare yourselves for the social revolution. Violence against violence! I say to you, the times will get even worse than they already are now, and we will be killed on the streets. You have built the palaces, you have made everything, but you yourselves have nothing. Call out for bread! It is your right to demand it, and if you are not able to get it, then you can take it." He concluded with the words; "Long live Anarchy!"

Speaking after him were Arthur Morton, F. Herschdorfer and Barnet Brave. The latter declared that they were called Anarchists because they were demanding bread, and that the police would be called in to arrest them. "If they arrest one person, they will have to take everyone along, all of our families. I have been told that I am supposed to be arrested. They might as well do it. I couldn't be any worse off in prison than I am now, for tomorrow I will be evicted. If we are not given bread, we will take it."

Emma Goldmann then spoke to the crowd, which eagerly devoured and thunderingly applauded the torrent of words from the Petroleuse.[5]

"This is the land of Thos. Jefferson, John Brown, Abe Lincoln,"[6] shouted the loudmouth in bad English, "and in it hundreds of thousands are crying out for bread. If those men could witness this meeting, they would blush in shame. The rich live splendidly and in their pleasures and their women have everything that the heart desires, but the wage slaves are worse off than the colored people in the time of slavery. These bad times are not due to the silver crisis, they have other roots. You demand bread, and if you cannot

chism. Many anarchists, including Peter Kropotkin, insisted upon retaining red to mark the anarchist movement's association with the socialist tradition, of which they considered themselves a legitimate part. Not until after the First World War would black be widely adopted as the predominant symbol. During the Spanish Civil War (1936–1939) both red and black were incorporated into anarchist flags and banners.

4. The reference is to Claus Timmermann, who was arrested, convicted of inciting to riot for this speech, and sentenced to six months imprisonment.

5. *Petroleuse* is the French word for "firebrand"; it was adopted during the Paris Commune of 1871 to identify the women who used petroleum to set fire to buildings.

6. EG, following a pattern set by the Chicago anarchists in the era of the Haymarket incident, often evoked the names of Thomas Jefferson, Thomas Paine, Wendell Phillips, and John Brown to demonstrate a perceived American anti-statist tradition. Chicago anarchists, in publications such as the *Alarm* and *Chicagoer Arbeiter-Zeitung*, frequently quoted the Declaration of Independence and alluded

acquire it through peaceful means you will get it by force. Unite and take it by force, if you cannot get it peacefully. It has been reported in the newspapers that workers want to go to Albany to make demands there; what will they get? Nothing. I no longer believe in such things. Rely upon your own strength, since the capitalist class has armed the police. Once again, if you cannot get any bread, then take it by force. Go forth into the social revolution!"

The wording of the incendiary speech is only worth mentioning because presumably the police will be concerned with its author.[7]

Only a few speakers came after Emma Goldmann. In the meantime the rumor had been spread that the police had decided to arrest Timmermann and Emma Goldmann because of their speeches, and this seemed all the more likely as a good dozen detectives were on the platform.

Suddenly Timmermann disappeared, and no one was able to learn whether he had been arrested or whether his friends had smuggled him away. After Emma Goldmann

---

favorably to a perceived anti-statism of the founders of the United States, particularly Thomas Jefferson. In his speech to the jury on 7 October 1886, August Spies named Paine, Jefferson, and Ralph Waldo Emerson as predecessors to his ideas.

7. The *New York World* gave the following account of EG's English-language speech (she addressed the gathering first in English and then in German):

"I would first like to appeal in English to the American workingmen. If Jefferson and Paine, who fought for freedom, Wendell Phillips and John Brown were here to see your misery they would be ashamed of their country. You have Senators and Congressmen who live in luxury while you have nothing to eat. Their children live in grand style. Their wives and mistresses wear silks and diamonds. You have thought that the liberty of America gives you freedom and bread. Now you know how very much mistaken you have been. You are not free citizens. You are worse than black slaves.

"Americans! if you really want to be free citizens, take your rights into your own hands. Go and fight with your brothers, no matter if they are foreigners. You are starving as well as they. Don't be prejudiced against these poor people who have come to this country. They are not responsible for the prevailing conditions. The capitalist class is responsible. The capitalist system is near its ruin.

"Unite and go from street to street. Go among the capitalists and rich people and ask for bread, and if they do not give it to you peacably, then take it by force. Do as the North did against the South! You will find your John Brown and your Wendell Phillips as the North did.

"If you do not get bread and freedom peacably, take it by force. As long as you are slaves, with nothing to eat; as long as you are dragged down, you cannot be human beings, respected by any nation. Unite with others. Go out in the street and fight for your bread, and take it if they will not give it to you."

The *World* translated EG's German-language speech as follows:

"Do not be afraid of the clubs of the police. The advice the Anarchists have given you is good. What they told you a few years ago would happen is now taking place. Do not be afraid of such creatures as the Pinkertons, the police and the reporters. They are all blood suckers. (Cheers.)

"You have as much right to arm yourselves as the police. (Cheers.) You have as much right to use arms as the police (cheers), and we know where to get the weapons, and you know! and what will the fat policemen do then? (Tremendous cheering.)

"Long live anarchy!

"Hurrah for revolution." (Cheers.)

The reporter was David G. Bailey. "A young Hebrew boy" in his employ translated EG's German-language speech (for other versions of EG's speech in German, see Excerpt from Trial Transcript, 4 October 1893, below). For Bailey's complete report of the Union Square meeting, see "Urging Men to Riot," *New York World*, 22 August 1893, *EGP*, reel 47.

finished, she withdrew slowly, accompanied by some friends. Several reporters followed, as well a small crowd of people. Moving through the park, the procession swelled in no time into the hundreds, and when it had reached the corner of 17th St. and 4th Ave. while going around the cottage, there were nearly a thousand people in Emma's following.

The crowd grew larger and larger. It went down 4th Ave. to 14th St., and by then there were at least 2,000 people in the procession. Suddenly the crowd came to a standstill. Emma had climbed onto a car driving in the westerly direction and a few people had sprung up after her. The car moved away and slowly the crowd dispersed. It was rumored that she would be arrested later.

During the course of the day two very calm mass meetings of the unemployed took place, one in Covenant Hall, No. 56 Orchard St., and the other in Pythagoras Hall on Canal St. near the Bowery. A. Jablinowski,[8] Jos. Lederer, M. Hillkowitz[9] and Jac. Milch spoke in the latter meeting, admonishing the audience not to disturb the peace. Emma Goldmann spoke in the former, recommending the opposite measures. [. . .]

New-Yorker Staats-Zeitung, 22 August 1893, p. 12. The excised remainder of this article reprints a resolution by the "Labor Conference," signed by Samuel Gompers and others, calling on government and private industry to come to the aid of the unemployed and for continuing peaceful struggle through unions. The article concludes with a description of a small workers' assembly organized by Ferdinand Levy, at which he warned his audience to remain calm and ignore anarchist pronouncements. The *New Yorker Staats-Zeitung* was a daily mainstream German-language paper published from 1834 to 1954 and edited by Oswald Ottendorfer from 1858 to 1900. Edward John Thimme, the reporter for this article, was called to testify at EG's 4 October 1893 trial on charges of unlawful assembly resulting from her 21 August speech. Translated from German.

8. Probably Ludwig Jablinowski. See note 6 in "Anarchists in Charge," Article in the *New York World,* 3 May 1892, above.
9. M. Hillkowitz is Morris Hillquit, a prominent member of the Socialist Labor Party and United Hebrew Trades as well as a labor lawyer.

Charles R. Young[1] of 11th Precinct Police Street,[2] occupation Police Officer being duly sworn, deposes and says, that on the 19th day of August 1893, at number 125 Rivington Street[3] in the City of New York, in the County of New York, one Emma Goldman being an evil disposed and pernicious person and of turbulent disposition, together with divers other evil disposed and pernicious persons to the number of fifty and upwards, unlawfully, wickedly and maliciously intending and contriving to disturb the public peace, and to excite the citizens of this State to hatred and contempt of its government and laws, and to raise and make riots, routs and unlawful assemblies within this State and to commit crimes against the laws of this State, with force and arms, did unlawfully wickedly, turbulently and maliciously assemble and gather together and being so then and there assembled and gathered together as aforesaid, the said Emma Goldman and the said other evil disposed and malicious persons did then and there unlawfully wickedly and maliciously threaten to raise insurrections, routs and riots in the Said City of New York, and did threaten to take steal and carry away the goods, chattels and personal property of the good citizens of the State of New York, and did make other wicked, malicious and unlawful threats.

Wherefore deponent prays that the said Emma Goldman be apprehended and dealt with as the law directs.

Sworn to before me

this 25 day of Aug. 1893

CHARLES R YOUNG

BERNARD MARTIN

POLICE JUSTICE

ADS, NNMA. "District Attorney's Office" is struck out on printed form, and "First District Police Court" inserted by hand.

1. The affidavits of three police officers pertaining to this case are extant. This one, by police officer Charles R. Young, purports to describe EG's address to a meeting at Golden Rule Hall on 19 August. The language of the three affidavits is virtually the same. The affidavits by police officers Morris Schwartz and Charles Jacobs, covering EG's activities on 21 August, added only one point of substance, that with others EG threatened "to procure arms, ammunition and weapons" to carry out "her most wicked and unlawful threats." The date of the infraction on the indictment originally was 19 August; it was subsequently changed by hand to 21 August. For these and other documents in the case, see *EGP*, reel 47.
2. "Street" is a printed element of the form; the author neglected to delete it and add "Station."
3. Located in the rear of a bar at 125 Rivington Street, Golden Rule Hall was a meeting hall and gathering place for anarchists. After leading a march with Adolph Ury from Golden Rule Hall to Union Square as part of an unemployment demonstration, EG spoke at Union Square on Saturday, 19 August (see *New York Times*, 20 August 1893).

Das Recht der freien Rede in Amerika.

Es ist schon lange nichts Neues mehr, daß die herrschende Klasse Amerikas unter dem Deckmantel der sog. freiheitlichen Institutionen einer Republik, die größten Niederträchtigkeiten und schamlosesten Vergewaltigungen dem arbeitenden Volke gegenüber begangen hat. Die Gefängnisse Amerikas bergen eine große Zahl von Menschen, die es gewagt hatten für ihre unveräußerlichen Rechte einzutreten; garnicht jener Zahlreichen zu gedenken, die von Seiten des herrschenden Raubgesindels auf feige und niederträchtige Art hingemordet wurden. Das Recht der freien Rede wurde zwar schon längst mit Füßen getreten, die herrschende Klasse konnte aber bisher die Ausrede gebrauchen, daß bei dieser oder jener Gelegenheit ihre Schergen von den Arbeitern attaquirt wurden, oder daß das Eigenthum irgend eines Blutsaugers gefährdet schien und sie daher das Recht hätte, dieselben zu bestrafen und Reden zu unterdrücken, die zu derartigen Handlungen aufreizen.

Das Elend der Arbeiterschaft Amerikas wächst von Jahr zu Jahr und niemals haben es noch die Hungernden gewagt, ihre Stimme laut werden zu lassen. In diesem Jahre aber wurde die Noth zu groß, der Hunger zu gräßlich und die Arbeiter wollen ihr Joch nicht länger mehr ertragen. Der Schrei der Unterdrückten und Hungernden ertönt aus allen Ecken und Enden Amerikas, und die Entrechteten versammelten sich zu Tausenden, um den Ausführungen der Redner mit Spannung und Aufmerksamkeit zuzuhören. Solches liegt abernicht im Interesse der herrschenden Blutsaugerbande—das wäre ja das Recht der freien Rede auf eine ganz sonderbare Art interpretirt. Wie, die Arbeiter, diese unsere Sklaven, unsere Ausbeutungs-Objekte, ihnen soll dieses Recht auch zugestanden werden? Nie und nimmermehr! In dem Momente wo die Arbeiter sich ihrer wahren Lage bewußt werden, derselben Ausdruck zu geben suchen und so an unseren Vorrechten rütteln, in diesem Momente ist unsere Existenz auf das Ernstlichste bedroht.

So und ähnlicher Art hat die capitalistische Bande in den letzten Tagen gedacht und gesprochen und in ihrer Angst und Bestürzung ihr Heer von Schergen auf diejenigen gehetzt, die es unternommen, die hungernden Arbeitslosen aufzuklären und denselben Mittel und Wege anzugeben—sich Brot zu verschaffen.

Nach Ansicht der herrschenden Capitalistenbande, haben also die Arbeiter, diese modernen Sklaven des neunzehnten Jahrhunderts, hierzulande nicht den geringsten Anspruch auf das Recht der freien Rede; sie haben kein Recht, ihre Forderungen um Brot geltend zu machen; sie haben kein Recht, über ihre Noth und ihr Elend und über die Mittel zur Beseitigung derselben zu sprechen: sie haben kein Recht, von der reich gedeckten Tafel des Lebens etwas für sich in Anspruch zu nehmen—sie haben nur ein Recht: das Recht, geduldig zu verhungern.

Von diesem Geiste beseelt, hetzten also die aus ihrer Ruhe und Behaglichkeit gescheuchten Volksbedrücker ihre Bluthunde auf einige der Redner, die in den Arbeitslosen-Versammlungen der letzten Zeit es versuchten, das gedrückte, entrechtete und ausgesogene Volk auf die richtige Bahn zu leiten und demselben zu zeigen, wie es sich von einem schmählichen Sklavenjoche befreien könne. Der ganze Büttel-Apparat von New York und Philadelphia wurde beispielsweise in Bewegung gesetzt und eine ganze Schaar von Spionen war in Thätigkeit um meiner Person habhaft zu werden, trotzdem ich nicht das Geringste unternahm mich vor den Häschern zu verbergen, vielmehr überall offen und frei meine Thätigkeit weiter entfaltete. Ich will mich über die mir seitens der Polizeibrut zu Thei gewordenen brutalen Behandlung und über die ganz niederträchtige Vergewaltigung, die mir von den Philadelphier Behörden wiederfuhr, hier nicht weiter ergehen—das eine nur will sagen, daß in meinen Augen der Leichenschänder des Schlachtfeldes ein ehrenwerter Mann ist im Vergleich zum Polizisten im Allgemeinen, und zum amerikanischen Polizisten im Besonderen.—Ich hatte es in ganz kurzer Zeit während meiner Haft in Philadelphia herausgefunden, daß man mich mit den angewandten raffinirten Torturen und niedrigen Anträgen zu demoralisiren suchte.

Bekanntlich soll das Weib hierzulande mehr Rechte haben. Ja, aber nicht das Proletarierweib, nicht eine Anarchistin. Mit Verachtung sieht der Amerikaner auf die Despotie Rußlands hin und doch werden hier unter dem Deckmantel der Freiheit dieselben Greuelthaten am Volke begangen. Nun wohl, wenn ich nicht frei meine Meinung sagen kann, so werde ich noch andere Mittel und Wege finden um dem Volke die Augen zu öffnen, zu ihm zu sprechen, daß den capitalistischen Cäsaren Amerikas das Herz im Leibe beben wird; ich werde der feigen Bande die Maske der Lüge noch vom Gesichte reißen. Die Idee der wahren Freiheit wird fortleben bis zum Tage der großen Abrechnung; an diesem Tage wird das jahrtausende lang getretene und gedrückte Volk zu neuem Leben erwachen—zum wahrhaft freien Leben in der Anarchie.

Emma Goldmann.

Essay in *DIE BRANDFACKEL*

Tombs Prison, New York, 13 September 1893

The Right of Free Speech in America.

It's a well-known fact that the ruling class in America has been committing the most despicable acts and most shameless assaults upon the working people using the so-called liberal institutions of a republic as a cover. The prisons of America hold a large number of people who dared to speak up for their inalienable rights,[1] not to mention the countless number who were executed in a cowardly and despicable manner by the ruling gang of robbers.[2] The right of free speech has been trampled upon for a long time, but until now the ruling class could use the excuse that in this or that case their lackeys were attacked by the workers, or that some bloodsucker's property seemed at risk and therefore they had the right to punish those same workers and suppress the speech that provoked such actions.

The misery of America's workers grows from year to year, and those who are going hungry have never dared to raise their voices. This year, however, the poverty is too great, the hunger too terrible, and the workers will not bear their yoke any longer.[3] The cry of the oppressed and hungry sounds from all corners of America, and those deprived of their rights have gathered by the thousands to listen to the pronouncements of speakers with excitement and attentiveness.[4] This, however, is not in the interest of the ruling

1. Along with her own arrest, EG may be referring to several free-speech advocates who had been prosecuted under the Comstock Act of 1873. Ezra Heywood, the publisher of *The Word*, a free love paper, was imprisoned in 1878 and 1890 for mailing material considered obscene. D. M. Bennett, editor of *The Truth Seeker*, served thirteen months of hard labor for mailing obscene material (the pamphlet *Cupid's Yokes*, which was Heywood's argument for free love) in 1879. In 1890, Moses Harman was found guilty of publishing obscene material in *Lucifer* and sentenced to five years in prison for publishing letters about sex education, women's liberation, and free speech. Many labor activists were also arrested and imprisoned during this time. The 16 July 1891 issue of *Twentieth Century Magazine*, for instance, reported at least eight recent arrests for union organizing and labor protests.
2. Among other incidents, EG is referring to the 6 July 1892 killing of striking and locked-out workers at Homestead.
3. EG refers to the current economic crisis, which could be traced back to the Sherman Silver Purchase Act of 1890. Some argued that the act had hurt the economy by undermining the value of gold and sending inflation soaring. The Wall Street Panic of 7 May 1893 had deepened the crisis as hundreds of banks and thousands of businesses failed, leaving between two and three million people unemployed.
4. In August 1893 several demonstrations by the unemployed took place in New York City. On 17 August 1893, a mass meeting of about five thousand unemployed Jews on the East Side at Walhalla Hall erupted into the streets. Three men were arrested—Abraham Rosenfarb, Jacob Gold, and Abram Simon. The speakers denounced the brutality of the New York police against the working-class demonstrators, and defended the right to speak on their condition. During the next several days EG spoke at a series of meetings of the unemployed, including on the 18th of August, the occasion of the first report quoting her advocacy of taking bread by force (see *New York Times*, 19 August 1893); on the 19th

DIE BRANDFACKEL

ANARCHISTISCHE MONATSCHRIFT.

Heft 1. Julie. 1893.

C. Timmermann, 209 E. 5. Str., New York.
Jährlich 50 Cts., Einzeln 5 Cts.

Cover from July 1893 issue of *Die Brandfackel,* German-language anarchist communist paper edited by Claus Timmermann, in which many of Goldman's earliest essays were published. (By permission of the Houghton Library, Harvard University)

band of bloodsuckers—that would be quite an unusual interpretation of the right of free speech. What, the workers, our slaves, our objects of exploitation, should also have this right granted to them? Never! At the moment in which the workers become aware of their true position, try to express it and thus threaten our privileges, at this moment our existence is in the most serious jeopardy.

In the last few days the capitalistic band has thought and spoken in this and similar ways, and in their fear and dismay have set their lackeys upon those who have undertaken

she participated in a march of over a thousand people, and she joined ongoing meetings on the 21st and the 23rd. Her speech on the 21st would lead to her arrest.

to enlighten the starving unemployed[5] and offer them ways and means to get hold of some bread.[6]

In the opinion of the ruling bands of capitalists, therefore, the workers, the modern slaves of the nineteenth century, do not have the least claim to the right of free speech; they have no right to assert their demands for bread; they have no right to speak about their poverty and their misery or about the means to eliminate these; they have no right to claim something for themselves from the richly set table of life. They have only one right: the right to die patiently of starvation.

Imbued with this spirit and driven from their comfort and contentment, the oppressors of the people set their bloodhounds on several of the speakers who have tried in recent workers' meetings to lead the oppressed, alienated, and exploited on the right path and show them how to free themselves from the despicable yoke of slavery. The whole lackey apparatus of New York and Philadelphia, for example, was set in motion and an entire army of spies were at work to apprehend me, even though I did not make the slightest attempt to hide myself from my pursuers and in fact continued to carry out my activities openly and freely.[7] I will not go on any further here about the at times brutal treatment inflicted upon me by the police and the vile assault coming from the Philadelphia authorities—I only want to say that in my eyes one who defiles corpses on a battlefield is an honorable man in comparison to policemen in general, and to American policemen in particular. I discovered in a very short time during my arrest in Philadelphia that they would try to demoralize me with refined tortures and vile requests.[8]

It is well known that women in this country are supposed to have more rights. Indeed, but not the proletarian woman, not an Anarchist woman. Americans look upon the despotism of Russia with disdain, yet here under the cover of freedom the same atrocities are committed against the people. Well, if I am not free to speak my opinion, then I will

---

5. Two hundred people marched in Rochester, New York, on 10 August 1893 to protest widespread unemployment. The mayor prohibited the marchers from carrying black flags and instead instructed them to carry American flags.

6. Bread as the most basic of people's needs and a reason for revolt was a fundamental theme of anarchism during this period. See for example the manifesto by Peter Kropotkin, Louise Michel, and other anarchists upon their arrest and trial in Lyon in 1883, in which they declared "Scoundrels that we are, we demand bread for all; for all equally independence and justice"; see also Kropotkin's *The Conquest of Bread* (1892).

7. After her Union Square speech, EG spoke in Long Island and Philadelphia. The New York City police told newspaper reporters that they were unable to locate EG and asserted that she was in hiding. EG was arrested in Philadelphia on 31 August, along with Otto H. Lieble and Albert Hanson, who attempted to shield and rescue her from detectives. Lieble and Hanson were held on $1,000 bail and eventually released.

8. In *Living My Life*, EG recalls that while awaiting extradition in Philadelphia she was allowed no mail, only the Bible to read, and was given towels to hem. She also claimed that Detective Sergeant Jacobs, who escorted her to New York, offered to pay her a large sum of money in return for periodic reports on the activities of radicals among the workers on the East Side, which she flatly refused (*LML*, pp. 125–26; see also Excerpt from Trial Transcript, 4 October 1893, below).

find other ways and means to open the eyes of the people and speak to them so that the hearts of the capitalist Caesars of America will tremble; I will yet rip the mask of lies from the faces of this cowardly band. The idea of true freedom will live on until the day of the great reckoning; on this day the people who have been trod upon and oppressed for thousands of years will awake to a new life—to a truly free life in Anarchy.

Emma Goldmann.

Die Brandfackel 1 (September 1893): 3–5. Translated from German.

Interview in the **NEW YORK WORLD**

New York, 17 September 1893

Nellie Bly Again.

She Interviews Emma Goldman and Other Anarchists.

[. . .]EMMA GOLDMAN.

Do you need an introduction to Emma Goldman? You have seen supposed pictures of her. You have read of her as a property-destroying, capitalist-killing, riot-promoting agitator. You see her in your mind a great raw-boned creature, with short hair and bloomers, a red flag in one hand, a burning torch in the other; both feet constantly off of the ground and "murder!" continually upon her lips.

That was my ideal of her, I confess,[1] and when the matron stood before me saying, "This is Emma Goldman," I gasped with surprise and then laughed.

A little bit of a girl, just 5 feet high,[2] including her bootheels, not showing her 120 pounds; with a saucy, turned-up nose and very expressive blue-gray eyes that gazed inquiringly at me through shell-rimmed glasses was Emma Goldman!

Her quiet little hands held rolled a recent copy of the *Illustrated American*.[3] The modest blue serge Eton suit, with a blue muslin shirtwaist and scarf, had no suggestion of bloomers, and the light brown hair, not banged but falling loosely over the forehead and gathered in a little knot behind, was very pretty and girlish.

The little feet were decorously upon the floor, and when the rather full lips parted, showing strong, white teeth within, a mild, pleasant voice, with a very fetching accent, said not "murder," but—

"What is it you wish, madam?"

I told her. I sat down beside her, and we talked for two hours.

"I do not want anything published about me," she said, "because people misjudge and exaggerate, and, besides, I do not think it looks well for me to say anything while I am in jail."

"But I want to know something about your former life; how you became an Anarchist, what your theories are, and how you mean to establish them."

1. Nellie Bly's was the first extensive interview of EG in the mainstream daily press. The interview, which took place while EG was awaiting trial in the Tombs jail, also marked Bly's return to the front pages of the *New York World* after a three-year hiatus.
2. Her 1893 Philadelphia arrest record gave EG's exact height as 4 feet 10 and 3/4 inches.
3. The recent issue contained an article entitled "Anarchism in New York," featuring a disparaging account of EG as a reckless agitator among the unemployed of the Lower East Side (see *Illustrated American*, 9 September 1893, pp. 295–98).

Nellie Bly in 1890, the *New York World* journalist whose 17 September 1893 front-page interview marked Goldman's debut in the American press as a serious political thinker with broad popular appeal, especially to a growing constituency of women. (Library of Congress)

SHE TELLS HER AGE.

She smiled at me, rather amused, but the smile was a very becoming one, lighting up the gravity of her face and making her look more girlish than ever.

"How old are you?" I asked as a beginning.

"Twenty-five last June," she replied without the faintest hesitancy.

What greater proof do I need that she is an unusual and extraordinary woman?

"But the month of roses has not brought many into my life," she added, with a little smile.

"When did you become an Anarchist, and what made you one?"

"Oh, I have been one all my life, but I never really entered into the work until after the Chicago riot, seven years ago."[4]

4. The aftermath of the Haymarket riots led to both fear and suspicion of anarchism and, interestingly, a resurgence of interest in anarchism in the United States. EG, AB, Voltairine de Cleyre, Bill Hay-

"Why are you one?" I asked. "What is your object? What did you hope to gain?"

She smiled again, and slowly smoothed her book upon her knee.

"We are all egotists,"[5] she answered. "There are some that, if asked why they are Anarchists, will say, 'for the good of the people.' It is not true, and I do not say it. I am an Anarchist because I am an egotist. It pains me to see others suffer. I cannot bear it. I never hurt a man in my life, and I don't think I could. So, because what others suffer makes me suffer, I am an Anarchist and give my life to the cause, for only through it can be ended all suffering and want and unhappiness.

A WORD ABOUT CAPITALISTS.

"Everything wrong, crime and sickness and all that, is the result of the system under which we live," she continued earnestly. "Were there no money and, as a result, no capitalists, people would not be over-worked, starved and illy housed, all of which makes them old before their time, diseases them and makes them criminals. To save a dollar the capitalists build their railroads poorly, and along comes a train, and loads of people are killed. What are their lives to him if by their sacrifice he has saved money? But those deaths mean misery, want and crime in many, many families. According to Anarchistic principles, we build the best of railroads, so there shall be no accidents. There is the Broadway cable, for instance.[6] Instead of running a few cars at a frightful speed, in order to save a larger expense, we should run many cars at slow speed, and so have no accidents."

"If you do away with money and employers, who will work upon your railroads?" I asked.

"Those that care for that kind of work. Then every one shall do that which he likes best, not merely a thing he is compelled to do to earn his daily bread."[7]

"What would you do with the lazy ones, who would not work?"

"No one is lazy. They grow hopeless from the misery of their present existence, and give up. Under our order of things, every man would do the work he liked, and would have as much as his neighbor, so could not be unhappy and discouraged."

"What will you do with your criminals if every one is free and prisons unheard of?"

---

wood, and others all point to the injustices of the trial and hangings of Albert Parsons, August Spies, George Engel, and Adolph Fischer as deeply influential in their own development as radicals. EG wrote in *Living My Life* that a speech about Haymarket made by Socialist Labor Party member Johanna Greie Cramer while EG was still living in Rochester had a great impact on her, as did articles written by Most in his paper *Freiheit*. Above all it was Louis Lingg's defiance during the trial and his taking of his own life before the scheduled hanging that resonated with EG and AB.

5. For discussion of anarchism and egoism, see note 3 to Letter from Alexander Berkman, 20 August 1892, above.

6. Fully operational in July 1893, the Broadway cable car line was the site of frequent accidents, particularly at Twenty-third and Fifty-third streets and at the segment along Fourteenth Street known as "Dead Man's Curve."

7. EG's comments on work under anarchism and the following discussion of crime and criminals are similar to those in Peter Kropotkin's pamphlet *Anarchist Communism: Its Basis and Principles* (London: Freedom Press, 1891).

WHY ARE THERE CRIMINALS?

She smiles, sadly.

"The subject takes a lifetime of study," she answered, "but we believe that we would not have a criminal. Why are there criminals to-day. Because some have everything, others nothing. Under our system it would be every man equal. The Bible says, 'Thou shalt not steal.' Now, to steal, it is granted, there must be something to steal. We do not grant there is anything to steal, for everything should be free."

"Do you believe in God, Miss Goldman?"

"Once I did. Until I was seventeen I was very devout, and all my people are so, even to-day. But when I began to read and study, I lost that belief. I believe in nature, nothing else."

"Where were you born?"

"I was born in Russia and afterwards my family removed to Germany. Although my people were of a good family, I was always in deep sympathy with the poor. I did not think of being an Anarchist then, but I was always trying to see some way to benefit the working classes. I was taught a trade. My father thought that no difference what one's position was, one should master a trade, so I learned dressmaking at a French school. I have worked at this for years, sometimes in my own rooms, and again in establishments."

SHE LIKES TO BATHE AND DRESS.

"Do you care for dress at all?"

"Oh, of course," she answered, laughing. "I like to look well, but I don't like very fussy dresses. I like my dresses to be plain and quiet, and, above all things," here she laughed as if recalling the oft-repeated declaration of Anarchists' hatred for soap, "I love my bath. I must be clean. Being a German, I was taught cleanliness with my youth, and I do not care how poor my room or my clothes are so long as they are clean."

"What did you do with the money you earned by sewing?"

"Spent it all for books," she said emphatically. "I kept myself in poverty buying books. I have a library of nearly three hundred volumes, and so long as I had something to read I did not mind hunger or shabby clothes."

Think of that, you girls who put every dollar upon your backs! Can you not testify to this woman's earnestness of purpose when she voluntarily sacrifices her looks for books?

Miss Goldman speaks Russian, German, French and English, and reads and writes Spanish and Italian.

HER IDEAS OF MARRIAGE.

"There is something else I must ask you. We look upon marriage as the foundation of everything that is good. We base everything upon it. You do not believe in marriage. What do you propose shall take its place?"

"I was married," she said, with a little sigh, "when I was scarcely seventeen.[8] I suffered—let me say no more about that. I believe in the marriage of affection. That is the only true marriage. If two people care for each other they have a right to live together so long as that love exists. When it is dead what base immorality for them still to keep together! Oh, I tell you the marriage ceremony is a terrible thing!

"Tell me," she added very seriously, "how can a woman go before a minister and take an oath to love 'this man' all her life? How can she tell but to-morrow, next week, she may get to know this man and hate him. Love is founded on respect, and a woman cannot tell what a man is until she lives with him. Instead of being free to end the relation when her feelings change, she lives on in a state that is the most depraved of all.

"Take the woman who marries for a home and for fine clothes. She goes to the man with a lie on her lips and in her heart. Still"—with a little uplifting of the hands—"she will not let her skirts touch the poor unfortunate upon the street who deceives no man, but is to him just what she appears! Do away with marriage. Let there be nothing but voluntary affection and there ceases to exist the prostitute wife and the prostitute street woman."

"But the children? What would you do with them? Men would desert; women and children would be left uncared for and destitute," I protested.

"On the contrary, then men would never desert, and if a couple decided to separate there would be public homes and schools for the children. Mothers who would rather do something else than care for their children could put them in the schools, where they would be cared for by women who preferred taking care of children to any other work. In this way we would never have diseased or disabled children from careless and incompetent mothers.

"Besides this," she went on, "in our free schools every child would have a chance to learn and pursue that for which it has ability. Can you imagine the number of children to-day, children of poor parents, who are born with ability for music or painting, or letters, whose abilities lie dormant for the lack of means and the necessity to work for their daily bread as soon as they are out of their cradles."

HER RELATIVES.

"Have you any brothers or sisters, Miss Goldman?"

"Yes; a married brother,[9] who does not bother about anything, and only reads the papers when there is something in them about me. My sister is also married and, while not

---

8. In February 1887 EG married fellow factory worker Jacob Kershner, thereby gaining U.S. citizenship. She divorced him between November 1887 and February 1888, then remarried him and was never officially divorced from Kershner after their remarriage.
9. Herman Goldman (1872–1934), EG's younger brother and a Rochester machinist, was interviewed about his sister at the time of AB's attempt on Frick. See *Rochester Union and Advertiser*, 28 July 1892, p. 5.

actively engaged in our cause, is bringing up her children to our principles.[10] My father and mother are also living, near Rochester, and, while not Anarchists, sympathize with me and do not interfere with my work."[11]

"What is your future?"

"I cannot say. I shall live to agitate to promote our ideas. I am willing to give my liberty and my life, if necessary, to further my cause. It is my mission and I shall not falter."

"Do you think that murder is going to help your cause?"

She looked grave; she shook her head slowly.

"That is a long subject to discuss. I don't believe that through murder we shall gain, but by war, labor against capital, masses against classes, which will not come in twenty or twenty-five years. But some day, I firmly believe, we shall gain, and until then I am satisfied to agitate to teach, and I only ask justice and freedom of speech."

And so I left the little Anarchist, the modern Joan of Arc, waiting patiently in the Tombs until her friends could secure bail for her.

"I shall certainly get a year or a year and a half,"[12] she said to me in parting, "not because my offense deserves it, but because I am an Anarchist."[. . .]

New York World, 17 September 1893, pp. 1, 3. Excised from the beginning of this article is Bly's declaration that the "labor wars" were the central issue of the period, since racial, regional, and religious tensions had "vanished." The excised remainder of the article includes interviews with Johann Most and Justus Schwab, and an account of EG's visit to Schwab's saloon Zum Großen Michel, a gathering place for radicals. Also included with the article are drawings of EG, Schwab, Most, and Claus Timmermann. For the complete article, see *EGP,* reel 47.

10. The sister EG refers to could be Lena Zodikow Cominsky (1862–1950), EG's half sister and the mother of six children, including two who would become close to EG, Stella (Cominsky) Comyn Ballantine (1886–1961) and Saxe Commins, born Isidore Cominsky (1892–1958); or EG could be referring to Helene Hochstein (1860–1920), who was a socialist and had three children, including the violinist David Hochstein (1892–1918).

11. EG's parents lived in Rochester, New York. Her father had a small furniture shop and her mother took an active part in Jewish philanthropy in that city.

12. EG was in fact sentenced to a year in prison and released after ten months for good behavior.

The People vs. EMMA GOLDMAN.

COURT OF GENERAL SESSIONS OF THE PEACE,
City and County of New York.[1]

Before, HON. RANDOLPH B. MARTINE,[2] and a Jury.

Tried, October 4th, etc., 1893.

Indicted for UNLAWFULLY ASSEMBLING.

Indictment filed SEPTEMBER 6TH, 1893.

APPEARANCES: ASSISTANT DISTRICT ATTORNEY
VERNON M. DAVIS,[3] For THE PEOPLE.

A. OAKEY HALL[4] and BENJAMIN F. DOURAS,[5] ESQRS.,
For THE DEFENSE.[6]

CHARLES JACOBS,[7] called by the People, being duly sworn, testified that he was a detective sergeant, connected with the Detective Bureau. He had been connected with that

---

1. The following court record is an excerpt from the official transcript of EG's 1893 trial. It does not offer a verbatim account of the proceedings, but only the government's summary of selected testimony. Newspaper coverage of the trial, some of which is excerpted in the following notes, provided verbatim reports of trial testimony not in the official court record. See also *LML*, pp. 129–32 for exculpatory court testimony omitted here.
2. Judge Randolph B. Martine (1844–1895), a prominent figure in Tammany Hall, presided over EG's trial.
3. In fact, Assistant District Attorney John F. McIntyre prosecuted the case.
4. Abraham Oakey Hall was a prominent New York attorney. EG's 1893 trial marked his return to the courtroom in New York, after nine years of practicing law in London. In her autobiography, EG gave a glowing account of Hall.
5. Benjamin F. Douras was a New York attorney and law partner in the firm of Oakey Hall, Douras and Bayer.
6. EG initially resisted the idea of hiring a defense lawyer, adhering to the anarchist position that justice was unattainable in capitalist courts. According to *Living My Life*, AB sent EG a letter suggesting that a lawyer could help her reap the propaganda value of the trial by protecting her right to speak during the process (see *LML*, p. 128).
7. New York City detective sergeant Charles Jacobs was the star witness at EG's 1893 trial. The jury convicted EG largely on the basis of Jacobs's firsthand account of her 21 August 1893 Union Square speech. He was also the key witness for the state in the trial of Claus Timmermann on 1 September 1893. Jacobs went to Philadelphia in August 1893 to serve EG with a warrant and, according to EG,

bureau about seven years, and had been on the police force about nine years. He knew the defendant. He first saw the defendant on the night of the 19th of August, 1893, at a meeting in Union Square. He next saw the defendant on the night of the 21st of August, on the stand at the Plaza, in Union Square. There was a labor meeting there that night, and about three or four thousand people were in the square. He, the witness, arrived at that place about 7 o'clock that night, accompanied by Detective Sergeants Krauch, Heidelberg, McNaught and Von Gerichten, Inspector McLaughlin, and Roundsman Schauwecker. The chairman of the meeting was a man named Joseph Levy.[8] He heard the defendant speak on that occasion, and he stood right behind her when she was speaking. He understood the German language; he could read and write German. On the night in question the defendant addressed the persons assembled, first in English and then in German. In the course of her English speech the defendant, "called the attention of the American workmen who were assembled in the crowd to the fact that that was a meeting held by the unemployed who were out of employment and wanted bread and were hungry. They were mostly all foreigners. She begged that the American workmen who were present would take some interest in it because it was a meeting for a good object, and she hoped that they would all give her their attention." While the defendant was speaking in German, he, the witness, took down what she said. He could not state, exactly, from memory, what she said. The witness then gave the following as a translation of what the defendant said, in her German speech, on that night: "My friends and Workmen: We have assembled here for the purpose of speaking about our condition, and to better our condition. But with idle talk you will accomplish very little. You must have courage. You want bread, but who will give it to you? No one. Nobody will give it to you. If you want it, you must take it. If you do not get it when you ask for it, upon your demands, take it by force." Immediately after the word "force," the crowd responded, "That is what we will do; that is what we will do." The defendant continued: "Go out into the street and prepare yourselves. The capitalists have prepared themselves with the police, who are armed—the capitalists have prepared themselves with the police, who are armed with clubs and pistols, but you can defend yourselves with clubs and stones, if you are attacked." After the word "attacked," the crowd cheered, and said, "That is what we will do." The defendant continued: "I tell you again, organize yourselves, and go out and demand what you want, and, if you do not get it, take it by force. And if you take bread alone, it will help you but very little." The crowd then cheered and shouted, "Hurrah! Hurrah! That is what we will do." The defendant continued: "Go to the houses of the capitalists and demand your rights, and, if you are refused them, take them by force. You will be attacked by the militia and the police. You must be prepared to defend yourselves with clubs and stones." The crowd shouted, "Yes, that is what we will have to do." The

---

tried to bribe her into becoming an informant on the activities of her fellow anarchists on the train ride back to New York City.

8. In the article "Badly Advised" (see *New-Yorker Staats-Zietung,* 22 August 1893, above), this "Joseph Levy" is identified as David Levy.

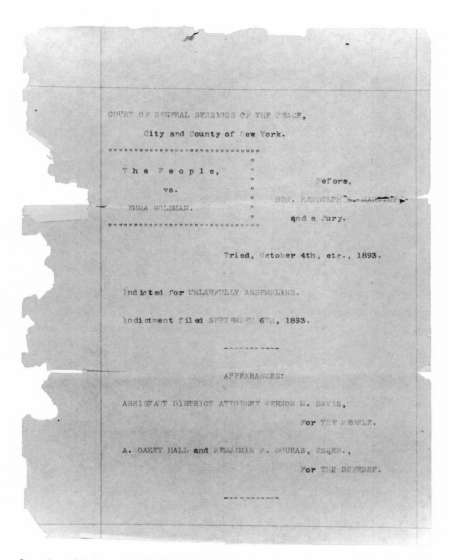

COURT OF GENERAL SESSIONS OF THE PEACE,

City and County of New York.

"""""""""""""""""""""""""""""""

          The People,   "
                                "
                  vs.   "   Before,
                                "
          EMMA GOLDMAN.   "   HON. RANDOLPH B. MARTINE
                                "   and a Jury.
"""""""""""""""""""""""""""""""

                        Tried, October 4th, etc., 1893.

            Indicted for UNLAWFULLY ASSEMBLING.

            Indictment filed SEPTEMBER 6TH, 1893.

                    APPEARANCES:

            ASSISTANT DISTRICT ATTORNEY VERNON M. DAVIS,

                                    For THE PEOPLE.

            A. OAKEY HALL and BENJAMIN F. DOURAS, ESQRS.,

                                    For THE DEFENSE.

Cover sheet of trial transcript, *The People vs. Emma Goldman,* 4 October 1893. (Municipal Archives, Department of Records and Information Services, City of New York)

defendant then said: "Prepare yourselves. Either you will do what I tell you or you can go home and lay down quietly and die of hunger. You cannot accomplish much by making speeches. You will have to act, and, if you want to act, you will have to prepare yourselves, so that you can defend yourselves." The crowd shouted, "She is right; we will have to be able to defend ourselves." The defendant continued: "It is true you are not prepared, but we know that the police are prepared with weapons, but we know where they can be got."

Police mug shot of Goldman, 31 August 1893, just after her arrest in Philadelphia on charges of unlawful assembly arising from the New York City demonstration of the unemployed on 21 August 1893. (Rogues' Gallery, Department of Records, City of Philadelphia)

The crowd shouted, "We know where to buy them." The defendant then said: "You are living in a time when you must act. The laws will not fill our empty stomachs. The rich live in luxury. Their wives and children have the nicest and best, while our wives and children roam about in rags." The crowd shouted, "We know that; she is right, she is right." Continuing, the defendant said: "Now, that you know what you have to do, prepare yourselves. Long live anarchy!" The defendant also made many references to the French Revolution and to the American Revolution, but he, the witness, at the time, did not think they were material, and he "didn't make copies of them." The defendant also referred to the riots in this country in 1863.[9] The defendant spoke about twenty-five minutes. At

9. The New York City Draft Riots in July of 1863 were a response to a recent draft lottery and a provision in the 1863 Conscription Act that allowed men to avoid military service if they sent a substitute or paid a $300 commutation fee. Complex sentiments were aroused against the act, especially from Democrats who opposed Republican President Lincoln's proclamation to free black slaves in the southern states. Many unskilled workers in northern states, who were mainly Irish and Democrats, feared that free blacks would move north and take away their jobs by working for less pay. Many among the working class also felt that they were being forced into war, while the rich could pay their way out. From 13 July to 16 July mobs rioted, destroying property, attacking prominent Republicans, and murdering free blacks. Labor unrest, inflation, and two years of the Civil War added to the tensions that started the riot.

Philadelphia police arrest record, labeling Goldman a "fugitive Anarchist" after her citation for unlawful assembly in connection with the New York demonstration of the unemployed on 21 August 1893. (Municipal Archives, Department of Records and Information Services, City of New York)

times, during the defendant's speech, hats were waved in the air, and the crowd appeared to get very much excited. When the defendant walked across the park, after her speech, she was followed by about fifty or a hundred people. He saw the defendant, about two weeks after that, in a cell in Police Headquarters, in Philadelphia. He had been looking for the defendant between the 21st of August and the time when he found her in Philadelphia. He brought the defendant back to New York.

In cross-examination the witness testified that the notes from which he had read the speech of the defendant were taken at the time of the meeting, and nothing had been added to them thereafter. He was instructed to take down anything of an incendiary nature that was said at that meeting. He was not instructed to arrest persons who made incendiary speeches. He was not in uniform at the time of the meeting. He was not a stenographer. He was not gratified when he heard what he thought was an incendiary speech; he had no interest in the matter, except an official interest. He supposed that he had left out of his notes some parts of the speech; he could not recall which part he had left out. The defendant did not say anything in her English speech that he thought was worthy of recognition in his book. The defendant's German speech was not a perfect German translation of the English speech. He, the witness, was born in this country. He went to a German school, in his youth, and, when he became a policeman, he was on duty in a German section of the city, where he acquired a good deal of German. He did not consider the meeting unlawful until the defendant spoke, in German, and then he thought it was very unlawful. He did not see any unlawful act committed there, aside from mere language; nor did he see any act that was against police discipline. So far as he knew, no arrests were made at the meeting. He had no feeling against the anarchists; but he did not believe in anarchism. He had been frequently detailed to report their meetings, but had never been instructed to arrest any of them. There were not more than twenty-five or thirty people on the platform. He didn't see any one jostled on the platform. He was prepared to take down any incendiary words in the defendant's English speech, had he heard any. If anybody testified that the defendant used incendiary terms in the English speech, he had not heard any such thing. His father and mother were Germans, and his wife was a German.[10]

CHARLES L. SCHAUWECKER, being duly sworn, testified that he was a Roundsman in the Police Department, in charge of the School of Instruction at Police Headquarters. He had been a police officer over nineteen years. He was born in Germany, and came to this country when he was ten years of age. He spoke the German language fluently, and could read and write it. He was acquainted, in an official way, with Detective Sergeants Jacobs, Krauch, Heidelberg and McNaught. He was detailed, on the night of the 21st of August, by the acting Superintendent, Inspector Conlin, to attend the Union Square meeting. He was on the speakers' stand, at the Plaza. There were about three or four thousand people at the meeting in the square. There were eleven speakers, including the chairman. He saw the defendant on that night, and heard her speak. The defendant first spoke in English, for about ten or twelve minutes, and then she changed into German. At that time, he, the witness, was standing a little to the right of the defendant, about four or five feet from her, on the stand from which she was speaking. He saw Detective Sergeants Jacobs, Heidelberg, Von Gerichten, McNaught, and others there. He saw Detective Jacobs standing behind the defendant, with a note-book in his hand, but he, the witness, was too busy himself to notice whether or not Jacobs was taking notes. He could testify to the defendant's words on that occasion from memory, but he could not remember particularly as to the rotation of the words. He took notes of the defendant's speech, in German, and he had the notes in his possession at the time of the trial. The witness then testified as follows: "Miss Goldman then opened her German speech by the following words: 'My Friends and Workmen: We are here assembled to-night to speak of the way of improving our condition, but with mere speaking we accomplish nothing, if you have no courage.' The speaker here digressed into relating the history of the French Revolution, and the self-sacrifice and courage that it took to bring about the over-throw of the then existing condition; and, after that, she also referred to John Brown and his advocating the abolition of slavery and the self-sacrifice that he was compelled to put up with in order to bring it about, through the war of the Rebellion, the abolition of slavery and other matters.

10. At the conclusion of Jacobs's testimony, on the first day (4 October), the judge denied continuation of EG's bail. She remained in custody throughout the trial and sentencing hearing.

Also, incidentally, she referred to the matter at Chicago, where the bomb was thrown, and then continued, in referring to the present condition of this assembly, and said, 'You want bread, but who will give it to you? No one will give it to you. If you want it, you must take it; if you do not get it on your demand, take it by force.' During the speech I heard responses from the crowd, such as approving, cheering, and an occasional voice, a little louder than the rest, that would declare they would, and so on, but I paid no special attention to them, because I was too busy keeping track of what she said. Then she continued: 'Go out into the social revolution. Prepare yourselves. The capitalists have prepared themselves with the police, who are armed with pistols and clubs.' There was another interval of applause and cries, and she continued, 'You can defend yourselves with sticks and stones, if assaulted, and, I say, again, organize and go out and demand what you want, and, if it is not given to you, take it by force; and if you only take bread, it will not help you much. Take all.' There was another interval here of applause, and cries from the crowd, during which time I caught up with her remarks. 'Go to the palaces of the capitalists. Demand your rights, and, if they are not given to you, take them by force. You will be assaulted by the soldiery and the police, and you must be able to defend yourselves. With sticks and with stones prepare yourselves. Either you must do what I tell you or you can go home and lie down quietly and die of hunger. You can't accomplish anything with holding speeches. You must act; and if you want to act, you must prepare yourselves in order to be able to defend yourselves. It is true, you are not prepared, and we know that the police are prepared with weapons. We know also where they are to be obtained. You are living in a time wherein you must act. The law will not fill your empty stomachs. The laws are made for the rich and not for the poor. The wealthy live in luxury. Their wives and children have the handsomest and best, while your wives and children are starving and running about in rags. Now that you know what you are to do, prepare yourselves.' Then, with a wave of the hand, she concluded her speech by saying, 'May Anarchy live!'" The defendant spoke on that for about thirty-five minutes. He took notes of one Timmerman, on the same night, and he had testified on Timmerman's trial.[11]

In cross-examination the witness testified that his instructions were to go to the meeting and take down such portions of the speeches, in writing, as would be serviceable as evidence, in case anything unlawful was spoken and the party apprehended. He had no instructions to arrest anybody who spoke in an incendiary manner. He took down the defendant's English speech, but had destroyed the copy, it was of so little importance. He was not a stenographer. He wrote in abbreviated long-hand. The crowd, as a body, was not disorderly. He did not arrest the defendant, because that was no part of his instructions, and his opinion was that an immediate arrest would have provoked acts of disorder. [. . .]

11. For a description of the trial of Claus Timmermann, see "Urging Men to Riot," *New York World*, 22 August 1893, *EGP*, reel 47.

FOR THE DEFENCE, <u>JOSEPH BARONDESS</u>, being duly sworn, testified that he was a cloak-maker, by trade. He remembered having been convicted of a misdemeanor, for which he had suffered imprisonment and been pardoned by the Governor.[12] He had secured a permit, from the proper authorities, for the meeting which was held in Union Square. The object of the meeting was to appeal to the local, state and federal government to inaugurate public works for the unemployed. He, the witness, was not present at that meeting on the 21st.

In cross-examination the witness testified that at the time of the trial he was an organizer of the Operators' and Cloakmakers' Union. He had last worked at his trade about three years before the trial. He was a married man and supported his family. He received seven dollars and a half a week as an organizer, but there was no one to take his place. He never extorted money from the firm of Popkin & Marks, Benjamin & Caspary or Fishel Brothers. He remembered being tried in the Court of Oyer & Terminer, found guilty, and sentenced to a year in State prison. He was pardoned by the Governor, upon the recommendation of the District Attorney. He was an anarchist. He believed in living up to the laws of the land, and believed in the proper administration of the laws. He had read the Constitution of the United States and of the State of New York, and he believed in them. He was a member of labor organizations, and believed in improving the condition of the toiling masses. He knew the defendant. He knew John Most. He had known the defendant about four years, and had seen her about three or four times during that period. He had never heard the defendant say, in any other speeches to the unemployed, that, if they could not get bread, they would be justified in taking it by force.

<u>EDWARD JOHN THIMME</u>, being duly sworn, testified that he was a reporter on the New York *Staats-Zeitung*.[13] He attended the meeting in Union Square, on the night of the 21st of August, in the pursuit of his occupation. He mingled with the crowd before going on the platform; it was a very peaceable crowd. He was on the platform when the defendant spoke. He heard the English speech of the defendant, and took notes of it. He was a German by birth. He had been a reporter since 1886. Before he was employed by the *Staats-Zeitung,* he was on the New York *Volks-Zeitung*.[14] He heard the defendant's German speech. He took notes of the defendant's English speech, and when the defendant started to speak in German he waited to see whether or not she was simply translating her English speech into German. When the defendant was about half-way through

---

12. Joseph Barondess was arrested in 1891 in New York for leading a cloakmakers' strike the previous year. Under allegations of accepting a bribe (he had accepted a check for $100 from the firm of Popkin and Marks as part of the settlement of a strike against the company, although he claimed the check was for the union), Barondess went to trial where he was convicted of extortion and sentenced to twenty-one months in jail. He fled to Canada while on bail, but soon after returned to New York, where he spent a few weeks in jail before being pardoned by Governor Sulzer.

13. The *New-Yorker Staats-Zeitung* was a German-language mainstream daily newspaper. See Thimme's reporting in the 22 August 1893 article "Badly Advised," above.

14. The New York *Volkszeitung* was the daily German-language organ of the Socialist Labor Party.

her German speech, he concluded that it was as close a repetition of her English speech as possible, without being literally a translation. While the defendant was speaking, he, the witness, did not hear any of the remarks which Detective Jacobs had testified were made by the crowd, but he thought he would have heard them if they had been made. The defendant spoke in a medium manner, neither very rapidly nor very slowly.

In cross-examination the witness testified that in taking notes he wrote in abbreviated long-hand, and sometimes with stenographic signs intermixed. The New York *Volks-Zeitung* was a paper of Socialistic tendencies. He, the witness, was certain he belonged to one of the schools of socialism. He was not connected with any Socialistic societies. He did not know the defendant personally. He approved of some of the defendant's utterances. If the defendant said, "If you do not get bread and freedom peaceably, take it by force," he would not approve of it. He did not remember seeing Jacobs on the platform that night, nor did he see Heidelberg or Krauch. He did see Officer Schauwecker on the stand. Schauwecker was not taking notes when he, the witness, saw him. He remembered hearing the defendant say that the workingmens' stomachs were empty, that they should be filled with bread, and that they ought to get bread and have bread, and if they could not get it by easy measures they should take it by forcible measures.

EDWARD BRADY,[15] being duly sworn, testified that he was a compositor. He was at the Union Square meeting on the night of the 21st. He was a German. He read and spoke German fluently. He went to the meeting with the defendant. He heard the defendant's English and German speeches. So far as he could remember, there was no difference in the spirit of the speeches. He heard common expressions of approval from the assembled people. He had heard the testimony of Detective Jacobs. He heard some of the sentences which Jacobs had testified to, at the meeting, but it seemed to him, the witness, that the defendant's language was misconstrued and contorted by the officers. He did not hear the defendant utter any threat at the meeting.

In cross-examination the witness testified that he had been in this country twelve months. He had [a] printing office of his own, and did any kind of printing that he could get. He printed a paper for a society of working men; he did not know who wrote the articles for the paper, but it was a Socialistic paper. He was an anarchist. He had known the defendant about six months. He made her acquaintance in a saloon in Fifth street,[16] where Anarchists were in the habit of meeting. He saw about half a dozen anarchists at the Union Square meeting, whom he recognized. He had heard the defendant say some of the things which Schauwecker testified she had said. The defendant did not say that the people would do right if they went to the palaces of the capitalists and took anything that they could get. The defendant spoke as though prophesying, "If certain things would

---

15. Edward Brady, an anarchist born in Vienna who immigrated to the United States in 1892, was EG's companion and mentor from 1893 to 1899.
16. Probably Zum Großen Michel, a saloon located in the basement of 209 Fifth Street and a gathering place for radicals.

happen, then the people would be compelled to do such and such a thing." He did not hear the defendant say, "I tell you again, organize; go and demand what you want, and, if it is not given to you, then take it by force. If you take bread alone, it will not help you; take everything. March to the palaces of the capitalists and demand your rights. If they are not given to you, take them by force." He did not hear the defendant say anything about getting weapons. He heard some persons in the crowd shout, "Bravo!" He did not hear any one in the crowd say, "She is right; we will do it." He did not remember seeing Officer Jacobs writing on that night. He had not read the Constitution of the United States or of the State of New York.

EDWARD JOHN THIMME, being recalled for further cross-examination, testified that he had a copy of the *Staats-Zeitung* of August 22 in his possession. He reported the story of the Union Square meeting for that paper. In the report of the defendant's English speech was the following language: "You demand bread, and, if you cannot get it in a peaceable way, you will get it by force. Unite, and take it by force, if you cannot get it peaceably." . . . "Again, if you cannot get bread, take it by force." That language was contained in the English speech, notwithstanding the testimony of the detectives that they had heard nothing incendiary in the English speech.

EMMA GOLDMAN, THE DEFENDANT, being duly sworn, testified, in her own behalf, that she had lived in this country eight years. She had delivered many public speeches in this country. She was in the habit of preparing her speeches and committing them to memory. She had written out the German speech which she delivered on the night of the 21st of August, 1893, and she had memorized it. She had made notes of the English speech which she delivered on that night, before she went to the meeting. There was not very much difference between the English speech and the German speech. She had been requested by several of the unemployed to speak at that meeting. She saw Detective Jacobs at the meeting. She had heard the testimony of Detective Jacobs, on the stand; she denied everything that he said, it was not true. She was arrested in Philadelphia. She left New York on Tuesday, the 22nd of August, at 4 o'clock in the afternoon, and went to Philadelphia. She went to Philadelphia for the purpose of forming a union and delivering a lecture. She had had that purpose in her mind before the 21st of August. She was not paid for her speeches. She did not leave New York from any apprehension of arrest. She was arrested, in Philadelphia, on the night of the 31st of August. She was willing to return to New York without the formality of a requisition, but she was held to await a requisition.[17] The defendant then read, from manuscript, in German, the following, which she stated was the speech delivered by her, in German, on the night in question, and which was written on the Sunday preceding the 21st:[18]

17. See *Living My Life* for EG's account of her Philadelphia arrest: "In the morning I was asked whether I was willing to go back with the detectives to New York. 'Not of my own free will,' I declared. 'Very well, we'll keep you until your extradition has been arranged'" (*LML*, p. 124).

18. The court interpreter, Professor Benedict Morossi, translated EG's speech into what one account described as "half an hour of pure, unadulterated fun." Another described him as "a born actor, [who]

"I see thousands of working men and working women before me who are assembled, driven by a common necessity. Hunger does not make any difference between nations—no, there is no difference between nations and races—and the cry of hunger re-echoes now in all the cities of America. Hunger is the incentive for workingmen since the millionaires are uttering sounds of abolishing them and the riots caused by hunger are repeating themselves oftener and oftener. Certain demagogues want to persuade us that the Silver bill is the cause of the crisis, but the Silver bill is only one of the links of the long chain of the system of spoilation.[19] They want to throw before us a morsel of bread. They want to give us alms. They want to give us alms in order to quell our excitement, but alms are not the means by which the capitalistic class can abolish need. The needs of the working class are not caused by universal improvidence but by the un-equal sub-division of goods, in so far as private property is concerned. A small group of oppressors, idle people, have seated themselves above the proletariat and they suck the blood from their veins. The monopolists, the rich people, are those who command all the treasures of the earth and who use the workingmen only as an animal—a beast of burden and the discouraged classes are the victims of such injustice. In this country nature has arrayed everything which is beautiful and magnificent for the benefit of the whole of mankind, and men have only to reach for and take everything which they need for the satisfaction of their wants, but a band of thieves stands by the State and by the Church and has taken everything to themselves, and you, workingmen, get nothing, only toil, year in and year out and carry the burden until you lose all your strength and until you drop down dead. Everything which is true and great to you you sacrifice to your despoilers. Your daughters and sons are like flowers who lose their freshness. They wither in the factories and your women are compelled to sell themselves in the street because you are not able to support your families. Nevertheless you have borne your misery with patience as long as you had a piece of bread, and now they take from you the very last thing and while you are starving your persecutors and tormentors are seated at a big table drinking champagne and squandering enormous amounts of money for their pleasures and servants. What for is there here a police? Look at them, those well-fed representatives of the others—how they are flourishing their clubs and how they lay in wait in order to throw themselves upon you at the first opportunity and kill you, but you ain't yet entirely deprived of all your strength by hunger. You still are possessed of your energy, of your courage, and you ought to gather up yourselves. You can not allow yourselves to be patiently killed. Think of your wives and children. There are yet those who advise you to

---

makes up in histrionic talents what he lacks in the knowledge of German." EG clashed repeatedly with Morossi over his translation; even jury members appeared to take exception to his rendering of lines from Schiller. See *New York World*, 6 October 1893, *EGP*, reel 47; and *New York Times*, 6 October 1893, *EGP*, reel 47.

19. A reference to the Cleveland administration's blame of the current economic crisis on the Sherman Silver Purchase Act of 1890. Cleveland succeeded in repealing the Silver Act in late 1893, and the economy gradually recovered.

keep patient and to go for alms. Already, for a time, did you allow yourselves to be led by the nose by demagogues and to be held as fools but you can not have been degraded as much as to go and ask for alms because to become a mendicant is a degradation both to men and women, and it is the desire of your oppressors to degrade you and to have you appear as idle people and mendicants. No, workmen, you ought to protect what belongs to you—what you yourselves have produced, and, in the first place, you ought to take bread, to procure bread in order to quench your momentary needs. Workmen, you must demand what belongs to you. Go forth into the streets where the rich dwell, before the palaces of your dominators because these dominators which otherwise are courageous, when they see you stand there single, they tremble before you as soon as they see you united and through your loud and energetic demands now we can see by the times those harmless people will be compelled to provide work for you. Why should they not do it? Workingmen were the delight of the poet Schiller for it was labor who attacked tyranny when the oppressed one could nowhere find right and justice. When the burden becomes insupportable, then he lifts up his hand with confidence towards the sky, or heaven, and he takes down from above—he is as indestructible as the stars themselves.[20] The pains of hunger know no boundaries or of no limits. If your depradators are not to help you then you will know how to find other means to procure bread, because you can not for a long time suffer under the pangs of hunger. But again, you have satisfied your hunger. Even then, you remain slaves, workingmen, and as long as you remain slaves the times will never change, not for the momentary satisfaction of hunger, but we are driven to distraction by the cause of hunger and this cause resides in slavery and in the spoilation of the people. We ought to deliver ourselves from our tyrants and dominators, because man is happy only when he is free and such happiness would only go down through a struggle with a people dispossessed of their rights and their oppressors. By means of the social revolution there is a possibility of a distribution of private property of State and Church for the benefit and the peace of the whole of mankind, and you unemployed, unite under the folds of a great banner and liberty will be your watchword."

The only reason she had for going to that meeting was to tell the unemployed the real reason for their starvation. She had no intention of creating a riot. She did not hear any ejaculations or exclamations from the crowd, except cheering and applause.

In cross-examination the defendant testified that she did not believe in a Supreme Being; she was an atheist.[21] She was twenty-five years of age, and was born in Russia. She left Russia because her parents did, and for no other reason. She first came to New York

20. From Schiller's *Wilhelm Tell*, act 2, scene 2.
21. Compare the account in the *New York World* (7 October 1893, *EGP*, reel 47; see also *New York Times*, 7 October 1893, *EGP*, reel 47):

Q—You don't believe the Church exercises a moral influence? A—No.
Q—Not any church? A—Not any church whatever.
Q—Do you believe in the tenets and precepts of Judaism? A—I do not. I only am an atheist. I believe in atheism.

to live in 1888. The first house she lived in in New York was in East Broadway, where she had a furnished room. After that she went to live in 44th street, with several young ladies. She was married, but had been separated from her husband six or seven years. An anarchist, Berkman, also lived in the house in 44th street. She knew that Berkman was the man who shot Frick, in Pittsburgh.[22] She was an anarchist. She understood anarchism to be "the establishment of a system without government of any kind, and perfect liberty to every individual to enjoy their life and cultivate their abilities as well as the attainment of the highest knowledge." She did not believe in any laws whatever. She knew John Most, and believed that he was a good agitator and educator. She knew that Most was an anarchist.[23] She heard Timmermann speak on the night of the 21st of August, and she approved of all she heard him say. She knew that he had been tried and convicted, but she did not believe that justice had been done to him. She did not receive any money for the lectures which she delivered. She was a dress-maker, by trade, and she worked at that. Her income was from $5.00 to $7.00 per week. Previous to her arrest she lived at 266 East 16th street. Her father and mother were not anarchists; they believed in a Supreme Being. She had two brothers, and a sister. Her sister was a socialist. Her brothers and sister lived in Rochester, New York. She did not know of any existing government which agreed with her views. She had read the Constitution of the United States. In answer to a question as to whether or not she believed in the Constitution of the United States, she replied: "If it should be quoted as it is there, I would believe in it, more or less." She had also read the Constitution of the State of New York, which she believed in, but she did not believe that the people lived up to it. Although she did not know positively that she was to be called upon to speak on the night in question, she expected to be, and, therefore, she had prepared her speech. She always reduced her speeches to writing before delivering them. She had made four or five speeches during the financial disturbance, and had prepared a different speech for each occasion. Various branches of industry were represented at the meeting on the night of the 21st of August. She destroyed the manuscript of speeches which she did not give for publication. She had the manuscript of the speech which she delivered on the 19th.[24] She preserved the manuscript of that speech, because she thought it would be published in some of their papers. She

22. At this point, according to the *New York Times* (7 October 1893, *EGP*, reel 47),

> The witness denied that she had ever lived with Berkmann as his wife. She also denied that she went to Homestead or Pittsburg with him.
>
> Q.—You approved of Berkmann's attempt to kill Frick? A.—I never approved of it.
> Q.—Don't you approve of his action now? A.—I have sympathy for him, and I admire his courage in doing what he did, but that is all.

23. The *New York Times* (7 October 1893, *EGP*, reel 47) recounted the exchange as follows:

> Q.—Do you believe in Most and his teachings? A.—Most is an Anarchist and I am an Anarchist, but we do not agree in a great many particulars.

24. On 19 August EG attended a meeting of the unemployed at Golden Rule Hall, where she spoke and helped lead a march of about a thousand people from the hall to Union Square.

could not recite the speech from memory at the time of the trial. She did not say, at the meeting on the 21st: "You want bread, and who will give it to you? No one will give it to you. If you want it, you must take it. If you do not get it at your demand, take it by force." She said exactly what was contained in the speech which she had testified to delivering, and she did not say anything else. She did not say anything that would inflame the minds of the people there assembled. She did not conclude her remarks by saying, "May anarchy live!" When she said, in her German speech, on the night of the 21st, "A band of thieves, sustained by Church and State, have taken everything," she meant that the monopolists and capitalists robbed the poor of what belonged to them. She thought if the unemployed were to organize and unite and march through the streets, to let the city authorities and the rich see their misery, that they would be compelled, by seeing their misery, and the great number of the unemployed, to help them. If the unemployed saw fit to rise up and violate the law, she would not encourage them, but she would not keep them back, because she had no right to do so. She knew that anarchists looked upon her with respect, but the anarchists did not compose all the unemployed of New York. She did not know that the people in the lower walks of life looked up to her with respect. If she saw those people banded together, to commit an unlawful act, she would not stop them. She thought if the tyrants would not give the unemployed bread or employment, starvation would drive them into taking bread, wherever they could find it. She remembered the Haymarket riots in Chicago; she did not think the anarchists threw the bomb which killed the officers; she thought the police themselves threw the bomb. She approved of the agitation of the anarchists at that time in Chicago. By "the tyrants" she meant the representatives of government, the rich, the monopolists, the upholders of any state—Vanderbilt, Gould, &c. She did not believe in the police system of this country, although she believed that, "under the present system, policemen might be necessary." She thought there was a great prejudice against her, as an anarchist. The peroration of her speech was, "Unite under the folds of the red banner, and then there will be liberty or death, and let that be your watch-word." By that, she meant that the people of education should become anarchists, and demand their rights under the flag of anarchy. There was no liberty in this country. She did say, in her English speech, "I would first appeal to the American workingmen. If Jefferson and Paine, who fought for freedom, Wendell Phillips and John Brown were here to see your misery, they would be ashamed of their country.[25] You have Senators and Congressmen, who live in luxury, while you have nothing to eat. Their children live in grand style; their wives and mistresses wear silks and diamonds. You have thought that the liberty of America gives you freedom and liberty. Now you know how very much mistaken you have been. You are not free citizens. You are worse than black slaves. Americans, if you really want to be free citizens, take your rights into your own

---

25. EG often evoked Thomas Jefferson, Thomas Paine, Wendell Phillips, and John Brown to ground her ideas within a perceived American anti-statist tradition.

hands. Go and fight with your brothers, no matter if they are foreigners. You are starving, as well as they. Don't be prejudiced against these poor people who have come to this country. They are not responsible for the prevailing conditions. The capitalist class is responsible. The capitalist system is near its ruin." She did not say, in that speech, "If you do not get bread and freedom peaceably, take it by force." The report of the speech was substantially correct, with the exception that she did not tell the people to take it by force. She did not tell the people to go out into the social revolution; that was impossible. She did not know the witness Thimme personally. After reading the report which he wrote, and which was published in the *Staats-Zeitung* the next day, she said that it was substantially correct, except that it stated that she said, "If they do not give it to you peaceably, take it by force," and she had said nothing of the kind. One of the purposes for which she went to Philadelphia was to organize a group of anarchists for their newspaper, the *Solidarity*.[26] She delivered a speech in Philadelphia on the night of the 28th. She had read in the newspapers that a warrant had been issued for her arrest, and she intended to return to New York as soon as she had finished in Philadelphia. The party at whose house she stopped in Philadelphia, was an anarchist; she would not give his name. She believed in the use of dynamite, if the time should come for it. She did not expect to live long enough to see the time come for the use of bombs, and she couldn't tell whether she would use them or not.

In re-direct-examination the defendant testified that she was not divorced from her husband; they had only separated. She was on good terms with her parents. She believed that there is a moral law which "obligates us not to misuse the liberty of the next one, not to do any harm to the one, nor to hurt him, or, at least, not to do any harm whatever to the person and to try by all possible means to help the next one, and to help as much as possible for the benefit of the other." She did not believe in murder, or theft, nor that which the laws of this country or the laws of any country make criminal. The press misrepresented anarchists, by trying to represent them as murderers, thieves and robbers, and as if they were only desirous of taking all the money of the capitalists and putting it in their own pockets. She did not believe in that. She denied the words that Officer Jacobs put into her mouth, although she did not deny the ideas. She wished it to be understood that she did not tell the workingmen to do anything at present, or to do it later, but she simply said that their terrible condition of starvation would drive them to do this and that.

In re-cross-examination the defendant testified that she approved of the course that was taken by the Communists, in France, in 1871.[27] Her object in going to all these meet-

---

26. *Solidarity*, based in New York, was then in difficult financial straits and suspended publication in August 1893, its last issue appearing on 23 August. EG traveled to Philadelphia in part to raise money for the paper. *Solidarity* would be revived in 1895 and 1898.
27. A reference to the Paris Commune, 18 March to 28 May 1871.

ings and addressing the meetings was that it was simply the use of her right of free speech, as she understood it had been granted here to every man and woman, and she had no other object than to use her right of free speech, and she knew it was honorable to use the right of free speech, so she did, and she had not done anything unlawful against the Constitution of the United States. [. . .][28]

TD, New York City Municipal Archives. Excised from this document is the testimony of three more police detectives for the prosecution and two unemployed workers for the defense as well as David Barly of the *New York World* in a rebuttal for the prosecution.

28. Defense attorney A. Oakey Hall's address to the jury rounded out the proceedings on Friday, 6 October. Prosecutor McIntyre's summation was held over to the following Monday. For accounts of Hall's closing address, see *New York World*, 7 October 1893, *EGP*, reel 47; and *New York Times*, 7 October 1893, *EGP*, reel 47; for McIntyre's summation, see *New York World*, 10 October 1893, p. 1; and *New York Times*, 10 October 1893, p. 1.

The Law's Limit.

Emma Goldman Is Sentenced to a Year's Imprisonment.

Anarchists Are Warned.

Judge Martine Says They Should Be Kept Out of the Country.

No Speech from the Prisoner.

But The World Presents in Full the Remarks That She Had Intended to Deliver.

Swore She Would, But Relented.

Emma Goldman, the Anarchist, who was convicted of "unlawful assembly" in General Sessions last week, was yesterday sentenced by Judge Martine to one year's imprisonment in the penitentiary. In sentencing the woman, Judge Martine intimated that he was sorry the Penal Code prohibited him from giving her a heavier sentence. When he had concluded his remarks, the spectators applauded, some cheering, others stamping their feet. There was no demonstration by the woman's compatriots, as threatened.

Miss Goldman was brought to General Sessions in company with a dozen other female prisoners. She demurred to the crowds staring at her and asked permission to walk alone. Of course, this was denied, and when the women reached the old brown court house, a crowd of fully four hundred people were at their heels. Emma was pointed out by the crowd and heard some very unpleasant remarks about herself.

OAKEY HALL GIVES UP.

As soon as Judge Martine took his seat Clerk Hall called Emma to the bar. In answer to the Clerk's questions regarding her pedigree, the woman responded loudly. She said that she was twenty-five years old.

"Where do you live?" inquired the Clerk.

"Why, in the Tombs,"[1] replied Emma loudly.

---

1. The Tombs was the popular name for the municipal jail—constructed in 1838 and occupying the block bounded by Center, Lafayette, Franklin, and Leonard streets—so-called for the Egyptian theme of its architecture. EG repeated this response as her city address during her trial. See "Only the Moral Laws," *New York World*, 7 October 1893, *EGP*, reel 47.

"Before that, I mean," explained Mr. Hall.

"Oh! At No. 422 East Fortieth street."

In answer to the Clerk's question as to what she had to say why sentence should not be pronounced, Emma started to speak, when ex-Mayor A. Oakey Hall, who defended her on her trial, arose. He surprised everybody by informing Judge Martine that, owing to a misunderstanding with his client, he would withdraw from the case. He said that he had advised her not to make a speech in court, but she had declared that she would.

Emma, who was standing then at the bar, awaiting her sentence, nodded her head. She again started to say something, when Judge Martine warned her to confine her remarks to the case in hand. Her face flushed and she grasped the railing in front of her.

She spoke in a rasping voice, humble and meek.

NO SPEECH AFTER ALL.

"Your Honor," she said nervously, "in view of the fact that the police have done everything they could to incite my friends, the Anarchists, to some demonstration, so that they could put them in jail also, I shall refrain from delivering any speech here."

That is all she said. When she had concluded she looked at her ex-counsel and smiled. Mr. Hall was watching her intently. He colored slightly and motioned to her to sit down. She started to do so when Judge Martine began to talk, and a court officer yanked her around to face the bench.

Judge Martine lost no time in sentencing her. This is what he said:

"In this case the Court has given much consideration as to what would be a just disposition to make of this defendant after this conviction. You were represented in this case by one who is as able to present the facts as any lawyer now at the bar. His vast experience and his ability as counsel were called upon to their utmost extent in your behalf. The facts were submitted to the jury. There were witnesses deemed worthy of credence by the jury who stated that they heard the remarks which you made. There is no question but that those remarks brought you clearly within the statute. Your language was such as to incite disorder, to incite to riot, and the language as interpreted by those who heard it was such that a riot might have ensued."

ANARCHISTS SHOULD BE EXCLUDED.

"You are a woman beyond the average in intelligence. What your advantages have been in the way of education I do not know, except as they were exhibited here in court. You are certainly an intelligent person. In the light of reason you must have known the effect of language such as you uttered on that occasion. Now you have testified in your own behalf, and you told us you did not believe in our institutions; that you did not believe in our laws, and that you have no respect for them. Such a person cannot be tolerated in this community by those who believe in law, and I am happy to say that the greater number of our people do believe in law. I think it very improper that the great strength of this nation is not exercised to the extent that you and those who entertain the same ideas should be met at the portal of our country to the end that they should not be allowed to enter here.

"We are proud of our institutions, and much money and much blood have been spent to build them up, and we do not propose that any person, man or woman, shall undertake to tear them down. We do not propose to allow you to bid defiance to our institutions without showing you that the strong arm of the law will take hold of you and that the law cannot be defied. I look upon you as a dangerous woman in your doctrine. Fortunately, there are only a few, compared with the great number of our citizens, who believe in your doctrines, but it is necessary that those who believe the way you do should be taught that the law will be vindicated."

THE LAW'S FULL PENALTY.

"I have no hope of doing any good for you. I am satisfied that you are depraved, and have no respect for law. The sentence of the Court is that you be confined for the full term allowed by law, which is one year in the penitentiary."

Miss Goldman paid no attention to Judge Martine's words. All the time he was talking she was smiling at several of her friends who sat within the inclosure. When Judge Martine concluded, she was led away to the Tombs. Outside the court room she met Justus Schwab.[2] She whispered something in his ear. Schwab smiled. Turning to a police officer, Schwab inquired the woman's sentence. He was told. "You've done your best," he replied.

The speech which Miss Goldman intended to deliver in court and which she abandoned at the last moment, was prepared in advance. This is it:

THE RIGHT OF FREE SPEECH.

"I speak not to defend myself, but to defend my right of free speech, trampled upon by those who have caused the curtailing of my liberty.

"I know that the right of free speech was once guaranteed to every man and woman in this land.

"What do those who have brought me here understand by the right of free speech? Does it give a right to all to say what appears to the individual good or bad, or has it been granted to permit the expression of only that which to a certain class of the citizens appears right?

"Is free speech solely for the purpose and use of the Government and its officers, are individuals prohibited from saying that which is true, even though hardly to the taste of a certain class or portion of the public? Can I only say that in which I do not concur, and must I say it?

"I am positive that the men who shed their blood for the independence of this land,

2. Justus Schwab, German-born anarchist, ran a popular Lower East Side saloon and was a close friend and supporter of EG.

and who offered up their lives to secure the liberty and rights of the American people, must have had a very different understanding of the right of free speech than those who to-day represent the Government, and who so interpret the right as to permit the expression only of that which is conducive to their benefit.[3]

"According to such an interpretation of the right of free speech I must call them despots, and as such, without the right to commemorate in celebrations the memory of those who fell in the fight for Independence, for the former deliberately trample under foot the principles of those heroes, and when decorating their graves commit blasphemy.

"Why don't the representatives of the State drop the so-called mantle of free speech, discard the mask of falsehood and admit that absolutism reigns here?

"Under such a condition of things the American citizen has no shadow of right in pointing the finger of contempt at European institutions and in speaking of the downtrodden hungry of the Old World.

"The sorrowful condition of the workingmen of the Old as well as the New World increases from day to day, and it reached a high point in its horizon this very year.

"Devoid of all means of sustenance, the workingmen assemble to consult, to devise means to remedy their need. Those who throughout the year utilize the people and gather riches at their cost perhaps feel that it would not go well with them should the workingmen become half conscious of their exigencies, and in their terror the latter seek the aid of government. Innumerable policemen and spies are sent into the meetings of the unemployed, to control all their deliberations, to control the speakers."

DEFENDING HER SPEECHES.

"I belonged to that class of speakers who endeavored to show the workingmen the real reason of their misfortune.

"The speeches made by me must have contained much that was unpleasant for the rich of the City of New York, because they set in motion whole bands of spies to cause my apprehension and confinement, for the reason, as the indictment reads, that I had offended against the law and exhorted those present at my speeches to acts of violence.

"If what I said at Golden Rule Hall and at Union Square was a violation of the laws, then all those who were present at those meetings, and who by protracted and loud applause evinced their approval of what I said, were equally guilty with me. Why, then, did the city authorities proceed against me alone? Why? Because the authorities know that no danger lies in the workingman's ignorance of the true cause of his privations.

"From the moment that I, as an Anarchist, showed them that the workingman could never expect relief from his despoilers, from that moment I made the ruling masses uncomfortable, and had to be put out of the way.

3. For a discussion of allusions to the founders of the United States by EG and preceding anarchists, see note 6 to "Badly Advised," Article in the *New-Yorker Staats-Zeitung*, 22 August 1893, above.

"I do not acknowledge laws made to protect the rich and oppress the poor. Who are the law makers? Senators, the great of the land? Capitalists. Capitalists who torture thousands to slow death in their factories they are people who live in affluence, robbing the workingman of his strength to deprive him of the results of his labor; they are men whose fortunes have been built upon a foundation formed by pyramids of children's corpses.

"The wealth, the luxury, the pomp and glory of power are bought at the price of murdered and disfigured mankind.

"Ever rises the voice of the disinherited people, a voice growing in volume, and to which the overbearing classes will not listen, and to still which they devise new laws intended to silence the masses. Bands of priests are sent out to teach subjection, to propagate superstition and keep the people in ignorance.

"The demands of the workingmen are met with the Winchester rifle and the Gatling gun,[4] and I must confess that my brethren and myself will ever oppose such a state of 'order,' an 'order' in which we do not believe, and whose representatives we will never be compelled to meet in the struggle for advancement."

AIM OF THE ANARCHISTS.

"I can fully understand that such people hate the Anarchists, for it is our endeavor to abolish private property, State and Church. In one word, we aim to free men from tyrants and government.

"The striving for freedom is not the creature of my brain, nor that of any other being; it lies rooted in the people, and the contentions of the past, the struggles between the people and their oppressors, show but too plainly that the people are desirous of being freed from their burdens.

"The burning at the stake and the gallows have been the reward of numberless men of advanced thought, and even to-day thousands feel the icy blasts of Siberia and the torrid breath of New Caledonia,[5] while others yield up their lives in the cause, hidden by the grim walls of dungeons deep. And yet the desire for freedom grew, and grows.

"The world is gliding ever nearer the fact that in Anarchy can be found the happiness and content of man.

"You will not be able to stifle Anarchy by the erection of gallows and of jails.

"You endeavor to make us appear to the public eye veritable murderers, wholly de-

---

4. EG's complaint that the legitimate demands of the workingmen were "met with the Winchester rifle and the Gatling gun" is similar to the words of Albert Parsons in his autobiography, *Life of Albert Parsons* (Chicago: Lucy E. Parsons, 1889), wherein he states that the capitalist press advised the use of militia bayonets and Gatling guns to suppress strikers and put down discontented laborers struggling for better pay and shorter work hours (p. 16).
5. EG refers to Siberia, where Russian political prisoners were exiled, and New Caledonia, the French penal colony where many Paris Communards were exiled, including Louise Michel, who lived there from 1873 to 1880.

praved, but when we show the people our true objects they find that we only desire the benefit of mankind.

"We seek the establishment of Anarchy, or, in other words, a freedom from government of any kind; a community of interests based upon common production of equal and necessary character; we seek a perfect liberty for each individual to enjoy the grand and glorious products of nature; we seek for each an equal liberty to cultivate the talents and abilities as well the attainments of the highest knowledge.

"All wrongs now perpetrated, such as theft, murder, lying and prostitution, are an outcome of the injustice at present obtaining in the social state, and will disappear with its downfall.

"I tell you, the day of reckoning is not far—a time when no concessions will be granted to the tyrants and despots.

"Such is my belief, spread by me among the workingmen, and this belief will cease only with my life.

"You have convicted me, you may pass sentence of imprisonment upon me, but I tell you that I hate your laws; that I hate your 'order,' for I know but one 'order'—it is the highest potency of order—Anarchy." [6]

WATCHED BY DETECTIVES.

On the way to the Tombs Miss Goldman was surrounded by a crowd of Central Office detectives. Her grandmother, Mrs. Fredrika Goldman, who attended her during the trial, followed her to the gates of the Tombs, where she kissed her an affectionate good-by. An old, gray-whiskered man, who looked every inch an Anarchist, followed Emma to the prison. The detectives watched him closely.

"Perhaps he's got a bomb," was suggested.

"If he raises his hand, he'll drop," a Central Office man replied.

Emma Goldman will be taken to the penitentiary to-morrow along with a number of other women. In the Tombs, when asked what she thought of her sentence, she replied:

"I have nothing to say to you. What I have to say shall be through my own paper." [7]

When asked what she thought of the spectators' applause of Judge Martine's remarks, she replied: "They were applauding me, not him."

Mr. Hall, when asked why he withdrew from the case, tapped his forehead and pointed at Miss Goldman. "She is like all fanatics," he said, "a little bit gone."

New York World, 17 October 1893, p. 7.

6. A German transcription of this speech appeared in *Die Brandfackel* 1 (November 1893): 4–6; and, with minor variations, in *Freiheit,* 21 October 1893, p. 2. *Free Society* reprinted it twice in 1904 during EG's attempt to speak in Philadelphia, the second time "by request for propaganda purposes" (*Free Society,* 17 April 1904, pp. 5–6, and 1 May 1904, p. 6).

7. EG's comments were published the following month in *Die Brandfackel;* see "American Justice," Article in *Die Brandfackel,* November 1893, below.

Essay in *DIE BRANDFACKEL*

New York, November 1893

Amerikanische Justiz.

Durch die Verurtheilung der Genossin Emma Goldmann kann es zum erstenmale in der Geschichte der Ver. Staaten verzeichnet werden, daß man eine Frau wegen eines sog. politischen Vergehens verurtheilt hat. Die Ehre dieser Priorität gebührt dem Staate New York, und im engeren Sinne der Stadt gleichen Namens.

Wenn wir den culturellen Entwicklungsgang der verschiedenen Völker und die mit demselben verbundenen Läuterungen der Rechtsbegriffe ins Auge fassen, dann können wir wahrnehmen, daß die Menschheit im Allgemeinen humaneren Ansichten über Verbrechen und Strafen huldigt. Es werden heutzutage in den sog. civilisirten Ländern keine Hexenprozesse aufgeführt; es werden nicht mehr Menschen wegen ihrer religiösen Überzeugung gefoltert, gerädert, geviertheilt oder verbrannt; nicht fürhrt man mehr den armen Sünder zur Richtstätte, weil er sich am Eigenthume des Nächsten vergangen; vorbei sind die Zeiten, wo es dem "Herrn" gestattet war, nach Belieben über die Freiheit und das Leben seines Knechtes zu schalten, und sein Mägde dem jus primae noctis zu unterwerfen.

Der Geist der Rachsucht, das Streben nach Wiedervergeltung der dem Einzelnen oder der Gemeinschaft zugefügten Unbill, ist wohl auch heute noch aus den Strafgesetzen aller Culturländer wahrzunehmen; es kann aber nicht abgeläugnet werden, daß dieser Geist nicht mehr jene unmenschlichen und barbarischen Formen der Wiedervergeltung heischt, wie dies in vergangenen Zeiten der Fall war; die Ansichten der Menschen haben sich in diesem Punkte eben gemildert.

Versetzen wir uns in die Denkungsart des Durchschnittsmenschen der heutigen Gesellschaft, behaftet mit all seinen Vorurtheilen und falschen Conceptionen über Ehre und Rechtlichkeit, dann werden wir ihm beipflichten müssen, wenn er in Fällen unzweifelhaft bewiesener Verletzung von Gesetzen, die er als den Ausfluß der lauteren Rechtsanschauungen und zum Schutze seiner persönlichen Sicherheit als nothwendig betrachtet, seiner Befriedigung über die Bestrafung eines Gesetzübertreters Ausdruck verleiht. Diesem Durchschnittsmenschen war es eben infolge seiner, durch Erziehung, Vererbung und durch die Macht des Einflusses seiner Umgebung erworbenen Ansichten nicht möglich, sich zu jener Höhe der Ethik aufzuschwingen, von der aus dem Menschen die Berechtigung abgesprochen werden muß, über die Menschen zu Gericht zu sitzen.

Es kann dem Unaufgeklärten nicht einleuchten, daß nicht das Individuum, sondern die bestehende Gesellschaft mit ihren grausam widerrechtlichen Einrichtungen die

Schuld am Verbrechen und dem Verbrecherthume trägt; daß jeder Missethäter ein beredtes Zeugnis der Schuld der bestehenden Gesellschaft ist, und daß nicht er, sondern eben diese Gesellschaft bestraft werden sollte.

Zu dieser Ansicht vermochten sich bisher nur verhältnismäßig wenige Menschen emporarbeiten: Einige ideal angehauchte Rechts-Philosophen der neueren Schulen und die wenigen Psychologen einer gewissen Richtung, die aber alle zusammen diese Ansicht nur vom Standpunkte der abstrakten Theorie aus verfechten; dann die Vertreter der anarchistischen Weltanschauung. Dem vorerwähnten Durchschnittsmenschen war dies, wie gesagt, nicht möglich und aus diesem Grunde können wir es ihm auch gar nicht verdenken, wenn er dem Urtheile eines Richters seine Zustimmung gibt, der mit ihm auf der gleichen Höhe der ethischen Rechtsbegriffe steht und seiner Überzeugung nach ebenso ehrlich ist, wie er selbst.

Ehrlich?!——Wo in aller Welt findet man dies seltene Thier, einen ehrlichen Richter? Sind wir denn nicht vollständig davon überzeugt, daß die Justiz aller Länder des Erdballs nur eine Klassenjustiz ist, die immer nur zum Vortheil der Besitzenden und zum Nachtheil der Nichtbesitzenden ausgeübt wird? Wissen wir es denn nicht ganz genau, daß die Phrase: "Gleichheit aller vor dem Gesetze" der größte Hohn ist, den je die Menschheit über sich ergehen ließ? Ist es denn überhaupt nur möglich, einen ehrlichen Richter zu finden?

Dennoch muß ich zugeben, daß, soweit die sog. gemeinen Verbrechen in Betracht kommen, die Strafrechtspflege selbst des despotischesten Landes der alten Welt eine Muster-Institution im Vergleich zur Gerichtsbarkeit in Amerika ist. Selbst in Rußland, mit seinen asiatisch barbarischen Einrichtungen, sieht sich der Richter gezwungen— wenn es sich um oben qualifizirte Vergehen handelt—gewisse Formen zu beachten; selbst in diesem fluchbeladenen Lande hat der Richter nicht die absolute Macht, so nach Willkür zu handeln wie—im "freien" Amerika!

Die scheußlichste Creatur, die je die Menschheit entwürdigt, kann nur ein amerikanischer Richter sein; bar aller wie immer gearteten Rechtsbegriffe, in den meisten Fällen ganz unwissend, fähig zu den gemeinsten Schandthaten, zum Betrug, zur Erpressung, zum Meuchelmord—erkennt diese im Dienste der capitalistischen Klasse stehende Hyäne nur eine Macht über sich: Den Mammon. Wehe Dir, wenn Du als armer Mensch einem amerikanischen Richter in die Hände geräthst! Das größte Verbrechen in den Augen dieses Scheusals ist es, wenn der Angeklagte arm ist—er kann ja doch die von ihm feilgehaltene "Gerechtigkeit" nicht kaufen und er wird deshalb, bevor er noch den Mund aufthut, für schuldig befunden. Insoweit ist der amerikanische Richter dem der anderen Länder voraus; seinesgleichen kannst Du in den europäischen Staaten finden, wenn es sich um ein Vergehen politischer Natur handelt und ganz besonders wenn ein Anarchist vor Gericht steht.

Trotzdem kann man aber behaupten, daß in keinem Gerichtshofe der Welt, Anarchisten-Prozesse von der Art aufgeführt werden können, wie wir sie in den letzten Jahren hierzulande erlebt haben. Der Chicagoer Anarchisten-Prozeß vom Jahre 1886 steht ohne Beispiel in der Geschichte aller Zeiten und Völker. Wie ich im Eingang dieser Zeilen anführte, wurden wohl in früheren Zeiten Menschen ihrer religiösen und politischen Anschauungen halber verfolgt und hingerichtet; die Rechtsanschauungen jener Zeiten ließen dies als gerechtfertigt erscheinen; es war damals nicht nothwendig, daß man erst Mitmenschen tödten mußte, um sein eigenes Leben zu verwirken; und schließlich mußte doch irgend eine Schuld vorliegen, die ein Todesurtheil in Einklang mit der Anschuldigung brachte. Dies war der Fall, wie gesagt, in denen finsteren Zeiten der Barbarei, die, wie ich ebenfalls bemerkte, nun vorbei sind. Vorbei?. . . . .

Nein, sie sind noch nicht für immer entschwunden, diese Zeiten; an der Neige des neunzehnten Jahrhunderts sehen wir sie wiederkehren, in ihrer ganzen schrecklichen Gestalt. Wir sehen, wie Menschen ihrer Ideen wegen und nur dieser wegen hingerichtet oder ihrer Freiheit beraubt werden. Im Jahre 1886 klagt man in Chicago eine Schaar Menschen des Mordes an, kann ihr dieses Verbrechen nicht im Geringsten nachweisen, verurtheilt sie aber dennoch zum Tode, nicht weil sie Menschen getödtet, sondern, eingestandenermaßen, weil sie Anarchisten sind. Aus demselben Grunde beraubt man an einem anderen Orte Amerikas zwei Menschen für Jahre hinaus ihrer Freiheit, denen ebenfalls nicht das Geringste bewiesen werden konnte, dessen sie angeklagt waren. Und erst in den jüngsten Tagen konnten wir dasselbe Schauspiel hier in New York aufgeführt sehen. Claus Timmermann und Emma Goldmann werden angeklagt "an einer ungesetzlichen Versammlung theilgenommen zu haben"; bei den inscenirten Gerichtscomödien stellt sich aber heraus, daß die Versammlung, an der die Beiden theilgenommen, ganz und gar nicht ungesetzlich war; daß dieselbe einen friedlichen Verlauf nahm und daß die Theilnehmer auch friedlich und ruhig auseinander gingen. Nichtsdestoweniger werden die beiden Genannten, Ersterer zu sechs Monaten und Letztere zu einem Jahre Zuchthaus verurtheilt; nicht weil sie an einer "ungesetzlichen Versammlung" theilgenommen, nein—weil sie Anarchisten sind, "weil sie eine Gefahr für den Bestand unserer Institutionen bilden, deren Erhaltung uns jährlich so viele Millionen kostet".— Das ist amerikanische Justiz im "Zeitalter der Aufklärung und Civilisation"!

Wenn nun der Culturhistoriker einen derartigen Rückschritt, der noch die Rechtsanschauungen der vergangenen Tage als die richtigeren erkennen läßt, damit motiviren will, daß die Culturetappen der Menschheit abwechslungsweise ein Vor- und Rückwärtsschreiten in der Entwicklung anzeigen, dann täuscht er sich in der Natur der heutigen Etappe—sie bedeutet kein Rückschritt mehr, sondern sie biethet das unzweideutigste Symphom einer Zersetzung und Auflösung des Gesellschaftskörpers; das erste Aufbrechen der Pestbeulen; das tollwüthige Wehren der Vertreter der heutigen Ordnung gegen die Verbreitung von Ideen, die darauf hinauslaufen, diesen Zersetzungs-Prozeß zu beschleunigen und die menschliche Gesellschaft einer Einrichtung zuzuführen, die zu ihrer Stütze keine Gesetze und keine Schergen benöthigt.

E. G.

Essay in *DIE BRANDFACKEL*

New York, November 1893

American Justice.

With the sentencing of Comrade Emma Goldmann it can be recorded for the first time in the history of the United States that a woman has been sentenced because of a so-called political offense.[1] The honor of this precedent can be claimed by the state of New York, and strictly speaking the city of the same name.

If we take a look at the cultural evolution of various peoples and the refinements of the legal principles connected with it, we can assert that people in general adhere to a humane point of view with respect to crimes and punishments. There are no witch trials being carried out in so-called civilized countries these days; people are no longer tortured, broken on the wheel, drawn and quartered, or burned because of their religious convictions; no longer is the poor sinner led to the place of execution because he committed an offense upon the property of his neighbor; gone are the times where the "lord" was allowed to command as he pleased over the freedom and life of his servants and subject the women among them to the *jus primae noctis*.[2]

The spirit of vengeance, the pursuit of retaliation for an injustice inflicted upon an individual or the community, is indeed still noticeable today in the criminal laws of all civilized countries. But it cannot be denied that this spirit no longer demands those inhuman and barbaric forms of retaliation as was the case in past times; the views of human beings have indeed softened in this area.

If we put ourselves in the position of the everyday man in today's society, afflicted with all his prejudices and false conceptions about honor and justice, then we must agree with him if he expresses satisfaction over the punishment of a lawbreaker in cases of a clear violation of laws that he regards as founded on established legal principles and as necessary for the protection of his personal security. Indeed, it was impossible for this every-

---

1. This statement is difficult to verify. Unlike Russia or Germany, for example, countries that had statutes criminalizing political affiliation or opposition, the idea of a "political" crime or prisoner in the United States up to and including this period is ambiguous at best. Even EG, in 1897, admitted that the United States did not recognize "such a specified class" as political criminal (see Letter to Augustin Hamon, 13 April 1897). By the same criterion used by *Die Brandfackel* in EG's case, Susan B. Anthony, who was arrested in 1872 for voting in New York, and Lillian Harman, arrested in 1886 for illicit cohabitation, could both be considered "political" prisoners because like EG, though they opposed current socio-political conventions, they were arrested under criminal and civil statutes.

2. "Jus primae noctis" or right of the first night, was in the European late medieval period a belief in the privilege of the lord to share the bed of his peasant women prior to their wedding night. However, historians debate how common this practice was.

Advertisement placed in the December 1893 issue of *Die Brandfackel* for a benefit concert to raise legal expense funds for the imprisoned Emma Goldman. (Labadie Collection, University of Michigan)

day man, owing to upbringing, heredity, and the powerful influence of his surroundings, to raise himself to that ethical height from which one must challenge man's right to sit in judgment over other men.

The unenlightened cannot be made to understand that it is not the individual, but rather the present society, with its cruel, unjust institutions, that bears the blame for crime and criminality; that every wrongdoer is eloquent testimony to the guilt of the present society, and that it is not the wrongdoer, but rather this society that should be punished.

Until now relatively few people have been able to arrive at this view: a few idealistic legal philosophers of the newer schools and the few psychologists of a particular slant who, however, all defended this view only from the standpoint of abstract theory; and then there are the representatives of the Anarchist worldview. For the above-mentioned everyday man this was, as I said, impossible, and for this reason we can hardly blame him if he gives his approval to the decision of a judge who is on the same level he is with respect to ethical notions of justice and who he is convinced is as honorable as he is.

Honorable?!——Where in the world does one find this strange animal, an honorable judge? Haven't we been completely convinced that justice in all countries of the globe is merely class justice, which is always carried out only to the advantage of the haves and to the disadvantage of the have-nots? Don't we know very well that the phrase "Equality of all before the law" is the greatest scorn that humanity has ever put up with? Is it therefore at all *possible* to find an honorable judge?

Nevertheless I must admit that as far as so-called common crimes are concerned, the practice of criminal law in the most despotic countries of the old world is a model institution compared to jurisprudence in America. Even in Russia, with its Asiatic, barbaric institutions, the judges are forced, when it comes to the above mentioned process, to observe certain forms; even in this curse-laden country the judge does not have the absolute power to act as arbitrarily as in "free" America!

The most atrocious creature ever to degrade humanity can only be an American judge; lacking in all legal understanding of any kind, completely ignorant in most cases, capable of the most cruelly shameful deeds, fraud, blackmail and assassination—this hyena, standing in the service of the capitalist class, recognizes only one power above himself: Mammon. Woe be to you if as a poor person you fall into the hands of an American judge! In the eyes of this monster the greatest crime is if the accused is poor—he cannot buy the "justice" put up for sale by the judge and will therefore, before he even opens his mouth, be found guilty. In this sense the American judge is ahead of judges in the other countries; you can find the likes of him in European states when it comes to an offense of a political nature, and especially if an Anarchist stands before the court.

However it can be said that in no court in the world can Anarchist trials be carried out as we have experienced them in this country in the last few years. The Chicago Anarchist trial of 1886 stands without precedent in the history of all epochs and peoples. As I stated in my opening lines, people in earlier times were tortured and executed owing to their religious and political views. The legal views of those times allowed this to appear justified. It was not necessary back then to have murdered fellow human beings in order to forfeit one's own life; and yet indeed some kind of guilt had to be present that would bring a judgment of death in accord with the accusation. This was the case, as I have said, in the darkest times of barbarism, which, as I have also pointed out, are now over. Over? . . .

No, they have not yet disappeared forever, those times; as the nineteenth century draws to a close we see their return in their entire, terrible form. We look on as people are executed or robbed of their freedom because of their ideals and only their ideals. In 1886 a group of people in Chicago were accused of murder; these crimes could not be substantiated in the slightest, yet nevertheless these people were sentenced to death not because they had committed murder but rather, admittedly, *because they were Anarchists.* For the same reason two people in another part of America are being robbed of their freedom for years, once again without any proof of that of which they had been accused.[3] And most recently we can observe the same spectacle being carried out here in New York. Claus Timmermann and Emma Goldmann are accused of "participating in an unlawful assembly"; at this staged judicial farce it became apparent, however, that the assembly in which both took part was not at all unlawful, that it proceeded peacefully and that the participants also departed peacefully and calmly. Nevertheless the aforementioned persons were found guilty and sentenced, the former to six months and the latter to a year in jail,

3. EG refers to Carl Nold and Henry Bauer, who began serving five-year sentences in the Western Penitentiary in February 1893 for incitement to riot and conspiracy in the attempted assassination of Henry C. Frick.

not because they took part in an "unlawful assembly," no—*because they are Anarchists,* "because they represent a danger to the existence of our institutions, whose maintenance costs us so many millions yearly."[4] The is American justice in the "era of enlightenment and civilization"!

If the cultural historian now wishes to offer as justification for this backward step, in which the legal views of bygone days are recognized as the more correct ones, that the cultural stages of humanity indicate varying forward and backward steps in its development, then he is deceiving himself about the nature of the current stage—it no longer indicates a backward step, but rather it represents the most irrefutable symptom of an undermining and dissolving of the social structure; the first bursting of plague-infested boils, the rabid resistance of the representatives of today's order to the dissemination of ideas that lead to an acceleration of the undermining process and bring a structure to human society that does not need to rely upon laws and lackeys for its support.

E. G.

Die Brandfackel 1 (November 1893): 1–3. Translated from German.

4. EG is paraphrasing Judge Martine's statements at her sentencing. See "The Law's Limit," Article in *New York World,* 17 October 1893, above.

LIEBER FREUND TIMMERMANN!

Zu meinem größten Bedauern vernehme ich von dem Unfalle der Ihnen begegnet—was Sie doch für ein Pechvogel sind! Kommt der Mensch vom Regen in die Traufe!—Ich war so froh als ich die letzten zwei Nummern der "Brandfackel" las, zu sehen, daß die regelmäßige Herausgabe des Blattes nun gesichert sei und daß auch der Inhalt desselben ein guter ist—hoffentlich werden Ihre Freunde Sie auch diesmal nicht im Stiche lassen und für das Erscheinen Ihres Blattes einstweilen Sorge tragen.

Dieser Tage habe ich wieder nach langer Zeit einige Nummern des von den "Vereinigten autonomen Gruppen Amerika's" (welch bombastischer, frech-verlogener Tam-Tam!) herausgegebenen Blattes zu Gesicht bekommen. Ich staune nur, wie dies Unternehmen denn noch vegetiren kann—na, die Zähigkeit und Härtnäckigkeit der Maulthiere kann man den jetzigen Herausgebern, deren Zahl, wie mir schon vor längerem berichtet wurde auf drei Nullen, Pardon, drei Stück gesunken, nicht absprechen; es ist ja aber auch so schwer, ein liebgewordenes Steckenpferd aufgeben zu sollen! Diese Ärmsten der Armen im Geiste begehen außer vielen anderen Irrthümern noch den, sich in ihren verrückten Bocksprüngen für "feurige" Pferde zu halten, eine Prätention, über die selbst ein Pferd lachen müßte; denn dieses Thier ist klug genug um herauszufinden, daß die intelektuellen Fähigkeiten der jetzigen Herausgeber der betreffenden Publikation höchstens gleich denen einer Schildkröte anzunehmen wären.—Was da aber auch für Geisteskoth in diesem Organ abgelagert wird! Leute, die als "Mistbauern" wohl in der Führung von Mistgabeln bewandert sein mögen, denen aber so jede Spur irgend eines positiven Wissens abgeht; denen die Wiedergabe der menschlichen Sprache durch die Schrift ein ewiges, ihnen tückisch scheinendes Mysterium bleiben wird; die in ihrer Verschrobenheit, Unduldsamkeit und niedrig-gemeinen Verläumdungssucht es dorthin gebracht haben wo sie nun stecken—im Unrath nählich, in welchem sie doch in kurzer Zeit ersticken werden; diese Leute wollen nun wie es scheint um jeden Preis ein von fähigen Elementen gegründetes und von solchen ehemals unterstütztes literarisches Unternehmen aufrechthalten.—Auf eine spezielle Critik der im betreffenden Blatte in letzter Zeit gebotenen Leistungen will ich gar nicht eingehen—mit solchem "Mist" sich länger zu befassen, wäre denn doch höchst überflüssig. Nur das Eine will ich noch bemerken: Solche Emanationen des unzweifelhaftesten Blödsinns können doch als nichts anderes als ein Attentat auf den menschlichen Verstand erachtet werden und geeignet erscheinen, den minder gebildeten aber wißbegierigen Leser zu verdummen; außerdem kann es nur als die reinste Beutelschneiderei bezeichnet werden, wenn man dem armen Arbeiter seine mühsam errungenen Cents für solch literarische Kost entlockt.—

Was die direkten Ihre Person anlangenden Angriffe dieses sauberen Trifoliums betrifft, rathe ich Ihnen, lieber Freund, dieselben ganz einfach zu ignoriren—"Wer da antwortet auf jedes Gespei, macht aus einem Übel zwei", sagt ein gutes deutsches Sprüchwort.

Ich befinde mich jetzt ziehmlich wohl, obschon die Umstände bisher darnach angethan waren mich zu biegen und zu brechen—aber es ist den verschiedenen Vertretern der "Ordnung" noch nicht gelungen und es wird ihnen auch nicht mehr gelingen mich zu "bekehren"; sie werden nur das erreicht haben, daß sich mein Haß gegen jegliche Tyranei und Unterdrückung noch vergrößert hat. Wie Ihnen bekannt ist, habe ich wenig Verkehr mit der Außenwelt; dennoch in der letzten Zeit von den muthigen Thaten unserer Genossen in Europa gehört. Wahrlich, solange es noch solche Männer giebt, die nicht von Solidaritätsdusel und "Moral" faseln sondern handeln, solange braucht man auch hinter Kerkermauern nicht verzagen! Nur noch 3 Monate etwa und ich werde wieder in der Lage sein, mit neuer und gesteigerter Kraft und Energie für die geliebte Freiheit zu kämpfen.

EMMA GOLDMANN.

Dear Friend Timmermann!

It is with the deepest regret that I learned of your accident[1]—what an unlucky fellow you are! It goes from bad to worse!—I was so happy when I read the two most recent issues of *Brandfackel* to see that the regular publication of the paper is now assured and also that its content is good—hopefully your friends will not abandon you this time and will take responsibility for the appearance of your paper for the time being.

Recently after a long time I once again saw several issues of the paper published by the "United Autonomy Group of America"[2] (what bombastic, brazenly dishonest drum-beating!). It surprises me that this undertaking can still vegetate—indeed the tenacity and stubbornness of mules must be attributed to the current editors, whose number, as I was informed long ago, has sunk to three nobodies, pardon, three people; yet it is indeed so difficult to have to give up a hobby one has grown fond of! Among the many other mistakes committed by these poorest of the poor in spirit, the old goats believe themselves in their crazy cavorting to be "fiery" horses, a pretension about which even a horse would have to laugh; for this animal is wise enough to discover that the intellectual abilities of the current editors of the publication in question would at most be assumed to be equal to those of a tortoise.—And what kind of spiritual dirt is deposited in this organ! People who as "dung farmers" may be well versed in the operation of pitchforks, but lack any trace of positive knowledge; for whom the rendering of human language in writing will remain an eternal, seemingly menacing mystery; who in their perverted-ness, impatience, and base and vulgar craving for slander have reached the point where they now find themselves—namely in dirt, in which they will soon suffocate; these people want to maintain at any price a literary undertaking founded and at one time supported by capable elements.—I will refrain completely from launching into a particular critique of the output offered lately in the paper in question—to deal with such "dung" any longer would indeed be utterly pointless. I will say only one more thing: such ema-nations of the most unquestionable nonsense can be considered nothing but an attack upon the human mind and seems designed to dull the mind of the reader who is poorly educated yet eager to learn; otherwise it can be labeled nothing but the purest racketeer-

1. Timmermann explains in an editorial note that he had broken his right arm and hence had to pre-pare the June 1894 issue of *Die Brandfackel* using only his left hand, which accounts for the issue be-ing shorter than usual (only eight pages).
2. *Der Anarchist* was published by the Autonomen Gruppen Amerikas (American Autonomy Group), whose members included Carl Masur, Otto Rinke, Joseph Peukert, and Joseph "Sepp" Oerter.

ing to worm out of the poor worker his painstakingly earned cents for such literary nourishment.—

As far as the attacks aimed directly for you by this fine trio are concerned, I advise you, dear friend, quite simply to ignore them.—"Wer da antwortet auf jedes Gespei, macht aus einem Übel zwei," says a good German proverb.[3]

I am quite well at the moment, although the circumstances until now were suitable to bend and break me—however the various representatives of "order" have not yet succeeded and they no longer stand a chance of "converting" me; all that they will have brought about is a deepening of my hatred for any kind of tyranny and oppression. As you know, I have little contact with the outside world; nevertheless I have heard recently of the brave deeds of our comrades in Europe.[4] Indeed, as long as there are still such men who act rather than blather about heady solidarity and "morale," one need not despair even behind prison walls! Only about 3 months more and I will once again be in the position to fight with renewed strength and energy for our beloved freedom.

EMMA GOLDMANN.

Die Brandfackel 2 (June 1894): 7–8. Translated from German.

3. The phrase means "He who answers every insult, makes out of one evil two."
4. EG refers to the rash of bombings in Paris in late 1893 and early 1894, and most recently Émile Henry's bombing of a Parisian café (Café Terminus) on 12 February 1894.

Article in the _NEW YORK WORLD_

New York, 18 August 1894

My Year in Stripes.

Emma Goldman, Anarchist, Describes Her Imprisonment on Blackwell's Island.

She Cannot Forget Its Horrors.

Her Life in the Women's Prison and the Sufferings
of the Miserable Ones Who Shared It.

Even More in Earnest Now, She Says.

Free Again, She Modestly Declares She Will Not Rest Until
Government Is Overturned and Anarchy Is on Top.

Emma Goldman, the Anarchist, was released from the penitentiary on Blackwell's Island yesterday. She was imprisoned there for delivering an incendiary speech a year ago. Miss Goldman wrote a letter relating her experiences and observations in prison, and the idea seized her that the letter had a certain commercial value. The _World_ bought it,[1] just as the _World_ would buy an unpublished poem by Tennyson or the description of a prize fight by John L. Sullivan. Besides being interesting to the few who agree with Miss Goldman's views touching society and government, this letter will appeal to the great body of the American people who like to hear both sides of a question.

Here it is:

To the Editor of the _World:_

The right of free speech and assembly has long been a dead letter, a farce.

Peaceful laborers are not safe from a policeman's club. Honest men are persecuted, imprisoned and legally murdered for giving utterance to their feelings. The crimes and outrages of the police committed during the past year prove only too well that despotism and tyranny have supplanted the freedom once guaranteed to every man and woman of America.

---

1. The _World_ paid EG $150 for the article, which she noted in her autobiography paid for the furnishing of the apartment she lived in with Ed Brady (_LML_, pp. 155–56).

My prosecution was conducted with such injustice, however, that many thinking men and women all over the country have not only noticed it but have assured me of their sympathy for the "terrible Emma Goldman."

Why was this prosecution conducted with so much venom and spite? Surely not because the accused was a woman!

I, this terrible Anarchist, was arrested, not for what I said, but on a trumped-up charge made by a few legalized blackmailers, detectives and spies—men who have sold their honor and their manhood for a petty mess of pottage.

The whole trial was conducted with the greatest unfairness. They proved neither my guilt nor my innocence.

SCARED BY THE GHOST OF ANARCHY.

I was convicted, not because of the lecture delivered on Aug. 21, but because it was an Anarchist that stood before them. It was not Emma Goldman that was tried in the Court of General Sessions, but the ideas she expressed. It was the red ghost of Anarchy that made the courageous "protectors of law and order" tremble—it was the fear of the future, their guilty conscience which told them that it was not wise to have Emma Goldman among the people. It was uncomfortable to have men and women who were able and willing to open the eyes of the oppressed and show them a way to a better condition. It is safer for corrupt people that such men and women should be out of the way even if perjury must be resorted to in order to accomplish it. What does it matter if Emma Goldman was brutally attacked by six ruffians—dragged through the streets, submitted to indignities that would make the most hardened criminal quail.

What does it matter how it is done, so she is disposed of?

JUSTICE SHE DID NOT EXPECT; MERCY SHE SCORNED.

What does it matter how many lies these Judases may tell, so the purpose is accomplished and the authorities are thereby enabled to rid themselves of one whose presence is disagreeable. I knew before the trial what the result would be, but engaged counsel not because I desired to sue for either justice or mercy. The former I did not expect, the latter I scorned.

Voltairine de Cleyre in 1891, prominent American anarchist and among the few women of stature in the anarchist movement; she visited Goldman in prison in 1893. (Labadie Collection, University of Michigan)

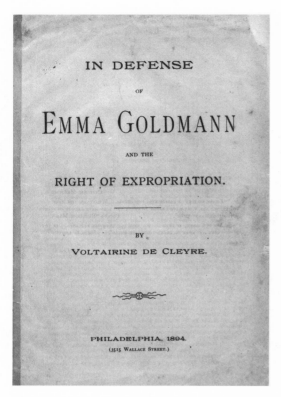

Cover page of Voltairine de Cleyre's 1894 pamphlet *In Defense of Emma Goldmann,* published in support of the ideas expressed in Goldman's 21 August 1893 speech at the New York City demonstration that led to her arrest and imprisonment. (Labadie Collection, University of Michigan)

It was to propagate my principles and prevent my enemies from hustling me off to prison without a hearing or a trial, as they did in the case of my comrade, Claus Timmermann.[2]

Well, Emma Goldman was disposed of. Not so her cause, you "noble knights," who tremble at the voice of Truth. You can imprison an Anarchist and legally slaughter our comrades, but you cannot kill Anarchy. It defies you, and will live on when judges, district attorneys, detectives, spies, tyrants and monsters of every description will be buried under the last fragment of private property, Church and State.

FROM THE TOMBS TO THE PENITENTIARY.

Two days after my trial I was sent to my new "residence," in which I was to spend the following ten months. After being confined for two weeks in the Tombs, this was a change, and any change was welcome. I enjoyed the trip immensely. When I reached the dock I saw several representatives of the press who had become my faithful knights and who stuck manfully by me all through my trouble. They seemed to think it their duty to stand by me to the last. I had never cared much for reporters, but I was very grateful for their company.

Blackwell's Island is beautifully situated, surrounded by water. Its grounds are lovely. It seems more like a place of enjoyment than of suffering, but one look at the gray, gloomy building is sufficient to chill the new prisoner.

"Beggars are not choosers" is the old proverb, and although I neither begged nor chose this place for my temporary "home," I was very much interested in it, and made a thorough examination of the outside of the palace.

DRIVEN THERE BY THEIR SURROUNDINGS.

American prisons compare favorably with foreign ones in cleanliness and order. On the whole, however, they are just as corrupt, just as miserable. And the food and cells are worse.

2. Claus Timmermann was convicted shortly after EG on the charge of incitement to riot for his part in the 21 August 1892 Union Square rally.

Most of the unfortunates in the penitentiary are victims of the pernicious conditions of society. They are driven either by need or circumstances to commit the offenses that place them there. Most of these offenses are of less importance than those committed daily and hourly by the rich and influential.

During my ten months' imprisonment I met no convicts that were at all well to do. All were poor, miserable, broken-down remnants of humanity. Reared in the streets of New York, surrounded from earliest infancy by the vilest associations, none of them is educated. All are aged long before their time by privations and poverty.

WHY SHE WRITES THIS.

Personally I cannot complain of my own treatment. From the time I entered I received much better treatment than the others. I was never punished. I had lighter work and was always treated with a certain amount of respect. It is not, therefore, any special spite I wish to vent that prompts me to place my experience before the public, but an earnest desire to call the attention of thinking people to the miserable conditions of the inmates there.

When I reached prison I was brought before the head matron, who has entire charge of the female portion of this institution. This lady is the sister-in-law of the warden, and, of course, has a "pull." The warden is an old, feeble man, and seems to be under the influence of four women—his wife, his sister-in-law and daughter and a cousin. They are the real managers, the poor old gentleman being only a puppet in their hands. He has, however, a certain amount of firmness, and if he knew how his sister-in-law abuses the position she holds she would not hold it a week.

"ALLOWED TO TAKE A BATH."

The matron is about fifty years of age, tall and very stout, with a cruel, hard face and a sensual mouth. She makes a chilling impression on the newcomer. To me she was more than usually kind. She gave me a more civil reception than prisoners usually get, and assisted me to undress myself. Then she gave me a blue and white striped dress and blue checked apron, the usual prison costume.

After my name, occupation and address were taken, I was allowed to take a bath, which was greatly refreshing after two weeks of the Tombs.

Prisoners are given a bath each week and furnished with a change of clothing.

"THE HOTEL," AS SHE CALLS IT.

The female wing consists of a large mess hall, with sixty-seven cells, a large room for the chapel and a ward for the sick. The cells are short and narrow, dark and damp. A piece of canvas stretched across two irons represents the bed, two blankets, a straw pillow and a pail completed the outfit.

It was near 5 o'clock when I retired to my "chamber." I sat down and commenced to think, "How shall I ever stand it in this hole?"

I fell asleep while meditating upon the subject, but suddenly I jumped to my feet, startled by a loud gong. One of the prisoners told me it was supper-time.

Supper consisted of a pan of a greasy black liquid called "coffee," which is a decoction made by pouring boiling water over burnt bread.

The "ladies" of the "hotel" seemed very hungry; they ate their portions in silence.

"Women are reforming," I thought, "for those seemed to have learned the lesson of keeping silent." Afterwards I found out that their silence was not due to improvement, but to the rules, which forbid talking at meals. This was one of the hardest rules for new female boarders to obey.

Supper did not last longer than five minutes. Then they all went back to their cells. Then a loud voice said "Close!" and all the doors slammed together. The cells were locked, and one day of misery had passed.

THE ROUTINE OF A DAY.

At 6 o'clock in the morning I was awakened again by the clang of a bell, at which signal the cells were unlocked and the "ladies" went down to make their toilets. The "ladies" are not very fastidious, for only five minutes are allowed for this purpose and they never are late.

After that they are driven like cattle to their cells again. Then the bell rings for breakfast and all the inmates march down to the mess-hall. This meal is a repetition of that on the night before; "coffee" and bread, then back they go to their cells, where they remain until 7.15 o'clock.

The air in those cells is choking and nauseating. The women remain in them until a bell calls them down for a walk. With their pails in their hands they all walk to the river, a short distance from the prison. The "line" or "gang" is led by two matrons.

There are usually about seventy women in this institution. About twenty-five women work in the laundry, which is considered the hardest work. Five serve at the warden's house. Two serve the deputy warden. The others, who are not in the sewing department, do chamberwork for the keepers.

MADE FOREWOMAN OF THE SEWERS.

I was made forewoman in the sewing-room. I had to give out the work, do all the folding and packing and keep the accounts of work sent in and out during the week. Here the women mend shirts, socks and pants for the male prisoners. The sewing women have to work very hard. Mine was not only a very disagreeable, but also a hard job. I had to be on my feet all day.

From 7.30 to 11.30 A.M. all is quiet. Then the washwomen come in and take their seats for dinner. The "menu" for the four days of the week is vegetable soup, with precious little meat in it. On two days there are corned beef and beans. On Friday there is a treat—fish and potatoes. A half hour is allowed for dinner and a half hour for rest. Then all start at work again until 5.30 P.M. On Saturdays the work is stopped at noon and the prisoners remain in their cells.

On Sundays those who are religiously inclined are allowed to leave their cells and attend church services.

IN THE HOSPITAL.

I remained on the floor two months, when I had an attack of rheumatism. But not until I could no longer work was I transferred to the hospital.

Until that time, although my work had been arduous, I had not seen the real horrors of prison life. But what I witnessed in that hospital made my blood run cold and filled me with indignation and horror.

The hospital is large and airy. There are sixteen beds, and it is kept exceedingly neat and clean—considering patients do all the scrubbing and cleaning. There are three doctors—house, senior and junior.

A doctor from the city visits the wards three or four times a week. The others visit them twice a day.

After a month's illness I was made orderly in the ward, after which time I had full charge of all the medicines and patients. I had to wait on the doctors who take care of the sick and attend all operations. Although one matron is on day duty and one at night, all the work was left to me, and for seven long months I worked night and day.

The day matron is old and too infirm to take proper care of the sick. She has also to attend to other duties. While her will is good, she is unable to do the work. The night matron, who is on duty four nights in the week, is a noble, generous woman, kind and good-hearted. She makes every effort to make the burden of those poor, sick women lighter.

CHARGES AGAINST THE HEAD MATRON.

The greatest pleasure of the head matron is to torment and plague both her assistant and the prisoners. Nothing satisfies her, nothing pleases her. Her harsh voice is heard from one end of the place to another, and she keeps it in an uproar from morning until night.

She encourages prisoners to gossip about each other and about the under matrons. She often requires prisoners to spy upon the under matrons and report to her—a duty I flatly refused to do.

She has, however, one unaccountable mania. She is very fond of colored people. While I see no difference in races, I think all should be regarded as human beings. The most depraved, ignorant, repulsive black woman is sure of a warm reception from this head matron and is placed above the most intelligent white woman. No matter what they do, she will never punish them, but will deprive white women of their food and other comforts for them. They abuse, insult and even beat their white sisters in misery.[3]

Some of this head matron's modes of punishment are as ridiculous as others are cruel. Fancy a full-grown woman standing all day facing a black-board! Prisoners receiv-

---

3. In her autobiography, EG wrote that New York City journalist and labor activist John Swinton construed these remarks to mean that EG shared "the white man's prejudice against the coloured race," an interpretation EG contested (*LML*, p. 154).

ing this punishment are also deprived of their dinner. If all these things fail then comes the dungeon, with its cold, dark dreariness—a most cruel and brutal punishment.

Many of the prisoners are kept in the dungeon for weeks.

SOME HORRORS OF THE PLACE.

My imprisonment is over now and I do not regret it. It has been a school of experience for me and my time was not altogether lost. For it was my privilege to make the lives of some of the poor, helpless ones more endurable.

I was often shocked by the cruelties of the place, and I remember one woman who was not allowed to see a doctor, though her temperature was 103.

Another woman begged to be taken out of the stifling cell. She was choking—the kind matron said she was only "faking." A few days after I was sent for and hurried down with restoratives. But I saw as soon as I reached her that she was no longer in the power of prison authorities. The doctors said she died of heart trouble.

Another woman seventy years of age came there sick, yet the brutal head matron put her to scrubbing. She was sick several days before the female Brockway[4] would admit that she was sick. When the doctor ordered her to be placed in the hospital the head matron still declared she was "faking," and continued to abuse her until for some reason she suddenly became all sympathy and attention. Poor old woman! The sympathy came too late, for she died just a day or so before she would have been free, legally murdered.

WHAT SHE SAW WILL HAUNT HER.

Again I say that I received no bad treatment. But that could not blind me to the sufferings of the poor inmates there. My friends were unremitting in their attention and gave me the tenderest care, and the head matron knew that if any harm had befallen me, even though the law did nothing, she would have had to account to my friends.

I can never forget the faces of the dead, pinched and distorted by suffering. I can never forget the haggard, worn look of the living. Those sights will haunt me to my dying day.

I do not know why, but our female monster seemed anxious to propitiate me, and used to send me meals from her own table, which I never tasted—and talked very confidentially to me. But I am not to be so taken in.

MORE OF AN ANARCHIST THAN EVER.

Yes, I am more of an Anarchist than ever.

I am more than ever determined to use every means in my power to spread my doctrines among the people.

4. EG compares the matron to Z. R. Brockway (1827–1920), superintendent of the Elmira Reformatory in New York. He was investigated (and acquitted) for cruelty to prisoners three times, in 1865, 1893, and 1894. In his retirement, he published his memoirs, *Fifty Years of Prison Service* (New York: Charities Publishing Commission, 1912), in which he defended and maintained his innocence against the charges leveled against his prison administration.

I defy prison and prosecution.

I could never content myself, now that I have seen the injustice of the law.

However pleasantly I might be situated, I could not banish from my mind the thousands who are oppressed and suffer from the injustice of the present system.

Society lies in its last convulsions. The people are awakening to their condition. Let them once fully realize it and the present system will go.

Men cannot be happy as long as they are slaves.

They cannot expect theft, murder, prostitution and oppression to be gotten rid of until the system which breeds rottenness is gone.

Mending of any kind won't do.

The earth must be swept of these parasites—human vampires, despots of crime.

As the last fragments of this system disappear, Anarchy will lift her proud head and spread out her blessings to all humanity.

For this I shall continue to work.

The true and loving mother of humanity, my motto is as ever, "Death to tyranny!"

Vive l'Anarchie!

EMMA GOLDMAN[5]

Before Warden Pilsbury, of the penitentiary, went away on his vacation, he left orders that no reporters should be admitted to Miss Goldman. Ordinarily, the prisoners released from the penitentiary leave Blackwell's Island on the 8 A.M. boat, which lands them at the foot of East Fifty-second street. But Miss Goldman, with the purpose of avoiding the newspaper men, who she knew would be waiting for her, was permitted to take the 6.30 A.M. boat, which carries back the officers who have been on night duty in the prison.

Arrived at East Fifty-second street, Miss Goldman was met by Edward Brady,[6] a German Anarchist, who was a witness for her at her trial. A few reporters were waiting for her, but she positively refused to speak to them. With Brady, she boarded a First avenue car and rode uptown a few blocks. Then alighting, they took an elevated railroad train downtown. She breakfasted at Dennett's, on Park Row.[7] Then she went home and yesterday afternoon and last night she visited her friends and received their congratulations on her release. The group of Anarchists in this city made no organized demonstration of joy at her return.

Miss Goldman was vivacious; her cheeks were red and her eyes were bright. She wore a new straw hat with gay flowers on it, a blue linen shirtwaist and a black dress skirt. She lost five pounds in weight during her incarceration.

5. The newspaper reproduced Emma Goldman's signature, as well as her salutation to this letter.
6. Edward Brady was EG's lover and companion at this time
7. Park Row was also known as "Newspaper Row." The *New York World, New York Times,* and *New York Staats-Zeitung* were among the newspapers located there.

"Physically I am pretty well," she said to a reporter of the *World*, "but the mental strain on me has been very great. It is a frightful thing for a woman of intelligence to be so placed that she cannot exercise her own free will; that she is a mere machine. But worse it was to be surrounded by such degraded wretches as are prisoners in the penitentiary. You must understand that I hold it is not their fault that they are what they are. But there they were in prison, and I was among them."

"Have you made any plans for the future?" asked the reporter.

"I cannot go backward," she answered. "I cannot go sideways. I must go forward."

Miss Goldman will speak in English at what is announced as a "grand concert, mass-meeting and reception," at the Thalia Theatre to-morrow night. John Swinton, Charles W. Mowbray and others will also make addresses.[8]

It was at a meeting of the unemployed at Union Square last August that Miss Goldman uttered the words that a jury decided were incendiary. Her trial was most sensational. It opened on Oct. 5, 1893,[9] and after four days her trial ended in a conviction. Her sentence of one year's imprisonment, which began on Oct. 16, was commuted by her good behavior to ten months.

New York World, 18 August 1894, pp. 1–2. Drawing of EG accompanies article.

8. Excerpts from addresses by EG and the English anarchist Charles Mowbray at this meeting were reprinted by the *New York World* (see "Hailed Emma Goldman," Article in *New York World*, 20 August 1894, below). There is no extant record of John Swinton having spoken at the meeting.
9. The trial began on 4 October.

Article in the *NEW YORK WORLD*

New York, 20 August 1894

Hailed Emma Goldman.

Anarchists Filled the Thalia Theatre to Celebrate Her Release from Jail.

But John Most Stayed Away.

Law, Government and Police Denounced in Several Languages, While the Audience Sweltered.

Marie Louise, Communist, Presided.

Police Made No Show, but Reserves Were Ready to Prevent an Outbreak— Goldman's and Mowbray's Fiery Words.

There was a polyglot assemblage in the Thalia Theatre[1] last night.

Twenty-eight hundred Anarchists of New York welcomed Emma Goldman, just released after ten months' imprisonment on Blackwell's Island.

A Frenchwoman presided. There were speeches in English, Italian, French, German, Spanish and a jargon[2] and a recitation in Russian.

In approbation of the speeches "vives," "vivas," "hochs," "bravas" and "bravos" rent the suffocating, humid air.

But there were no "hurrahs." It is doubtful if there were twenty people of American parentage in the big audience.

Incidentally the reception was turned into a source of revenue. It must have been profitable.

It is a nice question whether a short imprisonment does not pay a popular and accomplished Anarchist.

Those who paid ten cents each sweltered in the upper tier, those who paid fifteen cents sweltered in the balcony, those who paid twenty cents sweltered in the parquet. It was simply a question of sweltering at different altitudes.

Justus Schwab, his family and friends filled a box.

The police were very little in evidence. Inspector Williams was there in plain clothes, of course, and so was Capt. Berghold, who commands the precinct. But right back of the theatre, in Elizabeth street, all the reserves were on duty in the station-house.

1. The Thalia theater a frequent meeting place for Lower East Side radicals.
2. A reference to the Yiddish language.

ANARCHISTS IN ACTION.

MOWBRAY.   MARIE LOUISE.   MISS GOLDMAN'S FRIEND.   SCHWAB.   SHE INTRODUCED MISS GOLDMAN.   MISS GOLDMAN.

Growing interest from the mainstream press is marked by sketches of Goldman, including this one accompanying the *New York World's* 20 August 1894 coverage of the public celebration of her release after a ten-month imprisonment on Blackwell's Island.

Although the speakers called the police hard names, the police treated the audience with most distinguished consideration. They cleared the aisles, to be sure, but those who blocked the aisles violated the law. The fireman on duty at the theatre, a red-headed man, No. 819, was very nearly violent in his efforts to clear the aisles. But perhaps his professional eye saw more clearly the danger that threatened should fire break out.

The Frenchwoman who presided was Marie Louise. She was one of the Paris Commune.[3] She wore a black satin dress and a red necktie. She was as motherly a person as ever recommended the overthrow of all governments. She said in a weak voice that they were there for two purposes:

1. To welcome Emma Goldman.

2. "To protest against organized tyranny, which hides behind that convenient thing called law."

Charles W. Mowbray, the English tailor, was the first speaker. He said, privately, that he was very well but he did not look well. It will greatly rejoice the English police to learn that Mowbray has a much better opinion of them. They have improved by comparison with the police of this country.

"I always used to abuse the police of England," cried Mowbray. "They are gentlemen compared with your police."

This was a very popular sentiment.

3. Marie Louise David immigrated to the United States from London "a few months previous to the outbreak of the Franco-German war," by her own account, and hence could not have been a Communard. See her autobiographical introduction in the *Phrenological Journal* 99 (February 1895): 92–96. The reporter may well have confused her with the more well-known French anarchist Louise Michel.

THEY CHEERED MOWBRAY.

When the obese French Communist in black satin who presided, had introduced Mowbray, the British Anarchist received what he would call an "hovation." He did not look well. He needs new clothes, and he needs a rest.

"We are here," he said, "to welcome back to liberty a young woman whose crime was that she dared to tell the starving masses that they, who have created all that is valuable, all that is beautiful and all that is to be enjoyed, except that which nature has provided— that they had the right to enjoy life and their share of its comforts. She dared to tell the masses, as Cardinal Manning himself has said, that a starving man has a right to share his neighbor's food.[4] Emma Goldman suffered the tortures of Blackwell's Island for ten months for this alone, and there are many others who would do the same if the capitalists had their way.

"This young woman comes back to tell us that she is just the same at heart as she always was, to show the capitalists and their slaves, the authorities, that conviction and imprisonment make no difference to those who have truly accepted the principles of anarchy. (Cheers.) The ideas of anarchy are the only ideas which hold out hope to those who are now suffering for the necessaries of life. Those who rely on the policeman's bludgeon for power fail to understand what anarchy is, and they dare not put forward a man or woman to argue the issue with us.

"People are beginning to learn that government exists not for their protection, but for the protection of the thieving capitalists who have them by the throat and are throttling them."

POLICE EXIST FOR BOODLE.

"The police are here to protect the thieves of society in their work of plunder. It is just as well that those men who wear the blue coats and the brass buttons should know the dirty work they are doing, for there may perhaps be a spark of manhood left in their breasts which will bring them to say that too long they have been armed and fighting against their fathers, their brothers and their friends.

"You are all a lot of cowards. Yet they call this a civilized nation!

"Civilization, what does it mean? It means to you that in a country won by the blood

4. Cardinal Henry Edward Manning, in response to the Trafalgar Square "Bloody Sunday" deaths on 13 November 1887, wrote: "Necessity has no law, and a starving man has a natural right to his neighbour's bread" ("Distress in London: A Note on Outdoor Relief," *Fortnightly Review* 49, January– June 1888). There is no contemporary evidence that EG in fact cited Manning in the 1893 Union Square address that prompted her arrest for "inciting to riot." Other anarchists, including Charles Mowbray and Voltairine de Cleyre, did however cite Manning in this context. De Cleyre refers to Manning as early as 16 December 1893 (immediately before visiting EG in prison), in an address in New York City, "In Defense of Emma Goldmann and the Right of Expropriation," which was published as a pamphlet under the same title (Philadelphia, 1894), serialized in *Liberty* (London, November 1894– January 1895), and reprinted in *Herald of Revolt* (London, September 1913) and in the *Selected Works of Voltairine de Cleyre*, edited by AB (New York: Mother Earth Publishing Association, 1914).

of your fathers, shed for the cause of liberty, you have gradually permitted yourselves to degenerate into cowards and slaves. Until you get into yourselves some of the courage which your fathers had you will remain the slaves of the capitalistic classes. (Cheers.)

"Arouse yourselves! be men! (Shouts of 'We will.')

"Now give a hearty welcome to Emma Goldman, who comes to you to-night to [show] you and to show the capitalists [that] after imprisonment and torture she [will] not hesitate to say just what she [said] before and just what she was made [to] suffer for. (Cheers and shouts of 'Vive l'Anarchie!')"

THE ITALIAN SPEECH.

The crowd thought that this would bring Goldman to the front, but it did not.[5] Instead, the chairwoman brought her treble voice into play to present Maria Rhoda,[6] a black-haired, black-eyed, dark-skinned and black-gowned woman of uncertain age, but of no uncertain power of speech. She was a little woman, and spoke in Italian.

And this little woman worked herself up into a terrible passion, waving her arms and mopping her perspiring face with a red handkerchief. At least it looked like a handkerchief. But the crowd soon wearied of her.

"All the people who are grinding us down should suffer the vengeance!" she cried. "Do not use words, but strike! strike!

"All authority and all officials are rotten, from the dirtiest policeman up to the curs we call Presidents."

When she got through it was noted that her exertions had loosened her back hair and untied the bow of red ribbon she wore around her neck. She drank a tumbler of water and cooled off while stamping the floor with her foot.

HERE'S EMMA GOLDMAN.

Then came Emma Goldman, and her reception showed that her law-breaking and the punishment she received for it had almost deified her in the minds of her lawless admirers. When the fat Chairwoman had announced her as about to come on the stage pandemonium seemed to have broken loose. Nearly everybody who was sitting down stood up, and those who had been standing up jumped up in the air. The din and racket was worse than that on the baseball field when the home nine wins out on a tied score in the last inning.

She entered from the left wings and strutted to the front centre of the stage. There,

---

5. In *Living My Life*, EG remembers that she was to have addressed the room next, but grew faint and was unable to speak (*LML*, p. 149).
6. Marie Roda was an Italian anarchist, imprisoned after Sante Caserio, a member of her group, assassinated French president Carnot; Roda then emigrated to the United States, where she immediately took part in New York anarchist events.

dressed in simple black, save for a red ribbon at the neck, she stood with her head thrown back and glared up at the roof with her peculiar, half-closed eyes. The crowd was glad to see her. There was no doubt of that. There was whooping, howling, yelling and cheering, until finally she raised her arm and waved her handkerchief, while her countenance lost its expression of opera-bouffe hauteur and assumed one of weariness. That secured silence. Then she said:

"Friends and Comrades: I have come back to you after having served ten months in prison for talking. If the representatives of your Government intend to prosecute women for talking, they will have to begin with their mothers, wives, sisters and sweethearts, for they will never stop women from talking. (Cheers.) But it was not Emma Goldman who was prosecuted. It was the thoughts of Emma Goldman, the principles of Anarchy, that were prosecuted: the views held by thousands of brave men and women who have died and are ready to die as did Santo.[7]

"It was the right of free speech that was prosecuted in the Court of General Sessions, and not little Emma Goldman. (Shouts of 'Vive l'Anarchie!')

"The authorities are afraid of those who are trying to open the eyes of the people to their sufferings. I hate the tyrants of the present system too much to have pity on them, but when I sat before Judge Martine listening to the inflammatory speech of District-Attorney McIntyre I could but feel sorry for him. I said to myself, Oh, you coward District-Attorney. It is fear, a false fear of society that makes you try to convince those jurors of the terrible things that would happen if Emma Goldman was not convicted and imprisoned. (Cheers.)"

SHE LOATHES JUDGE MARTINE.

"I was found guilty, and then I was left to the tender mercy of Judge Martine. He gave me ten months because he could not give me any more. I loathe Judge Martine. (Cheers.)

"Oh, you Judges and you District-Attorneys, you can imprison and you can guillotine and send to the gallows all the Anarchists, but you need not delude yourselves with the idea that you can kill the spirit of Anarchy. (Cries of 'Never!' 'Vive l'Anarchie!')"

DEFIANT IN TWO LANGUAGES.

"The future will be ours, brothers and sisters. I am as loyal as ever to liberty, the loving mother of the poor, the wretched, the miserable. I defy the Judges, the District-Attorneys and the police, and so I say let them go on with their dastardly work. They are working on their own coffin. Every blow they strike drives a nail. Every Anarchist they send to jail or to death takes another spadeful of earth from the hole into which their carcasses will be placed. (Cheers.)

7. Sante Caserio assassinated French president Carnot on 24 June 1894 and was executed two months later, on 16 August.

"I am with you again under the red flag of Anarchy[8] and liberty, and under it we will march together until we get rid of poverty, of misery and of prostitution. We are children no longer. Our eyes are open now. They cannot tell us any more that the judges and the district attorneys are in office to protect us. They are there to protect those who are driving men to desperation, women to wretchedness and sweet young girls to sell themselves body and soul. 'Vive l'Anarchie' we will cry with our last breath."

There was another tornado of noise. Then Goldman repeated her harangue in German. When she had finished she strutted off in the same grotesque manner she had entered, but she had to come back and promise the crowd that they should hear again from her soon.

A very lady-like Anarchist then made an address in jargon. She was Miss Sarah Schmidt.[9] She wore a black lace dress trimmed with pink silk, as if her anarchistic ideas were not colored with the deepest Anarchist dye.

During John H. Edelman's[10] speech he said 2,000,000 tramps were wandering over the highways and byways of this country.

"What is a tramp?" indignantly interrupted a man who had paid 20 cents for a seat in the parquet.

"I will tell you," answered Edelmann, hastily. "A workingman who is out of work and waiting for another job. I know about tramps, for I tramped across the State of Iowa and studied them. My only surprise is that a workman, who can earn only enough to support life, does not throw down his tools when he finds he can support life without work."

Anarchist Estive[11] spoke in Spanish. Marie Louise then advanced to the footlights and said: "I now introduce you to an old friend—John Most."

(Loud and prolonged applause.)

But no John Most appeared,[12] and the audience went home, disappointed.

New York World, 20 August 1894, p. 8. Article includes pen and ink drawings of the speakers.

---

8. Though black had been associated with anarchism in France since 1883, the color red was the predominant symbol of anarchism throughout this period; only after the First World War was the color black widely adopted.
9. The 20 August 1894 account in the *New York Times* identifies this speaker as Sarah Edelstadt; the "jargon" was Yiddish.
10. John Edelmann was a New York anarchist and editor of *Solidarity.*
11. Spanish anarchist Pedro Esteve worked as a propagandist and labor organizer in Florida and New Jersey as well as New York.
12. The *New York Times* (20 August 1894) reported that Most was billed to speak, was present at the meeting, and at one point stuck his head through stage curtain to peek at the crowd, but never spoke.

Essay in *DIE BRANDFACKEL*

New York, October 1894

Anarchistengesetze

Ich las einst das Märchen von einem Gott, der den ersten Menschen geschaffen, ihn in einem herrlichen Garten voll prächtiger Fruchtbäume wohnen ließ, ihm aber ein Gebot gab, die Früchte von einem gewissen Baume nicht zu berühren. Als aber dieser Mensch, von Neugierde und Auflehnung gegen das Gebot seines Herrn getrieben, die Frucht des Baumes genaß, wurde Gott wüthend und vertriebe den armen Sünder aus dem Garten. Beim Lesen dieses Märchens erfaßte mich unwillkürlich ein Ärger gegen diesen Gott, der so herzlos verfahren konnte mit dem armen Adam, dessen Verbrechen ja nur darin bestand, der göttlichen Schöpfung seines Meisters Anerkennung zu zollen und sich an dem Safte der Frucht zu laben. Oft quälte mich die Frage, was wohl dem Gott, der mir als gütig und liebevoll geschildert wurde, veranlassen könnte, Schönes und Herrliches für den Menschen zu schaffen und dann Gesetze zu machen, die denselben verhindern sollten, es zu genießen? Damals war mir dieses Märchen noch ein Räthsel und mein kindlicher Geist wiegte sich schließlich in dem Glauben, daß alles was Gott thue, wohlgethan sei. Erst nachdem ich groß geworden und die "Güte" des Herrn selbst empfunden, konnte ich das Räthsel lösen; aber ich mußte der Lösung meinen naiven Glauben an einen Schöpfer opfern. Gott war ein Herrscher, und als socher verlangte er unbedingten Gehorsam von seinem Diener Adam; denn so lange er in Bewunderung und Andacht zu seinem Meister aufschaute, war Gott seiner Macht, seiner Gewalt über den hülflosen Menschen sicher; als aber dieser der Versuchung, Schönes und Gutes genießen zu wollen, nicht widerstehen konnte, als er trotz der Drohungen seines Schöpfers der Versuchung unterlag und vom Baume der Erkenntnis aß, da erfaßte den Herrn ein wilder Grimm ob der Frechheit des Dieners. Er sah seinen Einfluß schwinden und sich seiner göttlichen Macht beraubt. War schon die Willenskraft des unwissenden und hülflosen Knechtes so stark, um wie viel stärker die Kraft des zum Selbstbewußtsein erwachten Mannes. Darum mußte er fort von seinem Heimathsorte, verdammt, im Schweiße seines Angesichts das Brod zu verdienen, ruhelos umherzuziehen, von Ort zu Ort. Armer gehetzter Vorbote der leidenden Menschheit! Wie damals Adam, so sind heute seine "Nachkommen" verdammt, Lasten zu tragen, Paläste zu bauen, Schätze ans Tageslicht zu fördern und stöhnend und ächzend von Land zu Land zu ziehen. Die privilegirten Kinder des Herrn aber wandeln noch heute im Garten Eden, genießend, herrschend, befehlend und Verderben verbreitend für ihre enterbten Brüder.

Gleich damals finden sich heute Menschen von allen Herrlichkeiten der Natur umgeben, nur dürfen sie dieselben nicht genießen. Immer mehr Verbote und Gesetze für die Rechtlosen, immer mehr Gefängnisse, Galgen und Schaffote für jene die es wagen, sich gegen die Gesetze der Herren aufzulehnen und vom Baume der Erkenntnis zu genießen. Die bevorzugten Kinder wissen nur zu gut, daß ihre Macht, ihre Throne und ihr Reichthum auf Unwissenheit, Gehorsam und Geduld des größeren Theils der Menschheit erreicht sind; darum die Angst vor der Erkenntnis und der Überzeugung ihrer Diener und Sklaven. Zitternd und knieschlotternd steht sie da, die Macht der Dreieinigkeit, Gott Vater (der Geldsack), Gott Sohn (der Staat), und Gott heiliger Geist (die Kirche). Einer ist eifriger bemüht als der Andere, Mittel und Wege zu finden, den schrecklichen Feind (das Wissen und die Freiheit), zu vernichten.

Auch hier in Amerika, dem "freiesten" Lande der Welt, schlug ein Bluthund à la Bismarck ein Gestez gegen Anarchisten vor, um sich der verhaßten Freiheitskämpfer zu entledigen. Ein Anarchistengesetz, welcher Hohn! Wurde denn nicht schon längst der Versuch gemacht, das Brausen des herannahenden Sturmes zu unterdrücken und wurde nicht schon versucht, den Schrei der Entrechteten am Galgen zu Chicago zu ersticken? Versuchte man nicht den Muth und die Willenskraft eines Brutus zu brechen, indem man ihn auf 22 Jahre hinter Kerkermauern begrub, und wurden nicht schon zu weiderholten Malen die Forderungen der Hungernden mit Pulver und Blei beantwortet? Nicht zu reden von den unzähligen Menschen, die ihrer Liebe zur Freiheit wegen verfolgt, verhöhnt und ins Gefängnis geschleppt wurden. Sind noch immer nicht genug Gesetze vorhanden, um das rothe Gespenst zu bannen? Hill, die elende feige Memme, Hill, der als Gouverneurs-Candidat für den Staat N.Y. aufgestellt ist, dieser Beschutzer der Reichen schlug ein Gesetz vor, nach welchem man alle Ausländer, die auch nur im *Verdacht* stehen, Anarchisten zu sein, einkerkern und auf administrativen Wege ausweisen resp. an die europäischen Tyrannen *ausliefern* kann.

Verhülle dein Angesicht, 19. Jahrhundert vor der Schmach dieses "freien" Landes! Die Geldprotzen Amerika's schütteln die bluttriefenden Hände des wahnsinnigen Batuschka, des blöden Lümmels auf Deutschlands Thron und der alten Dirne Englands! "Freie" amerikanische Bürger rutschen vor den Mächten Europas auf dem Bauche!

Wohl ist das Gesetz noch nicht angenommen, aber nach dem was uns bis jetzt geboten wurde, läßt sich das Schlimmste erwarten. Sollte die Annahme des Gesetzes erfolgen, kann dies das Stürzen der Lawine aufhalten, die Verzweiflung der Geknechteten vermindern und den freien Gedanken hemmen? Nein! Der revolutionäre Geist lebt doch fort. Er wühlt und ruht nicht, er zerbricht alle Schranken bis die Bahn geebnet und die Freiheit sich erhebt, leuchtend und erwärmend, gleich der Sonne nach dem Gewitter.

Emma Goldmann.

Anarchist Laws.

I once read the fairy tale about a God who created the first human and let him live in a glorious garden full of splendid fruit trees but commanded him not to touch the fruits of a certain tree. When, however, this man, driven by curiosity and rebellion against the commandment of his God, ate the fruit of that tree, God became angry and expelled the poor sinner from the garden. While reading this fairy tale I was involuntarily gripped with anger against this God who could act so heartlessly with poor Adam, whose crimes indeed only involved showing appreciation for the divine creation of his master and obtaining refreshment from the juice of the fruit. I was often tormented by the question of what could have caused this God, who had been described to me as kind and loving, to create beautiful and glorious things for people and then make laws that are supposed to prevent these same people from enjoying them? Back then this fairy tale was a riddle to me and my youthful mind was lulled into the belief that everything God does is good. Only after I grew up and experienced for myself the "goodness" of the Lord could I solve the riddle; but for this solution I had to sacrifice my naive belief in a creator. God was a ruler, and as such he demanded unconditional obedience from his servant Adam; for as long as he looked up to his master in admiration and devotion, God was secure in his strength and power over helpless men. But when he was unable to resist the temptation of wanting to enjoy beautiful and good things, when he submitted to temptation and ate from the tree of knowledge in spite of the threats of his creator, a wild fury gripped the Lord over the impudence of his servant. He saw his influence dwindle and was robbed of his divine power. If the willpower of the ignorant and helpless slave was this strong, how much stronger would be the power of the man stirred to self-confidence. Therefore he had to leave his home, damned to earn his bread through the sweat of his brow and to wander restlessly from place to place. The poor, hunted forerunner of suffering humanity! Just as Adam was back then, so today his "descendants" are damned to carry burdens, build palaces, unearth treasures, and move moaning and groaning from land to land. Yet still today the privileged children of the Lord wander in the Garden of Eden, reveling, ruling, commanding, and spreading ruin for their disinherited brothers.

Just as back then, men find themselves surrounded by all the splendors of nature, yet they are not allowed to enjoy them. More and more commandments and laws for those without rights, more and more prisons, gallows, and scaffolds for those who dare to rebel against the laws of the rulers and eat from the tree of knowledge. The favored children know all too well that their power, their thrones, and their riches have been built upon the ignorance, obedience, and patience of the greater part of humanity; thus their fear of the knowledge and conviction of their servants and slaves. Trembling and weak-kneed they stand there, the power of the Trinity, God the Father (the Moneybag), God the Son (the State), and God the Holy Spirit (the Church). One endeavors more zealously than the other to find the ways and the means to destroy the frightful enemy (knowledge and freedom).[1]

Even here in America, the "freest" country in the world, a bloodhound à la Bismarck[2] has proposed a law against Anarchists in order to get rid of the hated freedom fighters. An Anarchist law, how scornful! Wasn't the attempt made long ago to suppress the roar of the approaching storm and wasn't there already an attempt to choke the cry of the disenfranchised at the gallows in Chicago?[3] Didn't they try to break the strength and will power of a Brutus by burying him for 22 years behind prison walls,[4] and haven't the demands of the starving people been answered repeatedly with gunpowder and lead? Not to mention the countless people persecuted, jeered, and dragged to prison due to their love of freedom. Are there not yet enough laws in existence to exorcise the red specter? Hill,[5] the interminably craven coward, Hill, who has been nominated as the gubernatorial candidate for N.Y. State, this protector of the rich has proposed a law according to which all foreigners who are even *suspected* of being Anarchists can be imprisoned and then *deported* by administrative means or handed over to European tyrants.[6]

Cover your face, 19th century, from the disgrace of this "free" country! The wealthy

---

1. The preceding passage is largely derived from Michael Bakunin's *God and the State*, first published in English in 1883.
2. Otto von Bismarck (1815–1898) served as the first chancellor of Germany for nineteen years under Emperor Wilhelm I. In the late 1870s, after two assassination attempts upon the emperor, Bismarck convinced the parliament to pass the anti-socialist "exceptional law," which banned the Social Democratic Party in 1878, a ban that lasted until 1890 and led to the emigration of many German radicals.
3. A reference to the Haymarket trial of eight anarchists, which resulted in the death by hanging of Albert Parsons, August Spies, George Engel, and Adolph Fischer; Louis Lingg, who was also slated to be hanged, killed himself in his prison cell the night before.
4. EG refers to AB's sentence of twenty-two years for his attempted assassination of Henry C. Frick.
5. The legislation EG excoriates was supported by David Bennett Hill (1843–1910), lawyer, Democrat, United States senator (1892–1897), and twice governor of New York (1885–1892). He was nominated for governor again in 1894 but lost the election.
6. As chair of the Senate Committee on Immigration, Hill supported an anti-anarchist law proposed in 1894. He argued on the Senate floor that "nearly all the principal European countries are now legislating against this class of people, and if they are not excluded from the United States this country will soon be the dumping ground of the anarchists of the world." Charles W. Mowbray's propaganda tour, under way while the bill was being debated in August, heightened the anxiety of the legislature. The proposed law barred anarchists or any person "not attached to the principles of the Constitution and well-disposed to the peace and good order of the same" from entering the United States and also called for the imprisonment and deportation of anyone convicted of illegal entry. The Senate and the House, however, each favored a different version of the bill, and thus it was never passed. See *Congressional Record*, 53rd Cong., 2nd sess., 1894, 26, pt. 8:8108–109, 8230–44, 8506, 8557–58.

show-offs of America are shaking the bloody hands of the mad Batuschka,[7] the stupid lout on Germany's throne[8] and England's old whore![9] "Free" American citizens squirm on their bellies before the powers of Europe!

To be sure, the law has not yet been passed, but given what has been presented to us up to now, we can only expect the worst. Should the acceptance of the law follow, can this halt the onrush of the avalanche, lessen the despair of the enslaved, and hamper free thought? No! The revolutionary spirit lives on. It fights on and does not rest, it breaks down all barriers until the path has been cleared and freedom has arisen, gleaming and radiant, just like the sun after a storm.

Emma Goldmann.

Die Brandfackel 2 (October 1894): 6–7. Translated from German.

7. *Batuschka,* or "Little father," was a nickname for the tsar, and was usually intended as an affectionate diminutive.
8. A reference to Emperor Wilhelm II.
9. A reference to Queen Victoria.

Article in the
PHRENOLOGICAL JOURNAL AND SCIENCE OF HEALTH
New York, February 1895

Character in Unconventional People.

A Pair of Anarchists.

From Personal Examinations by the Editor.

We trust that the readers of the *Journal*[1] will not be alarmed at the introduction of the two somewhat noted opponents of the existing order of society which we present herewith. We can vouch for their harmlessness in the shadows we print, however dangerous they may be in person and at short range.

As it is only by carefully studying and comparing all the elements of human nature, both agreeable and disagreeable, that we can hope to acquire accurate and comprehensive knowledge, we propose here to make a little excursion into the realm of unconventional mentality. Our purpose is to show a relation between peculiar ideas of life and certain types of organization. Of course we shall enter on no discussion as to the merits of the views held by the two subjects we have chosen, although it is only justice to say that both these women, especially Marie Louise, repudiate the commonly accepted idea that they advocate violence as a means of reform. Emma Goldman who recently served a year in one of the New York prisons for alleged utterances inciting to riot, is no doubt the more aggressive of the two, and is probably a fair representative of the radical class of anarchists. Marie Louise, on the other hand, professes to be what she calls a "scientific" anarchist. She is undoubtedly a scholar, while Miss Goldman is an enthusiast. Having recently interviewed and examined these two women, we hope to be able to point out certain facts about them which will be of interest.

Emma Goldman professes to be a Russian Jewess, although it is difficult to see any-

---

1. *Phrenological Journal* was published in New York and Philadelphia from 1838 to 1911 under a variety of titles. The Fowler and Wells Company, publishers of the journal, also published and distributed a number of editions of Walt Whitman's *Leaves of Grass*. The editor during the time this article was published would have been either Edgar C. Beall or Henry S. Drayton. Beall's book *The Life Sexual: A Study of the Physiology, Science, Art and Hygiene of Love* (New York: Vim Publishing, 1905) would later be suppressed by the Post Office under the Comstock Act. The phrenological study of EG followed an examination conducted after her conviction on 16 October 1893 (see "The Law's Limit," *New York World*, 17 October 1893, above). The journal's editorial introduction explained the relevance of the subject matter for phrenology and its enthusiasts. Still popular at the turn of the century, phrenology maintained that personality traits bore a direct relation to the shape and size of the skull.

thing in her face or head which we are accustomed to associate with the Hebrews. She is still a young woman, probably not over twenty-six or eight. She is only five feet in height but weighs about one hundred and twenty-five pounds. She has rather fine, soft, light brown hair, and blue-gray eyes of which the expression is very peculiar. Her head measures twenty-one and a half inches in basilar circumference, and the principal developments are above this line. The back head is rather long, showing friendship, domestic attachment and love of the opposite sex. There is considerable width just over the ears at destructiveness and appetite for food which the portrait does not clearly show, as it is copied from a crayon drawing. But with the further exception of the upper forehead, which in this picture is not square enough at causality, the likeness is remarkably correct. This is especially true as to the expression of the eyes and mouth. The facial signs of destructiveness and alimentiveness are very pronounced in the form of the mouth, and it is chiefly in the mouth and eyes that we may detect the signs of quality and temperament which account for the woman's disposition to attack the present social fabric.

There is a very considerable development in the rear of the crown. Approbativeness and firmness are especially strong. Conscientiousness is difficult to define. There is a latent sense of justice, but every thing in the organization points to a lack of discipline, and there are evidences of what might be called a habit of willfulness; an abandon to the dominant impulses. In that form of chin and mouth, with the large firmness in the brain, we have the phase of persistence that may be called tenacity, and which is often referred to in popular parlance by a comparison with the bull-dog. It means a deep-seated, ineradicable instinct to hold to an opinion, a purpose, or a passion. It is a vehement clutch which is never relaxed, and it differs from obstinacy or perseverance of the ordinary type in being independent of opposing forces or other external conditions. It nurses its joys or griefs whether anybody else is present to contradict or not. It does not depend on moods. It is always present in its activity and stamps the character with an indelible dye.

The incorrigibility of such a nature is also greatly augmented, as in the present instance, by the almost utter lack of reverence and faith. Hope is also weak. This combination leaves the intellect without incentive to search for evidences of optimism, and as such a nature readily finds itself at war with the conventionalities, ill adapted to compete in the struggle for existence with those more harmoniously constituted, a pessimistic view of life with a consequent desire to alter the existing conditions is the almost inevitable result. Of course there are thousands of people who have many of these peculiarities of feeling, but who are endowed with very ordinary intellect, so that they make no outcry, no protest, and indeed have few opinions beyond the consciousness that they are uncomfortable. But Emma Goldman, although obviously of a lineage far from aristocratic in tone, is endowed with a philosophical cast of mind which is very rare. Her upper forehead is beautifully developed and our portrait utterly fails to do her justice in this respect.

The development of causality and comparison, stimulated by her pessimistic emotions, renders her a radical thinker upon social problems. In her conversation she manifests that familiarity with the vocabulary of philosophy which is ordinarily expected only among cultivated professional men. However, her lower forehead is almost as defective as the upper portion is fine. The eyebrows are almost straight, and the space between them (the glabella) is depressed much more than appears in the engraving. This shows a want of observation, precision, accuracy and specification in her collection or application of data. In other words, she will reason profoundly but often upon insufficient evidence. After assuming certain premises she follows the rule of the syllogism in the most consistent, logical manner, but she is in danger of starting with premises which are false. As may be seen by the flattened outer angle of the eyebrow, she has scarcely a trace of order; and the eyes are deep set, showing little fondness for words or fluency in speech.

There are, doubtless, certain biases or tendencies in this woman which she owes to some marked peculiarities or habits of her ancestors. She says that her father was a man of an almost tyrannical disposition, and that her mother was very weak willed. Thus there is quite a difference between the indications in her head and those in her hand as regards firmness. Her hand is quite small, very flexible, but with a very poorly developed thumb, the first or nailed phalanx being very short. It is in this first joint that cheirognomists[2] locate willpower, while the second phalanx is, according to its length, a sign of logic. This imperfect first joint of the thumb is often found in people who are undeveloped or askew in some particular. This peculiarity in Miss Goldman shows how important it is to study the brain and not to rely upon any one isolated or remote sign. [. . .]

Phrenological Journal and Science of Health 99 (February 1895): 88–90. The omitted portion of this article includes an analysis of French anarchist Marie Louise David, who appended her own autobiographical sketch. A pencil portrait of EG and a photograph of Marie Louise David accompanied the article.

2. Cheirognomy was the science of reading character from the shape and type of the hand.

I beg to call the attention of the *Firebrand* comrades, and liberty loving men and women everywhere, to the fact that the friends of Alexander Berkman are getting ready to appeal for a commutation of the excessive sentence imposed upon him, in 1892, for attacking Frick, the superintendent of the Carnegie iron works, during the labor troubles of that time. Most of your readers will, no doubt, remember the outrageous treatment labor received at the hands of capital, during the Homestead strike; how Pinkerton's men were engaged by Frick, smuggled down there and armed with Winchester rifles, with instruction from this man Frick, to shoot to kill. Now these hired assassins charged upon a group of defenseless men and women, who were armed with nothing but their courage and honesty of purpose, killing eleven and wounding many more. As usual the attention of the strikers was directed to the poor scabs, who are ever through circumstances compelled to take their places, while Frick, who was directly responsible for the trouble, who gave the order to drive the sick wives and children of the strikers from their homes, and who expressed the desire to have the working men massacred, rather than to see them win the strike, was not in the least molested. Even the capitalist press joined with many law-abiding citizens in denouncing Frick, and sympathizing with the unfortunate workmen.

It was at this stage that Berkman appeared upon the field, July 23d., 1892. Though not a striker, and not suffering from the cruelty of Frick himself, he keenly felt the wrongs inflicted upon his brethren. Berkman, the noble youth, recognizing the man who was responsible for the sufferings of the strikers, determined to strike a blow at the cause of the evil, and the death of the eleven victims. The cries of starving mothers and innocent children gave him courage and will power to combat the enemy. He made an unsuccessful attack on Frick, slightly wounding him, but creating consternation in the enemy's camp. By the light of subsequent events it is shown that the act was not altogether in vain; Plutocracy has never raised its head so proudly since.

Utterly terrified, fearing a similar attack from other sources, the authorities hurried Berkman away to prison, where he was forced to remain two months, after which time he was brought before a prejudiced judge and jury, without council, or the least chance to defend himself. He was, on the 20th. of September sentenced to twenty-two years imprisonment;[1] such a trial being illegal and without a precedent in the history of jurisprudence.[2]

---

1. AB was sentenced on 19 September 1892.
2. The judge overrode the Pennsylvania law mandating a maximum of nine years in prison for AB's crime and compounded the charges, sentencing him instead to twenty-two years.

Today, while Frick, in perfect health, lives to enjoy his ill-gotten wealth, poor Berkman is languishing in a dark, musty cell, shut away from his friends and from the world, never enjoying a stray beam of sunshine; still dreaming of a dawn of perfect freedom, and a day when labor will no longer be crushed beneath the iron heel of wealth. For behind his prison bars his big warm heart still throbs with the hopes and fears of the downtrodden; he still keeps watch on the events of our times, and when permitted to write to his friends still encourages them not to give up the fight. Though but a boy in years, he has shown the philosophy and courage of a man; no word of complaint has ever passed his lips in all these three years, although he has been subjected to even more rigorous discipline than prisoners usually undergo.

Lovers of justice everywhere, even if not in sympathy with the feeling that prompted the act of 1892, must recognize the injustice of such a trial, under such circumstances, and by such a judge and jury, and must agree with us that when, according to the law he was accused of violating, the extreme penalty should have been seven years, the tactics pursued in order to sentence him for such a length of time were unlawful, as well as unjust and inhuman.

Berkman does not petition for a pardon, nor for a new trial, but simply for a reduction of sentence.[3] Comrades and friends that feel interested in this poor prisoner will bear in mind that money is required for every effort of this kind, and will help us all they can.

Those desiring further information, or desiring to contribute to the fund, should address, until further notice, Charles Schneider, 82 Hill street, 12th Ward, Allegheny, Pa.

EMMA GOLDMAN.[4]

Firebrand, 21 July 1895, p. 2. This letter also appeared in the *Torch* (London) 2 (September 1895), *EGP,* reel 1.

3. In early 1895, upon the advice of a friend, EG, Edward Brady, and others investigated the possibility of appealing AB's case to the Supreme Court. They discovered that no grounds for an appeal existed, since AB had made no formal objections to judicial rulings at his trial. Instead EG convinced AB to allow an appeal on his behalf before the Pennsylvania Board of Pardons, and began that summer to solicit funds and other aid for that purpose.
4. The newspaper's editorial annotation reads: "All our Exchanges who favor justice will please copy and request others to. The comrades everywhere will do well to exert themselves in Berkman's behalf. Get your local papers to mention this effort to free Comrade Berkman."

To the NEW YORK WORLD

New York, 2 August 1895

Emma Goldman's Attitude.

She Warns the Striking Tailors Against Their Leaders.

To the Editor of the *World:*

I beg to correct the statement published in your paper regarding the striking clothing-makers and myself. I have neither attended any of their meetings nor did I have the least intention of participating in the strike.[1]

I am, of course, greatly interested in labor troubles, and especially in the late strike of the tailors, and while I passed Walhalla Hall[2] one morning I went in to see how the strikers were getting on. I was directed to a room where several girls were chatting, and, not knowing that they were to have a private meeting, I entered to see Miss Persky.[3] She invited me to attend their mass-meeting in the afternoon, and while she was writing down my address up jumped one of the leaders and shouted that while he had no prejudice towards Miss Goldman, she was an Anarchist, and that was enough.

I quietly told him that he did not seem fit to be a leader, as he was afraid of the presence of a woman who is an Anarchist. Then I left the hall.

My sympathy is fully with the strikers, and I sincerely hope they will succeed in their efforts to better their condition, but they will do well not to put too much faith in their leaders or they will fail, as others have.

Emma Goldman.

New York World, 2 August 1895, p. 3.

1. On 28 July, members of the United Brotherhood of Tailors began a strike that soon involved 16,000 workers in New York, Brooklyn, and Newark. Called over the alleged failure of clothing contractors to comply with a previous union agreement, the strike ultimately succeeded in winning its demands.
2. Walhalla Hall, located at 52 Orchard Street, was also the site of the 17 August 1893 riot of unemployed workingmen for which anarchists (including EG) were blamed.
3. Lottie Persky (also spelled Perski) was a walking delegate of the Women's Branch of the United Brotherhood of Tailors, appointed as a trade union official to confer with local unions or to be a representative in negotiations between the union and the employer. The United Brotherhood of Tailors was active in the organization of the 1,800 union and non-union "girl tailors" on strike in New York and Brooklyn. On 31 July the *World* reported that EG had been escorted from a meeting of women tailors at Walhalla Hall by "a committee of ten" after she ignored a request to leave. "We don't want Anarchists here," the paper quoted Miss Persky as saying. "We are trades unionists and have no use for the sympathy or aid of such persons as Emma Goldman." See *New York World,* 29 July 1895, p. 5; 30 July 1895, p. 3; and 31 July 1895, p. 16.

According to a notice I received,[1] the anarchist Emma Goldmann intends in the near future to travel from New York to London,[2] and possibly from there to Germany.

The above-mentioned Goldmann is about 26–28 years old and Russian, but has a mastery of the German language.

For years she has been untiringly active in the United States of North America in the anarchist movement; there she has been imprisoned repeatedly for her unrestrained, anarchistic, inflammatory speeches,[3] and has managed many times to win comrades for the revival of propaganda for the cause which she fanatically follows. Another of Goldmann's lovers, the bookbinder Josef Oerter[4] who, together with her lover Berkmann, reportedly took part in the assassination attempt in 1892 against the director of the Carnegie plant in Pittsburg, came via England to Germany in 1893, financially supported by her. He was sentenced by a jury in Duisburg on October 25, 1893, for violations against §. 10 of the law of June 9th 1884 concerning criminal and dangerous use of explosives, and violations against §§. 110, 130, 128/129 of the criminal law code, to 8 years in prison, loss of civil rights, and placed under surveillance.—The above-mentioned Goldmann must be considered an exceedingly dangerous person.

I most devotedly beseech your honor to take the above-mentioned into custody in the event of her arrival, and, if possible, to notify me immediately by telegraph.

DER REGIERUNGS-PRÄSIDENT[5]

BY PROXY:

ZUCKER.

ALS, Hauptstaatsarchiv Düsseldorf. Marked "Confidential" and "Secret!" Translated from German.

1. Suspecting that EG, through Joseph "Sepp" Oerter, was involved in anarchist activities within Germany, the German Ministry of the Interior had its operatives compile the following information on EG and monitor her during her tour of England and Scotland. The Interior Ministry passed this information to the police, who in turn informed regional and local officials throughout Germany.
2. EG had left New York for London on 15 August 1895 to begin a speaking tour of England and Scotland.
3. EG was imprisoned once, in 1893, for her role in the unemployment demonstrations.
4. There is no extant evidence that Joseph "Sepp" Oerter was involved in AB's *attentat*.
5. An appointed office. The title is roughly equivalent to "chief regional administrator."

Article in *LIBERTY*

London, October 1895

Emma Goldman in London.

Public Meeting at South Place Institute, Finsbury.

Emma Goldman, the woman who voiced the sufferings of the unemployed in New York in 1892,[1] and who consequently suffered imprisonment for this so-called breach of the laws of the U.S.A., arrived in England on the 22nd of August. Her first appearance in public was in Regents Park, where she spoke to a large crowd. At later periods she addressed meetings at Hyde Park, Whitechapel, Canning Town, Barking, and Stratford, her speeches being received in every case with marked approval. And on Friday evening the 13th ultimo she delivered an interesting address in the South Place Institute, Finsbury.

The meeting was called to consider the subject "Political Justice in England and America." The chair was occupied by R. Peddie, and on the platform and amongst the audience were Louise Michel, Touzeau Parris,[2] E. Leggatt,[3] Henry Seymour, Amy Morant,[4] C. Morton, G. Lawrence, and James Tochatti.[5]

The Chairman having briefly stated the object for which the meeting had been called, Comrade Leggatt spoke on his imprisonment and said that a magistrate was always more severe on a man if he happened to be an Anarchist than upon an ordinary man, and that he as a working man would continue to assert his right to ride in comfort.

J. Tochatti said the question of Political Justice in England no one could afford to ignore, whatever their political views may be, nor could we allow the Continental system of "agents provocateur" to be introduced without strenuous opposition. Justice was not administered in accord with equity but used by the classes to suppress all advanced

---

1. The unemployed demonstration to which the article referred was in 1893.
2. Thomas Collins Touzeau Parris (1840–1907) was a member of the London Socialist League, an anarchist, and the owner of a gelatin manufacturing business. He lectured in 1881 to the National Secular Society, and by 1886 more widely on anarchism, often at outdoor meetings. He was a Hammersmith Socialist Society delegate to the 1896 London socialist conference. Occasionally contributing to the anarchist press, he took a stand against Christian anarchism and attempted to synthesize socialism and individualism.
3. "E. Leggat" was Ted Leggatt, a carman by trade and an anarchist and activist.
4. Amy Morant was a member of the British Independent Labour Party. She worked with the unemployed in London in 1887 and 1888 and served as a writer, translator, and organizer for the Women's Liberal Federation. She was author of *Carina Songs and Others* (Westminster: Roxburghe Press, 1895) and *The Crisis at Cardiff* (London: Independent Labour Party, 1895).
5. The London anarchist journal *Liberty* was edited by James Tochatti and published from January 1894 to December 1896.

Goldman's tour of England in 1895 was reported in the English anarchist press and highlighted here in *Liberty* (October 1895), an anarchist communist journal edited by James Tochatti. "W. M. Rowe," which appears as the cover artist's signature at lower right side of pedestal, is in fact a pseudonym for the illustrator Walter Crane. (By permission of the Kate Sharpley Library)

thought which threatened their interests. Acts of Parliament passed in panic had been strained in order to brutally punish men who had been trapped by the police. It had been admitted by ex-detective M'cIntyre that the Wallsall Anarchists were victims of a police plot. It was difficult to believe that in England men like Charles and Battola were suffering through the infamy of men like Coulon and the reptile detectives of Scotland Yard, but such was the case.[6]

Henry Seymour said the case of Berkmann, who got 22 years for a 7 years' offence because he happened to hold anarchistic views showed, according to American law, that if 7 years' imprisonment was a sufficient punishment for an attempt to kill, 15 years' imprisonment was the adequate penalty for daring to hold an opinion that American law was rotten. The case of the Chicago Anarchists made it manifest that the United States police were capable of every conceivable villainy. Turning our attention to our own country, the Wallsall Case showed that the Secret Service, in the light of the revelations of inspector M'cIntyre,[7] was an abomination not to be endured. Having recently taken an interest in the Maybrick Case, he said he was acquainted with its details, and could speak with assurance of the scandalous way in which the police manufactured evidence to secure a conviction, and an acquaintance with the case of John Hay revealed that Home Office officials were open to barefaced bribery. We might agitate and secure the reduction of unjust sentences in a few cases, but it must be understood that there is no radical remedy for this state of things except to put an end to the present inequitable economic conditions which permit the privileged few, who control the government, to live in opulence and ease at the expense of the degradation of the masses.

Emma Goldman dealt with the subject from an American point of view. She said three years had passed, since Alexander Berkmann, the noble youth, attempted to avenge the wrongs inflicted upon the strikers at Homestead, during the labor troubles of 1892. Three years of struggle, hardship and privation for the working class, and wealth, extravagance, amusements and pleasure, for a privileged few.

"What (she asked) was Berkmann's crime?" Had he stolen the wealth labor had created? Had he robbed mankind of the necessary means of life? Had he invested the hard earned pennies of widows and orphans in swindling schemes? Had he built factories, where men, women and half grown children, were slowly tortured to death? Had he

---

6. In January 1892, six anarchists were arrested in London and Walsall (in the English Midlands) and accused of conspiracy and possession of explosives. As the number of anarchist bombings and attacks in Europe increased, the possibility of a fair and objective trial became less likely. Three men, Jean Battola, Victor Cailes, and Fred Charles, were sentenced to ten years imprisonment. Joe Deakin was sentenced to five years while William Ditchfield and John Westley were acquitted. Many anarchists believed that the men had been set up by an agent provocateur, Auguste Coulon. The case sparked mutual suspicions, feuds, and bitterness within the English anarchist movement.

7. In April 1895 the London paper *Reynolds News* published the memoirs of former Detective Sergeant McIntyre, who affirmed the suspicion that an agent provocateur (Coulon) had been used to entrap the Walsall anarchists.

plagued, cheated, enslaved, and tyrannized humanity? No! Had he done all that, he might have remained a free man, he would have been honored and respected as a good citizen, have had a chance of being elected to Parliament, Senate, or Congress, or chosen as President of the U.S.A. Berkmann was in prison, because he hated and opposed all this, because he was strong, and let the act follow the thought, because he attempted to destroy the life of a man, who had brought disaster and privation upon thousands of people. The condition of the workers in America was just as miserable as in other countries, the strikes that had taken place within the last ten years demonstrated the long suppressed sufferings of the working classes. It was the Homestead strike of 1892, which revealed to the public the dreadful condition of the amalgamated steel and iron workers, and the brutal treatment they were subjected to by Frick, the superintendent; the workers were actually owned by Carnegie and Frick; the barracks they lived in belonged to Carnegie and Frick, the food, tools and clothing had to be bought at Carnegie's shops, and the prices they paid for these necessaries were enormous. The result of such tyrannical treatment was the strike of July 1892. The men were determined to fight for their homes and families, they were ready to die if necessary, they would not endure a life of drudgery any longer. Frick seeing the earnestness and seriousness of his slaves, engaged a number of Pinkerton's men at two dollars per day, smuggled them into Homestead and gave them the order to shoot and to kill. On the 6th of July these armed assassins charged upon a crowd of men and women, killing eleven and wounding many more. The strikers fought a brave battle, they energetically defended themselves and drove back the hired blood-hounds; Frick called upon the government to send the militia to his assistance. Of course the Government complied. What was the army in America for? what was an army kept for in England, or on the continent, if not to protect private property? But the militia would never have been permitted by the strikers to enter within the boundaries of Homestead, they would have had to pass over the bodies of the workers. The authorities saw the people were in earnest, they understood that to use force would mean a war, so they decided to use a trick. The strikers were promised full protection against Pinkerton's men and that "scabs" should not be put to work in the mines; the poor deluded and confiding strikers, did not see this trap and the militia were allowed to march into the town cheered and applauded by the people; those people afterwards shot down like dogs by the cowardly brutes in uniform. Frick who schemed all those things, and who gave the order to drive the sick wives and starving children of the strikers from their homes, he who caused the death of the eleven victims on the 6th of July, who expressed the intention to have the workers massacred, rather than let them win the strike, was not in the least molested. It was then that Berkmann appeared; though not a striker himself and not suffering from the brutality of Frick, he keenly felt the wrongs inflicted upon his brethren. Alexander Berkmann decided to strike a blow at the cause of the evil. His hatred of tyranny gave him the requisite courage, and on July 23rd, 1892, he made an unsuccessful attack on Frick, only wounding him but creating consternation in the enemy's camp. Utterly terrified and fearing a similar attack from other quarters the authorities hurried Berkmann away to prison, where he remained months without trial, after which time he was taken before a prejudiced judge and jury, and without counsel, or an opportunity to defend himself, was on the 20th of Sept. sentenced to 22 years' imprisonment. Such a trial was illegal and without precedent in the history of American jurisprudence. It was an open secret that America was ruled by a band of thieves who monopolized the land, machinery, rail-roads, mines and factories, in fact all the wealth of the country. All laws were made and enforced by the few. The rights of free speech, assembly and the press, were things of the past, so far as the interests of the workers were concerned, and the constitution which provided equality before the law, had never been observed in the U.S. Men who were in power and had the almighty dollar could commit any crime, seduction, theft, etc. and remain unpunished. Every official from the policeman to the President could be bribed; but those not possessing the means were lost— were helpless. Frick and Carnegie used their stolen money freely in order to obtain a long sentence for Berkmann, and they succeeded. Twenty-two years' imprisonment! Did it not make one's blood run cold to think of it? Could they imagine what it meant to be shut out from the world, to be buried alive for such a long term within prison walls? Could they grasp what it was to suppress one's feelings, wishes, passions and thoughts, to become a mere automatic machine, to see the same cold cruel faces of the watchmen, to hear the same harsh voices of the officials week after week, year after year—to have darkness around you all that time? No! no one who had not been in prison could understand it. Such however was the lot of hundreds of men and women in Siberia—in modern bastilles all over the world. Berkmann was one of the great army of free thinkers, revolutionists and Anarchists, who had sacrificed their life and liberty for the advancement and welfare of mankind. Frick to-day was in perfect health, was enjoying his ill-gotten wealth. The Brutus of the 19th Century was languishing in one of the prisons of America, but was dreaming of the dawn, of a day of perfect liberty when labor would no more be crushed beneath the iron heel of Capitalism. Behind the prison bars, his big warm heart still throbbed with the hopes and fears of the down-trodden, he still watched the events of our times and when permitted to write to his friends encouraged them to continue the fight. No word of complaint had escaped his lips during those three weary years, although he had been subjected to even more rigorous discipline than prisoners usually were. The pistol shot of the 23rd of July had found an echo in the hearts of the oppressed and opened the eyes of many people to the fact that the Anarchists were not a gang of ruffians, as Society was pleased to call them. Anarchism meant the destruction of the existing brutal system of exploitation and robbery of the masses, but not by unnecessarily violent means, and its aim was to establish a society of complete freedom, and respect for one another, free access to the means of life and to every individual unrestricted liberty to own the proceeds of his labor, and the right to learn, study, enjoy, love and live according to his own tastes and desires. The acts of Berkmann, Caserio,

In 1895 Goldman met Louise Michel, the French anarchist arrested in 1883 for urging the Parisian poor to take bread if they could not afford it—words echoed by the admiring Goldman in her address to the demonstration of the unemployed in New York on 21 August 1893. (Labadie Collection, University of Michigan)

Henry, Vaillant, Pallás,[8] and other brave heroes were but the heralds of the coming Social Revolution.

Louise Michel addressed the meeting in French to the effect that the speakers preceding her had spoken of English and American justice, but had not mentioned French justice, probably out of politeness as there was nothing good to be said of it. As she was not a patriot but an Internationalist she would complete the picture without talking politics, which is the art of deceiving others for your own benefit. When they saw the robberies committed in the Southern Railway scandals and other Panamas[9] known and unknown, and the immense Madagascar cemetery,[10] they found that French justice was very hard on the disinherited and most gentle towards the privileged. It was the most unequal justice in the world. And this we call a republic! Res publica, a public thing representing all, but this republic only represents capitalists acting against the workers who were condemned in advance, while the capitalists were absolved. All French statesmen were thieves, some murderers, yet justice crept before those offenders, it was bribed by those whose crimes were heaped as high as heaven. Even the Empire of bloody memory dared not have committed such injustice for fear of being destroyed. Tyrants did well in showing themselves in their true light. It was good for propaganda. The political farces are nearly played out. Anarchists despise weapons used by the enemy for human butchery. When an obstacle to the Social Revolution is to be removed it may sometimes be necessary to use violence. French potentates however, for the time being, may rest in peace.

8. Sante Caserio, Émile Henry, Auguste Vaillant, and Paulino Pallás were all anarchists who had been executed for committing *attentats* or causing explosions. EG's endorsement of the *attentater*, or the power of the individual act, echoes Peter Kropotkin's argument in his essay "The Spirit of Revolt," first published in *Le Révolté* in 1880 and reprinted in the June–July 1892 *Die Autonomie:* "by actions which compel general attention, the new idea seeps into people's minds and wins converts. One such act may, in a few days, make more propaganda than thousands of pamphlets."
9. "Other Panamas" is a reference to the 1889 Panama Canal company bankruptcy and subsequent scandal, involving charges of bribery and corruption among leading French government officials.
10. The colonial aspirations of the Third Republic had led to war and an anti-French movement in Madagascar that first began with the Franco-Merian war (1883–1885). The war ended with an ambiguous treaty, in which France was given a settlement in Madagascar, though not officially recognized as the colonial government. In 1890 the British government recognized Madagascar as a French protectorate, but the Madagascar government refused to submit to French rule. French troops landed in Madagascar in January 1895, and occupied the state on 30 September 1895, an act followed by an anti-foreign, anti-Christian rebellion that French troops suppressed in 1896.

They are too useful in showing the crimes that power commits for the Revolutionist to desire their immediate removal by any means, violent or otherwise.

T. Parris thought that the object of the meeting might have been more emphatically stated as "Legal Injustice" instead of "Political Justice." Unless the latter was intended to be sarcastic, and that was not apparent from the reading of the bill. He emphasised the fact that justice literally meant, what the law yielded us. Equity was usually meant when the word justice was used, but it was frequently proved that the laws were anything but equitable. However in the present case they had met to protest against punishments being given by Judges through prejudice, that even the law, that harshest of all taskmasters, had allotted for the offences charged against the prisoner Berkmann. The cause of this was class and social prejudices. Our rulers were the property class, and the laws were made and strained for the conservancy of their privileges. Our duty and work therefore was not to use their discredited means of coercion, but to educate the people in the principles of Socialistic Anarchism. And when so educated the power of the privileged classes would pass into the hands of the people, who would use it to destroy the present legal systems and promote equality of opportunity—the only possible basis of liberty.

Miss Amy C. Morant, of the Independent Labor Party, delivered an address which was received with considerable applause.

C. Morton told the audience that there had been a great deal of talk about brotherhood, but that he failed to see how that would improve matters, as brothers quarrelled and robbed each other. What was wanted was the abolition of government and exploitation.

Lawrence said that as those in possession of the wealth of the countries of Europe were the educated classes. It would be vain to preach the use of the weapons of brotherhood to the half educated workers, but seeing that the possessing classes are at all times prepared to use force to prevent the workers bettering their condition there was but one course open, and that was to teach resistance by like force.

A comrade having spoken in Russian, the meeting was brought to a close, having lasted three hours.

Liberty 2 (October 1895): 173–74. Immediately following the report of EG's lecture of 13 September, *Liberty* provided the following update on the rest of her tour: "Emma Goldman left London for Scotland on Saturday 14th of September, and on the following evening addressed a large audience in Bredalbane Hall, Glasgow. The welcome accorded her by Glasgow comrades was most hearty. During the week she was very busy, her engagements including meetings in Edinburgh, and Maybole, as well as in Glasgow. Her appeals on behalf of the Berkmann Release Fund were productive of good results—23/10 being collected by the cigarette makers of Glasgow, and at a social gathering 11/3 were subscribed. The various meetings were in every other way a great success, being largely attended, and the applause given to Emma Goldman and the other speakers most sympathetic. Our Comrade desires us to say that the reception she has met with in England and Scotland fills her with hope and energy for the strenuous continuance in the future of her labors for the cause of Liberty. We have a few 'Berkmann Subscription Lists,' and will gladly forward one to any comrade who will undertake to get it filled up."

Essay in the *TORCH OF ANARCHY*

London, England, 18 October 1895

The Condition of the Workers of America.

"Mind your own business" is a proverb very frequently used by every American. But, unfortunately, its real meaning has so far been misunderstood by the great majority. It has never cared for its own affairs, but has entrusted its business, its life and welfare, to the hands of a few land, mine, and railroad owners, and to merchants of every description.

This privileged minority, true to the teaching of Christ, "Love thy neighbor as thyself," has constantly robbed and exploited the people of America.

In fact only these "noble" gentlemen have grasped the meaning of the proverb "mind your own business." During the last century they have taken precious good care to get as much as possible out of the working class. They have cut down the wages of their employees at every favorable opportunity, driven them out of their homes, destroyed their happiness, suppressed all free thought, till at last they have reduced the country to a state of slavery and degradation.

The bourgeois class of America, which has increased its wealth year by year, battening on the toil of the people by an organized system of wholesale theft, blood-shed, and robbery, has had at its disposal a whole host of officials, superintendents, managers, and foremen, who have considered it their duty to assist their masters in the philanthropic work of tormenting the lives of those in their power.

While the Astors, the Goulds, the Vanderbilts, the Rockefellers, and the Dewits are spending their "valuable" time at the gambling tables of Monte Carlo, or trying to recruit their health, ruined by excessive drink and other vices, in Italy, Paris, or England, their humble servants are minding their affairs, inventing new schemes, and looking about for fresh means to delude and oppress the worker.

While the privileged few are getting richer and richer, the great mass of the people is sinking year by year lower and lower into poverty and distress. While millions of dollars are squandered in theatres, diamonds, dresses, and other luxuries, the downtrodden are leading lives of misery and starvation, working twelve, fourteen, and sixteen hours out of every twenty-four, in order to eke out a miserable existence.

I cannot deny the fact that a small proportion of the American workers are economically much better off than a great many of the workers of England and the Continent. But they are native-born American citizens who have banded themselves together for the purpose of excluding from the advantages they themselves enjoy all belonging to other

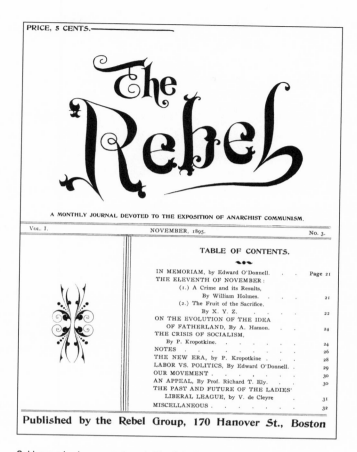

Goldman raised money to launch *The Rebel* (shown here, cover page from November 1895 issue), among the first anarchist communist newspapers in the United States and edited by, among others, American anarchist Harry Kelly. (By permission of the Kate Sharpley Library)

---

nationalities. They look down upon all foreigners, and consider that nobody is as smart, as witty, as capable as they themselves.[1]

Let us try to see who these brave, "free" Americans are.

We say in Russia "Scratch a Russian and you find a Tartar," but if you scratch an American citizen you find either an Englishman, Irishman, Dutchman, Frenchman, German, or a mixture of nationalities.

---

1. EG was most likely referring to the American Federation of Labor, a trade union whose membership was exclusively skilled laborers. She might also have been referring to those anarchists who were in-

The only true Americans were the native Indians, a kind and peaceful lot of people, who were cruelly robbed of their land and happiness by the ancestors of those who now rule the country. I should think myself disgraced had my ancestors been amongst those who mercilessly slaughtered the Indians wholesale, pretending to do so in the name of civilization.

Recently a few American missionaries were killed by an angry Chinese mob. According to the statement of one who escaped, the mob was provoked by the insolent, impertinent and overbearing behaviour of the missionaries; yet the American authorities were thrown into a state of terrible excitement by the "outrage," and the press joined with the clergy of every denomination in denouncing the poor Chinese as savages, and urged the government to demand immediate satisfaction from China.[2]

Were not the men who first settled down in America robbers and swindlers? Are the English, who are pretending to civilize Africa whilst killing hundreds of men and women, any better? Certainly not, and their conduct ought to be all the more strongly condemned inasmuch as they do it in the name of Christianity, whilst the Chinese and Negroes only act in self-defence when they resist the encroachments of the missionaries.

Let us now consider the condition of the American worker. As I said before, there is a small section which is in a good position, has comfortable houses, can afford to send their children to good schools, and so far has not felt the pangs of hunger.

Having inherited the business instincts of their Dutch, English, and Jewish ancestors, the Americans are first-rate business men. The average American is calculating, shrewd, and possesses wonderful skill, which enables him to cheat and swindle his neighbour of his hardly earned dollars. His chance of getting on in the world is, therefore, greater than that of his less smart competitor. Bar-keepers, cashiers, clerks, newspaper distributors and collectors are workers in a good position, but their numbers are so small that it would be unfair to judge the condition of the American worker by their example. The av-

---

volved in anti–foreign labor campaigns, like Henry Weismann, who, while in San Francisco, took an active role in the anti-Chinese campaigns in various Pacific Coast cities.

2. On 9 June 1895, the first reports from China of the destruction of Protestant and Catholic missions in Cheng Tu appeared in the *North China Daily News*. The viceroy of Szechwan province, Liu Ping Chang, was accused by the British and American governments and the press of orchestrating the attack. On 3 August another attack occurred in which Christians were killed at Kiucheng, followed a few days later by an attack on missionaries and their property in Foo-Choo, both in the Fukien province. On 17 August a commission of U.S. and British diplomats arrived in Kiucheng and began establishing order through arrests. The Chinese government refused to allow any inquiries into the Christian massacre; sentiment against foreigners in China was high, fueled by resentment of Britain's opium trade and murders of Chinese nationals in the United States. Not until 29 August did the Chinese government consent to help the commission. Seven prisoners convicted of complicity in the most recent massacres were executed at Kiucheng in the presence of foreign consuls, but the Chinese authorities refused to punish the viceroy. The U.S. State Department's response was thwarted by geographical distance and by the many errors and misspellings of Chinese place names, which served to confuse and exaggerate the issue.

erage wage of the working class in most branches is 6 dollars a week, for a working day of 12, 14, or even 16 hours. People working in the tailoring, cloak-making and cigarette trades do not earn more than 4 dollars a week, and there are thousands of people walking the streets of New York, Chicago and other great cities who would work for even less if they only could.

The unemployed movement of 1893 frightened the authorities to such an extent that, fearing a riot, they felt themselves compelled to do something for the people. But what these "charitable gentlemen" who feast on luxuriously prepared meats and drink sparkling wines actually did was but a mockery in the eyes of the starving unemployed.

They arrested first the speakers and leaders of the unemployed, sentencing them to rigorous terms of imprisonment in the hope of breaking the spirit of the people by so doing. After that they opened a few kitchens where coffee and tea could be obtained for 1 cent, but, as they needed the cent first, these kitchens did not prove of much use to the starving. Some land-owners gave a few hundred acres for the unemployed to work on, but the opportunities for work provided by it were but a few drops in the ocean of misery, especially as only a few families were supplied with the raw material and machinery necessary for tilling the soil.

Strange to say all this did not improve the condition of the unemployed. The number of people living in the slums of New York to-day is greater that it ever was before. Thousands of people live in the utmost poverty, surrounded by filth. They do not know where to turn for relief. Young women are compelled to sell their bodies on the street, and half-grown children, shivering with cold, without home or shelter of any kind, are forced to beg or steal, and some even to lie down in the streets and die.

Even the lot of those who have work is not much better.

Men, women, and children have to work from morn till night, never enjoying a breath of fresh air, never seeing the sun in the clear heavens, living on a few cents per day, and having everlastingly before their eyes the terrors of starvation. All this misery exists side-by-side with wealth and extravagance unequalled elsewhere. These horrors abound in nearly the richest country in the world, a country on which nature has bestowed its richest gifts. The people who have created all this wealth, who have built the mansions, found the gold, woven the silk and tilled the land are living in misery and degradation, whilst those who have robbed them of everything they have created are living in luxury, feasting, gambling, and generally enjoying themselves at the workers' expense.

If the stones of the mansions in which the rich live, the diamonds, silks and satins they wear could speak they would tell a horrible tale—a tale which would shake the nerves of the blood-suckers and exploiters of labour, and make them dread the day when the people, tired of their long sufferings, the wretchedness of their lot, will rise to revenge themselves on those who are responsible for it all.

And the apathy and indifference which have so long crippled the energy of the masses is at last beginning to disappear. The strikes at Homestead, Tennessee, Buffalo, Chicago,

Brooklyn and New York[3] have proved that the people of America are tired of leading the lives of dogs. The energy and enthusiasm displayed during these strikes, and the heroic way in which the worker has met death in the fights with the police and militia have shown what the people were capable of. They have been in earnest of what the workers will do when called upon to fight the great fight for the recovery of their rights and the welfare of all dear to them.

Of course, the authorities have used every means to sap the courage of the strikers. They have instructed the police and the militia to shoot down the strikers and show no mercy to anyone who dares to rebel against their power. We are told that the police and the military exist only for the protection of the people, but it is a fact that always and everywhere they have been used to protect property and to defend and uphold the powers that be.

But bullets and imprisonment cannot destroy an ideal. Five men were murdered in Chicago on the 11th of November, 1887. Lawfully and rightly, say the upholders of the present social order. But their deaths have not been able to silence their voices, which sound louder and louder from beyond the grave, and their ideas live on. Alexander Berkmann's brave act showed to all who wish to see the real cause of the people's misery. Anarchists are no longer looked upon as a set of fools or ruffians, and the principles of those who have died on the gallows or are languishing in prison are to-day discussed in the press, in the pulpit, and in the mansions of the rich. Hard work is before us, as it will not be easy to convince the American workman, who prides himself on his freedom, that he is a slave. But I see the day before me when the workers of America will unite with those of other countries, and the people rising in righteous wrath will wreck the system of brutality and tyranny which to-day crushes the life-blood out of them. It is a system which gives to the few the power to enslave the many, which upholds corruption, prostitution and degradation, and which must be destroyed before freedom be possible.

On the ruins of the rotten system Anarchy will be established, and Anarchy will render possible the welfare and happiness of all.

EMMA GOLDMANN.

Torch of Anarchy, 18 October 1895, pp. 75–77. Reprinted in the *Firebrand,* 17 November 1895, pp. 3–4.

---

3. In addition to the 1892 Homestead steel strike, EG refers to a coal miners' strike in Briceville, Tennessee, in 1891–1892; a railroad switchmen's strike in Buffalo in August 1892; the 1894 Pullman strike in Chicago; a cloakmakers' strike in Buffalo, New York, in the fall of 1894; and a strike of streetcar employees in Brooklyn in January 1895. Strikers at Homestead, Briceville, Buffalo, and Brooklyn were defeated when local authorities called in the National Guard; the Pullman strike was crushed after President Grover Cleveland sent in federal troops.

DEAR SIR!

You will be surprised to receive this lines, as I am a stranger to you,[1] still I think, you have heard my name. I am here for a short stay and would very much like to see you. Will you kindly inform me, when I can find you at home? If convinient Wednesday afternoon, I shall remain here only until Friday next.

SINSERLY YOURS.
EMMA GOLDMANN[2]

ALS, Augustin Hamon Archive, IISH. Addressed at top to "Mr Hamon." Return address given as Emma Goldmann, c/o Mdm. Resteger, St. André des Ars. 25.

1. EG met the French sociologist and anarchist Augustin Hamon for the first time in Paris in 1896.
2. The "n" in Goldman was written with a bar over it, the German language indicator for doubling a letter.

To AUGUSTIN HAMON

New York, 28 April 1896

DEAR COMRADE.

I promised to write to you occasonnally, but I am sorry I cann't furnish you many news at present.

There is not a subject important enough to write much upon, except that a London Anarchist, John Turner by name, (I think you must have met him during your soujourn in Engl.) is doing some propaganda here.[1] The anarchistic Idea's do not seem to meet with much success in this blessed Land, of the "free and the "brave." You rightly judged the American's as a practical people; they are always trying to find out the financial value of an Idea and do not care what the future will bring them, eagerly being after the "dividends" for the present time.

I doubt whether any Anarchist as a representative of his union will go to the London congress.[2] The Comrades have until recently not been in contact with the trades union movement of this country and the result is, that none of our people will be delegated.

I learned through the papers, that affairs are very lively in Paris, what is the truth about it?

I mailed copie's of several anarchistic papers to you, the *Alarm* is not in existence any more, neither is the *Brandfackel* nor the *Anarchist. Sturmglacken* is a new paper.[3]

A very good Friend of mine, has read two years ago, the first edition of your book; *Psychologie du Militaire Professionnel,* he has been delighted with it and at present, he is eagerly studying the "Défense" you prefixed the second edition of your oeuvre.[4]

---

1. See note 3 to "Eastern and European Propaganda," Essay in the *Firebrand,* 24 May 1895, below.
2. The London congress of the socialist Second International, held from 27 July through 3 August 1896, was the occasion for the expulsion of anarchist delegates by the socialist majority on the congress's second day. Anarchists had previously attempted to gain admittance at international congresses held in Brussels (1891) and in Zurich (1893), and had planned to hold their own meeting in 1896, in anticipation of the expulsion. Anarchist delegates included Peter Kropotkin, Errico Malatesta, Élisée Jean-Jacques Reclus, Gustav Landauer, Louise Michel, Charles Mowbray, Ted Leggatt, Jean Grave, Émile Pouget, Augustin Hamon, and Fernand Pelloutier.
3. The anarchist weekly *Alarm* was published in Chicago between 1884 and 1887 and in New York until 1888. The Chicago-based anarchist weekly *Sturmglocken (The Alarm Bell)* had a four-week run in March and April of 1896.
4. *Psychologie du militaire professionnel* (Paris: A. Savine, 1894) was vilified by reviewers, politicians, clergymen, and officers as unpatriotic, undermining of French society, and even treasonous. Their reactions sparked Hamon's preface to the second edition, which appeared in 1895, in defense of the book as a work of science, in which he drew on various examples of historical and textual precedents. Though the French military threatened legal action, it did not carry out a suit against Hamon.

I am very sorry, I cann't read it myself, but my knowledge of the French language does not go so far. I would highly appreciate to have La. P. du. M. P. in the German translation.[5]

I presume you are very busy, but should you find a few minute's of leisure, please let me know, something of the French movement.

FRATERNALLY

EMMA GOLDMAN

ALS, Augustin Hamon Archive, IISH.

5. *Psychologie des Berufssoldaten* (Leipzig, 1896). EG later called *Psychologie du militaire professionnel* (1894) a "brilliant work" and its author "the man who probably better than anyone else understands the psychology of the *Attentater*," in her essay "The Psychology of Political Violence" (1911).

Essay in the *FIREBRAND*

New York, 24 May 1896

Eastern and European Propaganda.

I was surprised to learn that you did not know of comrade John Turner's propaganda in this country.[1] I think it very important for the western friends to know how the propaganda is going on in the east.

I cannot say we have an Anarchistic movement of any importance in the east, but I am confident we could work one up if there were people both able and willing to participate in the work. Just what could be done we have seen by Comrades Mowbray[2] and Turner's visits[3] to the States. Mowbray has traveled as far west as St. Louis, holding good meetings all over, not to speak of the success met with in Boston. Thanks to his work, the Anarchists held a May day demonstration on the 3d and the Central Labor union arranged meetings for Comrade Turner[4]—things never before heard of here. We see that if a man is determined and has the ability to make his way he succeeds. It is foolish to say the American workingmen have no wish to study Anarchistic ideas. Give them a chance and they will do it. Of course our principles must be propagated in a plain and popular language, such as the *Firebrand* uses.

Comrade John Turner has left his work in London and come over to the "freest land in the world", though he was aware of the fact that the Americans are a hard lot, to preach Anarchism to. He is a very energetic and earnest fellow, a fine speaker and an excellent debater, and, above all, he is not conceited like many others who know less. We could suc-

---

1. EG's essay was an undated response to an announcement in the 26 April 1896 *Firebrand* on John Turner's first U.S. tour. One of the editors of the Portland, Oregon, anarchist-communist newspaper, Henry Addis, lamented that he only learned about the tour from an article in *Freiheit*: "It seems strange that none of the comrades were interested enough to send us word of comrade Turner's arrival, and his work and plans. We wish to make the *Firebrand* a journal of the movement, but to do this we must have the co-operation of the comrades everywhere. In order to give news of the movement it must be sent in by comrades"(*Firebrand*, 26 April 1896, p. 3).

2. English anarchist Charles Mowbray traveled to the United States in 1894, lectured on the East Coast, and eventually settled in Boston in 1895, where he was responsible for introducing Harry Kelly to anarchism.

3. English anarchist John Turner spent seven months in the United States beginning in April 1896, traveling as far west as Denver. He delivered approximately one hundred lectures, debating various political opponents including single-taxers, Tuckerite individualists, and free-silver advocates. EG helped organize Turner's New York lectures. For an interview with Turner about his American tour, reprinted from the London anarchist newspaper *The Alarm*, see "John Turner's View of the American Labor Movement," *Firebrand*, 20 December 1896, p. 4; see also "Personal Impressions of the United States," serialized in *Freedom* (London, March and May 1897).

4. The Boston Central Labor Union arranged meetings for Turner, from the 2nd to the 6th of May, including a large May Day meeting on the 3rd.

cessfully spread our ideas if he knew the localities and did not have to depend on those comrades who are willing enough to help, but who have not the least experience and understanding as to how to arrange meetings.

Comrade Turner has addressed three meetings in New York City, which have been well attended.[5] Not so those in Newark and Paterson;[6] but certainly Comrade Turner is not to blame for that. On the 30th of April we gave a farewell entertainment to our comrade. The hall was packed. A number of detectives and policemen were present, looking for a job. Comrades Edelmann, Mowbray, Turner, Withington and myself spoke,[7] but we did not seem to gratify the wishes of the officials, as they went away without running any of us in. I am sorry to state that the financial result of the affair was not satisfactory.

John Turner, the English anarchist and labor organizer, met Goldman in London in 1895. Turner was the first prominent European English-speaking anarchist to tour America; Goldman helped arrange his itinerary and chaired many of his meetings. (Labadie Collection, University of Michigan)

We have formed a group, meeting for the present at 50 E. First street.[8] Our work for the summer will be to raise a fund large enough to carry on propaganda next fall and winter. So far, we have issued an Anarchist May day manifesto of which several thousand were distributed on the 2d at the demonstration of workingmen at Union Square.

I can also inform the *Firebrand* readers that our brave Comrade Alex. Berkman's case is being pushed. No definite step can be taken until 1897. All we want to do now is to get money, and the more the better, as we will need about $1000. I beg the comrades of the *Firebrand* to appeal for aid; if all will help we are sure to liberate him some day.

I have made a trip through different countries on the continent, where I found our ideas marching on wonderfully. In England and Scotland meetings are held several times a week in halls and parks, thousands of workingmen and women listening eagerly

5. Turner spoke on 18 April to the Manhattan Single Tax Club on "Anarchist-Communism," on 19 April to the Socialist Labor Party on "The Class Struggle," and on 21 April to the Anarchist American Group of New York at Clarendon Hall on "Anarchy an Essential of Socialism," before traveling to Philadelphia where he lectured on the 22nd and 23rd of April. He then returned to New York City where he lectured on the 24th and 26th at Clarendon Hall on "The Policy of the Future" and "The Power of Capitalism."

6. On 27 April Turner spoke in Newark on "Church and State, Twin Enemies of the People" with Lothrop Withington, and on 29 April in Paterson he shared the platform at a meeting with Charles Mowbray.

7. On 30 April a farewell meeting was held for Turner at Clarendon Hall, replete with songs, recitations, a German choir, and speeches by John Edelmann, Lothrop Withington, Charles Mowbray, Turner, and EG. Turner then traveled to Boston, Buffalo, and Cleveland. EG noted that Turner's tour gave her her first real opportunity to address audiences in English (*LML*, p. 179).

8. Justus Schwab's saloon was located at 50 East First Street.

Masthead from 14 March 1897 issue of *Firebrand,* the U.S. English-language anarchist communist newspaper that featured Goldman's first explicitly feminist essay, "Marriage," in its 18 July 1897 issue. (By permission of the Kate Sharpley Library)

to the speeches, where leaflets, manifestos and papers are distributed in large quantities. In France the admirable acts of Ravachol, Henry, Vaillant, Caserio and others have done more for the spreading of our principles than ten years of writing and speaking.[9] *Les Temps Nouveaux* (formerly *La Révolte*) has increased its circulation from 8000 to 18,000, and *La Sociale* (formerly *Père Peinard*) from 8000 to 20,000. Anarchist publications are springing up in all parts of France. In Austria the comrades have to confine themselves to a clandestine propaganda, as the authorities make daily arrests, imprisoning or expelling everyone who takes any noted part in the movement. The plutocrats are confident now that they have annihilated Anarchistic propaganda, but they will soon find out that imprisonment and suffering cannot stop the tide from flowing on.

Firebrand, 24 May 1896, p. 2. Following the publication of her essay, EG wrote to the *Firebrand* protesting the omission of her name as author and offering to contribute an occasional report on anarchist activities. The editors defended their omission of her name on the basis that only her covering letter and not the essay itself was signed. "It was a matter of regret with us that your name was withheld, but supposed you had reasons for it. We would be glad to announce you as New York correspondent, and other well-known comrades as correspondents from other cities; then the comrades could report to you and we would get all the news in proper order and succinct form" (*Firebrand,* 14 June 1896, p. 4).

9. EG refers to François-Claudius Koenigstein (who was known by his pseudonym, Ravachol), Émile Henry, Auguste Vaillant, and Sante Caserio. For further discussion of the *attentater,* see "Emma Goldman in London," Article in *Liberty,* October 1895, above.

Dear Com.

I hope you will pardon my long silence.

I received your two postal-cards, the Journal *L'Aube*,[1] the German translation of your interesting book. *Psychologie du Militaire Professionel*,[2] also the newspaper *Paris* and a clipping of *Les temps nouveaux*[3] for which accept my thanks. I delighted very much in reading your Book. I think you have done great service to our cause with the work on the *Psychologie du Militaire professionel*. I am very pleased to learn of the energetic undertaking of the Carmeaux Workers,[4] you wrote about in the newspaper *Paris* and I shall have it translated for one of our english anarchist papers.

I have sent *L'Aube* to a Magazine, asking if they would accept contributions of your pen. As soon, as I will receive a reply, I will let you know.

I regret very much not to be in a position to attend the Congress, but I am satisfied to know, that you and other able Comrades will be there to represent our cause.

Do you ever think to visit our "glorious" country America

I should appreciate it a great favor, if you will drop me a line now and than, about the proceedings of the Congress. You might write in French if English gives you too much trouble.

I shall send you several copies of different anarchist papers and Pamphlates in a few day's.

With best greetings
Emma Goldman

ALS, Augustin Hamon Archive, IISH.

1. A French literary, political, and artistic journal with libertarian leanings, *L'Aube* was published in Paris from April 1896 to July 1897. Edited by Paul Adam, Pierre Guédy, Augustin Hamon, and André Ibels, among others, it was one of the most ambitious publications of its time, publishing articles by Edward Carpenter, André Gide, Knut Hamsun, Henrik Ibsen, Bernard Lazare, and August Strindberg, and illustrations by Toulouse-Lautrec and Edouard Vuillard. Most likely, EG is referring to one or more of the issues containing Hamon's "Notes de Voyage: En Angleterre," serialized in five installments between May 1896 and February 1897, which was based on his 1894 London diary.
2. In EG's letter of 28 April 1896 to Hamon, she asks for a German translation of his book.
3. An article by Hamon in *Les Temps Nouveaux* was reprinted in the *Firebrand*, 26 July 1896, p. 2, translated by "A.D" (possibly A. A. Davies); the article reports and comments on the manifesto of the Associated Anarchists group of Great Britain.
4. The livelihood of glassblowers was threatened in the 1890s by the introduction of continuous-flow gas ovens and mechanized bottle-turning, two improvements that meant factory owners could hire less-skilled workers for less pay. After an unsuccessful strike in 1895 in protest of wage cuts and the letting go of skilled glassblowers, Carmeaux glassworkers established a cooperative factory, the Verrerie Ouvrière, at Albi, about ten miles from Carmeaux, in 1896.

The Berkman Fund Again.

You have published an attack upon me written by a certain P. Franco,[1] in the *Firebrand* of July 26th,[2] and I hope you will not refuse to publish my reply.

First of all I must emphasize that I do not write these lines in order to satisfy the impudent inquisitiveness of P. Franco, or others like him, who would not hesitate a moment to besmirch one's honor at any cost.

The publishers of the *Firebrand* certainly have a right to publish whatever they please, but they have no right to publish any accusations without knowing whether they are false or true.

I did not expect the comrades of the *Firebrand* to defend me, as I can very well defend myself; nor did I ask them to make me acquainted with the contents of private letters, as that comrade Isaak[3] received from one of the *Firebrand* readers and which, according to Isaak was directed against me, stating that I had spent the money collected for Berkmann for my personal use, during my tour on the Continent. The man who has thus expressed himself about me to comrade Isaak has also written one to me, in which he says among other things; "Of course, I do not mean to say that you had used the money collected for Berkmann for yourself." This letter I have sent to comrade Isaak, which ought to convince him that the man has either written a falsehood to him, or has not moral courage

---

1. P. Franco was a London-based French anarchist possibly residing at the anarchist International School run by Louise Michel and Agnes Henry.
2. In the column in which Franco's letter, translated from French, appeared, J. H. Morris lamented that the *Firebrand* was being blamed by both sides in the dispute but acknowledged that the weekly had received other complaints about the solicitation and disposal of funds for AB; the column reasoned, "since we have published appeals for the fund it seems to us only fair, though we regret the occasion, to publish objections to the raising thereof and questions as to the disposal of moneys already obtained" (*Firebrand*, 26 July 1896, p. 2). Franco's letter read:

   During the twelve years that I have been in the Anarchist movement I have never seen anything more distasteful than the demand for money from all sides "for propaganda," especially the way it is carried on by Emma Goldman in the Berkman case, according to the *Firebrand* Nos. 10 and 19. She says some very fine things, and among others that $1000 should be raised for extricating Berkman from the toils, but says nothing about how this money is to be expended. And why is this time and money used for Berkman alone? are there not other comrades equally deserving of sympathy and assistance? For my part, all comrades who have sacrificed their liberty are as deserving as this one. The question here is, How many dollars did she get in Europe, and what did she do with them? No one seems to have courage enough to ask for an accounting. You may ask why I do not go to her for details regarding the matter. Among other reasons, I do not speak either English or German. I do not believe in using Anarchy as a good milch cow to be milked on all occasions.

3. Abe Isaak was editor of the *Firebrand*.

enough to uphold the same accusations in his letter to me. P. Franco in his letter to the *Firebrand* has lied, as well, as the man in his letter to Comrade Isaak. Franco says he did not ask me about the Berkmann fund, because he can speak neither English nor German. Now, those who know him are acquainted with the fact, that he can speak English enough to be understood, enough to make disturbance in meetings, as he did both in London and here, and that he knew enough English to spread false reports about Comrades Mowbray, Merlino, Cipriani[4] and other well known men who have suffered in the movement long before anyone knew of the existence of Franco. The reason why he did not ask me about the Berkmann fund is, because he is a coward, ready to admit this any time himself. Well, I do not care to take up too much space in talking of Franco; it is beneath any honest and decent person to spend time with such a miserable creature.

J. H. Morris, in his comment on Franco's letter says: "According to the principles of Anarchist association any member of the group, whose object is the release of Berkmann may know what is done with the fund to which he has subscribed." Certainly, and Comrade Morris could have saved himself the trouble to tell me that, as I claim to understand the principles of Anarchist association. According to my understanding of Anarchist principles, those who have *never* subscribed a cent, *never cared* for Berkmann's release, have no right to ask any accounts of whomsoever, and to poke noses into other people's affairs. I am the last one to give information to people like P. Franco or the conceited and impertinent fellow who wrote to Comrade Isaak.

To those who have assisted me in my work for my friend Alexander Berkmann, I say this: The money collected abroad by myself and other comrades amounts to about $20 and was sent to Charles Schneider, Pittsburg, Pa., who was appointed at the time as treasurer of the Berkmann fund by the Pittsburg comrades. Anyone wishing to know how the money was used will do well to address him.

As to Berkmann, he is not only my comrade, but also my friend and a very dear one, too. I shall continue to work for him as energetically as I have until now and all impertinent attacks and slanders will not induce me to give up the fight.

I am very sorry the *Firebrand* has taken up personal matters, and can only predict that if its publishers continue in the same way, they will only put nails to their own coffin.[5]

EMMA GOLDMANN.

4. EG refers to Charles Mowbray, Saverio Merlino, and Amilcare Cipriani.
5. Immediately below this letter J. H. Morris, speaking for the *Firebrand*, offered the following response: "We are glad to publish the above information in reply to inquiries received at this office, but we are sorry Comrade Goldmann takes the matter in the spirit here exhibited. We have published no accusations, and we could not know the truth or falsity of any we may have received without an accounting from her. The letter referred to as having been received by Comrade Isaak was not a private letter, but written to the *Firebrand*. In the most friendly spirit Comrade Goldmann was informed of the question raised as to the disposition of the fund, and we are sorry to say the reply consisted of bluster similar to the above. It was not our personal business to know the truth or falsity of any accusations or to settle matters between Comrade Goldmann and her questioners; but the *Firebrand*, as a representative of the movement, has been made a 'go-between' in the case, and however much we

Firebrand, 23 August 1896, p. 2. The *Firebrand* (and later, *Free Society*) frequently carried appeals for AB's expenses, especially his legal fees and the finance reports by the Berkman Defense Association from Pittsburgh. Similar reports appeared in other anarchist journals including *Lucifer, the Lightbearer.*

may regret it, we have been able to see no fair way to avoid it. Were we to follow her suggestion as to personalities, her own letter would furnish the first occasion for exclusion, because it is the first to indulge in personalities and hard names. Personal enmity may have prompted those letters of inquiry, but we are not omniscient and could have no knowledge of this. Personally, I want to say that what I said concerning the principles of Anarchist association was not intended for Comrade Goldmann's enlightenment, but was in the nature of a reason for publication of the inquiry coming, supposably, from a contributor to the fund; also as a hint to such inquirers as were not contributors. If, as appears from the above letter, the two inquirers mentioned are non-contributors, it is hoped they will have the good sense to keep still in the future. At any rate the matter closes here, so far as the *Firebrand* is concerned."

Article in the *PITTSBURG LEADER*

Pittsburgh, 22 November 1896

A Woman Anarchist.

Emma Goldman Teaches Anarchy to 250 Laboring People.

Her Lecture in German to an Audience in the Duquesne Dance Hall
on Wylie Avenue Last Night—She Pours Red Hot Anarchy Into the Mass
and Leaves It to Work—Her Criticisms of Politics.

A motley crew was the 250 men and women who assembled in the Duquesne dancing hall, on Wylie avenue, last night to listen to a lecture by Emma Goldman, the Anarchist. The men in the audience mostly kept their hats on and puffed industriously at vile-smelling stogies and cigarettes. The air was dense with smoke and reeking with fumes when Miss Goldman came in about 8:30 o'clock.

H. Gordon, president of the Pittsburg Socialistic society, opened the meeting with a short talk, and then introduced Miss Goldman.[1] The latter is a short and rather good-looking young woman, whose deep gray eyes and gold eyeglasses give her a decided air of intellectuality and finesse. Miss Goldman began at once her lecture, which was delivered in the German language, and in a full, clear voice she continued to exhort her audience for over an hour and a half.

In substance she said:

"Fellow-workmen and fellow-workwomen, you know it is an old saying that Anarchists do not believe in a God. Yet, were I a praying woman, I should certainly pray that God would take pity on the poor laborer and give us fair weather for our meeting to-morrow. Moses of old led the children for 40 long years through the wilderness, wanderers on the face of the globe, before they at last reached the land of promise, and from that day to this have the Jews been a persecuted race, hunted from land to land, until finally they turned to America, the new land of promise, where they can all do what they please, until a big policeman with a club comes along and tells them to desist. The difference between the life of the Jew in Russia and in America is that there he is under the surveillance of the gendarmes, who are a poor class like themselves, while here in Amer-

---

1. Immediately following EG's lectures in Pittsburgh, Harry Gordon, also the treasurer of AB's defense fund, wrote enthusiastically about her meetings to the *Firebrand*, complimenting the press for their fair and "polite" reportage, and criticizing the police and detectives in the audience for their attempts to verbally entrap EG during the discussion. He made a point of asserting that EG was an active and able comrade received with pleasure by her audiences, then he ended his article with an accounting of the receipts and expenses of the Berkman defense fund. See *Firebrand,* 20 December 1896, pp. 3–4.

ica they are ordered about by burly policemen who live at ease and draw fat salaries. There he must work like a galley slave whether he will or no. Here he is free—free to starve, free to be robbed and swindled on every hand. But the moment he seeks to organize labor, or assert his rights or strike for the defense of his dearest interests he is no longer free, but is apprehended and thrown in prison. The greatest hope of the few in this country is that he can save enough from his earnings to make him a wealthy man when he returns to his family in Europe. He forgets that here in this free land when he earns $5 he must at once spend it to feed and clothe himself.

"Most Jewish youths when they come to this country know no trade, for in Europe it is a disgrace for them to work at a trade—that is left to the lower classes among the Gentiles, while the Jews are the tradespeople. Consequently when he gets here and finds all mercantile pursuits filled by Americans, he is destitute of a means of support, and very soon learns that when it comes to cheating he is far outstripped by the American born.

"Are not the richest people here Americans? Is there any place in the 400[2] for a Jew? All the capital is in the hands of Americans and they control every interest. The Jew has every opportunity, according to law, of rising officially and can fill any office except that of President. Then why does he not rise unless because he is kept down and deprived of his rights by Americans? The Americans rail at the European and blame all our social evils on 'those foreigners.' They forget that their forefathers, the English, the Dutch, French, etc., came to this country and in the name of justice, of civilization, and of God, robbed and murdered the innocent savage, the sole possessor of the land for ages. Moses, when he came down from Mt. Sinai, brought us ten laws, one of which was 'Thou shalt not steal.' This law has come to be applied only to a certain class. For example, a poor, starving wretch, dying from hunger and cold, steals bread or clothing or money. Brought before a judge it is demanded of him if he did not know of the Divine prohibition of theft. Then he is given a so-called trial and imprisoned. If the man of wealth steals whole estates, whole factories, entire railroads or immense fortunes on change he is called a 'shrewd man' and honored with rank and title. (Applause.)

"If a rich woman is caught shoplifting, the wealthy court has a new word for her, and says she is afflicted with 'kleptomania' and pities her. (Applause and laughter.)

"We are told by the good Christians that we must live and endure these evils in Godlike patience, awaiting our reward in heaven. What do I care what awaits me in heaven! I have to live now on earth! They tell us laws will regulate these evils. Through study and education we are becoming more and more convinced that the more laws men have the more miserable is their condition.

"In politics there are no good parties. When these parties place their candidates before the public they fill their mouths with sweet-sounding promises of good to be done and reforms to be achieved, but when these selfsame men come to power they at once forget their good words and spurn the laboring man, who elected them, underfoot, call-

2. Originally a reference to the rich four hundred New York elites who would supposedly fit into Mrs. Astor's ballroom.

ing him a fool. Bryan is an intelligent man and an advocate of the people.[3] McKinley is also a good man, but his past record as governor is against him.[4] But you cannot put your trust in any of them, fellow-workmen! Cleveland was paid $200,000 for his four years' service to this country, and yet he became a multi-millionaire. Perhaps God was good, and rained down money like manna of old. No! Cleveland it is who made a contract with the Czar of Russia, the greatest tyrant on earth, stipulating for a consideration of a few million to send back suspect Nihilists to Russia, where they could be cast in prison or executed.[5] Cleveland it is who even now is receiving money from Spain for refusing to listen to the cry of distress from king-ridden Cuba.[6] From President to policeman it is the same, save that where the 'copper' is tipped a dollar Grover rakes in a million. I will not prophesy of McKinley, for he is not yet in the chair, and has not been tried, but let us hope he will not spend the time of his administration fishing and duck shooting. (Laughter.)

"It is not the inclination of any man in power to better the condition of the laboring man unless his own is greatly helped."

Miss Goldman then repeated in glowing details the story of the creation of the first man and woman, and their expulsion from the garden because they ate of fruit that gave them knowledge. "God was right," she said. "When He kept them in ignorance he had absolute control over them, and now our potentates are just as wise as God, and would forbid the mass of the people eating of the fruit of the tree of knowledge, for they know that then they will appreciate their degradation and rebel."

She likened the condition of the Anarchist now to that of the Saviour in His last days, when He said, "Whoso is not for Me is against Me." "Workmen of all lands, unite, and we shall be free," cried the lecturer. "What wonder we are despised and trodden down when we do not resist, but say: 'God will protect us.'"

3. Democratic candidate for president in 1896, William Jennings Bryan generally appealed more strongly to the rural population, who favored his free-silver policy, than to urban workers. His campaign rallies in the East were often organized and attended by radical groups.

4. William McKinley, with the help of Cleveland industrialist and politician Mark Hanna, was elected governor of Ohio in 1981 and reelected in 1893. In response to widespread strikes and social unrest, McKinley attempted to maintain order by calling the Ohio National Guard into constant service. State troops, often under the military supervision of the governor, forcefully suppressed the 1894 coal miners' strikes at Mount Sterling and in Guernsey County, among others. McKinley also sent militiamen to intervene in the march of J. S. Coxey's army of unemployed workingmen, as they traveled across Ohio in the summer of 1894 to Washington, D.C.

5. Article three of the U.S.-Russia extradition treaty, signed in March 1887, stipulated that any person who had attacked the tsar or a member of his family, or who had "attempted to commit or participate" in such an attack, was subject to extradition from the United States to Russia. Opponents of the treaty, who included George Kennan, Oscar Straus, and William Dean Howells, argued that under article three any Russian political dissident living in the United States could be extradited. Despite this opposition, the treaty was eventually ratified by Congress on 6 February 1893. Although the Cleveland administration negotiated the treaty, Benjamin Harrison signed it into law on 14 February 1893. Subsequent campaigns for abrogation of the treaty failed.

6. The insurrection in Cuba against Spanish rule began in 1895 and attracted considerable attention in the United States. To preserve peace with Spain and neutrality in the region, in 1895 the Cleveland administration maintained neutrality toward the Cuban insurgents. Cleveland's policies were unpopular among those who supported Cuban independence, particularly Republican party members and much of the press.

Continuing, Miss Goldman told the fable of the old, old man who was seen planting trees, and when asked why he did so when he could hope to eat none of their fruit, replied that he had posterity to provide for. So, she said, should the Socialist do who, though in ignorance himself, and consequently in poverty, should see to it that his children are educated, so that what they earn shall go to themselves and not be taken away to feed the rich. She made a bitter attack on Carnegie.[7] "He slaves you and robs you to feed his already fat purse and then turns about and to conciliate you, presents you with a fine library, music hall, and all that sort of thing when you are too poor to even pay to hear the music."

She urged upon her hearers that they fight for shorter hours and more pay. She bewailed the necessity of child labor and its results. "When such scenes of starvation as are daily noted about us become common it is time to cry 'Give us liberty or give us death,'" she said. Then lowering her voice from its high key of excitement to the modulated tones of a conversation she began to speak of Alexander Berkman, the Anarchist who is now serving a twenty-two year sentence in the Western penitentiary for attempting the life of H. C. Frick at the time of the Homestead strike. She pictured Frick in the enjoyment of health while Berkman languishes behind prison bars.

"To be an Anarchist is enough to get yourself hung in America for attempting even a small crime," she asserted. The judge, she said, knew Frick to be a millionaire, while his assailant was a hated Anarchist.

"Alexander Berkman," she exclaimed, "is good, brave, noble. What he did he did of his own accord, prompted only by a spirit of resentment against the brutality and mishandling he had suffered from the superintendent of the mills.[8] We Anarchists make no distinction as to race or color, so it is our duty to intercede for him because he stood for our interests. Therefore I appeal to you to contribute a little to alleviate the misery of his prison existence."

Miss Goldman herself took up the collection, which amounted to $10.78.

"When I was in prison, to my shame, for ten months, I did not find rich women ever confined. Only the poor are punished. The rich do not commit crimes. In the name of Berkman I thank you for your gift and will say that no one knows what may happen in this country before his long sentence expires. The day may come when he shall see the walls of his prison fall down, blown up by the hand of the revolutionist."

This closed the lecture after which followed a sort of question box, conducted by Miss Goldman. She announced for a meeting in the same place this afternoon at 3 o'clock to be addressed in English.

Pittsburg (Pa.) Leader, 22 November 1896, p. 6. EG was interviewed in the *Leader* two days earlier. See "Emma Goldman Here," *Pittsburg Leader*, 20 November 1896, *EGP*, reel 47.

7. Financier and steel magnate Andrew Carnegie was also a major benefactor to libraries, post offices, and cultural and scientific institutions.
8. AB, who never worked in the steel mills, was motivated by the brutality directed against the workers at Homestead rather than by any personal injury, and it is unlikely that EG meant to imply otherwise.

Article in the *PITTSBURG POST*

Pittsburgh, 27 November 1896

Goldman's Cry Against Society.

Noted Female Anarchist Deplores the Fate of the Haymarket Murderers.

Bombthrower's Noble Act.

Doesn't Believe in What She Calls the Ballot-Box Swindle.

A Collection for Berkmann.

Not much edified with the condition of anarchism in Allegheny county, but still hoping for the best, Emma Goldman left the city last night for the west. Emma's last words formed an appeal to local anarchists to join together and carry on the "good work," and to forget all personal differences and cease from bickering.

The famous anarchist's address was made in a hall at 1012 Penn avenue. The attendance was but sparse, applause was rare and there was not much enthusiasm. Once when Miss Goldman told what a shame it was that workingmen starved and were scantily clad while the store windows were filled with things good to eat and wear, that they might take by simply reaching out their hands, utter silence followed her remark. Pittsburg anarchists seem to approve of a law against taking what belongs to someone else, and they were not prepared to go to the length of taking unlawfully what is not theirs. So they did not applaud that part of Miss Goldman's speech.

Miss Goldman was introduced as one who would discuss the "murder of November 11, 1887,"[1] namely, the execution of the anarchists. Miss Goldman is a petite, blonde, good looking woman, to whom a pair of spectacles give a professorial look. She advanced to the platform and plunged right into her subject. Her address was in German.

"Jesus was crucified, Huss was burned, Bruno[2] was killed," she said, "because they were opposed to the order of things existing in their day and dared to advocate the rights of humanity."[3]

---

1. On 11 November 1887 Albert Parsons, August Spies, George Engel, and Adolph Fischer were executed for their alleged part in the bomb that exploded in Haymarket Square on 4 May 1886.
2. EG refers to Giordano Bruno, the 16th-century Dominican monk martyred by the Spanish Inquisition, and to Jan Hus, an early 15th-century religious reformer burnt at the stake for heresy.
3. EG echoes the words of August Spies at his 1886 trial after the Haymarket incident: "Truth crucified in Socrates, in Christ, in Giordano Bruno, in Huss, in Galileo, still lives—they and others whose number is legion have preceded us on this path. We are ready to follow!"

"The execution of the Chicago anarchists November 11, 1887," she continued, "was a horrible crime. What had those men done? Had they made widows and orphans, had they murdered, had they robbed?"

THEY COMMITTED NO CRIME.

"No," she continued, "I do not believe that anybody can say with a clear conscience that the Chicago anarchists committed a crime. They did one thing, a thing that from time immemorial had been punished by society with death and prison—they dared to think. They explained to the people in a popular way the writings of Rousseau, Paine and Jefferson, that all men are created free and equal and have equal rights.[4] They were simply anarchists, and because they were anarchists they were dragged to the scaffold on November 11, 1887.

"They were on a great strike for an eight-hour day, and patiently they waited to have their wrongs righted. They held a demonstration in the Haymarket. They were workingmen, they were quiet and they were peace-loving citizens. After most of the workingmen had gone home, and when nearly all the speeches were finished, Inspector Bonfield and his men threw themselves upon these men and began to shoot them down.[5]

"Although no one knows who threw that bomb; although the closest investigation has failed to disclose his identity, I must confess that I hold that he who threw the bomb did a deed that was great and holy. And that bomb was an echo of the miserable condition in which the workingmen of America find themselves.

"Eight policemen fell. Society doesn't care for the police. It considers them as its servants and slaves, but society thought: 'To-day they threw a bomb at the police; to-morrow they may direct a bomb at society itself.' Society knows it is sitting on a volcano; it knows that to-morrow the storm may break forth that will hurl it to destruction. Therefore, and for no other reason, it punished the Chicago anarchists."

BOMBTHROWER'S NOBLE DEED.

Miss Goldman's statement that the men gathered in the Haymarket were peace-loving citizens, followed by her praise of the man who threw the fatal bomb, coupled with the knowledge of the audience that the anarchists were hung, not because they had thrown the bomb, but because their teachings and speeches were directly responsible for the deed, proved a little too illogical for her auditors to stomach, and silence followed her remarks. She continued:

"Our murdered brothers now rest in Waldheim, but, as Spies predicted, their silence

4. Following a pattern set by Chicago anarchists a decade earlier, EG often evoked the names of Thomas Jefferson and Thomas Paine to highlight anti-statist ideas within the American political tradition.
5. Captain John Bonfield was commander of the Desplaines Street station; he shouldered much of the blame for the violence in Haymarket Square. He was known as "Black Jack" for his ruthless attitude toward demonstrations and picketers. Bonfield ordered his police to disperse the crowd in Haymarket just as the last speaker, Samuel Fielden, was concluding his talk.

in the grave is mightier than their speeches were upon earth.[6] Anarchy will live until society of to-day has been shattered to pieces and freedom reigns."

Miss Goldman then took up the case of Alexander Berkmann, who shot H. C. Frick. She said it was his belief that if the capitalists used Winchester rifles and bayonets on workingmen they should be answered with dynamite. Berkmann, she said, picked out the man who was responsible for the trouble at Homestead, the man who had hired the Pinkertons. She said Alexander Berkmann did not succeed in his attempt, and yet he was sent to the penitentiary for 22 years, although for his deed the laws of Pennsylvania prescribed a punishment of not more than seven years.[7]

While a collection was being taken up for Berkmann, Miss Goldman said he had not stepped into the breach for love of notoriety, but that it was his love for workingmen that led him to his deed. Whether his motives were noble or not, she claimed, it must be admitted that from the standpoint of law his sentence was unjust and excessive.

She spoke of the last election and the "parsons" who, with a full stomach and clad in broadcloth, had a good time calling on the poor to suffer patiently the ills of this life so that they could enjoy with greater zest the glories of the kingdom to come.

"It would make no difference to us anarchists if Bryan[8] had been elected," she said. "Of course an intelligent being admires intelligence. We sympathize with an intelligent man like Bryan. He is also energetic, and we must honor those qualities in anybody. Who could respect the little-souled McKinley, Mark Hanna's echo?[9] Nevertheless, the election of Bryan would not have benefited us anarchists, as the old order of society would have been maintained under him as well as under McKinley.[10]

"Why is it that while flour, groceries, meat and clothing are plentiful the workingman starves? He sees plenty everywhere. The stores are full of it. All the workingman needs

6. The words Spies uttered from the scaffold were engraved upon the Haymarket anarchists' monument in Chicago's Waldheim Cemetery: "The day will come when our silence will be more powerful than the voices you are throttling today."

7. Berkman was tried on six counts, including assault with attempt to kill both Carnegie steel company chairman Frick and John Leishmann, who was in the office when Berkman attacked Frick; three counts of felonious entry into the Carnegie offices; and illegally carrying concealed weapons. Berkman was found guilty on all charges. The judge multiplied the charges, and sentenced Berkman to twenty-one years in Western Penitentiary for assault, and one additional year in the Allegheny County Workhouse for the concealed weapon charge.

8. William Jennings Bryan was the Democratic party candidate for president in the 1896 election.

9. The 1896 Republican party candidate for president, William McKinley, was supported in his political aspirations by Cleveland industrialist and politician Mark Hanna.

10. The question of whether or not to coin silver currency, a policy that would benefit farmers and workers by easing the terms of credit, was central to the 1896 McKinley-Bryan presidential contest. When a Pittsburgh reporter asked for the anarchist position on the election, EG answered: "They were not exactly on either side, because it would be making a government in either case. But most of the Anarchists, I think, favored the silver question, as it tended much more to the alleviation of the workingmen's wrongs than the gold side, which was the upholding of the powers of monopolists and the rich classes." See "Emma Goldman Here," *Pittsburgh Leader*, 20 November 1896, *EGP*, reel 47.

is to stretch out his hand for it and take it, and yet he is such an ass that he does not grasp it, but says instead: 'There is no food, no clothing for me and my family.'"

Director J. O. Brown's[11] determination to arm the firemen and teach the police to shoot straight Miss Goldman ascribed to a desire to enable them to hit striking workingmen. She spoke of the "old, played out" cry that the ballot-box would right all ills, and remarked:

"I prophesy that the time will come when the workingmen will throw this whole ballot-box swindle overboard and right their wrongs in another way."

The collection for Berkmann amounted to $6.47, and Miss Goldman ordered that another be taken up, as the expenses of the hall in which the meeting was held had to be met.

After her speech Miss Goldman invited anybody who desired to defend the "ballot-box swindle" to step forward. She issued the invitation several times, but as no one accepted the meeting was adjourned.

To-morrow a meeting will be held in Turner hall at McKeesport. Herr Johann Most, the king bee of anarchists in this country and a noted advocate of the gold standard, will speak.

Pittsburg (Pa.) Post, 27 November 1896, p. 3. Copyright 2001 *Pittsburgh Post-Gazette.* All rights reserved. Reprinted with permission.

11. J. O. Brown was Pittsburgh's director of public safety. For a view of Brown and his career see Lincoln Steffens, "Pittsburgh: A City Ashamed," *McClure's Magazine,* May 1903.

To MAX METZKOW

New York, 2 December 1896

DEAR FRIEND METZKOW.

I come to you today with the Berk. matter. If I'm not mistaken, the Buffalo A-Z[1] has considerable influence in the unions there. Wouldn't it be possible to present the B matter in the CLU[2] there or in local unions? Let's say, a resolution which recommends a reduction of B's sentence? You'll understand that as long as B's case lies in the hands of anarchists we can never hope for success. It is a question of winning the organized workers for this. The CLU of Boston has adopted a resolution there,[3] the CLU of Providence[4] promised to do the same and I succeeded in gaining for the cause several representatives of local unions who will present a resolution in New York's CLU. You are undoubtedly aware that the A.F. of L holds its yearly convention on the 15th of this month in Cincinnati. Now, I have already won 2 delegates who will support B's case at the convention if one is brought forward. But it is important that the delegate who will introduce a resolution is not a known anarchist or socialist, otherwise there will already be prejudice against it.[5] Who will be sent by the Buffalo unions? and wouldn't it be possible to win the delegates in question for B's case, that is, would the people deign to support a possible

---

1. The *Buffaloer Arbeiter-Zeitung* was published in Buffalo, New York, from September 1887 to September 1897 and daily from September 1897 to December 1898, with a weekly edition, *Arbeiter-Zeitung und Buffalo "Herold,"* published from September to October 1898. From January 1899 until February 1918 it reverted to a weekly format as the *Arbeiter-Zeitung.* The organ of the socialist Vereinigten Deutschen Gewerkschaften (United German Trades), the journal was first edited by George M. Price; other editors included Max Baginski's brother, Richard Baginski (from February to September 1897), and Johann Most (from September 1897 to July 1898).
2. Central Labor Union.
3. Anarchists and Central Labor Union members Charles W. Mowbray and Harry M. Kelly were instrumental in gaining the Boston Central Labor Union's support.
4. Anarchist J. H. Cook was president of the Providence Central Labor Union.
5. The 16 December resolution was introduced by anarchist Henry Weismann of New York City, the delegate of the Journeymen Bakers' and Confectioners' International Union, and seconded by Henry Lloyd of Boston, general president of the United Brotherhood of Carpenters and Joiners and president of the Boston CLU. The resolution, directed to the Pennsylvania Board of Pardons, declared AB's sentence "excessive and far beyond the limit of the law, brought about by the excitement and prejudice prevailing at the time the offense was committed," and added that "the ends of justice have been fully satisfied with the four years of imprisonment . . . , considering the act was committed by a misguided youth, and that clemency could be extended in this case, as in many similar ones in times gone by." For the full text of the resolution, see *Proceedings of the American Federation of Labor: 1893–1896* (Bloomington, Ill., 1905), p. 52. In 1899, the week before a subsequent convening of the pardon board, AFL president Samuel Gompers personally followed up on the matter, writing to Pennsylvania senator Boies Penrose, asking him to intercede on AB's behalf. (See Gompers to Penrose, 19 April 1899, in Kaufman et al., *Samuel Gompers Papers,* 5:84–85.)

First page of letter written by Goldman on 2 December 1896 to Max Metzkow, Berlin-born anarchist and an anti-militarist. Active in support of the Homestead strikers, Metzkow worked as a compositor in Pittsburgh and then with the *Buffaloer Arbeiter-Zeitung*. (By permission of the Houghton Library, Harvard University) resolution or speak in favor of it? I beg you dear Metzkow, to take matters into your own hands and to let me know your opinion immediately.

It is a sad fact that very few people are interested in Berkmann and if I didn't constantly speak, write, and push the matter, B would have to end his life in prison. I know dear friend that you were one of the first ones who spoke up for B. and I hope that you won't deny me your help now either.

WITH REGARDS AND A HANDSHAKE.

E. GOLDMANN

ALS, Joseph Ishill Papers, MH-H. Translated from German. Reprinted by permission of the Houghton Library, Harvard University.

From ALEXANDER BERKMAN

Western Penitentiary, Allegheny City, Pa., 4 December 1896

My Dear Girl:

I have craved for a long, long time to have a free talk with you, but this is the first opportunity. A good friend, a "lover of horseflesh,"[1] promised to see this "birdie" through. I hope it will reach you safely.

In my local correspondence you have been christened the "Immutable." I realize how difficult it is to keep up letter-writing through the endless years, the points of mutual interest gradually waning. It is one of the tragedies in the existence of a prisoner. "K" and "G" have almost ceased to expect mail.[2] But I am more fortunate. The Twin[3] writes very seldom nowadays; the correspondence of other friends is fitful. But you are never disappointing. It is not so much the contents that matter: these increasingly sound like the language of a strange world, with its bewildering flurry and ferment, disturbing the calm of cell-life. But the very arrival of a letter is momentous. It brings a glow into the prisoner's heart to feel that he is remembered, actively, with that intimate interest which alone can support a regular correspondence. And then your letters are so vital, so palpitating with the throb of our common cause. I have greatly enjoyed your communications from Paris and Vienna, the accounts of the movement and of our European comrades. Your letters are so much part of yourself, they bring me nearer to you and to life.

The newspaper clippings you have referred to on various occasions, have been withheld from me. Nor are any radical publications permitted. I especially regret to miss *Solidarity*.[4] I have not seen a single copy since its resurrection two years ago. I have followed the activities of Chas. W. Mowbray and the recent tour of John Turner,[5] so far as the press accounts are concerned. I hope you'll write more about our English comrades.

I need not say much of the local life, dear. That you know from my official mail, and you can read between the lines. The action of the Pardon Board was a bitter disappointment to me. No less to you also, I suppose. Not that I was very enthusiastic as to a favor-

---

1. Robert Richards, the "Horsethief Bob" of AB's *Prison Memoirs*.
2. Carl Nold and Henry Bauer were code-named "K" and "G" respectively, to mask their identity as co-editors with AB of their handwritten, prison-produced, underground paper *Prison Blossoms* (also produced in a German-language version, titled *Zuchthausblüthen*). Based on their relative physical statures, "K" stood for "klein," the German word for small, while "G" stood for giant, or "gross" in German. AB was referred to by the initial "M" for "mittel" or medium (see Berkman, *Prison Memoirs of an Anarchist*, p. 182).
3. "The Twin" is AB's cousin Modest Stein.
4. *Solidarity* began publication again in 1895, after a two-year hiatus.
5. AB refers to English anarchists Charles Mowbray and John Turner; Turner undertook a seven-month lecture tour of the United States beginning in the spring of 1896.

able decision. But that they should so cynically evade the issue,—I was hardly prepared for *that*. I had hoped they would at least consider the case. But evidently they were averse to going on record, one way or another. The lawyers informed me that they were not even allowed an opportunity to present their arguments. The Board ruled that "the wrong complained of is not actual"; that is, that I am not yet serving the sentence we want remitted. A lawyer's quibble. It means that I must serve the first sentence of seven years, before applying for the remission of the other indictments. Discounting commutation time, I still have about a year to complete the first sentence. I doubt whether it is advisable to try again. Little justice can be expected from those quarters. But I want to submit another proposition to you; consult with our friends regarding it. It is this: there is a prisoner here who has just been pardoned by the Board, whose president, the Lieutenant-Governor, is indebted to the prisoner's lawyer for certain political services. The attorney's name is K— D— of Pittsburgh. He has intimated to his client that he will guarantee my release for $1,000.00, the sum to be deposited in safe hands and to be paid *only* in case of success. Of course, we cannot afford such a large fee. And I cannot say whether the offer is worth considering; still, you know that almost anything can be bought from politicians. I leave the matter in your hands.[6]

The question of my visits seems tacitly settled; I can procure no permit for my friends to see me. For some obscure reason, the Warden has conceived a great fear of an Anarchist plot against the prison. The local "trio" is under special surveillance and constantly discriminated against, though "K" and "G" are permitted to receive visits. You will smile at the infantile terror of the authorities: it is bruited about that a "certain Anarchist lady" (meaning you, I presume; in reality it was Henry's sweetheart, a jolly devil-may-care girl)[7] made a threat against the prison. The gossips have it that she visited Inspector Reed at his business place, and requested to see me. The Inspector refusing, she burst out: "We'll blow your dirty walls down." I could not determine whether there is any foundation for the story, but it is circulated here, and the prisoners firmly believe it explains my deprivation of visits.[8]

---

6. In 1896 EG and others began to look to legal means to release AB from prison. The first recommendation was to appeal AB's sentence, as he was given twenty-two years in prison instead of the seven allowable under Pennsylvania law. However, it was determined that because AB, without legal representation at his trial, had not appealed at the time of his sentence, he could not now appeal. Lawyers instead recommended that AB or his friends appeal to the Pennsylvania Board of Pardons for a reduction in his sentence. Although they were unsuccessful, EG and others continued to work to petition the state pardon board throughout 1897 and 1898 for a reduction.
7. Bauer's companion's name was Gretchen.
8. EG recounted a similar incident in *Living My Life*, but with herself as Inspector Reed's antagonist in 1892. Visiting him in his jewelry shop to obtain a pass to see AB, in a fury, EG ended by threatening Reed's life when he unilaterally denied her any further access to the prison and added his caveat that "Berkman will never get out alive!"

In my indignation and rage I swept everything to the floor—plates, coffee-pots and pitchers, jewellry and watches. I seized a heavy tray and was about to throw it at him when I was pulled back by one of the clerks, who shouted to

That is a characteristic instance of local conditions. Involuntarily I smile at Kennan's naïve indignation with the brutalities he thinks possible only in Russian and Siberian prisons.[9] He would find it almost impossible to learn the true conditions in the American prisons: he would be conducted the rounds of the "show" cells, always neat and clean for the purpose; he would not see the basket cell, nor the bull rings in the dungeon, where men are chained for days; nor would he be permitted to converse for hours, or whole evenings, with the prisoners, as he did with the exiles in Siberia. Yet if he succeeded in learning even half the truth, he would be forced to revise his views of American penal institutions, as he did in regard to Russian politicals. He would be horrified to witness the brutality that is practised here as a matter of routine, the abuse of the insane, the petty persecution. Inhumanity is the keynote of stupidity in power.

Your soul must have been harrowed by the reports of the terrible tortures in Montjuich.[10] What is all indignation and lamenting, in the face of the revival of the Inquisition? Is there no Nemesis in Spain?

Berkman, *Prison Memoirs of an Anarchist,* pp. 297–99. In AB's *Prison Memoirs,* this letter is dated 12 April 1896.The content of the letter strongly suggests, however, that this date is wrong. In particular, AB's reference in the last paragraph to the atrocities committed against political prisoners at Montjuich refers to events following the 7 June 1896 bombing of the Corpus Christi Day procession in Barcelona. The letter comes from AB's own transcription and the original is no longer extant, but it is possible that AB misread the date on the original, converting the numerals signifying the month and day (i.e., "12/4") from American style (month/day) to European style (day/month).

---

someone to run for the police. Reed, white with fear and frothing at the mouth, signalled to the clerk. "No police," I heard him say; "no scandal. Just kick her out." The clerk advanced towards me, then stopped. "Murderer, coward!" I cried; "if you harm Berkman, I will kill you with my own hands!" (*LML,* p. 113)

Afterward, according to EG, Metzkow and Nold expressed concern about the repercussions her outburst might have for AB. "I was shocked by the thought that Sasha might indeed have to suffer as a result of my outbreak," she continued. "But the threat of the Inspector that Sasha would never come out of prison alive had been too much for me. I was sure Sasha would understand" (*LML,* p. 113).

9. George Kennan was America's foremost authority on Russian political prisoners and penal conditions. His book *Siberia and the Exile System* (New York: Century, 1891) denounced the Russian exile system, and in 1893 he published *George Kennan on Russian Justice, and S. Stepniak's Appeal to President Cleveland* (New York: Russian American National League, 1893).

10. After the bombing by an unknown assailant of the Corpus Christi Day procession in Barcelona on 7 June 1896, the *Brigada Social,* the Spanish government's special anti-anarchist police unit under the command of General Weyler y Nicolau, arrested more than four hundred people including anarchists, labor militants, Republicans, and anti-clerics. Those arrested were held in Barcelona's Montjuich fortress. One of the detainees, Fernando Tárrida del Mármol, a Catalonian anarchist and director of the Barcelona Polytechnic Academy, published in exile a firsthand account of the tortures they suffered at the prison. The book, *Les Inquisiteurs d'Espagne: Montjuich, Cuba, Philippines* (Paris: P. V. Stock; *Bibliothèque sociologique,* no. 17, 1897), together with other reports smuggled out of Montjuich and printed in conservative as well as anarchist newspapers abroad, inspired international condemnation of the Spanish government. The 11 July 1897 issue of *Firebrand* published a special supplement, "The Modern Inquisition of Spain."

MY DEAR COMRADE.

Your letter and the book *Socialisme et Congrès de Londons*[1] to hand. Thank you very much for both.

I have not been able to look your valuable book through, as I have been very busy. You ask me to publish a critisism on your work in one of our papers, *Freiheit. Sturmglacken, Freie Gesellshaft,*[2] etc. *Sturmglacken,*[3] are not in existence any more, The *Freiheit,* will not accept anything of my pen and *Freie Gesellshaft,* is read only by the jewish populace, and is of miner importance.

I shall however try to insert a critisism in some other paper, if I will like the book. You also say, that you would be very happy, if I could publish an American edition in english. I certainly could publish it, If I had the means. You know, no doubt that in order to publish a book, one must have <u>money</u> something, I lack in, very badly. I have seen very little of the <u>Gold</u> which was to come in, after the election of McKinley.[4] Times are fearfully bad here and I think, that whithin the next four years, we will have a rebellion here. The American people are practical, as you remarked, at my visit, but when they find out that practicability is no policy, they also happen to loose their temper occasonnally, I am sorry to say they do not loose it too often.

I would like to hear your suggestion, about the publications of your 2 books, ~~do you intend~~ I can transalate both, but as I said before, I have no money to have it printed.

HOPING TO HEAR FROM YOU SOON. I REMAIN WITH FRATERNAL GREETINGS.
E GOLDMAN

ALS, Augustin Hamon Archive, IISH.

1. *Le socialisme et le congrès de Londres: étude historique* (Paris: P. V. Stock; *Bibliothèque sociologique,* no. 11, 1897).
2. A Yiddish-language anarchist monthly published in New York from 1895 to October 1900, *Freie Gesellschaft* (Free Society) provided literature and cultural commentary as well as political articles. The journal was edited by Lev Moiseev (under the pseudonym M. Leontieff), J. A. Maryson, Moishe Katz, and Hillel Solotaroff. From 1910 to 1911, Saul Yanovsky published a literary monthly of the same name.
3. *Sturmglocken,* edited by Max Baginski, ceased publication after its fourth issue, 18 April 1896.
4. A reference to President McKinley's support of the gold standard.

DEAR FRIEND.

That you have always been and will forever remain the brave, good comrade is something I have never doubted, and if I did not receive a prompt response to my letter I assume in that case that you were unable to write. I am extremely delighted by your success in the interest of our friend Berk. I have also submitted an appeal and resolution to the convention and am now awaiting an answer.[1]

You are right dear friend, I want to stage a far reaching movement for B., and even if we should not succeed in easing the burden on B. or liberating him, at least we will have made propaganda for our ideas. Indeed it is necessary, for at the moment we have damned little of a movement.

I ~~will~~ intend to make a tour through the countryside next month and rouse the sleeping brothers a little. What is going on in Buffalo? Are the comrades still with their bodies and souls so fond of Pope Hannes?[2] Please don't think I want to impose myself, dear friend, but I want to spread our ideas everywhere and set the movement, especially the English one, into some kind of motion. Write me your honest opinion on what you think about this business.

Bauer made 2 pictures out of colored tissue paper, for which he made use of 32,842 rolls of paper over

During late 1896, Goldman's speaking engagements grew. At the meeting reported in the 12 November 1896 *Pittsburg Post,* Goldman made a collection to help pay the costs of Berkman's proposed legal appeal.

---

1. See Letter to Max Metzkow, 2 December 1896, above, for EG and Metzkow's earlier correspondence on the issue of raising trade union support for the reduction of AB's sentence.
2. "Pope Hannes" is EG's sarcastic reference to Johann Most. He had been given this nickname, mocking his perceived autocratic nature, by supporters of *Die Autonomie,* including AB and EG.

3 months. He sent me the pictures for the raffle and the proceeds are supposed to go to the benefit of the trio Nold, Bauer Berk.[3] I am enclosing some tickets for you, could you sell some in B?[4] If so, please let me know how many I should send you.

I expect a really long, detailed letter from you and remain for today with sincere regards

EMMA GOLDMANN

ALS, Joseph Ishill Collection, MH-H. Translated from German. Reprinted by permission of the Houghton Library, Harvard University.

3. Henry Bauer and Carl Nold spent four years in the same prison with AB. The "trio"—Bauer, Nold, and Berkman (EG shortens his name to "Berk" here)—edited the handwritten journal *Prison Blossoms*.
4. Buffalo, where Metzkow lived.

DEAR FRIEND!

Sent you 100 tickets at your request. These cost only 10c apiece, and, as the "Freihei-tiener"[1] magnanimously declared themselves willing to take 50 tickets at 25c, I think that these "noble men" will also accept 100 tickets at 10c. The people will indeed still save 2.50D, which could then go to poor "Hannes." If, my friend, you could perhaps unload another 40 tickets in addition to the 100, I would send you some more. The money for the tickets must be sent to me, since I took 600 tickets from the L T.[2] to sell and will ac-count for all of them together. As far as the business related to the agitation tour is con-cerned, I am firmly resolved to travel on my own and also arrange meetings by myself. I want to go over my plans with you, dear friend—If I come to Pittsburg I will come at my own expense to Buffalo, and then, if you want to help me, we could get a hall for one or several meetings, properly announce them, and I am convinced that we would have a huge success. We could easily cover expenses from the collections. That is what I have done in Pittsburg, Baltimore and other cities and always with great success. What do you think about that? Of course we can not make this known for the time being or the whole thing would be botched. You offered me your hospitality, didn't you, I will make use of that in 4–6 weeks, the rest will work itself out. The business with the editor of the A Z is very regrettable,[3] but I should think that you and the other participants at the paper should be resolute enough to give the man his walking papers. Propaganda, in my opin-ion, is the most important thing, and whoever stands in the way of that must go. You may be surprised that I speak so categorically, but I know from bitter experience that consid-eration for one individual ruined the German movement here in this land. I don't have to explain myself any further, surely you understand me—

Your inquiry about Jac Fuchs is something I can respond to all too well. I know him very well and have seen in him a highly talented, capable and intelligent person, as well

1. *Freiheitiener* are "freedomites," or supporters of the prominent anarchist newspaper *Freiheit* edited by Johann Most. Justus Schwab was the paper's co-editor during its first year of publication in New York City.
2. That is, the Internationale Arbeiter Liedertafel (International Workers' Song Circle), which met every Wednesday evening at Faulhabers Hall, 1551 Second Avenue. The tickets to which she refers were for a lottery intended to raise money for AB (see Letter to Max Metzkow, 17 December 1896, above, for discussion of the lottery). A short note to Metzkow a month later registered a setback: "I must inform you that the A[rbeiter] L[ieder] Tafel has postponed the lottery until the 4th of April because we have not sold enough tickets. I would appreciate it if you would publish that in the *B[uffaloer] A[rbeiter-] Zeitung.*" EG to Metzkow, 1 February 1897, *EGP,* reel 1.
3. EG refers to Joseph Mostler, editor of the *Buffaloer Arbeiter-Zeitung* from September 1893, who left the paper due to a wage dispute and founded the *Buffalo Herold* in 1897.

as a noble character. He is not an Anarchist, but I like him a thousand times more than most of the "comrades." I think he would fit in very well as an editor, but I am afraid that this young man will not be especially liked, I mean by the comrades and the everyday lout. He has not made many friends even here because he is too radical, too open and, above all, too honest. However, perhaps with time he will become wiser and more experienced and will learn to close off his inner thoughts from the view of the everyday man. I can bear him the best witness and Justus Schwab will join in my opinion. He is an original mind and I am convinced that you will like him very much, dear friend. He is still very young indeed, only 23 yrs. and still can learn a lot, I mean in terms of doing right by all people, yet still for his age he knows more than a thousand others.

If you want to know more, dear friend, it would be best to hear from Justus Schwab, for perhaps you may think that I am too sanguine in my judgment. Jac Fuchs departed yesterday for Detroit and if you want to write to him you should send the letter to the A T.[4] The poor man has suffered terribly here and I would not begrudge it him if he would get the position at the B A Z.[5]

That final comment was meant only for you, dear friend. I wouldn't want anyone else to learn of the sad condition of my young friend.

In the hope of hearing from you soon, with revolut. greetings.

EMMA GOLDMANN

P.S. Best regards to your family.

ALS, Joseph Ishill Collection, MH-H. Translated from German. Reprinted by permission of the Houghton Library, Harvard University.

---

4. The initials "A T" refer to *Der arme Teufel*.
5. Jacob Fuchs edited the weekly paper *Der Herold* in Detroit from February 1897 to August 1897 and apparently did not go to Buffalo to work on the *Buffaloer Arbeiter-Zeitung;* in February 1897 Richard Baginski became its editor.

DEAR COMRADE AND FRIEND.

I hadn't responded to your most recent letter with the enclosed check because 1) I have been very busy and 2) I had nothing new to write about. The raffle is coming up soon, so I would like to ask you to send the money for the rest of the tickets since I have to settle the accounts. There is nothing new here; Most and the choral society[1] are quarrelling and nobody is doing anything. The Commune celebration arranged by the choral society was poorly attended because M worked against it with all his energy.[2] Both sides are distasteful to me and I prefer to go my own way. In a very short time I will publish a leaflet with Biedenkapp[3] and Timmerman and will also undertake a long trip to the West, mostly for Berkman but also for our ideas in general. Nold and Bauer are coming on May 25th, then there will be more life in this place.[4] How is Baginsky[5] doing at the paper? He is a capable fellow and a very good man indeed. Write soon and a lot.[6]

WITH GREETINGS AND A HANDSHAKE.

EMMA GOLDMAN

ALS, Joseph Ishill Collection, MH-H. Translated from German. Reprinted by permission of the Houghton Library, Harvard University.

1. By "choral society," EG refers to the Internationale Arbeiter Liedertafel (International Workers' Song Circle), a German anarchist choir of which Justus Schwab was a leader. The group had been selling raffle tickets to raise money for AB, hence Johann Most's attitude to the event.
2. A memorial festival to celebrate the Paris Commune, including lectures, a concert, and ball, was held 18 March 1897 in Germania Hall in New York City. The celebration was organized by the Internationale Arbeiter Liedertafel in association with the French and Italian groups of New York. Lectures were given in English, French, German, and Italian.
3. Georg Biedenkapp (1843–1924), a German-born socialist with anarchist sympathies, immigrated to New York from Germany in 1885; he founded and edited the satirical New York weekly *Der Tramp* (1888) with Wilhelm Rosenberg. He published books in German on scientific and historical topics, including *Friedrich Nietzsche und Friedrich Naumann als Politiker,* and works of poetry. He wrote a poem to AB, "In trüber Zeit" (In a gloomy time), that appeared in the September 1893 number of the anarchist paper *Die Brandfackel.* In 1895 Biedenkapp recited a poem at the Solidarity Group's Paris Commune Celebration in New York City. No extant record of the proposed leaflet EG refers to can be found.
4. Carl Nold and Henry Bauer were released from the Western Penitentiary on 25 May 1897, after four years of imprisonment in connection with AB's attempted assassination of Henry C. Frick.
5. Richard Baginski, Max Baginski's brother, began editing the *Buffaloer Arbeiter-Zeitung* in February 1897.
6. Metzkow did not respond, and EG wrote in German: "It appears as if you did not receive my letter from last week as no response has arrived thus far. I must write you again today with regard to the money for the lottery since I have to settle accounts. Thus I sincerely entreat you to send me either the money or the remaining tickets. The raffle did not take place yesterday because it was prohibited,

DEAR COMRADE.

Your favor of March 24th. to hand.

I regret very much that I am ever in such a position that provents me from carrying out your request and I fear that I shall not be able to do much better this time.

I will see that the publisher of *Freie Gesellshaft* forward you their paper.[1]

In regard to the publication of your book "Socialism & the London Congress" in the english language in this country, I can only tell you that no american publisher would consent to publish it, because the american public could not be interested in that.[2]

The Comrades of course would appreciate it, but I do not know of any of them that furnish the necessary funds for the publication.

I think, I might find a house, that would publish "Psychology du militaire professionel"

Please send me the origenal copy, (I mean in french of course) and let me know if it ever has been transelated in the english language before;[3] you will also have to send me a letter of special authority, otherwise the publishers might not accept me as your representative. Write the letter in french.

At present my time is too fully occupied to write an article for the *Humanité Nouvelle;*[4] later on perhaps I may be able to accomadate you. I could find out nothing about books, or any works, that deal with political criminals. As America does not admit the existence of such a specified class. Political criminals, are classed in the line of common criminals. They do not enjoy any other priveliges, nor are they treated differently. I have been told,

---

but it will be held in private in the next few days. What is R Baginsky up to and how is the movement in Buffalo doing generally. Our friends Nold and Bauer are coming out on the 25th of May. I intend to go to P at that time in order to work energetically with both of them for Berkmann's liberation" (EG to Metzkow, 5 April 1897, *EGP,* reel 1).

1. EG is volunteering to send to Hamon *Freie Gesellschaft* (Free Society), the New York City Yiddish-language anarchist monthly of cultural and political commentary. Hamon had requested that EG send him a number of American anarchist papers (for editorial details on *Freie Gesellschaft,* see note 2 to Letter to Augustin Hamon, 17 December 1896, above).
2. *Le socialisme et le congrès de Londres: étude historique* (Paris: P. V. Stock; *Bibliothèque sociologique,* no. 11, 1897). Hamon had requested that EG try and find an American publisher for this book (see Letter to Augustin Hamon, 17 December 1896, above). No English-language edition of the book was published.
3. Hamon's *Psychologie du militaire professionnel* (Paris: A. Savine, 1895) was never published in English.
4. The anarchist and cultural journal *L'Humanité Nouvelle* was founded and edited by Hamon between May 1897 and 1903.

that the place to find out anything on that subject is; the office de travail in Paris, of which, no doubt; you know. The president of the institution is Mons. Finance.[5] I suppose, you know all particularies about our Chicago Comrades, Spies, Parson[6] ect. If not, let me know and I will give you all the details, also about the Hoamstead affaire.[7] I would have gladly given you particularies in this letter, but my time is too limitted, as I am about to leave for Philadelphia and other cities on a lecturing tour.[8]

We no paper published in the english language on Anarchism Communism, in the East of N. A. Fultons paper,[9] I consider a very poor affaire.

The propaganda in this Country is at present very week. All circles reporte a general feeling of lethargy.

Times have never been worse, thousends and thousends are out of work and destitute, still they hope and wait and suffer. Even the radical element that knows the evil of our present system, lack the courage of action and try to satisfy the agonies of hunger of the people either with the ballot box, free coinage of Silver, tarif, or other rubbish. Those, who are willing to carry the torch of real aducation, in to the masses lack the means to carry on the work.

I assure you, it is not very pleasent to live in a country where the almighty dollar is all and love, passion, truth, honesty and earnestness are laught and scared at. Hoping to hear from you soon. I remain

FRATERNALLY.

E. GOLDMAN

ALS, Augustin Hamon Archive, IISH.

---

5. The Office du Travail was established in 1891 to investigate working conditions in France. Its first president was Isidore Finance, a house painter and militant positivist.
6. August Spies and Albert Parsons were two of the four anarchists executed in 1887 after the Haymarket affair in Chicago.
7. EG refers to AB's *attentat* at the offices of Carnegie Steel in Homestead, Pa., in July 1892.
8. EG spoke in Providence between the 23rd and 25th of April, before lecturing in Philadelphia in May.
9. Edward H. Fulton's individualist anarchist paper *Age of Thought* (published in Columbus Junction, Iowa, from 1896 to 1898) was influenced by Benjamin Tucker's prominent paper of anarchist individualism, *Liberty*. Fulton had shifted politically from anarchist communism.

CHER COMARADE.

Your letter of May 29 to hand. I could not answer it at once, because I was very ill from the effects of operation on my foot, at the time when your letter reached me. I am better now, but far from being well, and I therefore have to prospone the affair with your book until later. You need not send me a french copy of *Psychologie du militaire professionel*, because I have found the one you gave me. Together with this letter, I send you all the matirial for your lecture,[1] that I could get a hold of. The tings are as follow. a short Biography of Alex. Berkmann, Carl Nold, Henry Bauer with Photos. Than, a copy of the Chicago *Vorbote*[2] of 1887 with the pictures of the 8 Comrades and there Biography, I have not translated it, into English, since you have to translate it in to french. Now this copy, I must have returned, dear comrade, because that is the only copy left of that number. besides that, I send you, a pamphlet by Gen. M. M. Trumball,[3] Gov. John P. Altgeld's reason for pardoning our Comrade,[4] and a pamphlet by Prof. Edward W. Bemis of the Chicago University on the Hoamstead strike.[5] The last pamphlet does not belong to me, and I have promised to return it to the owner, I therefore beg of you to send this back to me, as soon as you are done with it, together with the copy of The *Vorbote*.[6]

The discription of the Hoamstead strike by Prof. E. W. Bemis is correct, only when hes critisism of Berkmann act and its influence on the strike, is wrong and from a prejudiced point of view.[7] The strike was not lost, because of B's act, but because the strikers were betrayed and soled by their leaders and because they did not have enough munition

1. Hamon had hoped to write a book on political violence and assassination, but never did. His collected research material, including what EG sent him, are in his archive at IISH. The enclosures reproduced here are EG's biographical sketches of Bauer, Nold, and Berkman, intended for Hamon's book.
2. *Der Vorbote* was the weekly edition of the *Chicagoer Arbeiter-Zeitung*.
3. EG probably enclosed *Was It a Fair Trial?* (1887), the first of two pamphlets by Chicago lawyer M. M. Trumbull defending the Haymarket anarchists and widely circulated.
4. John P. Altgeld, *Reasons for Pardoning Fielden, Neebe and Schwab* (Chicago, 1893).
5. Edward W. Bemis, "The Homestead Strike," *Journal of Political Economy* 2 (June 1894): 369–96.
6. Hamon never returned this material to EG.
7. Bemis wrote: "A final lesson of the strike is the great injury to the cause of organized labor resulting from anything savoring of anarchy. It is well known that the eight-hour movement was put back several years by the bomb-throwing of the anarchists at the Chicago Haymarket in 1886. Similarly the Homestead strikers in many ways lost some of the popular sympathy which previously was theirs by the shooting of Mr. Frick by the anarchist Berkman; while evidence has been presented above showing that the Carnegie Company might possibly have reopened the conference doors, when Berkman, acting wholly without the knowledge or desire of the strikers, shattered all their hopes" (Bemis, "Homestead Strike," pp. 395–96).

and money to continue the battle. I admit, that had B's act been successful, it would have made more propaganda, but the failure is not due to B. nor any body. I have been in Hoamstead after the act, and have found out that the sympathy of the strikers was with the act, their only regret was, that it did not kill Frick.

I will try to get specimen of writing of the Chicago Comrades later on, at present I can get nothing else. I am going to make a propaganda tour through the West next Septe and, as I also will visit Chicago,[8] I will try to get you more matirial in regard to the Com. from Mrs Parsons.[9] At What month in 1900 do you intend to lecture in Brussels? I am asking, because I intend to go to England and France the same year and I would like to meet you in Paris.

Hoping that the articles I sent you, will be of some use to you, I remain with

BEST GREETINGS

E GOLDMANN

P.S. Please reply, as soon, as you receive this letter and package, also be kind enough to send back, *Vorbote* and pamphlet of E. W. Bemis, as soon, as you will get done.

ENCLOSURE

Henry Bauer is the son of paysents and was born 28 April 1861 Grentel. (Hessen). He learned the Capenter trade and as he had to serve in the army, he preferred to go to America, he landed here Mai 1880 and went to Philadelphia, thand to Cumberland Md and finely to Pittsburg, he became foreman in a Capenter Shop, but this did not keep him from taking active part in the 8 hour movement during that time he got acquainted with the revolutionary Ideas. After his strike was lost, he was decharged and could from that time find no steady employment. The Chicago trial and the legal murder of our Comrades, has draughen him intirely in to the anarchistic ranks and since than he was one of the most active Comrade. In the Hoamstead strike he distributed revolutionary ~~leafl~~ leaflets and after Berkmans act he was arrest; ~~for~~ and at the beginning of 93 he was sentenced to 5 years penetentiaery, for distributing incendiary printing matter. Hes time expired last May 25th having received one year reduction for good behavior.

Carl Nold, was born 26 Sep, 1869 at Weingarten, Wurtenberg, he was a child of love, what is called to day an illegal child. His father was a phisician in the Army. He fought in the German-Franco war of 1870–1871 and after a long absence he came home ill and brokendown, he died soon afterwards. The mother of little Nold went to America and left the child with his grandparents, where he was brought up as a strict good Catholic. With 14 years he came to his mother, who meanwhile had married. He was sent to his oncle's to learn the trade of locksmith, but after one year he left his relatives, because he could

8. EG lectured in Chicago between 27 September and 13 October 1897, while on tour. She returned to Chicago and spoke at a Haymarket memorial meeting on 11 November 1897.

9. EG refers to Lucy Parsons, anarchist, labor activist, and widow of Haymarket anarchist Albert Parsons.

no longer stand the cruel and inhuman treatment. He first got acquainted with Socialistic and than with anarchistic Ideas and after having worked in different cities, he decided in 1889 to tramp to Chicago, but he did not come further than Pittsburg, where he settled down. He studied much and finely rendered great service to the cause, as a speaker and writer. He was well known to the police Authorities and after Berkmanns act, was arrested as a conspirater and was in Feb 1893 sentenced to 5 years Penetentiary, he also was released from prison the 25th of last May. Nold has a boy of 6 years and lives with his wife, of course in a free Union.

Alex. Berkmann My friend and Comrade. Was born the 24 November 1870 in Vilna, west russia. His father Joseph Berkman, was a merchand in leather and had a large business in St Petersburg, where to his family of 3 boys and a girl moved, right after Alex birth. His father was wealthy and gave all his children a first class aducation, first with private tutors and than he sent to gimanasium. He died, when Alex, was 12 years old and his mother with the 4 children moved to Kovno, in the western part of Russia. There Alex continued his studies in the Gimanasium, His one brother having left to Leipzig, to study medicin, his second brother studying pharmacy and his sister, was with Alex in Gimanasium. Soon Alex aroused the anger of the Authorities for his liberal and revolutionary Ideas and shortly before his graduation from the 6th class he was expelled from high scool and put on the black list, that means, that he could no more enter any college of Russia. After that, at the age of 17 year Alex sailed to America where he landed in 1888. Not being accustumed to phisical labor, he suffered very much and for over a year he lived one 5–7 c per day. Than he worked on different trades, as Cigarmaker, taylor and finely he lurned typesetting and went to work on the *Freiheit*, the german anarchist journal, with Most, as editor. During all this time, Berkman, studied the social question, political and economical. He was always a scolar and was well acquainted with all scientific work. he became an Anarchist and was very active, speaking, writing and asissting the movement financially. Alex. Berkman, was such an inthusiast, that he could go without propre food for days and give his earning for the cause, he was an Nihilist of the Bakunin type, he did acknowledge friendship love or any other feeling save the cause and this also led him to his act. He was of a very independend nature and would sumbit to no dogmas or rulership, he could not stand the dictator-ship of Most and left him in 1891. Berkmann, had somewhat of a ~~chara~~ caracter like Casario Santo. He went from New York to Pittsburg at the time of the Hoamstead strike, with 50 c in his pocket. No one accept one friend of his knew of his plan. His intention was to use dinamite, but he changed to a revolver, because the time was too limited and he could not optain the necessary quantity. On Saturday the 22 July 2 o'clock in the afternoon he entred Frick office and fired 5 times at, 3 times struck him, and two bullets went by. Frick was severly wounded, but through skilful medical attendence, he soon recovered. Alx Berk. After 2 month of imprisonement was, after a trial which lasted 1. 1/2 sentenced to 22 years imprisonement. He had refused legal deffence ~~and~~ hoping that he will be allowed to deffend himself, but this was not granted, as the whole trial was led on with the greatest of prejudice. There were

5 charges against him, carrying conceiled weepons, ~~entring the of~~ forcing his way into the Office of Frick, attempting to kill Frick, attempting to kill the Secretary of Frick, (which by the way was a lie) and comtempt of court. Had there not been so many charges against him, he could only have been given 7 years, that is the, highest limit of the law. of Penselvania. Berkmann has now served a term of 5 years, but according to the prison rules 7 years, that is 2 year counted for good behavior. We are ~~know~~ now working hard to get a reduction of sentence, and hope to get 10 years. Berkman, has used his imprisonement for active study and has accomplished great knowledge during this time. He is cheerful and inthusiastic as ever, only, as he calls himself, he has grow wiser.

ALS, Augustin Hamon Archive, IISH. On stationery of the *New York Recoder,* Editorial Department. The enclosure with biographical details of Bauer, Nold, and Berkman was handwritten by EG but unsigned.

Essay in the *FIREBRAND*

New York, 18 July 1897

Marriage

How much sorrow, misery, humiliation; how many tears and curses; what agony and suffering has this word brought to humanity. From its very birth, up to our present day, men and women groan under the iron yoke of our marriage institution, and there seems to be no relief, no way out of it.

At all times, and in all ages, have the suppressed striven to break the chains of mental and physical slavery. After thousands of noble lives have been sacrificed at the stake and on the gallows, and others have perished in prisons, or at the merciless hands of inquisitions, have the ideas of those brave heroes been accomplished. Thus have religious dogmas, feudalism and black slavery been abolished, and new ideas, more progressive, broader and clearer, have come to the front, and again we see poor downtrodden humanity fighting for its rights and independence. But the crudest, most tyrannical of all institutions—marriage, stands firm as ever, and woe unto those who dare to even doubt its sacredness. Its mere discussion is enough to infuriate not only Christians and conservatives alone, but even Liberals, Freethinkers, and Radicals. What is it that causes all these people to uphold marriage? What makes them cling to this prejudice? (for it is nothing else but prejudice). It is because marriage relations, are the foundation of private property, ergo, the foundation of our cruel and inhuman system. With wealth and superfluity on one side, and idleness, exploitation, poverty, starvation, and crime on the other, hence to abolish marriage, means to abolish everything above mentioned. Some progressive people are trying to reform and better our marriage laws. They no longer permit the church to interfere in their matrimonial relations, others even go further, they marry free, that is without the consent of the law,[1] but, nevertheless, this form of marriage is just as binding, just as "sacred", as the old form, because it is not the form or the kind of marriage relation we have, but the thing, the thing itself that is objectionable, hurtful and degrading. It always gives the man the right and power over his wife, not only over her body, but also over her actions, her wishes; in fact, over her whole life. And how can it be otherwise?

Behind the relations of any individual man and woman to each other, stands the historical age evolved relations between the two sexes in general, which have led up to the difference in the position and privileges of the two sexes today.

---

1. Probably a reference to the free marriage in 1886 of the sex radicals E. C. Walker and Lillian Harman, the latter the daughter of *Lucifer* editor Moses Harman. The couple were tried and sentenced to forty-five days in prison and fined for all the court fees. When they refused to pay the fines, Walker and Harman were imprisoned for six months.

Two young people come together, but their relation is largely determined by causes over which they have no control. They know little of each other, society has kept both sexes apart, the boy and the girl have been brought up along different lines. Like Olive Schreiner says in her Story of an African Farm "The boy has been taught to be, the girl to seem."[2] Exactly; the boy is taught to be intelligent, bright, clever, strong, athletic, independent and selfreliant; to develop his natural faculties, to follow his passions and desires. The girl has been taught to dress, to stand before the looking glass and admire herself, to control her emotions, her passions, her wishes, to hide her mental defects and to combine what little intelligence and ability she has on one point, and that is, the quickest and best way to angle a husband, to get profitably married. And so it has come that the two sexes hardly understand each other's nature, that their mental interest and occupations are different. Public opinion separates their rights and duties, their honor and dishonor very strictly from each other. The subject of sex is a sealed book to the girl, because she has been given to understand that it is impure, immoral and indecent to even mention the sex question. To the boy it is a book whose pages have brought him disease and secret vice, and in some cases ruin and death.[3]

Among the rich class it has long been out of fashion to fall in love. Men of society marry, after a life of debauchery and lust, to build up their ruined constitution. Others again have lost their capital, in gambling sports or business speculation, and decide that an heiress would be just the thing they need, knowing well, that the marriage tie will in no way hinder them from squandering the income of their wealthy bride. The rich girl having been brought up to be practical and sensible, and having been accustomed to live, breathe, eat, smile, walk and dress only according to fashion, holds out her millions to some title, or to a man with a good social standing. She has one consolation, and that is, that society allows more freedom of action to a married woman and should she be disappointed in marriage she will be in a position to gratify her wishes otherwise. We know, the walls of boudoirs and salons are deaf and dumb, and a little pleasure within these walls is no crime.

With the men and women among the working-class, marriage is quite a different thing. Love is not so rare as among the upper class, and very often helps both to endure disappointments and sorrows in life, but even here the majority of marriages, last only for a short while, to be swallowed up in the monotony of the every day life and the struggle for existence. Here also, the workingman marries because he grows tired of

2. EG is paraphrasing Lyndall, the heroine of Olive Schreiner's *Story of an African Farm* (London, 1883), who declares to a male listener: "We all enter the world little plastic beings, with so much natural force, perhaps, but for the rest—blank; and the world tells us what we are to be, and shapes us by the ends it sets before us. To you it says—*Work;* and to us it says—*Seem!*" Many turn-of-the-century European and American feminists saw Lyndall as a model for women's independence.

3. For a nearly contemporaneous elaboration on this theme, see the excerpt from EG's lecture entitled "Sex Problems," *Free Society,* 13 August 1899, *EGP,* reel 47.

a boardinghouse life, and out of a desire to build a home of his own, where he will find his comfort. His main object, therefore, is to find a girl that will make a good cook and housekeeper; one that will look out only for his happiness, for his pleasures; one that will look up to him as her lord, her master, her defender, her supporter; the only ideal worth while living for. Another man hopes that the girl he'll marry will be able to work and help to put away a few cents for rainy days, but after a few months of so-called happiness he awakens to the bitter reality that his wife is soon to become a mother, that she cannot work, that the expences grow bigger, and that while he before managed to get along with the small earning allowed him by his "kind" master, this earning is not sufficient to support a family.

The girl who has spent her childhood, and part of her womanhood, in the factory, feels her strength leaving her and pictures to herself the dreadful condition of ever having to remain a shopgirl, never certain of her work, she is, therefore, compelled to look out for a man, a good husband, which means one who can support her, and give her a good home. Both, the man and the girl, marry for the same purpose, with the only exception that the man is not expected to give up his individuality, his name, his independence, whereas, the girl has to sell herself, body and soul, for the pleasure of being someone's wife; hence they do not stand on equal terms, and where there is no equality there can be no harmony. The consequence is that shortly after the first few months, or to make all allowance possible, after the first year, both come to the conclusion that marriage is a failure.

As their conditions grow worse and worse, and with the increase of children the woman grows despondent, miserable, dissatisfied and weak. Her beauty soon leaves her, and from hard work, sleepless nights, worry about the little ones and disagreement and quarrels with her husband, she soon becomes a physical wreck and curses the moment that made her a poor man's wife. Such a dreary, miserable life is certainly not inclined to maintain love or respect for each other. The man can at least forget his misery in the company of a few friends; he can absorb himself in politics, or he can drown his misfortune in a glass of beer. The woman is chained to the house by a thousand duties; she cannot, like her husband, enjoy some recreation because she either has no means for it, or she is refused the same rights as her husband, by public opinion. She has to carry the cross with her until death, because our marriage laws know of no mercy, unless she wishes to lay bare her married life before the critical eye of Mrs. Grundy,[4] and even then she can only break the chains which tie her to the man she hates if she takes all the blame on her own shoulders, and if she has energy enough to stand before the world disgraced for the rest of her life. How many have the courage to do that? Very few. Only now and

4. EG refers to an off-stage character in Thomas Morton's *Speed the Plough* (1798), who represents the contemporary standards of respectability. "Mrs. Grundy" later came to signify prudishness, censorship, and the rigidity of social conventions.

then it comes like a flash of lightning that some woman, like the Princess De Chimay,[5] has had pluck enough to break the conventional barriers and follow her heart's desire. But this exception is a wealthy woman, dependent upon no one. The poor woman has to consider her little ones; she is less fortunate than her rich sister, and yet the woman who remains in bondage is called respectable: never mind if her whole life is a long chain of lies, deceit and treachery, she yet dares to look down with disgust upon her sisters who have been forced by society to sell their charms and affections on the street. No matter how poor, how miserable a married woman may be, she will yet think herself above the other, whom she calls a prostitute, who is an outcast, hated and despised by everyone, even those who do not hesitate to buy her embrace, look upon the poor wretch as a necessary evil, and some goody goody people even suggest to confine this evil to one district in New York, in order to "purify" all other districts of the city. What a farce! The reformers might as well demand that all the married inhabitants of New York be driven out because they certainly do not stand morally higher than the street woman. The sole difference between her and the married woman is, that the one has sold herself into chattel slavery during life, for a home or a title, and the other one sells herself for the length of time she desires; she has the right to choose the man she bestows her affections upon, whereas the married woman has no right whatsoever; she must submit to the embrace of her lord, no matter how lothsome this embrace may be to her, she must obey his commands; she has to bear him children, even at the cost of her own strength and health; in a word, she prostitutes herself every hour, every day of her life. I can find no other name for the horrid, humiliating and degrading condition of my married sisters than prostitution of the worst kind, with the only exception that the one is legal, the other illegal.[6]

I cannot deal with the few exceptional cases of marriage which are based on love, esteem and respect; these exceptions only verify the rule. But whether legal or illegal, prostitution in any form is unnatural, hurtful and despicable, and I know only too well that the conditions cannot be changed until this infernal system is abolished, but I also know that it is not only the economic dependence of women which has caused her enslavement, but also her ignorance and prejudice, and I also know that many of my sisters could be made free even now, were it not for our marriage institutions which keep them in ignorance, stupidity and prejudice. I therefore consider it my greatest duty to denounce marriage, not only the old form, but the so-called modern marriage, the idea of taking a wife and housekeeper, the idea of private possession of one sex by the other. I demand the independence of woman; her right to support herself; to live for herself; to

5. Princess Jeanne-Marie-Ignace-Theresa de Chimay (1773–1835) was known during the French Revolution as "Our Lady of Thermidor" for interceding on behalf of those sentenced to death. She was divorced by her husbands three times for committing adultery.
6. EG often compared marriage to prostitution, an idea current among anarchists of the period, especially in such papers as *Firebrand, Lucifer,* and *Liberty.* Compare this statement to EG's comments on marriage in her 1893 *New York World* interview ("Nellie Bly Again," Interview in the *New York World,* 17 September 1893, above).

love whomever she pleases, or as many as she pleases. I demand freedom for both sexes, freedom of action, freedom in love and freedom in motherhood.

Do not tell me that all this can only be accomplished under Anarchy; this is entirely wrong. If we want to accomplish Anarchy, we must first have free women at least, those women who are economically just as independent as their brothers are, and unless we have free women, we cannot have free mothers, and if mothers are not free, we cannot expect the young generation to assist us in the accomplishment of our aim, that is the establishment of an Anarchist society.

To you Freethinkers and Liberals who have abolished one God and created many whom you worship; you Radicals and Socialists, who still send your children to Sunday school, and all those who make concessions to the moral standard of today; to all of you I say that it is your lack of courage which makes you cling to and uphold marriage, and while you admit its absurdity in theory, you have not the energy to defy public opinion, and to live your own life practically.[7] You prate of equality of the sexes in a future Society, but you think it a necessary evil that the woman should suffer at present. You say women are inferior and weaker, and instead of assisting them to grow stronger you help to keep them in a degraded position. You demand exclusiveness for us, but you love variety and enjoy it wherever you can get a chance.

Marriage, the curse of so many centuries, the cause of jealousy, suicide and crime, must be abolished if we wish the young generation to grow to healthy, strong and free men and women.

E. GOLDMAN.

Firebrand, 18 July 1897, p. 2. This essay, probably the text of a lecture delivered in 1897, is the first version in print of EG's lecture on marriage, and the kernel of many such lectures delivered throughout her life. During this same period, her lecture series widened to include "Woman's Cause," "The Women in Present and Future," "Free Love," and "Prostitution." She reworked elements of her lecture on marriage into the essay "Love and Marriage," which appeared in her book *Anarchism and Other Essays* (1910).

7. Michael Bakunin, in *God and the State* (first English translation, 1883), makes a similar statement when criticizing "bourgeois Socialists" who have rejected the absurdity of religion but cannot reject the authority of god or state: "they have neither the power nor the wish nor the determination to follow out their thought and they waste their time and pains in constantly endeavoring to reconcile the irreconcilable."

Article in the *NEW YORK WORLD*

New York, 17 August 1897

Anarchy in Spain and in New York.

Anarchists Here Applaud the Assassination of Cánovas.

Golli Hailed as a Hero.

Emma Goldman Excites Cheers by a Wild, Bloodthirsty Harangue.

The Police Listen Inactive.

"I Glory in the Murder of Cánovas," Screamed the Frantic Woman.

President McKinley Assailed.

"We Are Enemies of Government; Government Is Tyranny,"
the Goldman Woman Said.

"President McKinley and Mark Hanna are shedding crocodile tears over the killing of Cánovas del Castillo.[1] In their own hearts they are saying 'Perhaps I will be the next.'

"I do not advise anybody to kill, but whether I advise it or you advise it fortunately makes no difference. Heroes like Golli do not ask permission of me or of anybody else to do their duty as they see it.

"So long as tyrants oppress mankind Gollis will be found to execute them.

"We are not enemies of society. We are enemies of government, for government is tyranny."

One thousand men and women cheered this sentiment uttered by Emma Goldman, the Anarchist, at a meeting held at Clarendon Hall, Thirteenth street, between Third and Fourth avenues, last night.

The crowd was not one upon which the hand of poverty seemed to rest very heavily. They were, as a rule, more than comfortably dressed, and they looked well fed.

Such a crowd could not have been brought together in any other American city than this. They listened to speeches in five languages—English, French, German, Italian and

---

1. On 8 August 1897, Italian anarchist Michele Angiolillo (mistakenly identified as "Golli" in the international press) shot and killed Spanish prime minister Antonio Cánovas del Castillo in retribution for the 4 May 1897 execution of five anarchists in the wake of the 7 June 1896 bombing in Barcelona of a Corpus Christi Day procession.

Spanish—and they interrupted the speakers with expressions not only in those languages, but in a variety of patois and dialects.

CELEBRATION OF A CRIME.

A circular that had been widely distributed brought the crowd together. The circular was really an invitation to rejoice over an assassination. It read:

MASS-MEETING TO
CELEBRATE
THE DEATH OF THE
LEADING DESPOT OF SPAIN,
CANOVAS DEL CASTILLO,
EXECUTED BY
ANARCHIST MICHEL ANGELO GOLLI.

The meeting was the first at which the spirit of anarchy as it exists in this city has dared to show itself with any strength since Herr Most, High Priest of the Order of Disorder, was made to serve a term in the penitentiary. He has been quiet since and was not present last night.[2]

POLICE WERE INFORMED.

The police were fully informed of the purpose of the meeting, and although Acting Captain Diamond, of the East Fifth Street Station, was present with twenty men, who had to stand by, and hear themselves called "dogs and thieves," the meeting was not broken up.

Emma Goldman evidently hoped that it would be, and did her utmost to say something that would cause the police to act.

The Goldman woman entered the big hall after it was crowded, accompanied by young and pretty girls, who seemed to idolize her. They were followed by as many young men, who wore red neckties and vainly tried to look unconcerned.

Cheers for Goldman swelled into frantic shouts of approval as she went to the platform and hung up two pictures. One was a picture of Pallás,[3] the Barcelona bomb thrower. The other was a picture of Sante,[4] who assassinated President Carnot, of France.

RED FLAG NOT DISPLAYED.

The red flag was not displayed in the hall, for the police had ordered that it should not be, but scores of the women wore flaming red shirt waists and the men waved red handkerchiefs.

2. Johann Most was released from Blackwell's Island penitentiary on 18 April 1892.
3. Spanish anarchist Paulino Pallás was executed 6 October 1893 for throwing two bombs at a Catalonia military commander who had suppressed the January 1892 Jerez uprising.
4. Italian anarchist Sante Caserio assassinated Carnot on 24 June 1894, in retaliation for the February 1894 execution of French anarchist Auguste Vaillant.

One queer feature of the meeting was that several of the women carried babies in arms and there were a great many boys and girls there.

A consumptive little man named H. M. Kelly was called upon to preside. He tried to make a fierce, bloodthirsty speech, but his feeble piccolo voice was not equal to the task, and the crowd shouted for something stronger.

HE DID HIS BEST.

Kelly struggled on though, and among other things, said:

"We are here to-night as Anarchists to express our emphatic indorsement of the execution of Cánovas by Golli on Aug. 8.

"We are so anxious to have peace all over the world that we celebrate and rejoice over the death of the Spanish despot. Cánovas has gone! May his like never be seen again!"

A German made a short speech in which he called Cánovas "a beast" who was "only fit for slaughter."

He was followed by a dark-bearded and dark-skinned man from Porto Rico named Abelardo A. Moscoso, who spoke in Spanish. His torrent of language, as interpreted by a friend, all went to show that the tortures inflicted upon the men arrested in connection with the Barcelona bomb throwing had of necessity signed the death warrant of Cánovas, and that Anarchists everywhere should rejoice that the warrant had been executed.

WENT INTO HYSTERICS.

An Italian named Pallavencini[5] claimed to speak as the delegate of the Italian Typographical Union. He became so excited in his speech that at times he laughed and cried hysterically. His countrymen in the hall went quite as wild.

"They say that we Anarchists are ferocious beasts, who should not be allowed to exist," he said. "Not so! Cánovas was a beast, and had no right to live in this enlightened age. I have seen documentary proof of his heinous acts.

"The man who killed Cánovas is a martyr to the cause of humanity and progress. The police knew fifteen days before the execution that the act was decreed,[6] for they know that anarchy works with precision and with certainty."

"JUST RETRIBUTION."

"The killing was an act of just retribution. The day of the emancipation of the world is not far away. Anarchists do not fear the guillotine or the gallows. Anarchy will soon be the religion of the world.

5. EG described Italian anarchist Salvatore Pallavencini as "a cultivated man, well-informed not only on the international labor movement, but also on the new tendencies in Italian art and letters" (*LML*, p. 238). Pallavencini hosted EG's visit in 1899 to Barre, Vermont, where he was editor of *Lo-Scalpellino* from 1896 to 1897. He moved to Paris in 1900 where, the same year, EG visited him and his family.

6. Following Cánovas's assassination, American and European newspapers printed rumors that it was no surprise. The *New York Times,* for example, reported that the Spanish government had word of an alleged meeting of anarchists in early July where it was decided to assassinate Cánovas by 15 August. See *New York Times,* 9 August 1897, p. 1 and 10 August 1897, p. 1.

"Anarchists think it is better to kill a ruler who is a tyrant than to have a revolution in which thousands have to die because of his acts.

"All honor to the Italian people for furnishing the assassin. They call us all assassins. Well, Italians do sometimes try their hand at that game.

"I am a peaceable man, but when I read of the torture of the Anarchists of Barcelona my blood boiled, and if there had been one hundred Cánovases I would have rejoiced to have killed them all."

AFTER BLOOD-MONEY.

The feeble voiced Kelly got up and plaintively announced that it cost money to hold Anarchist meetings, that bills for rent and printing had to be paid. He asked for $100. The rent of the hall alone was $40.

The pretty girls passed the collection baskets, with Emma Goldman directing them. When they got through and counted up they found that they had only $12.80.

Emma Goldman looked savagely through her gold-rimmed glasses at the big crowd, which just then was cheering the statement of a Spaniard named Arrango,[7] who said that the killing of Cánovas by Golli was the act of a slave rising against long oppression.

EMMA GOLDMAN SPEAKS.

Goldman was introduced. The woman talks with wonderful speed in a high pitched, harsh voice with a strong German accent. Although a small woman she is very masculine in her actions and manner, and seems to delight in saying risqué as well as blood-thirsty things in order to evoke applause.

"Some people think it cruel that we should celebrate the death of such a great and noble man as Cánovas," she said. "Those who have read history and know what Cánovas has done to the people of Spain, of Cuba and of other Spanish colonies will know, however, that we are perfectly justified in rejoicing over the death of such a beast.

"If it was an honest workingman who was dead we would be sorry for him, or sorry for his family, but we cannot even be sorry for the family when the dead man was nothing but a monster. He has spent his whole life devising methods of torturing and killing men."

"I GLORY IN THE DEATH OF CÁNOVAS."

"I glory in the death of Cánovas. I am ashamed of the Cuban patriots that they did not execute this monster long ago. I glorify the killing of Cánovas by Golli, the hero, because it removes an obstacle from the path of progress.

"They tell us that Cánovas was really not to blame for it all; that he was but an instrument in the hands of others. I say no. Cánovas was the tyrant and the tens of thousands of Spanish soldiers were his instruments. Down with all such!

"The tyrants of men are all cowards. Look at President Faure, of France. He hired a

7. Possibly Alfredo Arrango, a Spanish army colonel who fought on behalf of Cuban independence.

man to throw a bomb in order that he might become notorious, and then used his miserable scheme to try and punish and kill innocent men.[8]

"They tell us that by despatching one tyrant we will not change society; that another tyrant will take his place. Yes, my friends, that is true, and another Golli will come up to meet every such new tyrant. Wherever there is a Caesar there must be a Brutus."

A SHOT AT THE POLICE.

"It seems to me that this glorious and free country is in great sympathy with Cánovas. Otherwise they would not send so many policemen and detectives here to watch us tonight. I do not blame the policemen. They find it easier to stand around a corner twirling a club and watching for a chance to crack some honest man's skull with it than they do to go to work in the shops for twelve or fourteen hours a day. Some of them may be good men. There is honor even among thieves, you know.

"The authorities of this country, including President McKinley and Mark Hanna, who promised you prosperity a few months ago but are giving you starvation, are shedding crocodile tears over the death of Cánovas. In their minds they are perhaps saying to themselves, 'Maybe I will be the next.'"

ASSAILS THE PRESIDENT.

"This man McKinley said he had Cuba's cause at heart before he was elected. Now he is expressing his sorrow over the death of this Cánovas, who has killed thousands of our Cuban friends.

"If this man Cánovas believed in a heaven he is probably sitting on the right hand of the throne now telling the angels all about his life. All tyrants go there, I believe. All of us Anarchists, free-thinkers, revolutionists and philosophers go to hell, and we have a lively time there. When I die I would rather go to hell than to heaven.

"It is a shame, I say, that we cannot hold a peaceable meeting here unmolested. Look at the watchdogs around you. I understand that they are here to make an arrest if they find any excuse for doing it. Well, I will not bridle my tongue one bit, even at the risk of having one of them put his delicate hand on my shoulder and say 'Come with me.'"

MURDERS PREDICTED.

"Cánovas is not the only man who will have to die violently before the social revolution is accomplished. There are hundreds of people all over the world only waiting for the opportunity to show that they are tired of despotism and tyranny.

"It seems to me queer that such a contemptible wretch as Gen. Weyler[9] has been allowed to live so long. His atrocious acts, inhuman almost beyond conception, against

8. EG later wrote Hamon asking him if this staged bombing was actually true (see Letter to Augustin Hamon, 20 August 1897, below).
9. Spanish general Valeriano Weyler y Nicolau (1838–1930) became governor of Cuba in February 1896. In order to repress the Liberation Army, General Weyler y Nicolau initiated the "Reconcentration

Cubans and Americans, deserve death. He murdered Dr. Ruiz, an American citizen. What is America going to do about it? Sue Spain for $50,000.[10]

"Shame on such a cowardly country, I say!"

WOE UNTO TYRANTS!

"Do not think that if they kill the brave Golli they will put down Anarchy! The silence of the martyred anarchists of Chicago in their graves is more eloquent than were their voices when they lived. Woe unto the tyrants of the world! We have thousands of Gollis!"

The crowd had cheered itself hoarse by the time that Goldman finished speaking, but many remained to hear speeches by a Frenchman and another Spaniard. When Chairman Kelly got up to adjourn the meeting a big man got up and shouted in English:

"Long live Anarchy!"

The crowd echoed the sentiment in all tongues as it filed out of the hall.

New York World, 17 August 1897, pp. 1–2; includes sketch of EG addressing the meeting and portraits of other speakers. At a meeting of English-speaking anarchists on 22 August, EG defended the assassination against criticisms voiced by Charles B. Cooper and others. See "Her Comrades Rebuke Emma Goldman," *New York Tribune,* 23 August 1897, *EGP,* reel 47.

Plan," to separate local peasants from the insurgents, placing thousands of women and children in loosely organized concentration camps where disease and malnutrition spread, ultimately killing hundreds of thousands of people. In America, he was denounced by elements of the press who referred to him as "The Butcher." Recalled to Spain in the latter half of 1897, he continued his career and in July 1909, as captain-general of Catalonia, actively suppressed the anarchist uprising which ended with the execution of Spanish anarchist and Modern School educator Francisco Ferrer.

10. Ricardo Ruiz de Ugarrio y Salvador (d. 1897) was an Cuban American dentist living in Cuba. Part of the Cuban resistance, Ruiz was arrested 7 February 1897 and held in solitary confinement in Guanabacoa prison, charged with participation in the derailment, capture, and robbery of a passenger train in Cuba on 16 January 1897. Found dead in his cell some ten days later, the guards claimed he committed suicide. However, written in his own blood on a chair (the only piece of furniture in the cell) were found the words, "They intended to kill me." His suspicious death in prison prompted an international incident between the Spanish and U.S. governments the year preceding the Spanish-American War. At President McKinley's request, Judge William J. Calhoun of Danville, Illinois, conducted a judicial investigation in Cuba from 13 May to 7 June and determined that the Spanish government was responsible for Ruiz's death. EG's remark about "$50,000" is a reference to the $75,000 indemnity claim that the U.S. minister to Spain, Stewart Woodford, solicited from the Spanish government on behalf of the Ruiz family.

To AUGUSTIN HAMON

New York, 20 August 1897

DEAR COMRADE:

Your letter of July 10th received but have been unable to answer before. up to the present I have been unable to find any one to write the articles you desire. the following are a few names of Officers of some of the largest trade Unions, here Samuel Gompers Pres. American Federation of Labor Washington D.C. Frank Morrison[1] Secretary American Federation of Labor. Jas. R. Souverign[2] Grand Master Workman K. of L., Little Rock Arkeansaw. M. M. Garland[3] Pres. Amalgamated Association of Iron & Steel Workers. Pittsburg Pa. W. B. Prescott[4] Pres. International Typographical Union, Desoto Block Indianapolis Ind. M. D. Ratchford[5] Pres. United Mine Workers. Columbus Ohio G. W. Perkins[6] Pres. Cigar Makers International Union Chicago Ill. P. J. McGuire[7] General Sec.

1. Frank Morrison (1859–1949) was elected secretary of the American Federation of Labor in 1897, a post he occupied for more than forty years. He first joined the International Typographical Union in 1886.

2. James R. Sovereign (b. 1854) was grand master workman of the Knights of Labor from 1894 to 1897, having joined the Knights of Labor in 1881. An active labor journalist and lecturer, he was a member of the national executive committee of the People's Party in 1896.

3. Mahlon Morris Garland (1856–1920) was president of the National Amalgamated Association of Iron and Steel Workers from 1892 to 1898 and fourth vice-president of the American Federation of Labor from 1885 to 1898. Garland later served as a U.S. Congressman for the Republican party from 1915 until his death in 1920.

4. William Blair Prescott (1863–1916) joined the International Typographical Union in Toronto in 1883; he served as president of the union from 1891 to 1898.

5. Michael D. Ratchford (1860–1949) was president of the local Massillon, Ohio, branch of the United Mine Workers of America from 1890 to 1892, general organizer from 1893 to 1894, and president of the Ohio Miners from 1895 to 1896; he served as president of the United Mine Workers of America from 1897 to 1898 and went on to become a representative on the national Industrial Commission from 1898 to 1900.

6. A close associate of Samuel Gompers and the American Federation of Labor, George W. Perkins (1856–1934) was president of the Cigar Makers International Union. Serving first as vice-president of the union from 1885 to 1891, he acted as president for six months during 1888 and 1889. In 1891 he was elected president, a post he kept for thirty-five years.

7. Peter James McGuire (1852–1906) was chief executive officer of the United Brotherhood of Carpenters and Joiners of America from 1881 to 1901. A member of the International Working Men's Association, he helped organize the Social Democratic Workingmen's Party in 1874. McGuire was also a founder of the New York City Central Labor Union in 1882. In 1886, he was one of the founders of the American Federation of Labor and its first secretary. But he was forced to resign as vice president of the AFL in 1889 because of bad health and alcoholism, and then in 1902, when charges of embezzlement were brought against him, McGuire was forced to resign from the AFL.

Brotherhood of Carpenters & Joiners of A. Philadelphia Pa. and Jas. A. O'Connell[8] Pres. International Association of Machinsts, Monon Bldg. Chicago Ill. also write to Eugune V. Debs[9] Chicago Ill.

As to your book I have been to one of the largest publishing houses here. Scribners. and they could not handle it, several other publishers would not pass judgement on it until they saw an English translation of it and at the present time I can hardly tend to it as I start away on a three months propaganda tour in two weeks. still there is a Comrade in Boston who I will see about translating it and then try again.[10]

What effect did the death of the Canovas del Castillo[11] have on the general public in France, here in America it created a big sensation and it is safe to say that Anarchism has not been talked about by the newspapers and public at large since 1886 &-87[12] as during the past 10 days. pages of the daily press have been taken up by a description of the tortures and while all of the American Newspapers have admitted that Canovas was a monster, still when we held our meeting to celebrate the event on Monday night we were denounced as glorifing murder, the *New York Journal* the most sensational paper in American Daily papers, had some remarkable Editorals on the subject, which could hardly have been improved on by Anarchists, yet they turned tail when we had our meeting and denounced us in the most bitter terms. hypocrisy of the press is one of the features of American Journalism.

How do the Comrades in Paris regard the recent bomb explosions in Paris, as genuine attempts on Faure's life or police plots. the address of Mrs. Parsons[13] is as follows. Mrs. L. E. Parsons 1777 Troy st. Chicago Ill. U.S.A. with kind regards to all Comrades.

FRATERNALLY

E GOLDMANN

P.S. I send you by same mail clippings of N.Y. papers.

ALS, Augustin Hamon Archive, IISH. Except for the signature, the handwriting of this letter is not EG's; it may possibly be Edward Brady's.

8. James A. O'Connell (1858–1936) served as grand master machinist of the International Association of Machinists from 1893 to 1911. He first joined the union in 1889 and became a member of the executive board in 1891. O'Connell was the third vice-president of the AFL from 1895 to 1913 and second vice-president from 1914 to 1918.

9. As president of the American Railway Union, in 1897 Eugene Debs helped found the Social Democracy of America socialist organization.

10. EG had offered to help Hamon find an American publisher for his *Psychologie du militaire professionnel*. No English-language edition was ever published.

11. Spanish prime minister Cánovas del Castillo was assassinated by anarchist Michele Angiolillo on 8 August 1897.

12. EG refers to the tumult surrounding the Haymarket affair and subsequent execution of four anarchists in 1886 and 1887.

13. EG had promised in her 25 July 1897 letter to Hamon to get him more material on the "Chicago comrades" from Lucy Parsons, anarchist, labor activist, and widow of Haymarket anarchist Albert Parson.

> **Article in the *PROVIDENCE EVENING BULLETIN***
>
> *Providence, R.I., 4 September 1897*

Anarchy.

Emma Goldman Held Forth on Olneyville Square Last Night.

Addressed Her "Fellow Slaves" in Usual Strain.

There Were Rival Attractions, but They Were Completely Eclipsed
by the Little Dark-Complexioned Woman Mounted on a Dry-Goods Box,
Who Said Long Hair Was Not Necessary to be an Anarchist.

There were rival attractions on Olneyville square last night. They were the gospel wagon, a gentleman who sold everything from a shoestring to a complete shaving outfit and threw in a ventriloquistic entertainment free of charge, a series of pictures and advertisements thrown on a screen and finally Emma Goldman, whose Anarchistic beliefs are too well known to need much further description.

The gospel wagon was doing pretty well until the ventriloquist, alias shoestring salesman, arrived. When that gentleman proceeded to converse with a wooden dummy and exchange compliments with an invisible personage on a nearby roof the fickle crowd deserted the gospel wagon and flocked to the fakir's standard.

As soon as the dummy began to grow less voluble in his remarks and the peddler began to cry his wares the crowd gazed at the panoramic mixture of advertisements and pictures, principally advertisements, that were thrown on a screen stretched above the roof of a building.

Then Miss Goldman arrived. It was nearly 9 o'clock, and the crowd was looking for some new excitement. A packing box was improvised into a platform, and John H. Cook[1] of this city mounted upon it. Mr. Cook did this principally to draw the crowd. It did not draw very well at first. The fakir had renewed his seductive conversation with a gorgeously bedecked doll whose lower jaw worked on a hinge. It was a last effort to keep the crowd around him. The doll's lower jaw flapped to and fro frantically, and the ventriloquist wiped drops of perspiration from his forehead, although the night was cool.

Yet one by one the crowd went to the place where Mr. Cook was setting forth the object of the meeting.

---

1. John H. Cook was an anarchist and longtime labor activist in his hometown of Providence, R.I.

Finally a little woman, with a complexion that many of her sisters with less unpopular ideas might envy, and clad in a dress of some dark material, stepped upon the platform with head uncovered. Immediately the crowd, in a body, deserted the ventriloquist and surrounded the Anarchistic teacher.

The gospel wagon withdrew. The pictures on the screen quivered in indignation because of the lack of attention to their artistic details.

Miss Goldman's salutation was characteristic:

"Fellow slaves," she said. "I think you will all be indignant because I call you slaves." If any one was he did not say a word. Not even a bomb was forthcoming. The crowd was made up almost entirely of men. There were only one or two women in the audience.

Continuing, Miss Goldman said: "If you would only consider the question you would at once admit that I am right and give me credit for telling you the truth. I admit that you are not slaves in the sense that you are sold upon a block, but you are slaves nevertheless. The only difference is that you are hired slaves instead of block slaves. You have to dread the idea of being unemployed and of being compelled to support your masters."[2]

Miss Goldman then made a fierce onslaught on all clergymen, characterizing them as hypocrites, and the Gospel which they preached as something which ought not to be allowed the place in the minds of men that it is given.

"Christ said: 'I will love My neighbor as Myself.' The people do not do this—each one strives to put himself at the front, regardless of the rights of others. Under the present days of capital, poverty and wealth, to preach of love or of sympathy is simply a farce. You are but the working class, the common people. The capitalist says that if you don't have him you can't get along. He says you are dependent upon him, and that without him you would die on the street.

"This is not right. The police, the Government machine and all the officials are ruled by money. Can I call you anything less than slaves when you allow your right of free speech to be trampled under foot? I can't blame the police or the members of the police force. I look upon them as wage slaves as well as you. The only difference is that they have an easier job. They show their brotherly love by letting their clubs fall on your heads every once in a while.

"To believe in any labor leader who goes up on a platform and says 'I am your saviour' will keep you in slavery. It is only you that can help yourselves. It is only common sense you want. I don't preach robbery or death. I am against them both. Anarchy means nothing else than peace and happiness to all. The press has reported that only a man with long and unkempt hair and wild eyes and crazed speech can be an Anarchist. I was talk-

2. EG's comparison of the hired slave and the slave bought and sold on a block echoes Albert Parsons in his address to the jury in October 1886, reproduced in *The Accused, the Accusers* . . . (Chicago: Socialistic Publishing Society, [1886?]). In his speech Parsons stated, "The chattel slave of the past—the wage slave of today; what is the difference? The master selected under chattel slavery his own slaves. Under the wage slavery system the wage slave selects his master."

ing with a man to-night. I said: 'I am an Anarchist.' He said: 'You don't look like one.'
They have a false idea of us. If you wish to hold the right to the claim of being the freest
union in the world, you must allow the women to have equal rights with you. Then you
can hope for a free union. Till then I shall certainly have the right to call you slaves."

Miss Goldman will give another open-air meeting in Burgess square to-night [3] and
will hold a meeting in the Casino Sunday afternoon. [4]

Providence (R.I.) Evening Bulletin, 4 September 1897, p. 2.

3. EG's speech in Burgess Square on the evening of 4 September prompted Providence mayor Edwin
   McGuinness to threaten her arrest if she attempted to speak in a public plaza again. EG defied his orders, speaking three days later in Market Square, the principal open-air forum in Providence. She was
   arrested, the first time since 1893, and was held overnight at the central police station. See her account
   in "Letters from a Tour," no. 2 (1 January 1898), Series in *Sturmvogel,* 15 December 1897–15 February
   1898, below. Although EG suspected that her next visit to Providence would end in her arrest and trial,
   her return the next January passed without incident.
4. On 5 September, at the Providence Casino at 936 Westminster Street, EG spoke on the subject of the
   8 August 1897 assassination of Spanish prime minister Cánovas del Castillo by Italian anarchist
   Michele Angiolillo. A pamphlet entitled "The Modern Inquisition of Spain" (also issued as a supplement to the *Firebrand,* 11 July 1897) was distributed to everyone in attendance. See "More Anarchy,"
   Providence Daily Journal, 8 September 1897, and "Told to Get Out," *Providence Evening Bulletin,* 8 September 1897, *EGP,* reel 47. For EG's view of the assassination of Cánovas, see "Anarchy in Spain and
   New York," Article in the *New York World,* 17 August 1897, above.

Article in the *BOSTON DAILY GLOBE*

Boston, 13 September 1897

Advised Strenuous Measures.

Emma Goldmann Denounced Shooting of Miners and Advocated Resort to Arms to Obtain Rights.

Miss Emma Goldmann talked on "The Rights of the People" before 500 people in Phenix hall yesterday forenoon, and delivered a characteristic anarchistic address, which was liberally applauded.

She denounced the attack upon the striking miners at Hazleton by the deputy sheriffs,[1] and condemned the social system, advising strenuous measures to put it down, and crying out for revenge.

"When I think of this latest legalized murder," she began, "it seems like a mockery to the dead miners today to talk and talk, when it is necessary to act. The workingmen were fired upon because they were human beings who wanted bread for their children and homes for their families. They have been kept starving by the authorities and then fired upon because they peaceably asked for bread.

"You do not have to be an anarchist. If you want bread you are an enemy to society and must be put down. The order to kill the workingmen was given because they asked peaceably for the necessaries of life. If such a thing is a crime against society then society should be attacked and put down.

"I feel that nothing short of action is to be done today. If I am not with the widows of those miners today extending my sympathy to them it is because I have not the money to pay the railroad kings to take me there.

"My friends, you have free speech just so long as you say what the authorities desire that you should say, and they determine what constitutes free speech. You have this same kind of free speech in darkest Russia, in Germany, or even under the sultan, just as in enlightened America, where men are shot down like dogs. But I can tell you if this had been done in Russia the sheriff would not have lived 24 hours. Laws here are made by the capitalists and monopolists and enforced in the interest of capitalists and monopolists, against the people.

---

1. On 10 September 1897, at least 19 men died and between 35 and 50 were injured, most of them shot in the back, when deputies opened fire on a peaceful march of striking miners at Lattimer, near Hazleton, in the anthracite region of northeastern Pennsylvania. In March the following year, Sheriff James L. Martin and his deputies were acquitted of murder charges. Among anarchists and others on the left, "Hazleton" (historians now call it the Lattimer Massacre) became a symbol of the unpunished violence that could be meted out to organized labor.

EMMA GOLDMANN, ANARCHIST.

She Lectures in This City, Criticising Existing Social Conditions And Explaining the Theories of Her Cult.

EMMA GOLDMANN AND SOME TYPES IN HER AUDIENCE.

Sketches of Goldman and her audience speckled the pages of mainstream newspapers; this drawing appeared in the 6 September 1897 *Boston Daily Globe.* (Reprinted courtesy of *The Boston Globe*)

"If those strikers had been Americans the sheriff would not have dared to fire upon them. But they were foreigners, and foreigners do not amount to anything. The foreigner is good enough to build your elegant houses and your roads, sew your clothes and do everything for your comfort, but he is not good enough to enjoy the advantages that belong to the heads of the government. If you want to get your rights you must go armed; you must meet your oppressors with the sword. If that sheriff had known those miners were armed he would not have dared to act as he did. He would have feared the consequences. But he knew they were unarmed. They were Hungarians and Poles, and no one knew or understood what they wanted or for what they were peaceably asking.[2]

"It is time to act. I know how hard it is to arouse the Anglo-Saxon race. They are so phlegmatic, so cold, so slow to action. It is only when 100 of them are shot down that they will rise to defend themselves."

The greater part of Miss Goldmann's address was given to excoriations of the wealthy, the depicting of the attitude of the employer towards his workmen as a slave driver crushing a serf, and to a general denunciation of the laws and their enforcement. The militia, the police officers and every representative body charged with the enforcement of the statutes were the objects of her caustic criticism.

Boston Daily Globe, 13 September 1897, p. 6.

2. The unarmed marchers were approached by Sheriff Martin, who ordered them to stop marching and disperse. The marchers, most of whom were Polish, Slovakian, and Lithuanian immigrants and did not understand English, continued marching. The sheriff and his eighty-six deputies then opened fire.

Emma Goldman Has Her Say.

Regulated in Reform Convention She Speaks in a Hall All by Herself.

Emma Goldman, who found too much law and regulation in the reform convention[1] in this city, had a meeting all of her own at Union Hall, 45 North Clark street, last evening.

"I am not going to bring about a revolution," she said. "I have not the power, I am sorry to say, or I would do so tomorrow. I will be content if I sow the seeds of discontent."

Anarchists of the Social Democracy Branch 2 brand, she declared, were fit subjects for the insane asylum.[2]

"An Anarchist who believes in division of property, the killing of the rich, and the burning of fine houses is an idiot," she exclaimed.

Chicago Tribune, 30 September 1897, p. 5.

1. This national labor convention took place in Orpheus Hall in Chicago from the 27th to the 29th of September, bringing together representatives of reform clubs, trade unionists, and anarchists. It was actually the follow-up to a convention called by the striking United Mine Workers of America that took place at the end of August in St. Louis. The American Federation of Labor advised its unions not to attend because the miners' strike had been settled; consequently, the Chicago conference was sparsely attended. Led by EG, the anarchists walked out of the convention on 28 September, but not before EG expressed her opinion in a half-hour address to the group assembled. For EG's account, see "Letters from a Tour," no. 4 (1 February 1898), Series in *Sturmvogel,* 15 December 1897–15 February 1898, below.

2. In Chicago, Branch 2 of the Social Democracy of America responded to the Hazleton massacre by passing various resolutions on 12 September. It cast "plutocracy" as the real culprit in the shooting of strikers by police deputies, and urged that "for every miner killed and wounded a millionaire should be treated in the same manner." One resolution recommended "the torch as the most successful weapon to wield against them," a theme picked up by other Chicago radicals. Roy M. Goodwin, a member of the Social Democracy's national board of directors, speaking "for himself and not for his organization," said he "would burn every dollar's worth of their property" and "would destroy their fine palaces." Only Branch 2 passed such retaliatory resolutions, for which it had its charter suspended on 18 September by the executive council of the national office, headed by Eugene Debs (and including Roy Goodwin), after a four-hour meeting with Branch 2's board of directors. The leadership of Branch 2 included well-known anarchists, among them T. Putnam Quinn, Lucy Parsons, Jay Fox, and Eric B. Morton. Both Fox, a member of the special committee that drew up the resolutions, and Quinn, president of Branch 2, later defended in *Free Society* the actions of their branch and condemned Debs for bowing to pressure from the Chicago press and police and silencing Social Democracy's more radical voices. Debs defended the action of the executive council in the party's organ, the *Social Democrat,* as well as in the *Chicago Tribune* where he declared, "We believe in the ballot, not in bullets." See *Chicago Tribune,* 13 September 1897, pp. 1–2; *Chicago Tribune,* 19 September 1897, p. 1; *Free Society,* 14 November 1897, p. 6; *Free Society,* 3 July 1898, pp. 6–7; and *Social Democrat* (Chicago), 23 September 1897, p. 2, for reports of this controversy.

Interview in the
ST. LOUIS POST-DISPATCH SUNDAY MAGAZINE
St. Louis, 24 October 1897

What Is There in Anarchy for Woman?

By Emma Goldman.

"What does anarchy hold out to me—a woman?"

"More to woman than to anyone else—everything which she has not—freedom and equality."

Quickly, earnestly Emma Goldman, the priestess of anarchy, exiled from Russia, feared by police, and now a guest of St. Louis Anarchists,[1] gave this answer to my question.

I found her at No. 1722 Oregon avenue, an old-style two-story brick house, the home of a sympathizer[2]—not a relative as has been stated.

I was received by a good-natured, portly German woman, and taken back to a typical German dining-room—everything clean and neat as soap and water could make them. After carefully dusting a chair for me with her apron, she took my name back to the bold little free-thinker. I was welcome. I found Emma Goldman sipping her coffee and partaking of bread and jelly, as her morning's repast. She was neatly clad in a percale shirt waist and skirt, with white collar and cuffs, her feet encased in a loose pair of cloth slippers. She doesn't look like a Russian Nihilist who will be sent to Siberia if she ever crosses the frontier of her native land.

"Do you believe in marriage?" I asked.

"I do not," answered the fair little Anarchist, as promptly as before. "I believe that when two people love each other that no judge, minister or court, or body of people, have anything to do with it. They themselves are the ones to determine the relations which

---

1. EG's eight days in St. Louis, beginning 16 October 1897, were extensively covered by the local press and drew the keen interest of the authorities. When it was erroneously reported that she planned to speak at an open-air meeting on 19 October in front of the city's statue of President Ulysses Grant, Mayor Ziegenhein declared such a gathering illegal and ordered police to bar any attempt. Simultaneously, the city's House of Delegates passed a resolution approving the actions of the mayor and police department in stifling the "un-American" and "unpatriotic" teachings of a "notorious Anarchist." Under police surveillance, EG spoke the next night at Walhalla Hall to an overflow audience of hundreds. So successful were her meetings in St. Louis that her stay there the following year garnered no coverage at all since, according to *Solidarity*, "the dailies found out they were helping the Anarchists in their propaganda." See *St. Louis Post-Dispatch*, 20 October 1897, *EGP*, reel 47; and *Solidarity*, 1 May 1898, p. 4.
2. EG stayed at the home of August Sendlein, an anarchist and cheesemaker.

Front-page feature story on Goldman in the 24 October 1897 *St. Louis Post-Dispatch Sunday Magazine*. Journalist Miriam Michelson's interview departed from the usual mocking tone of the mainstream press and displayed intellectual curiosity and excitement about Goldman's ideas. (Reprinted with permission of the *St. Louis Post-Dispatch*, copyright 1897)

they shall hold with one another. When that relation becomes irksome to either party, or one of the parties, then it can be as quietly terminated as it was formed."

Miss Goldman gave a little nod of her head to emphasize her words, and quite a pretty head it was, crowned with soft brown hair, combed with a bang and brushed to one side. Her eyes are the honest blue, her complexion clear and white. Her nose though rather broad and of a Teutonic type, was well formed. She is short of stature, with a well-rounded figure. Her whole type is more German than Russian. The only serious physical failing that she has is in her eyes. She is so extremely nearsighted that with glasses she can scarcely distinguish print.

"The alliance should be formed," she continued, "not as it is now, to give the woman a support and home, but because the love is there, and that state of affairs can only be brought about by an internal revolution, in short, Anarchy."

She said this as calmly as though she had just expressed an ordinary every-day fact, but the glitter in her eyes showed the "internal revolutions" already at work in her busy brain.

"What does Anarchy promise woman?"

"It holds everything for woman—freedom, equality—everything that woman has not now."

"Isn't woman free?"

"Free! She is the slave of her husband and her children. She should take her part in the business world the same as the man; she should be his equal before the world, as she is in the reality. She is as capable as he, but when she labors she gets less wages. Why? Because she wears skirts instead of trousers."

"But what is to become of the ideal home life, and all that now surrounds the mother, according to a man's idea?"

"Ideal home life, indeed! The woman, instead of being the household queen, told about in story books, is the servant, the mistress, and the slave of both husband and children. She loses her own individuality entirely, even her name she is not allowed to keep. She is the mistress of John Brown or the mistress of Tom Jones; she is that and nothing else. That is the way I think of her."

Miss Goldman has a pleasant accent. She rolls her r's and changes her r's into v's and vice-versa, with a truly Russian pronunciation. She gesticulates a great deal. When she becomes excited her hands and feet and shoulders all help to illustrate her meanings.

"What would you do with the children of the Anarchistic era?"

"The children would be provided with common homes, big boarding schools, where they will be properly cared for and educated and in every way given as good, and in most cases better, care than they would receive in their own homes. Very few mothers know how to take proper care of their children, anyway. It is a science only a very few have learned."

"But the women that desire a home life and the care of their own children, the domestic woman, what of her?"

"Oh, of course, the women that desire could keep their children home and confine themselves as strictly to domestic duties as they desired. But it would give those women who desire something broader, a chance to attain any height they desired. With no poor, and no capitalists, and one common purse, this earth will afford the heaven that the Christians are looking for in another world."

She gazed contemplatively in the bottom of the empty coffee cup, as though she saw in imagination the ideal State, already an actuality.

"Who will take care of the children?" I asked, breaking in upon her reverie.

"Every one," she answered, "has tastes and qualifications suiting them to some occupation. I am a trained nurse. I like to care for the sick. So it will be with some women. They will want to care for and teach the children."

"Won't the children lose their love for their parents and feel the lack of their companionship?" A thought of the affectionate little darlings being relegated to a sort of an orphan asylum crossed my mind.

"The parents will have the same opportunities of gaining their confidences and affections as they have now. They can spend just as much time there as they please or have them with them just as often as desired. They will be the children of love—healthy, strong-minded—and not as now, in most cases, born of hate and domestic dissensions."

"What do you call love?"

"When a man or woman finds some quality or qualities in another that they admire and has an overweening desire to please that person, even to the sacrificing of personal feeling; when there is that subtle something drawing them together, that those who love recognize, and feel it in the inmost fiber of their being, then I call that love." She finished speaking and her face was suffused with a rosy blush.

"Can a person love more than one at a time?"

"I don't see why not—if they find the same lovable qualities in several persons. What should prevent one loving the same things in all of them?

"If we cease to love the man or woman and find some one else, as I said before, we talk it over together and quietly change the mode of living. The private affairs of the family need not then be talked over in the courts and become public property. No one can control the affections, therefore there should be no jealousies.

"Heartaches? Oh, yes," she said, sadly, "but not hatred because he or she has tired of the relations. The human race will always have heartaches as long as the heart beats in the breast.

"My religion," she laughingly repeated. "I was of the Hebrew faith when a girl—you know I am a Jewess—but now I am an atheist. No one has been able to prove either the inspiration of the Bible or the existence of a God to my satisfaction. I believe in no hereafter except the hereafter that is found by the physical matter existing in the human body. I think that lives again in some other form, and I don't think that anything once created over is lost—it goes on and on in first one shape, then another. There is no such thing as a soul—it is all the physical matter."

Pretty Miss Goldman finished speaking, and a delicate flush mounted to her cheek as I asked her if she intended to marry.

"No; I don't believe in marriage for others, and I certainly should not preach one thing and practice another."

She sat in an easy attitude with one leg crossed over the other. She is in every sense a womanly looking woman, with masculine mind and courage.

She laughed as she said there were fifty police at her lecture on Wednesday night, and she added, "If there had of been a bomb thrown I would surely have been blamed for it."

St. Louis Post-Dispatch Sunday Magazine, 24 October 1897, p. 9; includes three sketches of Goldman based on "photographs taken by the Sunday Post-Dispatch photographer for whom Miss Goldman posed." Reprinted with permission of the *St. Louis Post-Dispatch.*

Reise-Briefe.

I.

Es wurden in der letzten Zeit, sowohl in Europa als hierzulande, so viele Reisebriefe geschrieben, daß es eigentlich die reinste Nachahmung ist, meine Erlebnisse und Erfahrungen, die ich während meiner 14-wöchentlichen Bummelei im Westen gemacht habe, zu publizieren. Wer imitirt übrigens heutzutage nicht? Redner und Journalisten, Schriftsteller und Poeten, Sänger und Schauspieler. Alle wiederholen nur das, was schon Andere vor ihnen gesagt, geschrieben, gesungen und gespielt haben. Das Originelle wird nicht jeden Tag geschaffen, noch viel weniger Originale jeden Tag geboren. Es giebt zwar eine Menge von Leuten, die sich einbilden, große Geister, ja, sogar Genies zu sein; aber in Wirklichkeit sind diese armen Menschenkinder wie die Fliege, welche auf dem Felde sich gemütlich auf das Horn des Ochsen gesetzt, und nach vollbrachter Tageslast stolz mit dem Ausrufe in die Stadt kam: "Wir haben gepflügt!" Da ich weder eingebildet bin, noch mich je zu den Größen, oder gar Genies gerechnet habe, so mögen meine Freunde mir das Imitiren verzeihen, das heißt, wenn sie mir überhaupt etwas zu verzeihen haben.

Das Reisen ist gewiß eine schöne Sache, wenn man plenty cash in der Tasche hat und weder von Freunden noch Genossen abhängig ist. Aber reisen, wenn man gerade so viel hat um in die nächste Stadt zu gelangen, heute bei dem einen zu essen bekommt, (oder auch nicht), morgen bei dem andern entweder am Fußboden, oder im Familienbett, (mit Ausschluß des Hausvaters natürlich) schlafen muß, ist zwar nicht besonders angenehm, aber gerade solche Schwierig- und Widerwärtigkeiten verleihen meinen Reisen stets einen besonderen Reiz. Vielleicht weil ich, wie mein Freund, the Irish-dutchman sagt, eine geborene Vagabondin bin.

Es wurde mir oft gesagt, und wie ich es selbst am besten weiß, wie wenig ich mit meiner Rasse gemein habe; nicht daß mir dieser Umstand, zur besonderen Ehre gereichen soll—aber es ist nun einmal so, und da kann weder ich noch die Rasse dafür verantwortlich gemacht werden. Das Bedürfnis zu wandern; von Ort zu Ort zu ziehen, und wie der ewige Jude, nirgends Rast noch Ruhe zu finden, habe ich aber doch von den Juden geerbt. Meine Russengenossen konnten zwar ihren eigenen Willen selten in Anwendung bringen, denn sie wurden nie gefragt, ob sie gehen wollen oder nicht. Sie wurden einfach von Land zu Land, von Stelle zu Stelle gehetzt, gehaßt und gemieden gleich Aussätzigen. Selbst in diesem Jahrhundert der Intelligenz, des Wissens, des Fortschritts und der Aufklärung werden die Juden überall nur geduldet und es giebt wohl sehr wenige Arier, welche ganz frei von Vorurtheilen in diesem Punkte sind.

Mein Hang zum Vagabundieren, pour la vie bohème, wäre demnach genügend Beweis, daß mir nicht alle Eigenschaften der Semiten fehlen. Nicht die Nothwendigkeit, die Menschen von meinen Ansichten zu überzeugen oder die Welt aus den Angeln zu heben, veranlaßt mich, zeitweise von Stadt zu Stadt zu ziehen; sondern, wie gesagt, mein rastloser, unruhiger Geist, das Bedürfnis, neue Gesichter, andere Menschen und ihre Eigenschaften, Sitten und Gebräuche, Vorzüge und Mängel kennen zu lernen, treiben mich aus der gewohnten alltäglichen Umgebung. Monate-, jahrelang, ja vielleicht fürs ganze Leben an einem Platze weilen zu sollen, immer mit denselben Menschen verkehren zu müssen, in derselben Bierhöhle zu trinken—dieses trostlos öde Einerlei der Alltäglichkeit würde mich mit Entsetzen erfullen. Einer meiner Freunde, bei dem sich die Gewohnheit, den Handlungen anderer unlautere Motive zu unterschieben, zur Krankheit entwickelt hat, behauptet allerdings, die Sucht zur Masse zu sprechen, die Befriedigung, welche mir der Beifall der Zuhörer verschafft, das wären die eigentlichen Motive, welche mich von Zeit zu Zeit veranlassen, auszureißen. Gefehlt, mein Lieber. Ich glaube auch nicht einen Augenblick daran, daß ich durch mein Reden die Menschen ändern oder zu Anarchisten machen kann; gar keine Spur. Erstens reicht meine Rednergabe hierzu nicht aus; und zweitens bin ich längst zur Überzeugung gelangt, daß die Sprache zu armselig, zu ohnmächtig ist, um das wiederzugeben, was man empfindet. Will mir einer meiner sprachkundigen, intelligenten Freunde beweisen, daß sich die Liebe, der Haß, der Schmerz, die Freude, das Gemüths—und Seelenleben in Worte kleiden läßt? Empfindungen lassen sich nur durch die That, niemals aber durch die Sprache ausdrücken. Wenn ich von der Plattform aus zuweilen zu Tausenden meine Meinung auch noch so warm und begeistert gesprochen, empfinde ich nachträglich doch so etwas wie moralischen Kater; weiß ich doch, um das wiederzugeben was in meinem innern vorgeht, ich mir das Herz aus dem Leibe reißen und es den Anwesenden vor die Füße werfen müßte, überzeugt, daß sie mich auch dann noch nicht verstehen wurden. Ja, weshalb sprichst du denn überhaupt? wird mancher fragen. Wahrhaftig, nich des Redens, des Applauses oder der Notorität halber.

Jeder auch nur einigermaßen sensativ und selbständig veranlagte Mensch muß sich gegen die ihm umgebende Gemeinheit, Kleinlichkeit, gegen die Lügen und die Beschränkung seiner individuellen Freiheit auflehnen; und wenn er keine Gelegenheit hat, seinen Widerwillen gegen das Bestehende zu zeigen, so speichert sich der Haß, Zorn, Groll und die Verzweiflung in seiner Brust so lange auf, bis sie ihn zu ersticken drohen; dann muß er gleich dem Ertrinkenden, der den Strohhalm erfaßt, auf irgend einer Weise die ihm erdrückende Last abwerfen. Aus diesen Gründen rede ich, nur um mir Luft zu machen, um aufzuschreien gleich dem verwundeten Thiere; denn ich bilde mir ein, ein einziger von all den Tausenden muß mich ja doch hören, wird mich verstehen, wird meine Empörung begreifen, mit mir empfinden und die Gemeinheit, den Zwang und die Unterwürfigkeit hassen und dagegen kämpfen. Um den einzelnen war es und wird es mir zu thun sein, und da man unter vielen doch einen wahren edlen und großen Menschen finden kann, so gehe ich eben zu ihnen. Und ich habe gefunden wirklich wahre, herrliche Charaktere; ich habe denen in Pittsburgh, Chicago, St. Louis, Detroit,

Cleveland, Buffalo und anderen Plätzen getroffen: verborgene Edelsteine, welche ungekannt leben und leiden und doch so viel Licht ausstrahlen, um einem das bestehende Jammerthal auf Augenblicke vergessen zu machen.

Vorstehende Einleitung zum Bericht über meine Agitations-Tourist etwas weitläufig ausgefallen—ich wollte soeben mit dem eigentlichen Bericht beginnen, da kommt der Redacter, Sturm-, Pech- und Eisvogel, das Scheusal, oder wie er auch sonst noch von wohlwollenden Freunden benannt wird und befiehlt kategorisch Schluß. Ganz gegen meine Gewohnheit muß ich mich (aber nicht ohne Protest) also fügen, sonst wird mir noch die Gelegenheit entzogen in den nächsten "Sturmvögeln" meine Fortsetzung bringen zu dürfen, und das wäre schrecklich.——

III.

In Boston sprach ich in zwei gut besuchten Versammlungen; von da gings nach New Haven, wo ich ebefalls eine starke Versammlung adressirte. Von New Haven fuhr ich nach New York und von da nach Philadelphia. In N.Y. sprach ich in einer Protestversammlung gegen den Hazeltoner Mord von 21 Strikern. Ah, dieses Protestiren mit Worten nur, es ist die reinste Ironie! Ich möchte mich immer selber ohrfeigen, wenn ich nach einem geradezu bestialischen Gewaltakt, wie der vom Sheriff Martin verübte, nur dagegen rede, während jeder Nerv in mir zuckt, solch einen Bluthund zu erwürgen; und wäre es auch nur, um der herrschenden Klasse einen Beweis zu liefern, daß sie nicht immer ungestraft wehrlose Arbeiter morden kann . . .

In Philadelphia fanden sehr gut besuchte englische Versammlungen statt, welche von der Ladies Liberal League, Single Taxers und Friendship Liberal League, für mich arrangirt wurden. Von dort ging ich über Washington nach Pittsburgh.

In Washington fand keine Versammlung statt, aber ich machte dort Halt, um verschiedene Freunde des "Armen Teufel" kennen zu lernen. Ich konnte nur einige dieser Brüder treffen und ich muß gestehen, daß mich der Abstecher nach Wash. nicht reute, denn ich habe dort ein paar treffliche Menschen kennen gelernt.

Leider bleibt es einem in der Welt nicht erspart, neben wackeren Menschen auch solchen Gesellen zu begegnen, bei deren Zeugung ein unverzeihlicher Irrthum begangen wurde. Diese Leutschen hätten nämlich als Vierfüßler zur Welt kommen sollen; denn als Zweifüßler sind sie weder Menschen noch Thiere.

Da war unter anderen ein Architekt, alter Abonnent des "A.T.", ein Regierungsknecht, ein Mensch mit einem "Ohrfeigengesicht", wie Freund Reitzel sagt, der nicht begreifen konnte, daß ich als Anarchistin den Sinn für das Schöne und Gute im Menschen erwecken möchte. So ein Staatsverbrechen—der Masse begreiflich machen zu wollen, daß sie auch ein Recht zum Leben hat! . . . Es wollte diesem Patron gar nicht in den Schädel, daß ein Anarchist das Predigen von Entbehrung, Opfern, Geduld und Resignation den Pfaffen überläßt, um für den Genuß des einzelnen auf Kosten der anderen, sondern für das Wohlleben des Individuums, als auch für das der Gesammtheit. Was versteht übrigens so eine Regierungsseele vom Genuß?

Der zweite ähnlichen Schlages war ein dicker Bierbrauer aus Cincinnati, ebenfalls ein alter Leser des "A.T.", der sich gerade in Washington aufhielt und im Hotel Fritz Reuter wohnte, wo auch ich abstieg. Dieser schien zwar irgend welche Begriffe vom Genuß zu haben—seine stark geröthete Nase veranlaßte mich, einen solchen Schluß zu ziehen. Ein Riesenkerl mit einem Wanst, bei dessen Anblick ich mir meiner Mängel in der Mathematik bewußt wurde; denn um das Quantum Bier zu berechnen, das dieses Faß in sich barg, dazu gehörten die mathematischen Kenntnisse einer Kowalewska. Sein Schmalzgesicht glänzte nur so, als er hörte, daß ich die E.G. bin und er traktirte sogleich die ganze Gesellschaft; ich arme Seele aber mußte dafür alle seine Familiengeschichten hören, und da er schon Großvater ist, so kann man sich denken, wielang dieselben ausfielen. Er vertraute mir sogar die Nummer seines Zimmers an und frug so ganz nebenbei, welches Zimmer ich inne hätte. In der Hitze des Gefechts, oder des Gelages, um die Wahrheit zu gestehen, fiel mir die Frage gar nicht auf und ich sagte ihm meine Nummer.

Nach langem hin und her Discutiren über alle möglichen Tagesfragen, wurde es 2 Uhr Morgens und an der Zeit aufzubrechen. Ich war kaum eine halbe Stunde im Bett, als jemand ganz leise an meiner Thür klopfte. "Wer da?" rief ich; keine Antwort. "Who is there?" frug ich nochmals, indem ich glaubte, der Klopfer verstehe nicht Deutsch. Richtig war's mein dicker Bierbrauer aus Cincinnati. In meiner Empörung schnauzte ich den nicht übel an; höre dann wie der alte Sünder stammelt: "Not so loud, somebody may hear us; excuse me. I only was looking for the chambermaid." Diese freche, verlogene Antwort reizte mich noch mehr und ich brauche nicht erst zu betonen, daß ich dem Kerl einen solchen Sack voll Grobheiten sagte, daß er sich schleunigst trollte. Ich hätte die ganze Episode wohl kaum des Niederschreibens werth gehalten, würde dieselbe nicht Betrachtungen trauriger Natur in mir wachgerufen haben.

Seit Jahren liest dieser "ordnungsliebende" Bürger, (er sagte mir ganz stolz, daß er Republikaner und sein Ideal Carl Schurz ist) den "A.T.", pardon, ich wollte sagen, erhält den "A.T." Denn, wenn er den Inhalt desselben all die langen Jahre gelesen hätte, müßte doch ein wenig Freiheitssinn haften geblieben sein; er würde dann begreifen, daß eine Frau eben so viel Recht hat allein zu reisen, wie er, ohne Beleidigungen ausgesetzt zu sein. So weit reichen aber die Rechtsbegriffe dieses versoffenen und verspießerten Kaffern eben nicht.——

Pittsburgh—dieses traurige, rußige Nest mit seinen modernen Zwingburgen der Arbeit und seinem Gefängnis, weckt immer die trübsten Erinnerungen in mir;—weilt doch in letzterem seit Jahren einer meiner theuersten Freunde, Alex. Berkmann, den eine Bourgeois-Justiz nach einem leider mißglückten Vergeltungswerk an einem Scheusal, einer Geißel des arbeitenden Volkes, verdammt hat, seine jungen Jahre hinter grauen Wällen zu verbringen.

In P. wollte man dieses Mal keine Versammlungen für mich arrangiren, weil gerade Freund Berkmanns Angelegenheit vor the Board of Pardon gebracht werden sollte und die dortigen Genossen befürchteten, durch mein öffentliches Auftreten die Sache zu schädigen. Nachdem ich aber in Monaca, 27 Meilen von P., sprechen sollte und außerdem meine erst kürzlich aus dem Gefängnis entlassenen Freunde, Nold und Bauer, sehen wollte, so beschloß ich, einige Tage in P. zu bleiben.

Während meiner ganzen Fahrt von Washington nach Pittsburgh regnete es fortwährend und als ich meinen Bestimmungsort erreichte, goß es nur so, als ob eine zweite Sündfluth auf die Menschheit herniedergesandt werden sollte. Schaden würde es wahrhaftig nicht, denn nur durch solch ein Ereignis könnte die Welt von allerlei Ungeziefer befreit werden. Unser Nold, der angehende Dichter, (ach, wenn der nur das Dichten unterlassen würde—) und der große Bauernjunge mit dem goldenen Herzen, erwarteten mich am Bahnhof. "Bringt mich nur gleich auf mein altes Quartier zu Gordon," bat ich die Brüder, "denn ich bin totmüde." "Ja, ja, aber zuerst müssen wir einkehren!"

Ich war über das Wiedersehen mit meinen lieben Zuchthausvögeln so erfreut, daß ich nicht nein sagen konnte; zudem war meine Kehle ziemlich trocken und so ging es denn mit Sack und Pack bei gräßlichem Regen in eine Wirthschaft, deren Besitzer zur "A.T." Familie gehört; trotzdem fällt ihm aber doch das Herz in die Hosen, wenn ein Anarchist sein Lokal betritt, wie mir Freund N. sagte; mit einer Anarchistin könnte man übrigens schon eine Ausnahme machen, dachte ich mir. Der gute Mann schien über meinen Besuch erfreut zu sein und ließ gleich Essen und Trinken auftragen. Er war sehr aufgeräumt, rückte immer näher an meine Seite, zwinkerte mit den Augen, gleichzeitig ängstiche Blicke auf eine gegenüberliegende Thür werfend. "Was ist los, daß Sie immer nach der Thür blicken?" frug ich ihn. "Ja, wissen Sie, ich möchte gar zu gerne bei Ihnen bleiben, aber im anstoßenden Zimmer sitzt meine Alte mit noch einigen Klatschschwestern und wenn sie erfährt wer Sie sind, dann bin ich verloren. Um Gotteswillen, sprechen Sie nicht so laut." Trotzdem der Mann so gastfreundlich war, konnte ich doch nicht umhin, ihn wegen seiner Feigheit zu strafen; ich sprach und erzählte mit lauter Stimme, bis der arme Kerl es nicht mehr auf seinen Sitz aushalten konnte.

Gegessen und getrunken hatten wir ja, gekostet hatte es auch nichts und dazu noch die Schadenfreude. Die Karawane konnte nun getrost abschieben.

"Jetzt können wir Dich nicht mehr zu G. bringen, es ist zu spät", pustete Bauer, der sich noch immer vor Lachen über das Erlebte schüttelte. "Wir gehen jetzt in ein nahliegendes Boardinghouse, dessen Inhaber auch ein 'A.T.' Leser ist." "Na, hoffentlich nicht so einer als unser Wirth." "O nein, das ist einer von den Radikalen", riefen meine Begleiter unisono. Also los. Dort angekommen, wurden noch einige Gläser hinter die Binde gegossen, während das Bäuerlein mit dem Hauswirth betreffs eines Zimmers verhandelte. Endlich, nach langem warten, hieß es up stairs gehen. Im Begriffe, von meinen Cumpanen Abschied zu nehmen, höre ich dicht neben mir eine kreischende Stimme; "Wir haben keine Zimmer für Frauenzimmer!" Was war zu thun? Ich konnte doch gegen den Willen der züchtigen Hausfrau nicht dort bleiben. Also Bündel und Begleiter gepackt und weiter geschoben. Der Wirth, dem meine Freunde gehörig den Kopf gewaschen, war ganz trostlos, als er hörte, wer dieses Frauenzimmer eigentlich ist und er bat mich unter vielen Entschuldigungen, ja nur zu bleiben; aber ich hatte keine Lust, eine Keilerei zwischen Ehegesponsen zu verursachen und so blieb ich eben nicht. Wohin jetzt? "Weißt Du"—sagte Bauer, der den Mut noch nicht verloren hatte, während der arme weichherzige Nold ganz verzweifelt war—"jetzt führen wir Dich zu einem Genossen, da kannst Du übernachten." "Meinetwegen in die Hölle, wenn ich nur schon ein Unterkommen habe." Auf dem Wege zu diesem Genossen fiel mir mein kranker Freund R.R. mit seinem "A.T." ein. Was der für Augen machen würde, könnte er sich manche seiner Abonnenten aus der Nähe besehen; wüßte er, was das für Michel sind, wie wenig Einfluß sein Wirken auf diese Menschen ausgeübt hat.—Natürlich kannte ich bis dahin nur wenige Leser seines Blattes, sonst hätte ich nicht so urtheilen können. Ich habe mich während der übrigen Zeit meiner Reise überzeugt, daß der größte Theil der Freunde desselben wirklich liebe und freie Menschen sind, die mir durch ihre Güte und Liebenswürdigkeit die unangenehmen Erfahrungen mit "A.T." Lesern in Pittsburgh und anderen Plätzen leicht vergessen ließen.

Der Genosse, von dem Bauer sprach, wohnte in einem Zimmer, in welchem sich sein ganzes Eigenthum, Ehebett, Weib und Kind mit engeschlossen, befand. Die sog. bessere Hälfte, eine aus der Hefe hervorgegangene Deutsch-Amerikanerin, die ich schon von früher her als eine Zantyppe kannte, schien nicht sehr erbaut darüber zu sein, daß ihr Mann mir seine Stelle im Bette abtreten sollte. Unter solchen Umständen war mein Bleiben nicht sehr angenehm; aber ich war zu müde und abgespannt um erst lange zu überlegen; ich war froh, mich endlich meiner nassen Kleider entledigen und in ein warmes Nest krichen zu können, wo ich denn auch gleich in einen erquickenden Schlaf fiel.

Während ich nun von einer herrlichen Zukunft und freien, edlen Menschen träumte, brachte mich ein schrecklicher Lärm in die öde Wirklichkeit zurück. Ich war zu schlaftrunken, um im ersten Moment die Situation zu erfassen; dazu war es im Zimmer dunkel. Endlich konnte ich am Fußboden zwei Menschen unterscheiden, die sich gegenseitig mit Fäusten bearbeiteten und dazwischen die heisere, rauhe Stimme der Frau hören, die ihren Gatten, den theuren, meinen Gastwirth, in der gemeinsten Weise beschimpfte. Die ganze Situation war so horrend, dabei aber so komisch, daß ich eigentlich nicht wußte, ob ich weinen oder lachen sollte. Ich zog mich rasch an und stürzte in den peitschenden Regen hinaus um zu Bauer zu gehen, der in der Nähe wohnte.

Der arme Kerl, der schon längst schnarchte, kroch schnell in seine Unaussprechlichen und ging mit mir in Nacht und Nebel hinaus, ein Hotel suchen. Die traurige Affäre trug sich in Allegheny City zu, wo keine Hotels zu finden sind. Eine Car nach Pittsburgh war um diese Zeit, 3 Uhr Morgens, auch nicht mehr zu haben; also hieß es laufen; eine angenehme Sache bei dem Hundewetter.

Nach zwei Stunden kamen wir endlich an einen Platz, wo man auch für "Frauenzimmer Zimmer" hat. Ich konnte lange Zeit nicht zur Ruhe kommen, denn die Ereignisse des Abends und hauptsächlich die ekelhafte Familienscene, standen noch zu klar vor mir. Eigentlich hätte mich eine derartige Affäre nicht alteriren sollen. Geht es denn bei Eheleuten überhaupt anders zu? Wie ist es möglich, daß zwei Menschen, die absolut nicht für einander passen, ihr elendes Dasein doch zusammen dahinschleppen. Was hält sie denn vereint? Diese Fragen durchkreuzten mein müdes Gehirn. Die Liebe, werden manche sagen. Lächerlich! Menschen, die so wenig gegenseitig Achtung haben, und sich mit Schmutz und Koth bewerfen, die sich sogar soweit vergessen handreiflich zu werden; solche Geschöpfe wissen nichts von der Liebe. Es ist nur die verfluchte Gewohnheit und Feigheit des Mannes sowohl wie die der Frau, welches sie die größte Schmach viel eher ertragen läßt, als aus einander zu gehen, oder lieber den Tod einem solchen traurigen Leben vorzuziehen.

Ich war am nächsten Tage ganz zerschlagen und angeekelt von dem Schlamm, in dem sich die Menschheit wälzt. In diesem Zustande reiste ich nach Monaca, wo es mir in anderer Beziehung nicht viel besser erging.

Letters from a Tour.

I.

There have been so many travel letters written lately, both in Europe as well as in this country, that it is indeed the purest form of imitation to publish the experiences and ob- servations that I collected during my 14 weeks of loafing about in the West.[1] After all, who doesn't imitate these days? Speakers and journalists, authors and poets, singers and actors. They all only repeat that which others have said, written, sung, and performed be- fore them. The original is not created every day, and few original people are born every day. There are indeed a lot of people who think of themselves as great minds, indeed as geniuses; yet in reality these poor souls are like flies who sit comfortably on the horn of an ox in the field and come into the city after a long day's work with the cry, "We have been plowing!" As I am not conceited, nor do I count myself among people of greatness or indeed genius, may my friends forgive my imitation, that is, if they have anything at all to forgive me for.

Traveling is certainly a wonderful thing if you have plenty of cash in your pocket and are not dependent on friends or comrades. But traveling is indeed not especially pleas- ant when you have just enough to reach the next city, when you get something to eat from one person today (or perhaps not), and someone else tomorrow, when you have to sleep on the floor or in the family bed (without the father of the house, of course), yet exactly such difficulties and unpleasant circumstances lend a certain thrill to my travels. Perhaps because I am, as my friend the Irish Dutchman says, a born vagabond.

I am often told, and I myself know best, how little I have in common with my race. Not that this does me a particular justice, but it is simply so, and neither I nor the race can be held responsible for it. The urge to wander, to move from place to place, and, like the eternal Jew, never to find rest or peace, I have, however, inherited from the Jews. My fellow Jews were indeed rarely able to put their own desires into practice, for they were never asked whether they wanted to go or not. They were simply hounded from country to country, from place to place, hated and shunned like lepers. Even in this century of intelligence, knowledge, progress, and enlightenment, the Jews have only been tolerated, and there are indeed very few Aryans who are completely free of prejudices in this matter.

1. The five letters in which EG describes her Fall 1897 lecture tour of the Midwest were serialized in *Sturmvogel* between December 1897 and February 1898; the series appears here under the date of the first letter.

Sturmvogel

,,Lewwer dûad ues Slaav.''

NO. 2, JAHRGANG I.   NEW YORK.   15. NOVEMBER 1897.

Masthead from the 15 November 1897 issue of *Sturmvogel,* the German-language anarchist communist monthly based in New York, the first to publish Goldman's detailed lecture tour reports—a featured column Goldman later incorporated into her own magazine, *Mother Earth.* (By permission of the Kate Sharpley Library)

My inclination to the vagabond's life, *pour la vie bohème,* would therefore be enough proof that I am not completely lacking in Semitic qualities. It is not the need to convince people of my views or unhinge the world that leads me to move now and then from city to city; it is rather, as I have said, my restless, unsettled spirit, the need to get to know new faces, other people and their habits, customs and practices, strengths and weaknesses, that forces me out of my usual daily surroundings. Being obliged to stay in one place for months, years, or perhaps an entire life, always having to spend time with the same people, drink in the same beer dens—this disconsolately bleak monotony of everyday life would fill me with horror. One of my friends, for whom the habit of ascribing unfair motivations to the behavior of others has developed into a sickness, claims that the addiction to speaking to the masses and the satisfaction that the applause of the audience gives me are the actual motivations that cause me to go away from time to time. False, my dear. Neither do I believe for a moment that I can change people or turn them into Anarchists with my speeches; not at all. In the first place, my talent for speaking is not sufficient for that; and second, I long ago came to the conclusion that language is too weak, too powerless to express what one feels. Does one of my well spoken, intelligent friends want to prove to me that love, hate, pain, joy, the entire world of emotions can be clothed in words? Emotions are expressed only through deeds, never through language. After I voice my opinion to thousands from the platform with such warmth and spirit, I do indeed sense something like a moral hangover; yet I know that in order to render what is inside of me I would have to rip my heart out of my body and throw it at the feet of the audience, certain that even then they would not understand. Then why do you speak at all? many will ask. Truly not for the sake of speaking, the applause, or the notoriety.

Every person endowed with even a minimum of sensitivity and independence must rebel against the meanness and narrow-mindedness surrounding him, against the lies and the restrictions to his individual freedom; and if he has no opportunity to show his opposition to the present situation, then hatred, scorn, resentment and despair will build up in his breast until they threaten to smother him. Then, like the drowning man who grasps at straws, he must somehow shake off his overwhelming burden. For these reasons I speak to vent my anger, to cry out like a wounded animal; for I imagine that one single person out of all the thousands will indeed have to hear me, will understand me, will comprehend my outrage, will feel with me, and will hate and struggle against cruelty, coercion, and subjugation. It has been and will continue to be for this single person that I act, and I go to them precisely because among the many, one real, honorable and great person can be found. And I have found really genuine, marvelous characters. I have met them in Pittsburgh, Chicago, St. Louis, Detroit, Cleveland, Buffalo and other places: hidden gems, who live and suffer anonymously yet give out so much light that they make a person forget for a moment the vale of tears around us.

The above introduction to the report of my agitation tour is somewhat lengthy and odd—I wanted to start the actual report, but the editor, the stormy petrel, the unlucky fellow, the kingfisher, the monster, or whatever else he is called by his well-meaning friends, came and told me categorically to stop.[2] Completely against my custom I must therefore give in (but not without protest), otherwise the opportunity to be allowed to bring my continuation in the upcoming *Sturmvogel*s will be taken away, and that would be terrible.——

II.

On September 2nd I started my agitation tour with two dollars in my pocket. The first stop was Providence, Rhode Island,[3] a city of about 80,000 residents, mostly factory workers. Rhode Island, although a puritanical state, allowed its citizens until recently more freedom and privileges than Massachusetts or Connecticut. For example, parties of every orientation were allowed to hold meetings in the parks or squares of Providence without first getting the usual permission from the mayor, a privilege which no other city in this "free land" can show.

I had already been in Providence several times, had spoken before well attended meetings without ever being harassed by the police, but this time it was going to be different.

My comrades and friends, who were always very active, had arranged five meetings after it was agreed that this time I should stay an entire week. On September 3rd, 4th, and 5th, I spoke before three splendid meetings on street corners, in the afternoon of September 5th in a hall which was filled to the last seat. The police were everywhere heavily represented, naturally to "protect" me against the anger of the crowd. On the evening of the 7th, the last street meeting was supposed to take place. With a few friends I went to the square designated for that purpose, but when we arrived we found it occupied by

2. Claus Timmerman was the editor of *Sturmvogel* from 1897 to 1899.
3. EG spoke in Providence from the 3rd through the 8th of September.

a speaker of the S.L.P.[4] who tried to convince the audience from a wagon how wonderful everything in the world would be if De Lyon,[5] Sanial,[6] or Mcguire[7] were president of the United States.—So as not to disturb the vote catching, we went to another square. A comrade with a booming voice stood on a box and started to attract the public,[8] a job which only one who has to address those kinds of meetings knows to appreciate. Within 15 minutes, he gathered about 300 people. My herald left the box to me from where I began to work on the assembled troops. I had hardly started to speak when a 280 pound guardian of order tugged roughly on my sleeve and screamed with a drunken voice, "You have to stop immediately, you are not allowed to speak here." "What right do you have to interrupt me?" I asked the hippopotamus. "I am the law," screamed the lard-dripping monster. "And I have the right to speak here," and I proceeded leisurely with my talk. The crowd was extremely upset with the interference of the police and shouts like "damn the police, to hell with them" were heard from all sides. It would certainly have come to quite a clash between police and people had not four uniformed bulldogs packed me with brute force into a patrol wagon and made off with this "big criminal." Having arrived at the police station, I asked the captain why I was arrested in the first place. "You were arrested because you are Emma Goldman." Naturally I had not expected such an answer; how should I know that in this country things have gotten so bad that one arrests a person because of his name? To make an American policeman understand that a name could not possibly constitute a crime or an offense seemed to me superfluous in this situation, and with stoic calm I let them take me to the night quarters, a dirty cell whose furniture consisted of a wooden bench and a certain pot. I was very tired and already used to such hotels and would certainly soon have fallen into a deep sleep had a woman in the adjacent cell not constantly cried and wailed. The poor woman paced back and forth and cried and sobbed, "My six children, my little baby, who will nurse you; my poor, sick husband; let me go to my children; give me my beloved baby!" That's how it went all night. I tried to calm the woman down and started a conversation with her. It turned out that her husband had been sick and out of work for ten months, that she had six children of whom the oldest was fourteen, the youngest one year, and that she, in desperation, took a loaf of bread and a can of condensed milk from the table of a grocer whose laundry she

4. The initials "S.L.P." stand for the Socialist Labor Party, founded in 1876.
5. Daniel De Leon was a prominent and longtime leader in the Socialist Labor Party.
6. Lucien Sanial (1836–1927) was a French-born journalist and Socialist Labor Party leader. Sanial helped draft the SLP platform in 1889. He edited the *Workmen's Advocate* (1889–91) and *The People* (1891), both SLP propaganda organs. Sanial unsuccessfully ran for mayor of New York on the SLP ticket in 1894. He left the SLP and joined the Socialist Party of America soon after it was founded in 1901.
7. Peter J. McGuire was general secretary of the United Brotherhood of Carpenters and Joiners of America and a co-founder of the American Federation of Labor in 1886.
8. Probably John H. Cook (see description of his opening speech in "Anarchy," Article in the *Providence Evening Bulletin,* 4 September 1897, above).

used to do and was caught in the act . . . What an impression this sad story made on me can be easily imagined.

It is indeed nothing new that the person who takes a loaf of bread is locked up while those who steal millions go about freely as respected citizens, pious Christians, and good statesmen. It also is nothing new that thousands are hungry and walk around in rags and are desperate and do not know where to rest their heads. One becomes hardened if one has been dealing with the labor question for years, has gotten to know human misery in all its phases. One reads the daily reports about poverty, suicide, and crime and calmly drinks one's coffee, happy that for the time being one is not among these unfortunate people (because sooner or later, the same fate will overcome us). But the lament, the despair of that woman, the begging, pleading of the mother for her little ones could have melted a stone. Yet how much does empathy help if one is powerless, helpless and exposed to the arbitrariness and violence,—I did not dare to comfort the woman because, under the circumstances, it would have sounded like mockery.

The following morning, together with other involuntary inmates of this cozy house, I was brought before the judge who, after the usual questions, whether guilty or not guilty, placed me under bail, and because it could not be posted immediately, I, poor sinner, was taken away again.

At one o'clock I was led to the mayor at City Hall, who received me with the question whether I wanted to swear or promise not to speak in Providence for the next three months, and if so, he would let me go. I made it clear to him that I could neither swear nor promise anything; but to reassure him, I could tell him that I was on a tour to the West which would prevent me from honoring Providence with a visit in the near future anyway. After that, the local pasha let me go. Actually, he was glad to get rid of me, because my arrest evoked a lot of resentment and protest and because nothing emerged to allow pressing charges against me.

If the newspapers had already brought column-length reports about the meetings earlier, the day after my arrest they were full of sensational stories. The result of the comedy was that many people joined the anarchist groups that exist in Providence; the meetings are now well attended, and, in all circles, anarchism and Emma Goldman are discussed, a propaganda victory thanks to the police of Providence. I was not harmed by the few hours of arrest, to the contrary I am one experience richer.

Arrests and jail cells may under certain circumstances be considered pleasant shelters as one is protected against the inclemency of the weather in them. How it is with the state food is a different question. In the Providence police station, for example, the prisoners cannot complain about bad food because they simply do not get any. If someone is arrested in the afternoon or evening, he is brought only the next morning before the judge who either releases the accused on bail or imposes on him a monetary or prison penalty. If the prisoner does not have the necessary money to buy himself free from "justice," he has to wait until late afternoon before he will be brought to prison. During this time, he has not received a single bite to eat. Most of them arrive in any case with an empty stomach, and here they have the best opportunity to experience how caring the state is in terms of food.

After my so-called deportation from Providence, I spent a few hours in the merry company of friends there, and in the evening I drove to Boston, where a meeting had been arranged for September 12th, which I will report about in the next issue.

III.

In Boston I spoke before two well-attended meetings; from there I went to New Haven where I also addressed a large meeting. From New Haven I went to New York, and from there to Philadelphia. In N.Y., I spoke before a protest meeting against the murder of 21 Hazleton strikers.[9] Oh, this protesting with words only, it is the purest irony! I always want to slap myself when, after a downright bestial act of violence like the one committed by Sheriff Martin,[10] I only speak against it while every nerve in me twitches to strangle such a bloodhound, even if only to offer proof to the ruling class that it cannot always murder defenseless workers with impunity . . .

Very well attended English-language meetings took place in Philadelphia, arranged for me by the Ladies Liberal League,[11] Single Taxers[12] and Friendship Liberal League.[13] From there I went via Washington to Pittsburgh.

No meetings took place in Washington, but I stopped there in order to get to know various friends of *Der arme Teufe*.[14] I was only able to meet a few of these brothers, and I must admit that I did not regret the detour to Wash., for I got to know a few excellent people there.

Unfortunately in this world we are not spared from meeting, in addition to decent people, such fellows by whose conception an inexcusable error was committed. Such people should have been born as four-legged creatures, for as two-legged ones they are neither humans nor animals.

Among others there was an architect, an old subscriber to *AT*, a government slave, a

---

9. Though there are conflicting reports on how many were killed, at least nineteen strikers died at Hazleton.
10. EG refers to Sheriff James L. Martin.
11. Influenced by Voltairine de Cleyre and Natasha Notkin, the Ladies' Liberal League sponsored lectures on a wide variety of subjects and was an important forum for radical and feminist activity in Philadelphia. Prior to EG's visit, lecturers included Charles Mowbray, who was arrested after addressing the League in 1894, and Harry Kelly, who spoke to the group in 1896.
12. The Single Tax Society of Philadelphia included anarchist sympathizers G. Frank Stephens and A. Stevenson, and anarchists George Seldes and Arthur Pleydell.
13. The Friendship Liberal League was a freethought organization which sponsored lectures primarily on secularism, although several of its members, especially Voltairine de Cleyre and James B. Elliott, successfully lobbied to broaden the discussions to include anarchism. Charles Mowbray lectured in 1894, as did John Turner in 1896. EG would address the League five months later and again in 1901. See Letter to *Solidarity*, 15 March, 1898, below; and EG to James B. Elliott, 15 March 1901, *EGP*, reel 1.
14. EG abbreviates the journal name *Der arme Teufel* as *AT* in subsequent references.

man with an "Ohrfeigengesicht," [15] as our friend Reitzel puts it,[16] who could not understand that I, as an Anarchist, would like to awaken in people an appreciation for all that is beautiful and good. What a crime against the state—to want to make the masses aware that they too have a right to live! . . . This fellow could not get it into his skull that an Anarchist leaves the preaching of privation, sacrifice, patience, and resignation to the clergy in order to speak out in favor of the highest pleasures of all kinds. Of course not for the pleasure of the individual at the expense of others, but for the well-being of the individual as well as of the whole. What does such a governmental soul know about pleasure anyway?

The second of this ilk was a fat beer brewer from Cincinnati, also an old reader of *AT*, who happened to be in Washington and was staying in the Hotel Fritz Reuter, where I too was staying. This man seemed indeed to have some notion of pleasure—his heavily reddened nose caused me to draw such a conclusion. A huge man with a belly at the sight of which I became aware of my shortcomings in mathematics; for in order to calculate the amount of beer that this barrel held, one would need the mathematical skills of a Kowalewska.[17] His greasy face simply glistened when he heard that I was the E.G., and he immediately treated the entire party; I, poor soul, had to listen to all of his family stories, and as he was already a grandfather, one can imagine how long they turned out to be. He even confided his room number to me and casually asked me which room I had. In the heat of the action, or carousing, to tell the truth, I did not think much of this question, and I gave him my number.

After much back-and-forth discussion about every possible question of the day it had reached two in the morning and the time had come to cut things off. I was in bed for not quite half an hour when someone knocked very lightly on my door. "Who is there?" I called out; no answer. "Who is there?" [in English], I asked again, believing that the person knocking didn't understand German. Right, it was my fat beer brewer from Cincinnati. In my indignation I snarled at him not badly at all, then listened as the old sinner stammered: "Not so loud, somebody may hear us; excuse me. I was only looking for the chambermaid." This brazen, dishonest answer irritated me even more, and I do not need to emphasize that I hurled such a huge bag of insults at the fellow that he quickly retreated. I hardly would have considered this episode worth writing down if it had not evoked in me observations of a sad nature.

15. *Ohrfeigengesicht* is a colloquial German expression, roughly translated as "a face begging to be slapped."
16. EG refers to Robert Reitzel, editor of *Der arme Teufel*.
17. Sofia Kovalevskaia (1850–1891) was a prominent Russian mathematician, author, and pioneer of the early feminist movement. She fled to Germany in 1869 to escape the rigid gender norms of Russia that impaired her ability to direct the course of both her career and her relationships. Kovalevskaia was appointed professor of mathematics at Göttingen University in 1894. Her major works include *A Russian Childhood* (1890), and *Vera Branantzova* (1895; A Nihilist Girl, 2001). EG also refers to Kovalevskaia in her March 1906 essay in *Mother Earth* entitled "The Tragedy of Women's Emancipation" (see vol. 2).

For years this "order-loving" citizen (he told me with pride that he was a Republican and his idol was Carl Schurz [18]) had been reading *AT*, pardon, I mean to say that he received *AT*. For if he had read its contents all those years, at least a little sense of liberty would have had to stick; he would then understand that a woman has just as much right to travel alone as he does without being exposed to insults. Clearly the notions of justice held by this drunken, stodgy oaf did not extend that far.——

Pittsburgh—this sad, sooty nest with its modern fortresses of labor and its prison, always evokes the saddest memories in me; inside the latter is one of my dearest friends, Alex. Berkman, who was condemned by a bourgeois jury after a failed act of retaliation against a monster, a scourge of working people, to spend his young years behind gray walls. [19]

In P. no meetings were arranged for me this time because the matter of friend Berkman was about to be brought before the Board of Pardon, and the comrades there feared that my appearance in public would compromise the situation. But since I was supposed to speak in Monaca, 27 miles from P., and as I also wanted to see my friends Nold and Bauer, who had just recently been released from prison, [20] I decided to stay in P. for a few days.

It rained incessantly during my entire trip from Washington to Pittsburgh, and when I arrived at my destination it poured as if a second flood was being sent down upon humanity. That would truly not be such a shame, for only through such an event could the world be freed from all kinds of vermin. Our Nold, the budding poet (oh, if he only refrained from writing poetry), and the big farm boy with the heart of gold were waiting for me at the train station. "Take me immediately to my old quarters at Gordon's," [21] I asked the brothers, "because I'm dead tired." "Yes, yes, but first we must stop off for a drink!"

I was so delighted by the reunion with my dear jailbirds that I could not say no; furthermore, my throat was rather dry, and so we went with bag and baggage in terrible rain to an inn whose owner belonged to the *AT* family. [22] In spite of this his heart sinks whenever an Anarchist enters his place, as my friend N. told me; with a female Anarchist one could indeed make an exception, I thought. The good man seemed pleased with my visit and served food and drink. He was in very good spirits, moving closer and closer to me and winking, while at the same time casting fearful glances over at the door facing us. "Why are you always looking over at the door?" I asked him. "Well, you know, I would like to stay with you only too well, but my wife and a few other gossipy women are sitting

---

18. Carl Schurz immigrated to the United States from Germany after the 1848 revolution; a radical Republican, he served as a Missouri senator.
19. At this time, AB had been in prison for five years for his attack on Henry C. Frick, general manager of Carnegie's steel company at Homestead, Pa.
20. Carl Nold and Henry Bauer, who had been imprisoned for their alleged involvement in AB's assassination attempt, were released from prison on 25 May 1897.
21. EG had stayed at the home of Harry Gordon in November 1896.
22. EG is identifying the pub owner as a reader of *Der arme Teufel*.

in the next room, and if they find out who you are I'll be lost. For God's sake, don't speak so loudly." Although the man was very hospitable, I could not help but punish him for his cowardice; I talked and recounted with a loud voice until the poor fellow could not stand to remain in his seat any longer.

So we had eaten and drunk, and it had not cost us a thing and, moreover, we had our malicious joy. The caravan could now cheerfully shove off.

"Now we can't take you to G. anymore, it is too late," puffed Bauer, who was still shaking with laughter about the incident. "Let's go to a nearby boardinghouse whose owner is also an *AT* reader." "Well, hopefully not one like our innkeeper." "Oh no, he is one of the radicals," my companions said in unison. So we took off. Having arrived there we again wetted our whistle while little Bauer negotiated with the innkeeper about a room. Finally, after a long wait, I could go upstairs. While I was saying goodbye to my companions I heard a shrieking voice next to me. "We don't have any rooms for hussies!" What could be done? I could not stay there against the will of the chaste housewife. So with baggage and companions packed, we shoved off. The innkeeper, to whom my friends gave a piece of their minds, was inconsolable when he heard who this hussy actually was and begged me with many apologies to stay; but I did not feel like causing a fight between spouses and so I did not. Where to now? "You know," said Bauer, who had not yet lost courage, while poor soft-hearted Nold was totally desperate—"Now we'll take you to a comrade, there you'll be able to spend the night." "As far as I'm concerned you can take me to hell, as long as I have a place to stay." On the way to this comrade's, I remembered my sick friend Robert Reitzel with his *AT*. How he would roll his eyes if he could see some of his subscribers up close; if he knew what typical Germans they were, what little influence his efforts had on these people. Of course, up to then I only knew a few readers of his paper, otherwise I could not have made such a judgment. During the remaining part of my trip I have become convinced that the greatest number of its friends are truly dear and free people who through their kindness and hospitality caused me to forget the unpleasant experiences with *AT* readers in Pittsburgh and other places.

The comrade of whom Bauer had spoken lived in a room that contained his entire property, marriage bed, wife, and child included. The so-called better half, a German American from the dregs whom I already knew to be a Xanthippe,[23] did not seem very pleased that her husband should give up his place in the bed to me. Under such circumstances my stay was not very pleasant, but I was too tired and worn out to think about it for long; I was glad to finally get rid of my wet clothes and crawl into a warm nest where I immediately fell into a refreshing sleep.

While I dreamt of a wonderful future and noble human beings, a terrible noise brought me back into bleak reality. I was too drowsy to grasp the situation at first, and it

23. The name of Socrates' wife, Xanthippe, is used here in its colloquial sense to describe a shrewish wife.

was also dark in the room. Finally I could distinguish two human beings on the floor who were working each other over with their fists, and between blows heard the husky voice of the woman, who cursed her husband, my dear host, in the meanest manner. The whole situation was so horrendous, but at the same time so comical, that I did not know whether I should laugh or cry.[24] I quickly got dressed and ran out in the pounding rain to go to Bauer, who lived nearby.

The poor fellow, who was already snoring, quickly jumped into his unmentionables and went with me out into the darkness to find a hotel. This sad affair happened in Allegheny City, where no hotels were to be found. A car to Pittsburgh was at that time, three o'clock in the morning, also not available; that meant we had to walk, a pleasant thing in the wretched weather.

After two hours, we finally arrived at a place where there were "rooms for hussies." I could not calm down for a long time because of the events of the evening; in particular the disgusting family scene still stood before me all too clearly. Actually the whole affair should not have annoyed me. Isn't it always that way with married people? How is it possible that two human beings who absolutely do not match drag on their miserable existence together anyway? What keeps them united? These questions crossed my tired mind. Love, many will say. Ridiculous! Human beings who have so little mutual respect and throw dirt and muck at each other, who even forget themselves and become violent, such creatures do not know anything about love. It is only the cursed habit and cowardice of the man as well as the woman that lets them bear the greatest ignominy rather than separate or prefer death to such a sad life.

The next day I was totally shattered and disgusted with the mud in which humankind wallows. In this condition, I traveled to Monaca where in a different way I did not fare much better.

IV.

Encouraged by the *AT*, probably, I was invited by the gymnastic society in Monaca, Pa., to speak there on the topic "Woman, Marriage, and Prostitution," which led me to the belief that the gymnasts of Monaca were exceptionally progressive fellows.[25] Unfortunately, my assumption was premature. A day before the meeting, I was notified that it was canceled because half of the members had fled from the terrible, immoral hussy

---

24. In *Living My Life*, EG recalls this scuffle as having taken place at the home of Carl Nold, between him and his wife, Nellie (*LML*, pp. 199–200).

25. Gymnastic clubs (also known as *Turnvereine* or Turner societies) began in the early nineteenth century as nationalist organizations, incorporating both middle-class and working-class members. The first club was founded in Berlin in 1811 by Friedrich Ludwig Jahn. Gymnastic clubs were formed in the United States by German immigrants fleeing after the collapse of the 1848 revolution, during which the clubs had backed the antimonarchical factions. By the 1890s, Turner societies in the United States were almost exclusively middle-class with a factionalized split between socialists and conservatives. EG refers below to members of the fraternal clubs as "Jahn brothers."

E.G. Under different circumstances, I would have enjoyed such a case. However, as I had made a detour at the invitation of the Monaca gymnastic society, the news of the cowardice of the Jahn brothers did not exactly put me in a rosy mood. Despite these heroes, I went to Monaca and with the help of an old comrade and member of the club, the meeting was brought about all the same. The audience was comprised of 50 men and so instead of treating the topic: Woman, Marriage, and Prostitution, I talked about the idiocy of the gymnasts. That I did not spare the gentlemen is proven by the circumstance that the gymnasts convened a meeting to decide whom I had labeled an idiot. As the old comrade informed me, they dropped this matter from the agenda so as not to look even more ridiculous.

After my unpleasant experiences with the Monaca *Turnverein*, I drove to Chicago to participate in the workers' convention that took place there.[26]

Chicago is undoubtedly London in reduced scale; in no other city in America does gray misery stare you so glaringly in the face as here. As far as I have traveled throughout the country, I had not yet seen as many tattered creatures, crippled human beings, gaunt faces with sunken eyes, and indifferent countenances as in this so-called garden city. I don't know whether it was the dirt of the streets, the terrible smell of the Chicago River, the smoke of the factories, the human market on Clark Street where poor girls of all nationalities sell their sick, tired bodies for 25 and 50 cents, or whether it was the memory of the brutal murder of November 11, 1887, that made me see Chicago in such a dreary light,[27]—I only know that a longer stay in this city would awaken suicidal thoughts in me.

The friends and comrades will probably still remember what great success the workers everywhere hoped for from this convention. It was convened on the one side by Debs who so radically and energetically appeared in the St. Louis convention,[28] and on the other side by the representatives of the starving, desperate, striking coal miners.[29] I too ascribed importance to the convention, and since I had to speak at various meetings ar-

26. The three-day convention, which began 27 September 1897 and was held in Orpheus Hall of the Schiller Theater Building in Chicago, brought together reformers and trade unionists. EG's seating at the convention was challenged on the first day but finally allowed, since, it was argued, she did not represent a particular organization. EG was listed among the delegates to the convention as an affiliate of the New York Debating Club (an anarchist communist group that met regularly on Sunday evenings in Manhattan). See newspaper account of her address, "Emma Goldman Has Her Say," Article in the *Chicago Tribune*, 30 September 1897, above.
27. A reference to the Haymarket affair.
28. At the two-day labor conference in St. Louis, which began 30 August 1897, Eugene Debs outraged some trade unionists by urging them to halt their efforts to unseat AFL president Samuel Gompers. A full transcript of Debs's speech appeared in the *Social Democrat* (Chicago) on 2 September 1897.
29. EG refers to the three-month strike by the United Mine Workers of America, which resulted in the union's first national victory. The union won important gains for workers in the country's major coal regions (except West Virginia), including wage increases and eight-hour-day regulations. The confrontation, which began on 4 July 1897, was particularly violent in many regions, culminating in the massacre of strikers at Hazleton (Lattimer), and subsequent rioting.

ranged by the comrades, I went to Chicago several weeks earlier to participate in it. I can give my friends the reassurance that I was not delegated there at the expense of a group nor as representative. I had a mandate from a N.Y. workers' association merely for the purpose of being admitted to the negotiations.

To describe the convention in detail would take up too much space; I will therefore limit myself to say that all my life I had not participated in such a ridiculous, insignificant, meaningless affair. The convention opened with Gompers,[30] the great mogul of the American Federation of Labor, out of sheer envy and jealousy of Debs's notoriety, giving orders to the various organizations not to send any delegates there; and Eugene Debs, the new "Messiah," showed on that occasion that he was absolutely not master of the situation. He was frightened out of his wits by Gompers and he too called off all delegates of the social democracy;[31] consequently, the convention, with the exception of a few, rested in the hands of politicians and vote catchers of all shades. This rabble spent the time accusing each other and proposing the most absurd motions. Most of them arrived in the morning already drunk, (on their 5 dollars per day, which is how much every delegate received as a representative of his union, one can certainly afford quite a bit), and the screaming and yelling throughout the day was hair raising. Two days were wasted with the examination of the mandates and the rest of the time with proposals of the following nature: "To have free coinage of silver, to establish the Single Tax, to reform our government, to induce the legislature to pass such and such a law" etc. Not a word about the coal miners' strike, the brutal treatment of the workers by the mine owners. Not the slightest protest against the murder of defenseless workers in Hazleton, nothing at all about that. Just as someone would demand to be recognized, another person would jump up and cry out: "Mr. Chairman, I move that this man sit down, he is a fool, a goddamn fool, he is not a bona-fide delegate!" and other similar things. At the end of the second day, I got sick and tired of this spectacle. I wanted to get away from that atmosphere but first I had to make clear my point of view to these brutish, dirty fellows. I succeeded in taking the floor and the result of my half-hour long speech was that the better elements left the hall with me.

After all that, I believe nonetheless that my presence at the convention was not altogether futile. First, I had the opportunity to present my view on the coal miners' strike and the labor movement in general to people who otherwise never go to an anarchist meeting, as there were a number of guests from all sections of the population. Second, I could see for myself more than ever before how the workers are duped and exploited and cheated by their representatives. Third, I had the opportunity to get to know Debs

---

30. Samuel Gompers argued that with most of the miners back at work, the AFL's money would be better spent to aid miners and their families than to send delegates to the convention. He further argued that the organization of workers in trade unions, and not political conventions, would most help the working class.

31. By "delegates of the social democracy," EG is referring to supporters of Debs's organization, Social Democracy of America.

who promised a lot to the workers and kept very little. I am convinced that the woman who in a meeting said about Debs that he has a big heart but an empty skull was right. He is not the man of his time; he lacks energy and will and he collapses like a fly in the slightest gust of wind. Although he privately professes anarchism,[32] he believes all the same in having to use the ballot box as a means to attract the masses. There is no doubt that in his way he is honest and has good intentions, but what good does it do when a human being does not have the strength to stand up publicly, to show a bold front to the entire world, to break down all the barriers and to follow his own way?

The comrades in Chicago not only had not arranged a single meeting, although they had written to me that half a dozen of them were waiting for my arrival, but had not even arranged for a place for me to stay. Fortunately, I met an old dear friend in Chicago who occupied two rooms and immediately agreed to let one to me. To the horror of many philistines, old spinsters, and moralists, I accepted the hospitality of my friend and would have stayed with him during my stop in Chicago if his landlady, totally appalled at the indecency of her tenant putting up a woman in his room, had not objected to my staying any longer. Thus, I rented a room on my own where I could dwell undisturbed.

I stayed almost two weeks in Chicago. During that time, I spoke in six meetings which left much desired in regard to attendance. At one event, a celebration by the gymnastic society, where I spoke about the matter of friend Berkman, $35.50 was collected in his favor.

From Chicago I drove to Milwaukee, where I had three meetings; from there back again to Chicago to speak in a meeting that was convened in favor of the imprisoned "Firebrandians."[33] The success of the meeting was unfortunately weakened by Lucy Parsons who, instead of condemning the unjustified, vile arrest of the three comrades in Portland and the ever increasing censorship by Comstock and associates, took a stand against the editor of the *Firebrand*, H. Addis, because he tolerated articles about free love

---

32. In *Living My Life,* EG recalls speaking privately with Debs around this time: "Hearing his views, I could not help exclaiming, 'Why Mr. Debs, you're an anarchist!' 'Not Mister, but comrade,' he corrected me; 'won't you call me that?'" (*LML,* p. 220).

33. In September 1897, Abe Isaak, Henry Addis, and Abner J. Pope, editors of the Portland-based *Firebrand*, were jailed, charged under the Comstock Act with sending obscene literature through the mails, and the paper was banned. The materials deemed obscene included Walt Whitman's poem "A Woman Waits for Me" (long available in *Leaves of Grass*), and three articles on the subject of free love. The jury convicted them on one count only, based on back issues requested by and sent to the postal inspector under an assumed name and containing a letter entitled "It Depends on the Woman" (25 April 1897, p. 7) and the Whitman poem (14 March 1897, p. 1). On 1 March 1898, Pope, who had refused counsel and appeal, received a four-month sentence. The case against Isaak and Addis was dismissed on appeal on 20 June 1898, after the paper (renamed *Free Society*) had moved to San Francisco. The meeting EG attended to discuss the case was held on 13 October 1897, in Zepf's Hall, Chicago. In addition to EG, Lucy Parsons, Max Baginski, and Moses Harman spoke. The meeting sparked debate, when Parsons, while speaking at the meeting, made clear her distaste for free love and disapproval of the editorial policy of the *Firebrand*. Similar meetings were called around the country, including a rare meeting that combined English- and non-English-speaking anarchists in New York, as part of the widespread agitation on behalf of a free press generated by the *Firebrand* case. See *Lucifer,* 20 October 1897, p. 332.

in the columns of the *Firebrand*.[34] Apart from the fact that anarchism not only teaches freedom in economic and political areas, but also in social and sexual life, L. Parsons has the least cause to object to treatises on free love and in addition at a time when it is important to liberate comrades from the claws of the moral zealots. I spoke after Parsons and had a hard time changing the unpleasant mood that her remarks elicited, and I also succeeded in gaining the sympathy and the material support of the people present for the Portland trio.

I again came to Chicago after a few weeks in order to speak at the November 11th celebration and there too, as in the other meetings, I had the sad experience of seeing how impassive and indifferent most of the comrades are. The memory of the terrible murder of 1887, the sight of the shameful memorial[35] at the Haymarket and the repeated brutalities by the Chicago police should have left some enthusiasm and fire in the chest of the workers there. Nothing like that! On November 11 at least, a few thousand people will gather but not because they feel the need to remember the dead, not because they empathize with the strangling of our friends, but out of habit. That is why the previous Nov. 11th anniversary also turned out to be so tame and lame, and I believe that every Nov. 11th anniversary has had the same character since the workers quietly bowed to the order not to go en masse that day to Waldheim instead of fighting for the right to do so.[36]

One imagines such a celebration, beginning with the playing of hymns and songs like "The Star Spangled Banner" and "Tomorrow I will have to leave from here"; followed by a crow-, pardon me, a ladies' choir, cawing a song, "such a song that melts stone," etc; and after that a long-winded speech by the English-speaking speaker who for the umpteenth time dwelled on the story of the process and needlessly regaled those present with the recitation of one of his own, endless poems. On top of that the sight of the yawning, indifferent crowd—one can hardly imagine what impression such an affair must make on a sensitive and enthusiastically disposed human being. In order to keep awake the interest of the workers of this country, the Linggs[37] and others would have to die for their

34. Ironically it was Lucy Parsons, in a letter published in the 14 February 1897 issue, who sparked the debate in the *Firebrand* that led to the publication of articles deemed obscene by the Oregon postal inspector. Parsons's views on the "sex question" led to her decisive break at this time with a new generation of anarchists, including EG. Deeply rooted working-class values, the primacy of economic struggle in a revolutionary program, and apprehension about the effects of free love on the health of the family were the basis of Parson's hostility to those who attacked marriage, and the reason for her distancing herself from the label "anarchist" in association with "varietism." See *Free Society*, 21 November 1897, p. 1.

35. The bronze statue, depicting a single patrolman gesturing for order in the name of peace, was placed in Haymarket Square in 1889 by a group of Chicago businessmen to honor the policemen slain in the 4 May riot. The statue was moved many times and vandalized in protest over the years; twice rebuilt, it is now protected within the walls of the headquarters of the Chicago police department.

36. Chicago mayor John A. Roche had established strict conditions for the funeral procession to Waldheim Cemetery on 13 November 1887: no banners, no placards, no arms, no music except dirges, no revolutionary songs, no speeches, and no demonstrations were allowed. However, the number of mourners was not restricted and numbered more than twenty thousand.

37. A reference to Haymarket anarchist Louis Lingg.

conviction every day because in this country only that which is new counts; the old no longer has any appeal.

V.

My stay in St. Louis was already described in detail in No. 3 of "St."[38] I will only add that the newspapers stirred up the excitement which arose there so much that the common folk were shaking their knees and chattering their teeth in horror that the social revolution could break out at any moment. Unfortunately it does not lie in the power of a single person to bring about such a result, for I would certainly not have lacked the good will to make the fear of the philistines come true.

After St. Louis, I turned toward Caplinger Mills, a little farming town in the southwestern part of Missouri where an English comrade and her husband have lived for six years and have settled as farmers.[39] They sent me an invitation to speak there at several meetings that the two of them would arrange. After a twenty-hour trip by train and four hours of pain in a wagon drawn by two half-starved horses along a road where one is constantly close to breaking one's neck and legs, I finally arrived at my destination.

But it was worth the trouble because I have never met a more appreciative audience. All four meetings were attended very well for the circumstances there and so great was the interest of the people that many of them were not afraid to travel four to six miles in order to be present at the meeting.

During the day several farmers came to me to complain about their sorrow, the sorrow that distinguishes itself little from that of the factory worker and yet is unique in its kind.

Even with hard work they cannot scrape together enough to pay off their little piece of land so that they are in debt up to their necks; in addition, the quality of the soil there is poor and yields poor harvests. Fresh meat is considered the greatest luxury by farmers but they only seldom may enjoy it. The huts that were built before the Civil War are in such bad condition that they hardly protect the people from the inclemency of the weather. In addition, the state exploits these most destitute with regulation and high taxes. Under these miserable conditions human beings actually toil and drudge their entire lives for the landed proprietors. Small wonder if they start to rebel, if they revolt, if they welcome every means that could free them from their miserable situation. Always amid Nature, not surrounded by the corrupting influence of city life, the farmers have more courage than the factory workers, they are not as meek and content as the latter, and for that reason they would be the first to take up arms in a revolution. In view of such good material it is regrettable that, from the anarchist side, very little has been done up to now for the enlightenment of the American agrarian workers.

Accompanied by many good wishes and words of gratitude by the brave farmers, I

38. See *Sturmvogel* (1 December 1897), p. 3, for EG's report on a Haymarket commemoration on 11 November in Chicago and on 13 November in St. Louis, at which Lucy Parsons also spoke.
39. Kate Austin was born in Illinois and living in Missouri with her husband, Sam. Neither were English.

drove back to St. Louis. I spoke there at the November 11th celebration, which left much to be desired, and the following day at the Trades and Labor Council, a corporate body consisting of representatives of various unions.

Nevertheless, I very thoroughly exposed the cancer of trade unionism and the corruption of its leaders, and my speech seemed not to have been entirely without effect; because of it, I have since heard from a comrade in St. Louis, the gentlemen of these corporations now show more tolerance toward anarchists. They must have finally come to the realization that nowadays one cannot secure economic and political freedom for workers only by propagating strikes, eight-hour work days, May 1st celebrations, etc.——

A wish I have cherished for years has come true and I am finally in Detroit——. I have a lot of things to report about Detroit and the friends there; but as I would have to take up a lot of space in order to do justice to all and as I intend to close the reports from my journey with this issue (praised be God, many will exclaim), I will try to keep it as brief as possible. On my whole tour, this time as well as on earlier vagabond journeys, nowhere was so much hospitality, goodness, and kindness shown to me as in Detroit;—not only by my special friends of whom I had only a few when I arrived, but also by corporate bodies, among them the gymnasts, the Central Labor Union, etc., was I treated in the most attentive and courteous manner. The most loving and active support of all I received from friend Robert Reitzel of *Der arme Teufel*.

The great, blessed influence that this newspaper exerts for the propagation of liberal ideas and endeavors is noticeable not only in Detroit. Although the *AT* does not pretend to be an organ of the German anarchist tongue (it has its own and a damn sharp one at that), it works everywhere for individualism, free thinking, and the anarchist world view more than any newspaper which displays any bombastic motto.

The November 11th celebration which took place on Nov. 16th in the gymnastic hall there reminded me of the first huge meetings in the Cooper Union in N.Y., which were held after the murder of our Chicago comrades. There was fire and enthusiasm and everyone seemed, even if only for one evening, to remember the dead in a dignified manner. The second meeting, which was arranged the same day, was also very well attended, and the third and last, which took place in a church, topped them all. Hardly has there ever been a meeting that produced as much general attention as this one. That a priest should have the tolerance to offer his pulpit to a proponent of free ideas must be considered in itself a miracle; but that he made this offer even to an anarchist was simply unheard of; it goes without saying that I took the opportunity to proclaim from the pulpit not God's word, but anarchism. Wait till you hear this, the church, in which among others the sheep in Christ also attentively listened, still stands in the same place: neither brimstone nor pitch rained on the "desecrated house of God," nor did the devil take it with all the sinful brood that was in it.[40]

40. On Friday 19 November, EG spoke at the People's Tabernacle (Congregational) in Detroit, under the auspices of its pastor, Rev. H. S. McCowan, who was active in Detroit labor and reform circles, and whose congregation was predominantly working-class. EG lectured on the definition of anarchy, and

It was not the successes of the meetings in Detroit alone which gave me so much satisfaction. I remember also the pleasure which discussion with many dear human beings gave me and the pleasant, joyful hours I experienced in their company.

Saying good-bye was difficult, but since one has to part, I sailed by boat to Cleveland on Nov. 20th.

In Cleveland four meetings took place of which three were attended very well and the fourth only sparsely. There too I got to know a few superb human beings who showered me with goodness and kindness.

From Cleveland I went to Buffalo where despite all the obstacles that were put up by the other side a few friends managed to organize two English and one German meeting. One of the meetings held for me took place in the Spiritualist Temple, an honor that was given only, according to the spiritualists, to Comrade John Turner[41] besides me.

In Rochester, the last stop of my tour, I also spoke at three meetings.[42] And as R. is, so to speak, my native city, it is no surprise that all of "Jerusalem" was on its feet. But Americans and Germans also came in droves to view the strange animal that approximately nine years earlier had eked out a living for $2.50 per week as a factory worker.

One of my ex-exploiters, a multiple millionaire and factory owner who squeezed his entire fortune from the bones of workers, felt induced to pay me a visit. The old sinner probably feared that I would have an influence on his workers that would be personally disadvantageous for him. He was nervously eager to explain to me how humanely and justly he was treating his workers and how he showered them with benefits. I gave my opinion in an unequivocal manner to this deplorable creature, this German Jewish parvenu, after which he quickly toddled off like a wet poodle.

---

then fielded questions from a restless audience on more controversial subjects like free love and political assassination. The event spurred controversy, heightened by exaggerated early press reports about backlash in the form of mass resignation of the congregants. Later reports confirmed EG's claim that following her talk church attendance went up rather than down. According to Joseph Labadie, a Detroit labor activist and individualist anarchist, who introduced EG to McCowan and attended the lecture, the rumor of the formal demand for the pastor's resignation was untrue. Some local labor leaders and even the prominent freethinker Robert Ingersoll (in Detroit to lecture that week), joined with the city's conservative elite in condemning the event. Ingersoll objected to the address on the grounds that all anarchists are "insane" and "it is not commendable for a crazy man or woman to be invited to talk before any public assemblage." The Detroit correspondent for the *New York American Craftsman* criticized the EG spectacle for impugning the "dignity of labor" and giving ammunition to opponents who charge that the labor movement is led by irresponsible troublemakers. *Detroit Free Press*, 24 November 1897, p. 7; *Detroit Sentinel*, 27 November 1897, p. 2; *Detroit Sentinel*, 11 December 1897, p. 2; *Free Society*, 2 January 1898, p. 2.

41. John Turner spent two weeks lecturing in Buffalo in June 1896.

42. Local newspapers reported on at least two of these meetings. On 4 December, EG lectured on "Anarchy" in Germania Hall. She spoke the next day before the socialist Labor Lyceum on "The Aim of Humanity," after which she clarified her opposition to women's suffrage, standing armies, Christianity, and the vision of a socialist state. Both meetings drew crowds too large for the hall. See *Rochester Union and Advertiser*, 3 December 1897, p. 7; *Rochester Herald*, 6 December 1897, p. 6. While in Rochester EG visited her family for the first time since 1894.

On Dec. 14th, after an absence of fourteen weeks, I finally arrived again in New York. On the whole, I can be satisfied with the success of my journey. I visited eighteen cities and spoke at forty meetings, gained very many good and dear friends and had the opportunity to see for myself that the cries that America is no ground for anarchism were ridiculous and wrong. Americans are by nature independent and more than any other people capable of understanding the ideas of anarchism; it is therefore not their fault if up to now they know very little about it, but the fault of those who conducted the "movement" only in German and who have hindered however they could its explanation in English. To conduct the anarchist propaganda in the English language was and remains the most important issue; because only if the English-speaking element adopts our views is there hope for change in the situation in America.

Fortunately little has remained of a German movement; the elders now belong only to choral societies and lodges and withdraw to their drinking-corners where they rail against the immorality and disobedience of youth. The youth who have emancipated themselves from the anarchist-communist-autonomist dogmas and club fanaticism go their own way and independently spread the ideas of freedom.

Finally, I would like to thank all my friends and comrades as well the radical papers for their support, moral and otherwise.

See you soon!

Sturmvogel: letter no. 1—15 December 1897, pp. 1–3; letter no. 2—1 January 1898, p. 3; letter no. 3— 15 January 1898, pp. 2–3; letter no. 4—1 February 1898, pp. 2–3; letter no. 5—15 February 1898, pp. 2–3. Nos. 1–5 reprinted in *Der arme Konrad* (Berlin), 5 February, 5 March, 12 March, 26 March, and 2 April 1898. Translated from German.

Article in *LE PÈRE PEINARD*

Paris, 19–26 December 1897

American Post-Bag

Mon Vieux Peinard,

Anarchist ideas are making headway in the United States and if they have not spread more quickly it is because English-language propagandists have so far been too few and far between.

We would need lots of comrades of the calibre of Emma Goldmann who is presently making blessed propaganda wheresoever she goes.

This comrade does not know the meaning of tired! Scarcely has she been released from Blackwell Island prison in New York, after serving two years,[1] than she throws herself back into propaganda. She had been sentenced for letting her tongue run away with her unduly: at a workers' rally she had spoken too violently . . . and just to prove that freedom of speech no more exists in "America the free" than in the slick monarchies and republics in Europe, she was scooped.

Emma Goldman is of Russian extraction and Jewish parentage but she has long since renounced all religion and declared herself an atheist.

Tall, well-made, something like thirty five years old, she cuts a fine figure on the rostrum: she has a ringing voice, is given to gesticulation and speaks English and German alike with ease and eloquence. Also, she has enjoyed swelling success in the propaganda tour she has just made around the cities of the American continent.

Emma Goldmann's immediate objective is to whip up widespread agitation on behalf of comrade Bergmann who is serving twenty-five years' hard labour for having attempted in 1892 to blow the brains out of the martinet Frick, the manager of Carnegie's steelworks.

The exploiter Carnegie, the seventy-fold millionaire demon-crat who poses as a philanthropist was trying at the time to tighten the screws on the proles in his Homestead convict colonies, in Pennsylvania state. Since these good fellows would have none of it, this swine Carnegie mustered a gang of Pinkertons, volunteer police in the hire of their capitalist pay-master and unleashed them on Homestead. The moment they arrived, these Pinkertons worked wonders: they shot down the unarmed strikers and felled lots of them.

---

1. In fact, EG was arrested in 1893 at a demonstration of the unemployed for inciting to riot, found guilty, and sentenced to a year in prison, of which she served ten months.

Signaling her growing international stature, Goldman's activities were reported favorably in *Le Père Peinard* (shown here, 1897 almanac cover), a French anarchist scandal sheet edited by Émile Pouget. (By permission of the Kate Sharpley Library)

At which point, exasperated by the crimes of Carnegie and Frick, Bergmann tried to blow the brains out of one of the instigators of these craven actions.

Since when the poor fellow has been banged up!

And Emma Goldmann has rolled up her sleeves to secure his release.

Not that this means that in her talks Bergmann is all she has to talk about. In her most recent tour—which was also designed to revive memories of the execution of the Chicago anarchists—she spoke along general propaganda lines. Lucy Parsons, wife of Albert Parsons, one of the Chicago murder victims, accompanied her. She too is a belter of a propagandist! Since her husband's death she has not let up in her railing against the capitalist and government camp and reminding these nincompoops that they murdered an innocent man.

In addition to her clear and brilliant presentation of our ideas, Emma Goldmann never misses a chance to bait the police and there is not a meeting where she does not lay into the scum—which has the advantage of leaving the plain-clothed cops, plentiful at her meetings, to laugh on the other side of their faces.

Moreover, *mon vieux Peinard,* so that comrades may get some idea of the oratory of Emma Goldmann, let me offer you as best I can a summary of one of the talks[2] she gave in Saint-Louis to a packed hall and to frenzied applause from the public:

"In their utter ignorance, the masses have no knowledge of the reason for their existence.

"What is mankind's raison d'etre if not to enjoy the beauties and splendours of nature?

"But do human beings know such enjoyment? If the answer is yes, they ought to be satisfied and happy—and if it is no, they have been robbed of their legitimate inheritance and are entitled to reclaim it.

"The latter is the true state of affairs: so, are men making their claim?

"Few of them dare! Only a few have the audacity—the anarchists! And these are despised, hounded, mown down, cast into prison or hanged . . . All as punishment for their effrontery.

"As for the rest, the timorous slaves of the monopolies who bow and scrape, they do not possess the manly courage to make their minds known and demand that to which they are justly entitled.

"Religion, regardless of whatever it may go under, has always been the unfailing ally of the monopolists in oppressing the workers: it drums it into the poor ignorant slave that he should carry out the capitalist's instructions, obey the laws . . . and go in terror of the flames of Hell.

"To the devil with Religion! If the howlers the priests tell were true, I should rather go to Hell with my anarchist comrades than to Heaven with the cowards.

"The law is not made against the rich man, only against the long-suffering pauper. The rich man makes the laws and, of necessity, he looks to his own interests by legislating against the people.

"If a mother steals bread to save her children who are perishing of hunger, she commits a crime, an outrage against Society, and Society must come down hard on that! If, on the other hand, a lady bedecked in diamonds and living in luxury steals from a shop, although she is not really in need, she is a kleptomaniac, her plight is to be pitied and she gets away with it."

Then, looking at all of the mechanics of society, Emma Goldmann shows that the object of existing institutions is always to protect the rich and grind down the poor!

Then, turning to the Haymarket riots in Chicago in 1886 and to Homestead in 1892 and Hazleton just last month, she said:

"It is crimes like these that brought the people to a healthy appreciation of the task

2. The *Le Père Peinard* correspondent reports on EG's talk in St. Louis on 16 October 1897 in Harugari Hall, on "Anarchy."

facing it. These capitalist massacres have had the result of stirring the dormant manly feelings in the hearts of men.

"The Hazleton sheriff, Martin, who gunned down the miners, does he think that he will only ever be confronted by bleating sheep?

"And those of his ilk, do they think that things will always be this way?

"It is not, rather, evident that the massacres carried out by the capitalists and their henchmen will inspire the workers to arm themselves in order to resist by at least an equal, if not superior, force of arms . . . ?"

As for the likelihood of the Hazleton butcher, Sheriff Martin, being brought to trial, Emma Goldmann holds this as a mockery and she pokes fun at proles who imagine that the law, which he scrupulously observed, by ordering the massacre, will turn on him.

"Only a madman," she said, "could believe that! And anyway, why should we look to the law? . . . The law! We want no part of it! Each and every one of us is a living law and we claim for ourselves the right to right the wrongs and injustices foisted upon us. . . ."

"Furthermore," she added, "were X-rays able to delve into the recesses of the human mind, we should all be astonished at the numbers of anarchists in existence but unknown to one another, and who have simply not had a chance to break through the layer of prejudices by which they are cocooned. And the social system stifling us would not long survive!"

In conclusion, Emma Goldman points out that society will not be transformed through the ballot box but rather by force:

"And that may well come to pass before long," she cries, "for the warning tremors have already rattled capitalist society!"

Ah, *mon vieux,* you should have heard the stamping feet and frenzied applause once this comrade had finished!

It warmed the cockles of my heart, b'God!

Ah, if only she were right; what a blessing if the squall were to come soon. I cannot wait! It cannot come soon enough . . . , for me!

U<small>N</small> <small>VIEUX DE LA</small> C<small>OMMODE</small>[3]

Le Père Peinard, 19–26 December 1897, pp. 4–5. The paper's American correspondent wrote from St. Louis. Translated from French.

3. The signature of the letter, "Un Vieux de la Commode," translates as "an old hand from the furniture removal trade."

Transcript of Lecture in *FREE SOCIETY*

Providence, R.I., 13 February 1898

The New Woman.

An Address by Emma Goldman Before the
Liberal Progressive Society, of Providence, R.I.

The bible story of woman's inequality and inferiority is based on the declaration of her being created from the rib of man. Woman cannot without equal opportunity ever rise to equality with him, and hence women are slaves to society as a consequence, and intensified under the marriage code. Despotic rule causes people to revolt, and they will do so as a necessity. Woman is bred to be seen and for outside show, and hence the sham in society. Her only mission is to marry and to be a wife and mother, and to cater to a husband who for this will support her. She thus degrades herself. The present mothers are not so much to be blamed for this condition, this comes about by copying their mothers. The mother who is thus raised cannot have any conception of the true knowledge of the rearing of the children, i.e., of raising children as a profession, and she never can bring up the child as she ought to under this system. Mothers are conquered by the child, the exception being a good mother.

The duty of a wife is considered as an impure subject for consideration to the young, unmarried woman, and thus the ignorant girl is forced in the battle unprepared for life consequences. Another great error in the ideal new woman, and one that is to be condemned, is that of aping the male, seeking to become masculine, considering that man is superior to woman. No decent woman can emulate them. We must first have the New Man. In all things women are the equal of men, even in the productive field. Even radicals do not differ from the christians; they do not wish their wives to become radical; even they deem themselves necessary to her protection. So long as she needs protection she is not on equal footing, we need only to protect weaklings. One of the invasive points in the character of man is, that he is too authoritative for the forced progress in woman, and while he has evolved slowly he is making the fatal mistake of securing more liberty for woman through the very thing that was his own enslavement, i.e., authority. Opposition to this will correct this evil.

Contemptible marriage laws and the adherence to them tend to still farther increase the degradation. To assert that freedom of the sex relations is the natural law is interpreted to mean free lust. The law of love governs this as in all matters, love being the fulfillment of the law. Motherhood and its beauty, of which poets have sung and written, is a farce, and cannot be otherwise until we have freedom—economically.

A PERIODICAL OF ANARCHIST THOUGHT, WORK, AND LITERATURE.

VOL. IX. NO. 13.   CHICAGO, SUNDAY, MARCH 30, 1902.   WHOLE NO. 355.

Masthead from 30 March 1902 issue of *Free Society,* an anarchist communist newspaper, for which Goldman frequently wrote essays and political commentaries. She raised funds for the paper and rushed to aid its editors upon their arrest and false implication in the McKinley assassination of September 1901. (The Bancroft Library, University of California)

Men are all heroes at home, but cowards abroad. Women, too, would be as unjust at the ballot box as are the men. They are tyrants as well as are the men. Woman , to be free, must be the mutual friend and mate of man. The individual is the ideal liberty. We owe no duty to anyone, save ourselves. When universal woman once comprehends this ideal, then all protective laws, intended for protection, which is indeed her weakness, will disappear, and this adulterous system goes, and with it charity and all its attendant ills. In short, the new woman movement demands an equal advancement by the modern man.

Free Society, 13 February 1898, p. 2. Although there is no extant record of this lecture being delivered before any group (whether known by the name Liberal Progressive Society or by any other name), in Providence during her stay in that city, between 21 and 23 January 1898, the press reported that EG lectured on the topic "New Woman" before the Brooklyn Social Science Club on 15 January 1898 and before the Ladies' Liberal League in Philadelphia on 15 February 1898.

What Emma Says.

Anarchist Goldman on Maine Disaster and Dreyfus Case.

De Lome Letter and Blowing up of the Ship Should Not Cause War.
Scheming Politicians Trying to Cover the Real Grievances of the People—
Where France and the United States Are Alike.

The prominent woman Anarchist, Emma Goldman, is booked to deliver a number of lectures in Pittsburg and its vicinity, beginning to-morrow evening in Odd Fellows' hall, Eighteenth street, South Side.

She arrived in Pittsburg from New York yesterday. Since her last visit to this city Emma has lost none of her anarchistic tendencies, and if anything they have increased. In conversation with a *Leader* reporter, she discussed most of the leading events of the day, embracing the Maine disaster[1] and the Dreyfus case.[2] Of the former she said:

"In the event of war between Spain and the United States the position of the Anarchists will be a passive one. We do not believe in war between nations, but rather in a contest that will remove the causes that are responsible for misery and poverty as well as those questions that bring nations into bloody conflict. If the people of this country were to go to war it would mean that they would have to neglect home issues, which are of far more importance to their future welfare than a battle with Spain or any other power. There are enough issues at home that should be fought out. To my mind the present ten-

---

1. On 15 February 1898 the USS *Maine* exploded and sunk in the Havana harbor, killing over 260 men. The ship had been sent to protect American interests in Cuba during an insurrection against the Spanish government by Cuban rebels. Initial investigations claimed that the explosion had been caused by a mine placed under the ship. The sinking of the USS *Maine* led to a declaration of war by the United States against Spain on 25 April 1898, dated retroactively to 21 April (in response to Spain's declaration of war on 24 April); the Spanish-American War ended 12 August 1898. Later investigations questioned the assumption that a mine had caused the explosion.

2. French army captain Alfred Dreyfus was arrested on 15 October 1894 for espionage and sentenced to life imprisonment on the penal colony at Devil's Island, French Guiana. In 1896 the anarchist Bernard Lazare became interested in the case, regarding it as an outgrowth of anti-Semitism at the highest levels of the French state, and began to campaign for an appeal and reversal of Dreyfus's sentence, not only among anarchists but also among leading intellectuals convinced of Dreyfus's innocence. On 13 January 1898, *L'Aurore* printed "J'Accuse," Émile Zola's condemnation of the French government's conduct in the Dreyfus Affair. After another trial and guilty verdict in 1899 Dreyfus was pardoned by the French president later that year, and ultimately rehabilitated in July 1906.

sion has been caused by the designing tactics of politicians of both countries, who wish to detract from the people the real questions that confront them and that they should take up and pass upon. The real grievances of the people are buried under this war scare.

"The De Lome[3] letter," continued Emma, "was by no means a cause for war. While discussing it I might say that I agree with De Lome in classing McKinley as a low politician.[4] Neither can the blowing up of the Maine be regarded as a casus belli. It was the act of an individual or a subject, and the nation cannot be held responsible. Spain should be no more called to account for the act of an unauthorized person any more than that the United States should be held responsible for the killing of a king by one of its citizens."

Referring to the Dreyfus case Miss Goldman said:

"The French government is making a spectacle of justice and equality. There is no doubt of the innocence of Dreyfus. Still in this respect France is no worse than the United States or any other country as at present governed. Did not the United States hang the alleged rioters in the Haymarket square affair? They were put to death on the gallows without the shadow of evidence that they figured in the throwing of the bomb that caused the death of so many policemen. The only difference between France and the United States is that while Dreyfus still lives, alleged Haymarket rioters are dead."

Miss Goldman denies that she ever applied to Prison Inspector George A. Kelly for a permit to see Anarchist Berkmann, who is in the Western Penitentiary, nor is it her intention to ask for permission to see him at this time. She says the Anarchists now have a fund of $12,000[5] which will be used in an effort to secure his pardon.

As before stated, the woman Anarchist will lecture to-morrow night at Odd Fellows' hall, Eighteenth street and Larkins alley, South Side. It will be in English. She will speak in German Friday night at Vorwaerts' Saenger hall, Holmes street, Lawrenceville, and Saturday, at the Imperial Dancing academy. Sunday the lecture will be at Marion hall, Fifth avenue and Marion street, at 2 P.M., in English. Wednesday evening, March 2, she will speak at the North Side Turner hall, East street, Allegheny, and Sunday, March 6, again at the Imperial Dancing academy. The last two will be German. All but Saturday's lecture will be free.

Superintendent Leslie was asked to-day if his department would offer any objections to the lectures. "Not at all," was the response. "Mrs. Goldman has a perfect right to lecture, and certainly will not be interfered with, unless she commits a breach of the peace.

3. On 9 February 1898, William Randolph Hearst's *New York Journal* published a letter by Enrique Depuy de Lôme, Spanish minister to the United States, writing to a friend in Havana. The letter, printed under the headline "The Worst Insult to the United States in Its History," immediately increased public pressure for war with Spain. Stolen by Cuban insurgents and passed on to the newspaper, the letter unmasked the hypocrisy of Spanish promises for Cuban autonomy, and described McKinley in unfavorable terms.

4. In his letter, de Lôme wrote of McKinley, "McKinley is: weak and catering to the rabble, and besides, a low politician, who desires to leave a door open to me and to stand well with the jingoes of his party."

5. According to the statement published by the Berkman Defense Association in *Free Society* in February 1898, only $1,015.83 had been raised and the fund had $394.35 on hand.

If she does that, of course, she will be looked after just as anybody else would be." Asked if he would have any officers present to see that inflammable language and disorder was not indulged in, Superintendent Leslie answered that it was customary to have officers present to preserve order at all such entertainments, and that Mrs. Goldman's lecture would not be made an exception.

Pittsburg (Pa.) Leader, 23 February 1898, p. 1.

Article in the *PITTSBURG POST*

Pittsburgh, 25 February 1898

What Emma Goldman Thinks of Patriotism.

Female Anarchist Says the Meaning
of Word is Not Known in This Country.

Patriot is One Who Slays.

Shoots Down His Fellow-Man Under Law's Protection.

Series of Meetings Which Will Be Held in This Vicinity Opened
Last Night on the Southside.

Emma Goldman, anarchist, agitated in Odd Fellows' hall, South Eighteenth and Sarah streets, last night. It was the opening of a series of meetings which she contemplates holding in this vicinity during the next few weeks. She was brought here by the agitation committee of Western Pennsylvania, working under the direction of the International Workingmen's Association. Her subject last night was "Patriotism," and a large crowd was present to hear the fiery utterances as they fell, laden with molten metal, from the speaker's lips. Judging from the infrequency of any demonstration, however, the great majority of those present were there through curiosity more than sympathy with the cause which Miss Goldman represents.

"Patriotism," Miss Goldman thinks, is a word the meaning of which the vast majority of the people of the United States takes in entirely the contrary sense. "To be a patriot," she said, "one must wade ankle-deep in the blood of his fellow men. He must kill, slay, destroy in every conceivable manner and form, else he is not living up to the sacred meaning of that sacred word. The sheriff and deputies who ruthlessly shot down the miners at Hazleton were patriots in the strictest American sense. And as such, you may rest assured, they will be acquitted of the crime.[1]

"In Chicago, some years ago, someone threw a bomb into a crowd around the Haymarket. For this supposed crime the lives of five men paid the forfeit. And yet who knows who threw that bomb? Was it ever clearly proved? No, but the voice of capital cried aloud for the blood of the accused, and in this country the voice of capital is always heeded. The

---

1. On 10 September 1897, Sheriff Martin and his deputies shot and killed striking workers in Lattimer, Pennsylvania, near Hazleton. The sheriff and his deputies were arrested and charged with murder. The trial began in February 1898, lasted five weeks, and all were acquitted.

tragedy in Hazleton is not hidden by any cloaks of mystery. Men among those deputies have been heard to say, 'I killed five of them, and could have killed nine,' making no secret of the crime, and yet he will go unpunished, for the voice and influence and wealth of the mine owners is whispering insidiously into the ears of justice that these men who did the shooting did so in preservation of the law, and in so doing acted solely as patriots, and should be protected rather than condemned for a crime so brutal.

"What constitutes a good citizen in this beloved free country of America? I can tell you. If a man has the ability to rob his neighbor under the guise of a legitimate speculation. If by slipping stealthily up behind him and inserting the knife into his back he robs him of his life under the pretext that the crime was committed to preserve the integrity of the Nation, men in office, and, alas, even many of you here to-night, place a crown of laurel and roses on his brow, and he is at once crowned a public-spirited citizen and a patriot of the first water. Is it so with the man whose daily existence and the lives of his family depends on a crust? Hardly. Let him but purloin one loaf from the bakery of his neighbor and a cell yawns before him.

"There is talk of a war between America and Spain. I am not allied with either country, but I tell you it is unsafe, even dangerous, for America to war with any nation. Her own governmental props need bolstering; they totter and are likely to fall at any moment, and it is my candid belief that if war would ensue an uprising of thousands upon whom the country is now depending for support would follow."

At the conclusion Miss Goldman was asked how she expected to bring about the reforms in the labor question which she agitates. She replied that there was only one way in which it could be done: that was by a popular uprising of the people. A revolution such as that of more than a century ago was surely fomenting, and in time, a short time at that, the clouds were bound to break. That, she said, is the only solution, and that was a day to which she is confidently looking forward.

Pittsburg (Pa.) Post, 25 February 1898, p. 2. Copyright 2001 *Pittsburgh Post-Gazette.* All rights reserved. Reprinted with permission. The *Post* ran two subsequent, though shorter, reports of EG's Pittsburgh lectures. See "Emma Goldman Again" and "Again Emma Goldman," 26 February 1898 and 28 February 1898, *EGP,* reel 47.

To *SOLIDARITY*

Pittsburgh, 15 March 1898

DEAR COMRADES—

Hurrah for the new paper! Though I don't care for the name "Solidarity" (we have had experience with it before),[1] yet I hail its appearance, knowing how sadly a paper is needed in New York. After all, what's in a name? The principles and tendencies of a paper are all-important, and knowing the comrades who are to conduct *Solidarity*,[2] I am satisfied that our ideas will be ably set forth in its columns. I cannot tell you how many people are now interested in the philosophy of Anarchy. Even the most conservative clubs and organizations, that only a few years ago would have refused to listen to a professed Anarchist, are now inviting Anarchist lecturers. They have learned that conservatism is fast losing ground, and that nothing but advanced and radical ideas meet with popular approval. The Friendship Liberal League, of Philadelphia, for instance, has heretofore been controlled by its older members, who for twenty-five years have been killing God one night and reviving him the next; who have ceased to believe in a heavenly Lord, and yet have stood by without protest while earthly lords were robbing the people. Even these "pillars of society" have been taught the lesson that the old order changes and gives way to the new. The comrades of Philadelphia, who arranged five meetings for me in the city of Brotherly Love, had a hard battle with these gentlemen, who had decided that no Anarchist should speak from the platform of the League. The younger members, however, together with our energetic comrades, won the victory.[3] In spite of the strenuous opposition of the "respectable element," we had two glorious meetings at the League, in the afternoon and evening of Sunday, Feb. 20th. I lectured on "Patriotism" and on "Charity." The comrades have sent reports to *Free Society*[4] and other liberal papers, so I will refrain from telling you the details.

---

1. *Solidarity*, the first English-language anarchist communist paper in New York, had had many stops and starts since its founding in June 1892 by Italian anarchist Saverio Merlino and John H. Edelmann. When Merlino left for London at the beginning of 1893, Edelmann assumed most editorial responsibilities, keeping the journal going through August when it suspended publication. He revived it in January 1895, but within the year lack of funds once again forced it to close. Peter Kropotkin donated part of the proceeds from his 1897 U.S. lecture tour and Edelmann revived the paper once more in 1898, with the assistance of William C. Owen and Charles B. Cooper.
2. John H. Edelmann, William C. Owen, and Charles B. Cooper, among others.
3. EG spoke before the Friendship Liberal League during her Fall 1897 lecture tour. Although the Friendship Liberal League was a freethought organization that sponsored lectures primarily on secularism, Voltairine de Cleyre, James B. Elliott, and other members successfully influenced the group to broaden its topics to include anarchism.
4. See "Emma Goldman in Philadelphia," *Free Society*, 13 March 1898, pp. 2–3; and "A Short Campaign in Philadelphia," *Lucifer, the Lightbearer*, 16 March 1898, pp. 85–86.

In Pittsburg the comrades have arranged meetings for almost every night of the three weeks I expect to stay here, to try my endurance they say, but you know how much it takes to tire a woman of talking.

Here, too, I have had proof that our ideas are marching on. The Glass Blowers' Union, No. 36, of Monaca, Pa., the largest and most conservative labor organization of the country, had me down to speak on "Majority Rule," Saturday, Feb. 26th, at a meeting specially arranged for me. I must say that I was treated with unusual politeness by the committee, who showed me every attention. Of course, I care little for such formalities, but I think we have cause to be satisfied with the progress of the propaganda, when we, who have until recently been treated like criminals, or who, according to the "Christ of the Free Thinkers," Bob Ingersoll, ought to be treated like lunatics,[5] are invited to expound our doctrines, and are listened to with enthusiasm by people who a few years ago joined in the plutocratic cry "Hang the Anarchists!"

I will be able to give you a better report of my tour when I return home, which will be in the latter part of April. So far, meetings have been arranged until March 12th in this city. After that in Cleveland, Detroit, Chicago for two weeks; in Cincinnati by the Liberal League of Ohio,[6] another free thought society that has never invited an Anarchist speaker before; in St. Louis and other cities. In fact I think of extending my present tour as far as San Francisco, Cal.[7]

I need not assure you of my hearty co-operation; it is a matter of course that I will do my best for *Solidarity*. Please send me several hundred copies of the first number.

WITH HEARTIEST WISHES FOR THE SUCCESS

OF YOUR UNDERTAKING, FRATERNALLY,

EMMA GOLDMAN.

Solidarity, 15 March 1898, p. 3. EG's original is dated "March, 1898"; therefore, she must have written this letter between 1 March and 15 March, the date it was published.

5. EG lectured at the People's Tabernacle in Detroit on 19 November, under the auspices of its pastor, Rev. H. S. McCowan, on the definition of anarchy, and then fielded questions on more controversial subjects like free love and political assassination. Local labor leaders joined the city's conservative elite in condemning the event. The prominent freethinker Robert Ingersoll (visiting Detroit to lecture that week) objected to the address on the grounds that all anarchists are "insane" and "it is not commendable for a crazy man or woman to be invited to talk before any public assemblage."

6. EG spoke to the Ohio Liberal Society on 27 March 1898 on "The Aim of Humanity."

7. EG did travel to California, arriving in San Francisco in late April. She lectured throughout May in San Francisco and Los Angeles, before traveling to Portland where she lectured for three nights in early June.

Emma Goldman, Anarchist.

A little woman—she can't be five feet tall—her round, slender figure neatly dressed in black, a bunch of carnations at her belt and one glowing vividly in her brown hair, a white collar at her fair throat and white lace falling over her tiny hands. Her eyes are beautifully clear and gray, her forehead is fine and low, though the head itself seems narrow, the small nose is a bit blunt and the thin lips have an habitual disdainful curl that is far from pleasing.

This is Emma Goldman, the anarchist, who suffered a year's imprisonment in New York for "inciting to riot."[1]

"I didn't incite to riot," she said to me after last night's meeting was over. "I merely quoted Cardinal Manning's words: 'Necessity knows no law'."[2]

"But there was an implication, wasn't there? You meant them to riot?" I asked her. Incite to riot?

Why this five feet of feminine anarchy is the most dangerous enemy society has. Had she lived a century ago she'd have been beheaded. Two centuries ago Emma Goldman, anarchist, would have been given over to the loving embrace of the jungfrau;[3] while in the sixteenth century she would have been nicely boiled in oil or beheaded and then neatly broken on the wheel.

But this little Russian woman, with her thickened speech, her good rolling r's, her disdain of rhetorical rules, her vehemence of expression, her potent, unstudied postures, is the most interesting woman I ever met. She has life, she has courage, she has brains. She is fiercely consistent, unwaveringly true and, though I can't agree with her, I believe her to be absolutely sincere.

You should hear her talk. It doesn't matter whether you're socialist or anarchist or are endowed with a blessed indifference of isms in general. You can better afford to miss hearing Melba or even Bernhardt than listening to this genuine creature.[4] She is San

1. EG was sentenced to a year in prison in 1893 for inciting to riot at a demonstration of the unemployed. She was released after ten months for good behavior.
2. EG often attributed her statement to Cardinal Henry Edward Manning. See note 3 in "Hailed Emma Goldman," *New York World,* 20 August 1894, above.
3. The torture device known in English as the "iron maiden" (in German, *jungfrau*) was a metal casket, the inside of which was covered in sharpened metal pegs such that, when it closed around a body, the person was pierced by the pegs and slowly killed.
4. Reporter refers to Nellie Melba (1861–1931; née Helen Porter Mitchell), the world-renowned Australian opera singer; and to Sarah Bernhardt (1844–1923; née Rosine Bernard), the famous French actress, known for her strong female roles.

Francisco's sensation, as she was that of New York and Chicago; and next to the departure of the soldiers who marched off to Cuba, there is nothing so thrilling as listening to Emma Goldman. For nothing cows this woman, who alludes, in her full, strong contralto, to the Deity as "the old gentleman who employs full-stomached idlers, priests, rabbis and ministers to mind his business"; who attacks the Press, and charges it with the responsibility of the war with Spain; who speaks mockingly of President McKinley as "a low politician," and says that it was honesty among thieves that made De Lome so express himself;[5] and who then turns upon the people themselves present and taunts them with their ignorance, their helplessness, their gullibility.

"You—you—you fools," she cried, "you slaves, who prate of humanity! Did you interfere in humanity's name when Sheriff Martin and the other murderers, his deputies, shot the strikers down?[6] O, no, you did nothing of the kind! You believe what you're told to believe, you do what you're told to do. You stand like cattle before the bulletin boards with the war news. What for, my friends, what for? That the ruling classes may rejoice; that the yoke may press tighter upon you; that your blood and your body and your purse may suffer. And then you talk of freedom, of liberty!"

O, the contempt in this woman's voice! O, the power she has over this large audience that shouts bravos and stamps and roars in response to her fiery words!

"As if a workingman could ever be free! Why, you are slaves, slaves. And 'the brave boys, the brave boys,'" she went on, quoting sarcastically. "I say 'the brave boy' who goes to offer himself in battle while his father slaves and sweats at home and his sister sells herself in the streets deserves the lash—and I hope he gets it."

I asked Miss Goldman later whether she didn't fear to address men in such terms as this.

"Never," she answered. "I have talked to workingmen at the mines, in Chicago, during strikes and never once was molested."

She doesn't mince words, this fierce, scornful woman. She denounces the present war—all wars—as a relic of a barbarous time. She declares that the men we honor—Washington, Jefferson, and Wendell Phillips[7]—were not patriots, but rebels. She deplores love of country because it makes one intolerant.

"Do you mean to tell me," she demands, one little hand outstretched and the other braced upon her hip; "do you mean to tell me that it is wise and noble to throw yourselves like wild beasts upon the Spaniards, and that you'll believe it perfectly wise and perfectly legal and noble simply because you're told so by the press and the pulpit—the pulpit,"

5. EG refers to the letter written by Enrique Depuy de Lôme, Spanish minister to the United States, that revealed Spain's hypocrisy with regard to autonomy for Cuba. The *New York Journal* printed a pirated copy of the letter on 9 February 1898, inflaming war fever against Spain.
6. EG refers to the deaths of striking miners at Lattimer, near Hazleton, Pennsylvania, on 10 September 1897.
7. For a discussion of allusions by EG and preceding anarchists to presumed anti-statist sensibilities of founders of the United States, see note 6 in "Badly Advised," Article in the *New-Yorker Staats-Zeitung*, 22 August 1893.

she sneered, "for war!—and the monopolists and the Government that is not by the people and for the people? They tell you you'd tear yourselves to pieces if you had no leaders. Who does the lynching in the South—the white or the black?"

Miss Goldman's speech is epigrammatic; it is highly quotable. "The world is my country," she declares. "To do good is my only religion."[8] Freedom, freedom, is her cry. According to her creed every barrier is tyranny; every Government, all laws, an imposition.

And the remedy?

"I may be a fool; I am not a prophet," she answered a question from the gallery, with a swagger, the only betrayal of self-consciousness she was guilty of last night.

This small fire-brand will suggest no remedy save this:

"Truth is a dangerous weapon in the hands of working men and women. Your enemy is not in Spain, but in Washington; not in Madrid, but here in San Francisco, in New York, in Chicago. I believe in holding up a looking glass before you, so that you can see and know yourselves. When you are educated, when you realize your power, you'll need no bombs, and no dynamite or militia will hold you."

San Francisco Call, 27 April 1898, p. 16. The *San Francisco Examiner* reprinted an excerpt from this article on 28 September 1901 (with the headline "You Should Hear Her Talk"), in the wake of the McKinley assassination and extreme anti-anarchist sentiment, charging the *Call* with treating anarchism sympathetically. The two-paragraph excerpt began with "But this little Russian woman" and ended with "there is nothing so thrilling as listening to Emma Goldman." The *Call* responded by reprinting the entire article and accusing the *Examiner* of quoting it out of context.

8. The first half of EG's statement reiterates the words of Albert Parsons in his address to the jury in October 1886, reproduced in *The Accused, the Accusers . . .* (Chicago: Socialistic Publishing Society, [1886?]). In his discussion of the exploitation of workers by capitalism and governments in both industry and war, Parsons stated, "The world is my country, all mankind my countrymen." EG's statement also echoes Thomas Paine's in his 1792 *Rights of Man* (part 2, chap. 5): "My country is the world, and my religion is to do good."

To *FREE SOCIETY*

New York, 10 July 1898

"Ideas and Men."

Have just read Comrade Addis' article "Ideas and Men" and also A.I.'s comment.[1] The latter expressed my ideas on the subject so thoroughly that I would not have troubled to write the following, were it not for the fact that I am the cause of this discussion, or rather my criticism, during my last visit in Portland, of Anarchists taking part in politics.

He says among other things: "I have been told it is not best for me to make a lecturing trip to New York and the East, because of the highly colored and largely untrue reports of my private acts that have been assiduously circulated there." Why Comrade Addis has not stated who the person was that told him so, I do not know; but since he has failed to do so, I will tell the readers of *Free Society* that I spoke to Comrade Addis about it, therefore I will remind him that I did not say "it is not best for him to make a trip East," for none of the comrades whom I know paid any attention to the circulated reports about Addis and the rest of the *Firebrand* group. What I did say, was that many comrades in the East have, on learning that Addis stood in with the political gang, lost confidence in him and would not aid him to make his tour a success. Comrade Addis does not deny that he took money from some politicians for services rendered them; neither can he deny that while I was in Portland he again did work for some politicians, although, as he said, "only to give them pointers and advices." I am sure that very few of the Eastern comrades care much for Addis' private actions. For myself I can only say that I have suffered too much through Mrs. Grundy[2] in pants, in our own ranks, as to pay any attention to reports. I

---

1. See 26 June 1898 issue of *Free Society* (pp. 2, 4); Henry Addis had said, in part:

    I understand that Comrade Merlino and myself have greatly detracted from our usefulness by "dabbling in politics." That may be so, but, if it is it only shows how professed thinkers allow themselves to be influenced by prejudice, and by the sentiment that an advocate of a grand ideal should be above reproach personally. . . . [T]his asserting that it is wrong for an advocate to do so and so, or that propagandists destroy their influence by doing this or that, is an attempt to mould the action of the advocate or propagandist. It is connecting the theory to the man, and actions as though the theory was made good or bad by the personal acts of its advocate. Let's try to rid our minds of this false sentiment, and look at ideas as such, regardless of who advocates them.

    Abe Isaak's (EG refers to him by his initials, A.I.) comment in the 26 June 1898 issue of *Free Society* (p. 4) began: "It appears to me that Comrade Addis' contention that the actions of the individual 'should play no part in the acceptance or rejection of the theories advanced by him or her,' is synonymous with the vindication of a catholic priest requesting his flock to judge him not by his deeds but by his words, when it becomes known that he has been in the company of gay women in the back of a saloon." Isaak's comment ended with "If criticism of our actions is not admissible we might as well quit the propaganda of our ideal."

2. The character "Mrs. Grundy" in Thomas Morton's play *Speed the Plough* came to personify prudish censorship.

have been slandered and attacked in the most contemptible manner: and even now can be found all sorts of untrue denunciations of Emma Goldman in a German weekly.[3] Why? Because I have for years tried to destroy the impression of Anarchy in the heads of many people, that Anarchy means whisky and bombs, an impression produced by these very denunciators. I have never put myself up as judge or guardian over the acts of others.

But if an Anarchist enters the political field, this act is no longer private—it concerns me and all those interested in the success of our movement, for such inconsistency he or she does more harm to the movement than can be undone in years. Here we use all our energies to demonstrate that political action is a folly, that it corrupts the people and will never set them free; and the next moment this or the other comrade enters the political arena, helps nominating candidates—in one word, does all the political tricks necessary. Comrade Addis says "he never advised to vote." Of course he has not, but his actions remain the same. Just like the Jew calling a christian to light the candle on Saturday or kindle the fire, because some religious notions forbid him to do it himself. Now if it is right for the Jew to give to the christian girl the order to do the work, it must be right for him to do it himself. As prejudice and superstition knows no logic we may excuse the Jewish people, but there is no excuse for H. Addis entering the political field. Whether he advised people to vote or not, is not important: he helped the politicians and they finished the rest of the dirty job. Comrade Addis refers to Merlino. Ah, but there is a vast difference between Merlino's act in regard to politics and his.[4]

3. Most had reported on the Pacific Coast portion of EG's tour in the 18 June 1898 issue of *Freiheit* (p. 8; translated from German):

Several long-winded reports have reached us on the meetings held there by Emma Goldman. In general, they more or less sounded the same. From none of them can we gather anything about the *content* of the speeches held (the only thing that could interest larger circles), all are concerned almost exclusively with an exaggerated *cult of personality*, of which more than enough has been made already and which is not very suitable for anarchists. That is why we will *condense*.

In San Francisco, E. Goldmann spoke in several well-attended meetings, mostly in English. Comrade Rieger thinks she masters this language "better" than the German one, "although one immediately recognizes the foreigner in her hard accent." He also remarked that he tried to find out what impression these lectures made on outsiders and that he had to hear often: "What in the world is this woman getting at?" At a celebration of Reitzel, he says, Goldmann gave a speech "which didn't lack in inaccuracies or tactlessness." She said, for example: "If there were five men like Reitzel the world would be liberated in a short time from the bonds of slavery[.] . . ."

Comrade Doering from Portland, who compared Goldmann's agitation with a "tornado," which was suitable "to awaken in us the sense of guilt for having been asleep in recent times," informs us that the three meetings that took place there were only poorly attended because "the time to organize them was too short and the moment was poorly chosen." Finally he remarks that the speaker "was regretfully allowed to leave bedecked with flowers and accompanied by the best wishes."

Comrade Frenzel reports from San Jose that E. Goldmann had to speak on the street because the social democrats there, after having originally promised her their hall, took back their word.

Comrade Fäßler, from Los Angeles, is less delighted by the whole agitation that Goldmann engaged in there. He states that one had repeatedly written from the start not to come, but *nevertheless* was "honored" by her visit. Then he writes: "She can really boast to have spoken here for she left here unconcerned by the fact that she intensified the hatred against our ideas and the persecutional rage against our comrades."

4. In January 1896, Saverio Merlino advocated a strategic alliance with leftist forces in Italy, including participation in the 1896 election, as a necessary step in deposing the reactionary regime of Prime Minister Crispi.

Merlino openly and intelligently advocates the use of the ballot and political action. Now, whether I agree with him or not, I must at least admit that with Merlino it is a conviction, a principle; with H. Addis it is nothing of the kind, in fact he always has been opposing politics in the *Firebrand*. Why, then, did he assist the politicians? Because, he said himself, "there was money in it." And that is just the reason why I, and with me many others, deplore Comrade Addis' act. He says further, "I might be one of the vilest men, and yet be able to clearly and forcibly advocate the purest and most lofty ideas." Oh no, you cannot, Comrade Addis. The very fact of you being vile would never allow you to grasp the noble ideas.

It is time that we understand once for all that a rascal, a liar, a contemptible man or woman, never can be an Anarchist; and unless we do that we will make no headway in the future, as we have made but little in the past; and this only because we have had drunkards, liars, biggots and despots in our ranks, who delivered splendid speeches, talked about liberty, equality and other grand things, while as soon as they left the platform, they were cruel, mean, coarse and vile, ready to destroy everybody who dared to oppose them. Unless we reform ourselves, we have no right to reform others; unless we bring our acts in conformity with our ideas, we will never progress, never change conditions.

Of course Comrade Addis has a perfect right to do what he pleases, but if he so much insists on his right, he will kindly allow me the right to criticise his acts pertaining to the movement.

Comrade Addis has assisted me very much during my short stay in Portland. We have parted as friends, and he will therefore, I hope, not take these lines with ill feelings, for they have not been written in such a spirit. I have replied to his article because I wish the readers of *Free Society* to know what and whom he was aiming at, also state my position in regard to "men and ideas." [5]

E. GOLDMAN.

Free Society, 10 July 1898, pp. 4–5. EG dated her letter June 1898, but her reference later in this letter to "denunciations of Emma Goldman in a German weekly" implies that she wrote it on or after 18 June, the date of the *Freiheit* article.

5. Addis responded to EG in the next issue of *Free Society,* denying her allegations against him, claiming he neither wrote his original article with her in mind, nor had he taken work for politicians. He took offense at the personal nature of her attack: "Emma did not reply to my article, but tried to defend herself before she was attacked, and in so doing made a personal attack on me. I did not have her in mind when I wrote, in fact had no person in mind, only ideas. I have no more to say. When my theories will be criticised instead of my personality I will again enter the forum, but I positively refuse to mix in personal disputes" (*Free Society,* 24 July 1898, p. 2).

A Short Account of My Late Tour.

I had promised friends and comrades to give a detailed account of my tour through the States in the form of traveling notes, either in *Free Society* or in *Solidarity*. But on thinking the matter over, I concluded that this would be impossible, for if I should give a full history of all my experiences, all I encountered, and the many incidents which I recall, the people I met and their characteristics, during eighteen weeks on the road, it would fill a book of considerable size. As time and space will not permit me to do this now, I must beg my friends to accept a short account.

I left New York with $2 in my purse and a ticket to Philadelphia, my first stopping place. Through the kind assistance of various comrades I traveled to the Pacific Coast, South as far as Los Angeles, and North to Portland. I have visited in all eighteen cities, among them Philadelphia, Pittsburg, and in the Western Pennsylvania mining districts, McKeesport, Roscoe, Newton, Monaca, and Homestead, where six years ago the slaves of Carnegie's iron and steel mills fought like men to protect their lives and liberty for a time, only to return to greater hardships and humiliations than ever. I was in Cleveland, Detroit, Chicago, Milwaukee, Cincinnati, St. Louis, Denver, Salt Lake City, San Francisco, San Jose, Los Angeles and Portland, but was compelled to cancel engagements in Tacoma and Seattle and other places on account of misunderstandings. I addressed 66 meetings and conducted a debate with a leading Socialist in San Francisco.[1] On looking back over my tour I can say without flattering myself too much, that I have done good work. I have made friends for the cause of liberty, have done away with a good deal of prejudice formerly entertained by different people against Anarchy and Anarchists, and have won a number of personal friends. In fact I was received with open arms wherever I went, and the comrades did their utmost to make my visit pleasant in every respect. Of course I also made enemies. I do not understand why some people assert that America is a poor place for the spread of radical ideas. My experience in my last two trips has been that this country is an excellent field for them. I believe that if we only had a few able, en-

---

1. EG refers to Emil Liess, who was a German American socialist in San Francisco and editor of the labor daily *San Francisco Tageblatt* from 1894 to 1899. He debated EG in San Francisco on 4 May 1898, at Vorwärts Turner Hall. Later Liess assumed the editorship of the weekly organ of the San Francisco Socialist Party, *Vorwärts der Pacific Küste* (1911). A member of the German Free Thought Society in San Francisco, he shared the podium with James F. Morton, Jr., during an 11 November 1900 memorial meeting in San Francisco for the executed Haymarket anarchists.

ergetic workers going constantly back and forth between the Atlantic and Pacific we would have a strong movement in a short time.

It will surprise many of the comrades to learn that very little is known of Anarchy in the West. "Yet much money and time have been spent in literature, papers, pamphlets, etc.," some will exclaim. That is true, but unfortunately the papers, pamphlets and leaflets have only reached the few—not the many. It is only of late that a Western paper has been doing good work in propaganda, and that is *Free Society*. The Western people are ready to accept radical ideas, and *Free Society* is now paving the way for anarchy very rapidly.

The condition of the workers is, of course, much the same everywhere—poverty, lack of work, want of the necessaries of life, misery and starvation are at home in each large city; still, the West is not so much in the grip of politicians, bigots and hypocrites as the East. Sunday laws, moral laws, laws prohibiting speech in the open air, etc., are little known in the far West, and I hardly think ever will be. This alone makes life pleasanter on the Pacific than here, where every bluecoat exercises the power of a Czar.

Therefore, if the time, energy and money used in propaganda in the East had been devoted to the Pacific Slope we would have had a very different movement. However, better late than never. Philosophic Anarchy is still new to the American tongue. Let us continue our efforts, carry on an energetic propaganda, and we will soon see that intelligent Americans will join hands with the intelligent people of all countries in the battle for liberty.

I have often heard reformers say that the working class does not revolt because it is not yet wretched and starving enough, and that the sooner economic conditions get worse the sooner they will revolt. This is another wrong conception of men and conditions. Take the coal miners, the most ill paid and ill treated wage workers in existence. To try to describe the condition of the miners of Western Pennsylvania is to attempt the impossible. In many places grown men, with families, have not been able to earn more than $1.50 a week. They are herded together in miserable, filthy hovels, 12 or 15 people occupying one room; for how else can they pay rent? Yet these men do not revolt, and never will. They have not the strength. They are like animals—dumb, stupid, indifferent, ready to lick the hand that lashes them. But when I reached the districts where they earned $5 and $6 a week (a fortune (?) as they work), I found men carrying themselves with some pride and self respect, and open to ideas. It is therefore an unpardonable mistake to sit with folded hands awaiting the development of things to such a state that it will be too late to act. Men with empty stomachs do not fight for freedom. They fight for bread, and as soon as they get the crust, gnawing on it they forget their good intentions to fight for more. I have not spent 18 weeks in missionary work without learning that it is useless to appeal to the overfed, but still of less use to appeal to the underfed. To be successful we must reach that class whose brains have not yet been destroyed by starvation.

The convention of the Social Democracy, held in Chicago June 7th, which I attended as a visitor, was a fiasco, as many such have been. For the credit of the colonization side, however, be it said, that it was their intention to develop a sound, healthy, economic movement, leaving all politics to the politicians.[2] The will was strong, but the flesh was weak; not strong enough to maintain their position to the last, they compromised, that is, they dropped one, politics, but accepted the other, the colonization propaganda. I have no faith in either, for I know that nothing short of the propaganda against political control and against economic dependence will satisfy.

I will write no more of my tour, as most of the meetings have been reported in *Free Society* and in *Solidarity*. I will add that some of my lectures are to appear in *Free Society* shortly. Let me also add that before long I will start on another tour. Therefore, not good-by, but au revoir.

FRATERNALLY,

EMMA GOLDMAN.

Solidarity, 15 July 1898, p. 2. EG dated this travel letter "New York, July 1898."

2. The Social Democracy of America was formed by Eugene Debs in 1897. By the time of the 1898 convention, the organization was on the verge of collapse, internally divided over a colonization plan to settle workers in a western state where they would put their communitarian principles into practice. Their numbers, it was believed by some, would transform the state into a cooperative commonwealth, providing political leverage for a national transformation. Debs had adopted the project from the Brotherhood of the Cooperative Commonwealth, a communitarian socialist organization founded in 1896, and had made it the cornerstone of his Social Democracy movement. Leaders of an anti-colonization faction, however, turned Debs away from this idea. Headed by Milwaukee socialist Victor Berger, they opposed the plan as a distraction from the task of union building and political pursuit of immediate worker demands. Outvoted on the issue, these "political actionists" walked out of the 1898 convention and, with Debs in tow, immediately founded the Social Democratic Party, in effect spelling the end of the Social Democracy of America. Many anarchists were involved in the Social Democracy of America, especially in Chicago, where the anarchist Branch 2 had been thrown out of the Social Democracy for its radical rhetoric (see note 2, "Emma Goldman Has Her Say," Article in the *Chicago Tribune*, 30 September 1897, above).

Miss Emma Goldman

Replies to Questions Asked by Mr. F. B. Livezey.

She Does Not Favor Compulsory Education or Force as
Anarchistic Propaganda—Interesting Letter.

To the Editor of the *Sentinel:*

In your paper of July 2d I notice an item headed "Emma Goldman Wanted," in which
Mr. F. B. Livesey,[1] of Sykesville, Md., sends me his compliments and inquires whether I
am in favor of "compulsory education," and whether I advocate "force" in the propaganda of anarchy. He also states that he is in sympathy with my antagonism to marriage
and the clergy, and with my appreciation of Jesus Christ.[2]

May I ask that you be kind enough to publish this reply to Mr. Livesey's queries:

1. Francis Buck Livesey (1845–1925) was a reformer and correspondent ubiquitous in the pages of various radical and reform publications, including *Free Society* and *Lucifer, the Lightbearer*. Livesey was author of *Practical Religion* (West Friendship, Md., 1875) and was also active in the Press Writers Association, an organization dedicated to monitoring and corresponding with mainstream newspapers in
   an effort to gain fairer and more accurate coverage of radical philosophies and events. Other members included Kate Austin and James F. Morton, both anarchists, freethinkers, and advocates of free
   love. Livesey's later works, self-published in Sykesville, Maryland, include several broadsides attacking compulsory vaccination, compulsory education, prohibition, and child labor laws: *National Ruin
   and Vaccination, Virginia and Mississippi Legislators, the Great Gov. Vardaman* (1905); *Public Schools, Jack
   London, National Problems and Revolutions* (1905); *Schools, Socialism, Lynchings, Ministers, Catholics,
   Negroes, Revolution, England* (1906); and *Save the Country: Child Labor Laws, Compulsory Education,
   Prohibition . . . Will All Go Down As the People Rouse From the Slavery and Impoverishment These Things
   Have Brought Upon Them* (1908).
2. Livesey's request read (*Detroit Sentinel*, 2 July 1898, p. 1):

   I want somebody who knows where Emma Goldman is to send her my compliments and ask her if she has lectured
   favoring "compulsory education," and if she advocates "force" for the propaganda of anarchy. I want her to answer
   me these points publicly or privately, that I may in return answer her publicly. If she believes in compulsory education she is not a consistent anarchist, and if she believes in force she greatly hinders the spread of anarchy. I have
   all my life been a fighting boy or man in one way or another, but that anarchy's best weapon at the present is the pen
   I am ready to prove.
     Every reformer wants the changed opinion and not the forced man, even were force sufficient at hand to compel.
   From a description of Emma Goldman recently given in *Free Society*, of San Francisco, I have a high appreciation of
   her, and if she is in error in some of her points and methods I want to reason with her concerning them. I appreciate her antagonism to marriage and the clergy and her appreciation of Jesus Christ.

I do not favor compulsory education; nor have I ever lectured in favor of it. Not only do I not believe in it, but I am entirely opposed to our present school system, considering it injurious to the natural faculties of the child. I know by my own experience that instructors and teachers can seldom regard the individual abilities and inclinations of their pupils; they must follow the lines laid down by the board of education and stuff the children's heads with a lot of rubbish, which only burdens the little minds and which is of no benefit to the children. Until instructors will make it a special study to understand the nature of their pupils, their physical and mental wants, their trials and worries, their pleasures and sorrows, children will leave their schools automatic machines and not thinking and reasoning young men and women.

I have never advocated "force" for the propaganda of anarchy, nor do I know of any anarchist who has done so.

Every student of anarchist philosophy knows that anarchy has nothing to do with force and violence; that it denotes peace, safety and liberty, and does not recognize the right of one to rule, injure or coerce the others.

But every anarchist is also a student of history, and as such he or she must recognize that the ruling classes have never granted privileges to the oppressed until forced to do so by the latter.

Judging from the events of the past and present, there is no doubt in my mind that the struggling masses of the present century can expect nothing from their masters, and if they want to change their conditions and bring about a state of society in which no one shall enjoy the toil of his fellow man they will only succeed through the social revolution, never through peaceful methods.

As to individuals using force: well, whether we agree with them or not, whether we like them or not, such cases will occur from time to time, as a natural result of the causes existing in society. Let me give you an example. You will no doubt remember the shooting of Prime Minister del Castillo, of Spain, by the young student Angiolillo.

If Cánovas had not re-established the inquisition in Spain, if he had not caused 300 innocent workingmen to be tortured in the most barbarous and inhuman way in the prison of Montjuich,[3] the world had never heard of Angiolillo. He, whose heart was filled with love and sympathy for his fellow men, would not have thought of shooting Cánovas, as he was too gentle, refined and noble even to hurt a fly. But Cánovas del Castillo, with his murderous genius, has produced a Golli, just as Caesar produced a Brutus.[4]

We might as well fight against cyclones, earthquakes, tornadoes, lightning and other

---

3. The Corpus Christi Day bombing in Barcelona on 7 June 1896 led to the arrest and imprisonment of radicals, socialists, and anarchists at Montjuich.
4. After AB's *attentat* on Henry Clay Frick, EG also referred to AB as Brutus, a term later used by some anarchists to describe Leon Czolgosz. The reference stresses an interpretation of Brutus as the destroyer of a despotic power.

phenomena, as to fight against individual acts of violence. They have been and will be as long as we retain the causes which produce them; and I look upon such occurrences as warnings of the coming danger to the tyrants of the world.[5]

Of course I understand that violent acts do not change conditions unless a change has taken place in the minds of the people. Yet individual acts often set men to thinking and then books, papers, lectures and other methods of propaganda develop the first thought, which deeds like Angiolillo's, Sante Caserio's,[6] Alexander Berkman's[7] and others have first stimulated.

I hardly think Mr. Livesey will succeed in proving to me that the pen is anarchy's best weapon at present. It might have been so were it not for Boss Comstock.[8] Certainly Mr. Livesey must know by this time that free press and free speech are things of the past; that Comstockism is fast spreading in this country, destroying the liberty of each victim it reaches. True, Comstock has not succeeded in crushing the right of expressing one's opinion entirely, but the pen can no longer be used as openly as at the time when such biggots as Comstock were not known.

Every liberty-loving man or woman must be antagonistic to the clergy and our marriage institutions, and oppose them as obstacles in the way of freedom and as impertinent meddlers in private affairs.

I do not recollect ever having expressed my appreciation of Jesus Christ, and therefore I do not consider myself deserving of Mr. F. B. Livesey's compliments.

If Christ existed, of which I am not quite positive about, as there are so many pros and contras, he undoubtedly was a reformer; but unfortunately he advanced ideas based on sentiment and not on reason. I suppose this is the reason why priests, parsons and preachers have been able to use his teachings for their own benefit, causing humanity so much suffering. I prefer modern reformers, who base their philosophy both on sentiment and reason, knowing full well when people will learn to reason there will be no room for gods, devils or their emissaries, priests, Comstock and other parasites.

In conclusion I would like to thank Mr. Livesey for his high appreciation of me, but

---

5. EG's assertion that individual acts of violence are as inevitable as natural phenomena echoes August Spies's discussion of revolution in his address to the jury of 6 October 1886, reproduced in *The Accused, the Accusers* . . . (Chicago: Socialistic Publishing Society, [1886?]). In his speech Spies stated, "Revolutions are no more made than earthquakes and cyclones. Revolutions are the effect of certain causes and conditions." EG reiterates this idea in 1901 in regard to Leon Czolgosz. See "The Tragedy at Buffalo," Article in *Free Society*, 6 October 1901, below.

6. Sante Caserio assassinated French president Sadi Carnot on 24 June 1894, in retaliation for the execution of Auguste Vaillant.

7. AB attempted to assassinate Carnegie steel company manager Henry Clay Frick in 1892 in retaliation for Frick's ordering Pinkerton guards to shoot at striking workers during the strike and lockout at the Homestead plant.

8. In 1873 Anthony Comstock successfully lobbied Congress to pass a law, later known as the "Comstock Act," which gave the post office the power to exclude from the mails any material deemed obscene.

as he has gained this only from a description in *Free Society*, he may yet change in opinion should he ever meet the original of that description.

Emma Goldman.

Detroit (Mich.) Sentinel, 30 July 1898, p. 1. Robert Ingersoll's disparaging response to EG's lecture in a Detroit church in 1897 led to an exchange between Francis B. Livesey and individualist anarchist Joseph A. Labadie on the position of anarchist communists with respect to violence, citing EG in particular (see *Detroit Sentinel,* 7 May 1898, p. 1). In his 2 July letter to the *Detroit Sentinel,* Livesey invited EG to make her position clear, provoking this letter.

To *FREE SOCIETY*

New York, 31 July 1898

Gives Her Side.

T. P. Quinn in his article "Reflections on Debs," in *Free Society* of July 2, makes a statement concerning Debs and myself which I must correct.[1] Debs did not promise me the floor; he could not have done so as I had not applied for it. Now, whether Eugene V. Debs is guilty of all T. P. Quinn says or not I do not know (I personally have always believed, and still believe, him to be honest, though have always maintained that he lacks moral courage and energy),[2] I do not wish Debs to be accused of something he is not guilty of.

The truth of the whole thing is that I was requested by several Chicago delegates, R. Goodwin[3] and others, to stop over the convention, as they wanted me to speak there. Being on my way to New York and having nothing of greater importance to do I consented, but after attending the convention for two days I knew that I would not be able to speak before that body, as those in favor of political action would resist with all their power. In fact my very presence at the proceedings excited the political gang to a frenzy and they employed all the dirty tricks possible to exclude me from the convention, but they did not succeed of course.

On the third day of the convention I was informed by J. L. Lloyd, J. B. Ashorn and several others, that an entertainment was arranged for the evening and that I was expected to speak there, and that Debs had announced this from the platform. Before the close of the day's session Debs came over to me and asked whether I knew that I was expected to speak in the evening. I said yes. Debs promised to be present.

1. T. Putnam Quinn was an Irish American anarchist based first in New York and then in Chicago. A member of Chicago Branch 2 of the Social Democracy of America (SDA) in 1897, Quinn had attended an earlier St. Louis labor conference and was present at the September 1897 Chicago labor conference. The 3 July 1898 issue of *Free Society* included a report by Quinn on the 7–10 June SDA convention in Chicago: "Emma Goldman attended the recent convention and Debs promised her the floor, but the Socialists pressed from all sides and protested. It was then decided to have an entertainment on the evening of June 9, at which Miss Goldman could speak. When the evening came, Mr. Lloyd was deputed by the powers to announce that the committees were all in session, and thus excused the small attendance; but the bold Goldman arose and told the real reason for the non-attendance of the law-abiders to the audience in the straightest possible language" (p. 7).
2. In one of her "Letters from a Tour" (no. 4; *Sturmvogel*, 1 February 1898), EG comments on Debs's personality: "He is not the man of his time; he lacks energy and will and he collapses like a fly in the slightest gust of wind. . . . There is no doubt that in his way he is honest and has good intentions. . . ."
3. Roy M. Goodwin was an American anarchist and trade unionist and one of the directors of the American Railway Union along with Eugene Debs. Goodwin served a three-month prison term for his part in the 1894 Pullman strike. He was on the national board of directors of the Social Democracy of America, favored the colonization efforts, and was a member of the anarchist Branch 2 of the Social Democracy in Chicago.

When I arrived in the evening I found about two dozen people in the hall, among them but three delegates, the rest comrades and personal friends from Chicago. J. L. Lloyd tried hard to excuse his fellow colleagues, but he only made things worse,[4] and so when he called on me to speak I did not hesitate to express my opinion concerning the whole farce.[5]

E. GOLDMAN.

Free Society, 31 July 1898, p. 2.

4. According to Quinn's report, Lloyd announced that the missing delegates were all in committee sessions.
5. EG was one of a number of anarchists present among the seventy delegates at the 7 June 1898 SDA convention in Chicago; others included Lucy Parsons and T. P. Quinn. Shortly after the 1898 convention, EG wrote in *Solidarity* that she had no faith in the SDA: "I know that nothing short of the propaganda against political control and against economic dependence will satisfy." For more information on EG's involvement in the 1898 convention, see "A Short Account of My Late Tour," Letter to *Solidarity,* 15 July 1898, above.

To the **NEW YORK WORLD**

New York, 18 September 1898

New York Anarchist Leaders Denounce the Murder of Austria's Empress.

They Say that Lucchesi Is the Natural Result of Prevailing Conditions but They Do Not Excuse His Crime.

The New York Anarchists denounce and repudiate Luccheni,[1] the assassin of the Empress of Austria.[2] He had no "justification" according to their code for slaying a woman who was harmless, unhappy and not unkind.

No distinct nationality is recognized by the Anarchists; they call each other comrades. The story current of a distinct band of Italian Anarchists located in Zurich who plotted against the life of Humbert,[3] the Duke of Orleans[4] and the Austrian Empress[5] is discredited by the Swiss police, and also by well-known Anarchists here.

The name of Luccheni is not known by them, and while he may have called himself an Anarchist he did not, so far as New York members know, belong to a "group." Indeed, anarchy does not recognize a united assembly. With its votaries everything rests in the individual [. . . .]

1. The *New York World* headline misspells Luccheni's last name.
2. On 10 September 1898, the Empress Elizabeth of Austria was stabbed to death in Geneva by Italian anarchist Luigi Luccheni. Luccheni's act was prompted by the violent repression of demonstrations in Milan in the Fatti di Magio (Events of May) earlier that year. The assassination led to an international clampdown on anarchist activity by police authorities, and culminated in the International Conference for the Defense of Society against the Anarchists, convened in Rome on 24 November and attended by all twenty-one European powers. The conference marked the beginning of international cooperation in the surveillance of anarchists. On 11 September the *New York World* claimed the assassination of Empress Elizabeth was part of a world-wide anarchist conspiracy. This is presumably the charge to which EG and other New York anarchists felt obliged to respond (see "Assassins Plotted to Kill the European Sovereigns," *New York World,* 11 September 1898, p. 1). Accordingly, this letter was written between 11 September and the publication of EG's letter of 18 September.
3. The newspaper is referring to King Umberto of Italy.
4. Prince Henri d'Orleans was a French pretender to the throne.
5. Empress Elizabeth of Austria (1837–1898), the daughter of a Bavarian duke, became Empress Consort upon marrying Francis Joseph I, Emperor of Austria and King of Hungary and Bohemia, in 1854. Her first daughter, Sophie, died unexpectedly in 1857. Her son, Prince Rudolph, the heir to the throne, killed himself with his lover in 1889. The Empress was assassinated by Italian anarchist Luigi Luccheni in Geneva on 10 September 1898, when, although she was intending to travel incognito, her presence was announced by the local newspapers.

BY EMMA GOLDMAN.

To the Editor of the *World:*

Even if this man Luccheni declared himself an Anarchist, I would be the first one to say he is not one.

Any man who understands the philosophy of anarchy could never commit such folly. The philosophy of anarchy forbids the destruction of human life, particularly in a useless manner.

Had this man chosen Francis Joseph[6] for his victim I would have approved it, because he in his fifty years' reign has succeeded in bringing his empire nearly to dissolution.

While yet a young lad, in '48, he was the first one to set an example of cruelty by encircling the captive fighters for freedom and, without giving them a chance to defend themselves by arms or law, ordering them shot down like dogs.[7]

The most conservative people of his land opposed this act as unworthy of a monarch.

Had Luccheni immortalized his name by the dethronement of the Spanish Queen Regent it would also be accepted by me. She did not utter one word to prevent the Barcelona horrors.[8]

It was there that, during a religious procession last year, a bomb was thrown by a man whose identity remains hidden up to this day.

THE BARCELONA HORROR.

Yet for his crime more than three hundred radical workingmen, professional men and artisans were arrested and subjected to tortures too horrible to relate, a very repetition of the quondam Spanish inquisition.

All this was her work and the work of Cánovas del Castillo, who has since met retribution at the hands of Angelillo.

In my opinion, Luccheni was an individual who saw that life had nothing in store for him, and having nothing to lose he destroyed life.

Yet I would not consider him a crank nor insane. Rather say that he is a product of present economic, political and social injustices.

I formed this opinion when I heard of the Empress' death and before I learned anything about the man, who, as I heard later, did not know father or mother.

Just as little as the moon can dim its splendor at the barking of a dog, just as little will the philosophy of Anarchism lose of its grandeur because of acts committed by social outcasts.

---

6. EG refers to the Emperor of Austria and King of Hungary and Bohemia, who reigned from 1848 to 1916.
7. EG refers to the suppression of the 1848 Hungarian uprising and the resulting creation of a short-lived independent state. Austria regained control of Hungary in 1849, executing fourteen rebel leaders.
8. EG refers to the arrest and trial of anarchists and other radicals after the Corpus Christi Day bombing.

Because so many Italians have figured as political assassins, it does not follow that Anarchists would select Italians as martyrs.

Every man acts individually and the Italians happen to be very zealous. We have many Italian Anarchists in this country and none of them would approve of this murder.

Emma Goldman. [. . .]

New York World, 18 September 1898, p. 28; includes sketch of EG and other illustrations. For the excised portions of this article, including letters from New York Italian anarchists Salvatore Pallavencini, N. Blotto, C. Ferrara, and G. Imperato, see "New York Anarchist Leaders Denounce the Murder of Austria's Empress," *New York World,* 18 September 1898, *EGP,* reel 47.

An Undelivered Speech.

The following correspondence explains itself: [1]

7 December 1898

DEAR MR. TUCKER:

The Alexander Berkman Defence Association [2] is making an attempt and moving heaven and earth to have our friend, Alexander Berkman, pardoned.

It becomes necessary to plead with Mr. Carnegie, and solicit his aid for that purpose. Mr. Carnegie is reported to be in New York at present.

Will you kindly cooperate, select others you may choose, and act as spokesman?

If so, we will ever pray, etc.

FRATERNALLY YOURS, FOR THE COMMITTEE,

JUSTUS SCHWAB.

ED. BRADY.

EMMA GOLDMAN.

11 December 1898

To Justus Schwab, Ed. Brady, and Emma Goldman, representing the committee of the Alexander Berkman Defence Association:

FRIENDS,—

Answering your letter of December 7, honoring me with an invitation to act as your spokesman on the occasion of a proposed visit to Mr. Andrew Carnegie to solicit his aid in securing the release of Mr. Alexander Berkman, I hereby gratefully accept your trust,

---

1. Benjamin Tucker, editor and publisher of the leading journal of anarchist individualism, printed this exchange of letters in his January 1899 issue of *Liberty*.
2. After determining that the only hope for a reduction in AB's sentence was an appeal to the Pennsylvania Board of Pardons, attorneys for the Berkman Defense Association recommended that the pardon board's decision would rest upon the attitude of Andrew Carnegie. The idea of enlisting Tucker's help was apparently Justus Schwab's, who was close to Tucker.

Masthead from 1899 issue of *Liberty,* an anarchist individualist paper edited by Benjamin Tucker, which often printed sharp critiques of Goldman's activities. (By permission of the Kate Sharpley Library)

and I submit herewith a draft of the remarks which it is my intention to make to Mr. Carnegie, should the plan be carried out in the manner proposed.

I beg to add that, should the tenor of these remarks prove unacceptable to you, a withdrawal of your invitation would be received by me in perfect good part.

Awaiting your pleasure, I am

Yours sincerely,
Benj. R. Tucker.

Mr. Carnegie:

Mr. Alexander Berkman, who is now serving a sentence in a Pennsylvania prison for an attempt to kill your business partner, Mr. Henry C. Frick, in 1892, and the Alexander Berkman Defence Association, which is seeking to shorten that sentence, have asked me to solicit, on their behalf, the exercise of your influence with the Pennsylvania pardoning power, to the end that Mr. Berkman may go free. In compliance with their request I come to you.

You, in considering this petition, will be largely influenced, and very properly, by the attitude of your petitioners. In determining what that attitude is, you surely will take it for granted, as I take it for granted, that they approach you as penitent sinners, asking forgiveness and seeking remission of penalty. Their very appearance before you, in person or by proxy, on such an errand, must be taken to indicate that what they once regarded as a wise act of heroism they now regard as a foolish act of barbarism; that the method of reform by violence which they once thought efficacious they now think futile; that they keenly regret the attempt upon the life of Mr. Frick; that the six years of Mr. Berkman's imprisonment have convinced them of the error of their ways; and that henceforth they will neither commit, counsel, or approve any acts of violence whatsoever. Any other explanation of the prayer of these petitioners is inconsistent with their lofty character. Certainly it is not to be supposed for a moment that men and women of their courage and dignity, after shooting a man down deliberately and in cold blood, would then descend to the abject and basely humiliating course of begging their victim and his friends to leave them the freedom to assault him again. It is obvious, then, that they come here to-day in an attitude of sincere repentance,—no longer as reformers, but as reformed, and asking for liberty as a reward of their reformation. Now, sir, you are too close a student of social problems to need any argument of mine to convince you that punishment of the truly penitent is not politic on the part of society. In thus establishing the reality of their contrition, I am sure that I have commanded your assent to their petition.

But I cannot close without saying another word, no longer as their spokesman, but for myself. My own attitude in asking you to favor mercy for Alexander Berkman is not that of these petitioners. I do not appear here to-day as a repentant sinner. In my record on this matter there is nothing for which I have occasion to apologize. I reserve all my rights. In the past, in the exercise of my liberty, I have refused to commit, counsel, or sanction violence, but, since circumstances may arise when a policy of violence will seem advisable, I decline to surrender my liberty of choice. I have never so much favored force as to attempt assassination, and I have never so much opposed force as to be willing to pledge myself never to resort to it. If I, then, ask your intercession in favor of Mr. Berkman, I do so without occasion for penitence or promise, and less in his interest (although I shall be glad to see him free again) than in your own and that of good order, hoping that such a concession on the part of those who now have him in their power will lessen the temptation to a renewal of the policy of violence, and will induce a state of public feeling that will insure enlarged opportunity for that peaceful evolution of opinion which alone can avert social upheaval and all its attendant terrors. And, each in his respective way, your petitioners will ever pray.[3]

Anarchist individualist Benjamin Tucker, ca. 1887. (Labadie Collection, University of Michigan)

3. Tucker's original annotation reads: "It should be stated that my representation of the attitude of the petitioners does not justly apply to such of them as have steadily discountenanced propaganda by deed from a day ante-dating Berkman's act of violence. Justus Schwab certainly is one of these exceptions; perhaps Edward Brady also."

Mr. Benj. Tucker:

Dear Sir,—

Prompted by humane feelings, we may perhaps have gone too far to invite *you* to so excite the sympathy of Mr. Carnegie in an act of justice,—*viz.*, the pardon of Mr. Alexander Berkman.

We will by no means enlist the aid of Mr. Carnegie, the author of "Triumphant Democracy," [4] from your point of view, and therefore respectfully beg to withdraw the invitation sent you. [5]

Sincerely yours, for the committee,

Justus H. Schwab.

Edward Brady.

Emma Goldman.

Liberty 13 (January 1899): 8, *EGP,* reel 47.

---

4. Andrew Carnegie was the author of *Triumphant Democracy; or Fifty Years' March of the Republic* (New York: Scribner, 1886).
5. After withdrawing their offer to Tucker, EG, Brady, and Schwab next approached Ernest Crosby with the same request. "The matter finally ended with our decision not to apply to Carnegie at all. Sasha's case was not even brought before the Board of Pardons at the time intended. Its members were found to be too prejudiced against him, and it was hoped that the new Board, which was to take office in the following year, might prove more impartial." (*LML*, pp. 233–34).

Free Speech Suppressed in Barre, Vt.

We append here an extract from the undelivered speech[1] entitled "Authority vs. Liberty":

Have you ever, my friends, thought about the meaning of authority and about its injurious effects upon liberty? I doubt that you did, for else how could you continue to worship it, to kneel before its altars and offer such awful sacrifices to this insatiable monster. Let me show you what authority has done, look what it is doing today, be it exercised under the cloak of religion, government, paternal rights or public gossip. Let me impress you with the disastrous results it has produced, and some of you—those who think, those who love liberty—will agree that authority must be replaced by liberty.

There was a time, when to doubt the powers of God and his representatives meant death, horrible torture, agonizing persecution. Hideous and countless crimes were committed in the name of God, and his self-appointed earthly representatives perpetuated their existence by compelling implicit obedience to their authority. No one is able to tell all the struggles, all the sufferings, through which the rebellious minds went on account of the tyrannical absurdities of Church authority. Thousands, yea, millions of lives were sacrificed, the earth was deluged with the blood of heretics before the authority of gods and devils lost its hold upon the thinking men and women. Thousands refuse allegiance to religion today, they know that it is rooted in ignorance, fraud and humbug; and they combine their efforts to pull down the relics of Church authority. The growth of freedom from Church authority, Church despotism would be very encouraging indeed—but for the fact that a large number of unbelievers, freethinkers, atheists and infidels have not yet advanced far enough in freedom to benefit the world at large. Unfortunately they have only changed the form of authority; they have done away with the authority of the Bible and have replaced it with that of the statute book. They are ready to persecute and to condemn all those who refuse to acknowledge the right of the State to dictate to society just as quickly as the religious monomaniacs were to burn heretics and witches.

What is the statute book? Nothing else but the commands of earthly gods, monarchs, despots, czars, kings or presidents. True, to disregard heavenly authority meant perse-

---

1. In January 1899, EG delivered three lectures in Barre, Vermont, a center of Italian immigrant anarchism. Initially, she spoke unimpeded by the local authorities. At least two lectures were held at Tomasi's Hall, on "The New Woman" (26 January) and on "The Corrupting Influence of Politics on Man" (28 January). There is no extant record of the third meeting. On 31 January, Mayor Gordon, urged on by a committee of "leading citizens," ordered local police to prevent EG from delivering a fourth talk, on "Authority vs. Liberty." *Free Society* responded by printing a portion of EG's undelivered address, 5,000 copies of which were printed by local anarchists.

cution and death, yet it is still more dangerous to rebel against earthly authorities. They are so much more numerous, they have so much more power to back them, they can enforce their will in so many ways, that it sometimes seems as if there were no salvation for mankind. It is easy to convince a man nowadays that a supernatural being is an absurdity, that the story of creating the world out of nothing is ridiculous; science has demolished these fables; intelligent men and women do no longer spend their time in killing dead gods, nor are subject to Church authority.

Much more difficult it is to convince men that the authority of government, of the State, is injurious, and that man made laws are the worst foes of society. Abolish all laws? Do away with the State? You destroy society, people say when one enters into the discussion of the fallacy of belief in authority. No intelligent man or woman wants to destroy society, for society and State are not identical. Hear what Thomas Paine says: "Society has grown as necessity of man, but government out of folly of mankind."[2] He said it a hundred years ago, and we have learned that the State is really of recent date, while society exists since the world exists. I do not distinguish between monarchy and democracy, whether one man or a dozen of men backed by force represent authority; it has the same aim; the results are the same. They exercise their power at all cost and check every independent tendency. The statute book forbids theft, robbery and murder as crimes against the law, but those who worship these new gods profit by it. Thou shalt not kill, steal rob and cheat, says the law; at the same time under its very wing wars are carried on, whole nations are destroyed, prisons are crowded, armies enlarged, battleships built, thousands beheaded, garrotted, hung and sent to the electric chair, while a few are getting richer and richer, monopolizing half the earth, and the great mass of producers hunger, the army of the unemployed is on the increase and uncounted thousands of children die for lack of food and want of air.

And why all this misery? Because the State authority has taught you so long the sacred rights of property that you have learned to take it as truth. You do not recognize that it is the statute book by which capitalism is maintained; you do not understand that there is a new trinity: God, Capitalism—God, the State and God, the Church. So long have you submitted to this "worthy" trinity that you believe that authority is absolutely necessary—and that if it be abolished men would cut each other's throats. How little you know of human nature, how little you know its history. Says Kropotkin, the scientist: "You fail to recognize that the most glorious epochs in humanity were those, in which the liberties were not destroyed by the State and when masses of men lived in free communes and free federations."[3] Only those who do not think, who do not reason, who ac-

2. Compare Thomas Paine at the beginning of his *Common Sense:* "Society is produced by our wants, and government by our wickedness."
3. Quote is from Kropotkin's *The State: Its Historic Role;* originally, *L'État: Son Rôle Historique,* serialized in *Les Temps Nouveaux* beginning 19 December 1896. The first English-language version appeared in the London *Freedom* between May 1897 and June 1898, and was issued shortly thereafter as Freedom Pamphlet No. 11 (September 1898).

cept everything that is because they do not investigate still cling to authority. Intelligent people see clearly that authority in any form is but a check to development and growth, that it is but a chain tied to a man from cradle to grave which hinders the free use of his limbs. It has terrorized the mass of mankind into submission and slavery, it maintains itself by force only, producing cunning, shrewdness and violence.

Some I hear ask: "Do you not acknowledge authority in science, art and literature?" Most certainly I do. But that authority has no force to back it, it cannot compel my acception nor can it prevent my rejection of it. If, for example, I refuse to accept Spencer[4] as an authority on Communism, he cannot punish me, he cannot imprison me, he cannot hang me. He represents his thoughts only, and probably does not care one bit whether men accept his theories or not.[5] But should I refuse to recognize the order of the chief of police in Barre, which prevents my speaking to you,[6] I should find myself in your prison in short order. There lies the difference. Behind Spencer there is no force, behind your chief of police are the clubs and pistols of your policemen; and it is this brutal force that makes authority a curse to humanity.

Let us see, on the other hand, what liberty has brought us, and then choose together whether you prefer to bow your neck before authority or walk erect under the banner of liberty.

We have precious little of it and we are rapidly losing it; but even under the curse of government, side by side with despotism, the actions of individual free efforts are legion. Schools adopt free methods of instruction, they develop the liberal tendencies in their pupils; hundreds of societies spring up for self-improvement and the benefit of mankind. Societies for scientific research are founded without the aid of government and they produce the best works. Poets, artists, scientists and others have worked upon individual effort and not by dictation of government. Everything that is good and noble, grand and beautiful, wise and useful, has been done by the spirit of liberty, from the love of freedom, in spite and in the teeth of government and authority. When man will have recovered from the effects of authority, when he will understand that freedom is the most precious thing, when he will be free to live, to work, to act, to develop, to enter into social relations with whom he is in sympathy, then warfare, conquests, robbery, theft, corruption, poverty and all the ornaments of the State, all the burden of authority will be looked upon as relics of barbarism.

4. EG refers to English philosopher and sociologist Herbert Spencer, whose work was influential among individualist anarchists.
5. EG's discussion of her recognition of authority in matters of art, science, and literature echoes Michael Bakunin in *God and the State*, who also stated that he recognized authority when it was founded on knowledge and not propped by force, and when subscribing to such authority was an individual choice.
6. According to the May 1899 London *Freedom*, local anarchists immediately printed 5,000 copies of a four-page manifesto protesting the suppression of EG's lecture, along with a lengthy extract from "Authority vs. Liberty."

This, my friends, is a rough sketch of Anarchism, of the ideal you hate and persecute, the ideal of thousands of men and women in all spheres of life, who are proud of being called Anarchists. You are shocked when you hear that word, you shiver at its very sound. Your fear is but the result of authority, which has instilled into you the hatred for those who wish you well, who at the risk of their own lives and comforts try to free you from the clutches of your masters. You do not see our work in this light, you join in the cry of fools and knaves "Hang the Anarchists!" but I see the time coming when you'll understand that all efforts to check the growth of Anarchism are in vain. For its teachings are based upon the power of the individual within himself and not without. Its philosophy is based on that stern, undisputable logic that liberty is just as necessary for man as air, light and food.

Do not waste your time in trying to stop the waves of the ocean with a broom; it is useless. Already the elements are growing into immensity, tearing down every obstacle in the way; after the storm has passed the air will be calm and pure, and the world will be filled with the sweet odor of liberty.

Free Society, 5 March 1899, pp. 1, 3.

Interview in the *DETROIT EVENING NEWS*

Detroit, 14 March 1899

An Interrupted Interview . . . .

Emma Goldman, the High Priestess of Anarchism, Tries to Tell the Future of Her Cult, but is Interrupted by Songs of Her Companions.

It was a jovial, heart-and-soul little crowd that sat around two companionably-close tables in a rear room of the Hotel Randolph late last night. A few choice spirits had gathered to celebrate the visit of their guest of honor—their doctrinal saint—Emma Goldman. The incense of cigarettes were burned before her shrine. Long-necked, dark bottles gave forth pale Rhine wine, and white-aproned waiters carried in flagons of foaming beer. These people were Bohemians in all the sense conveys. Their simple, unrestrained enjoyment shamed the artificial apings of their American cousins. They lived in the land of Lotus, where carping care is left on the border, and all within is sunshine and happiness.

In the center of the circle sat the strange little woman who was born out of the social conditions of the period. About her were grouped a dozen of her Detroit disciples, and a contingent from the German dramatic company which is playing "Capt. Dreyfus" in town.

"Ich liebe dich,"[1] sang the merry-makers, as they clinked their glasses and added a hearty "Prost!"[2]

It was in this cheery circle that a News reporter came for the prosaic purpose of interviewing. But he was not treated as an intruder. He was greeted as a friend, and given a place and a glass. He could catch above the disturbing yet delightful revelry but few of the words to which the self-confessed anarchist gave ready utterance.

"Do I consider that anarchy has a future in this country?" she repeated. "Yes, indeed. It has a future, not only in this country but in the world. You will find in all classes people who are anarchists. When I say 'anarchist' I mean a person of higher independence—not the commonly mistaken enemy of law and order. The latter is not an anarchist. He is more often a 'bum.' The higher the education of a class, the more——"

Dreiunddreissig Jahre
Waehrt die Knechtschaft schon,
Nieder mit den Hunden
Von der Reaktion.[3]

---

1. "I love you."
2. "To your health!"
3. "Thirty-three years / The servitude has already lasted, / Down with the dogs / Of reaction."

In 1899, during her second lecture tour in England, Goldman joined a
host of prominent anarchist activists at a meeting to commemorate the
November 1887 execution of the Haymarket anarchists. (By permission
of the Kate Sharpley Library)

The chafing reins of restraint could be endured no longer. The others had broken into spontaneous song. Emma smiled indulgence for a moment, and even found herself joining in the chorus. Then she raised her magic hand. "Sh-sh!" she said, and the song stopped.

"As I was saying," she continued, "the higher the education of a class, the more anarchists it contains. Doctors, lawyers, professors, newspaper men, many of these are anarchists, but they dare not, perhaps, declare themselves. Even the freest man is tied to his surroundings. We are dependent upon one another, therefore we must make concessions. Yes, personally, I believe we should all have the courage of our convictions, but I would not condemn as cowards those who do not have that courage. Education——"

> Haerme dich, wenn ich mich haerme,
> Und sei wieder froh mit mir.[4]

"Education is the greatest promoter of anarchism. By education I do not mean the mere learning that comes from books—the simple training of the brain—I mean——"

> Und sollte ich auch dereinst noch in der Hoelle wimmern. So hat sich doch kein Mensch darum zu kuemmern.[5]

The crowd was becoming more boisterous. The singers this time laughed at the reproachful finger. A fine fellow, with a splendid voice, took advantage of the semi-silence to sing a tender love song:

> Bei einem Bach, der rauschend floss——[6]

When the last tremulous note had died away, two ladies and one gentleman of the Otis Skinner company,[7] who sat at an opposite table, clapped their hands and said "Bravo!"

"I mean," went on the nimble-witted little woman, turning once more to her task, "a healthy, natural education. The development of the mind by natural means. No, I certainly do not approve of violence——"

But violence was committed at this point. A waiter brought a cup of coffee, and with sugar and cream, placed it before the speaker. Her look of amazement was reflected in every face about the table. "Why, what did you bring this for?" cried the astonished missionary.

"He ordered it," said the waiter, indicating a German editor,[8] who sat next Miss Goldman and was holding her hand.

The disgraced journalist was loudly called upon to explain.

He raised his hands in piteous protest. Then he told what had caused the unseemly incident. In most uncertain English he had ordered a postal card, and had been misunderstood. A roar went up at his expense. Then Emma raised the cup to her lips, and swallowed the joke.

It was some time before she could resume.

---

4. "Grieve if I grieve, / And with me be happy again."
5. "And should I even someday yet whimper in hell. About that no one need worry."
6. "By a brook, which murmured along—"
7. The celebrated American stage actor and his company were performing *Rosemary* at the Detroit Opera House.
8. Max Baginski, a new friend, comrade, and, briefly, EG's lover.

"No, I do not approve of violence, but I never blame the one who commits it. There is always a cause—and it is the cause, not the person, we should blame. What is the condition which I hope to see anarchy bring about? A reform of systems that will drive misery out of and bring happiness into the world. A perfection? No. There is no such thing as perfection, and there never will be. It is contrast of sorrow and gladness that makes it possible——"

> Wo frohe Lieder sind, da lass dich ruhig nieder.
> Boese Menschen haben keine Lieder.[9]

"That makes it possible for us to know happiness. Peace and happiness in another life? No; there is no other life. When we leave this life, we leave life forever. It is the end of all. You know, I am an atheist. Would I rob those who never can know happiness here—of the peace, the comfort of their cherished religion? No; they can find the religion, the joy they crave, in the cathedral of the sky; in the music of the birds, in the poem of the brook, in the sermon of the forest, in the incense of the flowers."

Earlier in the evening Miss Goldman had appeared before a small audience in the hall at 224 Randolph street and discussed "The power of the idea." In the absence of a chairman, Miss Goldman introduced herself and sailed into her subject without hesitation. Religion, the church and the civil authorities came in for her special condemnation.

"You know nothing of freedom," she told her auditors, "when around the corner is a 260-pound policeman ready to club you if you resist the authority of government."

"I am not a Jesus, and I refuse to be one—consequently what I say is not given as gospel truth."

"The catholic church represents the greatest system of fellowship in the world, but it has a whole lot of bishops and other officials who live on the sweat of the toiler."

"Heaven is too lonesome a place for me to go to, because there everybody will think the same."

"When you lay down law you at the same time lay down the desire to do the thing prohibited."

"It is not peace but violence that needs a guardian."

"You are as ignorant as the politician and as bigoted as the minister and the priest."

"The down-trodden workingmen of this country are worse off than the Russian peasant."

"If another man have an idea different from mine and his motive is good, then the idea is good."

After an hour's talk she invited the audience to catechise her and sat down.

Geo. J. Eastman, the socialistic labor party's candidate for supreme court judge, objected to having socialism classed as "reform."

---

9. "Where there are happy songs, settle down calmly, / Wicked people have no songs."

"We do not propose reform, but revolution," said he. "Again, you say something cannot be created out of nothing. How about hypnotism?"

"On healthy minds there is no such force as hypnotism," replied Emma.

Tonight Miss Goldman speaks on "Criticism of ethics" in Trades Council hall.[10]

Detroit (Mich.) Evening News, 14 March 1899, p. 2.

10. In fact, Goldman spoke on "Trade Unionism: What It Is and What It Should Be."

An Anarchist Propagandist.

Emma Goldman Upon the Aim of Humanity.

Says It is For the Greatest Satisfaction at Smallest Exertion.

Declares That Absolute Freedom is Necessary
to the Development of Individuality.

The announcement that Emma Goldman, a real live anarchist, would lecture at Grand Army hall last evening, attracted an audience of 210 people, some of whom were in sympathy with the sentiments of the speaker, and others attracted through curiosity or in a desire to hear of this social philosophy from one of the cult. Before the speaker of the evening was introduced, the singing section of the Verein Eintracht[1] of Oakland rendered a chorus with fine effect. Miss Goldman, who has attained some prominence as a propagandist of the doctrines of the anarchist communists of the country, is a young woman who might be taken for a college student or an exponent of suffrage. She is of medium height, with hair tending toward the Titian, with strong features and wears eyeglasses. She speaks with a considerable vehemence and a foreign German accent. The topic of the speaker was The Aim of Humanity. She said that there are many people who think that life is fashioned by fate or shaped by divinity and not subject to human will. "We live in an age of doubt," she contended; "men actually have the audacity not to accept any political theory or religious doctrine upon authority. I myself have the audacity to differ from generally accepted political principles and think for myself. I believe that most human beings are striving for some purpose; have some end to attain. If men did not have some ideal or end human society could not exist. What, then, is the chief end of life? I have considered and investigated the subject and while I may not be infallible I think it is to reach the highest amount of happiness or satisfaction that most men strive to attain the greatest amount of happiness with the least expense of time and energy is the common end of human life. Men's conception of what real happiness is differ radically. Some are happy at the mere satisfaction of physical wants; some desire higher intellectual satisfaction; others have their highest delight in fighting for a cause or an ideal. Even to die

1. The Verein Eintracht was a German social group founded in San Francisco in 1868, and later expanded to Oakland, to foster musical and dramatic arts, offering social and literary entertainment to the community, and assisting its members in sickness and times of need.

ATHENÆUM HALL,

73, TOTTENHAM COURT ROAD.

EMMA GOLDMAN,

(Of New York)

THE ANARCHIST ORATOR,

will deliver the following Lectures at the
ATHENÆUM HALL.

SUNDAY, NOV. 19th. 1899,

AT 3 O'CLOCK,

"THE AIM OF HUMANITY."

SUNDAY, NOV. 26th, 1899,

AT 3 O'CLOCK,

"WOMAN."

Questions & Discussion Invited.

This 1899 handbill from Goldman's European tour represents a shift in her focus, away from the more narrowly anarchist and labor topics of her earlier lectures. (By permission of the Kate Sharpley Library)

for an ideal is happiness to some. For the realization of one's ideal of happiness there must be individual liberty. Our forefathers had a certain conception of liberty; they believed that the remedy for oppression was to get away from the conditions which created it, and they established what they called religious liberty in this country. But while theoretically religious liberty prevails, the church practically controls the education, the morals and the ethics of the country, and while persons who may differ from accepted beliefs are not subjected to the rack and thumbscrew they are often subjected to ostracism."

POPULAR UNREST.

"Why the great unrest of the people? Why the continual strife, battle and discontent? This is an evidence that there is life and growth. Stagnation follows the vegative existence. Content with more food and clothing develop conditions favorable for despotism. To whom shall those who desire a better condition of things look for direction and leadership if they do not inform themselves? Your Harvards and your Yales are not filled with the sons of the working classes, they are the show places of the sons of aristocrats. The rich send their sons to college simply because they desire the name of having a university education. These young men care little for the cause of the common people. They care little for the economics or the politics of the country.

"In the German universities during the stirring times from 1848 to 1880 the leaders of radical thought were the students. The same is true to-day of the universities of Russia and it is among the students that most of the reforms originate. This is because in these countries many of the poor people work nights that their children may be educated and many of the students come from the ranks of the common people and are in sympathy with them. To some extent conditions have changed in Germany, where at the present time the highest conception of liberty with many of the students is that of drinking beer and bowing to the monarch, the present representative of absolutism.

"We find the church under the domination of the capitalistic class and anxious to maintain its dominance over the thought of the people, but it will not permit liberty of thought.

"The newspapers are the least suitable sources of instruction for the people. They will give you full accounts of the Jeffries-Sharkey prize fight[2] and of the latest purchase of a European prince by an American millionaire's daughter, or the social doings of the aristocrats, but do the newspapers report the proceedings of labor meetings or speeches of those who are trying to better the conditions of the working classes. They are simply jumping jacks in the hands of capitalists who own them."

IDEALS OF LIBERTY.

"The average young man of the rising generation in this country has no real conception of what liberty means. If the American people realized what real liberty is, would they submit to the existing conditions for an instant? There can be no real equality without equality of opportunity. If you had no laws you would have equality: If you have laws you will not have equality. Only public freedom will permit the development of personality. Now position and importance attaches to a person not for what he is but for what he possesses. Society rests upon the basis of the almighty dollar. Wealth gives power and creates inequality before the law. The aspiration for wealth began when one man fenced in a piece of ground and said to the rest: 'This is mine; keep off the grass.'[3] There are those

2. World heavyweight boxing champion James J. Jeffries was in Oakland for an exhibition the same night as EG's lecture, drawing a large crowd. His opponent was not, however, contender Tom Sharkey, but Jeffries's brother Jack. The fight with Sharkey occurred 3 November at Coney Island.
3. From Rousseau's *Discourse on Inequality:* "The first man who, having fenced off a plot of land, thought of saying 'This is mine' and found people simple enough to believe him was the real founder of civil society."

among the working classes who are so dense that they think if the masters did not give them work they would have to lay down and die. It is a false idea that the beauties of nature were bestowed for the benefit of a few. The true conception of society is one of the interdependence of solidarity. That the happiness of each is based upon the happiness of all and that if your fellow man suffers you must suffer and if you suffer your fellow man must suffer. Let us try to become useful men and women and give what we have of ability and talent to educate and to help others. It is only through this that we will realize the true aim of life."

The lecture was followed by a number of questions which the speaker answered from her standpoint. During the evening there were distributed copies of *Free Society*, a publication issued in San Francisco, which is now in its fifth volume and is avowedly an exponent of anarchist communism.

Oakland (Calif.) Enquirer, 15 July 1899, p. 5.

The Red Queen Is Here.

Emma Goldman Says There Is No Prosperity in Pittsburg Except for the Employer.

She Is Going to Study Medicine Abroad.

"Prosperity! There's no prosperity here except for the employers. I find the miners just as poor as they were when I was here last. Prosperity and work are two different things; there is work, but not prosperity."

There was the sting of poignant sarcasm in the words as they came from the lips of Emma Goldman, the "Red Queen" of anarchism, as she made reply to the question of a representative of the Sunday *Leader,* "Why do you come to Pittsburg to speak when there is so much prosperity?"

Miss Goldman arrived in the city yesterday and is staying with friends, fellow-communists. She is just returning from an eight months' tour through the west and southwest, having spoken in the principal cities of California, Colorado, Kansas, Illinois and various other states. She is here now not so much to spread the propaganda as to "awaken the sleeping Anarchists." Last night she spoke in West Newton to a crowd of sympathizing workmen. This morning she is to be heard at Collinsburg, near West Newton; on Tuesday at Hope Church on Thursday at Columbia Turner hall in Lawrenceville; on Friday at Moorhead's hall, Grant street and Second avenue, under the auspices of the Molders' union; at Turner hall, Lawrenceville, on Saturday; Odd Fellows' hall, South Side, on October 1; McDonald on October 3 and 4; at 510 Wylie avenue, Pittsburg, on October 7; the following night at Fayette City; on the 9th at Roscoe; 10th at K. of L. hall, 432 Wood street. After a day or two of rest among her friends she will go to New York, whence on October 25 she will sail for Europe.[1] She expects to spend at least three years abroad, during which time she says she "will give America a rest." The first year abroad will be spent in spreading the red propaganda in England, Scotland and France, and the two remaining years in Switzerland, where Miss Goldman expects to pursue the study of medicine for the purpose of "ministering to the physical sufferings as well as the mental sufferings of humanity."[2] She has already graduated as a trained nurse, but believes

---

1. EG left New York for Europe on 3 November 1899.
2. Two wealthy benefactors, Herman Miller and Carl Stone, friends of Robert Reitzel in Detroit, promised EG forty dollars a month for five years to enable her to study medicine in Switzerland. Accord-

Goldman lectured regularly in Yiddish to Jewish audiences, although she much preferred and was more proficient in German, her mother tongue. This advertisement for Goldman's 1899 lecture "The Woman Question" appeared in the London Yiddish-language anarchist newspaper *Arbeter Freint,* then edited by Rudolf Rocker. (By permission of the Kate Sharpley Library)

she can be of better service to her fellows as a physician. She does not, however, entertain any idea of abandoning anarchy for medicine.

An Anarchist congress is to be held in Paris in 1900 during the World's fair, and to this Miss Goldman is accredited as American secretary and delegate from the American groups. The place of the meeting has not yet been designated, but the month of August

ing to *Living My Life,* when Stone learned that EG had been engaged in politics in Europe, he wrote that he and Miller would not support her. "'I am interested only in E. G. the woman—her ideas have no meaning whatever to me. Please choose,'" he wrote. She replied, "'E. G. the woman and her ideas are inseparable. She does not exist for the amusement of upstarts, nor will she permit anybody to dictate to her. Keep your money'" (*LML,* pp. 245–46, 268). On the subject of EG's decision to forgo studies in Switzerland, see Letter to Max Nettlau, 4 January 1900, below.

has been fixed upon as the time. This will be the first anarchistic congress held anywhere since 1878.[3] It is fathered by Dornelo Niewhenhas, editor of the *Free Socialist*, a German publication;[4] Pouget, editor of a French socialistic paper,[5] and Reclus,[6] the distinguished geographist of France. Speaking of the congress, Miss Goldman said:

"There may be trouble but if there is we are ready for it; we are prepared to fight to the bitter end."

She added that some effort may be made by France to prevent the assembly in Paris of foreign Anarchists in which events the Reds will make a determined stand. As for herself she apprehends no trouble. "I am an American citizen," she said seeming for the moment to forget that anarchy recognizes no form of government or order, "and that may carry me through all right." Then she added, in response to a query, that she had never had any trouble in Paris, although she had spent some time there at a period, however, when there were no disturbances.

Miss Goldman's speeches here will be upon such topics as "Patriotism," "Politics and Its Corrupting Effect Upon Men," "Trade Unionism" and "Why I Am an Anarchist-Communist."[7]

"I am here not so much to make a propaganda," she said to the *Leader* man, "as to awaken the people. I do not believe Anarchists are made; I think they are born. There is no prosperity for the workingman; there is work, 'tis true, but the toiler is not sharing in the fruits of his labor. Prosperity! That is for the employer. Why the miners are no better off to-day than they were when I was here before when there was so much talk of hard times."

An interrogatory as to what is being done in the case of Alexander Berkmann brought forth this explanation: "In the first place I was always opposed to any legal efforts in behalf of Berkmann because I knew in behalf of action was contrary to my views and principles. Still what I did for him was done in the name of humanity; I would not retard anything that others might think proper in his behalf.[8] The pardon board, you understand, has refused to hear the Berkmann case because Mr. Frick while he has not said 'nay' has intimated to the pardon board that it would not be to the interest of his class to do anything for the prisoner. So the Czar of Russia declares Berkmann shall not be pardoned. Nothing further is being done for Berkmann now."

Miss Goldman related her experience at Spring Valley, Ill., this month on the occasion on which she was alleged to have wished to baptize some children with beer. "There was

3. In fact, several anarchist congresses were held between 1881 and 1900. The International Social Revolutionary and Anarchist Congress was held in London 14–19 July 1881; a Social Revolutionary congress was held in Chicago 21–23 October 1881; the Pittsburgh congress was held 14–16 October 1883; and in New York City a Yiddish anarchist conference was held on 25 December 1890.
4. Domela Nieuwenhuis was actually the editor of the Dutch paper *De Vrije Socialist* (The Free Socialist, 1898–1919).
5. Émile Pouget was the editor of *Le Père Peinard*.
6. Élisée Reclus was a renowned geographer and anarchist communist.
7. It was reported in *Free Society* that EG gave thirteen lectures while in Pittsburgh.
8. See "An Undelivered Speech," Exchange of Letters in *Liberty*, 7–13 December 1898, above.

no truth whatever in the published reports," she said emphatically. "The facts of the matter are these: Between the time of my former visit to Spring Valley in May and the last one this month, 19 children had been born into Anarchist families. The women folks are not very far advanced and the men wanted to get them out to our meetings so I could talk to them on women's questions, so we played a little trick by inviting them to bring their children as a sort of reunion. I made a remark about the Christians baptizing with water and said if wine was good enough for them I was opposed to any adulteration and preferred the pure beer or wine. There was no reference to baptizing the children in beer, for in the first place we do not believe in baptism at all.[9]

"I had some trouble with the police in Spring Valley on September 6. We had arranged for a parade and meeting on the public square; I carried the red flag at the head of the procession and it was just like waving a red flag in the face of a bull. The mayor threatened to arrest me if I spoke, although he had already given permission for the meeting. I then reminded him of his promise, but he still insisted that I should not address the crowd and that they should disperse. I told him that the men were armed and were determined to hold the meeting; that if I were disposed to do so I could not influence them to leave, but that if he would not interfere with us I would guarantee that there would be no trouble; if, on the other hand, he did interfere I would not be responsible for what would happen. He finally said that I should be careful what I said. At all events we held the meeting and the newspapers roundly roasted the mayor for showing the white feather."[10]

Regarding the Dreyfus case, she said: "The Dreyfus case has done more for anarchy than twenty-five years of active propaganda; it has done more to show the world how rotten the government of France is than anything else in history. Of course, the Anarchists are all for Dreyfus; they did a great deal of work in his behalf. Personally I do not believe Dreyfus is a sympathetic character. What the Anarchists did, however, was from a humanitarian point of view—a principle."

Miss Goldman was with a group of fellow Anarchists when the writer talked to her, among the party being Messrs. Bauer and Gordon, who were active in the movement for Berkmann's pardon.[11] She looked remarkably well, and as she passed along Smithfield street the casual observer would never have suspected that an Anarchist of international notoriety was so close at hand. She wore a neat fitting black suit with tailor-made jacket and a small toque.

Pittsburg (Pa.) Leader, 24 September 1899, p. 1.

9. The 24 September 1899 issue of *Free Society* carried the baptism story. According to Joseph Corna, on 5 September the Italian, French, and German comrades had a picnic at which nineteen children of anarchists were "baptized" by EG. At the picnic EG gave a talk on the "freedom of the women and mothers and the necessity of the unhampered development of the child." There was no mention in the report of beer or anything else used ceremonially during the baptism.

10. From extant reports (*Princeton, Ill., Bureau County Tribune,* 14 and 15 September 1899; *Free Society,* 24 September 1899; and *Freedom,* November 1899), EG must have collapsed together several discrete events in Spring Valley between the 4th and 7th of September in this recounting.

11. EG refers to Henry Bauer and Harry Gordon, both active in the Berkman Defense Association.

DEAR FRIEND HAMON.

It is a long time, since we have corresponded, I hardly know, now, who was the last to write, at any rate I have not forgotten you. I am now, finishing an 8th months tour through the states, having delivered 210 lectures, on economic, sociological, ethical and sexual subjects, and am about to start for England & Scotland, at the latter part of Oct.[1] where I am to lecture also. I hope to reach Paris, by next March, to stay there for some times, and of course, I also hope to meet you, if you have not forgotten me. When I was in San Francisco, at the publishers of F S.[2] I saw the book, containing your lecture before the Bruxelles, University, which you wrote me about some time ago, I should very much like to have it, at least the english copy.[3] Will you kindly send it to me, either to my N.Y. address, 50 First street, if you will do it soon, or c/o H.M. Kelly[4]

> 266. Amhurst Rd
> London. N.
> England.

also *L'Humanité Nouvelle,* and the price of subscribtion, and the book; I will than forward the money; please send me the August number of *L'Humanit[é] Nouvelle.*—I would like to ask you for the following information, if not to troublesome for you to reply; it is this. A number of my friends, including, Artists musicians, journalists & other bohamians, have decided to come to Paris, for the ~~exhibi~~ exposition, 1900.[5] They send me as the amissary to obtain quaters for them, so I would like to rent a house, furnished if possible, somewhere's in the Country whithin 1/2 houre from Paris, of about 12−15 rooms. Can you tell me, if such a house can be rented, and what the possible expence could be? You would oblige me greatly, as I know no one in Paris except you, who could give me satisfactory information

1. EG did not sail for Europe until 3 November 1899.
2. The initials "F S" stand for the journal *Free Society.*
3. These lectures at the New University of Brussels appeared in English as *The Universal Illusion of Free Will and Criminal Responsibility* (London: University Press, 1899). Élisée Reclus taught geography at this university from 1895 until he died in 1905.
4. EG provides the London address for Harry Kelly, co-editor of the Boston anarchist monthly *Rebel,* who had returned to England in 1898.
5. The Paris Exposition Universelle opened 14 April 1900. The International Revolutionary Congress of the Working People was to be held in Paris in September 1900 to coincide with the world fair.

ATHENÆUM HALL,

73, TOTTENHAM COURT ROAD, W.

Saturday, 9th December 1899 at 8 p.m.

GRAND MEETING & CONCERT

for the benefit of the Agitation in favour of the polictical
victims in Italy.

SPEAKERS

A. PANIZZA — G. ROSSI — P. CALCAGNO — P. KRAPOKTINE
LUISE MICHEL — TCHERKESOFF
TOM MANN — EMMA GOLDMAN — TARRIDA DEL MARMOL
TCHECHOSKY.

PROGRAMME

FIRST PART.

I.   Italian Chorus   *(Hosanna to Crispi!)*
II. Piano   ...   (Four hands)   ...   Mrs. CINI and Miss DEFENDI.
III. Song   ...   By the celebrated singer   ...   Mrs. JENNY ATKINSON.
IV. Song   ...   .   Mr. GUERRA (Tenor.)
V.   Mandolinade.

SECOND PART.

I.   Politic Pantomine   *(A Detectif's Remorse)*
     Players : Mrs. EMILIA CARBONI — Mr. MAGNONI — COMOLLI BROS.
     — Mr. GALASSINI — Mr. FERRARONI.
II. Song   ...   *(The Grenadiers)*   ...   By Mr. COLLO (Barytone.)
III. Scientific illusionism   ...   By the celebrated EDISON GERMANO.
IV. Italian Chorus   *(1st May*, by P. Gori.)
V.   Song   ...   ...   (Opera *L'Ebreo*)   ...   Mr. COLLO.

THIRD PART.

I.   Lottery.   II.   Dancing.

TICKETS 6d EACH.

This program from the 9 December 1899 London "Grand Meeting and Concert" displays the
integration of music into political events and showcases Goldman's ascendance as a major
anarchist figure, sharing the stage with, among others, the French anarchist Louise Michel
and the Russian anarchist theorist Peter Kropotkin. (By permission of the Kate Sharpley
Library)

Hoping not to have asked too much, and that you would reply soon.[6]

SINCERLY.

E GOLDMAN

ALS, Augustin Hamon Archive, IISH.

6. Hamon replied to EG in London on 2 November, explaining he did not have a copy of his book on hand, directing her instead to the publisher, and requesting the subscription price of *L'Humanité Nouvelle* in advance. He also sent information on a house to rent, adding, "it is impossible to find cheaper principally during the exposition." The cost was too high for EG, who wrote back on 13 November thanking him for his trouble but declining the rooms. She added: "I have seen Tscherkessow [Cherkesov], yesterday, and he tells me, that I can get Flats, much cheaper, he has promised to write to friends in Paris, about the particulars." Concerning the book, EG responded she was "only too glad to pay for it, although I should have appreciated it a greater favor, if *you* had sent me the book complementary, and to tell the truth, I really hoped you would." She closed her letter with the comment, "I have been informed, that you too, are infected by the disease of Anti.-Semitism. Is it really true? I can hardly believe it—" (see Hamon to EG, 2 November 1899; and EG to Hamon, 13 November 1899, *EGP*, reel 1).

Dear Comrade Metzkow.

You were very angry in your letter as far as I could tell. Why? I don't know how N[1] learned what I wrote to you in the first letter, but he wrote to me that you had told him. The news concerning B's escape attempt you probably also know already. I don't think that he made an attempt to escape.[2] It is more likely that he exchanged words with the guard and that the latter shot at B. One can only find out if one goes to the prison personally. It is impossible for me to go now, as much as I would like to. How would it be if you went? You wouldn't be allowed to see B, but if you claim to be an uncle or other relative you will have the right to ask about his condition. If his injury is a dangerous one, then I will come even if I have to sell all I have to pay for my journey. Otherwise, if I am still in America at the end of November, I will go to P[3] then. I have written to N that I will not be able to go for the time being. I hope that you will be so kind as to make inquiries at the prison. Let me know immediately if you find out anything there.

With rev. greetings
EG

ALI, Joseph Ishill Collection, MH-H. Translated from German. Reprinted by permission of the Houghton Library, Harvard University.

1. EG uses the initial "N" to refer to Carl Nold.
2. EG would not have believed such a rumor, since she was privy to AB's true plans for escape and was involved in arranging for the construction of an escape tunnel. Neither *Prison Memoirs of an Anarchist* nor *Living My Life* make any public reference to AB's attempting an escape or being shot during this period. However, AB was put in solitary confinement on 25 December 1899 for attacking a fellow prisoner who kicked and killed his pet bird, Dick.
3. Pittsburgh, where AB was in prison.

DEAR NETLOW.[1]

Undoubtedly you already consider me an ungrateful person and have wondered if anything better can be expected from one of the "third" sex.[2] You were so kind as to send me catalogs and all kinds of conceivably useful information concerning universities,[3] even going to the trouble of indicating the cost of the various subjects, and I, the ungrateful one, haven't sent you words of either appreciation or gratitude. Indeed, I dare say, I have thanked you all the more in my mind, yet I could not write because I was ill.—

I developed a severe cold on my trip to Leeds; instead of staying in bed, I had to address the previously arranged meetings. I only stayed there for a week and came back to London with pleuritis which kept me confined to bed for two weeks and from which I have not yet recovered. Other than that, I am out of danger and rid of the inflammation, but a terrible cough still causes me great pain. Still, no rest for the wicked,[4] in spite of it all I had to speak Friday Saturday and Sunday and have to go to a meeting today too. Well, ill weeds grow apace, don't they? Following what you sent to me from the University of Berne, Berne is out of the question for me because I can hardly learn in one year everything necessary to fulfill the matriculation requirements. Especially Latin. Assuming I began work right away I still would not be finished by September; besides, I cannot concern myself with the preparations now. I must finish my agitation tour which has already started and which will take me till the end of Feb.[5] When I come to Paris, I want and will have to dedicate myself to the study of the French language and, because I want to learn

1. Nettlau went by the name Netlow in England. EG met him for the first time during this visit to London.
2. EG and Nettlau used the term "third sex" in an ongoing private joke to refer to a feminist or advocate of women's independence, not a homosexual. Nettlau, in his memoirs, elaborated on the significance of this ongoing reference to EG's feminist nature: "We talked often and much, but arrived most of the time at a point where we differed sharply. I said then, as a compliment, that after all she had a female logic, different from male logic, and that was something she didn't want to hear. We said that to each other up to the last time I saw her" (Nettlau, *Erinnerungen und Eindrücke,* 8:144).
3. That is, universities at which she might study medicine.
4. This first part of the sentence was written in English.
5. EG had arrived in London on 13 November 1899, where she lectured in English and German throughout December and January. She traveled to Leeds on 10 December, then back to London before continuing on to Scotland in January and finally leaving England after a farewell concert and ball on 26 February 1900. From England EG traveled to Paris.

it thoroughly, I cannot study Latin on the side. Furthermore, I will have to take care of the American correspondence regarding the congress[6] if the people over there should be induced to send a delegate. To be frank, Berne doesn't appeal to me because the contrast between my previous life and the tranquility in Berne would be too great and would produce in me a mental and emotional depression. Either Paris, Geneva, or back to Uncle "Sam."[7] In any case, from here I will first go back to Switzerland via Munich as I have already told you. Apropos, is it also so difficult to find a room in M.? You of course wouldn't know of anyone with whom I could stay <u>undisturbed</u> for a week?—I underline undisturbed because here I wasn't free for a minute. Miss Davies[8] wrote to me that I will get a copy of your essay,[9] I'm already very anxiously awaiting this.—She also said that you suggested I should make clear my position on the economic question. Unfortunately I can't do anything in my present gloomy mood but pace back and forth in my room; I enjoyed doing that in the cell, only my present cell is bigger; it's a comfort, isn't it?

Max Nettlau (ca. 1890s), the anarchist historian, writer, and lifelong Goldman correspondent. (IISH)

6. EG had been accredited as secretary and delegate from the American groups to the International Revolutionary Congress of the Working People in Paris, scheduled for September 1900.

7. On EG's decision not to study in Switzerland, Nettlau recounted in his memoirs that "Emma Goldman . . . spoke to me and wrote me about the possibility for her studying medicine in Vienna. She would have liked to become a doctor. I had to enquire for her about terms of admission, examinations, deadlines, costs, etc., ... It turned out with respect to Vienna, as was to be expected, that her education was not sufficient and that everything would have taken much longer than she thought. If she had earnestly wanted to study, Switzerland would have been suitable. But she wanted, because of her prospective clients, a degree from Vienna and she could not expect to achieve that without longer studies" (*Erinnerungen und Eindrücke*, 8:143).

8. EG refers to Ann A. Davies, who was then living in London and working with the paper *Freedom*.

9. Nettlau's essay "Responsibility and Solidarity in the Labor Struggle: Their Present Limits and Their Possible Extension" was based on an article he contributed to the November 1897 number of the London *Freedom*, entitled "New Tactics for Trade Unionists." The essay was originally read before the Freedom Discussion Group on 5 December 1899; first published in two installments in *Freedom* 14 (January–February 1900): 5–6 and (March–April 1900): 12–13; and issued in pamphlet form the same year, together with a second essay originally entitled "German Social Democracy and Edward Bernstein," and also published in *Freedom* 14 (January–February 1900): 2–3. See Max Nettlau, *Responsibility and Solidarity in the Labor Struggle, Also a Review of the Policy Lately Discussed by the German Social Democracy and Edward Bernstein* (London: Freedom Pamphlets, No. 12, May 1900). The pamphlet was also translated into Italian, *La Responsebilita' e las Solidariera nella Lotta Operaia* (Barre, Vt.: Cosa Editrice L'Azione, 1913) and was submitted by the *Freedom* Group to the International Revolutionary Congress of the Working People in Paris in 1900.

The concert to benefit the *Socialist*[10] was very beautiful, indeed extremely beautiful, Tschaikovsky[11] and Kahan[12] said. Also very well attended, but I don't think that there will be more than 3 pounds profit. We didn't take over the bar ourselves and that way lost at least 2 pounds. The main thing, however, is that the affair went better than is usually the case at workers' celebrations. I will travel to Scotland on the 18th, can hardly await the day.

Farewell and enjoy the good beer and good coffee, and think least of all of one who has been knitting a stocking for 2 years and hasn't finished yet, and who only every now and then thinks "too logically."

GREETINGS AND A HANDSHAKE.

EG.

HAPPY NEW YEAR——

ALI, Max Nettlau Archive, IISH. Translated from German.

10. Probably a fund-raising event for the German anarchist journal *Der Sozialist*, edited by Gustav Landauer, which had ceased publication in 1899. The paper was never revived. Its publishers soon launched *Der arme Teufel* (a literary journal named after Robert Reitzel's Detroit-based paper), but this time without Landauer, who remained critical of the venture.
11. EG refers to the Russian revolutionary Nikolai Chaikovsky, living in exile in London, where EG met him.
12. Possibly Zelda Kahan, a Russian Jewish socialist in London.

Dear Comrade.

Ihr Schreiben erhalten; besten Dank für Ihre Bereitwilligkeit, mir die Benützung der 3 Zimmer mit den fest verschlossenen Thüren, in Ihrer Wohnung, während des Tages zu überlassen. Ich wagte es gar nicht daran zu denken, daß Sie, der Frauen gegenüber so korrekt sind, wirklich so weit gehen werden, einer dieses Geschlechtes die Benützung einen Teil Ihrer Junggesellen Wohnung anzutragen. Freilich, gehöre ich zum Dritten Geschlecht u dann handelt es sich ja um den Aufenthalt am Tage, was ja schließlich den Anstand nicht verletzt. Nun, wen ich nach München komme, werde ich Ihre Güte schon in Anspruch nehmen, aber nur unter einer Bedingung, wen die Thüren <u>fest</u> verschlossen sind, <u>recht fest verschlossen</u> hören Sie, dear Comrade?—Ich sagte wenn ich nach München komme, bis vor Kurzem glaubte ich noch bestimmt daran, aber jetzt kommt so allerlei dazwischen. Ich habe nämlich erfahren, daß es von Zürich nach Genf u dann nach Paris, beinahe so viel kostet, als von hier nach Zürich über München, wenn dem so ist, dann freilich muß ich den Wunsch, nach München zu reisen aufgeben da meine Verhältnisse es nicht erlauben, solch riesige Summen auszugeben. In diesem Falle würde ich die Reise nach die Schweiz bis auf den Herbst verschieben, im Sep, gedenke ich Paris ja ohnedies zu verlassen, (d. h. wen ich dort die Kurse nicht besuchen kann) dann kann ich nach die Schweiz, u wenn ich in Genf auch nichts ausrichten kann, dann werde ich über Deutschland nach America reisen. Jedenfalls, würde ich Ihnen sehr dankbar sein, wenn Sie mir Auskunft geben ~~würden~~ könnten, was die Reise ~~nach Z~~ von Zürich nach Genf u von da nach Paris kostet, aber recht bald, bitte, ja?—

Sie täuschen sich, wenn Sie annehmen, daß ich die Ruhe verwerfe, oder unterschätze, gerade weil ich mich nach Ruhe sehne, will ich die Agitation eine zeitlang aufgeben u mich einem bestimmten Studium widmen. Freilich, bin ich der Ansicht, daß alle äußere Ruhe der Welt, einem die innere Ruhe nicht schaffen kann, außer man ist von der Natur mit ~~einem~~ Ihrem Temperament, gesegnet. Die Unruhe liegt mir im Blut, die habe ich von meinem Volke geerbt, u die wird auch mit mir selbst aufhören, aber jedenfalls weiß ich, daß nur die äußere Umgebung mir [*illegible word*] kann. Sie haben Recht. London muß auf jeden deprimierend wirken, u mich hat es vollständig gelähmt, vielleicht kommt es daher, daß ich gerade aus Californien hierherkam, u den Kontrast eben umso furchtbarer empfinde. Ich bin leider nicht in der Lage, Ihren Gruß an den Franzosen G. in Edinburgh, auszurichten, da ich nicht dahin komme. Meine Tour nach Schottland, ist ein ebensogroßer Fiasko, als die nach England. Überhaupt, scheint es mir als wenn ein Fluch auf dem ganzen ruhen würde, oder sagen wir, das ganze ist der Dummheit u Unfähigkeit derjenigen Genossen, die die Arrangements meiner Versamml. in Händen hatten. Ja, ja lieber N. the moral responcibility among the Anarchists, is even more lacking den among the workers at large, they would think twice, before they drag a persone from place to place, who's only misfortune is to be a speaker, or propagandist—Ja K. hat seinen Platz verloren, u vorläufig wenig Aussicht auf Beschäftigung, dazu kommt noch, daß er phisisch ziemlich auf den Grund ist.

Daß in Ihrer Wohnung nichts zur Bequemlichkeit fehlen wird, konnte ich mir schon denken, ebenso, daß Strick u Häkelnadeln vorhanden sein werden. Das alles, gehört sozusagen zu Ihnen, denn Sie, ein so großer Verfechter des Strickstrumpfes, u der bestimmten weiblichen Sphäre sind—die gütige Fee, die Ihnen 3 paar Strümpfe zu Weihnachten geschenkt hat, weiß vielleicht gar nicht, wie sehr sie Ihren sehnlichsten Wunsch erfüllt hat, was? Nein, ich kann jetzt nichts schreiben, am allerwenigstens etwas über die ökonomische Frage, die viel zu trocken u monoton für meine Stimmung ist. Endlich ist es mir gelungen, einen Abzug Ihres Artikels von Cantwell, zu erlangen, den ich gestern "FS." schickte, leider erscheint die Fortsetzung erst im Feb. "Freedom", somit wird auch "FS." warten müssen. Die einliegende Adresse habe ich Miss Davies übermittelt, sie wird Ihnen F. senden. Marie Isaak ist glücklich in [*illegible word*] angelangt u fühlt sich dort wohl. Gewiß nimmt sie ein Strickzeug zur Hand, denn sie ist eine sehr gediegene Hausfrau, das verhindert sie aber nicht sich auch anderweitig zu betätigen, eben weil sie nicht einseitig ist, die wie Menge, die das Weibe auf eine gewisse einseitige Sphäre, bestimmen wollen—

SIE HERZLICH GRÜßEND
EG.
ADRESSE DIESELBE

DEAR COMRADE.

Received your letter; many thanks for your willingness to grant me the use of the three rooms with firmly shut doors in your apartment during the day. I did not dare to think that you, who are so proper toward women, would really go so far as to propose the use of a part of your bachelor apartment for someone of this gender. Of course, I belong to the third sex,[1] and furthermore this has to do with my presence during the day, which really will not offend a sense of decency. Now if I come to Munich I will certainly make a claim on your goodness, but only under one condition, that the doors are <u>firmly</u> closed, <u>really firmly closed</u> do you hear, dear Comrade?—I said if I come to Munich, until recently I was certain of it, but now all kind of things are getting in the way. Namely I have discovered that to go from Zurich to Geneva and then to Paris costs nearly as much as it does from here to Zurich via Munich, if that is the case then I must obviously give up on my desire to travel to Munich as my circumstances do not permit me to spend such huge sums. In this case I would have to postpone the trip to Switzerland until the fall, in Sep. I plan to leave Paris in any case (that is if I can't attend the courses there) and then I can go to Switzerland, and if I can't accomplish anything in Geneva either, then I will travel to America via Germany. In any event, I would be very grateful to you if you ~~would~~ could provide me with information as to what the trip ~~to Z~~ from Zurich to Geneva and from there to Paris costs, and really soon yes?—

You are mistaken if you believe that I reject or undervalue tranquility, exactly because I yearn for tranquility I want to give up agitation for a time and devote myself to a particular study. Of course I am of the view that all the external calm in the world cannot create inner calm in a person, unless one is by his nature blessed with ~~a~~ your temperament. Restlessness is in my blood, I inherited it from my people, and it will die along with me, but in any event I know that the outside world can only [*illegible word*]. You are right. London must make everyone depressed, and it completely paralyzed me, perhaps it is because I came here straight from California, and indeed felt the contrast to be all the more terrible. I am unfortunately not in a position to pass on your regards to the Frenchman G[2] in Edinburgh, as I am not going to get there. My tour to Scotland is as great a fiasco

---

1. For explanation of EG and Nettlau's private joke with the term "third sex," see note 2 to Letter to Max Nettlau, 4 January 1900, above.
2. Possibly Lucien Louis Guérineau (1857–1940), a French cabinetmaker and anarchist militant. In 1884 Guérineau was a member of the Black Flag group and wrote for *Terre et Liberté*, published between October 1884 and February 1885. He was sentenced to two months in prison in August 1884 for fighting a police officer. In 1895, in the wake of a number of anarchist bombings, he was accused

as the one to England. Indeed, it seems to me as if the whole undertaking were cursed, or shall we say, the whole mess is due to the stupidity and incompetence of the comrades who held the arrangements of my meetings in their hands. Yes, yes dear N. the moral responsibility among the Anarchists, is even more lacking than among the workers at large, they would think twice, before they drag a person from place to place, whose only misfortune is to be a speaker, or propagandist[3]—Yes K.[4] has lost his position, and for the time being has little chance for employment, and on top of that comes the fact that he is physically rather run down.

I am certain that no comfort will be lacking in your apartment, and that knitting and crochet needles will also be available. All this is to be expected of you, so to speak, for you are such a great champion of knitted stockings and the <u>specifically</u> female sphere—perhaps the kind fairy who gave you three pair of stockings for Christmas had no idea how much they fulfilled your most ardent wish, could that be? No, I cannot write anything now, least of all something about the economic question, which is much too dry and monotone for my mood. I have finally succeeded in getting a copy of your article from Cantwell[5] which I sent yesterday to *FS*, unfortunately the continuation will appear first in the Feb. *Freedom,* and so *FS* will also have to wait. I transmitted the accompanying address to Miss Davies, she will send you F.[6] Marie Isaak[7] has arrived happily in [*illegible word*] and feels comfortable there. Of course she took knitting things, for she is a very devoted housewife, which however does not keep her from being active elsewhere, indeed because she is not one sided, like the crowd who want to assign women to a particular, one-sided sphere.

WITH WARM REGARDS TO YOU

EG.

SAME ADDRESS

ALI, Max Nettlau Archive, IISH. Translated from German.

---

of "criminal conspiracy" but acquitted; soon after he left for London. While in London, he corresponded with Jean Grave and contributed reports to *Les Temps Nouveaux.* He returned to Paris and in 1899 was among the contributors to the *Journal du Peuple* launched by Sébastien Faure during the Dreyfus Affair.

3. This sentence was written in English.

4. EG refers to Harry Kelly.

5. The article EG requested from Nettlau was his "Responsibility and Solidarity in the Labor Struggle," which she obtained from the English anarchist and compositor Thomas Cantwell and which she sent on to the journal *Free Society* (abbreviated *FS*).

6. EG uses the abbreviation "F" for the periodical *Freedom.*

7. Anarchist Mary Isaak was publisher with her husband, Abe Isaak, of both *Firebrand* and *Free Society* and traveled to England with EG.

DEAR COMRADE.

Endlich komme ich dazu Ihr Schreiben vom 20 Jan zu beantworten

Ich komme nicht nach München, da ich direckt nach Paris reise u zwar am 27ten d. M. Bis dahin habe ich viel zu thun. Große V. im Workingmens Club & Institute gegen den Krieg, morgen Abend wobei wir uns "a hot time" versprechen zwei sozialistische Versammlungen, wo Hyndman. sprechen sollte, waren von den Jingos gestört. Samstag Nachmittag die letzte Versammlung in White Chapel Sonntag Nachmittag letzte deutsche Versammlung in Atheneum Hall, u Montag Abschiedsfest, denn Dienstag nach Paris. Ich kann es kaum glauben daß ich bald von London von dem trüben schmutzigen grauenhaften London dort sein werde. Ich war bei Trunk Samstag, u er sagte mir, daß Sie seine Adresse für Briefe Packete u dengleichen angegeben haben, ich werde also Seaflote, Handbills, posters u was ich von Biller heißt der Mann, der Lydow ähnlich sieht, für Sie bekommen werde zu Trunk senden soll ich? Ich habe in den sozialistischen Monats-Hefte, die zwei Engelschen Article gelesen, die Sie ausgegraben haben. Sie sind eigentlich wunderbar im Wählen. Es wurde weder in Edinburgh noch Aberdeen etwas arrangiert ja nicht einmal in Glasgow fand ein englische Versammlung statt. Alles schläft im lieben England, nur die Dummheit nicht. Haben Sie ja von Claus Timmerman Antwort erhalten? Meine Adresse in Paris ist Vorläufig Mrs E Brady c/o P. McCabe 25 rue de Poliveau Paris France

E.G. wird jetzt einer zeitlang von der Oberfläche verschwinden—Wenn Sie nach Paris kommen werden Sie mich hoffentlich besuchen, nicht? Die Engländer sind mit Americaner gar nicht zu vergleichen. Der Patriotismus während des Spanish-American Krieges war gewiß groß, und doch wagte es niemand irgend einer Aussprache gegen den Krieg zu verhindern, denn, ob man mit dem Krieg einverstanden war oder nicht, Thatsache ist doch, daß das Motiv desselben schön war, zum mindestens seitens des amerikanischen Volkes, das wirklich aus Sympathy mit Cuba, Spanien bekämpfte. Aber in diesem Kriege, ist das Motiv Raub und Mord, und eine solche Brutalität, deren eben nur Engländer fähig sind. Einfach wahnsinnig sind die Menschen hier, und wenn jemand auch nur die leiseste Sympathy für die Boeren zeigt, oder ausspricht, denn hat er zu gewärtigen, daß er in der schmählichsten Weise molestiert wird! Die Boeren sind doch Prachtkerle, so eine Handvoll Menschen, und wie sie den Ball schütteln, grosßrtig einfach herrlich. Ich habe für morgen einen Vortrag ausgearbeitet, der den Stier gehörig wild machen wird, aber ich muß meine Empörung aussprechen ganz gleich, welches die Folgen sein sollten. Schreiben Sie bald wieder.

GRUß

E.G.

DEAR COMRADE.

I am finally getting around to answering your letter of 20 Jan.

I am not coming to Munich, as I am traveling directly to Paris on the 27th of this month. I have much to do before then. Big m[eeting] in the Workingmens Club & Institute against the war tomorrow evening[1] where we are promising "a hot time." Two socialist meetings where Hyndman[2] was supposed to speak were disrupted by the Jingos. Saturday afternoon the last meeting in White Chapel, Sunday afternoon the last German meeting in Athenaeum Hall, and on Monday the farewell party,[3] then Tuesday to Paris. I can hardly believe that I will soon be away from London, from dreary, dirty, horrible London. I was at Trunk's[4] on Saturday, and he told me that you gave his address for letters, parcels and the like, so I will send the leaflets, handbills, posters and whatever I receive from Biller, the man who resembles Lydow, to Trunk, is that right? I read in the

1. EG spoke on 20 February at the Workingmen's Club and Institute Hall, Clerkenwell Road, before a meeting of the Freedom Discussion Group on "The Effect of War on the Workers," later published in *Freedom* (March–April 1900) Other speakers included Tom Mann, Lothrop Withington, Sam Mainwaring, and Harry Kelly.

2. The English socialist Henry Mayers Hyndman (1842–1921) started his career as a journalist writing for the *Pall Mall Gazette*, but he was influenced by the writings of Karl Marx and in 1881 left journalism to form Britain's first socialist political organization, the Democratic Federation, later the Social Democratic Federation (SDF). Because of his earlier sympathies with the British Tory party and British imperialism, many were suspicious of Hyndman's dedication to socialism, a problem heightened by his autocratic leadership style. It was this which led to a schism in the SDF where the majority left the organization to form the Socialist League in 1884. Hyndman was criticized by other members for SDF involvement with the Tory party in the 1885 election. In 1900 the SDF, Fabian Society, and the Independent Labor Party met to form the Labor Representation Committee—the forerunner of the Labor Party. Hyndman was also a prolific author of political tracts, including *The Historical Basis of Socialism in England* (London: K. Paul, Tranch, 1883), *Commercial Crises of the Nineteenth Century* (London: S. Sonnenschein, 1892), and *The Future of Democracy* (London: G. Allen and Unwin, 1915).

3. On Sunday, 25 February, EG spoke at London's Athenaeum Hall on "Die Grundlagen Der Moral" (The Basis of Morality). On Monday, 26 February, there was a farewell concert and ball for EG also at Athenaeum Hall, which included addresses by EG, Peter Kropotkin, and Louise Michel.

4. Johann Sebastian Trunk was a German anarchist, cabinetmaker, editor, and advocate of propaganda of the deed who worked with Johann Most, Johann Neve, G. C. Uhly, F. J. Ehrhart, A. Benek, and others on *Freiheit* in London. Trunk edited the paper from 20 May to 3 June 1882 while Most was in prison for treason. Neve was also unavailable, being on the run for publishing the article "Der Rebellen Antwort" in the 13 May issue of *Freiheit* praising the murder of Lord Cavendish in Dublin by Irish nationalists. Trunk was a member of a group dedicated to propaganda by the deed organized by Victor Dave, which included Gustav Knauerhase, Otto Rinke, and Joseph Peukert. He also participated in the 14–19 July 1881 London Social Revolutionary Congress as a representative of the Kommunistischer Arbeiterbildungsverein, a German-speaking workers' association that included social-

Sozialistische Monatshefte the two articles by Engels that you dug up.[5] They were indeed wonderful choices. Nothing was arranged either in Edinburgh or Aberdeen, and even in Glasgow there were no English meetings. Everything is slumbering in dear old England except stupidity. Have you received an answer from Claus Timmerman? My address in Paris is

For the time being, Mrs E Brady[6]
c/o P. Mc Cabe
25 rue de Poliveau
Paris. France

E.G. will now disappear from the surface for a while—If you come to Paris, hopefully you will visit me, won't you? The English are simply not at all comparable to the Americans. The patriotism during the Spanish-American War was certainly great and yet no one dared prevent any talk against the war since, whether one agreed with the war or not, the fact is that intentions were good, at least on the part of the American people, who fought Spain truly out of sympathy with Cuba. But in this war[7] the motive is plunder and murder, and of such brutality as only the English are capable. The people here are simply insane, and if anyone shows even the slightest sympathy for the Boers, or speaks out, then he has to know that he will be handled in the most humiliating manner! The Boers are great people, such a wonderful group, and the way in which they are rocking the boat is fantastic, simply marvelous. I have prepared a lecture for tomorrow that may drive the beast thoroughly wild,[8] but I must express my anger regardless of the consequences.

Write again soon.

GREETINGS

E.G.

ALS, Max Nettlau Archive, IISH. Translated from German.

---

ists, anarchists, and other revolutionaries. Trunk played a secondary role in the Bruderkrieg (Brothers War) that plagued the German anarchist movement; eventually Trunk moved to an alignment with the anarchist communists around Joseph Peukert and Otto Rinke.

5. Nettlau had discovered two forgotten articles by Friedrich Engels in the paper *Das Volk*, published in London in 1859, and had edited them for re-publication, adding an introduction. See Nettlau, "Friedrich Engels über Karl Marx. Zwei Aufsätze aus dem Jahre 1859" (Friedrich Engels on Karl Marx. Two essays from the year 1859), *Sozialistische Monatshefte* (Berlin) 4 (January 1900): 38–46.

6. EG was traveling under the name of her former companion Edward Brady.

7. In the Anglo-Boer War (1899–1902), the British government fought two Boer republics for control of South Africa.

8. See "The Effect of War on the Workers," Transcript of Address in *Freedom*, 20 February 1900, immediately following.

The Effect of War on the Workers.

(Address by Emma Goldman on February 20, in London.)

Fellow Workers.—Let me begin my address with a quotation from one of England's greatest men; not the England of to day, the invading, murderous, crushing England, but the England of a time when Liberty and Hospitality were her main virtues—the England that has given the world the profoundest thinkers, the most brilliant writers, the most touching poets, from among whom Carlyle stands out like a shining star upon the firmament. It was he who said, when asked "What is the net purport of War?":

"There dwell and toil, in the English village of Dumdrudge, some five hundred souls. From these, by certain 'Natural Enemies' of the French, there are successively selected, during the French war, say thirty able-bodied men: Dumdrudge, at her own expense, has suckled and nursed them: she has, not without difficulty and sorrow, fed them up to manhood, and even trained them to crafts so that one can weave, another build, another hammer, and the weakest stand under thirty stone avoirdupois. Nevertheless, amid much weeping and swearing, they are selected; all dressed in red; and shipped away, at the public charges, some two thousand miles, or say only to the south of Spain; and fed there till wanted. And now to that same spot . . . are thirty similar French artisans, from a French Dumdrudge, in like manner wending; till at length, after infinite effort, the two parties come into actual juxtaposition: and Thirty stands fronting Thirty, each with a gun in his hand. Straightway the word 'Fire!' is given: and they blow the souls out of one another; and in place of sixty brisk, useful craftsmen, the world has sixty dead carcasses, which it must bury, and anew shed tears for. Had these men any quarrel? Busy as the Devil is, not the smallest! They lived far enough apart; were the entirest strangers; nay, in so wide a Universe, there was even, unconsciously, by Commerce, some mutual helpfulness between them. How then? Simpleton! their Governors had fallen out; and, instead of shooting one another, had the cunning to make these poor blockheads shoot." [1]

In these few pithy words of Carlyle, lies the whole secret of War and Militarism. Only a short while ago in what is called the greatest and freest land in the world (I mean America), from each Dumdrudge, thirty, nay, more, men were selected, dressed in uniform and shipped to a strange country; and the same was done in many Dumdrudges of

---

1. EG quotes from the eminent Scottish historian and writer Thomas Carlyle's *Sartor Resartus: The Life and Opinions of Herr Teufelsdröckh* (bk. 2, chap. 8). In *LML* (p. 256), Goldman describes a noticeably different version of this speech.

Spain. Both Spain and America had nursed and suckled their sons into strong and sturdy craftsmen. These same sons had children and wives to care for—often a mother and sister to support; but no amount of tears or prayers could keep them at home; they were told to go, and so they went to blow each other's brains out. Had they any quarrel? None whatever; they, too, lived far enough apart, and in this wide world there was rather a bond of helpfulness between them. What then? In the case of the American man, we were told that a beautiful sentiment, a deep moral, was the motive power; and so it was to some extent—at least, the American people thought so. It was the deep sympathy with the suffering Cubans, tortured and starved by the butcher Weyler[2] under the regime of the Spanish clergy and government; it was the just indignation of the American people over the atrocities committed in Cuba—I say: of the American people; I should say, of the American worker—and this noble sentiment, these humanitarian feelings, served the American governors as a good pretext for fighting Spain in order to get Cuba into their clutches.

Do you wish to know how the American-Spanish war affected the workers? I will tell you. First of all, America lost thousands of her sons—who either died of fever, lack of proper nourishment, or were killed by Spanish guns, or (as a reward for their patriotism and devotion to their country) by embalmed beef furnished by American capitalists.[3] Instead of those strong, able-bodied men who left their shores for the battlefield, we have today thousands of broken-hearted mothers, hungry widows and orphans, who swell the number of the unemployed and reduce the wages of the workers. Then we have the War Tax of Two Cents[4]—only a penny, you know; for the Government was kind to us—a penny War Tax that still, like the sword of Damocles, hangs over the workers' heads, that has increased the price of meat from 4d. to 6d., bread from 2d. to 2½d. per loaf, coals from 17s. to 25s., per ton, rent from 24s. to 30s. a month, beer, clothing and other necessities of life to still higher prices; it has ruined hundreds of small tradesmen, increased the ranks of the unemployed and reduced wages.

Still, all this suffering could be patiently borne if only one knew that the Cubans had

2. For more than a year, from February 1896 until he was recalled in 1897, Spanish general Valeriano Weyler y Nicolau served as governor of Cuba and attempted to deny local support for the insurgent Cuban Liberation Army by relocating peasants into loosely organized and poorly supplied concentration camps. Ultimately hundreds of thousands of people died from disease and malnutrition. In the United States, popular indignation at Weyler's methods encouraged support for the 1898 Spanish-American War.

3. EG refers to the canned beef rations served to soldiers in the war, often called "embalmed beef." The Armour meatpacking firm of Chicago sold the army 500,000 pounds of canned beef, much of which was tainted and rotting. The tainted beef is thought to have led to sickness and death among the soldiers. The overwhelming majority of casualties in the Spanish-American War were the result of diseases such as yellow fever, malaria, typhoid, and dysentery.

4. The War Revenue Act of 13 June 1898, enacted to "meet war expenditures," and repealed in 1902, imposed or increased taxes on a broad range of goods and services, including medicines, tobacco, beer, tea, mixed flours, telephone and telegraph service, inheritances (over $10,000), banking and other financial activities, and places of entertainment.

been helped. Were they helped? I deny it. I say that all the blood spilt, all the lives lost, all the money spent has been in vain; the Cubans have been freed from the atrocious government of Spain but only to fall into the hands of another almost as unscrupulous.[5] We have but to think of Homestead and its strike where eleven men were killed and some 30 wounded; of the coal strike in the Coeur d'Alene mines in Idaho, where 200 men were thrown to rot in the Bull Pen and confessions extorted at the point of the bayonet;[6] when we think of the atrocities rampant in the South, of the negroes lynched, tortured and burned by infuriated crowds without a hand being raised or a word said for their protection—when we think of all these things, then I say that the American Government is hardly an improvement upon that of the Spanish, signs of which can already be seen in Cuba, where, 12,000 workers being out on strike, the army was threatened to be called out.[7] We have saved the Cubans from the bullets of Spaniards, only, it seems to me, to expose them to the brutality of the bloodhounds of American capitalism. But as if this were not sufficient, there is a still more degrading, humiliating and brutal result of the late American-Spanish war—I allude to the invasion of the Philippine Islands and the crushing of the Filipinos, those noble rebels who are still defending their independence, though slaughtered by hundreds, their homes burned, their wealth destroyed, and their women ill-used by the very men who went to free the Cubans in the name of Liberty.[8] Co-

5. Cuba gained independence at the end of the war. However, U.S. troops occupied the country for the next five years, and in 1901, the Platt Amendment, which became part of Cuba's constitution in 1902, essentially made Cuba a U.S. protectorate.

6. In the spring of 1899 coal miners in Coeur d'Alene, Idaho, demanded a wage increase from the Bunker Hill and Sullivan Mining Company. The company agreed to raise wages but refused to recognize the union, the Western Federation of Miners. The WFM went on strike 23 April 1899. Then on 29 April a group of strikers and supporters, many armed, commandeered a train and attacked the mine, blowing it up and burning down the company offices. Governor Frank Steunenberg called for federal troops to intervene. As a result 700 miners were arrested and imprisoned in makeshift "bull-pen" prisons. The mine owners then forced miners who wanted to work to sign an oath renouncing the union. Federal troops remained in the area until 1901, and union leaders who had been in prison since 1899 were not released and pardoned until then. When Governor Steunenberg was murdered in a bomb explosion in 1905, authorities tried unsuccessfully to blame Western Federation of Miners leaders Charles Moyer, William Haywood, and George Pettibone. For further information, and EG's comments on these events, see "As to 'Crammers of Furnaces,'" Essay in *Mother Earth*, 20 November 1906, in vol. 2.

7. EG refers to the general strike in Havana in September 1899, which was called in support of the stonemasons' demand for an eight-hour day. Alarmed by local support for the strike, General William Ludlow, commander of U.S. occupation forces in the city, urged vigorous action by the police and arrested strike leaders, ultimately killing the strike.

8. At the end of the Spanish-American War, the United States bought the Philippines from Spain. However, the Filipino government had been fighting for independence from Spain since 1896, and soon fighting broke out between the United States and the Philippines. Though the war was declared over on 4 July 1902 by President Theodore Roosevelt, who was reacting to growing opposition to the war at home, fighting continued sporadically until 1913 when the United States established stable colonial control over the Philippines.

lumbia! cover your face under the shame of it; for you have become but a prostitute to the vice and greed of your sons!

Again we can say with Carlyle, out of every British and Irish Dumdrudge, men have been selected, dressed in khaki and sent to the Transvaal to blow out the souls of the Boers. Have these Englishmen quarrelled with the Boers? Why, no; on the contrary they were friends until a short time back. What then? In this case we cannot even say their Governors have fallen out, for the Governor of the Transvaal has certainly done more than any self-respecting man could or ought to do in the effort to prevent war, by yielding to the demands of Chamberlain, Cecil Rhodes and Alfred Milner.[9] No, it is not the Governors who have fallen out, but a few greedy and insatiable monsters, who have gone mad at the sight of the red Gold in the Transvaal like the proverbial bull at the sight of a red rag, and Britannia must sacrifice her sons at the demand of her sanguine traders. No fight so justifiable, no more righteous a defence, no nobler struggle for liberty, than that we see today on the side of the Boers, a handful of farmers who have known little of military drill or modern warfare, who, a peace-loving people, have taken to their guns only from sheer necessity and are showing the world that when a people fights for Liberty and independence it needs neither God nor King on its side. I see a report in one of your dailies, that a number of ministers have called upon you to repent; God because of your sins, having been against you no little in this war. Now I always believed the English were the most pious people on the earth; at least, they have always pretended to be such yet God has punished you; might it not be because you obeyed the call of your Governors to invade and slay a peaceful people? But no, your ministers call you to repent because God for once in their crude imagination is on the side of the righteous—otherwise he is too often on the side of the rascal. I hardly, however, think it necessary to go into details regarding the English-Boer War; enough has already been said from different sides as to the results likely to obtain on the workers; blind indeed are those who do not see them already. Aside of the increase of the cost of the coal and food, aside of your 50,000 children going to school without breakfast, you have sold your birthright for a mess of pottage; you stand before the world as willing slaves to the whims of robbers and thieves, and you have shown yourselves incapable (in spite of the gifts of chocolate from her gracious Majesty and plum-puddings from your aristocrats) of meeting and beating a handful of farmers!

Do not tell me Mr. Chamberlain is responsible for this war; it is you who are responsible. With Ruskin I can say: "There are two kinds of slaves—one are scourged to their work by the whip; others by their ignorance; some are bought with money, others with

9. EG refers to Joseph Chamberlain, the British colonial secretary from 1895 to 1903, who was responsible for British foreign policy during the Boer War. Cecil Rhodes, the diamond magnate, had been prime minister of Cape Colony from 1890 to 1896. Alfred Milner was the governor of Cape Colony and the British high commissioner of South Africa from 1897 to 1905.

praise (or promises of chocolate?) Again, it matters not what kind of work slaves do; some are set to digging fields, others graves; some press the juice out of vines, some the blood of men, but it is slavery just the same, because you do things at the bidding of others." [10]

Yes, fellow-workers, this is your curse—doing things at the bidding of others. When, oh when, will you learn to be yourselves, to think for yourselves, to act for yourselves? Not until you have learnt to understand the wrongs of War, of bloodshed, of legal murder and robbery; that all class and racial hatred is but the result of your ignorance, and that while you wilfully choose this ignorance you become the easy tools of your Governors, who are too cowardly to go out and fight themselves.

Freedom 14 (March–April 1900): 10–11.

10. EG paraphrases English writer, art historian, and social critic John Ruskin's discussion on "War" in *The Crown of Wild Olives: Three Lectures on Work, Traffic and War* (London, 1866).

I have the honor of informing you that the anarchist Emma Goldmann must have left London a few days ago for Paris, accompanied by the anarchist Havel. [1]

Emma Goldmann, whose somewhat old photograph I enclose, is of Russian nationality; she is approximately 32 or 33 years of age. She was in the United States of America a few years ago, where she worked very energetically at building up the anarchist movement; she was arrested and imprisoned several times because of the violence of her revolutionary speeches; [2] she has, by the way, succeeded on several occasions in recruiting comrades determined to carry out propaganda by the deed. In fact, I remember an attack with a revolver, which her lover, Mr. Alexander Berkman, committed in 1892 in Pittsburg against the Director of the Carnegie mines. [3] Another lover of Goldmann, [4] on her instructions, came from America to Germany via London; he was sentenced to 8 years in prison in 1893 in Duisburg for having violated the dynamite law.

Last spring, she reappeared in London, where she quietly made anarchist propaganda; there she got acquainted with an Austrian, Mr. Joseph-Hyp Havel, a waiter, born in Thabor (Austria) on August 13, 1871, [5] with whom she has lived with for some time.

Havel, of whom I am sending you a photograph taken in 1896, is an anarchist militant who has already been sentenced for attempts against property. He was interned in Austria in a mental hospital because of his extravagant behavior. In 1894, he was sentenced in Vienna to 18 months in prison for disturbing the peace. [6]

He is seen again in 1898 in Berlin, where he speaks at an anarchist meeting, then he goes to London where he starts to play a certain role in anarchist circles.

Until now, I have not been able to learn anything precise about the aim of this trip.

---

1. Hippolyte Havel, a Czech anarchist communist, met EG in London in 1899 and traveled with her to Paris.
2. She was arrested and imprisoned once in 1893 for a speech before the unemployed in New York City. Charged with "inciting to riot" she spent ten months in prison. This communiqué repeats much of the misinformation in the September 1895 report from the German Ministry of the Interior (see *Official Circular of the German Government*, 25 September 1895, above).
3. AB's *attentat* on Henry Clay Frick.
4. The reference is to Joseph Oerter, a German anarchist communist and, for a short time, companion of EG.
5. Havel was actually born in 1869.
6. According to Havel, he was imprisoned for eighteen months for making an inflammatory speech and then deported from Vienna.

ATHENÆUM HALL,
73, Tottenham Court Road, W.

Farewell Concert
for EMMA GOLDMAN,
26 FEBRUARY, 1900.

PROGRAMME:

1. OVERTURE ... ...
2. SONG ... ... *Barney O'Hea* ... ... LOVER.
   Mrs. ABBOTT.
3. RECITATION ... *Amelia's unfortunate young man.* ... MARK TWAIN.
   G. MEAD.
4. ADDRESS ... ... P. KROPOTKIN.
5. SONG ... ... *Der Lindenbaum.* ... ... SCHUBERT.
   MISS JENNY ATKINSON.
6. SELECTION ... ... *Souvenir de Boheme* ... ... PWRECK.
   THE SLAVONIC TAMBOURITZA ORCHESTRA.
7. SONG ... ... SELECTED.
   MISS ANNIE SCULL.
8. ADDRESS ... ... LOUISE MICHEL.
9. SLAVONIC DANCE ... ... *Kolo.* ... ... PETRAV.
   THE SLAVONIC TAMBOURITZA ORCHESTRA.
10. SONG ... ... *The Last Watch.* ... ...
    C. MORTON.
11. PAS DOUBLE ... ... *Kroatake.* ... ... ZARA.
    THE SLAVONIC TAMBOURITZA ORCHESTRA.
12. ADDRESS ... ... EMMA GOLDMAN.
13. DUETT ... ... *The Venetian Boat Song.* ... ... BLUMENTHAL.
    MISSES JENNY ATKINSON AND ANNIE SCULL.
14. GAVOTTE ... ... *Coquetterie.* ... ... CIBULKA.
    THE SLAVONIC TAMBOURITZA ORCHESTRA.
15. RECITATION ... *Parodies of the Balaclava Charge.* ... ...
    ARTHUR MEAD.

BALL.

PROGRAMME: ONE PENNY.

The 26 February 1900 farewell concert for Goldman, staged upon her departure from London to Paris for the planned anarchist conference, signaled her growing stature in the radical movement in Great Britain. (By permission of the Kate Sharpley Library)

But since Havel is to represent a group of London anarchists this year at the International Anarchist Congress, due to take place in Paris,[7] it is not unreasonable to think that this trip has to do with the organization of this congress. Given the character of these two individuals, and in particular that of the Goldman woman, it is not to be discounted that there may be a dangerous purpose behind this trip. This is why I thought it necessary to draw your attention to these two dangerous persons, and I would be very much obliged if you would keep me informed of their actions and movements, should you manage to find them.

Von Windheim

ALS, Dossier Emma Goldmann, Numéro 124786, Cote B/A 305, Archives de la Préfecture de Police, Paris. Marked "Confidential." Translated from French.

7. The International Revolutionary Congress of the Working People in Paris was scheduled for September 1900. EG later states that Havel has a mandate to "represent the Bohemian comrades from America at the congress" (see Letter to Max Nettlau," 15 May 1900 below).

Transcript of Address in *FREE SOCIETY*

Paris, 8 April 1900

The Propaganda and the Congress.

(Read before the organizing committee of the Anarchist Congress, Paris.)

COMRADES AND FRIENDS—

I have learned that the assistance received from the comrades in America and England in behalf of our congress, has not been very encouraging. I hope this has not led you to lose faith in the American or English Anarchistic movement, or that you have concluded the comrades in those countries are inactive or indifferent.

I have just finished an eight months' propaganda tour in America, having delivered 210 lectures, visited 60 cities, and addressed from 50,000 to 60,000 people, and a four months' tour in England and Scotland, which, although not as successful as the former, yet enables me to give you the assurance that the comrades, at least the English speaking of America and England, are heart and soul with you in your undertaking for the coming congress, and that they will assist you both materially and morally. The reason why you have heard so little from them so far is due to the various difficulties we have to deal with in the United States and Great Britain.

I shall try to give you an idea of how we stand in both countries just now, so that you may better understand our hard struggle. To begin with America, let me say: I am quite sure that many of you know more or less about the movement, I mean the Anarchist movement of the American people, not the foreigners, (for although the Italian, Spanish, French, Bohemian and Jewish Anarchists are larger and stronger in numbers, yet they are of no importance inasmuch as we must have the Americans interested in our philosophy, if we wish to succeed in the establishment of a free society in the United States), still you only know about it through our papers, and because of that you may not be aware of the fact that the American movement is yet in its infancy, not older than five or six years. Up to that period the movement was in the hands of the foreign speaking element, who themselves were either mostly Revolutionists only, or Anarchists by name, and Social Democrats in their tendencies. Only since the first issue of the *Firebrand*,[1] in Oregon, seized by the authorities, and now published under the name of *Free Society*, in San Francisco,[2] have we begun to make headway among the American people.

---

1. The first issue of *Firebrand* appeared 27 January 1895, in Portland, Ore.
2. In September 1897, Abe Isaak, Henry Addis, and Abner J. Pope, editors of the Portland-based *Firebrand*, were arrested and charged under the Comstock Act with sending obscene literature through

The best proof of my statement you will find in the fact that American trades unions, social and literary clubs, ethical and philosophical societies, no longer look upon us as bomb-throwers, wild beasts, drunkards, or uncombed and unwashed tramps, (this idea having been manufactured by our enemies, and their tool, the daily press), but meet us friendly, invite our lecturers and listen with interest to the exposition of the philosophy of Anarchist-Communism.

However, the American Anarchists not being numerous, and living in the far west, such as Colorado, Texas, and California,[3] it will be extremely difficult for them to raise 1500 francs ($300) to send a delegate to the congress, (it may even cost more than 1500 francs). But we have not abandoned the idea of sending one yet. Comrade Peter Kropotkin has recently sent an article to *Free Society*,[4] explaining the importance of the congress (this being absolutely necessary, as some of the German Anarchists in America have opened a crusade against the sending of a delegate, and have denounced the congress as parliamentarian),[5] and I shall soon have an article in the same journal proposing some of our ablest comrades as delegates,[6] at the same time opening up a subscription to raise the necessary sum, and with the assistance of the foreign speaking comrades, especially the Jewish Anarchists, who are the strongest and most active, we hope to send a delegate from America, if, however, we fail in our aim, we have decided to send reports about our propaganda, and the general outlook for our ideas at large. Comrade William Holmes,[7] James Morton,[8] Carl Nold,[9] and others, have begun to work out reports for California, Colorado, Texas, Missouri, Illinois, Michigan, Pennsylvania, New York, etc.

In England, the comrades have formed what is called a Congress Group, consisting of members of Freedom Group, including Comrade Kropotkin, Tscherkesoff,[10] Tschai-

---

the mails; the paper was banned. The materials deemed obscene included a Walt Whitman poem long available in *Leaves of Grass* and three articles on the subject of free love (for further details, see note 32 to "Letters from a Tour," Series in *Sturmvogel*, 15 December 1897, above). In November 1897, Isaak relocated to San Francisco and again began to publish his newspaper under the new name, *Free Society*, the first issue of which appeared on 14 November 1897.

3. EG most likely refers to anarchists William and Lizzie Holmes, who lived in Denver; Ross Winn, who lived in Texas; and James F. Morton, Jr. and the Isaaks, who were living in San Francisco.

4. See Peter Kropotkin, "The Revolutionary International Labor Congress," *Free Society*, 25 March 1900, p. 1.

5. EG refers to a series of remarks by Johann Most in *Freiheit*, criticizing congresses in general and the proposed anarchist congress in Paris in particular as a waste of time and resources. In a 21 April 1900 item in *Freiheit*, Most responds to EG's critique of his position with a personal attack on her political integrity. See note 3 in Letter to Max Nettlau, 15 May 1900, below.

6. The article, "Observations and Suggestions" (*Free Society*, 22 April 1900), appears immediately following.

7. William Holmes, previously of Chicago, was at this time living in Denver, Colorado.

8. James F. Morton, Jr. undertook a cross-country speaking tour from New York (where he had been based) to San Francisco during 1899–1900.

9. Carl Nold was, perhaps, writing the reports of Missouri, Michigan, and Pennsylvania, all places he had lived.

10. EG refers to Varlaam Cherkesov.

koffsky[11] and others. This group, with Comrade Charles, recently liberated from nine years hell in an English prison,[12] as secretary, is in communication with groups of a similar nature in Leeds, Glasgow, and other cities for the purpose of raising funds for the congress, and working out reports. Leeds has already raised 300 francs, and the group has prospects of raising more. In all, you may expect at least six delegates from England.

At present, the comrades in England must pay all their attention to getting up meetings, demonstrations, and manifestoes against the most cruel, brutal, inhuman, unjust and dastardly war, brought about by a gang of large thieves and money-mongers, and sanctioned by the insatiable monster—government, against a handful of brave, courageous farmers, who are fighting like lions for their independence and liberty. The first large protest meeting was held February 20, and I can assure you that a London meeting has not seen as much enthusiasm and honest indignation for a long time.[13]

As Anarchists it is our main aim to oppose and fight every form of injustice and oppression, and because of that, I hope you will join with me and the English comrades in the most vigorous protest against the cold blooded murder of the admirable Boer fighters by the English army, backed by robbers like Chamberlain, Cecil Rhodes, Milner, and other English capitalists who are anxious to get the gold mines in the Transvaal, over the bleeding and quivering bodies of the Boers and their families.

Down with all form of injustice; long live our love of independence and Anarchy!

Emma Goldman.

Free Society, 8 April 1900, p. 1. Reprinted in French, with the reports of other delegates, in *Les Temps Nouveaux* (Paris) *Supplément Littéraire,* 20 September 1900, pp. 189–90; and in German (translation by Hippolyte Havel) in supplement to *Neues Leben* (Berlin), 21 April 1900, pp. 67–68.

11. EG refers to Nikolai Chaikovsky.
12. Walsall anarchist Fred Charles, who was convicted and imprisoned on 4 April 1892, actually served seven and a half years of his ten-year sentence.
13. EG's address at this meeting was entitled "The Effect of War on the Workers" (see Transcript of Address in *Freedom,* 20 February 1900, above).

Observations and Suggestions.

DEAR COMRADES, FRIENDS AND SYMPATHIZERS OF *FREE SOCIETY*,—

Little has been heard of me in the columns of *Free Society,* and this may have led some of you to believe that I am inactive or out of the movement entirely; but I have been neither. True, I cannot boast of having been as active as I was during my tour through America, but I have done some propaganda after all, at the same time not leaving the progress of our American movement out of sight, especially devoting my attention to the health and growth of our brave little rebel, *Free Society.*

My tour has been reported in a previous number of *Free Society,*[1] so I will say little about it, only adding that while it did not turn out as successful as the one in the States, I do not think my trip fruitless.

I had occasion to join in a monster protest meeting against the brutal attempt of a few big thieves—Cecil Rhodes, Milner and Chamberlain—to rob the brave and marvelously courageous heroes of the Transvaal and the Free State of their independence and liberty.

Every Briton boasts of his freedom of speech, and in fact I myself with most radicals believed, up to my arrival in England, that freedom of speech was a reality in Britain. During my four months' touring in England and Scotland, however, I had ample opportunity to convince myself that freedom of speech is as much a farce there as elsewhere. The worst of it is that this sacred right is not suppressed by the government, like in our "blessed land," but by the people themselves. By the "people" I do not only mean the ignorant, whisky-saturated, patriotism-maddened workers, but also the mental wage slaves: clerks, bookkeepers, cashiers, typewriters, commercial travelers, and other flunkies to money and titles. We, too, have had to deal with a patriotic craze, but it was at least tinctured with humanitarian sentiments, and I cannot recollect one single instance of having been disturbed in any of my meetings against the Spanish-American war. The only disturbance came from the police and not the people; whereas in England, where patriotism in the present war is based upon nothing but commercialism, the brutality of the people is simply beyond any comprehension and rather discouraging. Yet the pleasure of an instructive association of comrades like Kropotkin, Tschaikoffsky, Tscherkesoff,[2] and others, together with the study of the lights and shadows of the English Anarchistic movement, overbalance the disagreeable features one meets with on a tour *hampered by obstacles of all kinds.*

---

1. See "The Propaganda and the Congress," Transcript of Address in *Free Society,* 8 April 1900, above.
2. Peter Kropotkin, Varlaam Cherkesov, and Nikolai Chaikovsky were all Russian exiles living in London.

Peter Kropotkin in 1890s. The Russian revolutionary, geographer, and principal theorist of anarchist communism was Goldman's ideological mentor and friend, in spite of their differing perspectives on personal relationships and sexuality. Their correspondence was launched in 1895. (Labadie Collection, University of Michigan)

I cannot close my short review of my tour without mentioning the kind and energetic assistance rendered me by comrades H. M. Kelly and A. Davies, both known to the comrades in America through *Solidarity, the Rebel, Free Society* and *Freedom.*[3] These two, themselves "foreigners" in England, like a faithful mate of a shipwrecked crew, are in a quiet and unassuming manner keeping the movement alive in London.[4]

It is a rather singular feature that both in England and America the energetic workers are foreigners, yet such is the case. Not that our ideas have failed to gain ground among the natives of either country, nay, on the contrary: the number of English Anarchists in London, for instance, is very large: but it seems the Anglo-Saxon character lacks that power of devotion and enthusiasm which forces one on and on, almost against oneself, to break the chains and to fearlessly climb over all obstacles; because of that one cannot but appreciate such workers as Kelly and Davies, and a few others, so much more.

Exceptional conditions produce exceptional characters, so I have not yet lost hopes that some day England and America may furnish us with a Kropotkin, Tschaikoffsky, Tscherkesoff, Perovskaya, Angelilio, Caserio[5] and other such wonderful men and women; indeed the beginning has been made in America by the appearance of a Parsons.[6]

The comrades in Paris and elsewhere are busily engaged in preparing for our congress; but why has so very little been heard from the comrades in America? Is it because the congress, when first proposed, was lightly treated by a few Anarchists, who either for personal reasons or because of lack of knowledge about the movement, have expressed themselves against the congress, and have denounced it as useless? If this be the case, I advise you to read Comrade Kropot-

3. *Solidarity, The Rebel, Free Society,* and *Freedom* were all English-language anarchist papers.
4. Both Harry Kelly and A. A. Davies (who was Irish) objected to EG's assertion that they alone were keeping alive the movement in London, noting that Thomas Cantwell, Ted Leggatt, Alfred Marsh, and David Nicoll, among others, were more deserving of such credit. See *Free Society,* 10 June 1900, p. 4; and 24 June 1900, p. 4.
5. EG refers to Sophia Perovskaya, Michele Angiolillo, and Sante Caserio.
6. EG refers to Albert Parsons, one of the Haymarket anarchists.

kin's article carefully, and I am sure any prejudices you may have hitherto entertained on the subject, will vanish.[7]

Of course, neither the organizers of the congress, Comrade Kropotkin, nor I believe that it will bring about a reconstruction in society, or a revolution in the methods of propaganda; but we do believe that there is not a better opportunity to let the world see that the Anarchists are very much alive, than the congress to be held during the Exhibition in Paris,[8] at a time when organized thieves, robbers, and legal and illegal prostitutes, will squander the sweat and blood-stained products of millions of workers. Or can you tell me of a more opportune occasion to send out a joint cry of protest against Church-sanctioned and State-legalized murder and exploitation? A protest against all forms of tyranny, not only in the ranks of the enemy, but even in those of so-called reformers, Socialists, nay, even Anarchists? I hardly think you can name one. And here I must not forget to mention the main object of importance of the congress, namely, that the last tie of relations between parliamentarian Socialism was broken at the congress in London in 1896,[9] and that from now on we must as much fight the narrowness, discipline and intolerance of parliamentarian Socialists as any other form of invasion and despotism, and show the workers that those who even without blushing rejoice over the success of one of their men as comrade of the murderer of 30,000 Communards,—Galliffet—have no claim to be the representatives of the workers' cause.[10]

It is an undisputable fact that our movement in America and Europe is not what it ought to and could be, but for the lack of co-operation and solidarity, and our enemies, including the leaders of the Socialist parties, have ever made use of this fact in attempting to show that "Anarchy is dead," and those Anarchists who are alive "work in obscurity." While they have willfully misrepresented us, it remains true that the majority of comrades in England, America and Germany seldom come to the front. I only refer you to a number of German groups, composed of Anarchists, wasting their time in singing and beer drinking, (I have no objection to either, if coupled with serious work), and discussing their next door neighbor; or some of our American parlor meetings, frequented by a number of middle-class people who have not the courage to be known as Anarchists;

7. In a letter to *Free Society*, Kropotkin called for anarchists everywhere to participate in the planned Paris congress, via printed essay if they could not attend in person. See "The Revolutionary International Labor Congress," *Free Society*, 25 March 1900, p. 1.

8. Announced in 1892, the Exposition Universelle, held in Paris between April and November 1900, was the largest of the world exhibitions to that time.

9. The London congress of the socialist Second International met 27 July through 3 August 1896. The anarchist delegates were expelled from the congress on 28 July. They then convened their own meeting that night. Delegates included Peter Kropotkin, Errico Malatesta, Pietro Gori, Louise Michel, Élisée Reclus, Jean Grave, Harry Kelly, and Charles Mowbray.

10. The "comrade" of General Gallifet was the socialist Etiennne-Alexandre Millerand (1859–1943), the first socialist to serve in French bourgeois government. He was minister of commerce from 1899 to 1902, under Rene Waldeck-Rousseau, and president of France from 1920 to 1924. EG also castigates Millerand in her 25 September report on the anarchist congress; see "The Paris Congress," To *Free Society*, 25 September 1900, below.

or some comrades who waste the precious space of our papers with the discussion of spooks and ghosts, Anarchist judges and jurors, or the consistency of prostituting oneself in politics,[11] which only tends to harm the movement instead of helping to lift the veil of ignorance from the eyes of the worker.

You may contend that we can protest against existing evils through our papers and public meetings; so we can, and do, but of what importance is it compared with an opportunity like that offered us in Paris? In the first place, our papers are read mostly by the comrades themselves, and our lectures reach only those who happen to attend meetings, the daily press either reporting nothing, or misrepresenting our speakers in the most shameless manner. I do not undervalue such methods of propaganda; yet I claim that by these methods we reach but the few and not the many, whereas bodies of men and women assembled in a congress have always been recognized by the press. It will be so with the coming Anarchist congress. The very fact that this is to be the first Anarchist congress since 1872;[12] that for the first time since then, men and women from different parts of the world bring tidings of international solidarity, deep love of liberty and hatred of tyranny, openly and fearlessly discuss the philosophy of Anarchy, and ways and means of a speedy spread of their ideas, and all this almost next door to the arena where international parasites celebrate one of their last orgies and dance a cancan upon the decayed pillars of a rotten society, would be of such grandeur, such importance that it could not pass unnoticed.

But there is still another reason why the comrades in America should take part in the congress. Since I have been in Europe, and especially in Paris, I have been dismayed to find how little is known of, or how little interest is shown here regarding the movement in America. This is due to the fact that very few French people know any language beside their own, and that very little is written about America in the French papers; unfortunately this is also the case in Italy, Austria, Germany and Holland. Now, in the face of the growth of imperialism, militarism and despotism, can we stand such lack of solidarity and unity? Can we hope to accomplish more in the future than we have in the past, unless we really become international, not only in theory, but also in practice? The congress is to serve as a medium of putting the comrades into communication with each other, and of suggesting ways and means of carrying on propaganda work co-operatively, and last but not least, to acquaint the comrades of all countries with the movements of each respective country.

The comrades in England and elsewhere have already formed groups for the purpose of raising funds to send delegates, and prepare reports and suggestions for the congress.

---

11. A reference to a debate sparked by an article by Henry Addis; see EG's letter to *Free Society* entitled "Ideas and Men," 10 July 1898, above.
12. After the schism between what the anarchists considered to be the authoritarians led by Karl Marx and the anarchists and mutualists grouped around Michael Bakunin in the Hague congress of the First International in 1872, the anarchist majority met at Saint-Imier to establish their own International. Comprising the majority of the rank-and-file membership of the First International, the Bakuninists of the Saint-Imier International considered theirs the true heir of the organization established in 1864. Besides the 1872 congress, a congress of the Anti-Authoritarian International took place 6–8 September 1877 in Verviers, Belgium, and an International Social Revolutionary Congress took place in London, 14–19 July 1881.

What are the comrades in America about? Surely they are not going to be silent and inactive in such a grave and important matter?

Permit me to make a few suggestions; first of all, a subscription should be opened to help make the congress a success, amounts temporarily to be sent to *Free Society*. I hereby contribute $5 to the same to make a start. With a little effort and the assistance of our Jewish comrades, we can raise enough to send an American delegate. The Bohemian and Italian comrades will also send delegates. We have a few able and competent Americans who could represent our cause, (I say cause and not comrades, because I wish to avoid misunderstanding). There is, for instance, Borland,[13] who has not been heard of much of late, yet who understands the movement and Anarchist-Communism thoroughly. There is Comrade Edelman, known as an able worker for years, who may be well enough to go to Paris.[14] There is Comrade Cooper,[15] certainly one of our most intellectual writers, and there is Voltairine de Cleyre, a fearless and brilliant exponent of Anarchism. Of course, Addis objects to her as a lecturer, claiming that she opposes Communism, yet that is a mistake; she does not oppose Communism "because she favors Individualism," but rather because she wants to be known as an Anarchist without a tag.[16] That ought not to influence any one. She may not be so well posted on Communism as Addis, but she has the advantage of having a clean past—I mean in regard to her devotion and faithfulness to the cause, and her hatred for politics and politicians. I venture to say that she would rather do scrubbing than make common cause with politicians, a quality which Addis seems to value very little. She may not know as much of economics as some of our other workers, but, as she says herself, she is all right in the philosophy of Anarchy, and certainly perfectly competent to represent the Anarchistic movement of America.

Of course I have suggested these comrades merely because I think them the fittest as delegates. I have done so without their consent, leaving it for you to ascertain whether they would like to accept a delegation or not, or to suggest others, if you know. At any rate, I hope the congress will be discussed and reports prepared. Should it be absolutely impossible to raise enough money to send a delegate, Comrade Kelly and myself will gladly submit any of your suggestions or wishes to the congress, but the groups should send us credentials for that purpose. I should like to recommend Harry Kelly to your attention as he is an American. I shall be there at all events. But I beg you to leave nothing undone to raise the necessary means for a delegate directly to be sent from America, as Harry Kelly has been away for two years.

Emma Goldman.

Free Society, 22 April 1900, pp. 1–3. The return address on EG's letter was "140 rue Mouffetard, care of *Les Temps Nouveau.*" The French anarchist communist paper was published from the attic of editor Jean Grave's apartment; Grave was dubbed the "pope of Mouffetard."

13. EG refers to American anarchist and trade unionist Wilfred P. Borland, who lectured frequently in Chicago.
14. John H. Edelmann died 12 July 1900.
15. EG refers to British-born anarchist Charles B. Cooper, who was an active lecturer in New York City.
16. Voltairine de Cleyre called herself an anarchist without a hyphen.

> **To *FREE SOCIETY***
>
> *Paris, 29 April 1900*

Some More Observations.

I welcome the readiness of our comrades to raise a fund for the purpose of importing a speaker from England, for it is a sign of revived energy, although I am convinced that naught will come of it. I need not assure the comrades that my whole heart is in the American movement and that I would give much to see it prosper, yet I must take issue with the proposed importation of a speaker from England; and this not because of a *lack* of international feeling, but because of a preponderance of it. For that reason I would not like the movement of one country to grow at the expense of another; and that would certainly be the case should you succeed in getting Comrade Turner over.[1] He is the only able speaker in England at the present time, and even he cannot do much straight Anarchist propaganda, because his whole time is taken up with the Trades-Union movement. Mark you, I do not undervalue the good he is doing in his present position, but I only wish to show that England is even more in need of speakers than America and that to take away John Turner would in my opinion be a very uncomradely act, to say the least. Besides, it is idle to talk about importing Comrade Turner: *he cannot nor will he go to America*, and if he ever does go, it will be in an independent way. This I can say with full authority. Since there are no other comrades in England capable of carrying on effective work in America (for we must not forget that to make a successful tour, one must not only be a good speaker, but also have a reputation as well, otherwise one may be an Antony and yet not draw a crowd in our "blessed land"), why not turn to domestic goods?

Comrade Morton is struggling hard to reach 'Frisco, and were it not for liberal assistance of a few individuals, and James' wonderful ability to feast on the "luxury" of a dish of Boston baked beans and two slices of bread a day, he might never have gotten as far as he did.[2] Were our comrades so eager to have paid speakers in the field, why did they not help him? There is Voltairine de Cleyre who was ready to make a tour last spring, urged

---

1. John Turner would not return to the United States until 1903. EG's opinion about Turner's prospective visit was published along with comments by others; the question of the effectiveness of propaganda tours by anarchists from outside the United States was debated for several months in *Free Society*.
2. James F. Morton, Jr.'s national speaking tour (1899–1900) concluded in San Francisco, where for a time he edited *Free Society*. Reports of his tour in *Free Society*, after little initial coverage, began appearing on 4 February. Morton's chronicle was serially published in 1900 from 25 March through 24 June.

by Comrades Nold and Burmin[3] who did their utmost to raise money for the purpose, and being unsuccessful in their efforts, the idea of her tour abandoned. Where were these comrades then? Comrade Southworth,[4] a newly acquired power in our movement, an intellectual, highly cultured and brilliant speaker, who told me he would start out on the route at once, if he could but have $6 per week. Why not invite him to tour? Are we Anarchists going to adopt the old and foolish notion that "prophets are seldom recognized in their own land," a notion that has driven many able men and women from the cradle of their birth to struggle and starve in the cold of strange lands, until they made a fame for themselves? Let me call your attention to Heine, Boerne,[5] and scores of others who hated their people because of the cruel indifference they met with from their side. Let us Anarchists not be guilty of gross neglect of those in our own midst, because we can only appreciate the talents of comrades in other countries when we have helped to develop the abilities of those in our own ranks. In fact, how can those who are so anxious to import a speaker, expect that one would trust their promises, seeing how little they have done in aid of those who are right at their next door.

As to the idea of employing a speaker and paying him a fixed salary, I think this a thing for each one to decide for himself. I for one would never consent to make a business of lecturing. It seems to me that the work of a true propagandist cannot be paid; that the very thought of being paid for what one says, must rob one of the enthusiasm and devotion for our cause. I claim that one can only give the best of one's self when actuated by love to the thing one gives, out of one's innermost desire to be useful, to oppose that which one considers wrong, and such a product of one's thoughts, nerves, blood, and the whole make-up, is above any remuneration. I am aware that a propagandist cannot live on ideals, yet if the comrades would only extend more of the precious articles, so rarely found, *hospitality* and *solidarity,* and through voluntary contributions pay railway fares, one could easily tour from five to six months in the year, and that is more than any one ought to do, if he really is desirous to serve the cause.

And then, too, no comrade with individuality and sensitiveness would consent to become a wage slave of one's own kind. It is bad enough to have the enemy as a boss, tyrant and dictator, but I shudder when I think of having comrades as such; and I am sorry to say that we have already too many among us who perform the job of bosses and invaders to perfection.

What has happened to my friend Willie Holmes? He of all the people in the world to advocate Anarchistic judges and lawyers,—he whose whole nature would shrink from

---

3. EG refers to Carl Nold and Nahum H. Berman.
4. Victor E. Southworth was an anarchist and poet based in Alcott, Colorado. A former Unitarian minister, he organized regular Sunday anarchist discussion groups in Alcott in 1899 and 1900, and frequently contributed to *Free Society.*
5. Heinrich Heine's (1797–1856) and Ludwig Boerne's (1786–1837) works were suppressed in Germany because of their political content. Little public support was offered to these writers when this happened.

the thought of being employed as such himself to go so far as to cite a case of a man re-maining an Anarchist, although he had become a proprietor of a house of prostitution![6] What is up? Has Willie's logic forsaken him? If, as an Anarchist, one may be a judge, ju-ror and lawyer, why not a policeman, sheriff, hangman, spy, prostitute, politician, in fact, anything? And if so, why combat the capitalist regime, why oppose Vanderbilt, Spreckles, Rockefeller, Cecil Rhodes?[7] What an absurd thing to say that if an Anarchist cannot con-sistently be a judge, he cannot be a wage slave! Holmes seems to forget that in one case no choice is left, in the other one can either remain true to himself or get a comfortable life at the expense of his fellow men and his real self, which is even worse.

I understand Anarchy to mean the negation of all forms of authority, invasion and robbery; an Anarchist, therefore, to be one who abhors all existing wrongs, because un-der no circumstances would he voluntarily consent to do the same. If I was mistaken, then I never knew the meaning of Anarchism. But I claim to understand Anarchy, and I am sure Holmes does, yet it seems his logic failed him and so leaped from the sublime to the ridiculous, which is but one step. Let us hope he will soon come back to the old heights. Really, I cannot understand the arguments of Holmes, unless he means the so-called Individualists when he speaks of Anarchist judges. If this is the case, I fully agree with him. Since they believe in private property, they must also believe in a force to pro-tect their property; thus they are perfectly justified in becoming judges, lawyers and po-licemen. And outside of their opposition to compulsion, it must be borne in mind that the Individualists believe in a voluntary police. (Who laughs??) I for one could never see the logic of their claim to the term "Anarchists." I mean from a theoretical standpoint; for their practices differ as much from their theory as a blizzard from a warm summer breeze. Their actions are humane, warm-blooded, kind, noble, very sympathetic and con-

6. William T. Holmes, himself a lawyer, had asserted: "Why a person cannot be a good Anarchist be-cause he practices law is beyond my comprehension" (*Free Society*, 14 January 1900, p. 3), sparking a debate in the pages of *Free Society* on tactics and doctrinal "consistency" that lasted half a year, and in which Abe Isaak, Henry Addis, Kate Austin, Lucy Parsons, and Philadelphia anarchist Susan Patton (ca. 1866–1901; she corresponded with AB while he was in prison), in addition to EG and others, par-ticipated. EG's reference to an anarchist brothel-keeper was rooted in Holmes's claim to have known an Illinois anarchist "who afterward went to Wisconsin and became the keeper of a public house of prostitution, and I never heard that he was any the less an Anarchist for doing so" (*Free Society*, 25 Feb-ruary 1900, p. 2). Complaining that "every criticism of my position has been dictated by prejudice," Holmes attempted to end the discussion in the 10 June number, claiming that no argument had been advanced "to show why a lawyer cannot be a good Anarchist or why a good Anarchist cannot be a lawyer or serve on a jury, or why certain tactics . . . are not proper to use under special conditions"; adding that the "ability to make rabid speeches, in which wholesale denunciation plays the chief part, is no longer the test of devotion to Anarchism" (*Free Society*, 10 June 1900, p. 3).

7. EG refers to the American industrialists Cornelius Vanderbilt, John D. Rockefeller, and Claus Spreck-les. Spreckles (1828–1908) was a California sugar magnate and railroad operator, who emigrated to the United States from Germany in 1848 and made his fortune in the sugar business by building lu-crative trade alliances in Hawaii. In 1907, Spreckles began construction on the San Diego and Ari-zona Railroad to facilitate cheap distribution of his products.

siderate; but no sooner do they leave the realm of life and wander into their theory than they become cold, calculating, bloodless, mere automatic machines. Such beings can be "Anarchistic judges," or anything you please, but never one whose heart throbs for mankind, and who is so full of the sentiment of solidarity that the very idea of pain or sorrow reflects upon his whole being.

EMMA GOLDMAN.

Free Society, 29 April 1900, p. 1.

LIEBER NETLAU

Wollte Ihnen schon längst schreiben, aber kam nicht dazu, dafür habe ich oft an Sie gedacht, hauptsächlich als ich durch den Louvre ging u schrecklich viel Zeit verlor, weil mir ein solch guter Führer wie sie fehlte. Nein, Paris hat mich nicht absorbiert, obgleich das Leben hier sehr flott ist und einem keine Zeit läßt sich mit der Vergangenheit oder Zukunft zu beschäftigen. Leider bin ich zu deutsch, um von einem Pariser Leben verschlungen zu werden oder gar dadurch meine alten Freunde u Genossen zu vergessen. Ich sage leider, denn glücklich sind sie doch, die Pariser Kinder, die leicht u oberflächlich das Leben genießen, während solche Menschen, die über Alles grübeln logisch sein wollen, die, die Vergangenheit nicht vergessen können u sich mit Problemen der Zukunft befassen, am Leben vorbeigehen oder für das Vergnügen teuer bezahlen müssen.

Ich habe Gesellschaft aus America bekommen, bin somit nicht mehr so isoliert wie früher, französische Genossen kenne ich wenige, u habe auch kein Bedürfnis sie zu kennen, da sie mir mit wenigen Ausnahmen sehr oberflächlich scheinen. Die glücklichsten Momente in Paris habe in Gesellschaft Daves verlebt. Welch ein herrlicher Mensch, so kindlich gut so teilnahmsvoll vielseitig u dieser Mann wurde so furchtbar verleumdet? Es ist einfach gräßlich ~~wen~~ daß gerade die besten Menschen, verleumdet u bekämpft werden. Ich habe hier weder Bücher noch Zeitschriften gekauft einfach weil ich kein Geld habe. Meine Luftschlösser mit Schriftstellern etwas verdienen zu können sind zerfallen. Die hiesigen Blätter nehmen von Fremden keine Artikel an, u die Amerikanischen haben ihre eigenen Verträter in Paris. Somit blieb mir kein anderer Weg, als mich mit Stunden-Geben zu beschäftigen, u wenn ich Ihnen sage, daß jeder zweite Student in P. Stunden giebt, so können Sie sich vorstellen, wie glänzend mein Einkommen ist. Jedoch würde ich noch mit Wenigerem eher zufrieden sein als irgend einer der Genossen in Anspruch nehmen. Ach, diese Genossen nur graut vor ihnen: Solidarität, Freiheit, Gegenseitigkeit, Moralische-Verantwortung, alles sehr schön in Theorie, aber weh wenn man im praktischen Leben davon abhängig wäre. Unter Kirchenanfänger, oder den unwissendsten Bauern herrscht mehr menschliches Empfinden, als unter den Genossen, ganz gleich, ob sie Franzosen oder weiß ich was waren. Jedoch glaube ich, daß gerade die Franzosen am allerwenigsten Begriff von Solidarität oder Genossenschafts-Gefühl haben, noch nirgends habe ich solch eine Oberflächlichkeit u Gleichgültigkeit gefunden, als gerade hier, es ist einfach schrecklich—Wie gesagt, ich habe außer Dave keinen einzigen Genossen getroffen, der auch nur einen Funken von Menschlichkeit hätte.

Ja, ich habe viel mit Dave über längst Vergangene Zeiten gesprochen, vergangene Zeiten? Als wenn sie jetzt nicht ebenso wären; der Süffel-Hannes schimpft immer weiter, nennt mich eine politische Hochstaplerin u noch andere schöne Namen, u hat es soweit gebracht, daß die deutsch-sozialdemokratische Presse in America über mich hergefallen sind, wie die wilden Hunde. Ein wahres Glück, daß ich nicht eingebildet bin, hätte sonst mit Recht annehmen können daß ich viel wert bin, sonst würden sich die Wolfe nicht so um mich reißen. Na, ich sende Ihnen nächstens einige Ausschnitte aus der "F." u verschiedenen sozialistischen Zeitungen, die man mir neulich aus America zugeschickt hat.

Der Congress findet in der ersten Hälfte des Sep. statt, wenn Sie ohnedies nach P. kommen wollen, kommen Sie doch recht bald, erstlich möchte ich Sie schon gerne wiedersehen, u dann würde mir Ihre Anwesenheit Gelegenheit geben Französisch zu sprechen, was ich jetzt leider nicht kann, da ich mit äußerst wenig Franzosen verkehre. Ob ich überhaupt nach die Schweiz komme ist jetzt sehr fraglich. Studieren werde ich in Europa nicht u nur zur Erholung oder zum Vergnügen hinzureisen fehlen mir leider die Mittel.

Der junge Czeche von dem Ihnen D schrieb ist Havel, derselbe der Ihnen Ihren Artikel im S. nicht verzeihen konnte. Es ging ihm furchtbar schlecht in London u da er noch dazu eine schrecklich traurige Vergangenheit hat, so ersuchte ich ihn mit nach Paris zu kommen, leider hat sich seine Lage nur in so fern verbessert, als das Hungern zu zweit, leichter ist, als wenn man es allein besorgen muß——

Er wird die böhmischen Genossen von America zum Congress verträten, hat auch schon das Mandat. Grave ist schon hier, habe ihn nur einmal flüchtig gesehen. Es ist jetzt wunderschön hier, die Sonne spendet ihre Wärme allen gleich, u doch können viele sich nicht erwärmen. Warum? Ja wer das ergründen könnte.

Frau Ruedebusch, die Frau des Verfassers vom Old & New Ideal!! ist jetzt hier u die auch schon fröhlicher scheinen.

Herzlichen Gruß
E.G.

DEAR NETLAU

Wanted to write you for a long time but didn't come to it, so I have been thinking about you a lot, especially as I was going through the Louvre and lost a terribly great amount of time because I was missing a guide as good as you. No, Paris has not absorbed me although life here is very gay and doesn't leave one any time to concern oneself with the past or the future. Unfortunately I am too German to be consumed by a Parisian life or forget my old friends and comrades. I say unfortunately, for happy are they indeed, the Parisian children, who enjoy life in an easy and superficial way, while such people who can't forget the past and concern themselves with the problems of the future pass life by or must pay dearly for pleasure.

I received visitors from America,[1] and am therefore no longer as isolated as before, I know few French comrades and have no desire to know them since to me they seem, with few exceptions, very superficial. My happiest moments in Paris have been spent in the company of Dave. What a wonderful person, of such childlike goodness and solicitous versatility, and this man has been so horribly slandered?[2] It is simply disgusting that the best people are always the ones being slandered and attacked. I have bought neither books nor journals simply because I have no money. My castle in the air, being able to earn money by writing, has disintegrated. The local papers don't accept articles by foreigners, and the Americans have their own representatives in Paris. Thus I was left with no other choice than to devote myself to tutoring, and when I tell you that every other student in P. gives lessons, you can imagine how splendid my income is. However I would sooner be satisfied with less than demand anything of one of the comrades. Oh, I shudder at these comrades: solidarity, freedom, mutual aid, moral responsibility, all very nice in theory, but woe to anyone who would be dependent on those things in practical life. More human feeling exists among church novices or the most ignorant farmer than among the comrades, regardless of whether they are French or whatever else. However I believe that it is really the French who have the least idea of solidarity or sense of camaraderie, nowhere else have I come across such superficiality and indifference as right here, it is simply horrible—As I said, except for Dave I have met not one comrade who possesses even a spark of humanity.

Yes, I have spoken a lot with Dave over times long past, times past? As if the times were any different now; the tippler Hannes continues to be abusive, calling me a politi-

---

1. EG refers to German-born sex reformer Emil Ruedebusch and his wife, Julie, who lived in Mayville, Wisconsin.
2. EG met Victor Dave, anarchist and close associate of Johann Most, in Paris. For further discussion of Dave and his affairs, see Augustin Hamon to EG, 27 November 1901, *EGP*, reel 1.

cal swindler[3] and other beautiful names, and has taken things so far that the German social democratic press in America has fallen on me like wild dogs. It is truly fortunate that I am not educated, as in that case I could rightly assume that I am worth a lot, for otherwise the wolves would not be scrambling for me so much. Well, I will soon send you a few clippings from the *F*[4] and various socialist newspapers that were sent to me from America.

The congress takes place in the first half of Sep., if you want to come to P. in any case you should indeed come very soon, firstly I would very much like to see you again, and then your presence would give me the opportunity to speak French, which I unfortunately can't do now as I associate with very few Frenchmen. Whether I will come to Switzerland at all is now very questionable. I will not study in Europe and I unfortunately don't have the means to travel there simply for relaxation or pleasure.[5]

The young Czech about whom D wrote you is Havel, the same man who could not forgive you for your article in *S*.[6] He was doing terribly badly in London and, as he also has a terribly sad past, I entreated him to come to Paris with me, unfortunately his situation has improved only insofar as having to go without food with someone else is easier than having to care for oneself all alone——

He will represent the Bohemian comrades from America at the congress, he already has a mandate. Grave[7] is here already, saw him fleetingly only once. It is beautiful here now, the sun bestows its warmth equally to all, and yet many can't warm themselves. Why? Indeed who could get to the bottom of that. Frau Ruedebusch, the wife of the author of the *Old & New Ideal*!! is here now, and they already seem happier as well.[8]

VERY SINCERELY YOURS,

E.G.

ALI, Max Nettlau Archive, IISH. Translated from German.

3. Johann Most, nicknamed "Pope Hannes," had announced his opposition to sending an American delegate to the proposed anarchist congress in Paris, in a series of remarks in *Freiheit* criticizing such congresses. In a short notice in the "Letter Box" column in *Freiheit*, Most continues his personal attack on EG: "For the time being we protest here against the fact that you take as the truth the misrepresentation of the anarchist movement of America by a political imposter and circulate it further. By letter we will inform you further about the swindle" (*Freiheit*, 21 April 1900, in German Police File, *EGP*, reel 67).
4. EG refers to the journal *Freiheit*.
5. EG had originally planned to study medicine in Europe.
6. EG abbreviates Victor Dave's name as "D" and the journal *Der Sozialist* as "S"; Hippolyte Havel is the Czech anarchist who met EG in London in 1899 and accompanied EG to Paris. Nettlau had published an article in an 1897 issue of *Der Sozialist* attacking Count Badeni and the role played by minorities (including Czechs) in Austro-Hungarian politics.
7. EG refers to Jean Grave, French anarchist and editor of *La Révolte* until the government shut it down in 1894; after his release from prison a year later, Grave resumed the publication with a new title, *Les Temps Nouveaux*.
8. Julie Ruedebusch (neé Shernberger) was a German American daughter of a German "48er" who emigrated to Wisconsin after the failed revolution of 1848. Her husband, Emil Ruedebusch, was the author of *The Old and New Ideal*, a defense of sexual varietism, which was published in both German and English versions in 1895 and 1896; two thousand copies were sold before a Wisconsin court banned the book in 1898.

In keeping with my report dated May 18, which indicated that the anarchist <u>Goldman</u> Emma dwelled, under the name <u>Brady</u>[1] and with her lover Havel,[2] in the furnished accommodation located 50 Avenue des Gobelins, I have ordered an investigation about the above named.

The named Goldman (a.k.a. Brady) resides at this address since March 2 of this year, with a monthly rent of Fr. 25.

She lives alone in her room, although she has relations with the named Havel whom she presented as one of her relatives when she rented.

She is seen as very intelligent.

She entertains a friendship with a Protestant minister from the rue des Sts-Pères, and receives quite a few visitors during the day, notably foreigners.

She gets much foreign mail, some letters being registered.

She usually goes out around 6:00 p.m.

Her landlord does not have the knowledge that she is involved in anarchist propaganda, however he believes she has very progressive ideas, because she very much reveres Karl Marx.

She attends the meetings accompanied by the named Havel and the named Ruedebusch,[3] who is the subject of a special report.

On May 17 of this year, she gave a lecture at the libertarian library, 26 rue Titon, where I had her followed.

On May 19, she gave another lecture at the Harmonie Hall, 94 rue d'Angoulême, about woman's emancipation.

Herewith enclosed is the notification for this latter meeting, printed in German, with its translation.

The named Havel John, 29 years old, is not employed; he seems to live at the expense of his mistress.

The landlord, who seems very well disposed toward the Authorities, gave the enclosed list of the newspapers received by the above named as well as the notification to attend the meeting rue d'Angoulême.

1. EG was traveling under the name of her former companion, anarchist Edward Brady.
2. The document later refers to Hippolyte Havel as "Havel John."
3. Most likely this is Julie Ruedebusch, since the French adjective is in the feminine form. She and her husband had recently arrived in Paris.

In summary, the named Goldman seems to be dangerous as far as theoretical propaganda is concerned.

The Chief of Police,

E. André.

ADS, Dossier Emma Goldmann, Numéro 124786, Cote B/A 305, Archives de la Préfecture de Police, Paris. The address line on this report read "From the Police Chief, 3rd Brigade, to the Chief Executive Officer of Investigations." Translated from French.

L<small>IEBER</small> N<small>ETLAU</small>.

Ihr Schreiben habe ich natürlich erhalten, u wenn ich bis jetzt nicht geantwortet habe, so ist es, weil ich nichts vom Interesse mitzutheilen hatte. Nicht daß ich in Paris, nicht schon viel erlebt hätte, aber da meine Erlebnisse, in traurigen Erfahrungen über den Kampf ums Dasein u sonstigen persönlichen Widerwärtigkeiten waren, so wollte ich Sie nicht damit belästigen, u Dinge von allgemeinem Interesse habe ich leider nicht erlebt. Sie sind doch ein glücklicher Mensch mit Ihrer Fähigkeit sich in eine Arbeit vertiefen zu können, wie die, die Sie jetzt in Händen haben, dazu gehört eine Ausdauer u Zähigkeit deren ich mich leider nicht rühmen kann. Ich bin viel zu viel Zigeunerin um überhaupt, etwas, was der Geduld bedarf, ausführen zu können, wenn ich es doch fertig bringe, so geschieht es nur weil ich mich zwinge, gehe aber dabei innerlich zu Grunde wie alles, was sich nicht frei u ungezwungen gestalten kann. Das Nachforschen, woher auf einmal all die grünen Blätter kommen, ist freilich eine angenehmere Beschäftigung, als 347 Seiten zu schreiben, das würde auch meinem unruhigen Geist entsprechen, leider konnte ich so etwa nie thun, weil ich in den Großstadt leben, u das zum Leben Notwendige verdienen mußte.—Ich kann mir schon denken, daß das Material über Bakunins Wirken u Schaffen, noch lange nicht zu Ende ist, giebt es doch Wenige, die ein solch reiches Leben geführt, so unendlich viel geleistet haben für das allgemeine Wohl u dabei in so ganz eigener individueller Art. Ich bin kein neidische Natur, aber ein bißchen beneide ich Sie doch, um die vielen Reisen, die die Sammlung von Material über B.s Leben, mit sich brachten, hauptsächlich aber weil Sie vielleicht nach Rußland kommen werden, wohin ich so gerne wieder hin möchte, aber nicht kann. Sie sagen Sie wären zu schwach, um am Umsturz der Gegenwarth zu helfen; das ist doch aber nicht ganz wahr; d. h. wenn wir annehmen, daß nur die am Umsturz der Gegenwarth helfen, die Reden halten, dann dürfen Sie ja vielleicht Recht haben, aber ich finde, daß gerade durch das Reden leistet man am allerwenigsten, u diese Thatsache ist es auch, die mich so furchtbar elend macht, fühle ich doch, daß ich mit meiner Agitation in 14 Jahren wenig geleistet habe, u jetzt noch viel weniger leiste, denn durch Vorträge ist noch kein Mensch Anarchist oder Revolutionär geworden, während das durch literarisches Werken schon eher der Fall ist, u im Letzteren gerade, habe Sie doch gewiß viel gethan. Auch ich habe gefunden, daß jeder Mensch von Natur aus Communist ist, das Traurige aber ist, daß die Natur des Menschen verkrüppelt wird, ehe sie überhaupt zur Geltung kommt, daher kommt es auch, daß viele den Communismus verstehen, aber viel zu wenig innere Größe haben, um ihn auszuüben. Und, wenn die, die denselben verstehen, ihn nicht üben, wie sollten, diejenigen die ihn nicht verstehen jemals überzeugt werden, daß der Communismus realisierbar ist?—

Daß ich im Louvre an Sie gedacht habe, wenn auch an der langweiligsten Stelle, wie Sie sagen, dürfte Ihnen nur als Beweis dienen, daß ich Ihre Führerfähigkeiten sehr schätze, denn [wären?] Sie mit mir, dann wäre es im Louvre überhaupt gar nicht langweilig. Ich bin auch seitdem nicht mehr im Louvre gewesen, den im Palais de beaux Arts auf der Ausstellung, giebt es so unendlich viel Schönes u Herrliches, u da dann ich auch ohne Führer auskommen. Zwar sind die Gemälde u Statuen im Palais de beaux Arts moderne Leistungen, aber umso werthvoller für mich, denn ich habe für das Dagewesene wenig Sinn. Ich will das Leben, das Reale, u nicht, das was einst war. Das kleine Venus-Zimmer ist entschieden großartig, aber wenn ich die Venus betrachte u an meine armen [ver]krüppelten Schwestern [denke] dann wird mir das kleine Zimmer zu klein, ich [muß] dann in die frische Luft [hinaus] u wieder etwas athmen können. Daß ich unter den Genossen in Paris nicht die Richtigen getroffen habe, [kann] ja sein, u ich würde micht gewiß freuen, wenn dem so wäre, aber wo sind die Richtigen zu treffen? Sie nennen Gerineau, das ist aber gerade einer von denen, die sich mir gegenüber sehr unsolidarisch benommen haben. Ich kann Ihnen die Geschichte hier nicht auseinandersetzen, aber ich bin überzeugt, daß Sie mir beipflichten würden, wenn Sie wüßten wie sich Gerineau benommen hat: Grave, habe ich nur einmal gesehen, aber er ist krank u viel beschäftigt u ich liebe es nicht zu stören. Ich bin sicher, daß die Bewegung in Paris einstens groß war u vielleicht auch später [groß] sein wird aber jedenfalls nur quantitative, niemals qualitative, denn ich kann mir nicht denken, daß die Franzosen tief empfinden, oder sich in etwas vertiefen können sie sind zu oberflächlich und zu genußsüchtig. Die Genossen die ich getroffen habe sind für mich ein Greuel weil sie gräßliche Fanatiker sind und darum engherzig, intollerant u blind in ihrem Urtheil, dazu sind sie furchtbar vulgär, ich meine weniger moralisch, als aestetisch, u was am Schlimmsten ist, sie haben auch kein Fünkschen von Menschlichkeit, u vermuthen in jeden einen Spitzel, von dem man sich fern halten muß. Unter diesen Umständen, werden Sie begreifen, wie einsam ich mich hier fühlen muß, u [w]as das für eine active Natur wie die Meinige bedeutet. Ich habe es zwar versucht [hier] unter den jüdischen Arbeit zu agitieren, aber erstlich ist das Material sehr [arm]selig, weil die Juden für nicht anderem als den Zionismus zu haben sind, u dann ließ man mir sagen, daß ich mich ruhig verhalten muß sonst werde ich ausgewiesen. Da es nun definitiv ist, daß kein Delegat von America zum Congress kommt so ist es für mich wichtig hier bleiben zu können, u darum [. . . .]

DEAR NETLAU.

I received your letter of course, and if I haven't responded until now it is only because I had nothing interesting to report. Not that I haven't had many experiences in Paris already, but I didn't want to burden you since my experiences had to do with the sad realities of the struggle for existence and other personal troubles, and I have unfortunately not experienced anything of general interest. You are certainly a lucky man with your ability to become absorbed in work such as that which you currently have in your hands; that requires a level of perseverance and tenacity of which I unfortunately cannot boast. I am much too much of a gypsy to carry out anything that requires patience; even when I do complete something it is only because I force myself, yet as a consequence I collapse internally as does everything that was not formed freely and without pressure. The hunting around for what suddenly all the green leaves grow from is most certainly a more pleasant activity than writing 347 pages; that would also suit my restless spirit, yet I could never do anything like it because I live in the big city and must earn what is necessary to survive.—I can certainly imagine that the material about Bakunin's[1] life and work still has a long way to go; there are few people who have led such a rich life and have contributed so unendingly to the general good in such a unique, individual manner. I do not have a jealous nature, yet in a small way I do envy your many trips connected to collecting material about B's life, mainly because you might go to Russia, where I would so much like to go but can't. You say you would be too weak to help with the overthrow of the status quo; yet that indeed is not entirely true; that is, if we assume that only those who give speeches are contributing to the overthrow of the status quo, then perhaps you would be correct. But I think that speeches are actually the least effective route, and the fact is, much as it makes me so completely miserable, I feel as if I have contributed very little with my fourteen years of agitating thus far, and currently am contributing even less, as not one person has become an Anarchist or a revolutionary through lectures, while such is more likely to be the case through literary works, and in the latter you have certainly accomplished a great deal. I have found that every person is a communist by nature; the sad thing is, however, that the nature of man is stunted before it ever can be expressed. Thus it is the case that many understand communism, yet far too few have the inner greatness to practice it. And, if those who understand it do not practice it, how should those who don't understand it ever be convinced that communism is attainable?—

---

1. Nettlau was working on a biography of Michael Bakunin. Between 1896 and 1900 he produced by hand 50 copies of this huge work.

The fact that I thought of you in the Louvre, albeit in the most boring place, as you say, should only serve as proof that I treasure your abilities as a guide, for if you [had been] with me, it wouldn't have been boring at all in the Louvre. Since then I have not been back to the Louvre because in the exhibit in the Palais des Beaux Arts[2] there is an endless amount of beautiful and glorious works, and I can manage there without a guide. Indeed the paintings and statues in the Palais des Beaux Arts are modern creations, but this is all the more valuable to me as I have little interest in things of the past. I want life, the real, and not what once was. The little Venus room is certainly wonderful, but as I looked upon the Venus and thought of my poor crippled sisters the small room became too small, and I had to go out into the fresh air in order to catch my breath. It could well be that I have not met the right people among the comrades in Paris, and I would certainly be glad if that were the case, yet where does one run into the right people? You mention Gerineau,[3] but he is precisely one of those who have demonstrated a lack of solidarity toward me. I can't get into that story here, but I am convinced that you would agree with me if you knew how Gerineau behaved. I have only seen Grave[4] once, but he is sick and very busy and I don't want to disturb him. I am sure that the movement in Paris was once very big and perhaps will be big in the future, but only in a quantitative, never in a qualitative sense. I can't imagine that the French could ever feel deeply or become absorbed in something, they are too superficial and pleasure-seeking. The comrades I have met have been for me an abomination, as they are disgusting fanatics and therefore petty, intolerant, and blind in their judgments. In addition they are horribly vulgar, not so much in a moral as in an aesthetic sense, and worst of all they possess not an ounce of humanity and consider everyone to be a spy from whom they must keep their distance. Under these circumstances you should understand how lonely I must feel here, and what that means for such an active nature as mine. Indeed I have tried to agitate among the Jews here, but first of all the material is extremely paltry since the Jews have no time for anything other than Zionism, and then I've been told that I have to keep quiet or otherwise I would be deported.[5] Since it is now certain that no other delegate from America is coming to the congress, it is important for me to be able to stay here, and therefore [. . . .]

ALf, Max Nettlau Archive, IISH. Translated from German.

2. The Grand Palais, designed by affiliates of the École des Beaux-Arts, was a major and lasting architectural contribution of the 1900 Paris Exposition Universelle. It housed a retrospective of nineteenth-century French paintings, and an almost equally conservative international exhibition of fin-de-siècle art that excluded impressionist and postimpressionist works, but did incorporate foreign entries by Gustav Klimt and James Ensor, among other modernists.
3. EG refers to Lucien Guérineau, who she may also mention in a previous letter to Nettlau (see note 3, Letter to Max Nettlau, 24 January 1900, above).
4. EG refers to Jean Grave, editor of *Les Temps Nouveaux*.
5. The French Interior Ministry ordered EG's expulsion in March 1901, four months after her departure. See Extradition Order from the French Government, 26 March 1901, below.

Yours of the 2 & 14th inst to hand, thanks for your readyness offer of your quaters. The date you gave me July 20th until August 10th would suit me nicely were I to know difinitely whether I am going at all, and this I can not possibly tell until I receive the news, I am waiting for. All I know at present is, that the party I <u>must</u> and will have to meet is expected in Munich either the latter part of this, or the begining of next month,[1] and as soon, as that party arrives I will be notyfied by wire and leave on the same day. It is only because of this that I intend to go to M at all, other wise, I could not do it owing to my limitted means. I do not wish to inconvience you in the least and I beg of you to dispose of your time and arrange your plans to suit yourself. When I know difinitely if you can expect me I will write, and should my coming give you any trouble I will stop at a cheep Hotel. I know from my own experience, the trouble of having a house and furniture on one s back and I therefore rejoice with you, that you are soon to be a free man. Next to freeing ones self from a the burden of a husband or wife, this is really the hardest.[2] Why do you hate ~~the~~ russian writing, is it because you do not know the language, as well as other languages or because B[3] had a poor handwriting. Now, I do not know of another language I like so well, as the russian, as for diciphern handwritings, I have to admit, that I am no good at all. For instance, I have great difficulty to get through with your letters,[4] although I think, that yours is really not a difficult one.

Die Ausstellung wird im Ock jedenfals noch offen sein, bestimmt weiß ich es freilich nicht, aber wollen Sie es doch nicht noch möglich machen bis zum 19ten Sep. (anfang des Congresses) hier zu sein? Ich sehe erst, daß ich angefangen habe Deutsch zu schreiben (das kommt aber daran, wen man während des Schreiben, an Kartoffel-

---

1. EG is referring to AB, who, in 1899, planned an escape via a tunnel dug under the prison wall. With funds raised by an advertisement calling for financial support for new legal moves on AB's behalf, in *Freie Arbeiter Stimme* and other papers, work began in the fall from a rented house opposite the Western Penitentiary and was directed by AB's former prison mate, a German anarchist, identified only as "Tony" in AB's *Prison Memoirs,* who communicated with AB through smuggled notes written in code. Norwegian-born anarchist Eric B. Morton, code-named "Ibsen," dug the tunnel with the help of another anarchist code-named "Yankee," and Chicago anarchist Vella Kinsella, who sang and played the piano to cover the noise of the digging. As the digging proceeded, EG toured Europe, planning to meet AB in Munich as soon as he was free. The tunnel was discovered on 26 July 1900. Prison officials suspected AB and placed him in solitary confinement. Both he and EG later blamed the plan's failure on Tony's stubborn refusal to heed AB's instructions about the tunnel's direction. See *Prison Memoirs of an Anarchist,* pp. 355–62.
2. Nettlau inserted three question marks at this point.
3. EG refers to Michael Bakunin, the subject of Nettlau's voluminous biography.
4. Above this line Nettlau wrote: "& I with yours."

Fliesen denkt, die ich heute noch braten u essen will, 2 Freunde sind gerade daran die Kartoffel zu schählen u reiben, verzeihen Sie die Prose).[5] Firstly, because it is really of the greatest importance to have as many people as possible, participate in the Congress. Secondly, you can be of great service, because of the number of languge you know, and thirdly, ~~you~~ I will not be able to see you in Oct, and unless I should go to M, will have to leave Europe without seeing you again, which I should not like at all.

The art exhibits, at the exhibition is gloreous, I greater and finer collection never was placed in one house. I too like some of the old painters, but the modern school represented at the Exhibition appeals to me more, because it represents life in every phase. So you too are getting pessimistic with our inner circle, I am glad to hear it, as sad as it is, at least, I am not the only one, who has lost faith[6] in our so called Com. Yes, men like B, are born but once in a century, and such women, maybe never yet the~~i~~re is no hope for the future, unless such men will turn up. I had again an opportunity to see, how insignificant we are, at the Fete Nationale and the military display; how can we ever hope to accomplish anything, with such a drilled disciplinised mack of soldiers and with a hand full of confused, disharmonious set, who take big mouth, but lack of the necessary intergrety for action? Nothing at all; I feel very, very dispondent, more so, since I have lived on European grounds.

Au revoir—

I will write again, ~~when~~ as soon as I know when you may expect me.

E.G.

ALI, Max Nettlau Archive, IISH. Accompanying envelope addressed to Vienna.

5. EG switches to German, which may be translated as follows: "The exhibition will in any case still be open in Oct, of course I don't know that for certain, but would it be possible for you to be here by the 19th of Sep. (beginning of the Congress)? I see only now that I have begun to write in German (this happens when, while writing, one is thinking of potatoes which I want to bake and eat today, 2 friends are at this moment at work peeling and grating the potatoes, excuse the prose)."
6. Nettlau bracketed "lost faith" with several question marks.

To *FREE SOCIETY*

Paris, 25 September 1900

The Paris Congress.

COMRADES AND FRIENDS:—

The greatest enemies of improvement and progress will agree with me that the modern means of communication have done the world a lot of good; of course we must also take into the bargain the evil that some improvements carry with them. This is especially true of the cable system, which carries news as quick as lightning from one part of the globe to the other. It was already on the 19th inst. that the comrades of America were startled by the news of the suppression of our Congress;[1] and only weeks later will they find out how and by whom it was done, as well as all other details. However, I hardly think that the suppression was much of a surprise to many people; rather would it have been surprising, if our Congress were not interfered with. A German proverb says: "It is unwise to mention rope in the home of one just hanged." So we may well say about all in any way connected with the system of robbery and despotism. Just mention the word Anarchy; and terror seizes everyone, from the throne to the commonest policeman, from the multimillionaire down to the lowest shopkeeper living on the sweat of the people. Is it because they really think that every Anarchist is a bombthrower, or necessarily carries a dagger in his belt? Oh, no, they know better; they know too well that the majority of Anarchists by temperament detest bloodshed in every form. The real reason for the dread of all organized tyranny toward Anarchy, lies in the fact that Anarchism undermines the system of power maintained by each and every means, no matter at what cost; and therefore it must not be allowed to spread. "What fools these mortals be!" Here the champions of authority go on suppressing the growth of Anarchy, persecuting Anarchists, and in all their glorious idiocy failing to see that thereby they are doing more to provoke interest in the ideas they are so anxious to kill, than the ablest man in our movement.

That an Anarchist Congress was called at all, is really due to our naivete, to our childlike belief that some governments are better than others; that if our gatherings are suppressed in Germany, Italy, Spain, and Russia, they surely must be permitted in France, the country of which every wall reechoed with the cry "à la Bastille," "à bas le roi," "vive la Liberté, Egalité, Fraternité," "ni Dieu, ni Maitre," etc; that it would be allowed in Paris, the city of revolution, the history of which has been written with the blood of its people, the sons and daughters of which have stood on the barricades, days, nights, weeks, fight-

---

1. The Paris congress was suppressed on 18 September 1900.

ing and dying for Liberty; the city which holds out a warning to all crowned heads, in the Place de la Concorde, upon which Louis XVI and the beautiful Marie Antoinette were beheaded; the city which has built a monument on the site of the once hideous Bastille, to the memory of Camille Desmoulins,[2] and the innumerable unknown who threw down the black walls in which France's grandest men lay buried for life; Paris, that can boast of a Montmartre, upon which the sons of the Commune bathed in the light of the setting sun, that is nowhere seen so beautiful as here, in all their grand and noble zeal, fought the last battle for Liberty;[3] Paris, with its Père la Chaise and the wall of the federals killed there by the whiskey and absinthe brutalized soldiers of Thiers and Galliffet,[4] buried in one hole, and even now after thirty years kept alive by wreaths of flowers, ribbons and inscriptions of all those whose hearts throb for Freedom;[5] Paris, whose boys and girls from fifteen to sixteen years up to snowhaired men and women, vibrate with the memory of the past and the hope of the future; Paris, whose children have given the world all that human skill, ability, and genius can produce, gathered in the Exhibition; and last but not least, Paris, the only city that is ruled by a "radical" government and a Socialistic minister.[6]

Surely in this city, in which thousands of people from all over the world hold counsel with each other, we, the Anarchists, could come together and peacefully discuss. That must have been the thought of the comrades who signed the first call for the Congress, and all those who helped to organize and make it a success. Poor naive Pouget,[7] you who know, like no one else, how to reach the common people in their own tongue, and you Pelloutier,[8] young genius that you are, with your success in organizing 300,000 men in a body to hold together and stand up for the principle of human independence, and you Domela Nieuwenhuis,[9] with the Christ-like head, and the temperament of a child, loved and honored by all who know you, you who have raised your children as workingmen, although you have devoted your wealth to our cause, and all of you, who have worked for a year to make the Congress a success, you were wise enough to choose the Paris of the

2. Camille Desmoulins (1760–1794) was a French revolutionary, whose 12 July 1789 speech contributed to the storming of the Bastille two days later. He was executed on 3 April 1794.
3. A reference to the Paris Commune, 18 March to 28 May 1871.
4. The Paris Commune was suppressed by Adolphe Thiers (1797–1877), chief executive of the National Assembly, and by Gaston Gallifet (1830–1909), the general who carried out Thiers's orders in Paris. Gallifet's army was responsible for the deaths of over 25,000 Communards.
5. The Mur des Fédérés in the Père Lachaise Cemetery marks the site where 147 Communards were executed by the Versailles forces under the command of Adolphe Thiers on 28 May 1871.
6. EG refers to the Radical Republicans and to Alexandre Millerand (1859–1943), who was the first socialist to serve in French bourgeois government and was minister of commerce from 1899 to 1902, under Rene Waldeck-Rousseau. Millerand served as president of France from 1920 to 1924.
7. Émile Pouget was one of the organizers of the Paris congress.
8. Fernand Pelloutier was general secretary of the Fédération Nationale des Bourse du Travail (National Federation of Labor Exchange).
9. Domela Nieuwenhuis was a Dutch freethinker who began his career as a Lutheran pastor, moved into parliamentary politics as a socialist, and edited two pacifist journals between 1898 and 1919.

revolutionary spirit; but you were very unwise to forget the Socialistic ministry. Therefore you and I and all of us must stand the consequences.

The fact of the matter is, that no consequences of an unpleasant character have arisen. True, the Congress was prohibited; but what are prohibitions for, if not to be broken? And so the Congress took place, in spite of all and every order; on a smaller scale, that is true, but by no means less important. This will be seen by the results, of which some are already in print, and the others to follow.

The difference between a Socialistic and any other government is the hypocritical liberalism of the former, and the open despotism of the latter. Any other government would have suppressed our Congress in its embryo, or at least given some sign of its intent to suppress it; but the Socialistic ministry with "Comrade" Millerand at its head, who, in order to gain and keep his post, not only showed that he is just like his colleagues, but even worse than they, the same Millerand who has broken his promise as a Socialist by the very acceptance of the ministry, and who has proven a traitor to the cause of "class consciousness," at the shooting of the strikers at Martinique and Chalons-sur-Saône,[10] and on many other occasions. Millerand and his ministry went the ordinary government one better. They let us go for a whole year; did not even watch over the arrangements carried on for seven months by the committee; waited until reports were sent from all parts of the world, all delegates were in Paris, and the last finishing touch given to the Congress, and the social arranged for the evening previous; and then came down with an order suppressing the Congress, and all meetings protesting against such infamy.

One must be blind not to see that the intention of Galliffet's partner was not so much to hurt Anarchism; for he is really too insignificant a figure to succeed in something in which the united despots have failed; but to prove to the French bourgeois, that they are really safer with a Socialistic ministry, than with one of their own.

As I have already said, no other government would have waited until the last moment, the more so, as it is absolutely against the French law to suppress a peaceful meeting openly held; but Millerand knew how to get over this difficulty. He simply searched out the "*lois scélérates,*"[11] issued in 1894, during the number of acts of violence committed; against all Anarchistic meetings and publications, setting them down as criminal. At that

10. On 9 February 1900, in Martinique, French soldiers killed ten strikers during a demonstration; for examples of the commentary in the French anarchist press, see *Le Père Peinard,* 5 March 1900, p. 4, and 12 March 1900, p. 1. On 2 June 1900, French local police fired on strikers at Chalon-sur-Saône, killing three.

11. The *lois scélérates,* or "villainous laws," were a series of acts passed by the French parliament in response to a rash of violent protest in France (1891–1892 and 1893–1894) instigated by the actions of Ravachol (pseudonym of François-Claudius Koenigstein), Auguste Vaillant, Émile Henry, and others. The first, an amendment to the press law of 1881, was passed on 12 December 1893; the second, concerning *associations de malfaiteurs* (associations of wrongdoers), on 18 December; and the third, *pour réprimer les menées anarchistes* (to quell anarchist schemes), on 28 July 1894. As a result of the laws, hundreds of workers, mainly anarchists, were given long prison terms and deportation orders, forcing many radicals into exile. Rigorously applied for less than a year, the laws remained a permanent threat.

time, Jaurès[12] was deputy; and he was among the most vigorous opponents of such an infernal law. He since then helped Millerand to the ministry; and Millerand uses the same outrageous law his comrade and bosom friend opposed, as an excuse to suppress our Congress. Such are the ironies of life.

Tuesday morning the 18th inst. our secretary, Comrade Rémy,[13] was called to the prefecture de police, police headquarters; and there he was told, that neither the social nor the Congress could take place, by order of the ministry. (By the way, here it is not like in our own "free land," where every captain or policeman can stop a meeting; the police here do not enjoy such power, they only act upon the order of the ministry.)

Comrade Rémy immediately notified all those comrades he could reach; and the others, unaware of the ukase, went to the social; and found the doors of the hall locked and the street blocked by police. We called a secret meeting for Wednesday afternoon, at which only a few could be present owing to the danger involved, and more to the lack of space, as we were to meet outside of Paris in a small room. Here, then, huddled together in a stuffy room, in danger of being surprised by government hirelings, but with a zeal which knows no fear, were a few men and women, who have given the best years of their life for the cause, some having undergone years of privation, imprisonment, persecution and want, old in years and experience, but young in heart and spirit, ever ready to continue the fight for final human emancipation. Here we decided to hold several secret meetings, in order to discuss a few subjects of the many on the program for the Congress. But one of the first decisions was to protest most vigorously against the suppression of our Congress. In accordance with this, several French comrades arranged two meetings for Thursday afternoon and evening, in a hall called Maison du Peuple; but when we got there, the street was blocked by police, and one comrade, Libertas,[14] arrested and brutally taken to the station. In the evening, the same spectacle of force and brutality, an increased force of police and detectives, with hidden cameras behind the windows of the hall, to photograph all those who came to protest.

Here I cannot help giving you a funny incident. M. Sully-Prudhomme,[15] a member of the Academy, the house of the forty immortals, into which a Zola[16] is refused admission, a reactionary and hater of all progress, was driven to the Maison du Peuple by curiosity, and photographed. Now his glorious image hangs in the rogues' gallery at the prefecture

12. Jean Jaurès (1859–1914) was a French left-wing socialist politician.
13. EG refers to Léon Rémy, the French anarchist who edited the reports in *Les Temps Nouveaux* on the 1900 Paris congress. Rémy later moved to socialism and syndicalism.
14. EG refers to A. A. Davies.
15. M. Sully-Prudhomme (1839–1907), French poet, philosopher, and essayist, a member of the Académie Française (elected 1881) and winner of the Nobel Prize for Literature (1901). His publications include *Le Bonheur* (Paris: Alphonse Lemerre, 1888) and *A. Alfred de Vigny* (Paris: Pelletan, 1898).
16. The Académie Française was the national arbiter of French language and literature. Often accused of literary conservatism, it refused to admit the authors Émile Zola, Molière, Jean-Jacques Rousseau, Honoré de Balzac, Gustave Flaubert, and Marcel Proust, among others.

de police, along with the pictures of the bravest and noblest men of France. Undoubtedly M. Sully-Prudhomme never dreamed of such an honor; and in the future he will surely take care not to give way to curiosity, which is rather out of place for a man, especially a member of the Academy de France.

While we had our secret meeting outside of Paris, one of the trade unions of our Congress, the Bronze Workers, called a meeting of their own to protest against the suppression; but their meeting, too, was stopped, and the crowd dispersed by force. They have since manifested their protest through large posters posted all through Paris, denouncing the government, and declaring their intention of continuing the work of education and enlightenment, until the last vestige of tyranny is gone.

Another manifesto, of which I send you a copy for translation, and signed by the best known comrades of Paris, was issued on Friday, September 21, and spread all over town. As I already said, the public Congress of the International Revolutionary Workers was suppressed. Instead of that, four sessions were held secrectly, to the peace of mind of all governmental cowards. However, be it said that no dynamite was fabricated, nor dagger sharpened at those meetings. The Revolutionists gathered from all over the world had really more important work to do, and higher aims to achieve than the removal of the heads of a few rotten kings.

At the meetings, we discussed and organized a Bureau of International Correspondence, or International Federation, based upon national federation, for the purpose of better acquainting each other with the economic, political and ethical state of the movement in each country, and the practice of the principle of solidarity. To accomplish the former, each country is to issue a quarterly bulletin, to be sent to all countries, and those to do the same. In this way, it is hoped, the comrades will keep in touch with each other, which has so far not been the case. As to the latter, it certainly has been sadly neglected so far. Comrades came to a strange land, the language of which they did not know; and without means or friends, they often have been near starvation. This is to be done away with through the International Bureau. So when a comrade comes to Paris, London, Madrid, or Constantinople, he will know where to find friends. I cannot dwell upon this matter elaborately in this report; but I can promise the comrades, they will learn more about it soon.

The second matter discussed and decided upon, was the publication of all the reports sent to the Congress in book form; but as we have not enough money to do it right now, the reports will be published in the supplement of *Les Temps Nouveaux*,[17] the plates set aside and a book made out of all the plates when ready. For this, money is needed; and I herewith appeal to all the comrades in America, to put their hands into their pockets, and send on their mite to the secretary, whose name and address will be given in a week or so.

17. The report of the Paris congress appeared in *Les Temps Nouveaux Supplément Littéraire*, vol. 3, nos. 23 and 31, in November 1900.

We have received ninety reports on all possible subjects; and although only twenty or twenty-five are in the form of an essay; yet the others are not less interesting, and will be published in a resume.

The third and last thing decided was to issue a manifesto, together with all the subjects on the program for the Congress, the names of all reports and the nationalities of those who have taken part, to be published in *L'Aurore*,[18] a radical daily in Paris, *Les Temps Nouveaux* and *Le Libertaire*. These are to be sent to all the trades unions, that were to participate, with a request to send on the papers to the trades unions of the world, asking them to protest with us against the suppression of the Congress of the International Revolutionary Workers of the World.

To give you an idea of the vast amount of work done for the Congress, a list of subjects for discussion and reports sent in will be given next week.

E. GOLDMAN.

Free Society, 21 October 1900, pp. 1, 3.

---

18. *L'Aurore* was a major French daily paper founded in 1897 by leading Radical politician and journalist Georges Clemenceau. *L'Aurore* in its 13 January 1898 issue printed "J'Accuse," Émile Zola's condemnation of the French state's conduct in the Dreyfus Affair. An extended report on the Paris congress was not published in *L'Aurore*.

Rented by Emma Goldman.

Proprietor of Everett Hall Warned Social Science Meeting Against Anarchy.

At the Social Science mass meeting in Everett Hall, 31 East Fourth Street, last night, the proprietor of the hall, Harry Bimberg, threatened to turn out the lights should the meeting develop into one of Anarchistic tendencies.[1] He said that Emma Goldman had rented the hall from him by concealing her identity. The hall was crowded and the announcement of the proprietor was received with a howl of protest.

Emma Goldman said Bimberg was influenced by fear of the police.[2] She stated that this only went to prove her contention that there was no liberty, personal or otherwise, in America, and that under "your Platts, your Crokers, and your Hannas[3] there can be no such thing as liberty, any more than there is in the Republic of France to-day."[4]

"King Humbert," she said, "was justly put to death by a brave man,[5] who dared to act for the good of his fellow-men, among whom he considered himself but a unit in a universe." She said she should hate to be in the shoes of a monarch or of President McKinley, owing to the "fickleness of the masses."

New York Times, 12 December 1900, p. 2.

1. EG, who had returned to New York from Paris in early December, spoke at this meeting, as did Spanish anarchist Pedro Esteve.
2. According to the *New York Tribune* of 12 December 1900, the police were present at this meeting, including Captain Thompson of the Mercer St. Station and seven plainclothes detectives.
3. Thomas Collier Platt, Richard Crocker, and Mark Hanna were all Republican party members. Thomas Collier Platt (1833–1910) was a U.S. senator and Republican political boss in New York State, U.S. representative from New York (from 1873 to 1877), and U.S. senator from New York (1881 and 1897 to 1909). Also the president of the Tioga County National Bank, Platt possessed considerable commercial interests (including in the lumbering business in Michigan), and was the president of the United States Express Company from 1880 to 1901. In 1881 he resigned his senatorial seat after only three months in office over a disagreement with President James Garfield about federal appointments in New York. He regained his senate seat in 1896, remaining there until shortly before his death. Richard Crocker (1843–1922) was a New York City political boss; an Irish American, he was associated with Tammany Hall for four decades and was for sixteen years its "chief." Mark Hanna was a Cleveland industrialist and politician who managed William McKinley's rise to the presidency.
4. A reference to the suppression of the International Revolutionary Congress of the Working People in Paris.
5. Gaetano Bresci, an Italian American anarchist, assassinated King Umberto of Italy on 29 July 1900. The 12 December 1900 account in the *New York Tribune* of the anarchist meeting in Everett Hall quotes EG as follows: "The King of Italy was justly sent to his account by a brave man. We have other brave men left for a New York tyrant."

Interview in the *NEW YORK SUN*

New York, 6 January 1901

Talk with Emma Goldman

Woman Anarchist Declares She Opposes Violence.

She Tells a *Sun* Reporter the Stages by Which She Reached Her Present Way
of Thinking—Declares Anarchists Are Greatly Misunderstood and Maligned,
and That the Hope of the World Lies in Adherence to Their Social and
Moral Doctrines—She Thinks American Women Will Greatly
Advance the Propaganda of Anarchy.

"I was born a revolutionist." Emma Goldman leaned her elbows on the little table in the back room of Justus Schwab's saloon and looked calmly at the *Sun* reporter,[1] across a glass of Rhine wine and seltzer. At first glance there was so little of the revolutionary in her appearance that her statement seemed a trifle absurd. A second glance changed the impression. A short sturdy figure, a pale face whose cheeks flush warmly under the influence of excitement, a determined chin and firm mouth, brown hair brushed smoothly, from a low, broad forehead, earnest dilating gray eyes under straight, heavily marked brows. There is Emma Goldman, the Anarchist. She has the mouth of a worker and the eyes of an enthusiast. Her face is quiet, but it is the face of a Slav, and the quiet means self-control, not indifference. No one would think of calling the woman handsome. She would pass unnoticed in a crowd, but no one who had talked with her and studied her would forget her. One sees many such faces among the girl students of Russia. Intelligent, desperately earnest, lighted from within by an ideal and a purpose, yet calm as a mask, save for the eyes.

When Emma Goldman was upon trial for inciting to riot, in 1897, Assistant District Attorney McIntyre besought the jury not to be deceived by the innocent face of the prisoner, who would make the streets of New York run with blood, were she turned loose upon the community.[2] One must allow some rhetorical license to a public prosecutor, but brooding innocence calculated to mislead twelve good men and true seems as inappro-

---

1. The interview generated criticism of EG from within the anarchist movement because in it she seemed to renounce propaganda by deed. As Abe Isaak commented, "It is hardly credible that Comrade E.G. should have made the statements which now circulate in the daily press; but I suppose we shall soon hear from herself." Indeed, soon afterward EG clarified her position on violence. See Letter to *Free Society*, 17 February 1901; and Letter to Marie Goldsmith, 8 February 1901, below.
2. In fact, 1893. There is no corroboration of Attorney McIntyre having said these words at the trial.

priate to a description of Miss Goldman, as seas of gore seem foreign to her native element. She looks like what she is, a forceful woman of brains and experience, under the influence of a great enthusiasm. The fact that she is unpopular with a large element of her own party, is due to her disbelief in bloody streets as a pathway to the millennium. But then, as the woman for whom the Assistant District Attorney's eloquence won a year in prison says: "One must say something imposing, when one wishes to send a woman to prison for quoting Cardinal Manning." [3]

"You are Russian?" asked the reporter, although the answer was a foregone conclusion. The gray eyes lighted suddenly. One thing besides anarchy is sure to bring the illumination. It is the mention of Russia.

"Yes, I am Russian, Russian through and through, although very little of my life was spent there. I was born in Russia, but brought up in Germany and graduated in a German school. All that didn't make a German of me. My ideas, my feelings, my sympathies, my tastes remained Russian, and when we went back to St. Petersburg the year I was 15 it was going home for me.[4] My family was orthodox. None of my revolutionary tendencies was inherited. At least my parents were not responsible for them and were horrified by them. I did have an uncle, my mother's brother, who was mixed up with the revolutionary party at one time. He was a very distinguished lawyer and though he did not do any active work for the nihilists he had advanced ideas and talked them. He was hurried off to Siberia, but after awhile it was proved that he wasn't guilty of the offence for which he was condemned, so he was allowed to return.[5] Perhaps I inherited some of my ideas from him. At any rate it is true. I was born a revolutionist. In Germany I did not think much about such things. German women do not take naturally to anarchy. But then I went back to St. Petersburg. Russia changed my whole attitude toward life and I went into radicalism with all my heart and soul.

"You see things are different in Russia from what they are here or anywhere else. One breathes in revolutionary thought with the air, without being at all definitely interested in anarchy one learns its principles. There were reading circles among the young students. There was discussion and thought and enthusiasm all around me, and something in me responded to it all. There is no other place in the world where woman has what

3. EG often attributed her words to Cardinal Manning; see note 3 to "Hailed Emma Goldman," Article in *New York World*, 20 August 1894, above.

4. EG also elaborated on this Russian revolutionary influence in an 1899 interview in the *Seattle Post-Intelligencer*. Elsewhere EG recalled her return to St. Petersburg as having occurred shortly after the assassination of Alexander II on 13 March 1881, when she would have been twelve or thirteen. Compare this account with the one she gave to Frank Harris in 1923: "I was too young to understand and grasp the theories that carried Russia's youth onward. But my soul became imbued with the humanitarian ideas everywhere in the air." See *Seattle Post-Intelligencer*, 28 May 1899, *EGP*, reel 67, and Frank Harris, "Emma Goldman," *Contemporary Portraits* (New York, 1923); reprinted as "Biographical Sketch," in EG, *My Disillusionment in Russia* (New York, 1925), pp. xvii–xviii.

5. According to *Living My Life*, Yegor Bienowitch was arrested, imprisoned in the Peter and Paul Fortress, and sent to Siberia until EG's mother successfully pleaded with the governor-general of St. Petersburg on his behalf. See *LML*, pp. 27–28.

she has in Russia. American women have great freedom. The American men bow down to them, but there is no such equality between sexes here as there is in Russia. There the women have not only the same rights in law as the men, they have the same liberties, the same social and intellectual freedom.

"The man respects woman, looks upon her as his equal, is her good chum—yes, that is the word. Nowhere are men and women chums as they are in Russia. This isn't so true in the aristocracy, where French influence has corrupted conditions, though even in that class the women have great freedom, but it is absolutely true in the middle class, in the student world, the intellectual world of Russia. A woman student in Russia may receive visitors all day and most of the night, discuss all vital subjects with them, go with men when and where she pleases, and yet she will not be criticised and no landlady would dream of insinuating that there was anything wrong with her morals. What is more there wouldn't be anything wrong with them. The standard of morals in that class is phenomenally high and the average intelligent Russian woman's mind is as pure as it is broad. There is great help for her in the *camaraderie* with thinking men. The feminine mind needs rubbing against masculine mind. The Russian woman student is met with respect and honor by the men, and she studies hard to deserve the granted equality. The relation between the sexes in Russia is the most ideal of any I know about. That is why young Russian women learn to think. And because they think they become Anarchists.

"I was an Anarchist when I left Russia to come to America, but I had hardly formulated my belief. The final influence that crystallized my views was the hanging of the Chicago Anarchists in 1887.[6] I followed that case carefully and it made me an active Anarchist. I was living with my family in Rochester then, and the nearest thing to a radical society the town had was a social Democratic society, tame as a house cat. I came away to New York and went to work in a factory. That showed me a new side of life. My family had been well-to-do, and I hadn't come in actual contact with the want and suffering of the world until I joined the wage earners.

"Of course the experience strengthened my revolutionary ideas. When the Waist and Shirtmaker Girls' Union went out in 1888 I led the strike.[7] That is, in a way I led it. I have never been an Anarchist leader. I cannot afford it. A leader must be a diplomat. I am not a diplomat. A leader of a party makes concessions to his party, for the sake of holding his power. He must give way to his followers in order to be sure they will sustain him. I can't do all that. I am an Anarchist because I love individual freedom, and I will not surrender that freedom. A leader must sooner or later be the victim of the masses he thinks he controls.

6. EG refers to the Haymarket anarchists, who were executed in 1887.
7. Possibly a reference to EG's involvement in the 1890 strike of the Dress and Cloakmaker's Union organized by Joseph Barondess. In 1888 EG was working in garment factories, first in New Haven and then in Rochester. No record of her involvement in a strike in either city has been found. EG mentioned the same incident in an 1899 interview (see *Seattle Post-Intelligencer*, 28 May 1899, *EGP*, reel 67).

"When I went into the work I was an enthusiast. I felt more than I thought. I was an Anarchist from sentiment, not from reason. I thought that man ought not to suffer and I saw suffering. So I was an Anarchist. But when I definitely entered the work I gave myself a solemn pledge that I would study, that I would make passion bow to wisdom, that I would not be carried away from the truth by sentiment. I soon saw that the safest and wisest way to keep myself free was not to be a leader. That is why I am connected with no party. I am a member of no group. I stand outside. I take no pay. I accept no favors. What I do I do individually, for love of the cause. There is no party to back me, but there is no party to say, 'You must do this and you must not do that. You are paid. You owe it to us. You must bow to the majority.' I bow to nothing except my idea of right. I am free and I will stay free. Individual freedom and responsibility—there is the basis for true anarchy."

The plain face was transfigured. The sturdy little figure seemed to expand and grow imposing. Emma Goldman may be mistaken. The courts of New York have said that she is, but she is in earnest, desperately in earnest, and she is an idealist such as only the Slav race produces.

"But do you pay your own expenses when you go about the country settling strikes or lecturing?" asked the reporter.

"I accept only my railway fare when I go on definite work, that is, in case of a strike or other disturbance. When I am on a lecture tour an admission fee pays my expenses, or, in some cases, my expenses have been paid by individual friends—wealthy people who are interested in the cause and yet have not come out openly as Anarchists. I have a few friends like that and they have occasionally helped me because they believe in me and in my influence. I don't approve of their attitude. I believe they would do infinitely more good if they would come out and declare themselves Anarchists and be consistent. Personally I cannot understand compromise, but we are not all made alike, and it is encouraging to see that the wealthy and the educated class in America is at last getting a glimmering idea that anarchy isn't bomb throwing—that it is philosophy. The old anarchistic method, which was merely a kick against anything and everything, is giving way to the true anarchy. Americans who insisted on believing that anarchy was foreign revolution are finding out that it is universal philosophy, and that their own Emerson and Thoreau[8] said more sensible anarchical things than any of our professed Anarchists.

"I have never propagated violence, in spite of Mr. McIntyre's rivers of blood theory. I don't know of a single truly great Anarchist leader who ever did advocate violence. Where violence comes with anarchy it is a result of the conditions, not of anarchy. The Russians were not terrorists by nature—no people further from it. Gross abuses produced sporadic violence. The same thing is true in Italy. The biggest fallacy going is the idea that

8. EG often evoked figures such as Henry David Thoreau and Ralph Waldo Emerson to bring attention to a perceived undercurrent in the American political tradition that supported individual freedom and cautioned against the power of the state, which echoed the sentiments and beliefs of anarchism.

Anarchists as a body band together and order violence, assassinations of rulers, and all that. I ought to know something about anarchy, and I tell you that is false—absolutely false. The gross misrepresentation in that regard makes my blood boil. There is ignorance, cruelty, starvation, poverty, suffering, and some victim grows tired of waiting. He believes a decisive blow will call public attention to the wrongs of his country and may hasten the remedy. He and perhaps one or two intimate friends or relatives make a plan. They do not have orders. They do not consult other Anarchists. If a man came to me and told me he was planning an assassination I would think him an utter fool and refuse to pay any attention to him. The man who has such a plan, if he is earnest and honest, knows no secret is safe when told. He does the deed himself; runs the risk himself; pays the penalty himself. I honor him for the spirit that prompts him. It is no small thing for a man to be willing to lay down his life for the cause of humanity. The act is noble, but it is mistaken.

"No: I have never advocated violence, but neither do I condemn the Anarchist who resorts to it. I look behind him for the conditions that made him possible, and my horror is swallowed up in pity. Perhaps under the same conditions I would have done the same. If I had been starving in Milan and had raised my starving baby in the air as an appeal for justice, and had had that baby shot in my arms by a brutal soldiery, who knows what I might have done.[9] I might have changed from a philosophical Anarchist to a fighting Anarchist. Even in the worst Russian times, before the death of Alexander II, there was no commanded assassination in anarchy. The novels and plays and stories about that sort of thing make me sick. The plot to kill the Czar was planned by a little individual group of Anarchists, and they didn't do the killing after all. Their bomb only killed a horse, and then an unknown young man stepped up and threw a bomb between the Czar and himself, killing both. The Anarchists themselves, didn't find out until long afterward who the assassin was.[10] Do you suppose if Santo Caserio had had Anarchist organization back of him he would have tramped all the weary way to Paris, without money, in order to kill Carnot?[11] If Bresci[12] had been sent out from us, would he have had to scrape together

9. A reference to the Fatti di Maggio, the events of 5–8 May 1898, when public demonstrations in Milan against economic hardship were suppressed by government troops; the incident was considered by anarchists to be the immediate precursor to Luigi Lucheni's assassination of the Empress of Austria.
10. Alexander II's assassins were members of Narodnaya Volya (People's Will), a clandestine revolutionary group that emerged out of a split in the populist Zemlya i Volya (Land and Freedom) and focused its political strategy on assassination; it planned its 1881 attack for two years. The bomb thrower was Ignaty Grinevetsky, who died in the explosion. Also involved were Sophia Perovskaya, Alexander Mikhailov, Nikolai Kibalchich, and Andrei Zhelyabov, all of whom were executed. Another conspirator, Nikolai Sablin, committed suicide before he could be arrested; Gesia Gelfman died in prison. After the tsar's death, Narodnaya Volya issued manifestos claiming shared responsibility for the assassination, in accordance with the organization's philosophy.
11. French president Marie François-Sadi Carnot was assassinated by Sante Caserio on 24 June 1894.
12. EG refers to Gaetano Bresci, who assassinated King Umberto of Italy on 29 July 1900, and died in prison the following year.

every cent he could, even forcing one of his Anarchist friends to pawn some of his clothes in order to repay a loan Bresci had made him. The friend curses Bresci for a hard-hearted creditor, but Bresci never told why he needed money so desperately.

"We in America, haven't yet reached conditions—economic conditions I mean—that necessarily breed violence. I am thankful for that; but we are nearer such conditions than the old-time Americans ever dreamed we would be, and unless something is done to stop it, the time will come. I have great faith in America. Anarchy's best future lies in America. The people here have finer innate ideas of freedom. I have faith in Anglo-Saxon blood, too. It takes a long time to make an Englishman or American think, but when he gets started he will not stop. He isn't fickle. When he gives his heart to a cause, he is capable of sticking to it. Then the American woman ought to help our cause. She has freedom and intelligence and opportunity for education, and influence. The trouble with the American girls is that they are frivolous. That is particularly true of the girls of the working class. The ordinary American working girl doesn't care for any serious ideas or study. She only wants to amuse herself. It is a pity, but it is true. I realize that more and more.

"In our American work—I mean our English propaganda here, as opposed to the propaganda carried on in foreign languages—there are very few young girls. Russian girl Anarchists of 16 are common enough, but the American woman Anarchist under 35 years of age is most unusual. The moral education of the young working girl here is bad. As I said she cares only for showy clothes and frivolity. Her one aim in life is matrimony. It isn't until she finds out that life isn't all dancing and flirting, until she learns sorrow and bitterness and pain, that she begins to think. We have a great many American women in our ranks now, but they are almost all in the 30s or older.

"The able women Anarchists here do little speaking. Almost all of them confine themselves to circulating literature, obtaining subscriptions and writing.[13] Many of our ablest writers are women. You see, when a woman becomes an Anarchist comparatively late in life she has already contracted obligations and has entered into economic conditions that hold her. She can do for the cause only what is consistent with the life she seems compelled to lead. Some of the women do great work though."

Miss Goldman's English is the careful English of a well educated foreigner and save for its burring would usually show no trace of her foreign origin save in its precision. So, when she occasionally drops into American slang, the effect is a trifle odd.

"I know a woman Anarchist in Missouri who is a hustler," she went on. "She lives on a farm twenty-two miles from a railroad, and she has a husband and five sons who have all gone over to her theories with heart and soul.[14] What's more, she has interested all the farming population around her. I went there on my last tour and I found that one woman's individual influence had been simply wonderful. Voltairine de Cleyre and I are

13. Perhaps a reference to anarchists such as Natasha Notkin, who did not lecture but instead circulated newspapers and literature in various languages from her pharmacy in Philadelphia.
14. Kate Austin, who in fact had two sons and three daughters.

the only professional women speakers of our party in this country. She is a wonderful woman, musician, poetess, philosopher. She has great ability and great influence, but she is tied down in Philadelphia so her field of work is not what it ought to be.

"The ordinary American woman is an obstacle to progress. The average working-man's wife in this country has little profound feeling. It isn't her fault. It is the fault of her training. What she spent on a showy, shoddy hat and paste jewelry as a girl, she spends on baby's clothes that will make the neighbors talk, as a woman. She is shallow and a principle means nothing to her. Still I insist that the American woman will help on the cause greatly. The movement will come from the middle class, but it will spread. There are few women Anarchists in Germany, and those few are Anarchists because their husbands are. Of course there are exceptions. In the ranks of the women doctors, journalists and lawyers of Germany there are Anarchists, but not in the working class. The Italian women are rebels by nature, but too ignorant for intelligent anarchy. The French women are winning their freedom but it is an uphill fight. It is a matter of course for the American woman to be free, but the French woman must tear herself free. And then she works under one frightful disadvantage. The Frenchman sees the woman first and the worker afterward. It is always so—among radicals as among all other French classes. The French women workers themselves admit it and it is a frightful handicap. The English women are slow to take up advanced thought. It is their awful English prudence that holds them back. Modesty is a good thing in woman, but the English woman has an overdose. Still she is taking a place in social work.

"But it is the American woman who has the opportunity for freedom—for anarchy. She hasn't so much idealism as the Russian, but the Russian woman is hampered by despotism. The American woman has liberty—home, public, social, educational, religious. She is bound to forward our cause. A woman can do so much for anarchy, if she goes at it right. I believe I owe my success to my being a woman. The audience, in this country, will grant a woman a hearing because she is a woman. Then she must hold them. She must not talk to them as a woman, but as a comrade. This is not France. I can be a worker first, a woman afterward here, as I could in Russia. I have never been made to feel before any American man, however rough, that my sex impressed him before my argument. I do not make the mistake that most of your strong-minded women make. I do not want to topple men off their pedestal in order to take it. I am contented to share it. The woman's suffragists get up and rave against man and exalt woman. That is nonsense. I wish to be fair. I do not talk against man as a sex. I criticise my own sex quite as freely as I criticise the other. The question of sex has no place in a great movement toward truth, save as women accomplished certain forms of work better than men, and vice versa. When men find a woman does not abuse them and howl for her rights and theirs too; when she meets them on logical ground, is rational and fair, and able, they welcome her generously. I have always found it so, and I have worked more among men than among women, because there are more men to work among.

"I have been devoting my time to the English propaganda, because I speak good English and because I have made a close study of conditions purely American; and, as I told you, there are as yet comparatively few American women Anarchists. Most of the girl Anarchists here have to be worked with in Yiddish, and I do not speak Yiddish. Still, I do speak German and Russian, and since I came back from Europe last fall I've been getting into touch with the girls' organizations. I went to Europe after I came out of prison. You know I am a professional nurse. It has always been the dream of my life to be a doctor, but I could never manage it—could not get means for the study. My factory work undermined my health, so I thought that if I couldn't be a doctor I could at least be a little part of the profession. I went through the training for a nurse, did the hospital work and now nurse private cases. While I was in prison on Blackwell's Island I had plenty of chance to get experience. Except in extreme cases they don't have a trained nurse there. The sick prisoner is left to the ignorant mercies of other prisoners, except when the city physician demands a trained nurse. Having me there was handy, and I was glad to be useful, so the doctor worked me hard that year. I had all sorts of cases, but I used up my strength and was a nervous wreck when I came out. I'm not usually nervous."

The reporter looked at the firm, well-shaped hands that had been clasping and unclasping themselves all through the interview.

"Oh, yes; I suppose I am nervous in my temperament and involuntary motions, but I can usually keep myself well in hand. I have been in many trying situations, and I do not lose my nerve. The worse the ordeal, the cooler I become. But I was nervous when I came out of prison. I decided to try a change and go to Europe for a year. I could lecture for the cause and take a course in massage and in midwivery in Vienna. There is no good training for either here, though we have the best training schools for nurses in the world. Well, I went and did my studying and then went to Paris to study and wait for the Anarchists' Congress.[15] You know the Government prohibited the Congress. We had it all the same, but the meetings were secret. It was tremendously interesting and of great value, but it is a pity the meetings could not have been open and have reached more people. Famous radicals from all over the world were there. I was surprised to meet so many. The French authorities were in a terrible flutter. At another time they would never have allowed us to stay, but they were determined to have the Exposition go off smoothly, with no alarms or commotion, so they didn't stir up trouble, but contented themselves with watching us closely.[16] I received the honor or dishonor of especially strict surveillance. I was to give a series of lectures, but after the third the authorities warned me that if I gave any more I must leave France, and as I wanted to attend the Congress I kept quiet. Finally detectives escorted me to the station and saw my luggage checked to the steamer, and then notified the Government that the dangerous woman was on her way out of France."

15. EG traveled to Europe twice, once after her release from prison in 1895, when she went to England and Scotland to lecture and to Vienna to study, and once in 1889–1900, to London and then Paris for the International Revolutionary Congress of the Working People.

16. For more detail on the suppression of the Paris congress, see EG's article in *Free Society*, 25 September 1900, above.

Miss Goldman smiled, and when she smiles her likeable, crooked little smile, one can't regard her as a dangerous and incendiary young person.

"It's all too absurdly silly," she said, with a quiet little laugh, "this talk about my being dangerous. Half my fellow believers think me a fool because I am always talking against violence and advocating individual work. I really work very little with the masses—not that I am not in sympathy with concerted action, but I believe our ends are reached more quickly by educating the individual. There is an entirely mistaken conception of the purpose of anarchy, even among many Anarchists, so called. A great many people seem to think that in order to be an Anarchist all one has to do is to kick against everything, private property in particular, and hosts of the individuals opposed to the present system would do the same thing the rich are doing now if a chance for wealth came their way. The man who enters the Anarchist movement only because he has nothing is a menace to the cause, though one understands his feelings. The men who consider economic conditions the cause of all the evils in society are absolutely wrong. They say man is on a low level because of oppressive conditions. Upset everything, set him free, and things will adjust themselves. They will do nothing of the kind. I don't deny that economic conditions are important, but they are not a cause. They are a result—a result of the lack of responsibility in the individual man. Man has given up his birthright because he didn't understand himself, his responsibility, his powers.

"The individual man must develop until he is fit to be free. The individual must be free morally, intellectually, spiritually, or no amount of turning social conditions topsy turvy will better anything. That is my creed—and yet they call me a dangerous woman and talk about my drowning New York in blood. I am no prophet, but I am no fool, and I believe that the next ten years will see a wonderful spreading of the true principles of anarchy in this country. The progress will come through the irresistible force of truth, not through bomb throwing; but the part of the public that doesn't know anything about the real meaning of anarchy insists upon thinking we all carry bombs in our coat pockets."

A group of comrades were waiting for the little woman in the outer room of the saloon—genial, mild-mannered men, with no hint of dynamite and infernal machines about them. As Paul Verlaine [17] was "chez soi" in the Paris café, so Emma Goldman is at home in the First street saloon. Her mail is sent there, and when Justus Schwab died recently she lost one of her oldest and most loyal friends, as did many another East Side advocates of Schwab's way of thinking. [18]

New York Sun, 6 January 1901, p. 5.

17. The French symbolist poet Paul Verlaine (1844–1896) took part in the Paris Commune. After publication of his *Poèmes saturniens* (1866) and *Fêtes galantes* (1869), Verlaine became an important figure in the Paris bohemian literary scene. Imprisoned for wounding fellow poet Arthur Rimbaud, his return to his Catholic faith was reflected in his poetry published in *Sagesse* (1881).
18. Justus Schwab, whose Lower East Side saloon was a popular gathering place for radicals, died in 1900.

My dear Comrade Goldschmidt.

You will be surprised, to hear from me after so long a time,[1] I intended writing to you on my arrival in America, but many events prevented me from do so, but as I believing that it is better to be late, than never, I write, hoping, you will not receive my letter unkindly. First of all, I have a little business to transact, I took some literature of you, but not knowing how much I owe for it, I inclose 2D.10.P. of which, pleace take out the amount I owe, and the rest can go as a payment on the lot, which, I am now going to order. Please send me, as soon, as possible 50 copies of each of the russian pamphlates you have on, hand, or you can get for me, make them up in small packages, so I will not have to pay duty on them. I want you to send the literature to the above address, also the bill, and I will forward the money on receipt of the pamphlates. You understand dear Comrade, I want 50 copies of each, but if you can not send as many, send all you can, only the russian literature for the present. The movement in America is slowly progressing, the best proof for it is, that even the daily papers, are beginning to treat the Anarchists decently. I inclose a report of an interview, I have had with a reporter from one of our "respectable" capitalistic papers[2] you can judge for yourself, if it is not favorable, of course, the reporter had to misrepresent some, that is in regard, to my being against force, I never said anything of the sort, and the reporter has already corrected his mistake. I have been very busy since I returned, as I told you, when I was in Paris, we have very few lecturers in our ranks and since Comrade Edelman died,[3] we have still less, so on my return I found more work to do, than one individual can do, especially, when one work 12 hours daily, as I do in my profession, as nurse. However, I have managed to address a numbre of meetings in this and neighboring Cities, including Philadelphia, where the Comrades are very active. In this City the jewish Anarchists are the most active, but we also hold weekly english meetings, attended chiefly by Americans.[4] *Free Society* has been removed

1. Though there is no record of their meeting, EG likely met Marie Goldsmith in Paris in 1900.
2. EG refers to interview entitled "Talk with Emma Goldman" in *New York Sun*, 6 January 1901.
3. John Edelmann died 12 July 1900.
4. According to a report published in the February 1901 *Freedom*, Voltairine de Cleyre had recently organized the Social Science Club in Philadelphia, which included among its members many who had previously participated in the Ladies' Liberal League. The club had been holding weekly open air meetings, and when the weather changed the meetings continued indoors. Reporting about the activities of young Jewish anarchists holding meetings in New York, Brooklyn, and Newark, including lectures by EG and Hillel Solotaroff, *Freedom* also notes that the revival of meetings at the Social Science Club in New York upon EG's return marked a change in its constituency to mostly American-born anarchists.

from San Francisco to Chicago, and appears 8 pages instead of four.[5] I intended making a propaganda tour extending to Calif, but owing to a numbre of things, I have prosponed it for the present, I may start out in April or next Fall meanwhile I am working to pay my debts and save money for my tour. I hear, that our jewish Comrades have raised 150 D. 750 Francs for the publication of the reports in English, which is to take place in London; outside of that little has been done to accomplish the organisation of a Bureau of Correspondence. Had I goen on a tour, I should have made this, my main work, but as it is little interest is shown in that; I have not given up hopes, however, and I think that sooner or later we will succeed in organising a National Bureau of Correspondence.[6] How are you and your mother? Well, I hope; and how are the new groups progressing? I know you are very busy, but I would appriciate a long letter very much.

Give my regards to your mother, Remy and the Cornellissons.[7] Hoping to hear from you soon and to get the literature

FRATERNALLY

EMMA GOLDMAN

ALS, GA RF fond 5969, opis' 1, ed. khr. 77, listyl-4. On stationery of Emma Goldman, 50 First Street.

5. *Free Society* moved from San Francisco to Chicago in 1901, upon the invitation of Chicago anarchists, who hoped the publication's news and propaganda would reach all parts of the country faster from the Midwest. The first Chicago issue was published on 3 February.

6. After the 1907 anarchist congress in Amsterdam the idea of a Bureau of Correspondence was considered again.

7. Marie Goldsmith lived in Paris with her mother, Sofia Goldsmith; the family had fled Russia in 1884. EG also extends her regards to the French anarchist Léon Rémy, who had served as secretary to the suppressed 1900 Paris congress, and to the Dutch anarchist Christianus Cornelissen, who had been living in Paris since 1898.

An Open Letter.

I have of late received several postals and letters of inquiry respecting the reports in the daily press, that I am against force, or propaganda by deed.[1] I should have paid little attention to these reports, for I thought that my personal friends would not believe anything said in the newspapers about me; and those comrades who believe them, simply show how little they know of the capitalistic press. But it was the reply Comrade Isaak gave to someone in the last issue of *Free Society,* that induced me to make this statement.[2]

I have never opposed force or propaganda by deed, either publicly or privately. I demand and acknowledge the right of an individual, or a number of individuals, to strike back at organized power, and to defend themselves against invasion; and I have and always will stand on the side of the one who has been courageous enough to give his own life in taking or attempting to take the life of a tyrant, whether industrial or political. I am on the side of every rebel, whether his act has been beneficial or detrimental to our cause; for I do not judge an act by its result, but by its cause;[3] and the cause of each and every rebellious act has been organized despotism, robbery and exploitation on the part of society, and the innate sense of justice and a rebellious spirit on the part of the individual.

What I said, and shall repeat again and again, is that violence is not a phase of Anarchism. The philosophy of Anarchy is based on harmony, on peace; and it recognizes the right of every individual to life, liberty and development, and opposes all forms of invasion;[4] consequently the philosophy of Anarchy is an absolute foe to violence, therefore I

1. See EG's disavowal of having ever advocated violence in "Talk with Emma Goldman, Interview in the *New York Sun,* 6 January 1901, above.
2. Responding to "J.C." of Marion, Indiana, editor Abe Isaak had stated: "It is hardly credible that Comrade E.G. should have made the statements which now circulate in the daily press; but I suppose we shall soon hear from herself . . ." (*Free Society,* 3 February 1901, p. 8).
3. Note AB's similar discussion of his *attentat* on Henry Clay Frick in his underground, prison-produced publication *Prison Blossoms* : "[the meaning of] a deed, such as mine . . . in no way depend[s] upon the physical consequences (to the parties concerned) incidental to that act, but must have for its criterion the purpose underlying the deed and should be estimated according to the moral effect." For full quote of AB's motives for his *attentat,* see note 3, Letter from Alexander Berkman, 19 October 1892, above.
4. EG's use of the term "invasion" suggests that she was familiar with Max Stirner's *Der Einzige und Sein Eigentum* (The Ego and His Own), which was first published in German in 1844. A constant theme

do not advocate violence. An Anarchist who advocates violence as a part of the teachings of Anarchy, has never properly understood its doctrines. If I stand on the side of the rebel, or if I approve of an act of violence, it is only because I know that organized force—government—leaves us no other method of propaganda—because we are the invaded, and not the invaders.

The mass of mankind can remain indifferent in the face of every injustice; but fortunately for humanity, there are men and women whose whole beings rebel against injustice, whose social instincts are so strongly developed that they feel every blow which the present economic and political system strikes at society. Such men and women can no more stand quietly by and see workers shot, children starved, women outraged, and thousands of the social family ruined, destroyed and killed, than one's breathing functions can work without pure air; but they are not necessarily Anarchists; they have existed and rebelled as long as the world exists, long before Anarchists or Anarchism was known; and it is well that they exist, otherwise despots would reign supreme, and life be unbearable. Let us therefore understand that violence is a product of oppression, of need, of suffering, and man's innate sense of justice and social instinct—if not crushed by commercialism—on one side, and greed on the other. Incidentally I want to say that it is this sense of justice and social rebellion that have produced the philosophy of liberty, of Anarchism, and not as some of my worthy comrades insist, that it is Anarchism that makes or will make men good and just. The philosophy of Anarchy has no such metaphysical power; it cannot make pure that which is impure, nor can it make anything just which is essentially unjust. The teachings of Anarchy are a product of man's sense of justice and craving for righteousness, based upon man's recognition of the fact that justice and righteousness are only possible in freedom, under non-invasion; and not under government, dictum, interference of man with man, either economically, politically, morally or ethically, consequently only in an Anarchistic mode of living, which is not a child of the future, but a life which each and every liberty-loving man must begin now, because it is man who makes society, and not society that makes the man.

I think I need say no more about my position towards individual or collective revolt; so I will only repeat that I am a revolutionist by nature and temperament, and as such I claim the right for myself and all those who feel with me, to rebel and resist invasion by all means, force included, consequently a destructionist. But I am also an Anarchist, and as such a constructionist. In order to construct a new sanitary building, fit for human beings to live in, I must, if I do not find cleared ground, tear down the old, rotten decayed obstacle which stands in the way of that beautiful and magnificent mansion called Anarchy.

---

in the work, which was widely read in anarchist circles, addresses the right of the individual to protect the self from invasion by the state or any outside force.

In conclusion, I would also like to correct a statement which circulated in the daily press shortly after I left for Europe. The mouthpieces of capitalism reported, after I had been two weeks in England, that I had just sailed, and, on leaving, had told a reporter that I was disgusted with the American workers; that I considered them a lot of fools and blockheads, and a thankless crew; that I was dissatisfied with my own comrades, and that I said there were not more than a dozen Anarchists in America.[5]

While I had not seen a single one of the press sharks, and hence could not have spoken to them, the report contained some truth. I know the responsible party, in fact every one in New York knows him; but as he is out of the movement, and has done a lot of mischief, I do not think it necessary to disclose his name. However, while it was absolutely false that I had expressed my views before I left, he often heard me say from the platform that "if the American workers were not such fools and slaves, they could not quietly submit to the growth of imperialism; they could not and would not allow the decayed institutions of Europe to replace the liberal and independent principles laid down by their fore-fathers." This I maintain now; and add that the American worker is not only a fool, but a conceited fool, which is still worse. He believes himself free, whereas the chains of slavery make his limbs bleed; he thinks himself independent, while his back is bent with the burden of dependency; he boasts of his right to choose his master, not knowing that he thereby foreifeits his right to be his own master; he claims to be charitable and ready to help his neighbor, while his only help consists in helping himself to his neighbor's property, and then to take possession of his neighbor also, as has been done in Cuba, and as is now being done in the Philippines.[6]

Well, but is he worse than the European worker? some one may ask. No, he is not; but the European worker is the product of centuries of despotic rule; he is a born slave—he had no choice in the matter. The American worker is born a "free man," with the right to life, liberty, and the pursuit of happiness; but he makes no use of his freedom; he cannot see that liberty is like a delicate plant, and needs proper care and attention, or it fades away. Of course, all this refers to the average worker. The intelligent worker of America is the intelligent worker of the world; he stands up for his rights, and works with those whose aim in life is the establishment of equal liberty in all phases of life.

The reports said that I considered the workers "thankless." This is absolutely false. I could not consistently say so, because I do not believe in gratitude or obligation, since

5. See, for example, *New York Times*, 23 November 1899, p. 7; and *New York World*, 23 November 1899, p. 4.
6. EG refers to the role of the United States in the occupation of Cuba and in the annexation of the Philippines following the Spanish-American War. Although Cuba gained independence from Spain in 1898, the United States occupied the country for the next five years, and the Platt Amendment of 1901 in effect made Cuba a U.S. protectorate. In late 1898 the United States bought the Philippines as part of the Treaty of Paris, but the Philippine Revolution against Spain, begun in 1896, led to fighting between the United States and the Philippines. Though the war was declared over on 4 July 1902 by President Theodore Roosevelt, fighting continued until 1913 when the United States established stable colonial control over the Philippines.

I am only acting according to the dictum of my inner self. No one owes me anything for my work in the movement.

Further: that I believe we have but a dozen Anarchists in America. Well, there is some truth in that, although I have not said so to any newspaper representative. Theoretical Anarchists—men and women who understand the teachings of our philosophy—we have thousands of in America, and still a larger number of those who are Anarchists without knowing it; but those who not only think, but act, who practice Anarchism in their every day life, who are consistent, who defy the world, maintain their personal liberty and consider the liberty of others, such Anarchists are indeed few, not only in America, but all over the world. Yet if liberty is ever to bless mankind, it is only when the example set by the few will be followed by the many.

Now that I have explained my position, I hope the readers of *Free Society* will not misunderstand me again; and will believe only that which has my signature.

Emma Goldman.

Free Society, 17 February 1901, p. 3.

DEAR FRIEND

Just got your letter

As to the reporters. I must see the reporters of <u>all</u> the N. York Press, as was done last time, or none. It seems to me an absolute condition. All the middle class papers are for an elite, and this is the only way to show no preferences and to avoid being hunted afterwards by reporters of the excluded papers.

As to articles, I have much more demands than I could write, and such offers as no daily paper will ever pay—but have no time to write.[1]

So let us have all reporters from all the dailies, as we had last time.[2] That will guarantee <u>good reports of all the lectures</u>,[3] and save a lot of trouble. Even —[4] from the <u>Journal</u> which, after all, rectified its nonsense, was mystified by an occasional reporter. Let all come at noon on Friday—

FRATERNALLY YOURS

P.K.

ALI, Emma Goldman Archive, IISH. On stationery of the Colonial Club. Letter is undated but most likely was written between 24 and 29 March, when Kropotkin departed from Cambridge.

1. In a letter to Robert E. Ely, EG had arranged for an exclusive interview for Kropotkin with an unnamed New York City newspaper. In exchange for the interivew, the newspaper agreed to pay for a subsequent article to be written by Kropotkin. See EG to Robert Ely, 23 March 1901, *EGP*, reel 1.
2. Kropotkin toured the United States for the first time in 1897.
3. Kropotkin's second tour of the United States began in February 1901 and ended in early May. Speaking in both Russian and English, he lectured at Boston's Lowell Institute, the Labor Lyceum in New York, and Chicago's Hull House, among other venues. Both anarchist and popular newspapers reported on his tour, which ultimately raised hundreds of dollars for *Freedom, Les Temps Nouveaux, Free Society,* and *Discontent.* His comments here refer to his forthcoming New York dates.
4. Kropotkin inserted a dash in place of the name at this point.

Whereas article 7 of the law of November 13–21 and December 3, 1849, states: The Minister of the Interior can, by police measures, enjoin any foreigner traveling through or residing in France to immediately leave the French territory and have him taken to the border.

Whereas article 8 of the same law, states: Any stranger who would have absconded from the execution of the measures set forth in the preceding article, or who, after having exited France following these measures, would have re-entered without Government permission, will be brought before the court and sentenced to one to six months imprisonment.

After expiration of his punishment, he will be taken back to the border.

Considering that the presence on the territory of the Republic of the named Goldmann, Emma, of Russian nationality is of such nature as to compromise public security;

On the proposition of the Chief of Police, Orders:

Article One

It is enjoined to the named Goldmann, Emma, to exit the French territory.[1]

Article 2

The Chief of Police is assigned the execution of the present order.

Executed in Paris, March 26, 1901.

SIGNED: WALDECK-ROUSSEAU[2]

Certified copy

To the Chief Officer of General Security

The Chief of the 4th Bureau

ADS, Dossier Emma Golkmann, Numéro 124786, Cote B/A 305, Archives de la Préfecture de Police. Document is addressed to "Minister of the Interior and of Religions" and is written in a different hand than that of the signatory, Prime Minister Rene Waldeck-Rousseau. Translated from French.

1. EG was apparently never aware of this extradition order from the French government, having left France before it was issued. Neither was she notified of such an order in subsequent visits to France. Compare EG to Theodore Dreiser in 1929: "I was never driven from France. I lived in Paris from Feb, 1900 to the end of Nov. of the same year and then returned to the States. . . . No, it was left for America to drive me from pillar to poste and then kick me out" (EG to Dreiser, 20 January 1929, *EGP,* reel 20). Compare, also, her account of her departure from France in "Talk with Emma Goldman," Interview in the *New York Sun,* 6 January 1901, above.
2. Rene Waldeck-Rousseau (1846–1904) served twice as minister of the interior (1881, 1883–1885), and was later appointed prime minister (1899–1902). Although he signed the extradition order ejecting EG from France in 1901, he was considered a member of the republican left.

Interview in the *PHILADELPHIA NORTH AMERICAN*

Philadelphia, 11 April 1901

A Character Study of Emma Goldman

By Miriam Michelson

"I shall speak in Philadelphia."

Emma Goldman said this to me yesterday.[1] Her hands, a workingwoman's hands, were crossed on her knee. She was sitting in a rocking chair in an ordinary little Philadelphia parlor, but her voice, which becomes guttural and strongly accentuated in its Teutonic quality when she speaks earnestly, had nothing of the commonplace in it.

Somehow, I believed her when she said it. There is so much force, as well as sincerity, in this woman's speech that one must find very good reason in one's own mind for differing with her. And when Emma Goldman says she will, a little matter like the "she won't" of the Mayor,[2] the Director of Public Safety[3] and the police force of Philadelphia seems hardly an obstacle worth considering.

"I shall speak in Philadelphia," she repeated, the line between her eyebrows growing more marked as her voice became firmer. "I may have to suffer the consequences, but speak I will. Perhaps the Mayor and Director English will come to their senses. No one would be gladder than I if they come to understand how foolish they have been. But whether they do or not, I shall speak."

"On what subject?"

"The methods of Russia in America," she answered with a smile. "The methods of Russia are of the tenth century; the intellectual development of America is of the twentieth. They don't go very well together, do they?"

1. Miriam Michelson (1870–1942), who was given a byline for her interview of EG, was an American novelist, playwright, drama critic, and contributor to mainstream newspapers in Philadelphia and San Francisco. She would go on to become a well-known author. Her best-known works include *In the Bishop's Carriage* (New York: Grosset and Dunlap, 1904), *The Madigans* (New York: Century, 1904), *Anthony Overman* (New York: Doubleday, Page, 1906), and *The Motherlode of Gold and Silver* (Boston: Stratford, 1934).

2. Samuel Howell Ashbridge (1849–1906), mayor of Philadelphia from 1899 to 1903, was entrenched in the Republican machine that controlled Philadelphia politics at the end of the nineteenth century. His term of office was marked by allegations of graft, corruption, and intimidation of the press. In April 1901, Ashbridge refused EG the right to speak in Philadelphia, a decision that generated publicity and support that EG welcomed. Public opinion ultimately forced Ashbridge to lift the prohibition against her.

3. Abraham Lincoln English (1864–1913) was director of Philadelphia's Department of Public Safety in 1901, under Mayor Samuel H. Ashbridge.

SHE IS A CREATURE OF MOODS.

The photograph of Miss Goldman which accompanies this article will not give you an altogether truthful impression of this remarkable woman. To realize her personality you must know that this awful Anarchist is a creature of moods.

When she speaks, when she is interested, when she is delivering an address, the face which on the first page looks sad and rather weary and a bit heavy, is lighted up till it is almost pretty. Miss Goldman would rather face Lieutenant Wood,[4] of the Philadelphia police force, than the camera.

"Newspaper sketches always make me look vulgar," she said, when we were planning her photographs. "I am not vain. I have no reason to be. But I cannot bear to be made to appear vulgar."

Vulgarity is the last characteristic one would think of in connection with Miss Goldman. You must imagine this strong face softened and femininized by its pretty coloring, by a very fair skin, and cheeks and the tip of the chin pink with excitement.

The great, column-like throat is beautifully white. The hair is a fair brown, and, though the eyebrows and lashes are darker, the small, deep-set eyes are a clear gray that looks blue when Miss Goldman's speech becomes emphatic. And this happens pretty often.

"It is my nature to be what I am," she says. "As long as I live I must be a crusader. What I think, what I feel, I must speak. Not for a hundred, not for five hundred years, perhaps, will the principles of anarchy triumph. But what has that to do with it? 'Is it right?' not 'Is it hopeless?' is the touchstone of courage and principle."

"I AM NOT HOPELESS."

"If all the world was at peace and happy, and in one small village there lived a man who was a toiling slave, a woman who was suffering, a child condemned to degrading labor, I could know no rest. It is my temperament to propagate opinions. As a matter of fact, I am not hopeless.

"I see the world improving. I know that fifteen years ago no audience in America would listen to the doctrines I advocate. I know that to-day in every town all over the country there is a society formed to disseminate those ideas. I know that when Krapotkin came to America there was but one college in all the country courageous enough, enlightened enough, to listen to him.[5] And to-day he is besieged by offers for his lectures, offers of $75 and $100 for each address from institutions of learning in every great city of America."

---

4. In fact, Wood was "Acting Lieutenant" (in the following article from the *Philadelphia North American*, his name is spelled as Woods); dressed in plain clothes, he led a group of six officers from the police station on Second and Christian streets to block EG's passage into Standard Hall. See *Philadelphia North American*, 10 April 1901, p. 1; and *Philadelphia Public Ledger*, 10 April 1901, p. 3.
5. In 1897 Kropotkin spoke at the Lowell Institute in Cambridge, Massachusetts, and to the Prospect Union, a group of Harvard students and local workers. At the time of this interview, Kropotkin was on his second U.S. tour.

Miss Goldman was born in St. Petersburg, but was educated mainly in Germany. She is a little body, this famous Anarchist, who has roused in the Mayor and the Director of Public Safety and the whole police force a desperate desire to stifle free speech in Philadelphia. She is stout, though, and broad-hipped, a sturdy-looking, quick-moving, intense woman.

"I very well understand," she said with quiet scorn, "why your Mayor and your Director English object to my speaking in Philadelphia. It is not because of my Anarchistic opinions—what do they know of these? They do not know what an Anarchist is. Besides, I have delivered speeches in Philadelphia two months ago,[6] and often I have spoken here.

"But it occurs to your Mayor that he has a very nasty, a very black record.[7] He will do something to show the people that he is not so black as he is painted. He says to them: 'See what it is I am doing for you. See how careful I am of Philadelphia's pure morals. Here comes a shocking woman, an Anarchist, a wretched creature, a bomb-thrower. See how I stifle her. See how I forbid her speech. Philadelphia shall not be corrupted by her anarchistic doctrines!'

"And as Anarchy is not understood, as it is a bogy to the ordinary so-called respectable community, your Mayor gets the credit of being a very wise, very courageous man, whereas he is only very foolish."

FREE PRESS IS IN DANGER.

"For he cannot prevent my speaking. It is not Emma Goldman, it is not anarchy, he attacks. It is liberty of speech. Let the newspapers take care. The next thing attacked will be the freedom of the press. For me, I must press this case. I must see just how far the enlightened public opinion of the independent city of Philadelphia will let its Mayor go.

"Do you realize that Lieutenant Wood, of your police force, came at me with his fist at my breast? I have been treated by this man—an officer, a lieutenant of police—with such brutality and vulgarity as Russia would be ashamed of. I am an impulsive woman. I could control myself only by remembering that there were two young girl students with me just ready for their diplomas. I would face arrest—though I assure you I know the discomfort of prison life—but arrest for them in my company would have hurt their careers. But a brute like that Wood—"

She stretched out her hand, closing her fist and bringing it down upon her knee. We went on talking about herself and her opinions, among other things her opposition to prisons, and her contention that no human being, however degraded, is irredeemable.

---

6. EG tells Marie Goldsmith of speaking before "very active" comrades in Philadelphia (see particularly note 3 in Letter to Marie Goldsmith, 8 February 1901, above).

7. The Ashbridge administration distinguished itself for lawlessness in a city already widely known as the most corrupt in the nation. In addition to graft, the scandals during the Ashbridge administration included intimidation of the press (specifically, threats against the *Philadelphia North American*), the growth of prostitution and speakeasies, and gambling in Philadelphia schools.

"Even Wood—even Lieutenant Wood," she said, hurried by her interest in her subject past the point where her sense of humor usually stands guard, "there is hope even for such a man as that. It is his position that holds him. Let him once break from the fear of losing his little political job; let him cut loose from a corrupt municipal machine that corrupts all who benefit by it, and he can again become a man who dares to think and dares to feel."

There is vigor in this woman's speech. She is utterly fearless, utterly free from restraint. There is no "no thoroughfare" for her mind. She dares to follow wherever conviction leads.

No one who has not heard her deliver an address can conceive of the force there is in this Russian free thinker. No care of the prettinesses of manner or speech can stay her. Her voice may break, her knowledge of English may fail her; but she is more effective than art could possibly make her, more eloquent than the completest elegance of speech could give. She snarls, she sneers, she thunders at her audience, and she is as indifferent to their rage as to their approval.

HAS NO FAITH IN THE MOB.

"I know the mob," she said, yesterday, "and I do not count upon it—no, not a bit. I looked at the crowd that followed hurrahing for me the other night, and I said in my mind to them, 'You cheer for me, you follow me, but you'd hang me if your mood changed.'

"It is not in the laboring man, the lowest classes, that I find my hope. It is the middle class and the professional people that are being educated to whom theories of life like mine appeal. Just so long as there remain in the world men and women ready to die for principle, there will be hope for mankind. It is from the minority that the strength to uplift the world has always come. In America we are becoming more and more imperialistic. We shall become more like Russia before we become less like her.

"But so far as the spread of anarchy goes, let me tell you that a little political move like this of your Mayor's—yes, or one policeman like Lieutenant Wood—goes further to make Anarchists than all the speeches I have ever delivered. It would have been different if there had been some excuse, if there had been a strike or if the public mind was heated and excited. But as it is, it is your Mayor who is inciting to riot; it is your Lieutenant Wood who appeals to violence. For me, I do not admit that I ever incited men to riot."[8]

But I'll admit for you that what you say is enough to incite them to riot, Emma Goldman. If during a strike, when bitterness and poverty and excitement combine to upset men's reason, a fire brand like yourself were thrown among them the damage done might be incalculable.

8. EG was convicted of inciting to riot in 1893, for which she spent ten months in prison. See her disavowal of incendiary speech attributed to her by police witnesses in "The People vs. Emma Goldman," Excerpt from Trial Transcript, 4 October 1893, above.

If I were a guardian of the peace, I'd rather Johann Most[9] himself would tell the strikers of their wrongs than that a woman like yourself, with your clear intelligence, your impetuous tongue, and your ardent heart, should heap contempt last arbitrament, or encourage them to battle for their rights.

I should fear your influence, Emma Goldman. I should fear your cleverness. I should fear your courage. I should fear your capacity to rouse the sleeping devil in the mob that stirs uneasily when your uncompromising voice rings out.

All of which has nothing to do with the case in point, of course.

Emma Goldman is not a fanatic; nor is she a cruel-hearted monster; nor is she a dreamer.

"The man who joins a movement because his stomach is empty," she says in rude epigram, "will leave it as soon as he is better off. We Anarchists want people who think to listen to us—not the people who only feel. Enlightened public opinion will come to know us in time, not as bomb throwers, but as free men and women, who want the world to be free, who hope to teach the people to govern themselves, not to be governed like children by the rod of the law."

"I wonder, Miss Goldman, whether you'd approve of Mrs. Nation?" I asked.[10]

"As a woman who is willing to sacrifice herself for a principle? Yes. As a one-idead reformer, who foolishly expects to make men abstain from drink by smashing saloons—no. And then—I am sorry—I have been unable to convince myself of her sincerity, for she accepts money for what she does."

"And you?"

"I? I am a trained nurse. I support myself by my work. I was to have come here some time ago, but I had an important case which I could not leave.

"Do you suppose I would accept money for my work? Never. It would spoil it all. My traveling expenses, yes; my hotel bill, if I do not stop with friends. But to speak, to work, to propagate the truth I feel—I love that. I could not take money for that."

Does it not occur to you that there's something rather lofty about this point of view—for an Anarchist? As a lecturer, this woman could make more money than half a dozen trained nurses. Her work would be infinitely easier, and, as she says, she loves it. But she loves it too well to make money out of it.

"I am not conceited," she said, "but I am not blind to the fact that I can work, that I can do things. I could make what goody-goody people call an honest living in other ways, but there is no other life than just this for me."

As a property Anarchist, to be used by the Mayor as a bogy, Emma Goldman is not a success. She likes "women to be feminine," she told me. She loves "flowers and pretty things, although I cannot have them, for there are other uses I must put money to."

9. Refers to German-born anarchist orator, editor, and publisher Johann Most.
10. Carry Amelia Moore Nation (1846–1911) was the American temperance crusader and women's rights advocate known for her violent methods (including the use of a hatchet) in closing down saloons across the country beginning in 1900.

WORKED IN A PRISON HOSPITAL.

In the car, as we came uptown together she glanced across to a pretty girl, stylishly dressed, and told me how she enjoyed looking at her. As we walked along the street together she noticed the pretty things in the shop windows and commented upon them impersonally as desirable things for the adornment of other women. When she was imprisoned for a year in New York she served all that time in the prison hospital, and you could not have made the degraded women who learned to adore her believe that she was an Anarchist. She went to Europe last year, because she wanted to study to become a physician. But she is back in America working still at the hardest profession a woman can adopt, and her young brother is going through Columbia College at her expense.[11]

No, if even the Mayor and Director English and Lieutenant Wood were to go to call upon Emma Goldman, the Anarchist, they would find her too human, too kindly, too tolerant, too straightforward and honest and altogether too clever for their purpose.

"Wait, and you will see that I shall speak. It is a small matter, of course, if Emma Goldman is denied the right of speech. But if I am denied that right other Anarchists in this city will also be denied it. For this I must fight. And I will carry it through the courts, and into the prison, if I must, but I will speak before I go back to New York. New York is more cosmopolitan. One can breathe freer there. Philadelphia is narrow, of course. It is the cradle of conventionality. Still, I shall speak here."[12]

I have engaged a seat for Miss Goldman's lecture. I am sure that if the Mayor and the Director of Public Safety and a certain lieutenant of police express a wish to hear it, they can also be accommodated, and they might learn something from this Russian woman of the difference between tenth and twentieth century methods of governing.

Philadelphia North American, 11 April 1901, p. 2.

11. Morris Goldman (b. 1879) is EG's younger brother, Moe, who is referred to in *Living My Life* as Yegor. He moved to New York City in 1898, where he lived with EG, who helped finance his studies at Columbia University. He later became a doctor based in Iowa. EG had hoped to obtain a medical degree in Europe but gave up her plan because of the time required to meet matriculation requirements, including learning Latin (see particularly note 7, Letter to Max Nettlau, 4 January 1900, above). Five years earlier, she had apparently studied nursing and midwifery in Vienna for five months.

12. EG did speak in Philadelphia on the same day as this interview, 11 April, at a secret meeting to the Single Tax Society (see "Tyranny of Police Publicly Denounced," Article in the *Philadelphia North American,* 12 April 1901, below). Then on 14 April she spoke with Voltairine de Cleyre before a large crowd at the Industrial Art Hall. The meeting was sponsored by the Social Science Club, whose participants passed a resolution protesting the violation of EG's right to free speech. Ending her Philadelphia tour on 17 April, EG spoke with de Cleyre at the Bricklayer's Hall to a meeting sponsored by the United Labor League.

Article in the *PHILADELPHIA NORTH AMERICAN*

Philadelphia, 12 April 1901

Tyranny of Police Publicly Denounced

Addresses Made at a Mass Meeting Under
the Auspices of the Single Tax Society.

Emma Goldman Carries Out Her Promise to Speak
in This City Despite the Police.

She Denounces Ashbridge and English and Says
Their Acts Would Shame the Czar.

Despite the orders, threats and warnings of Director English,[1] Emma Goldman, Anarchist, made a public address last night in the very shadow of the City Hall, and the police authorities knew nothing about it until an hour or more after the meeting had ended.

She spoke to the Single Tax Society[2] of Philadelphia, in Mercantile Library Hall, Tenth street, above Chestnut. About 200 persons heard her, for the hall was crowded to its capacity, and her every utterance was greeted with unanimous applause.

Although no public announcement of her coming had been made, it was generally understood by those in attendance that she would be there, and at exactly 9.15 o'clock she appeared.

Arthur Pleydell, editor of Justice, a Single Tax paper of Delaware,[3] was discussing the attempts of the local Administration to suppress free speech, when he was interrupted by the demonstration which met Miss Goldman's arrival. She took a seat in the front part of the room, and Mr. Pleydell presently closed his address.[4]

Percy Marcellus, who was presiding, then announced that the "floor was open," and instantly there were calls for Miss Goldman from all over the hall. She stepped up to the platform and began with composure and deliberation, but as she progressed in her bitter denunciation of Director English and his men, she warmed almost to passion, and the words fell from her lips in torrents.

---

1. Both the director of Philadelphia's public safety, Abraham Lincoln English, and the mayor, Samuel Howell Ashbridge, had prohibited EG from speaking in the city.
2. A number of prominent single-taxers in Philadelphia were anarchist sympathizers.
3. Arthur Pleydell (1872–1932), was an anarchist, single-taxer, and editor of *Justice*, the Delaware single-tax paper, until November 1901.
4. In addition to Pleydell, architect William L. Price and G. Frank Stephens, single-taxers, and anarchist George Brown each addressed the meeting before EG's arrival.

MISS GOLDMAN'S SPEECH.

"Mr. Chairman, ladies and gentlemen," she said, when a second outburst of applause had subsided, "I thank you for this kind reception. I did not at first intend to come here to-night—not that I doubted that you would receive me as you have, but because I hesitated to take advantage of your hospitality in the face of the action of the law and order people of your city, who say they will not let me speak.

"I can think of no other word than absurd to characterize that action. It is enough to set not only people like yourselves thinking, but every half-intelligent man or woman—even the 'dummies,' as we call them, for these two gentlemen, your Mayor Ashbridge and your Director English, are attempting in these free United States such a willful act as, even if free speech were tolerated in Russia, the Czar would be ashamed of.

"These authorities of your government say that I shall not speak. As I do not believe in government, I shall ignore them. I have decided to take up the fight here and to fight it out to the end. I do not want to go to prison. I want to walk under the sky, under the stars—but not the Stars and Stripes—but prison or no prison I will not be silenced.

"If you are willing to stand quietly by and permit the freedom of speech to be taken from you, then you might as well go back forty years and restore slavery, for what good can be accomplished for society if expression is denied, and if a man like English is to dictate what you shall say and what not?

"He has gone further than that, though. He has taken to himself the potency of the Pope of Rome to decide what is going to be said before it is spoken. This is not, as I first thought, vanity. It is insanity! I certainly shall oppose it on every occasion and find out how far they will go. It is Emma Goldman to-day, but it may be you to-morrow and somebody else the next day."

"AMERICA IS AROUSED."

"I notice that all America is aroused and indignant over the outrages now being perpetrated in Russia, but when it happens in America, in your free America, you are all quiet. If, on last Tuesday night, I had dared, not to use a bomb or a dagger, as they do in Russia, but if I had dared to touch with the tip of my finger a button on the precious person of this Lieutenant Woods he would have lashed me as the serfs are lashed by the Cossacks, because I could see that he is a brute, although he was drunk beyond his capacity and perhaps did not know what he was doing.

"The trouble is that these men, Ashbridge, English and Woods, know that we are telling the truth. Nothing is more dangerous than the truth, and that's why they want to silence us. But their action has done more for Anarchism than I and my comrades have done in ten years. I am thankful to them, and I think I'll take up a collection and send them flowers or cigars or whisky, which they would rather have, perhaps.

"The authorities have seized upon this as a pretext. I know that your Mayor is a man with a past, and he is trying to get the admiration of the so-called respectable people of the community by saying that he and English are always looking after their safety,[5] and that they know better what these people need than they know themselves.

"But what does it mean to be one of the 'respectable' people to-day? It means to be one who never objects to anything, who pays his taxes, who submits to fraud and oppression, who goes to church on Sunday and during the sermon thinks up a way to beat somebody on Monday. To be a 'respectable' person nowadays is to place men in positions to guard your safety who are least fitted to do so—it is to be an idiot. I am glad to say that I do not belong to that 'respectable' community.

"In these times in America, as soon as a man commits a crime, no matter how black or treacherous, if he is backed by the government everybody falls on his knees and they erect arches to him or smother him with kisses. I am sure that English has received hundreds of letters of congratulations from these old maids."

ASHBRIDGE AND ENGLISH TOOLS.

"That is the root of it all. Ashbridge and English are only the tools in the hands of those behind them. It is the community that keeps such men in office that is guilty of the outrage.

"These men have made a mistake, and they have not the courage to admit it. In face of the fact that a paper like The North American and all thinking people are opposing their action, they say they will go right on and continue to stop free speech.

"To me it is a settled question that free speech does not exist in America unless it suits the government. If the people of Philadelphia do not take immediate action to oppose the outrages committed in their city this week, they will sacrifice their freedom on the altar of greed, robbery, fraud and all that represents government.

"I repeat that I shall speak in Philadelphia. If I cannot get a hall I will speak nevertheless, if I have to do so from the City Hall tower. If this is to be a fight for my principles, the Mayor will find that I am more courageous than he, and that I can die for them if need be." [. . .]

Philadelphia North American, 12 April 1901, pp. 1–2. Excised from this article, following the report on EG's address, is a description of the closing remarks of a workman, after which "nearly everybody there shook hands with Miss Goldman, and the meeting ended." The article also reports on the speeches preceding EG's by prominent Philadelphia anarchist George Brown and Arthur Pleydell, editor of the Delaware single-tax paper *Justice,* who denounced the suppression of free speech and detailed the resolutions adopted by the Single Tax Society deeming the action of the Philadelphia authorities "tyrannical" and "a gross usurpation of power," and calling "upon all who value their liberties to resist the attempts made to Russianize our city government." Reprinted in part, with editorial comment, in "Free Speech Strangled," *Free Society,* 21 April 1901, pp. 1–2, *EGP,* reel 47.

5. Political scandals of the Ashbridge administration are detailed in note 7, "A Character Study of Emma Goldman," Interview in the *Philadelphia North American,* 11 April 1901, above.

Body Cremated, Goldman Spoke.

Anarchists Wept in Taking Leave of Paita, the Italian Self Slayer.

Speech Defended Suicide.

Goldman Said the Dead Man Had Too Fine a Nature to Bear With Life.

Ashes Are to Be Preserved.

After a long address by Emma Goldman, in which she endeavored to show that an idealist, who finds the world unbearable is justified in committing suicide, the body of Joseph Paita, the Italian anarchist, who shot himself at 1221 Penn avenue on Friday, was cremated at Samson's mortuary yesterday afternoon. The function was attended by from 75 to 100 anarchists, most of whom saw the body shoved into the furnace at the conclusion of Miss Goldman's address. Some of them shed tears when invited to look for the last time upon the face of the dead man. Miss Goldman herself, appeared to be deeply affected, and admitted in her speech that notwithstanding all the reasons she had advanced in favor of suicide, affection was stronger than philosophy.

The body of Paita was taken to the undertaking establishment in the forenoon and lay for some time in the little chapel before the assembling of the anarchist mourners. It had been neatly dressed and placed in a plain wooden coffin upon the lid of which some friends of the deceased placed a large bunch of red carnations, bound together with a broad red ribbon, the flowers and the ribbon being the only touches of the symbolical anarchist color anywhere in evidence,[1] except the fire in the furnace. Slowly the anarchists gathered, until nearly 3 o'clock, the hour set for the delivery of Miss Goldman's address. One of the last to come was Henry Bauer, of Allegheny. The audience consisted partly of Italians, but there was probably a majority of Russian Hebrews, doubtless on account of Miss Goldman being of that nationality. There was a fair sprinkling of women in the audience. A few had children with them. Shortly after 3 o'clock Miss Goldman took a position at the head of the coffin and began a speech which lasted nearly half an hour. It was almost entirely devoted to a justification of the dead man's act of self-destruction. She said in part:

---

1. On the symbolism of the color red to the anarchist movement, see note 4 to "Badly Advised," Article in the *New-Yorker Staats-Zeitung*, 22 August 1893, above.

CHEAP MOTIVES ASSIGNED.

"When a man takes his life the world speculates upon the motive for his act. Generally the motives assigned are small and cheap. I know that our friend, who lies here took his life because he could not endure the sufferings of the world. His nature was high and noble. He was intelligent and physically strong. He was able to make a good living for himself, had he chosen to walk in the narrow paths that most men take. But he could not live so. Society with its meanness set bounds to his activities which he could not endure. He saw on all sides of him thousands carelessly laughing and dancing, rich, happy and gay, while beside them other thousands were bleeding to death. With his sensitive nature he felt the sufferings of the miserable in the world. He was not able to bear it and he could do little to relieve it. He was too sensitive for the world and so he was justified in taking his life. He is better off dead. The dead know nothing, feel nothing, while the living who are endowed with a noble nature that pines for liberty of action amid an environment of slavery must suffer as long as life lasts.

"Yet while reason and philosophy tell us he is better as he is, there is something stronger. Affection will not in a long time cease to regret that he did not choose to live. We shall miss him from our midst and regret the absence of the high ideal, by which he was inspired. Let us then over his body resolve, not swearing as the Christians do, but swearing by our own energy and our own honesty of purpose to carry forward his work as he would wish it to be carried."

SOME WEPT BITTERLY.

Miss Goldman stated in conclusion that it had been expected to have an anarchist come from New York to speak in Italian, but the time had been too short and the local Italians were too much overcome by emotion to do any speaking. Her address would therefore be the only one. She invited the friends of the deceased to look for a last time upon his face, which most of them did, a few of the men and several of the women weeping bitterly as they took the last farewell. The undertaker then took charge of the body and moved it to the basement to be placed in the retort. When it was ready the audience was allowed to see it consigned to the flames. Wrapped from head to foot in heavy white cloths, it was quickly shoved into the furnace before the gaze of all and the ceremonies of the funeral were over. The furnace was heated to a temperature of 1,200 degrees. It was stated that about four hours would be required for the body to be consumed, but that it will not be taken from the furnace until this morning. The ashes will be turned over to the personal friends of the dead man's among the Italians.

Previous to the cremation yesterday Miss Goldman gave out for publication the letter which Paita addressed to her before killing himself. It read as follows:

"I am tired of existing conditions, and for that reason I have decided to commit suicide. My last request to you is to give my love to all friends and the comrades. While in theory I believe the anarchist should live for the purpose of propagating the cause and trying so far as possible to eliminate the iniquities that surround and permeate the social system, thus assisting toward the grand ideals when the oppressed shall be raised up and liberty be known in its fullest and greatest sense, nevertheless I am compelled to acknowledge my weakness and unfitness for the struggle, for I cannot stand the strain of battling against the obstacles in life. Therefore, I relieve the comrades of the incubus of my inutility. Love to friends and the camaraderie. Long live anarchy!"

Miss Goldman left at 5 o'clock yesterday evening for Cleveland, where she will give a series of lectures, beginning this evening.[2]

Pittsburg (Pa.) Post, 5 May 1901, p. 2. Copyright 2001 *Pittsburgh Post-Gazette.* All rights reserved. Reprinted with permission.

---

2. EG lectured on 5 May 1901 in Cleveland on "The Modern Phase of Anarchy" before the Franklin Liberal Club. She also spoke later that evening on "The Cause and Effect of Vice."

Defends Acts of Bomb Throwers.

Woman Praises Motives Leading Up to Many Terrible Crimes.

Speaker Arraigns Police Who Attend an Anarchist Meeting.

Emma Goldman, the famous anarchist orator and propagandist, addressed a meeting at Memorial hall yesterday afternoon.[1] While the hall was not crowded, a good sized audience was in attendance and evidenced its approval of the speaker's sentiments by frequent and vigorous applause.

Officers Bernhart and Thorpe of the citizens' squad formed a portion of the audience, while Patrolman Gibbons lingered around on the sidewalk in front of the hall, just to be handy in case of emergency. Nothing at all exciting happened, however, and the plain clothes men up stairs never turned a hair as the orator entered upon a scathing arraignment of policemen, and especially detectives. "Soldiers are bad enough," she said, "but policemen are worse, and a detective is the meanest and most despicable creature in the universe." It is said that Miss Goldman had been informed that the "plain clothes" men were to be among her auditors, and she considerately intended to include them in the class of "detectives."

Miss Goldman is of small stature, but is a woman of wonderful vigor. She has a strong and resonant voice, and her command of English is excellent, although she has a slight German accent. She spoke entirely without reference to notes, and never for a moment hesitated or stumbled in her delivery. She has a fine vocabulary and also shows evidence of careful and systematic reading.

Miss Goldman outlined the principles of anarchism and detailed the methods by which she hoped for their accomplishment. Her talk was full of forceful passages, in some cases more notable for their strength than for their elegance.

"Men under the present state of society are mere products of circumstances," she said. "Under the galling yoke of government, ecclesiasticism and the bonds of custom and prejudice it is impossible for the individual to work out his own career as he could

1. EG addressed the Franklin Club in Cleveland on 5 May, traveling there from Pittsburgh, where she had delivered the eulogy at Joseph Paita's funeral the day before (see "Body Cremated, Goldman Spoke," Article in the *Pittsburgh Post*, 5 May 1901, above). In attendance was Leon Czolgosz. EG later recognized Czolgosz as the young man who approached her at intermission and asked her to suggest something for him to read.

wish. Anarchism aims at a new and complete freedom. It strives to bring about a freedom which is not only a freedom from within but also a freedom from without, which will prevent any man having the desire to interfere in any way with the liberty of his neighbor. Vanderbilt says, 'I am a free man within myself, but the others be damned.'[2] This is not the freedom that we are striving for. We merely desire complete individual liberty and this can never be obtained as long as there is an existing government.

"We do not favor the Socialist idea of converting men and women into mere producing machines under the eye of a paternal government. We go to the opposite extreme and demand the fullest and most complete liberty for each and every person to work out his own salvation upon any line that he pleases so long as he does not interfere with the happiness of others. The degrading notion of men and women as breeding machines is far from our ideals of life.

"Anarchism has nothing to do with future governments or economic arrangements. We do not favor any particular settlement in this line, but merely seek to do away with the present evils. The future will provide for these arrangements after our work has been done. Anarchism deals merely with social relations and not with economic arrangements."

The speaker deprecated the idea that all Anarchists were in favor of violence and bomb throwing. She declared that nothing was further from the principles which they support. She then went on, however, into a detailed explanation of the different crimes committed by Anarchists lately, declaring that the motive was good in each case, and that these acts were merely a matter of temperament. Some men were so constituted, she said, that they were unable to stand idly by and see the wrongs that were being endured by their fellow mortals. She herself did not believe in these methods, but she did not think that they should be too severely condemned in view of the high and noble motives which prompted their perpetration. "We must have education before we can have power," declared Miss Goldman. "Some believe that we should first obtain the force and let the intelligence and education come afterwards. Nothing could be more fallacious. If we get the education and intelligence first among the people the power will come to us without a struggle."

In the evening Miss Goldman spoke on "The Cause and Effect of Vice." She dwelt in detail upon the most revolting forms of social evil, and assigned to each their cause. Some of the vices which are most abhorrent to the sense of modern civilization were upheld by Miss Goldman.

She bitterly attacked the churches and the modern system of education as responsible for most of the social evil. She did not hesitate to put forward a number of senti-

2. EG paraphrases railroad magnate William Henry Vanderbilt who in 1879 eliminated a popular but unprofitable railroad line between New York and Chicago. When asked if he should not take a loss in order to provide a public service, Vanderbilt replied, "The public be damned. I am working for my stockholders."

ments far more radical and sensational than anything ever before publicly advanced in Cleveland.

She was warmly applauded throughout her remarks by a crowd fully twice as big as that of the afternoon. Patrolmen Wilmore, Martinec and Smith of the citizens' dress squad were present during the address, but did not deem it necessary to interfere.

Gaetano Bresci.

Gaetano Bresci, the Italian rebel and Anarchist, whose overflowing sympathy with human suffering prompted him to strike down one of the world's tyrants, is dead (at least such is the report circulated in the daily press).[1] All tyrants, despots, rulers, parasites, Pharisees, and hypocrites, can now breathe freely once more. What does it matter to them that they have added another tear and blood-stained page to the history of crime and misery; that they have tortured a man into insanity; that they have bought their safety through the agony and despair of a man whose only sin consisted in rebelling against wrong? He is dead; and tyranny reigns supreme.

"After all the man was only an Anarchist, an enemy to law and order, an outcast; why care about him?" echoes the thoughtless multitude.

Fortunately the world is not inhabited by tyrants and slaves only; there are a vast number of men and women whose hearts, even as Bresci's, throb with love for those whom power and greed has condemned to everlasting ignorance and despair. Men and women, in all stations of life, who see the injustice and cruelty around them; and who feel that Bresci's awful death is but another indictment against those institutions in society that are being maintained at the cost of human lives.

A society which destroys myriads of its members, must give birth to men like Bresci. It is violence and force upon which the whole system is based, and that begets force. How could it be otherwise?

Bresci is the child of Italy, where the masses of the people toil and sweat, yet never enjoy the beauties that mother nature has so abundantly bestowed upon that country; Italy, whose strong, healthy, and stalwart men must leave their native soil to wander in strange lands in search of bread; Italy, where women are wrecks at the age of twenty, and whose children, dirty, filthy, ragged, and starved, are degraded to beggars. The few have robbed the country to gain their accumulated wealth, and are now suppressing every sound of protest, celebrating orgies to drown the voices of agony coming from the prisons, where the daring spirits are confined to a life of hell. It was here where he first imbibed the spirit of discontent and hatred against a society which endures such awful conditions; it

---

1. Sentenced to life imprisonment on 29 August 1900 for his assassination of King Umberto of Italy a month earlier, Gaetano Bresci was held in the penitentiary on Santo Stefano Island, having received the severest sentence allowable under Italian law. News of his apparent suicide reached the United States on 24 May 1901. Most anarchists, including Bresci's widow, suspected that he had been murdered by his jailors.

was here where he learned to understand and to love the idea that is to bring the dawn of the day, and establish human happiness.

Since man has dictated terms to his brother, the spirit of righteous indignation has been afloat; and it is well that it should be so. Were it not for the spirit of discontent, of indignation and protest against wrong, the spirit that feels every blow, pain, and sorrow that suffering and starving humanity has to endure, progress would be impossible. It was this spirit that moved man to become helpful, good, and generous; to tear down the old institutions of darkness and ignorance, and build new ones. It was this spirit that has given to past generations the power of endurance, determination, and enthusiasm in their fight for man's highest treasure—liberty.

Each age has had its John Browns, its Perovskayas, its Parsons, Spies, Angiolillos, and its Brescis,[2] who were misunderstood, persecuted, mobbed, tortured, and killed, by those who could not reach the sublime heights attained by these men. Yet they have not lived in vain, for it is to them that we owe all that is good and noble, grand and useful in the world.

It is therefore useless to assert that the science of life, the philosophy of liberty and human independence, are responsible for the acts of violence. This may satisfy sensational minds; but earnest men and women are beginning to understand that the philosophy of Anarchism, which occupies the most intellectual minds of our time, which has given to the world a Tolstoy, a Kropotkin, and many others, which permeates the literature, art, science, and every branch of human knowledge, which aims at the deliverance of mankind from a life of tragedy and despair, which is based upon harmony, and the recognition of the equal rights of every individual to all that his intelligence, skill, and ingenuity can produce, certainly can have nothing to do with violence, nor have the representatives of this idea ever advocated it.

Bresci has paid the penalty of his crime. And a crime indeed it was to have loved one's kind, to have felt the existing wrongs in the world, and to have dared to strike a blow at organized authority. He has lived and died true to himself; and the world will have to learn that while one Bresci is killed, hundreds are born ready to lay down their lives to free mankind from tyranny, power, ignorance, and poverty.

EMMA GOLDMAN.

Free Society, 2 June 1901, p. 1.

2. In addition to the American rebel John Brown, EG refers to Russian revolutionary activist Sophia Perovskaya, the Chicago Haymarket anarchists Albert Parsons and August Spies, and Italian anarchist Michele Angiolillo.

Dear Girl:

This is from the hospital, *sub rosa*. Just out of the strait-jacket, after eight days.

For over a year I was in the strictest solitary; for a long time mail and reading matter were denied me. I have no words to describe the horror of the last months . . . . I have passed through a great crisis. Two of my best friends died in a frightful manner. The death of Russell,[1] especially, affected me. He was very young, and my dearest and most devoted friend, and he died a terrible death. The doctor charged the boy with shamming, but now he says it was spinal meningitis. I cannot tell you the awful truth,—it was nothing short of murder, and my poor friend rotted away by inches. When he died they found his back one mass of bedsores. If you could read the pitiful letters he wrote, begging to see me, and to be nursed by me! But the Warden wouldn't permit it. In some manner his agony seemed to affect me, and I began to experience the pains and symptoms that Russell described in his notes. I knew it was my sick fancy; I strove against it, but presently my legs showed signs of paralysis, and I suffered excruciating pain in the spinal column, just like Russell. I was afraid that I would be done to death like my poor friend. I grew suspicious of every guard, and would barely touch the food, for fear of its being poisoned. My "head was workin'," they said. And all the time I knew it was my diseased imagination, and I was in terror of going mad . . . . I tried so hard to fight it, but it would always creep up, and get hold of me stronger and stronger. Another week of solitary would have killed me.

I was on the verge of suicide. I demanded to be relieved from the cell, and the Warden ordered me punished. I was put in the strait-jacket. They bound my body in canvas, strapped my arms to the bed, and chained my feet to the posts. I was kept that way eight days, unable to move, rotting in my own excrement. Released prisoners called the attention of our new Inspector to my case. He refused to believe that such things were being done in the penitentiary. Reports spread that I was going blind and insane. Then the Inspector visited the hospital and had me released from the jacket.

I am in pretty bad shape, but they put me in the general ward now, and I am glad of the chance to send you this note.

Sasha.

Berkman, *Prison Memoirs of an Anarchist*, pp. 424–25.

---

1. Russell Schroyer died on 25 April. A young man of nineteen years, Schroyer was portrayed by AB as full of impractical plans to escape the Western Penitentiary. He took part in one abortive escape attempt with AB and was privy to the escape tunnel being dug to free AB. He died as a result of apparent medical malpractice. AB gave no details of Schroyer's sentence, except that it was a short one and he was about to be released when he died. See Berkman, *Prison Memoirs of an Anarchist*, pp. 368–70.

DEAR SONYA:

I cannot tell you how happy I am to be allowed to write to you again. My privileges have been restored by our new Inspector, a very kindly man. He has relieved me from the cell, and now I am again on the range. The Inspector requested me to deny to my friends the reports which have recently appeared in the papers concerning my condition. I have not been well of late, but now I hope to improve. My eyes are very poor. The Inspector has given me permission to have a specialist examine them. Please arrange for it through our local comrades.

There is another piece of very good news, dear friend. A new commutation law has been passed,[1] which reduces my sentence by $2^1/_2$ years. It still leaves me a long time, of course; almost 4 years here, and another year to the workhouse. However, it is a considerable gain, and if I should not get into solitary again, I may—I am almost afraid to utter the thought—I may live to come out. I feel as if I am being resurrected.

The new law benefits the short-timers proportionately much more than the men with longer sentences. Only the poor lifers do not share in it. We were very anxious for a while, as there were many rumors that the law would be declared unconstitutional. Fortunately, the attempt to nullify its benefits proved ineffectual. Think of men who will see something unconstitutional in allowing the prisoners a little more good time than the commutation statute of 40 years ago. As if a little kindness to the unfortunates—really justice—is incompatible with the spirit of Jefferson! We were greatly worried over the fate of this statute, but at last the first batch has been released, and there is much rejoicing over it.

There is a peculiar history about this new law, which may interest you; it sheds a significant side light. It was especially designed for the benefit of a high Federal officer who was recently convicted of aiding two wealthy Philadelphia tobacco manufacturers to defraud the government of a few millions, by using counterfeit tax stamps. Their influence secured the introduction of the commutation bill and its hasty passage. The law would have cut their sentences almost in two, but certain newspapers seem to have

---

1. Pennsylvania's Commutation Act of 1901 repealed an earlier act of 21 May 1869. The 1901 act allowed for reducing a prison sentence for good behavior: shaving off two months for the first year, three months for the second year, four months each for the third and fourth years, and five months for each subsequent year. Upon intake, prisoners were informed of their right to the reduction of sentence based upon good behavior. Monthly reports were issued by prison officials to the governor for reduction recommendations; if a prisoner was not recommended, the officials had to provide justification; the governor, however, could override the recommendation.

taken offence at having been kept in ignorance of the "deal," and protests began to be voiced. The matter finally came up before the Attorney General of the United States,[2] who decided that the men in whose special interest the law was engineered, could not benefit by it, because a State law does not affect U.S. prisoners, the latter being subject to the Federal commutation act.[3] Imagine the discomfiture of the politicians! An attempt was even made to suspend the operation of the statute. Fortunately it failed, and now the "common" State prisoners, who were not at all meant to profit, are being released. The legislature has unwittingly given some unfortunates here much happiness.

I was interrupted in this writing by being called out for a visit. I could hardly credit it: the first comrade I have been allowed to see in nine years! It was Harry Gordon,[4] and I was so overcome by the sight of the dear friend, I could barely speak. He must have prevailed upon the new Inspector to issue a permit. The latter is now Acting Warden, owing to the serious illness of Captain Wright.[5] Perhaps he will allow me to see my sister.[6] Will you kindly communicate with her at once? Meantime I shall try to secure a pass.

WITH RENEWED HOPE, AND ALWAYS WITH GREEN MEMORY OF YOU,
ALEX.

Berkman, *Prison Memoirs of an Anarchist,* pp. 410–11.

---

2. In fact, AB is referring to the Pennsylvania state attorney general in 1901, John P. Elkin, who had run unsuccessfully for governor of Indiana in 1896. He then served as president of the Pennsylvania State Association of School Directors until 1901. He again ran unsuccessfully for governor, this time of Pennsylvania in 1902, and was elected as a Pennsylvania state supreme court justice in 1905.

3. Attorney General Elkin noted that the 1901 act was constitutional in that every constitutional requirement for granting of a pardon had been set out in the act; he declared that the act could be applied retroactively and did not fall within *ex post facto* considerations prohibited by the Constitution. He clarified that as a state law, it applied only to prisoners convicted in state courts, not to federal prisoners incarcerated in state prisons.

4. A Lithuanian-born anarchist living in Pittsburgh, Harry Gordon had served as both secretary and treasurer of the Berkman Defense Association.

5. According to a note in AB's *Prison Memoirs of an Anarchist* (p. 419), Warden E. S. Wright forced officer Robert G. Hunter to testify against men who Hunter knew were innocent. Upon disclosure of this coerced testimony, Warden Wright had fallen ill. Hunter later committed suicide.

6. "Sister" was AB's code for EG.

Article in the *SAN FRANCISCO CHRONICLE*

San Francisco, 8 September 1901

Assassin's Trail of Crime
from Chicago to the Pacific Coast.

Assassin Tells of His Crime.

Czolgosz Declares Emma Goldman's Words Drove Him to Murder.

Chicago, September 7—A special to the Daily News from Buffalo says: The statement of Leon Czolgosz,[1] made to the police, transcribed and signed by the prisoner, is as follows: "I was born in Detroit nearly twenty-nine years ago. My parents were Russian Poles. They came here forty-two years ago. I got my education in the public schools of Detroit, and then went to Cleveland, where I got work. In Cleveland I read books on socialism and met a great many Socialists. I was pretty well known as a Socialist in the West. After being in Cleveland for several years I went to Chicago, where I remained seven months, after which I went to Newburg, on the outskirts of Cleveland, and went to work in the Newburg wire mills.

"During the last five years I have had as friends, anarchists in Chicago, Cleveland, Detroit and other Western cities, and I suppose I became more or less bitter. Yes, I know I was bitter. I never had much luck at anything and this preyed upon me. It made me morose and envious, but what started the craze to kill was a lecture I heard some time ago by Emma Goldman.[2] She was in Cleveland, and I and other anarchists went to hear her. She set me on fire.

"Her doctrine that all rulers should be exterminated was what set me to thinking so that my head nearly split with the pain. Miss Goldman's words went right through me,

---

1. On 6 September 1901, Leon Czolgosz shot President William McKinley at the Pan-American Exposition in Buffalo, New York. McKinley died from complications of his wounds eight days later, and Czolgosz was sentenced to death on 26 September, barely three weeks later. A factory worker and son of Polish immigrants, Czolgosz had been influenced by the Haymarket incident and the 1893 strike in Cleveland, had attended socialist meetings in Cleveland, and been in contact with Cleveland anarchist Emil Schilling, who had warned readers in *Free Society*, 1 September 1901, that Czolgosz had been asking suspicious questions and may be an agent provocateur. Czolgosz had also attended a lecture by EG in Cleveland on 5 May 1901. (For a report of this lecture, see "Defends Acts of Bomb Throwers," Article in the *Cleveland Plain Dealer*, 6 May 1901, above.)
2. EG lectured on 5 May 1901 at the Franklin Liberal Club in Cleveland on "Modern Phases of Anarchy," where Czolgosz asked for suggestions on reading material (see note 1, "Defends Acts of Bomb Throwers," Article in the *Cleveland Plain Dealer*, 6 May 1901, above).

EMMA GOLDMAN, HIGH PRIESTESS OF ANARCHY,
WHOSE SPEECHES INSPIRED CZOLGOSZ TO HIS CRIME.

EMMA GOLDMAN

SPEECH THAT PROMPTED MURDEROUS ASSAULT ON THE PRESIDENT.

In the wake of the assassination of President McKinley, this newspaper photo embellished with drawing of flames demonized Goldman, both reinforcing and fostering the public's fear of anarchists. (Copyright 1901. Chicago Tribune Co. All rights reserved. Used with permission.)

and when I left the lecture I had made up my mind that I would have to do something heroic for the cause I loved.

"Eight days ago, while I was in Chicago, I read in a Chicago newspaper of President McKinley's visit to the Pan American Exposition at Buffalo. That day I bought a ticket for Buffalo and got here with the determination to do something, but I did not know just what. I thought of shooting the President, but I had not formed a plan.

"I went to live at 1078 Broadway, which is a saloon and hotel. John Nowak,[3] a Pole, a sort of politician, who has led his people here for years, owns it. I told Nowak that I came to see the fair. He knew nothing about what was setting me crazy. I went to the exposition grounds a couple of times a day.

"Not until Tuesday morning did the resolution to shoot the President take hold of me. It was in my heart; there was no escape for me. I could not have conquered it had my life been at stake. There were thousands of people in town on Tuesday. I heard it was the President's day. All of these people seemed bowing to the great ruler. I made up my mind to kill that ruler. I bought a 32-caliber revolver and loaded it. On Tuesday night I went to the fair grounds and was near the railroad gate when the Presidential party arrived. I tried to get near him, but the police forced me back. They forced everybody back so that the great ruler could pass. I was close to the President when he got into the grounds, but was afraid to attempt the assassination because there were so many men in the body-guard that watched him. I was not afraid of them or that I should get hurt, but afraid I might be seized and that my chance would be gone forever.

"Well, he went away that time and I went home. On Wednesday I went to the grounds and stood right near the President, right under him, near the stand from which he spoke. I thought half a dozen times of shooting while he was speaking, but I could not get close enough. I was afraid I might miss, and then the great crowd was always jostling, and I was afraid lest my aim fail. I waited Wednesday, and the President got into his carriage again, and a lot of men were about him and formed a cordon that I could not get through. I was tossed about by the crowd, and my spirits were getting pretty low. I was almost hopeless that night as I went home.

"Yesterday morning I went again to the exposition grounds. Emma Goldman's speech was still burning me up. I waited near the central entrance for the President, who was to board his special train from that gate, but the police allowed nobody but the President's party to pass where the train waited, so I stayed at the grounds all day waiting.

"During yesterday I first thought of hiding my pistol under my handkerchief. I was afraid if I had to draw it from my pocket I would be seen and seized by the guards. I got to the Temple of Music the first one, and waited at the spot where the reception was to be held. Then he came—the President—the ruler, and I got in line and trembled until I got right up to him, and then I shot him twice through my white handkerchief. I would have fired more, but I was stunned by a blow in the face—a frightful blow that knocked me down—and then everybody jumped on me. I thought I would be killed, and was surprised the way they treated me."[4]

3. Walter Nowak went to the police to speak with Czolgosz following his act.
4. Czolgosz waited in a reception line on Friday, 6 September, at the Pan-American Exposition's Temple of Music, ostensibly to shake hands with McKinley. When he reached the front of the line, Czolgosz shot McKinley, leaving the president severely wounded. Czolgosz was arrested immediately and later that night signed a confession, in which he stated that the last person he heard speaking was EG, but that she did not tell him to kill the president.

Czolgosz ended his story in utter exhaustion. When he had concluded, he was asked: "Did you really mean to kill the President?"

"I did," was the cold-blooded reply.

"What was your motive, what good could it do you?" he was asked.

"I am an anarchist. I am a disciple of Emma Goldman. Her words set me on fire," he replied, with not the slightest tremor. "I deny that I have had an accomplice at any time," Czolgosz told District Attorney Tenney. "I don't regret my act, because I was doing what I could for the great cause. I am not connected with the Patterson group, or with those anarchists who sent Bresci to Italy to kill Humbert.[5] I had no confidants; no one to help me. I was alone absolutely."

San Francisco Chronicle, 8 September 1901, p. 2.

5. Paterson, New Jersey, was a stronghold of Italian American anarchism. The Italian American Gaetano Bresci, who traveled to Italy and assassinated King Umberto (styled "Humbert" in the American press) on 29 July 1901, was a member of an anarchist group whose members were militant believers in propaganda by the deed. On 9 September, Secret Service men searched the office of the Italian-language anarchist paper, *La Questione Social,* in Paterson, questioning editor Pedro Esteve, in an effort to link Paterson anarchists to a plot to assassinate the president.

Interview in the *NEW YORK WORLD*

Chicago, 11 September 1901

Story of the Arrest of Anarchist Queen.

CHICAGO, Sept. 10 — Miss Goldman[1] arrived in Chicago Sunday morning, registered in a downtown hotel under an assumed name, and yesterday engaged a room in the Sheffield avenue flat.[2]

C. G. Norris,[3] who owns the flat, was later taken into custody. An hour before the woman's arrest the Chief of Police received from a source outside the department news regarding her whereabouts. Capt. Schuettler,[4] a famous Anarchist-hunter of the Haymarket days, was in the office. Schuettler and Detective Hertz were ordered to go to the flat and bring in all persons found there.

The building is within the shadow of the Sheffield Avenue Police Station and contains three flats. In the top flat, so ran the information, the queen of Anarchy was in hiding.

DENIED HER IDENTITY.

"Who are you and what do you want?" she asked.

"We are policemen and we want you, Miss Goldman," replied Schuettler.

"I am not Miss Goldman, my name is Thorsen, and I am Swedish," she said.

Schuettler, who had been examining the apartment, picked up a fountain pen and began spelling "Emma Goldman."

---

1. After the 6 September assassination attempt on President McKinley, much of the press held EG and anarchists responsible for Czolgosz's act and initiated a widespread campaign for the arrest of EG, and the punishment of anarchists in general.
2. EG first found out about Czolgosz's act on Saturday, 7 September, while in St. Louis, through a local newspaper. At the same time she was alerted to the arrest of local Chicago anarchists Abe and Mary Isaak, their son and daughter, as well as Hippolyte Havel, Enrico Travaglio, Clemens Pfuetzner, Julia Mechanic, Alfred Schneider, Jay Fox, Martin Rasnick, and Michael Roz, all of whom were connected, in some way, with the journal *Free Society;* there was country-wide sentiment calling for EG's own arrest. In *Living My Life* she writes of her decision to go to Chicago and be arrested with her comrades: "it became clear to me that I must immediately go to Chicago. The Isaak family, Hippolyte, our old comrade Jay Fox, a most active man in the labor movement, and a number of others were being held without bail until I should be found. It was plainly my duty to surrender myself. I knew there was neither reason nor the least proof to connect me with the shooting. I would go to Chicago" (*LML*, p. 296). According to the *New York World* interview (datelined Wednesday, 10 September), EG arrived in Chicago on Sunday morning, 8 September.
3. Charles Goldsmith Norris was a Canadian-born Chicago insurance agent.
4. Hermann Schuettler was a Chicago detective, known for his dramatic arrest of Louis Lingg; Schuettler was later promoted to assistant chief of police.

Sensationalist reportage in the 11 September 1901 *San Francisco Call* typified negative representations of Goldman as Leon Czolgosz's accomplice and as a force of evil.

"You are a smart policeman," she laughed. "Yes, I am Emma Goldman, and I was just thinking of going down to police headquarters and give myself up. If you had come an hour later I would have been gone. If you will excuse me while I change my waist I will go with you."

The suspicious policeman balked at Miss Goldman's desire to close the door of her bedroom during the toilet proceedings. A compromise was reached by leaving the door half open. Finally she emerged carrying a book, *Towards Democracy*,[5] and announced herself ready to go.

"Why, this is all nonsense and I am innocent as a babe, as far as conspiring to kill the President or inspiring others to do it,"[6] she said to Schuettler.

TO HEADQUARTERS IN STREET CAR.

The trip to headquarters was made in a street car. Miss Goldman read her book, and once looked up to the two men sitting beside her and said:

"Do I look like the woman they paint me?"

In a jaunty white sailor hat, white waist, blue skirt, belt and necktie she looked anything but bloodthirsty. She was calm and good humored when the City Hall was reached. Ushered into the chief's office she sat down and began reading her book. Chief O'Neill summoned Mayor Harrison[7] and an inquisition began, which lasted an hour. Although she maintained her self control she could not refrain at times from weeping.

Soon after her arrest she sent the following telegram:

H. Hochstein,[8] No. 213 Joseph ave., Rochester, N. Y.:
Don't worry. Am arrested. Will be out soon. Comfort mother.
    E

Miss Goldman told her story as follows:

"While in Buffalo I stopped with Hattie Lang[9] and left for the home of my sister in Rochester at noon on July 15. I stayed in Rochester until Aug. 17 or 18, and during the time I was there I wrote five letters to Havel,[10] which I suppose are now in the hands of

---

5. Edward Carpenter's *Towards Democracy* (London: J. Heywood, 1883) is a long prose poem reflecting the influence of Walt Whitman and expressing Carpenter's belief in the movement of humanity toward freedom and happiness.

6. In a similar article published in the *New York Times* of the same date, EG was quoted as saying, "Am I accountable because some crack-brained person put a wrong construction on my words? Leon Czolgosz, I am convinced, planned the deed unaided and entirely alone" (*New York Times*, 11 September 1901).

7. Carter H. Harrison, Jr. (1860–1953) was mayor of Chicago from 1897 to 1905 and the son of Carter Harrison, who had been mayor of Chicago for five terms, one of which encompassed the Haymarket riot and trial. After the McKinley assassination, he prevented EG from speaking in Chicago.

8. EG's sister, Helene Hochstein.

9. Hattie Lang was a Buffalo anarchist and the local distribution agent for *Free Society*. EG stayed with her in Buffalo in 1901.

10. After traveling to the United States with EG, Hippolyte Havel settled in Chicago.

the police. From Rochester I went to a number of other cities, accompanied by relatives. I was taking a short vacation and visiting my friends. I stopped in Buffalo, Pittsburg, Cincinnati and St. Louis. I came to Chicago, as I had intended, and was to have gone from here to Detroit, Cleveland, Pittsburg, Buffalo and New York. In these various cities I sold office supplies to pay my expenses." [11]

HEARD THE NEWS IN ST. LOUIS.

"I first heard of the President's attempted assassination Friday afternoon. The newsboys of St. Louis were crying it. I was riding on a Tower Grove line car at the time, and was on my way to my boarding-house at No. 1350 South Thirteenth street. I did not buy a paper, because I did not believe the news to be true. They print so many things that are not true! This is especially the case whenever a ruler travels. They are always finding plots and bombs on those occasions.

"I did not read a paper until Saturday noon. I had got through with my business, and when I went to lunch I thought I would see what was causing all the excitement. I never was more surprised in my life than when I saw that I had been connected with the affair.

"That afternoon I sent a telegram to some friends in Chicago asking if the Isaaks [12] were in trouble. The newspapers said they were under arrest, but I would not believe them. I wanted to get information from persons who tell the truth. I received a reply to my telegram, stating that the newspaper account was true and that the Isaaks were being held.

"This information caused me to determine to come to Chicago and help them if I could. I left St. Louis Saturday night by the Wabash, and arrived at the Polk Street Depot about 8 o'clock Sunday morning. I was dressed as I am to-day, except that I was not wearing my glasses. I do not always wear them. They become painful after I wear them a while. I had a wrap and a small handbag, which I gave to the porter. I came from the train with a crowd. A woman preceded me and a woman followed me. I saw a detective—you know you can't miss them if you ever have had any experience with them."

NEVER SAW MISS GOLDMAN.

"He was about as intelligent as the usual one of his profession. He looked at the woman ahead and the woman behind, but never a glance did he give to me. I called a cab and went to a hotel, the name of which I do not care to give. I registered under an assumed name, so it's no use to try to find the place.

"Sunday I walked about town and Monday I went shopping at Field's, walked up and down State street and passed the City Hall two or three times. Monday evening I went to

11. EG worked for Edward Brady's firm as a traveling salesperson to supplement her income while on lecture tours.

12. Abe and Mary Isaak were arrested directly after the assassination along with their son, Abe Jr., daughter Mary, and others. The women were released on 10 September, and the men were charged with conspiracy to commit an illegal act and held until 23 September 1901.

No. 303 Sheffield avenue. I had known Mr. Norris in a business way. I did not know his mother or sister. I told him the situation and asked him to take me in. This he did and said he was glad to give me shelter. I do not know even if he is a believer in my faith. I never talked to him about it. I simply met him when he was a travelling salesman and I have known him about a year. I could think of no place else to go, so I went there, sure of a welcome.

"If the police had been half an hour later I would have given them a surprise. I intended as soon as I saw that the women arrested at Isaak's[13] were turned loose to give myself up. I knew if the police wanted me it was only a question of a short time when they would get me."

WANTED TO "HAVE FUN."

"I was amused when Capt. Schuettler and his detectives came. I was dressed in a loose wrapper, and it occurred to me to have some fun with them. I wanted to see how smart they were.

"'We are looking for Miss Goldman,' said the handsome captain.

"'I do not know her,' I replied in a Swedish accent. 'I am sure there is no such woman here.'

"'And who are you?' he asked.

"'My name is Thorsen,' I answered. 'I am a domestic here.'

"Then he began a search in the closets and under the beds and all over the premises. When nothing had been found except a pen-holder with my name on it the Captain said he would have to leave one of his detectives with me until he could make a further search. I took a good look at the detective and told the Captain that he need go no further, that I was Miss Goldman. He allowed me to dress, and I came to the station with them."

Mayor Harrison here said:

"Miss Goldman, are you sure that fellow Czolgosz didn't talk plots and assassinations to you?"

"I am certain he did not," came the impetuous reply, "but I heard he talked 'plots' and 'inner circles' to Mr. Isaak and for that reason was denounced as a spy."[14]

"Did any person write to you about this man?" asked the Mayor.

Miss Goldman answered in the negative.

"Suppose a Democrat had shot the President," Miss Goldman suddenly burst forth, "would you arrest every Democrat in the land and drag their children to prison as you have done with us?"

"Why did you come back here," she was asked.

13. Julia Mechanic was arrested along with Isaak's wife and daughter.
14. Abe Isaak became suspicious of Czolgosz after his appearance in Chicago when he began inquiring about anarchist secret societies and talked of violence. After receiving a warning from Cleveland anarchist Emil Schilling, who had similar suspicions, Isaak printed a warning in *Free Society* calling "the attention of the comrades . . . to another police spy" who had recently attended anarchist meetings in Cleveland and Chicago (see *Free Society*, 1 September 1901).

SOUGHT TO HELP THE ISAAKS.

"I came to get the Isaaks out. I was at the house at No. 303 Sheffield avenue since yesterday. I wanted to know if bail would be allowed to get them out of prison."

"Where would you get the money to bail them out?"

"I have seen certain people."

"Who were they?"

"You would not expect me to tell that," she replied with a smile.

"I have nothing to fear from your officers and your law," Miss Goldman continued. "I did not hide from you more than suited my own convenience. I went about the neighborhood where I was staying and yesterday I came downtown. I also walked around the City Hall and I saw your policemen, but they did not see me. It speaks volumes for the freedom of this country to see the way myself and my friends are deprived of liberty simply because we exercise the right of free speech."

Miss Goldman almost burst into tears at this point.

WAS HUNGRY, SHE SAID.

Then she smiled on all about her and said: "Mr. Mayor, if the State can afford it I would like to have something to eat. I am awfully hungry. I have ate nothing since 7 o'clock this morning."

"You shall have a good dinner because you are an obliging little woman," said Chief O'Neill.

"But first," continued the Chief, "you are such a good-looking woman I really must have a picture of you."

The woman smiled and said: "You shall have it."

Then she burst into tears, but controlled herself in a moment. A carriage was called and Capt. Schuettler escorted his prisoner to a restaurant, where she ate a hearty dinner. From there she was driven to the Harrison Street Police Station, where she sat for two negatives. Then she was turned over to the matron and given the best room in the annex. Once in the matron's rooms she again gave way to tears, but soon composed herself and received all callers.

Obstacles confront the Federal and State authorities in Chicago in the possible prosecution of Emma Goldman. It is the opinion of several lawyers that she cannot be taken for trial in New York unless she and Czolgosz are charged with an offense under the Federal statutes.

QUESTION OF EXTRADITION.

The suggestion that the assassin must be tried under the State laws of New York for assault with intent to kill would, it is said, preclude the possibility of Miss Goldman's being extradited as an accessory before the fact, as her alleged incendiary statements were not made in New York, and she is not a fugitive from justice from that State.

It is stated, however, that she and Czolgosz might be charged with an offense under section 5508 of the Federal statutes, which fixes a ten-year term of imprisonment and a

$5,000 fine for two or more persons who conspire to injure any citizen in the exercise of any right secured to him by the Constitution and laws of the United States. The enforcement of this statute against Miss Goldman and Czolgosz would, it is said, permit of the former's extradition from any State.

"TIP" CAME FROM A WOMAN.

The "tip" that caused the arrest of Emma Goldman came from a woman. She lives close to the Norris flat in Sheffield avenue, and while not an Anarchist, is acquainted with many of them. She saw Emma Goldman enter the flat yesterday, and while not certain of her identity suspected it. This morning she saw the Goldman woman again and instantly hastened to Police Headquarters with the information.

Charles Goldsmith Norris, with his mother and sister, Mrs. Stella Thorndale, occupy the flat. They have lived in it since May and have been puzzles to their neighbors. Norris is an insurance agent, twenty-nine years old, a Canadian by birth.

"I have known Miss Goldman about a year," he said. "I met her when she was here in June. When she asked me for a room I took her in."

"Why did you not notify the police?" asked the chief. "You knew she was wanted."

"I don't want to talk about it until I consult an attorney," said Norris. "I did not and don't think now that she is guilty of anything."

Percival Verral, a clerk, and Miss Edith Unealt, a relative of Norris, also lived in the flat. Norris was the only one arrested.

New York World, 11 September 1901, pp. 1, 3.

The Tragedy at Buffalo.

For they starve the little frightened child
  Till it weeps both night and day:
And they scourge the weak, and flog the fool,
  And gibe the old and gray,
And some grow mad, and all grow bad,
  And none a word may say.

Oscar Wilde[1]

Never before in the history of governments has the sound of a pistol shot so startled, terrorized, and horrified the self-satisfied, indifferent, contented, and indolent public, as has the one fired by Leon Czolgosz when he struck down William McKinley,[2] president of the money kings and trust magnates of this country.

Not that this modern Caesar was the first to die at the hands of a Brutus.[3] Oh, no! Since man has trampled upon the rights of his fellowmen, rebellious spirits have been afloat in the atmosphere. Not that William McKinley was a greater man than those who throned upon the fettered form of Liberty. He did not compare either in intellect, ability, personality, or force of character with those who had to pay the penalty of their power. Nor will history be able to record his extraordinary kindness, generosity, and sympathy with those whom ignorance and greed have condemned to a life of misery, hopelessness, and despair.

Why, then, were the mighty and powerful thrown into such consternation by the deed of September 6? Why this howl of a hired press? Why such blood-thirsty and violent utterances from the clergy, whose usual business it is to preach "peace on earth and good-will to all"? Why the mad ravings of the mob, the demand for rigid laws to curtail freedom of press and speech?[4]

---

1. From Oscar Wilde's *Ballad of Reading Gaol* (London, 1898), part 5.
2. Leon Czolgosz shot President William McKinley on 6 September 1901, severely wounding but not killing him. Suffering from two bullet wounds to his abdomen (surgeons were able to remove only one of the bullets), McKinley died as a result of gangrene in both the stomach and pancreas on 14 September 1901.
3. EG also referred to AB as a "Brutus," a positive term among anarchists for one who destroyed despotic power, for his *attentat* on Henry Clay Frick.
4. Following Czolgosz's assassination attempt there was a strong wave of anti-anarchist hysteria among the press, various community leaders, and law enforcement officers. Almost immediately after the as-

For more than thirty years a small band of parasites have robbed the American people, and trampled upon the fundamental principles laid down by the forefathers of this country, guaranteeing to every man, woman, and child, "Life, liberty, and the pursuit of happiness." For thirty years they have been increasing their wealth and power at the expense of the vast mass of workers, thereby enlarging the army of the unemployed, the hungry, homeless, and friendless portion of humanity, tramping the country from east to west and north to south, in a vain search for work. For many years the home has been left to the care of the little ones, while the parents are working their life and strength away for a small pittance. For thirty years the sturdy sons of America were sacrificed on the battlefield of industrial war, and the daughters outraged in corrupt factory surroundings. For long and weary years this process of undermining the nation's health, vigor, and pride, without much protest from the disinherited and oppressed, has been going on. Maddened by success and victory, the money-powers of this "free land of our's" became more and more audacious in their heartless, cruel efforts to compete with rotten and decayed European tyrannies in supremacy of power.

With the minds of the young poisoned with a perverted conception of patriotism, and the fallacious notion that all are equal and that each one has the same opportunity to become a millionaire (provided he can steal the first hundred thousand dollars), it was an easy matter indeed to check the discontent of the people; one is therefore not surprised when one hears Americans say, "We can understand why the poor Russians kill their czar, or the Italians their king, for think of the conditions that prevail there; but he who lives in a republic, where each one has the opportunity to become president of the United States, (provided he has a powerful party back of him); we are the people, and acts of violence in our country are impossible."

And now that the impossible has happened, that even America has given birth to the

---

sassination attempt the press began to associate all anarchists, and especially EG, with the crime. As early as 7 September, the day after McKinley was shot, newspapers across the country were linking EG's words with Czolgosz's deed. Headlines claimed "Czolgosz Declares Emma Goldman's Words Drove Him to Murder" (*San Francisco Chronicle*, 8 September 1901); "Nieman's Crime Expected to Result in Movement to Rid Country of Red Conspirators" (*Chicago Tribune*, 7 September 1901); "Police Dragnet Out for Emma Goldman, Vigorous Search for Her in Chicago and Other Cities" (*New York World*, 9 September 1901); "All Are Guilty, Punishment Is in Store for Anarchist Who Advised Violence Against the President" (*Buffalo Commercial*, 9 September 1901); and the most sensational, "Czolgosz's Portrait in Emma Goldman's Room, Police Are Confident That She Was a Party to the Attempted Assassination of the President" (*San Francisco Examiner*, 10 September 1901). As early as 10 September, a Chicago group, the National Association of Merchants and Travelers, adopted resolutions to prevent anarchists from entering the United States. In California, Representative Metcalf proposed an anti-anarchist immigration law, and in New York the police commissioner ordered a careful census of all anarchists in the city to "make conditions disagreeable for those named." Also in New York the Marquette Club organized a committee to "extirpate Anarchists." See *Free Society*, 6 October 1901, for a sampling of unsolicited letters sent to the paper in the wake of McKinley's death. Reports of EG being hung in effigy were also circulated.

Police mug shot of Goldman in Chicago on 10 September 1901, taken upon her arrest based on circumstantial evidence in relation to President McKinley's assassination. With no official charges, she was released on 24 September. (Library of Congress)

man who struck down the king of the republic, they have lost their heads, and are shouting vengeance upon those who for years have shown that the conditions here were beginning to be alarming, and unless a halt be called, despotism would set its heavy foot on the hitherto relatively free limbs of the people.

In vain have the mouthpieces of wealth denounced Leon Czolgosz as a foreigner;[5] in

5. Leon Czolgosz was an American-born citizen, his parents were Polish immigrants.

METROPOLITAN POLICE DEPARTMENT,
WASHINGTON, D. C.

Name *Emma Goldman* — Reg. No. *1786½*

Alias — Color *White*

Residence, *New York City* — Date of Arrest *Sept 10"* 19 01

Crime *Conspiracy to Kill* — Criminal Specialty *None*

Officer

Disposition of Case *Discl in Police court for want of evidence.*

Known or Admitted Former Imprisonment *1 year at Blackwells Island NY*
Charg Inciting Disch. Aug 17-1894

Num'l Order	MARKS, SCARS AND MOLES
I	*Small brown mole at wrist, rear.*
	2nd pha. Thumb very short.
II	*Scar of 1½ obl. 2nd pha. Thumb, rear.*
III	*" " 4½ × 1. left side of neck back of ear.*
	Flesh mole ½ × ½ at 2. to front of left lobe.
	Pit scar at right temple at 8 from M.L.

YAWMAN & ERBE MFG. CO., ROCHESTER, N. Y.   63024

Police intake report describing Goldman's physical characteristics at her 10 September 1901 arrest in Chicago. (Library of Congress)

vain they are making the world believe that he is the product of European conditions, and influenced by European ideas. This time the assassin happens to be the child of Columbia, who lulled him to sleep with

> "My country, 't is of thee,
> Sweet land of liberty," etc.,

and who held out the hope to him that he too could become president of the country. Who can tell how many times this American child had gloried in the celebration of the

4th of July, or on Decoration Day, when he faithfully honored the nation's dead? Who knows but what he too was willing to "fight for his country and die for her liberty"; until it dawned on him that those he belonged to have no country, because they have been robbed of all that they have produced; until he saw that all the liberty and independence of his youthful dreams are but a farce. Perhaps he also learned that it is nonsense to talk of equality between those who have all and those who have nothing, hence he rebelled.

"But his act was mad and cowardly," say the ruling class. "It was foolish and impractical," echo all petty reformers, Socialists, and even some Anarchists.[6]

What absurdity! As if an act of this kind can be measured by its usefulness, expediency, or practicability. We might as well ask ourselves of the usefulness of a cyclone, tornado, a violent thunderstorm, or the ceaseless fall of the Niagara waters. All these forces are the natural results of natural causes, which we may not yet have been able to explain, but which are nevertheless a part of nature, just as all force is natural and part of man and beast, developed or checked, according to the pressure of conditions and man's understanding. An act of violence is therefore not only the result of conditions, but also of man's psychical and physical nature, and his susceptibility to the world surrounding him.[7]

Does not the summer fight against the winter, does it not resist, mourn, and weep oceans of tears in its eager attempt to shield its children from the icy grip of frost? And does not the winter enshroud mother earth with a white, hard cover, lest the warm spring sunshine should melt the heart of the hardened old gentleman? And does he not gather his last forces for a bitter and fierce battle for supremacy, until the burning rays of the sun disperse his rank?

Resistance against force is a fact all through nature. Man being part of nature, he, too, is swayed by the same force to defend himself against invasion. Force will continue to be a natural factor just so long as economic slavery, social superiority, inequality, exploitation, and war continue to destroy all that is good and noble in man.

That the economic and political conditions of this country have been pregnant with the embryo of greed and despotism, no one who thinks and has closely watched events can deny. It was therefore but a question of time for the first signs of labor pains to be-

---

6. Immediately following Czolgosz's act there was general confusion and debate in anarchist circles. Some anarchists, including Saul Yanovsky, editor of *Freie Arbeiter Stimme*, whose offices in New York were attacked on 15 September, denounced Czolgosz's act. Some, such as EG and Kate Austin, defended Czolgosz in *Free Society*, while others, including Abe Isaak, Jr., tried to explain and interpret his actions; still others, such as C. L. James, argued that attempts made by police and government officials to suppress anarchism actually did more to further anarchist propaganda than anarchists themselves could ever accomplish. Some individualist anarchists, including Joseph Labadie, were appalled by the affair and considered Czolgosz insane.

7. EG's comparison of individual acts of violence to natural phenomena echoes August Spies's discussion of revolution in his address to the jury on 6 October 1886, reproduced in *The Accused, the Accusers . . .* (Chicago: Socialist Publishing Society, [1886?]). For another example of EG's use of Spies's analogy, see Letter to the *Detroit Sentinel*, 25 July 1898.

gin. And they began when McKinley, more than any other president, had betrayed the trust of the people, and became the tool of the moneyed kings. They began when he and his class had stained the memory of the men who produced the Declaration of Independence, through the blood of the massacred Filipinos.[8] They grew more violent at the recollection of Hazleton,[9] Virden,[10] Idaho,[11] and other places, where capital has waged war on labor; until on the 6th of September the child begotten, nourished and reared by violence, was born.

That violence is not the result of conditions only, but also largely depends upon man's inner nature, is best proven by the fact that while thousands loathe tyranny, but one will strike down a tyrant. What is it that drives him to commit the act, while others pass quietly by? It is because the one is of such a sensitive nature that he will feel a wrong more keenly and with greater intensity than others.

It is, therefore, not cruelty, or a thirst for blood, or any other criminal tendency, that induces such a man to strike a blow at organized power. On the contrary, it is mostly because of a strong social instinct, because of an abundance of love and an overflow of sympathy with the pain and sorrow around us, a love which seeks refuge in the embrace of mankind, a love so strong that it shrinks before no consequence, a love so broad that it can never be wrapped up in one object, as long as thousands perish, a love so all-absorbing that it can neither calculate, reason, investigate, but only dare at all costs.

It is generally believed that men prompted to put the dagger or bullet in the cowardly heart of government, were men conceited enough to think that they will thereby liberate the world from the fetters of despotism. As far as I have studied the psychology of an act of violence, I find that nothing could be further away from the thought of such a man than that if the king were dead, the mob will cease to shout, "Long live the king!"

The cause for such an act lies deeper, far too deep for the shallow multitude to comprehend. It lies in the fact that the world within the individual, and the world around him, are two antagonistic forces, and therefore must clash.

Do I say that Czolgosz is made of that material? No. Neither can I say that he was not. Nor am I in a position to say whether or not he is an Anarchist; I did not know the man; no one as far as I am aware seems to have known him, but from his attitude and behavior so far, (I hope that no reader of *Free Society* has believed the newspaper lies), I feel that he was a soul in pain, a soul that could find no abode in this cruel world of ours, a soul "impractical," inexpedient, lacking in caution, (according to the dictum of the wise); but daring just the same, and I cannot help but bow in reverenced silence before the power

8. EG refers to the independence movement in the Philippines where, after the Spanish-American War, the United States fought for colonial control of the country for a decade.
9. EG refers to the 10 September 1897 massacre of peacefully striking coal miners in Pennsylvania.
10. EG refers to the 13 October 1898 coal strike at Virden, Illinois, where armed guards of the Chicago-Virden Coal Company killed seven miners; four guards also died.
11. EG refers to the strike at the Bunker Hill and Sullivan Mining Company in Coeur d'Alene, Idaho in 1899, organized by the Western Federation of Miners.

of such a soul, that has broken the narrow walls of its prison, and has taken a daring leap into the unknown.

Having shown that violence is not the result of personal influence, or one particular ideal, I deem it unnecessary to go into a lengthy theoretical discussion as to whether Anarchism contains the element of force or not. The question has been discussed time and again, and it is proven that Anarchism and violence are as far apart from each other as liberty and tyranny. I care not what the rabble says; but to those who are still capable of understanding I would say that Anarchism, being a philosophy of life, aims to establish a state of society in which man's inner make-up and the conditions around him, can blend harmoniously together, so that he will be able to utilize all the forces to enlarge and beautify the life about him. To those I would also say that I do not advocate violence; government does this, and force begets force.[12] It is a fact which cannot be done away with through the prosecution of a few men and women, or by more stringent laws—this only tends to increase it.

Violence will die a natural death when man will learn to understand that each unit has its place in the universe, and while being closely linked together, it must remain free to grow and expand.

Some people have hastily said that Czolgosz's act was foolish and will check the growth of progress. Those worthy people are wrong in forming hasty conclusions. What results the act of September 6 will have no one can say; one thing, however, is certain: he has wounded government in its most vital spot. As to stopping the wheel of progress, that is absurd. Ideas cannot be retarded by restraint. And as to petty police persecution, what matter?

As I write this, my thoughts wander to the death cell at Auburn,[13] to the young man with the girlish face, about to be put to death by the coarse, brutal hands of the law, walking up and down the narrow cell, with cold, cruel eyes following him,

> "Who watch him when he tries to weep
> And when he tries to pray;
> Who watch him lest himself should rob
> The prison of its prey."[14]

And my heart goes out to him in deep sympathy, and to all those victims of a system of inequality, and the many who will die the forerunners of a better, nobler, grander life.

EMMA GOLDMAN.

---

12. These words would be echoed by Hippolyte Havel, Harry Kelly, and AB in 1912, after EG's and Ben Reitman's brutal experience with vigilantes in San Diego during the IWW's free speech fights there. In a letter written on 14 May and published in the 18 May 1912 *New York World* they write, "Violence begets violence. Terror from above breeds terror from below."
13. After Czolgosz was sentenced to death on 26 September, he was transferred to the Auburn prison in Cayuga County, New York, where on 29 October he was executed.
14. Wilde, *Ballad of Reading Gaol*, part 1.

Free Society, 6 October 1901, pp. 1–2. Reprinted in *Mother Earth* 1 (October 1906): 11–16. This essay appeared in the first issue of *Free Society* published after the arrest of its editor, Abe Isaak, following Czolgosz's assassination of McKinley. The article caused some of EG's associates to distance themselves from her, while others, including Kate Austin, joined her in defending Czolgosz's act in the pages of *Free Society* (see "Who Are the Guilty," 13 October 1901, p. 4, and "Why Not Be Logical," 8 December 1901, p. 1). Other anarchists offered more staunch support for Czolgosz's act; see, for example, the article "Czolgosz," published in the 26 October 1906 issue of *L'Aurora* (an Italian-language anarchist paper from Spring Valley, Illinois), written by the paper's editor, Guiseppi Ciancabilla, who was also arrested in the wake of McKinley's death. EG's essay builds on her earlier lectures and writings on political violence (see, for example, EG's discussion of Michele Angiolillo and Gaetano Bresci). EG later incorporated part of her description of Czolgosz and his *attentat* into her essay "The Psychology of Political Violence" (1911).

To **LUCIFER, THE LIGHTBEARER**

New York, 11 November 1901

Emma Goldman Defines Her Position.

In *Lucifer* No. 889 was printed a report that at a meeting of the Manhattan Liberal Club I deplored the assassination of McKinley.[1] This is a misrepresentation, for at that particular meeting there was no particular occasion to either deplore or applaud the assassination, consequently I made no such statements. Besides, in my article on the Buffalo tragedy in *Free Society* of Oct. 6 I plainly and emphatically stated my position,[2] and instead of retracting I could only add that I have since come to the firm conclusion that Czolgosz was a man with the beautiful soul of a child and the energy of a giant. I have observed with great sorrow that the majority of Anarchists have utterly failed to comprehend the depth of that soul, that was put to death by organized authority on Oct. 29.[3]

Methinks that Anarchy is the philosophy of life, and as such it includes every branch of human knowledge pertaining to life. If this be so, and I know of no Anarchists who would deny it, Anarchists ought to be students of psychology and honestly endeavor to explain certain phenomena, not only from a politico-economic but also from a psychological standpoint. Had they done so, they would not have joined the thoughtless rabble in its superficial denunciation of Leon Czolgosz as a lunatic and a villain. Do not we know that every act which ignorant minds have failed to explain, have ever been stamped as insane or villainous?

Surely it does not behoove thinking people to adopt such methods in their search for a cause for certain acts. Besides, is it not time to perceive that the act of Sept. 6,[4] like many previous acts, was but the result of the elements pent up and stifled in the human heart through a false and pernicious system and bound to leap through the heavy walls of organized authority sooner or later?

Of course I believe that each individual has a right to his opinion, but I do not wish to be a party in the vain endeavor of some of our Anarchists to bow before respectability by sacrificing their ideas to its altar.

It has taken all my time for the past fourteen years to deplore human misery in all its awful forms, so I have not a moment left to deplore the assassination of one, who has ignored all rights of the people, and bowed before the dictum of a privileged few; then, too,

1. EG refers to a meeting on 8 October, which *Lucifer* summarized in its report as follows: "Emma Goldman is quoted as saying that, as an Anarchist, she was opposed to violence. She deplored the assassination of McKinley, and said that if the people want to do away with assassins they must do away with the conditions which produce murderers" (*Lucifer*, 31 October 1901, p. 338).
2. See "The Tragedy at Buffalo," Article in *Free Society*, 6 October 1901, above.
3. Leon Czolgosz was executed on 29 October 1901.
4. Czolgosz shot President McKinley on 6 September 1901.

Following President McKinley's assassination, wide-ranging and unsubstantiated accusations against Goldman permeated the mainstream press; this front-page feature article in the 10 September 1901 *New York World* is among the most strikingly negative representations.

I am kept busy regretting the fact that so many even in the radical ranks have lost their manhood and womanhood at the sight of Government and Power let loose, and have denounced the man, who was so pitiful in his loneliness and yet so sublime in his silence and superiority over his enemies.

EMMA GOLDMAN.

Lucifer, the Lightbearer, 21 November 1901, p. 366.

DEAR COMRADE NETLAU.

You have undoubtedly been amazed by my lack of punctuality, but you should not believe that lack of punctuality also belongs to my many other faults. I am otherwise always very prompt, but this time I wanted to wait until I could provide you with something certain about the book. Unfortunately I can not do that even now, as I have yet to hear anything definite about the book up to this point, but I believe that nothing will come from the whole affair. The good man lost his courage at the last moment, for it would truly take courage to publish an anarchist work, or indeed the "Life of E.G.," at this time.[1] You can imagine how great the prejudice is, fabricated by a dishonest and rotten press, that would make an American pass up material gain, for there is no doubt that thousands of copies of the book would be sold. Indeed no one would have worried about prejudice if I had given my approval to let the book appear in a truly shrill and sensational form, but something soberly instructional and objective, according to the esteemed publisher, "not in the interest of our middle class people." And thus the matter appears to have fallen through. For my part I am happy about it, as it would have been very difficult for me to have written objectively about my life. One has to be able to stand above one's life in order to do that, or at least outside of the events. But when one is standing right in the middle of the battlefield surrounded by enemy fire, as I am, one can not judge things objectively, and thus I am happy not to have to report about my life at this time. For propaganda it would clearly be of great significance if a series of essays about Anarchism would appear at this moment, indeed if it would appear in book form and out of a publishing house, for you would not believe what nonsense is being spread about A., simply hair-raising and without even one voice raised in objection. There is a complete and utter lack of truly great minds here who possess not only talent but also courage and a sense of justice. Men such as Dean Howell,[2] Crosby[3] and Hawthorne,[4] who on other oc-

---

1. No book on EG was published during this period, nor any prospective publisher identified.
2. William Dean Howells (1837–1920), American novelist and critic, was editor of the *Atlantic Monthly* from 1871 to 1881. Howells publicly defended the Haymarket anarchists in 1887, attempting to win support for a stay of execution. Howells became discouraged by the prevailing attitude in the country and ceased submitting editorials to newspapers. His sympathy for the Haymarket anarchists influenced his later writings, considered by many to be identified with socialism, most notably *Annie Kilburn* (New York: Harper, 1889), *A Hazard of New Fortunes* (New York: Harper and Brothers, 1890), and *A Traveler From Altruria* (New York: Harper and Brothers, 1894). He was also a member of the Society of Friends of Russian Freedom.
3. EG refers to Ernest Crosby, who was the leading U.S. proponent of Tolstoyan anarchism; he offered to help EG secure a pardon for AB.
4. In his novels, Nathaniel Hawthorne (1804–1864) explored the conflict between social constraints and human passions, and featured complex female protagonists, especially evident in *The Scarlet Letter*

casions have had a good word for us, have drawn back in a cowardly fashion, and what of our own people? Well, firstly there are only a small number of people of any importance here, and secondly these people lack courage and I am telling you, one could despair if one listens to the whimpering of these comrades, their convulsive exertions [*several words illegible*] it was simply horrible. These same people who could exalt Bresci, Luccheni and Ravachal[5] as martyrs have shamefully abandoned poor Leon C.[6] and have denounced him. Fortunately he belongs to the small number of people who bear a never-failing source of strength, energy and conviction and can manage without the world; otherwise he would have to despair of everything and everyone.—Have you read my article in *FS* from Oct 6th?[7] How I was attacked over this article in our own ranks, and what confusion came into view. I am telling you if we need $\frac{1}{2}$ a century to bring clarity to our own ranks, how much longer to lift the cloud which hangs over the spirit of the masses?

I do not have your letter on hand, since I am writing from the bedside of a patient who is sleeping,[8] and thus can not respond to it. Heartfelt thanks for the sources you sent me; even if I can't make use of them now, I will use them at a later date. I would also like to hold on to your essays which I received yesterday, may I? HK[9] wrote me that he sent me the manuscript of the Congress-reports;[10] up till now with the exception of W. Holme's[11] report I have not received anything and can not understand why the committee did not send the material a long time ago. The money for the printing has been available for many months and we are only waiting for the material. It is precisely at this moment that the Congress-reports would be of great importance. You say people are not well disposed toward me here, now that is nothing new. They are always the same, followers of Most;[12] consisting of Jews and Germans, but what does that have to do with the reports? Our good D[13] wrote me immediately after receiving your letter expressing his willingness to write something for the book, but that is no longer necessary and I have written to him

---

(1850). His *Blithedale Romance* (1851) was a fictional study of a socialist community based on his six-month stay at Brook Farm, an early experiment in communal living, in West Roxbury, Massachusetts.

5. EG refers to Gaetano Bresci, who assassinated King Umberto of Italy in 1900; Luigi Luccheni, who assassinated Empress Elizabeth of Austria in 1898; and Ravachol, the French anarchist executed in 1892 for the murder of an elderly, rich man.

6. EG refers to Leon Czolgosz, who was executed 29 October 1901, less than two months after he shot President McKinley.

7. See "The Tragedy at Buffalo," Article in *Free Society*, 6 October 1901, above.

8. EG was working as a private practical nurse during this period, often on the night shift.

9. EG refers to the American anarchist Harry Kelly, who worked in London on the anarchist communist paper *Freedom* and who aided EG in lobbying for a commutation of AB's sentence.

10. Apart from the individual reports published in *Free Society*, no English-language version of the reports to the Paris congress ever appeared. Only *Les Temps Nouveaux* published a comprehensive edition of the reports, first serially in its *Supplément Littéraire* (vol. 3, nos. 23 and 31) and then together under a separate cover.

11. Anarchist William T. Holmes wrote a report on the history of the anarchist movement in the United States.

12. EG refers to Johann Most.

13. EG refers to Victor Dave.

accordingly. His address is still Rue des Boulainvilliers, right? Dear N, would it be possible for you to obtain Bakunin's letters to Alex Herzen for me, either in Russian or German,[14] I would be most obliged. Everything is in a state of paralysis here, the comrades have not yet recovered from their fright over the recent affair, and thus their reactions could take on even further dimensions.—On Monday we are opening the Social Science Club,[15] and if the police don't interfere I intend a rather lively agitation this winter. Nothing more for today, please write back very soon, even if I was not as punctual. I am working 14 hours a day now, and am taking care of a neurotic, so you can imagine that I am in frightfully great demand.

GREETINGS,
EG

ALI, Max Nettlau Archive, IISH. Translated from German.

14. A volume of collected letters from Bakunin to Alexander Herzen and Nicholas Ogarev, edited by M. P. Dragomanov, had appeared in German as *Michael Bakunin's Socialpolitischer Briefwechsel mit Alexander Iw.Herzen und Ogarjow* (Stuttgart, 1895), and in Russian as *Pisma M.A. Bakunina k. A.I. Gertsenu i N.P. Ogarevu* (Geneva, 1896). Alexander Herzen (1812–1870) was an influential radical author and editor of the newspaper *Kolokol* (The Bell; 1857–1865). An associate of Bakunin, he argued for a free Russia and believed in small cooperatives for landowners and regional self-government.
15. The Social Science Club met weekly at 250 West 23rd Street in New York City.

DEAREST GIRL:

I know how your visit[1] and my strange behavior have affected you . . . . The sight of your face after all the years completely unnerved me. I could not think, I could not speak. It was as if all my dreams of freedom, the whole world of the living, were concentrated in the shiny little trinket that was dangling from your watch chain . . . . I couldn't take my eyes off it, I couldn't keep my hand from playing with it. It absorbed my whole being . . . . And all the time I felt how nervous you were at my silence, and I couldn't utter a word.

Perhaps it would have been better for us not to have seen each other under the present conditions. It was lucky they did not recognize you: they took you for my "sister," though I believe your identity was suspected after you had left. You would surely not have been permitted the visit, had the old Warden been here. He was ill at the time. He never got over the shock of the tunnel, and finally he has been persuaded by the prison physician (who has secret aspirations to the Wardenship) that the anxieties of his position are a menace to his advanced age. Considerable dissatisfaction has also developed of late against the Warden among the Inspectors. Well, he has resigned at last, thank goodness! The prisoners have been praying for it for years, and some of the boys on the range celebrated the event by getting drunk on wood alcohol. The new Warden has just assumed charge, and we hope for improvement. He is a physician by profession, with the title of Major in the Pennsylvania militia.

It was entirely uncalled for on the part of the officious friend, whoever he may have been, to cause you unnecessary worry over my health, and my renewed persecution. You remember that in July the new Inspector released me from the strait-jacket and assigned me to work on the range. But I was locked up again in October, after the McKinley incident.[2] The President of the Board of Inspectors was at the time in New York. He inquired by wire what I was doing. Upon being informed that I was working on the range, he ordered me into solitary. The new Warden, on assuming office, sent for me. "They give you a bad reputation," he said; "but I will let you out of the cell if you'll promise to do what is right by me." He spoke brusquely, in the manner of a man closing a business deal, with the power of dictating terms. He reminded me of Bismark at Versailles. Yet he did not seem unkind; the thought of escape was probably in his mind. But the new law has germinated the hope of survival; my weakened condition and the unexpected shortening of

---

1. EG visited AB sometime between the 19th and 24th of August 1901, her first visit since November 1892.
2. AB refers to the assassination of William McKinley by Leon Czolgosz on 6 September 1901.

my sentence have at last decided me to abandon the idea of escape.[3] I therefore replied to the Warden: "I will do what is right by you, if you treat *me* right." Thereupon he assigned me to work on the range. It is almost like liberty to have the freedom of the cellhouse after the close solitary.

And you, dear friend? In your letters I feel how terribly torn you are by the events of the recent months. I lived in great fear for your safety, and I can barely credit the good news that you are at liberty. It seems almost a miracle.

I followed the newspapers with great anxiety. The whole country seemed to be swept with the fury of revenge. To a considerable extent the press fanned the fires of persecution. Here in the prison very little sincere grief was manifested. Out of hearing of the guards, the men passed very uncomplimentary remarks about the dead president. The average prisoner corresponds to the average citizen—their patriotism is very passive, except when stimulated by personal interest, or artificially excited. But if the press mirrored the sentiment of the people, the Nation must have suddenly relapsed into cannibalism. There were moments when I was in mortal dread for your very life, and for the safety of the other arrested comrades.[4] In previous letters you hinted that it was official rivalry and jealousy, and your absence from New York, to which you owe your release. You may be right; yet I believe that your attitude of proud self-respect and your admirable self-control contributed much to the result. You were splendid, dear; and I was especially moved by your remark that you would faithfully nurse the wounded man, if he required your services, but that the poor boy, condemned and deserted by all, needed and deserved your sympathy and aid more than the president. More strikingly than your letters, that remark discovered to me the great change wrought in us by the ripening years. Yes, in us, in both, for my heart echoed your beautiful sentiment. How impossible such a thought would have been to us in the days of a decade ago! We should have considered it treason to the spirit of revolution; it would have outraged all our traditions even to admit the humanity of an official representative of capitalism. Is it not very significant that we two—you living in the very heart of Anarchist thought and activity, and I in the atmosphere of absolute suppression and solitude—should have arrived at the same evolutionary point after a decade of divergent paths?

You have alluded in a recent letter to the ennobling and broadening influence of sorrow. Yet not upon every one does it exert a similar effect. Some natures grow embittered, and shrink with the poison of misery. I often wonder at my lack of bitterness and enmity, even against the old Warden—and surely I have good cause to hate him. Is it because of greater maturity? I rather think it is temperamentally conditioned. The love of the

3. A commutation law passed by the Pennsylvania legislature enabled AB to appeal his sentence on 18 November 1901. His term was reduced by two and a half years. See Letter from Alexander Berkman, 25 July 1901, above.
4. In Chicago, anarchists including the Isaak family, Hippolyte Havel, Clemens Pfuetzner, Alfred Schneider, Julia Mechanic, Martin Rasnick, Jay Fox, and Enrico Travaglio were arrested, suspected of conspiring with Czolgosz.

people, the hatred of oppression of our younger days, vital as these sentiments were with us, were mental rather than emotional. Fortunately so, I think. For those like Fedya and Lewis and Pauline,[5] and numerous others, soon have their emotionally inflated idealism punctured on the thorny path of the social protestant. Only aspirations that spontaneously leap from the depths of our soul persist in the face of antagonistic forces. The revolutionist is born. Beneath our love and hatred of former days lay inherent rebellion, and the passionate desire for liberty and life.

In the long years of isolation I have looked deeply into my heart. With open mind and sincere purpose, I have revised every emotion and every thought. Away from my former atmosphere and the disturbing influence of the world's turmoil, I have divested myself of all traditions and accepted beliefs. I have studied the sciences and the humanities, contemplated life, and pondered over human destiny. For weeks and months I would be absorbed in the domain of "pure reason," or discuss with Leibnitz[6] the question of free will, and seek to penetrate, beyond Spencer,[7] into the Unknowable. Political science and economics, law and criminology—I studied them with unprejudiced mind, and sought to slacken my soul's thirst by delving deeply into religion and theology, seeking the "Key to Life" at the feet of Mrs. Eddy,[8] expectantly listening for the voice of the disembodied, studying Koreshanity[9] and Theosophy,[10] absorbing the *prana*[11] of knowledge and power, and concentrating upon the wisdom of the Yogi. And after years of contemplation and study, chastened by much sorrow and suffering, I arise from the broken fetters of the world's folly and delusions, to behold the threshold of a new life of liberty and equality. My youth's ideal of a free humanity in the vague future has become clarified and crystallized into the living truth of Anarchy, as the sustaining elemental force of my everyday existence.

Often I have wondered in the years gone by, was not wisdom dear at the price of enthusiasm? At 30 one is not so reckless, not so fanatical and one-sided as at 20. With maturity we become more universal; but life is a Shylock that cannot be cheated of his due. For every lesson it teaches us, we have a wound or a scar to show. We grow broader; but too often the heart contracts as the mind expands, and the fires are burning down while we are learning. At such moments my mind would revert to the days when the momen-

---

5. AB refers to his cousin Modest Stein, Roman Lewis, and possibly Pauline Sieger, who spoke with EG and other anarchists at the 1893 Union Square demonstration on unemployment, for which EG was sentenced for inciting to riot. All had moved away from anarchism by this time.

6. German philosopher and mathematician Gottfried Wilhelm Leibnitz (1646–1716).

7. English sociologist Herbert Spencer (1820–1903).

8. Mary Baker Eddy (1821–1910) was the founder of Christian Science. In 1866, she believed that she had been healed from a serious illness through spiritual means alone and developed a religious alternative to science that encouraged healing through divine law to overcome sin, disease, and death, which she believed were evils alien to God.

9. An American physician, Cyrus Read Teed (1839–1908), developed a pseudo-scientific doctrine called the Universology of Koreshanity (from the Hebrew name "Koresh," for Cyrus).

10. Incorporating aspects of Buddhism and Brahmanism, Theosophy became widely known in the United States after the founding of the Theosophical Society in 1875.

11. Sanskrit word for "life force."

tarily expected approach of the Social Revolution absorbed our exclusive interest. The raging present and its conflicting currents passed us by, while our eyes were riveted upon the Dawn, in thrilling expectancy of the sunrise. Life and its manifold expressions were vexatious to the spirit of revolt; and poetry, literature, and art were scorned as hindrances to progress, unless they sounded the tocsin of immediate revolution. Humanity was sharply divided in two warring camps,—the noble People, the producers, who yearned for the light of the new gospel, and the hated oppressors, the exploiters, who craftily strove to obscure the rising day that was to give back to man his heritage. If only "the good People" were given an opportunity to hear the great truth, how joyfully they would embrace Anarchy and walk in triumph into the promised land!

The splendid naivety of the days that resented as a personal reflection the least misgiving of the future; the enthusiasm that discounted the power of inherent prejudice and predilection! Magnificent was the day of hearts on fire with the hatred of oppression and the love of liberty! Woe indeed to the man or the people whose soul never warmed with the spark of Prometheus,—for it is youth that has climbed the heights . . . . But maturity has clarified the way, and the stupendous task of human regeneration will be accomplished only by the purified vision of hearts that grow not cold.

And you, my dear friend, with the deeper insight of time, you have yet happily kept your heart young. I have rejoiced at it in your letters of recent years, and it is especially evident from the sentiments you have expressed regarding the happening at Buffalo. I share your view entirely; for that very reason, it is the more distressing to disagree with you in one very important particular: the value of Leon's act. I know the terrible ordeal you have passed through, the fiendish persecution to which you have been subjected. Worse than all must have been to you the general lack of understanding for such phenomena; and, sadder yet, the despicable attitude of some would-be radicals in denouncing the man and his act. But I am confident you will not mistake my expressed disagreement for condemnation.

We need not discuss the phase of the *Attentat* which manifested the rebellion of a tortured soul, the individual protest against social wrong. Such phenomena are the natural result of evil conditions, as inevitable as the flooding of the river banks by the swelling mountain torrents. But I cannot agree with you regarding the social value of Leon's act.

I have read of the beautiful personality of the youth, of his inability to adapt himself to brutal conditions, and the rebellion of his soul. It throws a significant light upon the causes of the *Attentat*. Indeed, it is at once the greatest tragedy of martyrdom, and the most terrible indictment of society, that it forces the noblest men and women to shed human blood, though their souls shrink from it. But the more imperative it is that drastic methods of this character be resorted to only as a last extremity. To prove of value, they must be motived by social rather than individual necessity, and be directed against a real and immediate enemy of the people. The significance of such a deed is understood by the popular mind—and in that alone is the propagandistic, educational importance of an *Attentat*, except if it is exclusively an act of terrorism.

Now, I do not believe that this deed was terroristic; and I doubt whether it was educational, because the social necessity for its performance was not manifest. That you may not misunderstand, I repeat: as an expression of personal revolt it was inevitable, and in itself an indictment of existing conditions. But the background of social necessity was lacking, and therefore the value of the act was to a great extent nullified.

In Russia, where political oppression is popularly felt, such a deed would be of great value. But the scheme of political subjection is more subtle in America. And though McKinley was the chief representative of our modern slavery, he could not be considered in the light of a direct and immediate enemy of the people; while in an absolutism, the autocrat is visible and tangible. The real despotism of republican institutions is far deeper, more insidious, because it rests on the popular delusion of self-government and independence. That is the subtle source of democratic tyranny, and, as such, it cannot be reached with a bullet.

In modern capitalism, exploitation rather than oppression is the real enemy of the people. Oppression is but its handmaid. Hence the battle is to be waged in the economic rather than the political field. It is therefore that I regard my own act as far more significant and educational than Leon's. It was directed against a tangible, real oppressor, visualized as such by the people.[12]

As long as misery and tyranny fill the world, social contrasts and consequent hatreds will persist, and the noblest of the race—our Czolgoszes—burst forth in "rockets of iron." But does this lightning really illumine the social horizon, or merely confuse minds with the succeeding darkness? The struggle of labor against capital is a class war, essentially and chiefly economic. In that arena the battles must be fought.

It was not these considerations, of course, that inspired the nation-wide man-hunt, or the attitude even of alleged radicals. Their cowardice has filled me with loathing and sadness. The brutal farce of the trial, the hypocrisy of the whole proceeding, the thirst for the blood of the martyr,—these make one almost despair of humanity.

I must close. The friend to smuggle out this letter will be uneasy about its bulk. Send me sign of receipt, and I hope that you may be permitted a little rest and peace, to recover from the nightmare of the last months.

Sasha.

Berkman, *Prison Memoirs of an Anarchist,* pp. 412–17.

---

12. EG strongly disagreed with AB's position on Czolgosz's act. In his *Prison Memoirs,* AB recalled EG's reaction to his stance: "Continued correspondence with the Girl accentuates the divergences of our views, painfully discovering the fundamental difference of attitude underlying even common conclusions. By degrees the stress of activities reacts upon my friend's correspondence. Our discussion lags, and soon ceases entirely." Many years later EG wrote AB: "That you could sit down and cold-bloodedly analyse an act of violence nine years after your own, actually implying that your act was more important was the most terrible thing I had yet experienced . . ." (see Berkman, *Prison Memoirs of an Anarchist,* p. 418; and EG to AB, 23 November 1928, *EGP,* reel 20).

CHRONOLOGY

1869

JUNE 27

EG born to Taube Bienowitch and Abraham Goldman in **Kovno, Lithuania,** a province of the Russian empire.

1870

Ezra Heywood published *Uncivil Liberty,* in support of suffrage and against marriage, which later served as the introduction to *Cupid's Yokes,* the harbinger of free speech and obscenity cases for years to come.

NOVEMBER 21

Alexander Berkman born in Vilna, Lithuania.

1871

MARCH 18–MAY 28

Paris Commune.

1872

SEPTEMBER

The congress at Saint-Imier, Switzerland, marked the beginning of the Anti-Authoritarian International, following the split in the First International at The Hague. Among the delegates in attendance were Michael Bakunin, Carlo Cafiero, and Errico Malatesta.

1873

MARCH 3

Comstock Act signed into law in the United States.

DECEMBER 7

National Free-Love Convention held in Ravenna, Ohio. Ezra and Angela Heywood and Benjamin Tucker attended.

1874

Lassallean Social Democratic Working-Men's Party of North America (SDWMPNA) formed with Adolph Strasser as head of executive board.

1876

Comstock Act amended.

Ezra Heywood published *Cupid's Yokes.*

JULY 4

In Philadelphia, the National Liberal League founded the First Centennial Congress of Liberals, called by the Free Religious Association and attended by freethought advocates. Opposition to the Comstock laws of 1873 (amended 1876) was organized.

JULY 19–23

At a Unity Convention in Philadelphia, the Working Men's Party of the United States was founded when American delegates of the International Working Men's Association dissolved their party and merged with the Workingmen's Party of Illinois, the Social Political Workingmen's Society of Cincinnati, and the Social Democratic Working-Men's Party of North America.

OCTOBER 21

At their secret congress held in the village of Tosti (near Florence), the Italian Federation of the Anti-Authoritarian International formally adopted the ideas of anarchist communism, breaking with Bakunin's collectivist ideology.

1877

JULY 16

First in series of strikes, later known as Great Railway Strikes. Baltimore and Ohio freight fireman and brakemen halt work after learning that lucrative dividends were paid to company shareholders, on the heels of another 10 percent cut in wages. Albert Parsons blacklisted for speaking at rally for Working-Mens Party of the United States in Chicago's Market Square.

SEPTEMBER 6–8

At the final congress of the Anti-Authoritarian International in Verviers, Belgium, European anarchists groups were represented, as well as anarchist groups from Mexico, Uruguay, and Argentina. Peter Kropotkin was among the delegates.

NOVEMBER 2

Anthony Comstock personally arrested Ezra Heywood at meeting of the New England Free Love League in Boston; Heywood was charged with mailing two obscene publications, *Cupid's Yokes* and R. T. Trall's *Sexual Physiology* pamphlet.

DECEMBER

The Working-Mens Party of the United States became the Socialist Labor Party of North America (SLP) at its convention in Newark, New Jersey.

1878

JANUARY 22

Ezra Heywood's trial began. *Cupid's Yokes* deemed obscene by the jury, while *Sexual Physiology* was not. Sentencing postponed pending Heywood's appeal.

FEBRUARY

National Liberal League presented petition

(with 70,000 signatures) to Congress protesting the Comstock Act and calling for its repeal.

JUNE 12

National Defense Association formed by E. B. Foote, A. L. Rawson, Edward Chamberlain, and others. Heywood, Benjamin Tucker, and Flora Tilton joined its executive committee.

JUNE 25

Heywood's appeal scheduled but delayed pending the outcome of a Supreme Court decision of the constitutionality of the Comstock laws. Sentenced to two years imprisonment and a $100 fine when the Supreme Court upheld the Comstock Act.

AUGUST 1

Mass meeting to protest Heywood's conviction held in Boston by National Defense Association, which petitioned President Hayes for pardon.

OCTOBER

Anti-socialist laws passed in Germany.

DECEMBER 10

D. M. Bennett, the editor of *The Truth Seeker,* arrested on obscenity charges under Comstock Act for sending *Cupid's Yokes* through the mail.

DECEMBER 16

President Hayes pardoned Heywood.

DECEMBER 19

Heywood released from prison.

1879

MARCH 18

Bennett's case set to begin. He was found guilty of mailing obscenity.

MAY 15

The ruling against Bennett upheld.

JUNE 5

Bennett sentenced to thirteen months at hard labor and a $300 fine.

1880

APRIL

Bennett released from prison.

OCTOBER

In Switzerland, Peter Kropotkin's definition

of anarchist communism was adopted at the Congress of La Chaux-de-Fonds of the Jura Federation.

1881

MARCH 13 (NEW STYLE; MARCH 1, GREGORIAN CALENDAR)

Alexander II mortally wounded by bomb in St. Petersburg set by the revolutionary group Narodnaya Volya (People's Will).

MARCH 30

Johann Most arrested in London for endorsing the assassination of Alexander II in 19 March *Freiheit*. Held for three months during his arraignment and trial (25–26 May); after an unsuccessful appeal (18 June), was sentenced (29 June) to sixteen months at hard labor.

APRIL–MAY

Pogroms in Russia, tolerated and in some areas abetted by the authorities; instigated by rumors that the tsar's assassins were Jews.

APRIL 15

N. I. Kibalchich, Alexander Mikhailov, Sophia Perovskaya, Ivanovich Rysakov, and Andrei Ivanovich Zhelyabov, members of Narodnaya Volya, hanged for their part in the assassination of Alexander II.

JULY 14–19

International Social Revolutionary and Anarchist Congress in London. Delegates overwhelmingly endorsed propaganda by the deed. Among the participants were Victor Dave, Frank Kitz, Peter Kropotkin, Errico Malatesta, Saverio Merlino, Louise Michel, Johann Neve, and Joseph Peukert. Several American revolutionary groups were represented, including the Social Revolutionary Club of New York, Social Revolutionary Group of Philadelphia, and Socialist Labor Party of New York, German Branch; Gustave Brocher represented the Iowa Icarians; Miss M. P. LeCompte, associate editor of the *Labor Standard,* represented the Boston Revolutionists. Closed sessions were followed by a public meeting on 20 July.

AUGUST

Liberty founded, Boston, Massachusetts.

OCTOBER 21–23

Congress of Social Revolutionary Groups in Chicago. Proceedings led by Albert Parsons, Michael Schwab, and August Spies. The Revolutionary Socialistic Party was formed, the first national anarchist association in the United States.

1882

OCTOBER 25

Johann Most released from prison.

OCTOBER 26

Ezra Heywood arrested by Anthony Comstock for mailing *Cupid's Yokes* and also mailing a special issue of *The Word,* featuring two poems by Walt Whitman including "A Woman Waits for Me" and an advertisement for a contraceptive syringe called by Heywood "the Comstock syringe."

DECEMBER 18

Most arrives in the United States; *Freiheit* reestablished in New York.

1883

APRIL 12

Ezra Heywood found not guilty of charges arising from his arrest on 26 October 1881.

AUGUST 24

Lucifer, the Lightbearer founded, Valley Falls, Kansas.

OCTOBER 14–16

Pittsburgh congress convened in Pittsburgh, Pennsylvania; Pittsburgh Manifesto written largely by Johann Most but amended by Victor Drury, Albert Parsons, Joseph Reifgraber, and August Spies; document served as the ideological and programmatic basis of the International Working People's Association. This was the first and last congress of the IWPA.

1884

OCTOBER 4

The Alarm founded, Chicago, Illinois.

DECEMBER 6

Der arme Teufel founded, Detroit, Michigan.

1885

DECEMBER 29

EG arrived in the United States with her sister Helene; they settle in **Rochester**, New York, with their sister Lena.

1886

EG found work as a garment worker. The rest of EG's family immigrated to Rochester from St. Petersburg.

APRIL 26

The Alarm is suppressed in Chicago.

MAY 1

Several hundred thousand workers across United States struck for eight-hour workday.

MAY 3

In Chicago, striking workers of McCormick Harvester plant clashed with police; four workers killed, several wounded.

MAY 4

At a rally in Chicago's Haymarket Square, bomb was thrown into midst of police. One officer was killed, several officers wounded. When police fired into the crowd, six police-men died from their wounds, and an un-known number of civilians. Casualties totaled 67, most from police bullets rather than bomb fragments. The identity of the bomb thrower was never determined but prominent Chicago anarchists subsequently arrested and tried for murder.

MAY 11

Johann Most arrested for incendiary nature of speech given to Workingmen's Rifle Club in New York.

JUNE 2

Most sentenced to one year in prison on Blackwell's Island for inciting to riot as a re-sult of his speech on 11 May.

AUGUST 20

Seven of the Haymarket anarchists found

guilty and sentenced to death (George Engel, Samuel Fielden, Adolph Fischer, Louis Lingg, Albert Parsons, Michael Schwab, and August Spies). Oscar Neebe was also found guilty of murder but sentenced to fifteen years in prison.

1887

Comstock again arrested Heywood and charged him with mailing obscene materials; the case, however, was not prosecuted.

EG heard New York socialist Johanna Greie Cramer speak in **Rochester** on the Haymarket case. See *LML*, p. 7.

FEBRUARY

EG married Jacob Kershner, gaining U.S. citizenship.

APRIL 1

Most released from Blackwell's Island.

SEPTEMBER

Buffaloer Arbeiter-Zeitung founded, Buffalo, New York.

SEPTEMBER 21

After a year of appeals, the Illinois Supreme Court upheld the verdict of the Haymarket anarchists.

NOVEMBER 5

The Alarm resumes publication under Dyer D. Lum's editorship.

NOVEMBER 10

Refusing to let the state take his life, Haymar-ket anarchist Louis Lingg committed suicide by exploding in his mouth a dynamite car-tridge that had been smuggled in by Dyer D. Lum in a cigar.

Illinois Governor Oglesby commuted Fielden's and Schwab's death sentences to life in prison.

NOVEMBER 11

Haymarket anarchists George Engel, Adolph Fischer, Albert Parsons, and August Spies executed.

NOVEMBER 16

Most arrested in New York for illegal assem-

bly and incitement to riot, later sentenced to
one year on Blackwell's Island; but out on bail
pending appeal until 1891.

1888

Between November 1887 and February 1888,
EG and husband, Jacob Kershner, were divorced, and EG left Rochester for **New Haven,**
Connecticut; met Russian socialists and anarchists, including Hillel Solotaroff; found work
at a corset factory. Returned to **Rochester,** living with sister Helene's family, and worked in
sewing factory. According to *LML* (pp. 23–25),
EG remarried Kershner, remained with him
for three months, and then was shunned by
her parents when she left Kershner for good.

FEBRUARY

AB immigrated to the United States.

JUNE 16

According to its masthead, *The Alarm* began
publication in both Chicago and New York until its cessation in February 1889.

OCTOBER

Lucy Parsons left for speaking tour of England.

1889

FEBRUARY 2

The Alarm ceased publication.

AUGUST

Der Anarchist founded, St. Louis, Missouri.

AUGUST 15

EG arrived in **New York**; met AB at Sachs's
restaurant and later met Johann Most at a
meeting. Later in the month she found work
first in a corset factory, then in a silk waist factory. See *LML*, pp. 25–29, 37.

AUGUST–DECEMBER

EG worked at *Freiheit* office, helped organize
11 November Haymarket commemoration.
EG and AB became lovers. They shared an
apartment with Modest Stein, and the sisters Helene and Anna Minkin. See *LML*,
pp. 43–44.

1890

JANUARY

Most arranged EG's first public lecture tour to
Rochester, Buffalo, and **Cleveland** to speak on
the limitations of the eight-hour movement.
See *LML*, p. 46.

JANUARY 25

Most arrested in New York on 16 November
1887 charge but then released, pending second appeal.

FEBRUARY

Joseph Barondess asked EG to recruit women
workers for the cloakmakers. See *LML*,
p. 55.

EG became ill and forced to spend several
weeks convalescing; had a brief affair with
Modest Stein.

Although she and AB contemplated returning to Russia to help with revolutionary activities, EG instead accompanied Most on a two-
week lecture tour of **New England.** See *LML*,
pp. 63, 70.

FEBRUARY 16

EG spoke to Group 1 of the IWPA in Clarendon Hall, **New York.**

FEBRUARY 18

EG gave a talk at the home of J. Kuirim, 443
Pearl, **New York,** sponsored by IWPA, Agitation Committee.

FEBRUARY 22

EG spoke to Group 1 of IWPA in **New York.**

MARCH 16

Spoke on the Paris Commune to a Newark
branch of the IWPA in Phoenix Park Hall,
Newark, New Jersey.

APRIL 12

Spoke on "The Right to Be Lazy" in **New York**
at Matthei's, organized by IWPA.

APRIL 20

Scheduled to speak to Group 1 of IWPA, **New
York.**

MAY

Ezra Heywood arrested for sending obscene
material through the mail in his March 1890

publication of *The Word*. Two articles, one a "Letter from a Mother" on the topic of sexual education, and the other an article written by Angela Heywood charging Anthony Comstock with discrimination against women, were cited as obscene.

MAY 1

Demonstrations celebrating the labor holiday in Andalusia, Spain, end in reprisals by government authorities. In the wave of arrests that followed, over 150 anarchists and labor militants jailed.

MAY 3

EG spoke on "The Pittsburgh Proclamation of 1883" to the IWPA, West Side Group, **New York.**

MID-MAY

Heywood's trial began; found guilty and sentenced to two years at hard labor, without appeal.

JUNE 15

AB attended talk in Clarendon Hall by Joseph Peukert, sponsored by Radikaler Arbeiter-Bund.

JULY 4

First issue of *Freie Arbeiter Stimme*, New York.

SUMMER

To earn money to return to Russia and join the revolutionary work there, EG moved with AB, Stein, and Helene and Anna Minkin to **New Haven** to start a dressmaking cooperative. Until they built a clientele, EG worked temporarily at the corset factory where she had worked in 1888. AB gained employment in the printing trade.

They helped organize an anarchist educational group that attracted German, Russian, and Jewish immigrants; among the invited speakers were Most and Hillel Solotaroff. See *LML*, pp. 70–71.

FALL

EG and AB moved back to **New York** and began attending meetings of the Gruppe Autonomie, led by Joseph Peukert. See *LML*, pp. 74–75.

OCTOBER 12

EG lectured in German before German- and Yiddish-speaking workers' societies in **Elizabeth**, New Jersey.

OCTOBER 19

EG spoke in **Baltimore** to members of IWPA in the afternoon. Later spoke in German to Workers' Educational Society at Canmakers' Hall. Michael Cohn and William Harvey also spoke.

NOVEMBER 7

Most arrested in New York along with others, including Lucy Parsons and Hugh O. Pentecost, speaking on the Haymarket anarchists.

DECEMBER 25

Conference of Yiddish anarchists held in Clarendon Hall, **New York;** called by *Freie Arbeiter Stimme*. AB attended and proposed an investigation of the charges by Johann Most against Joseph Peukert.

1891

MARCH 8

EG spoke at mass meeting of the International Working Men's Association in **New Haven**, Connecticut, Trades Council Hall.

MARCH 16

Spoke at a "Great Commune Celebration" sponsored by the International Working Men's Association in **New Haven**, Connecticut, Trades Council Hall.

MAY 1

Marched with the Working Women's Society of the United Hebrew Trades at May Day parade in **New York**. See *LML*, pp. 79–80.

At a May Day demonstration in Clichy Levallois, France, two anarchists were arrested after violent clashes with the police and sentenced to three and five years, respectively, although the prosecutor had asked for the death sentence.

JUNE 16

Most began second term on Blackwell's Island.

JUNE 18

EG addressed a mass meeting held to protest the Supreme Court's upholding of Most's 1887 conviction for illegal assembly and incitement to riot.

1892

WINTER AND SPRING

EG moved to **Springfield**, Massachusetts; worked in a photography studio with Modest Stein. In **Worcester**, AB, Stein, and EG opened their own studio. When this failed, they opened an ice cream parlor; when the ice cream parlor opened "it was spring and not yet warm enough for an ice-cream rush" (*LML*, p. 82). They planned to raise money to return to Russia to respond to the political repression under Alexander III.

Socialist League of New York founded during the early part of this year.

JANUARY

Der Anarchist moved to New York from St. Louis, Missouri.

JANUARY 6

Joe Deakin arrested in London. First arrest in the Walsall case.

JANUARY 8

As a result of the government persecutions in 1890, uprising of Spanish peasants in Jerez. Hundreds were arrested and beaten by government agents. Sixteen men tried and convicted; their sentences ranged from ten years to life. Anarchist Fermín Salvochea, known as the "saint," was later tried for inciting the "riot," although he had been imprisoned in Cadiz during the incident.

FEBRUARY 16

Four anarchists, arrested in the wake of the Jerez uprising, executed in Jerez.

FEBRUARY 18

A meeting was held at Cooper Union, organized by New York anarchist communists to protest against the execution of Spanish comrades in Jerez. John Edelmann, Henry Weismann, and Roman Lewis all spoke.

MARCH 11

Ravachol bombed house of the judge who conducted the trial against the Clichy Levallois anarchists involved in 1 May 1891 incident; also bombed the prosecutor's house on 27 March; there were no injuries from either bomb.

MARCH 30

Ravachol arrested in Paris for bombings. Trial of Walsall anarchists began.

APRIL

Liberty moved to New York.

APRIL 4

Four of the six Walsall anarchists (Fred Charles, Jean Battola, Victor Cailes, and Joe Deakin) found guilty in an English court of conspiracy to make a bomb. William Ditchfield and John Westley found innocent and released.

APRIL 18

Most released from Blackwell's Island.

APRIL 26

Ravachol sentenced to life for bombings.

APRIL 30

Liberty's first issue in New York.

MAY

Freie Arbeiter Stimme ceased publication.

MAY 1

EG, Most, and other anarchists attempted to speak at the Central Labor Union's May Day celebration in Union Square, **New York.**

JUNE

Solidarity (John Edelmann, editor) founded, New York.

JUNE 22

Ravachol found guilty of murder of French miser (unconnected with bombings).

JUNE 30

Workforce locked out of Homestead steel works.

JULY 6

In a battle with Pinkerton strikebreakers, at least nine striking Homestead steel plant workers and three Pinkerton detectives killed.

JULY 8

Henry Bauer and two others attacked by strikers at Homestead, who "want nothing to do with the agents of Most."

JULY 10

EG composed an appeal to workers in English and German. See *LML*, p. 86.

JULY 11

Ravachol executed by guillotine.

JULY 12

AB left New York for Pittsburgh, arrived 11 p.m. on 13 July.

JULY 13

AB registered at the Merchants Hotel near the train depot as Mr. Rakhmetov.

JULY 14

At 10 a.m., AB went to Carl Nold's home, where he stayed for eight days. Met Bauer through Nold.

JULY 23

AB shot and stabbed Carnegie's steel company manager, Henry C. Frick, wounding but not killing him.

In the aftermath, EG suspected of complicity but not charged; police raided her apartment, seizing her papers. The press refer to EG as the "Queen of the Anarchists."

Debate over AB's act began within anarchist and radical circles.

JULY 25

Nold arrested.

JULY 26

Bauer arrested.

JULY 27

In an interview with the *New York World,* Most criticized AB's action.

JULY 30

EG attacked Most in *Der Anarchist.*

AUGUST 1

EG chaired meeting at Military Hall, 193 Bowery, **New York,** in defense of AB's act. Speakers included Dyer D. Lum, Saverio Merlino, and Joseph Peukert.

AUGUST 5

EG spoke at meeting of Gruppe Autonomie, along with Joseph Peukert at the Zum Großen Michel saloon, 209 Fifth Street, **New York.**

AUGUST 27

Most's article "Attentats-Reflexionen," criticizing AB's action yet praising his courage, written 31 July, appears in *Freiheit.*

SEPTEMBER 19

AB sentenced to twenty-two years in prison; EG learns about his sentence while lecturing in **Baltimore.** Announcement prompts audience alarm, police action, and EG's arrest.

NOVEMBER

Simon Wing and Charles H. Matchett received 21,164 votes for president and vice-president, respectively, on the SLP ticket, marking the first time the socialist movement entered the national political scene.

NOVEMBER 24

EG visited AB at the Western Penitentiary, **Allegheny City,** Pennsylvania. See *LML,* p. 111.

DECEMBER

Met Robert Reitzel in **Detroit.** Lectures intermittently. Met Edward Brady.

DECEMBER 4

Spoke in Clarendon Hall, **New York,** at a meeting denouncing congressional schemes to restrict immigration. John Edelmann, Pedro Esteve, and Saverio Merlino also spoke.

DECEMBER 18

EG struck Johann Most in the face with a small horsewhip at a meeting at 98 Forsyth Street, **New York.**

1893

SPRING

EG begins her relationship with Ed Brady.

MARCH

Freie Arbeiter Stimme resumes publication.

MAY

New York stock market crashed. In a series of events, beginning with the failure of a major railroad, the Panic of 1893 began. U.S. Treasury will be bankrupted for first time in its history, threatening collapse of U.S. government. Events lead to public panic and subsequent rush to withdraw money. By end of year, close to 500 banking institutions and 16,000 businesses declared bankruptcy and hundreds of thousands out of work.

JUNE 20

At a meeting at Ulrich's Hall in Chicago, the American Railway Union was officially launched, with Eugene Debs as president.

JUNE 25

Approximately 8,000 attended dedication of monument to Haymarket anarchists at Chicago's Waldheim Cemetery.

JUNE 26

Illinois Governor Altgeld unconditionally pardoned the remaining Haymarket anarchists —Samuel Fielden, Oscar Neebe, and Michael Schwab—condemning the Haymarket affair as judicial murder, and effectively ending his political career.

JUNE–JULY

EG returned to **Rochester** to recuperate from illness. See *LML,* p. 120.

JULY

Die Brandfackel began publication, New York.

AUGUST

Solidarity ceased publication.

AUGUST 8

Anarchists in attendance at the Zurich congress of the socialist Second International were excluded, and a resolution was passed stating that only those who regarded political action as a necessary strategy would be permitted into the proceedings.

AUGUST 17

Unemployed rioted at Walhalla Hall in New York.

AUGUST 18

EG addressed a meeting at Golden Rule Hall, **New York,** urging the needy to take bread if they are hungry.

AUGUST 19

After speaking at a demonstration in **Newark,** EG led procession of several hundred to

Union Square, **New York,** where she and others addressed a crowd of the unemployed.

AUGUST 21

EG spoke to a large crowd at Union Square, **New York,** in German and English.

AUGUST 23

EG lectured in the Brownsville section of **Brooklyn;** went to **Philadelphia** where she met Max Baginski and Voltairine de Cleyre. See *LML,* pp. 123–24, 216.

AUGUST 25

Warrants issued at Essex Market Police in New York for the arrest of six of the speakers at the 21 August Union Square meeting. EG, Joseph Barondess, Julius Bodansky, Pauline Sieger, Claus Timmermann, and Adolph Ury were charged with incitement to riot.

AUGUST 26

Claus Timmermann arrested and held on $5,000 bail. Charged with unlawful assembly.

AUGUST 31

As she was about to address a rally of the unemployed in Buffalo Hall in **Philadelphia,** EG arrested on the New York warrant.

SEPTEMBER 1

Claus Timmermann tried for inciting to riot at the 21 August Union Square demonstration; sentenced to six months on Blackwell's Island.

SEPTEMBER 6

A New York grand jury indicted EG on charges stemming from her 21 August speech.

SEPTEMBER 9

EG returned from Philadelphia to **New York** by police.

SEPTEMBER 11

Pled not guilty

SEPTEMBER 14

Bail set at $1,000; released on bail.

SEPTEMBER 23

Benefit concert held at New Irving Hall in **New York** to raise money for EG's defense.

SEPTEMBER 24

In retaliation for the Jerez executions, on 16 February 1982, Paulino Pallás attempted to kill the captain general of Catalonia, Arsenio Martínez de Campos, wounding him slightly, killing 2 and wounding 12. He was immediately arrested, subsequently convicted, and sentenced to death within days of the incident.

SEPTEMBER 30 – OCTOBER 8
The International Anarchist Convention, Chicago, coinciding with the world's fair, was banned by the police but held anyway, on the premises of the *Chicago Times*. Broad range of anarchist opinion was represented by the twenty-five in attendance, including William Holmes, Voltairine de Cleyre, and C. L. James.

OCTOBER 4 – 9
EG tried; defended by ex-New York mayor A. Oakey Hall; found guilty of inciting to riot.

OCTOBER 6
Paulino Pallás executed by firing squad.

OCTOBER 16
EG sentenced to **Blackwell's Island** for one year.

OCTOBER 18
EG began serving her term; worked first in the prison's sewing department and later as an orderly in the prison hospital.

NOVEMBER 7
Avenging Pallás's execution, Santiago Salvador French, an associate, bombed a Barcelona opera house, killing 22 and injuring almost 50. Spanish government suspended constitutional liberties; many suspected radicals detained, tortured. Seven anarchists, including French, later executed, four given life terms.

DECEMBER 9
Auguste Vaillant threw bomb of nails into the French Chamber of Deputies; no one killed; Vaillant injured in the blast, later confessed while in hospital.

DECEMBER 12
The French government passed the first of the three *lois scélérates,* making provocation of violence, possession of explosives, and conspiratorial associations punishable by long prison terms. The other two laws were passed on 18 December 1893 and 28 July 1894.

DECEMBER 16
A "Grand Concert and Ball" held at New York's Clarendon Hall for the benefit of EG "and others now suffering for freedom of speech." Features performance by the Internationale Arbeiter Liedertafel. Voltairine de Cleyre delivered "In Defense of Emma Goldmann and the Right of Expropriation." Afterward de Cleyre visited EG in prison.

1894

JANUARY 10
Vaillant on trial for bombing of Chamber of Deputies, found guilty and sentenced to death.

FEBRUARY 5
Vaillant executed.

FEBRUARY 12
In response to the *lois scélérates* (the "draconian" measures of the French government against anarchists) and the execution of Vaillant, Émile Henry bombed Café Terminus in Paris, killing one person, and injuring many.

MARCH 8
Claus Timmermann released from Blackwell's Island.

MAY 10
Strike breaks out at Pullman railroad car plants in Chicago over savage wage cuts.

MAY 21
Émile Henry executed.

JUNE 24
French president Marie François-Sadi Carnot assassinated in Lyons by Sante Caserio, in retaliation for Vaillant's execution.

JUNE 26
American Railway Union (ARU) servicemen, under the leadership of Eugene Debs, began refusing to service trains with Pullman cars in support of the striking Pullman workers.

JULY 2
A federal injunction issued against the leaders of ARU over their actions.

JULY 3

President Grover Cleveland sent federal troops into Chicago.

JULY 6

Fires caused by 6,000 protesters destroyed 700 railcars and caused $340,000 of damage in South Chicago Panhandle railway yards.

JULY 7

National Guardsmen fired into crowd of strikers in Chicago, several people killed. Eugene Debs and other ARU leaders arrested for disobeying the federal injunction.

AUGUST 2

Pullman plants reopened; the strike broken.

AUGUST 16

Sante Caserio executed.

AUGUST 17

EG released after serving ten months. Her account of her experience, "My Year in Stripes," appeared in the *New York World* on 18 August.

AUGUST 19

A meeting at the Thalia Theatre, **New York,** welcomed EG back; Sarah Edelstadt, John Edelmann, Pedro Esteve, Charles Mowbray, and Maria Roda also spoke.

AUGUST 21

EG spoke on "The Right of Free Speech" at a mass meeting in Phoenix Park Hall in **Newark** called by the American Labor Union, Branches 1 and 2. Voltairine de Cleyre, John Edelmann, and Charles Mowbray also spoke.

SEPTEMBER

Met with John and Orsena Swinton (both had visited her at Blackwell's Island), and resolved to conduct more propaganda in English. Spoke in **Baltimore.** Moved into an apartment with Edward Brady. See *LML*, pp. 154–56.

OCTOBER

Began a new campaign for the commutation of AB's sentence; worked as a nurse. See *LML*, p. 157.

OCTOBER 15

Alfred Dreyfus, member of the French War

Ministry, arrested and accused of selling military secrets to the Germans.

NOVEMBER

The 15 October arrest of French officer Alfred Dreyfus for espionage publicly announced in the antisemitic paper *La Libre Parole.*

NOVEMBER 11

EG spoke at a Haymarket commemoration in **New York;** Max Baginski, Voltairine de Cleyre, John Edelmann, Charles Mowbray, and Justus Schwab also spoke.

NOVEMBER 13

Spoke with Charles Mowbray in **West Hoboken,** New Jersey.

NOVEMBER 16

Left New York for **Pittsburgh.**

NOVEMBER 17

Spoke in **Pittsburgh.**

NOVEMBER 18

Spoke in German in **Baltimore** at Canmakers' Hall. Mowbray also spoke, in English.

NOVEMBER 21

Santiago Salvador French executed.

DECEMBER 22

Alfred Dreyfus court-martialed, convicted, and sentenced to life in prison on Devil's Island, French Guiana. The controversy surrounding his case, known as *l'Affaire,* will grow over the next ten years, dividing the country and sparking debate internationally.

DECEMBER 28

C. W. Mowbray arrested and charged with inciting to riot and sedition against the Commonwealth of Pennsylvania.

1895

JANUARY

Die Brandfackel ceased publication.

JANUARY 5

EG helped organize a ball at Clarendon Hall, **New York,** sponsored by the Joint Anarchist Groups of New York. Proceeds went to *Solidarity,* which was struggling financially.

JANUARY 24

Lectured in hall on 54 East St., **New York,** on

"Strikes." Landlord at first barred EG from hall but later relented for one lecture only and returned a three-month rent deposit.

JANUARY 27

The Firebrand founded, Portland, Oregon.

APRIL 13

Alfred Dreyfus transferred to Devil's Island, where he was placed in solitary confinement.

SPRING

EG, Claus Timmermann, and Ed Brady opened an ice cream parlor in **Brownsville, Brooklyn;** the venture failed within three weeks.

SUMMER

AB's appeal to the U.S. Supreme Court proved legally impossible; EG began soliciting funds for an appeal to the Pennsylvania Board of Pardons. See *LML,* p. 175.

JUNE

Der Anarchist ceases publication.

JUNE 12

Debs begins a six-month sentence for conspiracy over the Pullman strike in McHenry County Jail, Woodstock, Illinois.

JULY 15

La Questione Sociale, Italian-language anarchist paper, founded, Paterson, New Jersey.

AUGUST 15–22

EG traveled to **England,** arrived in **London** on 22nd.

AUGUST 25

Reception in London for EG sponsored by French anarchists. EG met Louise Michel.

FALL

EG addressed crowds at open air meetings in **London**'s Hyde Park; spoke in **Whitechapel, Canning Town, Barking,** and **Stratford.** Topics included "The Futility of Politics and Its Corrupting Influence." Met Kropotkin and Malatesta. German police monitored her movements in London, prepared to arrest her if she entered Germany.

SEPTEMBER

The Rebel founded, Boston.

SEPTEMBER 13

EG appeared at the South Place Institute in **Finsbury** with James Tochatti and Louise Michel, among others. Spoke on "Political Justice in England and America," highlighting AB's case.

SEPTEMBER 14

EG traveled to **Scotland;** during her stay lectured in **Glasgow, Edinburgh,** and **Maybole.**

OCTOBER

Freie Gesellschaft, Yiddish-language anarchist cultural and literary journal, founded, New York.

OCTOBER 1

EG traveled to **Vienna** to begin formal training in nursing and midwifery at the Allgemeines Krankenhaus. While there read works by Friedrich Nietzsche, attended Richard Wagner operas, saw Elenora Duse perform, and attended lectures by Sigmund Freud. Delivered lectures on Saturdays in the circle of the independent socialists. See *LML,* p. 170.

NOVEMBER 22

Debs released from prison.

1896

MARCH

Left Vienna for **Paris;** there met Augustin Hamon.

Die Sturmglocken founded, Chicago. Ceased publication in April.

MARCH–APRIL

The Rebel ceased publication.

APRIL

Lucifer, the Lightbearer moved to Chicago from Kansas.

EG back in **New York,** continued to live with Ed Brady on Eleventh Street; worked as midwife and nurse; solicited Voltairine de Cleyre's support on AB's behalf; helped arrange lectures for John Turner. See *LML,* pp. 176–78.

APRIL 30

Spoke at Clarendon Hall at John Turner's last **New York** lecture (before he traveled to Boston). Speakers included John Edelmann, Charles Mowbray, and Lothrop Withington.

MAY 1

At a demonstration in Union Square, helped distribute a manifesto written by her and a group of American-born comrades in **New York.**

JUNE 7

Bomb exploded during the Corpus Christi Day procession in Barcelona killing 11, wounding approximately 40; Spanish authorities imprisoned hundreds of anarchists and radicals suspected of involvement. Subsequent reports of torture in Montjuich Prison sparked international protests.

JULY 27–AUGUST 3

London congress of the socialist Second International.

JULY 28

Anarchist delegates expelled from the London congress of the Second International; anarchists and social revolutionaries convened their own meeting that night. Delegates included Peter Kropotkin, Errico Malatesta, Pietro Gori, Louise Michel, Élisée Reclus, Jean Grave, Harry Kelly, and Charles Mowbray. Final break between anarchism and organized international socialism.

OCTOBER 12

EG acted as chief usher at a debate in Clarendon Hall, **New York,** between John Turner and Charles H. Cook on "Will Free Coinage of Silver Benefit the People?" During EG's speech advertising a commemoration meeting for the Haymarket anarchists she was interrupted by an abusive and drunken Johann Most.

NOVEMBER 4

EG spoke before the **Philadelphia** Ladies' Liberal League on her experiences on Blackwell's Island.

NOVEMBER 8

EG spoke before a mass meeting called by a **Philadelphia** Jewish group to honor the Haymarket anarchists and raise money for AB; spoke later that evening on "Woman's Cause" to the Young Men's Liberal League.

NOVEMBER 11–15

EG lectured in **Baltimore;** raised money for AB's appeal.

NOVEMBER 20–26

Lectured in **Pittsburgh,** primarily in German; raised money for AB. Aided by Harry Gordon. Topics included "The Jews in America," "Anarchism in America," and "The Effect of the Recent Election on the Condition of the Workingman." Her concluding lecture addressed the Haymarket affair.

DECEMBER 11

Eighty-seven Spanish anarchists on trial for the Corpus Christi Day bombing.

DECEMBER 20

Sentences handed down in Corpus Christi Day bombings. Eighteen given long prison terms, five sentenced to death.

1897

APRIL 23–25

EG gave several lectures in **Providence,** Rhode Island, including "What Is Anarchism?" and "Is It Possible to Realize Anarchism?" Police prevented her from addressing a second open-air meeting on the grounds that she had no permit. Local socialists disavowed connection to EG.

MAY

EG spoke in **Philadelphia** on the topic "The Women in the Present and the Future." Back in New York EG underwent an operation on her foot, requiring several months of recuperation.

MAY 4

Five Spanish anarchists executed in connection with the Corpus Christi Day bombing.

MAY 25

Carl Nold and Henry Bauer released from prison. See *LML*, p. 197.

JUNE 15

Social Democracy of America was organized at the final convention in Chicago of the American Railway Union. Leading members included Eugene Debs and Victor Berger.

AUGUST 8

Michele Angiolillo assassinated Spanish prime minister Cánovas del Castillo in retaliation for the deaths of the five Spanish anarchists executed 4 May.

AUGUST 16

EG spoke at meeting of 1,000 at Clarendon Hall in **New York** celebrating Cánovas's death. Harry Kelly and Salvatore Pallavencini also spoke.

AUGUST 22

At a public meeting in Clarendon Hall, **New York**, EG faced criticism from Charles B. Cooper and other anarchists for glorifying Cánovas's death rather than advancing the cause of anarchy by explaining the reasons for his assassination.

SEPTEMBER 3

Beginning a four-month lecture tour, EG spoke at an open air meeting in Olneyville Square, **Providence,** Rhode Island.

SEPTEMBER 4

Spoke at an open air meeting in Burgess Square, **Providence.**

SEPTEMBER 5

Spoke in **Boston** on the topic "Must We Become Angels to Live in an Anarchist Society?"; collected money for victims of Spanish repression. That evening spoke on Cánovas's assassination at Providence Casino. John H. Cook chaired meeting.

SEPTEMBER 8

Having been warned by Providence's mayor that she would be arrested if she spoke outdoors again, EG held an open-air lecture at Market Square, **Providence**, Rhode Island, in opposition to his warning. She was prevented by the police from continuing her speech, taken to the police station, held overnight, and released the next day at noon, but was threatened with three months imprisonment if she did not leave town within 24 hours.

SEPTEMBER 10

At least 19 striking coal miners shot and killed at Hazleton, Pennsylvania; close to 40 others seriously injured.

SEPTEMBER 12

EG spoke in **Boston** at Phoenix Hall. Her original lecture topic was "Free Speech." In response to the Hazleton massacre, she spoke instead on "The Rights of the People."

SEPTEMBER 13–14

Scheduled to speak in **New Haven** and **New York** on the Hazleton massacre.

SEPTEMBER 15

Spoke on "Free Love" before the **Philadelphia** Ladies' Liberal League.

Spoke to the Philadelphia Single Tax Society on "Anarchist-Communism."

SEPTEMBER 17

Firebrand editor A. J. Pope arrested for sending obscene material through the mail, including Walt Whitman's poem "A Woman Waits for Me"; co-editors Abe Isaak and Henry Addis arrested soon thereafter on same charge. *Firebrand* ceased publication that month.

SEPTEMBER 19

EG delivered an afternoon and evening lecture before the **Philadelphia** Friendship Liberal League.

LATE SEPTEMBER

EG in **Pittsburgh;** met Nold and Bauer, who informed her that AB planned to escape from prison if his appeal failed. Spoke before a Turner gymnastic society in **Monaca,** Pennsylvania.

SEPTEMBER 27–29

EG addressed convention of reform clubs and trade unions in **Chicago.** Eugene Debs, Ross Winn, and Jay Fox were also in attendance.

SEPTEMBER 29

EG held her own meeting after walking out of the convention on the 28th.

SEPTEMBER 30

Spoke in **Chicago** to the *Lucifer* Circle on "Prostitution: Its Causes and Cure."

OCTOBER 7

Spoke in **Chicago** to the *Lucifer* Circle on "Free Love" at 1394 Congress Street.

MID-OCTOBER–NOVEMBER 23

Kropotkin toured the United States for the first time.

OCTOBER 13

EG spoke with Max Baginski, Moses Harman, and Lucy Parsons at Zepf's Hall in **Chicago** at a fundraiser for imprisoned *Firebrand* editors.

OCTOBER 16

EG gave lecture in German in **St. Louis** at Harugari Hall on "Anarchy."

OCTOBER 17

Spoke in German at Ohlman's Hall, **St. Louis.**

OCTOBER 19

St. Louis's House of Delegates supported mayor's ban on EG's open-air meetings; her lectures, including "Revolution" and "Why I Am an Anarchist and Communist," were held in private halls under police surveillance.

OCTOBER 20

Spoke at Walhalla Hall in **St. Louis.**

LATE OCTOBER

EG in **Caplinger Mills**, Missouri; meetings arranged by Kate and Sam Austin; topics included "The Aim of Humanity," "Religion," "Anarchy," and "Free Love." Told a St. Louis reporter she planned to lecture next in Kansas City, Topeka, and Denver.

NOVEMBER

Sturmvogel founded, New York.

NOVEMBER 11

EG spoke at a commemoration of the Haymarket anarchists in German in Turner Hall in **Chicago.** Meeting chaired by Jay Fox and Theodore Appel.

NOVEMBER 14

Free Society founded, San Francisco.

NOVEMBER 16

EG spoke in German at Turner Hall, **Detroit,** Michigan; meeting commemorated Haymarket, organized by Central Labor Union.

NOVEMBER 19

Having been invited by its pastor, Reverend McCowan, despite considerable opposition,

EG spoke at the **Detroit** People's Tabernacle. Jo Labadie helped arrange the meeting. It was reported in local newspapers that the following day a majority of its congregants and deacons asked McGowan to resign and threatened to leave the church.

NOVEMBER 21

Lectured in **Cleveland** on "What Anarchy Means"; collected money for *Firebrand* editors. Meeting arranged by Fred Schulder.

NOVEMBER 28

Spoke at Council Hall, **Buffalo,** New York.

DECEMBER

AB's hearing before Pennsylvania Board of Pardons postponed.

DECEMBER 1

EG spoke in **Buffalo**, New York, at Spiritualists Tabernacle on "Anarchy."

DECEMBER 4

Spoke in **Rochester**, New York, at Germania Hall.

DECEMBER 5

Lectured on "The Aim of Humanity," at the Labor Lyceum in **Rochester.**

MID-DECEMBER

EG returned to **New York.**

1898

JANUARY

EG's brother Morris Goldman moved into EG and Brady's New York apartment.

JANUARY 5

Lectured in German on "The New Woman" to the **Brooklyn** Social Science Club.

JANUARY 13

In the French journal *L'Aurore*, Émile Zola published an open letter to the French president of the Republic, accusing the officials involved in the Dreyfus case of meddling with the truth. Zola's letter became known as *J'Accuse,* coined by the owner/editor of *L'Aurore*, Georges Clemenceau.

JANUARY 15

EG announced lecture topics for the coming year in *Sturmvogel:* "Charity," "Patriotism," "Authority," "Majority Rule," "The New Woman," "The Woman Question," and "The Inquisition of Our Postal Service."

JANUARY 21–23

Returned to **Providence**, Rhode Island; lectured without interference from the mayor or police; assisted by John H. Cook. James F. Morton, Jr. also spoke.

To defray traveling expenses, EG made sales for Brady's stationery business while on tour.

JANUARY 24

Lectured on "Authority" to economics students in Phoenix Hall, **Boston**. James F. Morton, Jr. also spoke.

FEBRUARY–JUNE

Addressed 66 meetings in 12 states and 18 cities; participated in one debate. Reporters noted EG's improved command of English.

FEBRUARY 13

Spoke before the **Brooklyn** Philosophical Society.

FEBRUARY 15

The USS *Maine* exploded and sank in Havana harbor.

FEBRUARY 16–20

EG lectured in **Philadelphia** before Ladies' Liberal League, Single Tax Society, Society of Ethical Research, and German Anarchist Society; lectured twice before Friendship Liberal League. Topics included "The Absurdity of Non-resistance to Evil," "The Basis of Morality," "Freedom," "Patriotism," and "Charity."

FEBRUARY 23–MARCH 12

Nold and Bauer invited EG to lecture in **Pittsburgh** and nearby mining towns. Topics included "Patriotism," the Hazleton massacre, and "The Coming War with Spain."

EG suffered "nervous attacks" from the strain of continuous lecturing.

FEBRUARY 24

Lectured at Odd Fellows Hall in **Pittsburgh** in English.

FEBRUARY 25

Lectured in German at Vorwaerts Saenger Hall in **Lawrenceville**, Pa.

FEBRUARY 26

Lectured in **Monaca**, Pennsylvania, in front of the Glass Blowers' Union local.

FEBRUARY 27

Lectured in **Beaver Falls**, Pa., and in Marion Hall in **Pittsburgh** in English.

MARCH 1

Lectured in **Carnegie**, Pa.

MARCH 2

Scheduled to speak in **Allegheny City** but the lecture was canceled when the owners of Northside Turner Hall refused to let her speak.

MARCH 4

Lectured in **Duquesne**, Pa.

MARCH 5

Spoke in **McKeesport**, Pa.

MARCH 6

Spoke in **Pittsburgh**, Pa. in German at the Imperial Dancing Academy.

MARCH 7

Lectured in **Challeroi**, Pa.

MARCH 8

Spoke in **Roscoe**, Pa.

MARCH 10

Spoke in **Newton**, Pa..

MARCH 11

Lectured in **Tarentum**, Pa.

MARCH 12

Spoke with Nold and Harry Gordon in **Pittsburgh** at a twenty-seventh anniversary celebration of the Paris Commune at the Imperial Dancing Academy on Wylie Avenue.

MARCH 13

Traveled to **Cleveland**, Ohio, lectured before the Franklin Club on the "Basis of Morality."

MARCH 14

Lectured at Glessen's Hall in **Cleveland** on "Charity."

MARCH 15

Lectured again before the Franklin Club in **Cleveland** on "The New Woman."

MID-MARCH

Visited the ailing Robert Reitzel in **Detroit**.

MARCH 20–26

Gave several lectures before **Chicago** labor unions, aided by Joseph Peukert. Visited Max Baginski at the *Chicagoer Arbeiter-Zeitung* office; discussed women's emancipation with Moses Harman. Visited Michael Schwab, who was hospitalized with tuberculosis.

MARCH 20

Lectured in front of the Economic Educational Club in **Chicago** on "Authority."

MARCH 21

Spoke to the Brewers' and Malters' Union in **Chicago** on "Trade Unionism."

MARCH 22

Spoke in **Chicago** to the Painters and Decorators Union on "Trade Unionism."

MARCH 23

Addressed the Cooperative College of Citizenship group of the IWA in **Chicago** on "Patriotism."

MARCH 24

Spoke in **Chicago** to the Turnverein (Turner Gymnastic Society) of the *Vorwärts* newspaper on the "New Woman."

MARCH 26

Spoke on "Passive Resistance" to the Bakers' and Confectioners' Union in **Chicago.**

MARCH 27–28

Lectured before Ohio Liberal Society in **Cincinnati.**

MARCH 29

Returned to **Chicago**; lectured on "Charity."

MARCH 30

Spoke in **Chicago** to the International Group on "The Basis of Morality."

MARCH 31

Lectured in **Chicago** on "The Inquisition of Our Postal Service" to a Bohemian workers group, addressing the *Firebrand* case; group unanimously adopted a resolution protesting postal censorship.

Robert Reitzel died in **Detroit.**

APRIL 2

EG honored at a farewell meeting held by the Committee on Agitation of the Progressive Labor Organization of **Chicago.** Moses Harman also spoke.

APRIL 3–4

Spoke in **Milwaukee** at Central Park and Garten Falls on the 3rd; and at Ragger's Hall on the 4th.

APRIL 6–10

Delivered five lectures in **St. Louis**; no interference by mayor or police.

APRIL 6

Spoke on "Patriotism" in **St. Louis.**

APRIL 7

Spoke on "Authority vs. Liberty" in **St. Louis.**

APRIL 8

Spoke on "Basis of Morality" in **St. Louis.**

APRIL 9

Spoke on "The Absurdity of Non-Resistance" in **St. Louis.**

APRIL 10

Final lecture in **St. Louis** on "Charity."

APRIL 13–18

William and Lizzie Holmes arranged EG's five lectures in **Denver,** Colorado; William rated "The Basis of Morality" her best. Sponsors included the Denver Educational Club, a Jewish group.

APRIL 24

Spain declared war on the United States.

APRIL 25

United States Congress declared war on Spain and made the declaration retroactive to 21 April.

LATE APRIL–EARLY MAY

EG in **San Francisco.** While in town stayed with Abe Isaak; met socialist Anna Strunsky and, through Strunsky, writer and socialist Jack London.

APRIL 26

Spoke on "Patriotism" at the Turk Street Temple in **San Francisco.**

MAY 1

Spoke at a May Day rally with socialist Emil Liess and others in **San Francisco.**

MAY 4

Debated Emil Liess in **San Francisco.**

MAY 5–8

Violent demonstrations in Milan over taxes, rising food prices; martial law declared. Death toll was over 80, including 2 policemen; approximately 450 wounded. King Umberto awarded General Fiorenzo Bava Beccaris Italy's highest award for his role in suppressing the riots. Incident given the name Fatti di Maggio.

MAY

EG spoke in **San Jose** and **Los Angeles.** Returned to **San Francisco** for additional lectures.

EARLY JUNE

EG's three **Portland** lectures arranged by Henry Addis.

JUNE 7–10

In Ulrich's Hall, **Chicago,** EG attended first convention of Eugene Debs's Social Democracy, held 7–10 June, and labeled the event a "fiasco." At the end of the conference a large group of members walked out, including Eugene Debs and Victor Berger, who proceeded to form the Social Democratic Party.

JUNE 20

Firebrand case dismissed by United States District Court in Portland, Oregon.

JUNE 29

Michael Schwab died.

JULY

EG returned to **New York**. Supported textile strike in Summit, New Jersey, with Salvatore Pallavencini and other Italian anarchists.

SEPTEMBER 10

Empress Elizabeth of Austria stabbed to death by Luigi Luccheni.

SEPTEMBER 18

EG lectured in **Boston** on "Charity."

SEPTEMBER 20

EG lectured in **Lynn**, Massachusetts, on "Authority vs. Liberty."

NOVEMBER–DECEMBER

With Justus Schwab and Brady, EG sought

Andrew Carnegie's influence in granting AB a pardon. They approached Benjamin Tucker to act as intermediary but withdrew their request after reading Tucker's proposed letter to Carnegie; plan was eventually abandoned.

NOVEMBER 24–DECEMBER 21

International Anti-Anarchist Conference convened in Rome by the Italian government under international pressure after the assassination of the Austrian empress by Luigi Luccheni. Organized to coordinate international efforts to police and punish anarchist activity, the conference was attended by diplomats, ambassadors, and law enforcement agents. The delegates represented twenty-one countries, including all of Europe as well as Russia and Turkey. Among the items discussed at the conference were methods for identifying anarchists (including the *portrait parlé*, a system based on criminal anthropometry), and extradition and deportation tactics, including the deportation of anarchists to their countries of origin. The network of international police communication created during the conference contributed to the development of the International Criminal Police Organization, or Interpol.

DECEMBER 10

President McKinley signed peace treaty with Spain. As part of the treaty, United States acquired Puerto Rico, Guam, and the Philippines; Spain relinquished claim to Cuba.

DECEMBER 21

EG scheduled to lecture at Lear's Hall, 61 E. 4th Street, **New York**, on "The Power of the Idea."

1899

JANUARY

EG ended relationship with Edward Brady.

JANUARY 5

Spoke at a large meeting at Cooper Union, **New York**, protesting the Anti-Anarchist Conference in Rome. Other speakers included George Brown, J. H. Cook, Pedro Esteve, and Saul Yanovsky.

LATE JANUARY–SEPTEMBER

EG conducted nine-month lecture tour of eleven states, beginning in **Barre,** Vermont, where she was hosted by Salvatore Pallavencini. Met Luigi Galleani.

JANUARY 21

Gave lecture in **Barre** on "Authority v. Liberty" at Tomasis Hall, Mairs Street.

JANUARY 25

Gave another lecture in Tomasis Hall, **Barre,** on "Trades Unionism—What It Is and What It Ought To Be."

JANUARY 28

Third lecture at Tomasis Hall, **Barre;** spoke on "The New Woman."

JANUARY 31

Final lecture in **Barre** at Tomasis Hall, on "Authority vs. Liberty" suppressed by police. Local anarchists printed and distributed copies of the speech she was to deliver.

FEBRUARY 4

Insurgent forces began rebellion against rule of United States in Philippines.

FEBRUARY 6

Congress approved treaty with Spain by one-vote margin, after Senate opposition.

MID-FEBRUARY

EG delivered lectures in German and English in **Philadelphia;** spoke before Friendship Liberal League, Ladies' Liberal League, Fellowship for Ethical Research, Knights of Liberty, and Radikaler Arbeiter-Bund.

LATE FEBRUARY

Spoke in **Cleveland.**

MARCH 13

EG scheduled to speak in **Detroit** at 224 Randolph Street on "The Dying Republic."

MARCH 14

EG scheduled to speak in **Detroit** at the Trade Council Hall on "Trade Unionism: What It Is and What It Should Be."

MARCH 16

EG scheduled to speak in **Detroit** at Turner Hall, Sherman Street, in German.

LATE MARCH

In **Cincinnati** spoke on trade unionism before the Ohio Liberal Society; in **St. Louis** gave ten lectures, including one before the Bricklayers' Union; two lectures in the nearby mining town of Mount Olive, including "The Eight-Hour Struggle and the Condition of the Miners of the Whole World."

APRIL–MAY

Spent over a month in **Chicago;** delivered about twenty-five lectures in German and English; topics included "Religion," "Women's Emancipation," "Origins of Evil," and "Politics and Its Corrupting Influence on Man." Aided by Max Baginski and other German comrades, spoke before trade unions, philosophical and social societies, and women's clubs; English lectures included "Trade-Unionism and What It Should Be." Her address before the conservative Amalgamated Wood Workers Union was the first by an anarchist.

MAY

EG spent a few days visiting miners in **Spring Valley,** Illinois.

Sturmvogel ceased publication.

MAY 20

In **Tacoma,** Washington, debated "Socialism versus Anarchism." Spiritualist temple was offered to EG free of charge for her lecture series, but offer withdrawn when she proposed to lecture on "Free Love."

MAY 28

Lectured at the Germania Hall in **Seattle,** Washington, on "Anarchism: Its Philosophy and Ideas."

MAY 29

Lectured at the Germania Hall in **Seattle** on "Politics and its Corrupting Effects."

JUNE

Visited the anarchist Home Colony, near **Lakebay,** Washington.

JUNE 5

French Court of Appeal overturned the 1894 sentence of Alfred Dreyfus.

JUNE 10–17

Supported by Henry Addis, lectured in **Portland,** Oregon, and in the farming town of **Scio** met Gertie Vose, Donald Vose's mother, where town marshal offered her use of city hall.

JUNE 22

Arrived in **San Francisco;** began seven-week lecture series in **San Francisco, Oakland, San Jose,** and **Stockton,** California. Topics included "Why I Am an Anarchist Communist," "The Aim of Humanity," "The Development of Trades-Unionism," and "Charity." Socialists were antagonistic to her on several occasions. "Sex Problems" talk stirred debate.

JULY 14

Lectured on "The Aim of Humanity" at Grand Army Hall, **Oakland.**

AUGUST 7

Second trial of Alfred Dreyfus began before a French court martial.

MID- TO LATE AUGUST

EG delivered three lectures arranged by William Holmes in **Ouray,** Colorado; in **Denver,** lectures included "The Power of the Idea," "Education," and an open air meeting on "Patriotism." Traveled to the farming town of **Caplinger Mills,** Missouri, as the guest of Kate and Sam Austin; delivered three lectures, including "Patriotism."

SEPTEMBER 4

In the mining town of **Spring Valley,** Illinois, headed a Labor Day procession. Afterwards spoke in defiance of the mayor's injunction at a meeting arranged by the miners' union.

SEPTEMBER 7

Spoke in **Pittsburgh.**

SEPTEMBER 8

Spoke in **Fayette City,** Pa.

SEPTEMBER 9

Alfred Dreyfus found guilty of treason once

again, with extenuating circumstances, and sentenced to ten years' detention.

SEPTEMBER 10

Spoke in **Pittsburgh.**

SEPTEMBER 19

Alfred Dreyfus formally pardoned.

SEPTEMBER 23

Spoke in **West Newton,** Pa.

SEPTEMBER 24

Spoke in **Collinsburg,** Pa.

SEPTEMBER 26

Spoke in **Hope Church,** Pa.

SEPTEMBER 28

Spoke in **Lawrenceville,** Pa.

FALL

EG arranged for work to begin on AB's escape tunnel.

OCTOBER 3–4

Spoke in **McDonald,** Pa.

OCTOBER 9

Spoke in **Roscoe,** Pa.

OCTOBER 11

Anglo-Boer War began.

MID-OCTOBER

Returned to **New York.** With Saul Yanovsky and others, raised money for AB's escape tunnel under the guise of pursuing new legal action on AB's behalf.

NOVEMBER 3

Traveled with Mary Isaak to **Europe** via London with the intention of attending the 1900 International Revolutionary Congress of the Working People in **Paris,** and then to study medicine in **Zurich,** Switzerland. Also planned to meet AB in Europe after his escape from prison.

NOVEMBER 13–DECEMBER 9

In **London** stayed with Harry Kelly and family; lectured in English and German. Topics included "America: The Land of the Free and the Home of the Brave," "Strikes and Their Effect on the American Worker," and "Marriage." Visited Peter Kropotkin at his home in Bromley, met Nicholas Chaikovsky. Argued with Kropotkin over political significance of "the sex problem." Met Hippolyte Havel; met German anarchist Rudolf Rocker, editor of the Yiddish anarchist *Arbeter Fraint*.

DECEMBER 9

Spoke with Louise Michel, Kropotkin, Varlaam Cherkesov, Tom Mann, and Tarrida del Mármol at a **London** meeting on behalf of victims of Italian political repression.

DECEMBER 10

Traveled to Leeds to deliver several lectures. Scheduled to remain until the 23rd, she left after a week, returning with pleuritis to **London** where she was confined to bed for two weeks.

1900

Freie Gesellschaft ceases publication.

EARLY JANUARY

EG attended a Russian New Year party in **London**; met Russian revolutionary exiles. Cherkezov, Chaikovsky, and Kropotkin present. See *LML*, p. 262.

MID TO LATE JANUARY

Scheduled to lecture in **Glasgow, Dundee**, and **Edinburgh,** where she met anarchist Thomas Bell.

JANUARY 19

Lectured in **Glasgow.**

JANUARY 21

Gave two lectures in **Dundee.** The afternoon lecture was entitled "Authority vs. Liberty"; the evening lecture was entitled "The Aim of Humanity."

FEBRUARY 20

Back in **London**, spoke out against the Anglo-Boer War in "The Effect of War on the Workers" at a meeting of the Freedom Discussion Group in the Club and Institute Hall, Clerkenwell. Other speakers include Harry Kelly, Samuel Mainwaring, Tom Mann, and Lothrop Withington.

FEBRUARY 26

Honored at a farewell concert and ball; Peter Kropotkin and Louise Michel spoke.

MARCH

With Havel, traveled to **Paris** to prepare for the International Revolutionary Congress of the Working People, scheduled to begin 19 September. Decided against pursuing medicine to concentrate on political activity. Addressed organizing committee of the Paris congress on the state of the American movement.

EG presented papers on behalf of Lizzie Holmes and William Holmes, Abe Isaak, Susan Patton, Kate Austin, and others.

MAY 17

EG lectured at the Libertarian Library, 26 rue Titon, **Paris.**

MAY 19

EG spoke on women's emancipation at the Harmonie Hall, 94 rue Angoulême, **Paris.**

JUNE 14

French police surveillance noted presence of EG and Havel at a women's congress in **Paris.**

JULY 9

SDP and Hillquit's section of the Socialist Labor Party merged to form SDP based in **Springfield**, Massachusetts. There remained another SDP that disfavored the union being headquartered in Chicago. They decided to form tacit truce in order to present a unified campaign in upcoming presidential elections.

JULY 26

AB's escape tunnel discovered. Shortly thereafter, Eric Morton left for Paris.

JULY 29

King Umberto of Italy assassinated by Gaetano Bresci to avenge the victims of Fatti di Maggio, 5–8 May 1898.

AUGUST 4–6

International Conference of Neo-Malthusians held in **Paris**. Representatives attended from Holland, England, France, and Germany. EG obtained birth control literature and contraceptives to take back to the United States and informed participants on the illegal status of birth control dissemination in America.

SEPTEMBER 6

Der arme Teufel ceased publication.

SEPTEMBER 18

The primarily anarchist International Revolutionary Congress of the Working People, scheduled to begin the following day, was prohibited by the French Council of Ministers. That evening a protest meeting was prevented by the police.

OCTOBER 8

EG attended two secret meetings held by anarchists at 26 rue Vitou in **Paris** regarding the barred International Revolutionary Congress of the Working People.

NOVEMBER

The socialist ticket of Debs and Job Harriman as president and vice president, respectively, gains 96,978 votes.

NOVEMBER 1

EG reported by French police as departing Paris for **Boulogne** with Havel and John Leroy (Eric B. Morton), en route back to the United States.

EARLY DECEMBER

Arrived in **New York** with Havel and Eric Morton.

DECEMBER 11

EG addressed Social Science meeting at Everett Hall in **New York.** Owner threatened to "turn out lights" if meeting took anarchistic turn. Pedro Esteve addressed meeting in Spanish.

DECEMBER 23

Spoke to the Italian group of **New London,** Connecticut. Pedro Esteve also spoke.

1901

JANUARY–MARCH

Worked as a nurse; re-established friendship with Ed Brady. See *LML,* pp. 283, 288.

JANUARY 15

Dutch anarchist Douwe Boersma charged EG as the instigator of slanders against Most in Domela Nieuwenhuis's paper, *De Vrije Socialist,* prompting debate about EG's character and her role in the anarchist movement.

JANUARY 20

Salvatore Pallavencini died in Paris.

FEBRUARY

Free Society moved to Chicago from San Francisco.

FEBRUARY–MAY

Kropotkin's second U.S. tour. EG helped with arrangements.

MARCH 4

McKinley inaugurated for second term.

MARCH 8

EG lectured at the Manhattan Liberal Club in **New York** at 8:00 p.m. on "What Will Lessen Vice."

APRIL 2–JUNE 13

Spoke in **Lynn,** Massachusetts; **Boston, Pittsburgh, Cleveland, St. Louis, Chicago, Philadelphia,** and **Spring Valley,** Illinois. Topics included "Anarchism and Trade Unionism," "The Cause of Vice," and "Cooperation a Factor in the Industrial Struggle."

APRIL 6

A letter in defense of EG (with regard to attacks on her character and charges that she has unfairly incited attacks against Johann Most), dated 30 March, appears in *De Vrije Socialist.* Letter signed by Victor Dave, Christiaan and Lily Cornelissen, Tárrida del Marmol, Max Nettlau, Albert Zibelin, Marie Goldsmith, Marc Pierrot, and Léon Rémy.

APRIL 7

EG in **Philadelphia.** She gave one lecture in the afternoon under the auspices of the Workingmen's Cooperative Association on the subject "The Necessity of Cooperation among Labor Organizations." A second lecture under the auspices of the Social Science Club was prohibited by the police.

APRIL 9

EG forcibly prevented from speaking on "Trade Unionism" at Standard Hall in **Philadelphia.** The meeting was sponsored by the Shirt Makers Union, and EG was accompanied by Natasha Notkin before being barred entry by the police.

APRIL 11

EG spoke to an audience of 200 at the Single Tax Society of **Philadelphia** at Mercantile Library Hall. The police were unaware of the meeting until it ended.

APRIL 14

Spoke at the Social Science Club in **Philadelphia** with Voltairine de Cleyre and others before 2,000 people at the Industrial Art Hall; Social Science Club passes a resolution protesting the violation of her right to free speech. The police did not attempt to stop EG from speaking on this occasion.

APRIL 17

Lectured with Voltairine de Cleyre at Bricklayer's Hall, **Philadelphia**, sponsored by United Labor League.

APRIL 26 – MAY 4

Spoke in **Pittsburgh**; gave four lectures: "Modern Phases of Anarchism," "Anarchism and Trades Unionism," "The Causes of Vice," and "Cooperation a Factor in the Industrial Struggle." She also gave a lecture in **Cecil**, Pennsylvania, during this time.

MAY 4

Delivered eulogy in **Pittsburgh** at the funeral of a young Italian anarchist who had committed suicide.

MAY 5

Lectured on "The Modern Phase of Anarchy" before the Liberty Association of the Franklin Liberal Club in **Cleveland**. Leon Czolgosz in attendance. EG later recognized Czolgosz as the young man who approached her at the intermission and asked her recommendation for books to read. Later that evening EG spoke on the "Cause and Effect of Vice."

MAY 11

Pennsylvania's Commutation Act of 1901 passed. The act allowed for the reduction of prison sentences for good behavior and shortened AB's sentence to just five more years.

MAY 19

Czolgosz visited Cleveland anarchist Emil

Schilling to ask for suggested readings and information on "secret" anarchist societies. He visited Schilling three more times by early August.

MAY 21

The brothers Jesús and Ricardo Flores Magón arrested in Mexico City office of *Regeneración*, charged with writing an inflammatory article, sentenced to eleven months.

EG spoke in **Chicago** to the Scandinavian Painters Union on "Cooperation an Important Factor in the Industrial Struggle."

MAY 23

Bresci died in prison, reportedly by suicide.

MAY 25

Spoke before the Blacksmith Helpers Union in **Chicago** on "Trade Unionism from an Anarchist Standpoint."

MAY 26

Spoke before the Anthropological Society in **Chicago** at 3:00 p.m. on "Modern Phases of Anarchism."

MAY 30

EG delivered address at Decoration Day gathering in **Chicago**'s Waldheim Cemetery.

JUNE 22

Spoke in German on "Trades Unionism from an Anarchist Standpoint" in front of the Brewers' and Malters' Union at 122 West Lake Street, **Chicago.**

JUNE 25

Spoke to the *Lucifer* Circle in **Chicago**, 500 Fulton Street, on "Failure of So-called Free Unions."

JULY 2

Spoke in German before the German Painters Union in Lauterbach's Hall in **Chicago**. Lecture entitled "Cooperation an Important Factor in the Industrial Struggle."

JULY 11

Czolgosz left Cleveland for Chicago.

JULY 12

Czolgosz attempted to visit office of *Free Society* in Chicago, came back later the same day and introduced himself as Mr. Nieman from Cleveland. Havel, Max Baginski, and others from the office were leaving for the train station to see EG off to **Buffalo** and **Rochester.** Czolgosz joined them. After EG left Chicago, her comrades became suspicious of Nieman's repeated references to acts of violence. A letter (from Emil Schilling) later arrived at the *Free Society* office from Cleveland warning that "Nieman" was an assumed name and that Czolgosz was probably a spy.

JULY 15

EG left Buffalo for **Rochester,** where she stayed for the next five weeks. During her stay with her sister, she took short trips to **Niagara Falls** and **New York.** While in Rochester, EG learned that AB's sentence had been commuted by two and one-half years and he was permitted to receive visitors.

JULY 29

At the Socialist Unity Convention in Indianapolis, in what was the largest gathering of socialists in the United States at that time, the two SDPs voted to unite and the Socialist Party was created, based in St. Louis and led by Eugene Debs and Victor Berger.

AUGUST 15

EG left Rochester for **Buffalo.**

AUGUST 18

EG visited Pan American Exposition in **Buffalo** with Marie Isaak, Abe Isaak's sixteen-year-old daughter.

AUGUST 19

EG went to **Pittsburgh** to work as a traveling saleswoman for a New York firm (Ed Brady's stationery and office supply company). During her stay in Pittsburgh she visits AB for the first time in nine years at the Western Penitentiary, **Allegheny City.**

AUGUST 24

EG left Pittsburgh for **Cincinnati**, Ohio.

LATE AUGUST

In Chicago, Czolgosz read in the paper that President McKinley would be visiting the Pan American Exposition in Buffalo. He immedi-

ately bought a train ticket for Buffalo, although he was not yet planning to kill the president.

AUGUST 31

Czolgosz called on his friend Walter Nowak and asked to stay with him. Began visiting the exposition grounds a few times each day.

SEPTEMBER 1

EG in **Cincinnati.** Left that night for St. Louis. Abe Isaak's *Free Society* carried a notice warning people against an agent provocateur who is "soliciting aid for acts of contemplated violence." This is Leon Czolgosz.

SEPTEMBER 2

EG arrived in **St. Louis**, where she worked for Ed Brady's firm until after Czolgosz shot McKinley.

SEPTEMBER 3–5

Czolgosz followed McKinley around to public appearances, waiting for a chance to shoot him.

SEPTEMBER 6

Czolgosz waited in line for the president at the Temple of Music during the Pan American Exposition in Buffalo. He shot and severely wounded McKinley. Czolgosz was arrested immediately and later confessed to the crime. EG was canvassing stores in **St. Louis** for Ed Brady's firm when she first heard of the McKinley shooting.

Czolgosz signed a statement at 10:20 p.m. saying that the last public speaker he had heard was EG, but that she had never told him to kill the president.

Secret Service officers in Buffalo sent a telegram to Chicago officials, asking them to investigate and find the location of *Free Society*'s headquarters. Abe Isaak, Abe Isaak, Jr., Hippolyte Havel, Enrico Travaglio, Clemens Pfeutzner, Julia Mechanic, Mary Isaak, Mary Isaak, Jr., and Alfred Schneider were arrested and charged as accomplices in the plot to assassinate the president. The men were subjected to all-night interrogations and held without bail; the women were released three days later.

EG left St. Louis for **Chicago** to help Isaak, Havel, and the other anarchists arrested after McKinley's assassination.

Secret Service launched a search for any anarchists implicated in the assassination attempt.

Police ransacked *Free Society*'s headquarters again and arrested Jay Fox, Martin Rasnick, and Michael Roz.

Czolgosz admitted in a statement that he had met EG in Chicago, but insisted that EG had not spoken to him.

"Murder against Murder," an old article by Karl Heinzen praising tyrannicide, appeared in *Freiheit* No. 36, ironically used as a space filler by Most, who was short of copy.

SEPTEMBER 8

EG arrived in **Chicago,** was met by Max Baginski, and went into hiding at the home of Charles Norris. According to the *Chicago Tribune,* she registered in a hotel under a fictitious name before going to Norris's home.

The *Chicago Tribune* let it be known it was prepared to give EG $5,000 for an exclusive interview; she however needed to stay in hiding long enough to secure the money for the defense of the *Free Society* anarchists.

Czolgosz named EG and another free-love proponent as influential to him.

SEPTEMBER 9

The *Buffalo Commercial* reported that "according to the law as construed by the Illinois supreme court in the case of the Chicago anarchists involved in the Haymarket riot some years ago, Emma Goldman and all the other anarchists who belonged to the anarchistic society with which Czolgosz was affiliated, or whose addresses or writings in any way might tend to induce Czolgosz to shoot the President, are equally guilty with him."

Cleveland police issued an official statement to the Associated Press regarding the alleged anarchist plot to kill the president: they found no definitive proof of a plot.

Harry Gordon and Carl Nold arrested in Pittsburgh.

Hearing for *Free Society* arrestees. Women allowed $3,000 bail and released later in the day at the prosecution's request. Case postponed to the 17th and then to the 23rd.

Secret Service men in Paterson, New Jersey, searched office of *La Questione Sociale* and questioned editor Pedro Esteve, trying to determine if anarchists there were involved in the plot to kill the president.

SEPTEMBER 10

Warrant issued for EG's arrest. Police go to Norris's house where EG was hiding; she posed as Swedish maid to evade them but eventually gave herself up. She was subjected to intensive interrogation. Though initially denied, bail was set at $20,000.

Cases against *Free Society* women (Julia Mechanic, Mary Isaak, and daughter Mary Isaak, Jr.) dropped for lack of evidence.

The National Association of Merchants and Travelers, a Chicago group, adopted resolutions to prevent anarchists from entering the United States. Representative Metcalf of California proposed an anti-anarchist immigration law.

New York police commissioner ordered a "careful census" of all anarchists in the city to be compiled and turned over to the detective bureau to "make conditions disagreeable" for those named.

SEPTEMBER 11

EG arraigned in **Chicago,** denied bail and hearing date set for the 19th.

Gordon and Nold released for lack of evidence.

SEPTEMBER 12

Buffalo district attorney announced he had no evidence to warrant EG's extradition.

Johann Most arrested for publication of Heinzen's article on political violence in *Freiheit.* Despite past differences, EG later supported Most and helped raise funds for his defense.

SEPTEMBER 13

Managers of the musical comedy *The New*

Yorkers announced they had to rewrite the comic opera, omitting the three anarchist characters because of bitter public sentiment against anarchists.

Most was arraigned and his bail set at $1,000. He was sent to the Tombs in default of bail.

SEPTEMBER 14

President McKinley died from gangrenous infection stemming from his wounds.

SEPTEMBER 15

EG received wire in jail from Ed Brady promising the backing of his firm. In the evening she was questioned by Chief O'Neill, whom she claimed in *Living My Life* (p. 302) said he believed her innocent.

Offices of *Freie Arbeiter Stimme* attacked by mob.

Anarchist settlement Guffey Hollow, Pennsylvania, raided and 25 anarchist families forced to leave the area.

SEPTEMBER 16

Article appeared in *New York Journal* suggesting EG had been a tsarist spy since 1891.

Johann Most arraigned and released on bail.

Czolgosz arraigned.

Gaetano Bresci's widow asked to leave Cliffside Park, New Jersey, by mayor.

SEPTEMBER 17

Wife of Bresci's alleged co-conspirator, Quintevallo, forced to leave Union Hill, New Jersey.

SEPTEMBER 18

EG's bail set at $20,000, and her hearing for the 24th.

SEPTEMBER 19

McKinley's funeral held.

SEPTEMBER 23

EG transferred to **Chicago**'s Cook County Jail, claimed she was struck by a guard and lost a tooth.

Czolgosz's trial began in Buffalo Supreme Court. He was charged with first degree murder.

Free Society arrestees discharged by judge.

SEPTEMBER 24

EG released after a two-week incarceration;

case dropped for lack of evidence. She was never officially charged with a crime.

Czolgosz found guilty of first-degree murder.

James E. Larkin, Charles L. Govan, G. Morong, and James W. Adams, all connected to the anarchist paper *Discontent*, charged with using the mail to distribute obscene literature.

SEPTEMBER 26

Czolgosz sentenced to death.

SEPTEMBER 27

Czolgosz moved from Buffalo to Auburn prison. When his train arrived at 3:10 a.m., he was brutally dragged from the train through a crowd of several hundred.

OCTOBER

AB locked up again in solitary confinement in aftermath of McKinley's assassination.

OCTOBER 3

EG scheduled but prevented from delivering the same lecture that allegedly inspired Czolgosz.

OCTOBER 6

EG's "The Tragedy at Buffalo" appeared in *Free Society*.

OCTOBER 6–29

Finding it difficult to secure an apartment or job, EG adopted the pseudonym "E. G. Smith."

OCTOBER 8

EG spoke at the Manhattan Liberal Club, **New York.**

OCTOBER 13

Free Society printed statement of apology to Czolgosz, retracting previous accusation of his being a spy.

OCTOBER 14

Most convicted for publication of "Murder against Murder." Sentenced to one year for violating section 675 of New York penal code.

OCTOBER 29

Czolgosz executed.

Most released pending appeal.

NOVEMBER 18

Berkman appealed to Pittsburgh Superior Court for release. His appeal was based upon the argument that his lesser indictments, including entering Frick's office, carrying concealed weapons, and carrying firearms, should have been merged under the greater indictment of felonious assault, that he should have been sentenced to ten years not twenty-one, and that under the new commutation law passed in Pennsylvania his time should expire on 2 December 1901. Although the appeal was in Berkman's name, it was carried out without his permission.

DECEMBER 9

EG spoke at meeting of Social Science Club in Civic Hall, **New York**; Rudolph Grossman also spoke on "Anarchism and Communism."

DECEMBER 18

Discontent publishers discovered six issues had been held by Tacoma post office.

Addis, Henry (1864–1934) American anarchist, writer, editor, and lecturer. Formerly a resident of Colorado, Addis settled in Portland in 1890. He published the anarchist paper *Freedom* (1893–1894). A leading Portland anarchist, Addis co-founded the *Firebrand* in 1895. Addis was tried with fellow *Firebrand* editors Abe Isaak and A. J. Pope on obscenity charges in the fall of 1897 (for publishing, among other articles, Walt Whitman's "A Woman Waits for Me" in the 14 March 1897 issue); all three were convicted. While Pope spent four months in prison, Addis's and Isaak's convictions were overturned on appeal in 1898. Addis remained in Portland after Isaak relocated *Firebrand* to San Francisco. Addis later moved to Home Colony in Washington State and continued to write for the paper, re-named *Free Society*. Writing from Holland from 1903 to 1904, he contributed to *Free Society*. Among his published works are *Receptive and Imperative Wants and Their Gratification through Labor Exchange* (Portland: Morris-Jones, 1894), *Essays on the Social Problem* (San Francisco: Free Society Publishing, 1898), and *Communism*, published in a single pamphlet with Jay Fox's *Roosevelt, Czolgosz and Anarchy* (New York: New York Anarchists, 1902).

Altgeld, John Peter (1847–1902) Democratic governor of Illinois (1892–1896). Born in Germany and raised in Ohio, Altgeld at the time of his election was a successful real estate developer in Chicago, a superior court judge, and a leading advocate of penal reform. In June 1893 he pardoned the surviving anarchists convicted in the Haymarket affair, releasing Samuel Fielden, Oscar Neebe, and Michael Schwab from prison. In a detailed statement in a pamphlet titled *Reasons for Pardoning Fielden, Neebe, and Schwab*, Altgeld attacked the legality of the original trial, addressing the illegitimacy of jury selection, the conduct of the police and prosecution, and the bias of Judge Joseph E. Gary, and concluded that the proceedings were a clear miscarriage of justice. Issued along with the texts of the pardons, Altgeld's 1893 pamphlet circulated for years among anarchists and socialists (publishers included Free Society Publishing, Lucy E. Parsons, C. H. Kerr, and New York Labor News). During the 1894 Pullman strike in Chicago, Altgeld supported the striking American Railroad Union and protested President Grover Cleveland's dispatch of federal troops to Chicago to stop the strike. After losing his re-election campaign in 1896, he returned to the practice of law in partnership with Clarence Darrow. Altgeld's writings include *Our Penal Machinery and Its Victims* (Chicago: Jansen, McClurg, 1884), *The Eight Hour Labor Movement* (Boston: Labor Leader Publishing, 1890), *Organized Labor's Demands* with Eugene Debs (New York: Morning Advertiser, 1894), *Oratory: Its Requirements and Rewards* (Chicago: C. H. Kerr, 1901), and *The Cost of Something for Nothing* (Chicago: Hammersmark Publishing, 1904).

Angiolillo, Michele (1871–1897) Italian anarchist. Angiolillo (often referred to in newspapers as "Golli") shot and killed Antonio Cánovas del Castillo, the prime minister of Spain, on 8 August 1897, at the Santa Agueda baths in the Basque region of Spain. Born in Foggia, Italy, Angiolillo attended technical school and was reported to have become interested in anarchism while serving in the military. He worked as a printer until 1895, when he was forced to flee Italy for printing an antigovernment manifesto. In the interim between leaving Italy and shooting Cánovas del Castillo, he lived in Spain, France, Belgium, and England. Reportedly, Angiolillo committed the act to avenge the tortures and deaths of the Montjuich prisoners. He was executed by garrote on 20 August 1897.

Aronstam, Modest *see* Stein, Modest.

Austin, Kate (1864–1902) American anarchist, advocate of women's independence, and free-thinker. Born Catherine Cooper in La Salle, Illinois, she settled with her husband, Sam Austin, on a farm near Caplinger Mills, Missouri. She was an early freethought and free-love advocate, and a lifelong anarchist communist influenced by the trial and execution of the Haymarket anarchists. Kate Austin was a friend and correspondent of William Holmes and Carl Nold. She and Sam arranged EG's Missouri lectures in 1897 and 1899. According to *Living My Life*, EG intended to, but was barred from, delivering Austin's report on "The Question of the Sexes," on the history of the free-love movement in the United States, at the 1900 International Revolutionary Congress of the Working People in Paris; a group of French anarchists feared "that any discussion of sex would only serve to increase the misconceptions of anarchism" (*LML*, p. 271). The text of Austin's paper did however appear in the official reports of the 1900 Paris congress in *Les Temps Nouveaux*, as well as in the Italian-American anarchist newspaper *La Protesta Humana*. In 1901 Austin joined EG in defending Czolgosz's act in the pages of *Free Society*. Austin was a contributor to *Free Society*, *Firebrand*, *Lucifer the Lightbearer*, and *Discontent* and a regular correspondent to a variety of papers. She died of consumption in Kingman, Kansas, on 28 October 1902 while traveling to Denver. Austin was memorialized in obituaries by both EG and Voltairine de Cleyre.

Baginski, Max (1864–1943) German American anarchist and editor. Baginski was a member of the German Social Democratic Party and became a follower of Johann Most. By 1891 he was a member of Youth, the anarchistic group in the Social Democratic Party, and editor-in-chief of *Proletarier aus dem Eulengebirge*. Baginski was also a member of the New Free Popular Theater in Berlin and in 1891 guided his roommate Gerhardt Hauptmann (*see vol. 2*) through Silesia, which Hauptmann later depicted in his drama *The Weavers* (1892). Baginski left Berlin after a thirty-month prison term for press violations, traveled through Zurich and London, arriving in New York in 1893 with his brother Richard Baginski. Max Baginski first met EG in Philadelphia in August 1893; he settled in Chicago where he became lovers with EG in 1898. Baginski later married Emilie (Millie) Schumm. Honoring their lifelong friendship, EG later wrote, "Max showed greater breadth, sympathy, and understanding than I had found among even the best of the German anarchists" (*LML*, p. 217). Baginski lived for a short time in Paris with his companion Millie Schumm in 1900, returning to the United States in 1901. Baginski wrote for *Freiheit* in New York and edited the *Chicagoer Arbeiter-Zeitung* from 1894 to approximately 1907, as well as its two weeklies, *Die Fackel* and *Der Verbote* (from 1893 to [?]), and published four issues of his own journal, *Die Sturmglocken* (in 1896). *See also vols. 2, 3.*

Bakunin, Michael (1814–1876) Russian revolutionary and theorist of anarchism. Bakunin was born into the aristocracy of Premukhino, in Tver province, and later was a part of the Russian intelligentsia. Radicalized under the repressive regime of Nicholas I, Bakunin found in Western Enlightenment philosophy, especially in the works of Johann G. Fichte and Georg W. F. Hegel, a theoretical basis for opposition to tsarist autocracy. He moved to Berlin in 1840 and joined the circle of the Young Hegelians. In Paris in 1844 Bakunin met and was influenced by Karl Marx, who would later become his political adversary, and by the anarchist Pierre-Joseph Proudhon, with whom he became fast friends. After his arrest in Dresden, Bakunin was condemned to death for his part in the revolutionary activity of 1848 and 1849; he was transferred to Russia, placed under government custody, and his sentence commuted to life imprisonment. In 1861 Bakunin escaped from exile in Siberia, traveling to Japan, the United States, England, Italy, and ultimately to Switzerland. Bakunin first joined the International in 1864, and by 1872, when Marx succeeded in expelling him from the International, Bakuninists probably constituted a majority of the organization's members. As a leading force in the anti-authoritarian opposition to Marx in the First International, Bakunin first described himself verbally as an anarchist in the mid-1860s, and in writing in 1867. His writings explored the idea of anarchist collectivism, an ideology later adopted by Victor Dave and Johann Most. Bakunin, preferring the life of an activist more than that of a theoretician, never wrote complete polemical tracts, with most of his writings unfinished fragments. His principal works are *Statism and Anarchy* (1873) and *God and the State* (1882), originally translated into English by Benjamin Tucker (Boston: Benjamin Tucker, 1883). *God and the State* was reprinted in 1896 by E. H. Fulton (Columbus Junction, Iowa: E. H. Fulton, 1896) and again in 1900 by Abe Isaak (San Francisco: A. Isaak, 1900). Tucker also serialized Bakunin's *The Political Theology of Mazzini and the International,* translated by Sarah E. Holmes, in *Liberty* in 1886 and 1887. Bakunin died in Berne, Switzerland, on 1 July 1876.

Barondess, Joseph (1867–1928) Russian-born trade union organizer. Barondess was born in Kamenets-Podolsk, Russia, the son of a rabbi; he immigrated first to England where he was an active trade unionist, and in 1888 to the United States. Barondess was employed in New York City as a kneepants maker, while attending night school at New York University Law School. He quickly became a popular labor leader and worked with the United Hebrew Trades in the 1890s, after leading the striking cloakmakers in New York City in 1890. In 1893 charges of extortion were brought against Barondess by a group of employers allegedly intent on slandering union officials. He was convicted and briefly fled to Canada; upon his return he spent a short time in jail before being pardoned by the governor of New York. In 1895 he led an unsuccessful general strike of cloakmakers that weakened both the union and his leadership. Barondess was sympathetic to anarchism and was an occasional contributor to *Freie Arbeiter Stimme* during the 1890s. In 1894 he left New York City and his work for the cloakmakers union, moving to Baltimore where he started the short-lived Yiddish paper *Free Press*. By the late 1890s he had gravitated toward socialism, and in 1897 he co-founded the *Jewish Daily Forward,* a socialist paper opposed to the Socialist Labor Party. In 1898 Barondess joined Eugene Debs and Victor Berger in the Social Democratic party and contributed articles to the *Social Democratic Herald*. A force in founding the International Ladies Garment Workers' Union in 1900, Barondess was invited to join the National Civic Federation that same year. *See also vol. 2.*

Battola, Jean (dates unknown) Italian anarchist exile living in England, shoemaker. A Walsall anarchist, Battola was arrested in January 1892 and charged with conspiracy to make explosives. He was sentenced to ten years in prison on 4 April 1892.

Bauer, Henry (1861–1934) German-born anarchist. Bauer immigrated to the United States in 1880 and settled in Pittsburgh, where he took part in the movement for an eight-hour workday. Bauer was drawn to anarchism in response to the Haymarket trial and executions. AB stayed with Bauer and Carl Nold in Pittsburgh before his attempted assassination of Henry Clay Frick. With Nold, Bauer was sentenced to five years, and served four, in prison on two charges: incitement to riot (stemming from their distribution of a handbill addressed to striking Homestead workers on 8 July); and conspiracy (with AB) to commit murder. Bauer was also charged $50 and sixty days in county jail for contempt of court when he refused to name the other men involved in distributing the leaflets (one of whom was Max Metzkow). Bauer corresponded with AB through the journal *Prison Blossoms*, created within the walls of the Western Penitentiary in Pennsylvania. After his release, Bauer served as secretary of the Berkman Defense Committee. Settling in Pittsburgh, he became western Pennsylvania's distributor of English- and German-language anarchist books, pamphlets, and newspapers, including *Firebrand, Free Society,* and *Freiheit*. He contributed to *Freedom* (1892, on the consequences of the Frick shooting) and to *Free Society* (25 December 1898, "Can Anarchism Be Killed?" a reprint of an interview first published in the *Pittsburg Leader*).

Berkman, Alexander (Ovsej Berkman) (1870–1936) Lithuanian-born anarchist and early mentor, lover, and lifelong comrade of EG. Berkman, whose legal name was Alexander Schmidt Bergmann and nickname was "Sasha," was born into a middle-class Jewish family in Lithuania (then a part of Russia). Berkman's uncle, Mark Natanson, was a founder of the Chaikovsky Circle and the Zemlya i Volya (Land and Liberty) society, the largest Russian populist group in the 1870s; Natanson would become an important figure in the Socialist Revolutionary Party and at various times in his life supported the strategy of terrorism. AB's interest in anarchism was first aroused upon reading an article on the hanging of the Haymarket anarchists in 1887. He immigrated to the United States just a few months later, at the age of 17 in February 1888, and frequented Jewish and German anarchist groups. Berkman joined and became an active member of Pionere der Frayhayt (Pioneers of Liberty). He worked as a cigar maker and tailor before learning typesetting, a skill he exercised in his work on Johann Most's paper, *Freiheit*. Gradually AB distanced himself ideologically from Most and *Freiheit*, gravitating toward the anarchism of Joseph Peukert and the Autonomy Group associated with the anarchist communist paper *Die Autonomie*. AB and EG first met in August 1889, upon her moving to New York, and within a short time they began to live together communally with Modest Stein and the sisters Anna and Helene Minkin. In 1890 the group moved to New Haven, Connecticut, to open a dressmaking co-operative modeled after that in N. G. Chernyshevsky's novel entitled *What Is to Be Done?* (Boston: Benjamin Tucker, 1886). Then in 1891 AB, EG, and Stein moved to Worcester, Massachusetts, where for a short time they operated an ice cream parlor. Upon hearing the news of the Homestead strike and lockout, however, they returned to New York in a effort to find a way to help the steel workers. AB, EG, and Stein planned AB's *attentat* in early July 1892. AB then traveled to Pittsburgh, arriving on 13 July and staying with Henry Bauer and Carl Nold. While in Pittsburgh he used the name Rahkmetov, a central character from *What Is to Be Done?* On 23 July 1892, AB made an unsuccessful attempt on the life of Henry Clay Frick, for which he was sentenced to twenty-two years in prison, although his act under Pennsylvania law only called for seven years in prison. He edited the journal *Prison Blossoms* with Henry Bauer and Carl Nold from inside Western Penitentiary. In 1900 Berkman, with the help of Eric B. Morton and others, organized an escape; the plan was to tunnel into the prison and rescue Berkman. While EG was in Paris, the plot was discovered and thus abandoned. The Berkman Defense Association was formed shortly after AB's imprisonment to work for AB's release, a reduction in his sentence, and at one time as a cover to raise funds for his tunnel escape. Harry Gordon, Henry Bauer, Carl Nold, Ed Brady, Harry Kelly, and EG were the driving forces behind these efforts. Although instinctively sympathetic to Leon Czolgosz, Berkman was critical of his act, believing the assassination would neither help the working people nor further the cause of anarchist propaganda.

Berman, Nahum H. (also Burmin) (d. 1900) Russian-born Jewish anarchist communist. Berman immigrated to the United States in 1885 and worked on *Freiheit, Solidarity,* and the *Alarm* before he anonymously helped edit the *Rebel* from 1895 to 1896. A close friend of Harry Kelly and Charles Mowbray, and a one-time lover of Voltairine de Cleyre, Berman helped start the short-lived anarchist paper *Match* in 1896. He died insane in Chicago; de Cleyre wrote his obituary for *Free Society.*

Bly, Nellie (1864–1922) American journalist. Writing under a *nom de plume,* Bly (who was born Elizabeth Jane Cochrane Seaman) began her career with the *New York World* in 1887 with an exposé of abuses at the Women's Insane Asylum on Blackwell's Island, to which she had herself committed in order to get the story. This investigative style of reportage soon became Bly's trademark. Bly left the *New York World* staff following her celebrated trek around the world in under eighty days in the winter of 1889–90, returning to the paper in 1893 when she interviewed EG. She wrote *Around the World in Seventy-Two Days* (New York: The Pictorial Weeklies Co., 1890).

Borland, Wilfred P. (b. ca. 1830) Michigan and then Chicago anarchist communist and trade unionist. Borland, a frequent lecturer in Chicago around the turn of the century, worked with Eugene Debs on the *Brotherhood of Locomotive Fireman's Magazine* and was a member of the colonization commission of the Social Democracy of America in 1898. An occasional contributor to the *Firebrand,* Borland also acted as a Chicago subscription agent for *Free Society.*

Brady, Edward (1852–1903) Austrian anarchist born in Vienna. Arrested in Munich in 1885 for distributing anarchist literature and deported to Vienna, Brady served eight years of a twelve-year prison sentence at hard labor. Upon his release, Brady emigrated to the United States in 1892. He met EG in December 1892 at a meeting for the commutation of AB's sentence. Brady soon became EG's teacher, mentor, and lover, and introduced her to the classics of European literature. His resentment of EG's singular devotion to the anarchist cause ultimately ended their intimate relationship in 1897, although they remained close friends and comrades. Brady served as treasurer of the Workingmen's Defense Association in 1901, working to appeal the imprisonment of Johann Most in the wake of the McKinley assassination; and for a brief time he also published *Der Anarchist.* Harry Kelly wrote the obituary for Brady in the May 1903 *Freedom.*

Bresci, Gaetano (1869–1901) Italian American anarchist. Born in Prato, Tuscany, Bresci apprenticed as a silk weaver in Milan, where he first joined the anarchist movement. Bresci settled in early 1898 in Paterson, New Jersey, where he worked as a silk weaver. He was drawn to the *antiorganizzatori* (anti-organization) affinity group in Paterson, where he became a subscriber and benefactor of the paper *La Questione Sociale*. In May 1900, to avenge the victims of government repression in Milan and Sicily, he left his home in New Jersey to assassinate King Umberto of Italy at Monza on 29 July 1900. He died in prison the following year, reportedly by suicide, and was considered a martyr of heroic significance to many within the American and European anarchist movement.

Brown, John (1800–1859) American abolitionist. Brown attacked the national government for its link to slavery and led the raid on Harpers Ferry in 1859, in an attempt to secure arms and distribute them to slaves for rebellion. Brown was tried for murder, slave insurrection, and treason in the state of Virginia, and was hanged 2 December 1859. He was regarded as a martyr and a hero for the bravery he exercised at his trial before facing death. EG and other anarchists identified with his willingness to die for his principles, and for adhering to a law of ethics while challenging the state in pursuit of a more just society.

Bruno, Giordano (1548–1600) Italian philosopher, Dominican monk. A victim of the Spanish Inquisition, Bruno was venerated by anarchists, among others, as a martyr to freedom of thought. *Lucifer* used the death of Bruno, rather than the birth of Jesus, to serially date issues of the paper.

Cailes, Victor (1858–1926) French anarchist. Cailes was convicted in the Walsall affair. Wanted in France for incitement to "incendiarism, murder and pillage" after a riot in Nantes, he arrived in England in 1890. Cailes was arrested with Fred Charles on 7 January 1892, at the Walsall Socialist Club, and later served seven and a half years of a ten-year sentence.

Cánovas del Castillo, Antonio (1828–1897) Spanish prime minister, historian, and writer. Cánovas was assassinated by Italian anarchist Michele Angiolillo after ordering the execution of five anarchists and the torture of hundreds of anarchists and radicals for their alleged involvement in the 7 June 1896 bombing of a Corpus Christi Day parade in Barcelona.

Cantwell, Thomas Edward (1864–1906) English anarchist, compositor. A member of the London branch of the Socialist League, Cantwell was the compositor and printer for *The Commonweal* from 1890 to 1894, except for the six months he spent in prison in 1893 after an anti-royalist demonstration at Tower Bridge. He was the compositor for *Freedom* from 1895 to 1902.

Carnegie, Andrew (1835–1919) Scottish-born American industrialist, philanthropist. Carnegie immigrated with his family in 1848 and settled in Allegheny City, Pennsylvania, where he began working at the age of 13. By his twenties Carnegie had become a financier with a fortune amassed from his investments. In the 1860s he founded an iron and steel works business and by 1889 had consolidated his interests into the Carnegie Steel Company. In April 1892, with Henry C. Frick acting as his proxy, Carnegie declared that the mills at Homestead, Pennsylvania, would become non-union in June of that year. Frick was given carte blanche authority to implement Carnegie's decision, the results of which led both to the Homestead lockout and to Berkman's failed *attentat* on Frick's life. In a letter printed in the November 1911 edition of the London anarchist newspaper *Freedom*, AB claimed that "it was universally understood that Carnegie arranged the Homestead lock-out and absented himself merely to shift responsibility for the troubles which he knew would follow." In 1901 Carnegie transferred his steel trust to the United States Steel Corporation and retired with significant reserves of wealth, which he later distributed according to the philosophy of his book, *The Gospel of Wealth* (London: F. C. Hagen, 1889), donating huge sums to educational and scientific institutions.

Carnot, Marie François-Sadi (1837–1894) French president, the fourth (1887–1894) during the Third Republic. Carnot was stabbed to death by Italian anarchist Sante Caserio on 24 June 1894, in retaliation for his refusal to pardon Auguste Vaillant, who was executed on 6 February 1894 for attempting to blow up the Chamber of Deputies on 9 December 1893.

Caserio, Sante (1873–1894) Italian anarchist. Caserio was from Motta Visconti, near Pavia, and a baker by trade. Caserio sought to avenge the execution of Auguste Vaillant on 6 February 1894 by assassinating French president Sadi Carnot in Lyon on 24 June 1894, which led to the passage of the third of three anti-socialist "Exceptional Laws" (also known as *lois scélérates*) on 26 and 27 July 1894.

Chaikovsky, Nikolai (1851–1926) Russian revolutionary. In St. Petersburg in 1869 he founded with Mark Natanson (AB's uncle) what became known as the Chaikovsky Circle, a group of radical students and intellectuals, including Peter Kropotkin and Sophia Perovskaya, who devoted themselves to a populist program of studying political and social issues, publishing radical literature, and propagandizing among workers and peasants. Chaikovsky left Russia in 1874, and apart from two trips to the United States (1875–1879, 1882–1885), spent his exile years in London. As an authority on Russian politics, he was well known among those British intellectuals who were critical of the tsarist regime. Chaikovsky was a delegate to the July 1881 anarchist meeting in London (the International Social Revolutionary Congress) and member of the *Freedom* Group. EG met him in 1900 in London at Kropotkin's house. Chaikovsky joined the Russian Socialist Revolutionary Party when it was organized during 1901 and 1902. *See also vol. 2.*

Chamberlain, Joseph (1836–1914) British politician and prominent member of the Liberal Party. Chamberlain became town councilor in 1868 and mayor of Birmingham in 1873. He won a seat in the House of Commons in 1876 and in 1880 was appointed president of the Board of Trade. His strong opposition to Irish Home Rule, symptomatic of his strong support of British imperialism, led him to form the Liberal Unionist faction, which broke with the Liberals and allied with the Conservative Party. For his support of the Irish Act of Union, he was appointed British colonial secretary from 1895 to 1903, responsible for British policy during the Boer War. By 1906, his proposed system of protective tariffs within the British empire failed, and after serious illness that same year he withdrew from public life.

Charles, Fred (original name F. C. Slaughter) (1864–1934) British anarchist. Born in Norwich, England, he was a leading member of the Socialist League between 1885 and 1892; he attended the 1887 international socialist conference in Paris and co-founded the *Sheffield Anarchist* in May 1891. Arrested 7 January 1892 and convicted on 4 April of conspiracy in connection with the Walsall case, Slaughter served seven and a half years of a ten-year sentence. He changed his name after his release.

Cherkesov, Varlaam N. (1846–1925) Georgian anarchist and revolutionary. Born to nobility, Cherkesov joined Russian revolutionary circles in the 1860s, conspiring against the tsar's life in 1866. Arrested in 1869 and exiled to Siberia, Cherkesov escaped in January 1876 to London where he befriended Peter Kropotkin, becoming one of his closest collaborators. A member of the *Free-*

dom Group, Cherkesov contributed articles to *Freedom, Liberty* (London), and *Les Temps Nouveaux.* Cherkesov also wrote *Let Us Be Just* (London: Liberty Press, 1896), *Pages of Socialist History: Teachings and Acts of Social Democracy* (New York: Charles B. Cooper, 1902), and *Concentration of Capital, A Marxian Fallacy* (London: Freedom Press, 1911). He returned to his native Georgia briefly in 1905 and again in 1917, dying in London in 1925.

Cipriani, Amilcare (1844–1918) Italian revolutionary. Cipriani was born in Anzio and served under Giuseppe Garibaldi between 1860 and 1870. A member of the general staff of the Paris Commune, Cipriani spent eight years in a French penal colony before being granted amnesty in 1880. Returning to Italy, Cipriani joined other revolutionaries, including the anarchist Carlo Cafiero, in organizing a revolt against the monarchy after which the government arrested him for an 1867 murder that it had earlier deemed to have been in self-defense, sentencing him to twenty-five years in prison. A popular revolutionary leader, Cipriani's case became a cause célèbre for the Italian left, which mounted a sustained campaign for his release, including helping elect Cipriani to the Italian parliament four times. Widespread public sympathy won him a pardon in July 1888. Cipriani and Errico Malatesta were the leading speakers at a conference of anarchists at Ticino in January 1891. His imprisonment again for participating in Rome's May Day riots of 1891 sealed Cipriani's legacy as a heroic figure for many nineteenth- and twentieth-century anarchists.

Cleveland, Grover (1837–1908) United States president (1885–1889, 1893–1897) and New York governor (1882–1884), the only president elected to two nonconsecutive terms, and the first Democrat elected after the Civil War. Under the auspices of the Sherman Antitrust Act of 1890, Cleveland ordered federal troops to Chicago on 3 July 1894. He claimed that the Pullman strike interfered with the delivery of the mail; the arrival of federal troops sparked rioting, bloodshed, and led to the strike's eventual collapse. EG, in the 22 November 1896 *Pittsburg Leader,* criticized Cleveland for signing the extradition treaty negotiated with Russia in June 1893, which stipulated that Russian political dissidents living in the United States could be subject to extradition.

Cohn, Michael Alexander (1867–1939) Russian-born Jewish anarchist, physician, and lifelong friend and financial supporter of both EG and AB. Cohn spent two years in rabbinical training before deciding to study mathematics and the Russian language in Warsaw. Instead of graduating, he emigrated in 1886 to Boston where he worked as a tailor and began writing for the Yiddish periodical *New Yorker Volkszeitung.* Cohn studied medicine at New York University and in Baltimore, while remaining an active anarchist. Deeply affected by the execution of the Haymarket anarchists, by 1890 he had become a regular contributor to *Freie Arbeiter Stimme.* His first wife, Annie, was also a strong supporter of the anarchist movement and highly regarded by EG (in 1916 both Cohn and his wife would work with EG in the fight for birth control). From 1890 Cohn practiced medicine in Brooklyn and continued to contribute intellectually and financially to the Jewish anarchist movement. He helped work for AB's release from prison. Cohn attended the 1900 International Revolutionary Congress of the Working People in Paris with EG, where he gave a report on "The History of the Jewish Movement in America." In addition to *Freie Arbeiter Stimme,* Cohn contributed to *Twentieth Century Magazine* and *Free Society,* including a series of European reports during his 1900 trip. *See also vols. 3, 4.*

Comstock, Anthony (1844–1915) American reformer, founder of the Society for the Suppression of Vice in 1872. In 1873, Comstock successfully lobbied Congress for passage of a law giving the postal service unprecedented powers to exclude "obscene, lewd, or lascivious" material from the mails. Offenders were subject to prison terms of up to ten years. As the postal official charged with enforcing the law, which was known as the Comstock Act, Comstock prosecuted a wide range of progressive and radical publications. A frequent target of Comstock's attention, EG sharply criticized his role as censor in many of her talks and essays. Comstock's published works included *Frauds Exposed* (New York: J. H. Brown, 1880), *Traps for the Young* (New York: Funk and Wagnalls, 1883), *Morals versus Art* (Chicago: J. S. Ogilvie, 1887), and *Gambling Outrages; Or Improving the Breed of Horses at the Expense of Public Morals* (New York: American News, 1887). *See also vols. 2, 3.*

Cook, John H. (d. 1931) American anarchist. A socialist until his late twenties, he was a mainstay of the labor movement in his home city of Providence, Rhode Island, involved in the city's Wendell Phillips Educational Club, and served as founding secretary of the local carpenters' union for fifty years and for several years as the president of the Central Labor Union. The local subscription agent for *Free Society* as well as a contributor, Cook was also a contributor to *Twentieth Century Magazine.* Cook was arrested on several occasions for holding street meetings in defiance of local ordinances. He regularly arranged and introduced EG's Providence meetings beginning in the 1890s. The Providence press identified Cook as the leader of the local anarchists.

Cooper, Charles B. (1852–1930) British-born anarchist, active lecturer in New York City. Cooper worked on *Solidarity* when it was briefly revived in 1898, contributing articles and acting as treasurer for the *Solidarity* Group; he also contributed to *Free Society* and *Lucifer, the Lightbearer.* Cooper published Varlaam Cherkesov's *Pages of Socialist History* (New York: Charles B. Cooper, 1902). Cooper shared an apartment with anarchist Alex Horr in New York City in 1902.

Cornelissen, Christianus Gerardus (Christiaan) (1864–1942) Dutch anti-parliamentarian socialist and syndicalist; close associate of Ferdinand Domela Nieuwenhuis. While Nieuwenhuis was concerned with intellectual emancipation through education, Cornelissen stressed industrial labor organization and the educational potential of syndicalism. Cornelissen published the journal *Recht voor Allen* (from 1892) with Nieuwenhuis and organized syndicates through the Nationaal Arbeids-Secretariaat in 1893. Cornelissen also organized anarchists, syndicalists, and anti-Marxists against the social democratic faction at the 1896 London congress of the socialist Second International—a cooperative effort taken with Fernand Pelloutier, Émile Pouget, Errico Malatesta, Gustav Landauer, and others. Moving to France in 1898, Cornelissen contributed to various socialist, anarchist, and syndicalist publications, including *Les Temps Nouveaux* and his own journal, *Bulletin International du Mouvement Syndicaliste* (Paris, 1907). Cornelissen's written works in this period include *Les diverses tendances du Parti Ouvrier International* (1896), *Le Communisme révolutionnaire: Projet pour une entente et pour l'action commune de socialistes révolutionnaires et communistes anarchistes* (1896), and *Het revolutionaire Kommunisme: zijn Beginselen en zijn Taktiek* (1897). EG befriended Cornelissen and his wife, Lily, in Paris in 1900. *See also vol. 2.*

Coulon, Auguste (dates unknown) French anarchist. Coulon worked at the libertarian International Sunday School in London founded by Louise Michel and contributed regularly to *The Commonweal.* A central co-conspirator in the 1892 Walsall affair and the only one not arrested, subsequent events suggested he was an agent provocateur, later exposed by David Nicoll, among others.

Crosby, Ernest Howard (1856–1907) American social reformer, single-taxer, lecturer, author. A leading proponent of Tolstoyan anarchism in the United States, Crosby was also profoundly influenced by the ideas of abolitionist William Lloyd Garrison and the poet Walt Whitman. He succeeded his friend Theodore Roosevelt in 1887 as a representative to the New York state assembly, and in 1889 was appointed to the International Court in Egypt as a judge. In 1894, Crosby, influenced by the ideas of Tolstoy, gave up his judgeship to advocate pacifism and anti-militarism as chairman of the New York branch of the Friends of Russian Freedom (*see vol. 2*) and president of the New York Anti-Militarist League (1900–1904). Crosby was also one of the founders and first president of the Social Reform Club of New York and president of the Anti-Imperialism League in New York as well as serving on the executive committee of the Brotherhood of the Kingdom, an interdenominational group formed to establish a "Kingdom of God on Earth" in 1896. He offered to assist EG in her attempt to secure a pardon for Berkman in 1898 and 1899 by acting as Berkman's spokesman and applying to Andrew Carnegie for his support, a plan which was eventually abandoned. Crosby was associate editor of the Christian Socialist journal *Social Gospel* (from 1898 to 1901) and editor of *The Whim*, "a periodical with several tendencies" (from 1901 to 1904), and contributed a series of articles to *The Kingdom* (1895) on the abolitionist William Lloyd Garrison, in which he developed a seven-point program for a revolutionary movement, which included nonviolent resistance with a working class base. Crosby's publications from this period include *Plain Talk in Psalm and Parable* (London: Brotherhood Publishing, 1898), *Edward Carpenter: Poet and Prophet* (Philadelphia: The Conservator, 1901), and *The Absurdities of Militarism* (Boston: American Peace Society, 1901). *See also vol. 2.*

Czolgosz, Leon (1873–1901) American laborer, self-proclaimed anarchist, and assassin of President William McKinley. Born near Detroit of Polish-immigrant parents, Czolgosz supported his family upon his mother's death when he was young, working at a glass factory in Pennsylvania, and later at a wire mill in Cleveland, Ohio, where after participating in a strike at the mill, he first used the alias "Fred Nieman" in 1893 to circumvent the company blacklist. In the fall of 1897, Czolgosz suffered a nervous breakdown and returned to the family farm in Ohio. He began reading radical publications and traveling to Cleveland to attend various socialist and anarchist meetings. Czolgosz was greatly influenced by Gaetano Bresci's assassination of King Umberto of Italy in July 1900, an event glorified in anarchist publications, including *Free Society*. Czolgosz heard EG speak in Cleveland on 5 May 1901, while he was traveling, under the Nieman alias, between Chicago, Cleveland, and Buffalo. He contacted EG and the publishers of *Free Society* in Chicago in July 1901. Upon receiving a warning from Cleveland anarchist Emil Schilling about Czolgosz's suspicious demeanor and his repeated questions about anarchist secret societies and acts of violence, editor Abe Isaak printed an alert in *Free Society* on 1 September 1901 labeling "Nieman" an agent provocateur. On 6 September 1901, after tailing President McKinley for several days at the Pan American Exposition in Buffalo, New York, and hearing him speak the previous day, Czolgosz shot him. Eight days later McKinley died. Czolgosz, who had been arrested and beaten immediately after his assassination attempt, was charged with first-degree murder. Accused by some of being involved in a large anarchist conspiracy, his act was linked in the press to the influence of EG's speeches. Despite Czolgosz's claims that he had acted independently, the assassination ignited a fierce wave of anti-anarchist sentiment in the United States, resulting in the arrests of many prominent anarchists (including EG, Johann Most, Abe Isaak, Hippolyte Havel, and others), several criminal anarchy acts, and the passage in 1903 of an immigration law that excluded alien anarchists from entering the country. Czolgosz's trial began 23 September 1901; he was convicted the following day, sentenced to death on 26 September, and electrocuted at Auburn, New York, on 29 October 1901.

Darrow, Clarence Seward (1857–1938) American socialist, freethinker, single taxer, and lawyer. A friend and associate of John Altgeld, Darrow served on the Haymarket amnesty committee petitioning Governor Altgeld, but later he criticized Altgeld's pardon of the three anarchists as a personal attack on the court. Relinquishing his position as legal counsel for the Chicago and Northwestern railway, Darrow gained national repute as a labor lawyer defending Eugene Debs and the American Railway Union during the 1894 Pullman strike. In 1901 he won the release of Abe Isaak and other anarchists arrested after McKinley's assassination. Darrow ran unsuccessfully for Congress in 1896. During this period his publications included *A Persian Pearl: And Other Essays* (East Aurora, N.Y.: Roycroft Shop, 1899), *Realism in Literature and Art* (Girard, Kans.: Haldeman-Julius Co., 1899), and *The Skeleton in the Closet* (Girard, Kans.: Haldeman-Julius Co., 1899).

Dave, Victor (1845–1922) Belgian-born anarchist writer, editor, sometime advocate of propaganda by the deed. The son of the president of Belgium's Revenue Court, Dave attended the University of Liège and the University of Brussels. Drawn to the libertarian wing of the First International as a student, Dave was an associate of Michael Bakunin, Peter Kropotkin, and Johann Most, as well as one of Max Nettlau's confidants. In 1869 he became a member of the General Council of the First International. In 1873 he took part in the uprising in Catalonia and represented the Verviers branch at the congress of the Anti-Authoritarian International held in Geneva. He settled in Paris and married in 1878. Deported for his activism, he relocated to London in 1880. After spending two years in a German prison for high treason and violating the 1878 anti-socialist law, Dave returned to London in 1884. Dave became the leader of the opposition to Joseph Peukert and his followers in the Bruderkrieg (Brothers War), the infighting that plagued the German anarchist movement; he was also a strong proponent of propaganda by the deed. In what was essentially a struggle for ideological and personal control of the movement, Most and Dave stood for Bakuninist collectivism while Peukert advocated Kropotkin's anarchist communism. Dave contributed to Augustin Hamon's *L'Humanité nouvelle* and became secretary of its editorial board in 1897. He met EG in Paris in 1900, where they both came to attend the banned International Revolutionary Congress of the Working People. Dave wrote, with E. Belfort Bax and William Morris, *A Short Account of the Commune of Paris* (London: Socialist League Office, 1886).

David, Marie Louise (b. 1840s) French individualist anarchist. A delegate to the General Council of the First International in London (1868), she immigrated to the United States in 1870. David's articles were published in a variety of radical publications, including *The Alarm*, *Individualist* (Denver, 1889–1890), *Twentieth Century Magazine* (New York), and *Liberty* (Boston and New York). In the early 1890s she was a regular speaker at Socialist League meetings in New York. In 1895 she and EG were the featured subjects of a comparative phrenological analysis of political activists in the *Phrenological Journal*.

Davies, Ann A. (pseudonym Libertas, most often referred to as Miss Davies) (dates unknown) Irish and American anarchist. For many years Davies was associated with the London paper *Freedom*. She became an anarchist while living in New York City in the 1890s. With John Edelmann, Saverio Merlino, and others, she was part of the circle around the New York Socialist League and the anarchist paper *Solidarity*. Her interest in Irish independence led her to London in 1897. In 1898 she joined the *Freedom* Group, helping to print the paper as well as working with Max Nettlau to compile its "International Notes" section, and occasionally contributing articles under her pseudonym. She also founded the Libertarian Lecture Society, in the spirit of the *Freedom* Discussion Group, as a weekly (later biweekly) anarchist forum on contemporary thought, art, and politics. Both ventures lasted until 1902. She attended the suppressed International Revolutionary Congress of the Working People in Paris in 1900. From February to April 1905 her story "The King and the Anarchist" was serialized in *Freedom* (under her pseudonym, Libertas) and issued in May of that year as Freedom Pamphlet No. 25. Around 1910 Davies left the *Freedom* Group and joined the suffrage movement, still maintaining contact with her anarchist circle well into the 1920s.

Deakin, Joe (dates unknown) English anarchist, secretary of the Walsall Socialist Club. Arrested on 6 January 1892 and, although he later claimed he had been tricked, Deakin confessed to the charge of manufacturing explosives and was subsequently denounced in *The Commonweal* as an informer. It was, however, this confession that revealed the depth of Auguste Coulon's complicity. Deakin was found guilty of possessing explosives on 4 April 1892, and sentenced to five years imprisonment.

Debs, Eugene Victor (1855–1926) American socialist, labor leader, five-time presidential candidate. In February 1875 Debs joined the Brotherhood of Locomotive Firemen and in 1880 he accepted the editorship of the *Brotherhood of Locomotive Fireman's Magazine*. Debs was elected to the Indiana legislature in 1884 as a Democrat. In 1893 he was elected the first president of the American Railway Union and helped lead the new organization to a successful strike against the Great Northern Railroad in 1894. Then in May 1894 Debs led the Pullman strike, calling for railway workers nationwide to boycott all trains carrying Pullman cars. On 3 July President Grover Cleveland ordered federal troops to Chicago and the strike was defeated. Debs was arrested for contempt of a court injunction and sentenced to six months imprisonment. During his imprisonment, Debs gravitated toward socialism and in 1897 formed, with Victor Berger and others, the Social Democracy of America (SDA), which supported policies of both electoral political action and utopian colonization. EG met him for the first time that September at a Chicago labor convention. The SDA split the following year, with Debs leading a faction, along with Berger, to form the Social Democratic Party, which subsequently merged in 1901 with Morris Hillquit's New York branch of the Socialist Labor Party to form the Socialist Party of America. His works include *Liberty: A Speech Delivered at Battery D, Chicago, on Release from Woodstock Jail November 22, 1895* (Terre Haute, Ind.: E. V. Debs and Co., 1895) and *Prison Labor* (Terre Haute, Ind.: E.V. Debs and Co., 1899).

de Cleyre, Voltairine (1866–1912) American anarchist, freethinker, advocate of women's independence, poet, essayist. De Cleyre was one of very few women anarchist lecturers of her time. Born in Michigan and named after the French philosopher Voltaire, she spent four years in a convent school, though she would later reject religion. Like EG, she became an anarchist after the Haymarket hangings in 1887. In 1889, she moved to Philadelphia, where she taught English to Russian Jewish immigrants and became a mainstay of the city's radical life, often speaking at meetings and organizing, with Natasha Notkin, the Ladies' Liberal League. She first met EG in Philadelphia in August 1893 and, later that year, visited her in prison in New York. Though she consistently defended EG in public, privately the more austere de Cleyre maintained a critical view of EG's flamboyant political style. De Cleyre began her correspondence with AB in prison from 1893. She traveled to England in June 1897, where she stayed with John Turner and met the entire *Freedom* Group, including Peter Kropotkin, Max Nettlau, and others, and returned to the United States in October. Soon after de Cleyre began contributing a column, "American Notes," to *Freedom* in London (November 1897 to January 1899). In 1900 she wrote a report on the state of the anarchist movement in Philadelphia slated for delivery at the banned International Revolutionary Congress of the Working People in Paris. A member of the American Secular Union, in 1901, de Cleyre organized the Social Science Club of Philadelphia, whose reading list at de Cleyre's suggestion was compiled by C. L. James. Also in 1901 she and anarchist George Brown initiated a series of open air meetings and distributed occasional handbills and leaflets, all of which were suppressed in the wake of the McKinley assassination. De Cleyre was a frequent contributor to anarchist and free-thought periodicals, including *The Boston Investigator, Firebrand, Freedom* (both the Chicago and London papers), *Free Society, Free Thinkers Magazine, Freie Arbeiter Stimme, Liberty, Lucifer,* and *The Rebel.* She also translated Yiddish and French anarchist literature into English, including Jean Grave's *Moribund Society and Anarchy* (San Francisco: A. Isaak, 1899). De Cleyre's works of this period include *The Drama of the Nineteenth Century* (Pittsburgh: R. Staley, 1889), *The Gods and the People* (London: Liberty Press, 1897; also published by Abe Isaak in San Francisco in 1898), *In Defense of Emma Goldman* (Philadelphia: V. de Cleyre, 1894; lecture originally given on 16 December 1893), *The Past and Future of the Ladies Liberal League* (Philadelphia: Ladies' Liberal League, 1895; serialized in *The Rebel,* 20 October 1895 through January 1896), and *The Worm Turns* (Philadelphia: Innes and Sons, 1900). *See also vols. 2, 3.*

De Leon, Daniel (1852–1914) Socialist, journalist, and polemicist. Born in Curacao in the Dutch West Indies, De Leon studied medicine in Amsterdam before graduating from Columbia University Law School in New York City in 1876. After working as a lawyer and a university law lecturer, De Leon became involved in Henry George's single-tax plan and then in the promotion of Edward Bellamy's ideas about nationalism. In 1890 De Leon joined the Socialist Labor Party (SLP) and quickly rose through the ranks, becoming editor of its daily paper, the *Daily People,* and its undisputed leader. De Leon would dominate and transform the party for the next twenty-four years. In 1895 De Leon launched the Socialist Trade and Labor Alliance to serve as an alternative labor federation to the AFL. His rigid leadership style elicited numerous enemies within socialist ranks and resulted in a split within the party in 1899 when Morris Hillquit's faction formed a rival SLP based in Rochester. *See also vol. 2.*

Ditchfield, William (dates unknown) English anarchist, brushmaker. One of the Walsall anarchists arrested in January 1892, Ditchfield was charged with conspiracy to make explosives; he was released in April 1892 when the court pronounced him "not guilty."

Dreyfus, Alfred (1859–1935) French army captain court-martialed for treason; later cleared of all suspicion of wrongdoing. Dreyfus was arrested on 15 October 1894, charged with passing military secrets to Germany, and sentenced to life in prison at Devil's Island, French Guiana. His trial was accompanied by virulent antisemitic reporting. Doubts about his sentence grew, however, when another officer was found guilty of espionage and when it was discovered that much of the evidence against Dreyfus had been forged. Anarchists, especially Bernard Lazare, were instrumental in reopening the extremely divisive case. On 13 January 1898, *L'Aurore* printed "J'Accuse," Émile Zola's condemnation of the French state's misconduct in the Dreyfus Affair. Dreyfus was granted a retrial on 5 June 1899 and left Devil's Island on 9 June. On 20 July 1906, with his innocence firmly established, Dreyfus was reinstated in the army and received the Legion of Honor medal.

Edelmann, John H. (1852–1900) American anarchist. The son of German immigrants, Edelmann was an architect in Louis Sullivan's Chicago firm in the 1870s. A supporter of Henry George and the single tax, Edelmann managed George's New York mayoral campaign in 1886. Edelmann was a member of the Anti-Poverty Society (1890). Edelmann became a regular lecturer of the American Branch of the New York City Socialist Labor Party. In 1892 Edelmann, along with John C. Kenworthy, William C. Owen, and others, founded the Socialist League, a New York anarchist organization modeled after the Socialist League of England. He edited the anarchist communist journal *Solidarity* (in the years 1892, 1893, 1895, 1898). In a letter appearing on the front page of the 1 March 1895 issue of *Solidarity*, Edelmann renounced and criticized George and the single-tax movement, asserting that the scheme would merely shift economic bondage from the control of landlords to politicians. Edelmann hosted Kropotkin in New York during his 1897 visit and often spoke on the same platform as EG in the 1890s.

Engel, George (1836–1887) German-born American anarchist, Haymarket defendant. Engel was co-editor with Adolph Fischer of *Der Anarchist* (Chicago, 1886); both men were executed after the Haymarket affair. Apprenticed to a painter at age fourteen, Engel married in 1868 and immigrated to the United States in 1872, arriving in Philadelphia on 8 January 1873 and settling by the end of the year in Chicago. There he became interested in socialism, opened a toy shop in 1876, and joined the SLP. In 1883 he became a member of the North West Side Group of the IWPA. Engel's and Fischer's anarchist communist paper *Der Anarchist* promoted all forms of violent resistance.

Engels, Friedrich (1820–1895) German Socialist, political theorist, and associate of Karl Marx. After spending time in Manchester, England, Engels wrote *The Condition of the Working Class in England in 1844* (1845) to expose the poverty of the city and the shockingly harsh condition of the workers, a book on which Marx collaborated, inserting in it ideas that would become the foundations of revolutionary materialist socialism. In 1846, Engels joined, with Marx, the secret Communist League, and represented the Paris communists at the two League congresses in London in 1847. He collaborated with Marx on the *Communist Manifesto* (1848) and after Marx's death, edited the second and third volumes of *Das Kapital* (1885, 1894) from Marx's notes and drafts. Engels's own works include *Socialism: Utopian and Scientific* (1880; New York: New York Labor News Co., 1892) and *The Origin of Family, Private Property and the State* (1884; Chicago: C. H. Kerr, 1902).

Esteve, Pedro (1865–1925) Spanish and American anarchist, editor. Trained as a typesetter, Esteve worked for a leading newspaper of Spanish anarchism, *El Productor* (Barcelona, 1887–1893). Esteve was already a prominent anarchist when he embarked on a propaganda tour of Spain with Errico Malatesta in 1891–1892. He left for North America in the wake of the 1892 Jerez uprising. Fluent in Italian as well as Spanish, Esteve distinguished himself among anarchist propagandists and labor organizers within a wide range of groups from Spanish and Cuban cigar makers in Tampa and Ybor City, Florida, Spanish sailors and dockworkers in New York, to Italian silkworkers in Paterson, New Jersey. Esteve edited *El Despertar* (New York, 1891–1902), *El Esclavo* (Tampa, 1894–1898), *La Questione Sociale* (Paterson, 1895–1908), and *Cultura Obrera* (New York, 1911–1927). His works include *Reflexiones sobre el movimiento obrero en Mexico* (1911) and *Reformismo, dictadura, federalismo*

(1922). A friend of EG, Esteve often shared the platform with her and acted as her interpreter. Esteve married Italian anarchist Maria Roda.

Fielden, Samuel (1847–1922) English-born American anarchist, manual laborer, Haymarket defendant. Fielden grew up in a Chartist household, arriving in New York in 1868. Except for a visit to England in 1879, he lived in Chicago from 1871, working at a variety of manual jobs, the last as a hauler of stone. Fielden joined the Chicago Teamsters Union in 1880 and soon became its vice president. A freethinker, Fielden was vice president of the Chicago Liberal League and its delegate to the national congress of the American Secular Union in Milwaukee in 1883. A frequent and effective speaker at radical meetings, Fielden joined the American Group of the IWPA in 1884 and served as its treasurer. Fielden was sentenced to death at the Haymarket trial; a petition for commutation of his sentence resulted in its reduction to life imprisonment. Pardoned in June 1893 by Governor John Altgeld, Fielden returned to his former job. Upon inheriting money, he purchased an isolated ranch in Colorado. He was still in contact with his old comrade William Holmes when he died on 7 February 1922. *See also vol. 3.*

Fischer, Adolph (1858–1887) German-born American anarchist; Haymarket defendant. Fischer was co-editor with George Engel of *Der Anarchist* (Chicago, 1886); both men were executed after the Haymarket affair. Fischer arrived in the United States in 1873, trained as a compositor, and moved to Chicago in 1883 where he worked as a printer on the *Chicagoer Arbeiter-Zeitung*. He joined the IWPA in 1883 and also the Lehr-und-Wehr Verein (Education and Defense Society), an armed workers' defense group. With fellow Haymarket defendant George Engel, Fischer was part of the autonomist-leaning Chicago North West Side Group of the IWPA. He was also a member of Typographical Union, Branch Number 9. Influenced by the writings of Pierre-Joseph Proudhon and sympathetic to individualism, Fischer, who was not a public speaker, was reputed for the gentleness of his character. With George Engel, he co-edited *Der Anarchist,* an organ of the autonomist and anarchist communist faction, which ran for four issues beginning in January 1886. The paper advocated propaganda by deed (influenced by Most's *Revolutionary War Science*) as a tactic for destroying capitalism and promoted autonomy in workers' organizations. It was Fischer who arranged the printing of handbills and solicited speakers for the Haymarket rally. Fischer was arrested on 5 May, the day after the bombing. He continued to assert his belief in violence as a means of social change, refusing to petition for his life and reacting angrily to attempts by supporters to water down the militancy of anarchist ideas.

Fox, Jay (1870–1961) Irish-born American anarchist, labor organizer, and syndicalist. A prominent Chicago anarchist who had been present at the 1886 Haymarket affair, Fox joined Lucy Parsons and others in forming local Branch 2 of Debs's short-lived Social Democracy of America, played a major part in the publication of *Free Society* in Chicago, and was among those arrested in 1901 after the McKinley assassination. *See also vols. 2, 3.*

Francis Joseph I (1830–1916) Hapsburg dynasty emperor of Austria (1848–1916). Known for his conservativism, Francis Joseph I assumed the throne in the aftermath of the nationalist revolution of 1848 and was thrust into coping with a growing, violent nationalist movement. In the Austro-Prussian War of 1866, Austria's influence over German affairs waned, and in 1867 pressure from Hungary led to the reorganization of the empire as an Austro-Hungarian dual monarchy. Hungary became an independent kingdom—whose ruler was also the emperor of Austria. Francis Joseph

I's policies for maintaining order generally included harsh punishment for social and political dissent, and legislation discouraging the organization of workers. Although he survived an assassination attempt in 1853, his wife, Elizabeth (known as "Sisi"), was assassinated by an anarchist in 1898 and his son and heir, Francis Ferdinand, shot by a nationalist in 1914.

Frick, Henry Clay (1849–1919) American industrialist. Frick was a coal mine owner, whose company, Frick Coke, was established in 1871 and controlled 80 percent of the coal output in Pennsylvania. Frick became partners with Andrew Carnegie, and in 1889, became chairman of the Carnegie Company. Frick played a central role in organizing and establishing Carnegie Steel Company in 1892. Frick's decision to increase profits by lowering the piecework wage rate led to the 1892 call to strike by the Amalgamated Iron and Steel Workers Union. His strong anti-union policies during the Homestead strike and his decision to employ 300 Pinkerton strikebreakers, leading to the death of nine workers, was the impetus for AB's *attentat*.

Fulton, Edward H. (dates unknown) American anarchist communist, later individualist anarchist. A land reformer, Fulton contributed occasionally to *Firebrand* and published several journals, including the *Age of Thought* (1896–1898), as well as a series of *Liberty Library Monthly* publications, including his own *Land, Money and Property* (Columbus Junction, Iowa: E. H. Fulton, 1896). Fulton also reprinted classic anarchist texts, including Michael Bakunin's *God and the State* (Columbus Junction, Iowa: E. H. Fulton, 1896) and Élisée Reclus's *An Anarchist on Anarchy* (Columbus Junction, Iowa: E. H. Fulton, 1896).

George, Henry (1839–1897) American economist, writer, and leader of the single-tax movement. Co-founder of the *San Francisco Evening Post* (1871–1875) and editor of the New York weekly *The Standard* (1887–1891), George also authored several works on economics and politics, including *Progress and Poverty* (San Francisco: W. M. Hilton, 1879), the best-selling book on economics of its time; *The Irish Land Question* (New York: D. Appleton, 1881); *Social Problems* (National Single Tax League, 1883); *Protection or Free Trade* (New York: H. George and Co., 1886); *The Condition of Labor. An Open Letter to Pope Leo XIII* (New York: Doubleday, 1891); and *A Perplexed Philosopher* (1892). His *Science of Political Economy* (New York: Doubleday and McClure, 1898), a summary of his philosophical and economic views, unfinished at his death, was published posthumously. George ran unsuccessfully for mayor of New York City in 1887 and for president of the United States the following year. Supported by a wide coalition of labor interests including the Central Labor Union, he ran again for mayor in 1897, but died suddenly four days before the election. EG and other anarchists were bitterly angered by his renunciation of support for the executed Haymarket anarchists during his 1888 presidential campaign, a topic addressed in pamphlet form by Benjamin Tucker (*Henry George, Traitor*, 1896).

Goldsmith, Marie (aliases M. Isidine, M. Korn) (1873–1933) Russian anarchist and scientist living in Paris. Goldsmith was an associate, friend, and regular correspondent of Peter Kropotkin after 1897. Her father, Isidor, published radical journals in St. Petersburg and after her mother, Sofia, completed medical studies, the family joined various proscribed associations. In 1884, the family fled Russia and settled in Paris, where, in 1886, Isidor died. EG probably met Goldsmith during her visit to Europe from 1895 to 1896. Goldsmith was awarded a doctorate in biology at the Sorbonne in 1915 and published numerous scientific papers. She was an active and well-respected figure in Russian anarchist circles who maintained strong relationships with the broad Russian revolutionary movement. She wrote regularly for the anarchist press, often under the pseudonym M. Korn, in English, French, Italian, and Russian, and also for the Yiddish periodical *Freie Arbeiter Stimme*. The Paris apartment she shared with her mother was an important meeting place for Russian anarchists of the city. Just hours after her mother fell ill and died, Goldsmith committed suicide. *See also vol. 2.*

Gompers, Samuel (1850–1924) English-born American labor organizer. Elected as the first president of the newly organized American Federation of Labor in December 1886, Gompers held this position, with the exception of the year 1895, until he died in 1924. Early in life, Gompers worked as a shoemaker and then as a cigar maker, a trade which he pursued when he immigrated to New York with his parents in 1863. As president of the AFL, Gompers wrote to Pennsylvania senator Boles Penrose on 19 April 1899, asking him to intercede with the pardon board on AB's behalf. Publications include *The Philosophy of the Labor Movement: A Paper Read before the International Labor Congress* (Washington, D.C.: American Federation of Labor, 1893); *The Eight-Hour Workday: Its Inauguration, Enforcement, and Influences* (Washington, D.C.: American Federation of Labor, 1897); and *Address of Samuel Gompers, President, American Federation of Labor, Before the Arbitration Conference, Held at Chicago, Ill., Dec. 17, 1900, Under the Auspices of the National Civic Federation* (Washington, D.C.: American Federation of Labor, 1901).

Gordon, Harry (1866–1941) Lithuanian-born Jewish American anarchist and machinist. Born to a prosperous family, Gordon settled in Pittsburgh. EG described him as "one of our best workers, a faithful and enthusiastic friend." Gordon served as secretary and treasurer of the Berkman Defense Association, and in 1901, was the first person allowed to visit AB in prison in nine years.

Grave, Jean (1854–1939) French anarchist communist, participant in the Paris Commune, writer, and editor. A shoemaker by trade, Grave was attracted to anarchism in 1879. In 1880 Grave cofounded the Social Study Group, the first significant anarchist group in Paris after the fall of the Commune; it was attended by Errico Malatesta and Carlo Cafiero. In 1882 Grave wrote for *Le Droit Social*. In 1883, Grave's *Organisation de la propagande révoltionnaire* called for propaganda by the deed carried out by small, clandestine, spontaneously organized groups. In the same year, after Kropotkin's arrest and imprisonment for belonging to the International, Élisée Reclus asked Grave to assume the editorship of the leading anarchist paper *Le Révolté*. Grave moved the paper from Geneva to Paris in 1885, and changed the name to *La Révolte* in 1887, adding a popular literary supplement. In March 1894 French authorities banned the paper and imprisoned Grave under the *lois scélérates*. Upon his release, Grave began publishing *Les Temps Nouveaux*, until it ceased publication in August 1914. One of the four primary anarchist newspapers in France at the time, with an auxiliary press that published numerous pamphlets (at least eighty-eight between 1895 and 1914), its combined circulation reached into the millions. Grave attended the congress of the socialist Second International in London in 1896 that led to the final split between the anarchists and socialists. In 1900, Grave published *Enseignement bourgeois et enseignement libertaire*, a brochure contrasting libertarian education with bourgeois education. His *La Société mourante et l'anarchi* (Moribund society and anarchy; San Francisco: The Free Society Library, 1899) was translated into English by Voltairine de Cleyre.

Hall, Abraham Oakey (1826–1898) New York lawyer, lecturer, journalist, and Tammany Hall politician. Part of the notorious Tweed Ring (the corrupt Democratic political machine that controlled New York City under William Mercy "Boss" Tweed) during the 1860s, Hall served as district attorney and then mayor of New York (1868–1872). After nine years in London, practicing law and representing the *New York Herald* there, Hall returned to New York at the end of 1892. EG's 1893 trial marked his reentry into the courtroom. In her autobiography, EG commented on his engagement with party politics, remembering him as far "too humane and democratic for the politicians."

Hamon, Augustin (1862–1945) French sociologist, critic, and editor. An anarchist during the 1890s, Hamon was a delegate to the London congress of the socialist Second International in 1896; his early attachment to anarchism influenced his four decades of activity in the Socialist Party in Brittany and his participation in the French Resistance during World War II. He founded and edited *L'Humanité nouvelle* (1897–1903), was a translator and critic of George Bernard Shaw, contributed to *The Free Review* (London), and authored, among other books, *Psychologie de l'anarchiste-socialiste* (1895), *Psychologie du militaire professionel* (1894), *Le Socialisme et le congrès de Londres* (1897), and *The Universal Illusion of Free Will and Criminal Responsibility* (London: The University Press, 1899). EG met Hamon in Paris in 1896.

Hanna, Marcus Alonzo (nickname Mark) (1837–1904) Cleveland industrialist, politician. Hanna was involved in industrial businesses including lake shipping, iron and coal mines, and shipbuilding; he also owned the *Cleveland Herald*. First elected as a delegate to the Republican National Convention in 1884, Hanna managed the party's funds in 1888, as well as William McKinley's successful gubernatorial campaigns in 1891 and 1893, and rose to chairman of the Republican Party in 1896. In this post, Hanna engineered the presidential nomination of his fellow Ohioan William McKinley, as well as McKinley's victory over William Jennings Bryan in the general election. Hanna was later appointed to the Ohio Senate seat vacated in 1897, and elected to the seat in 1898. Throughout his political career, Hanna promoted political support of business interests and was commonly portrayed in the radical press as being the real power behind the McKinley administration.

Harman, Lillian (1870–1929) American sex radical and anarchist editor, daughter of Moses Harman. She assisted her father in publication of *Lucifer, the Lightbearer* and *Our New Humanity* (1895–1897), and assumed editorial and publishing duties for *American Journal of Eugenics* after his death, with the single and final issue, "Memorial to Moses Harman" (30 January 1910). Harman then transferred the subscriptions of *American Journal of Eugenics* to *Mother Earth* when she was no longer able to continue publication. Harman also edited *Fair Play* (1888–1891) with E. C. Walker, and contributed to *The Adult* (1898) during her 1898 tour of England, where in 1897 she had been elected president of the Legitimation League. Her writings include *Some Problems of Social Freedom, etc* (London: Office of the Adult, 1898), *Marriage and Morality* (Chicago: M. Harman, 1900), and *The Regeneration of Society* (Chicago: M. Harman, 1900).

Harman, Moses (1830–1910) American sex radical, anarchist, editor, and publisher. Harman, a prominent early free-love, women's rights, and "family limitation" (birth control) advocate, was an abolitionist and liberal and freethought editor before he moved to sex radicalism and anarchism. His journal *Lucifer, the Lightbearer* (1883–1907), like Ezra Heywood's *The Word* (1872–1893), helped define sex radicalism for many anarchists in late nineteenth- and early twentieth-century America. Harman suffered repeated persecution for obscenity violations under the Comstock Act of 1873. In 1890 he was sentenced to five years in prison based on a previous arrest in 1887 for printing obscene material in his journal, then released after four months on a technicality. Harman was again arrested and tried under the Comstock Act; sentenced to a year, he served eight months before his release but was soon re-sentenced in 1895 to a year of hard labor for his first conviction. After serving a year, he was finally released in April 1896. EG first met Harman in the fall of 1897 in Chicago. His publications during this period include *Free Press: Arguments in Support of Demurrer to the Indictment of M. Harman, E. C. Walker, and Geo. Harman* (Valley Falls, Kans.: Lucifer Publishing, 1889), *The Next Revolution: or Women's Emancipation from Sex Slavery* (four pamphlets; Valley Falls, Kans.: Lucifer Publishing, 1890–1891), *Love in Freedom* (Chicago, 1900), *Motherhood in Freedom* (Chicago, 1900), and *Institutional Marriage* (Chicago, 1901), as well as editing the monthly journal *Our New Humanity* (1895–1897) with his daughter Lillian Harman.

Havel, Hippolyte (1869–1950) Czech anarchist communist, journalist, and editor. Havel was arrested in Vienna in 1893 or 1894 for delivering an inflammatory speech, imprisoned for eighteen months, and deported. Upon returning to Vienna to visit his family, he again faced a short period of incarceration. Via Zurich, Paris, and Berlin, he arrived in London where he met EG in 1899. They became lovers and the following year he accompanied her to the International Revolutionary Congress of the Working People in Paris. Havel returned with EG to the United States and settled in Chicago, where he was briefly arrested with the Isaaks, EG, and others after the assassination of McKinley. In *Living My Life* EG describes him as "a veritable encyclopedia" of the movement, but rather changeable in his moods (*LML*, p. 259).

Henry, Émile (1872–1894) French anarchist, advocate of propaganda by the deed. The son of a Communard, Henry won a scholarship in 1888 to the Ecole Polytechnique, where he became an anarchist. He wrote articles for *Le Père Peinard* (Paris) and *La Révolte* (Paris). On 8 November 1892, Henry carried out an attack against the management of the Carmaux mining company, which recently had violently quashed a strike. A year later, on 12 February 1894, Henry threw a bomb into the Café Terminus at the Gare Saint-Lazare in Paris to avenge the execution of Auguste Vaillant, who was convicted for throwing a bomb into the Chamber of Deputies the previous December. (Henry's act was also to protest the *lois scélérates*.) Taken to court on 25 April, he delivered what became a widely circulated speech, first published by *The Times* on 30 April, and subsequently in the May 1894 issue of *Freedom*. Henry's speech was later issued as a pamphlet, published and translated into many languages. Henry was executed on 21 May 1894.

Hill, David Bennett (1843–1910) U.S. senator (1892–1897), twice governor of New York (1885–1892), nominated for governor but defeated in 1894. Hill, a Democrat and a lawyer, as chair of the Committee on Immigration brought for debate to the Senate floor in August 1894 a bill designed to bar anarchists from entering the United States.

Hillquit, Morris (born Moishe Hillkowitz) (1869–1933) Russian Jewish immigrant socialist, trade unionist, politician, and labor lawyer. Hillquit joined the Socialist Labor Party (SLP) in 1887 and was a founder and corresponding secretary of the United Hebrew Trades Organization, initially an umbrella group of Jewish trade unions formed by two Jewish sections of the SLP, the United German Trades, and three small Jewish trade unions (1888). Hillquit helped found the Yiddish-language, socialist *Arbeiter Zeitung* (Workers' Paper) in March 1890, which often published articles and commentary in opposition to anarchism; he worked as both business manager and editorial contributor for the paper. In 1891 Hillquit began attending law school at New York University, prompted by his belief that social revolution did not require mass violent action and his desire to reform the legal structure of the state from within. During this time his participation in the SLP and the UHT was minimal. After passing the bar exam in 1893, however, he served as a lawyer for several UHT locals. Hillquit transferred his membership from the all-Jewish, Russian-speaking branch of the SLP to the American section of the New York party. In 1898 Hillquit led the opposition within the SLP to the party's leader Daniel De Leon, criticizing his authoritarian style, unwillingness to "Americanize" the SLP, and his Socialist Trade and Labor Alliance, an industrial union aimed at organizing unorganized workers. Instead, Hillquit favored the tactic of "boring from within," working with the already established American Federation of Labor. This culminated in the split of the party in 1899 into two competing factions, one led by De Leon and the other by Hillquit. After a court ruled the De Leon faction was the only legal executive of the party, Hillquit's group moved its headquarters to Rochester and in 1900 merged with Eugene Debs's Social Democratic Party. In 1901 Hillquit became a prominent member of the newly formed Socialist Party and defended Most after McKinley's assassination.

Hochstein, Helena (1860–1920) EG's older and the most protective of her half-sisters, with whom she immigrated to the United States in 1886. Helena, a socialist, had attended socialist meetings with EG in Rochester, where both had first settled. In 1892, EG wrote to her sister to secure money, which Helena gave, for AB's attempt on Frick. In the late 1890s Hochstein subscribed to both *Free Society* and *Lucifer,* and collected funds for the Berkman Defense Association. She had three children with Hyman Hochstein, including David Hochstein, a violinist, whose performances EG would promote among her substantial circle of acquaintances. *See also vol. 3.*

Holmes, Lizzie (born Lizzie May Swank) (1850–1926) American anarchist and journalist, dressmaker. Co-editor with Albert Parsons of the *Alarm,* Holmes was arrested with the other anarchist leaders of the movement for the eight-hour workday in the wake of the Haymarket riot, but released before trial. Holmes helped re-launch the *Alarm* with Dyer D. Lum in 1887. She contributed to *Freedom, Free Society, The Labor Enquirer, Wilshire's Magazine, Our New Humanity* (1895–1897), and *Lucifer, the Lightbearer,* among other papers, as well as writing for the Associated Labor Press. Together with her husband, William, she co-edited the *Labor Exchange Guide* (Denver, 1897).

Holmes, William T. (1850–1928) English-born American anarchist. Holmes immigrated to the United States with his family as a child. He was an early member of the Socialist Labor Party and a close friend of Albert Parsons in Chicago in the 1880s. In 1883 he joined the American Group of the IWPA with Parsons in Chicago, where he immediately became secretary of the group. In support of the Haymarket defense and amnesty campaigns, Holmes initiated his own speaking tour of the Midwest and West to raise support for the condemned men. After the execution of the Haymarket anarchists, William and Lizzie remained active in the anarchist movement in Chicago, helping to organize the city's 1893 anarchist conference, for which Holmes served as secretary. In the mid-1890s they moved to La Veta, Colorado, and later to Denver, where he practiced law. He arranged EG's lectures in Colorado in 1898 and 1899. In 1900 Holmes was asked to write the report on the state of the American anarchist movement for the anarchist congress in Paris. The paper, "A Short History of the Movement in America," was later published in the report of the congress in *Les Temps Nouveaux.* He wrote articles for the *Alarm, Firebrand, Free Society, Labor Enquirer, Liberty, Solidarity,* and was the editor, with his wife, of the *Labor Exchange Guide* (Denver, 1897), and the author of a Liberty Library Monthly pamphlet, *The Historical, Philosophical, and Economical Bases of Anarchy* (Columbus Junction, Iowa: E. H. Fulton, 1895). *See also vol. 3.*

Isaak, Abe (1856–1937) Russian-born American anarchist, editor. Raised in a Mennonite colony, Isaak moved to Odessa as a young man, joining the movement against the tsar. To avoid arrest he fled first to South America and then the United States with his wife, Mary Dyck Isaak. In 1889 Isaak settled with his wife and three children in Portland, Oregon. In January 1895, along with Henry Addis, J. H. Morris, Abner J. Pope, John Pawson, Ezekiel Slabs, and Mary Squire, he started the *Firebrand,* a weekly paper that succeeded in its mission to introduce anarchist communist ideas to English-speaking radicals. An early member of the Socialist Labor Party, Isaak resigned when the 1896 London congress of the socialist Second International ejected anarchists. The *Firebrand* ceased publication in September 1897 after its editors were indicted on obscenity charges stemming from the paper's longstanding emphasis on free love, including its reprinting of Walt Whitman's poem "A Woman Waits for Me." Isaak, his wife, Mary, and their children, Abe, Jr., Mary, and Peter, moved to San Francisco where he reestablished the paper in November as *Free Society.* In 1900 Isaak moved the paper to Chicago, where in 1901 after meeting Leon Czolgosz and responding to a warning by Cleveland anarchist Emil Schilling, he placed a notice in *Free Society* warning readers that Czolgosz may be a police spy. In the wake of the McKinley assassination, Isaak and his family were arrested on conspiracy charges, along with other Chicago anarchists, and eventually freed.

Isaak, Mary (born Marie Dyck) (1861–1934) Russian-born American anarchist, publisher, and editor. Mary Isaak was born into a Dutch family of Mennonites in Russia. She married Abe Isaak in 1879 in Russia and immigrated in 1889, living first in Portland, then San Francisco, Chicago, and New York, where she helped publish, with her husband and others, both the *Firebrand* and *Free Society. Free Society* was published from their home by the entire family, including children, Abe, Jr., Mary, and Peter. Their house was also a gathering place for local anarchists and radicals. EG met her in San Francisco in 1897, and in 1900 they went to England together, where Mary met Peter Kropotkin. All four of the Isaaks were arrested in September 1901 after the McKinley assassination. In 1904 the family moved *Free Society* to New York; Mary and Abe later moved to a cooperative agricultural colony in Lincoln, California, where she died in 1934.

Jefferson, Thomas (1743–1826) Third president of the United States. Jefferson founded the Republican Party to limit the power of federal government. Though a drafter of the Declaration of Independence, Jefferson was a wary supporter of the Constitution in 1787. In 1787 he wrote a letter to James Madison warning that the Constitution concentrated too much power in the federal government. Jefferson also drafted the 1799 Kentucky Resolution, asserting the power of local state government and protesting the alien and sedition laws enacted by Congress, which the Kentucky assembly viewed as unconstitutional. Jefferson was often evoked by EG to place anarchism in a political tradition of American anti-statism.

Kelly, Henry May (nickname Harry) (1871–1953) American anarchist, printer, lecturer. An active trade unionist in St. Louis, Chicago, and Boston, Kelly was drawn to anarchism in 1894 after hearing a lecture by English anarchist Charles Mowbray. Kelly traveled to England in 1895 with a letter of introduction from Mowbray to John Turner, with whom Kelly later became friends. (It was Kelly who persuaded Turner to embark on his first speaking tour of the United States in 1896, and who then helped to organize it.) Kelly also met Peter Kropotkin as well as Errico Malatesta, Louise Michel, Frank Kitz, and Alfred Marsh, among other members of the *Freedom* Group. In Boston

Kelly co-edited, with Mowbray and Nahum Berman, an anarchist monthly, *The Rebel* (1895–1896), and the smaller and more ephemeral *Match*. Around this time Kelly introduced a petition to the Boston Central Labor Union (of which he served as financial secretary) calling for the commutation of AB's sentence. The resolution passed and was sent to the governor of Pennsylvania, eliciting a letter of thanks and an offer of friendship from EG, who a short time later asked Kelly if he would help arrange her Boston lectures. In 1897 at Harry Gordon's call, Kelly traveled to Pittsburgh to aid in the agitation on AB's behalf. He lobbied workers' organizations to pass resolutions supporting a reduction in AB's sentence. En route to England, Kelly stopped in New York where EG and Ed Brady persuaded him to continue working for AB's release through the end of the year. In January 1898 Kelly was in London and working with the *Freedom* Group, helping to publish the paper and lecturing at meetings. While in England he became involved in the obscenity trial of George Bedborough and the Free Press Defense Committee, reporting on the events in the pages of *Free Society* in December 1898. Kelly remained in England until 1904. Besides editing *The Rebel* and *The Match,* he contributed to *Freedom* and *Free Society. See also vols. 2, 3.*

Kennan, George (1845–1924) American journalist, lecturer. Kennan, a leading authority on Russia and Siberia, recounted his experiences as part of a survey team investigating a possible telegraph line route across Siberia to Europe in *Tent Life in Siberia* (New York: G. P. Putnam and Sons, 1870). After a fifteen-month investigation of the Russian government's system of Siberian exile for political prisoners from 1885 to 1886 (which included meetings with Russian émigrés in London), Kennan reversed his earlier stance of support for the regime in an influential series of articles for *Century* magazine, beginning in May 1888; the articles were later published in book form under the title *Siberia and the Exile System* (New York: Century, 1891). On this trip Kennan met, among other political prisoners and refugees of the tsarist state, Catherine Breshkovskaya and Peter Kropotkin, then in Siberian and London exile, respectively. His other publications include *Campaigning in Cuba* (New York: Century, 1899), which covers the Spanish-American War.

Kenworthy, John Coleman (b. 1863) English Christian anarchist, writer, popularized Tolstoy in England. While visiting the United States between 1890 and 1892, Kenworthy, along with W. C. Owen and John Edelmann, helped organize the New York Socialist League in 1892. Kenworthy visited Tolstoy in 1895 and in 1900, publishing *Tolstoy: His Life and Works* in 1902. Active in the effort to prevent anarchist exclusion from the 1896 London congress of the socialist Second International, Kenworthy also contributed to James Tochatti's *Liberty.*

Kershner, Jacob A. (also Kersner) (1865?–1919) Russian-born tailor. Kershner came to the United States from Odessa in 1881, settling in Rochester. He met EG in Leopold Garson's factory and, as EG remembers, he "filled a void in my life, and I was strongly attracted to him" (*LML*, p. 20). They were married in a Jewish traditional ceremony in February 1887. According to *Living My Life,* they later separated, due in part to Kershner's impotence, divorcing shortly after the Haymarket executions in November 1887. EG then moved to New Haven to work in a corset factory. She returned shortly to Rochester due to poor health and almost immediately remarried Kershner after he threatened suicide (*LML*, p. 25). EG remained with him for three months, then moved to New York City, though she and Kershner never officially divorced after EG left the second time. Kershner continued to live in Rochester until 1907, then moved to Chicago under the name Jacob Lewis (the name on his death certificate). *See also vols. 2, 4.*

Kitz, Frank (born Francis Kitz Platt) (1849–1923) English anarchist. Kitz was a member of radical working-class clubs in the 1870s and a delegate to the International Social Revolutionary Congress in 1881. Fluent in German, he had strong ties to German exiles in London and served as secretary of the *Freiheit* Defense Committee and editor of its English-language version of *Freiheit* published while Johann Most was in prison between 1881 and 1882. A dyer by trade, Kitz was the delegate of the Garment Dyers Union to the 1896 London congress of the socialist Second International. He joined the Socialist League in the 1880s, became a member of its general council, served as its secretary between 1888 and 1891, and co-edited its organ, *The Commonweal*, with David Nicoll after May 1890. In 1891 Kitz was accused of embezzling Socialist League funds and subsequently expelled, but continued to work and lecture in and around anarchist circles, moving increasingly toward the ideology of syndicalism. In 1907 he contributed an article on "slums" to the *Voice of Labor*. Kitz's "Recollections and Reflections" were printed in *Freedom* between January and July 1912.

Kropotkin, Peter (1842–1921) Russian revolutionary, geographer, geologist, and principal theorist of anarchist communism. Born into the Russian aristocracy in Moscow, Kropotkin spent his youth in Alexander II's Corps of Pages, subsequently serving as an officer in Siberia, where his experiences helped form his radical consciousness and lay the foundation of his scientific career. Kropotkin traveled to Switzerland in 1872 where he met Bakunin's associate, James Guillaume, and visited the anarchist Jura Federation of workers, returning to Russia a convert to Bakunin's revolutionary collectivism. Joining the Chaikovsky Circle, Kropotkin was arrested in 1874 for revolutionary activity but escaped in 1876, settling in Switzerland. There in 1879 he founded *Le Révolté* (changed to *La Révolte* in 1887), the editorship of which was taken over by Jean Grave in 1883. In July of 1881 Kropotkin attended the London International Social Revolutionary Congress where support for propaganda by the deed was one among several resolutions adopted. Expelled from Switzerland in 1881, Kropotkin went to France, where he was arrested and imprisoned (1882–1886) for membership in the International. From 1886 until his return to Russia in 1917, he lived in England, where he met EG in 1895. A founder of *Freedom* and a regular contributor to *La Révolte* and *Les Temps Nouveaux,* Kropotkin spent his years in England developing and refining his theory of anarchist communism. Although the major concepts of anarchist communism had been circulating throughout anarchist and socialist circles since the 1870s, Kropotkin formalized them into a broad theory of economics, society, culture, and ethics, with particular emphasis on the development of a scientific basis for anarchist communism. Kropotkin posited that evolutionary theory proved that cooperation, and not competition, was the law of nature, a perspective at odds with fellow evolutionists including T. H. Huxley and Herbert Spencer.

Kropotkin played an active role in the protests against the trial of the Haymarket anarchists in 1886. Together with Stepniak, William Morris, and George Bernard Shaw, he addressed a mass rally in London against the Haymarket death sentence.

Kropotkin visited the United States twice (1897 and 1901), lecturing at the Lowell Institute in Boston, the National Geographic Society in Washington, D.C., the Association for the Advancement of Science, and various universities, as well as to anarchist audiences. He donated $249 from the proceeds from his 1897 U.S. lecture tour to *Solidarity,* and his 1901 tour helped finance many other anarchist newspapers, generating large sums for *Free Society, Freedom,* and *Discontent.* An admirer of American federalism, Kropotkin extolled the American Revolution and Declaration of Independence, in spite of his strong criticism of capitalism and the U.S. government's abuses of power. Kropotkin met leading American anarchists, including Johann Most, Benjamin Tucker,

Joseph Labadie, Harry Kelly, Saul Yanovsky, Voltairine de Cleyre, and EG, who helped arrange the New York segment of his second visit (although he failed in his attempt to visit AB in prison); he also met a variety of American progressives including Jane Addams and Lillian Wald. He also visited the tomb of the Haymarket anarchists. He would remain EG's ideological mentor for the next decade, although they would continue to disagree over the emphasis anarchists should place on personal and sexual issues.

At the urging of Robert Erskine Ely and other American friends, Kropotkin wrote his memoirs, first serialized in the *Atlantic Monthly* (from September 1898 to September 1899) and then revised and published in book form as *Memoirs of a Revolutionist* (Boston: Houghton, Mifflin, 1899). His other major works written during this period include *Fields, Factories, and Workshops* (Boston: Houghton, Mifflin, 1899) and *La Conquête du Pain* (Paris: Tresse et Stock, 1892; first English translation, London: Chapmann and Hall, 1906). Besides these major works, Kropotkin also published numerous articles, many later published as pamphlets, including "An Appeal to the Young" (first English translation by H. M. Hyndman serialized in *Justice* [London], 1885; published in pamphlet form by both Modern Press [London] and International Workmen's Association [San Francisco], 1885), "Law and Authority: An Anarchist Essay" (first English translation published as a pamphlet by International Publishers [London], 1886), "Communism and the Wage System" (serialized in *Freedom*, 1888), "Anarchist Communism: Its Basis and Principles" (London: Freedom Pamphlet No. 4, 1891), "Revolutionary Government" (first English translation serialized in *The Commonweal*, 1892; pamphlet published by the Socialist League/*The Commonweal* [London], 1892), "Anarchist Morality" (serialized in *Die Autonomie* and *Freiheit*, 1891; pamphlet published by *Die Autonomie* [London], 1891; first English translation serialized in *Freedom*, 1892, and published as Freedom Pamphlet no. 6 [London], 1892), "Expropriation" (serialized in *Die Autonomie* and *Freiheit* [New York], 1892), and "The Spirit of Revolt" (first English translation serialized in *The Commonweal*, 1892), as well as the numerous articles published in *The Nineteenth Century*, beginning in 1890, which would make up his *Mutual Aid: A Factor of Evolution* (London: William Heinemann, 1902).

Landauer, Gustav (1870–1919) German anarchist. Landauer wrote for *Der Sozialist*, organ of the libertarian group Jungen (Youth), from the time it was founded in 1891 to its termination in 1899 and again from 1909, when the paper was resurrected under Landauer's editorship, to 1915. At the 1893 congress of the socialist Second International in Zurich, Landauer and other anarchists were excluded for arguing that parliamentarian politics only serve the bourgeois state. Landauer was also present at the London Conference of 1896 where the anarchists were expelled. Several issues of *Der Sozialist* expressed the groups' objections to Marxism, including the Jungen call for "free, ruler-less socialism." Landauer also voiced his differences with the "collectivist anarchists," remarking "there are only individuals." He was responsible for facilitating the accessibility of Proudhon and Kropotkin to the German-reading public. His translations of Proudhon were preserved in the *Der Sozialist* issues published after 1909. Landauer's works during this period include the pamphlets *An den Zuricher Kongress: Bericht uber die deutsche Arbeiterbewegung* (Berlin: W. Werner Verlag, 1893) and *Von Zurich bis London* (Paris, 1896).

Lavrov, Peter L. (1823–1900) Russian populist, writer, philosopher, and mathematician. Lavrov was convicted of treason in 1866 and exiled to Vologda, escaping to western Europe in 1870. Influential in revolutionary circles in and outside of Russia for his political writings, especially his *Historical Letters* (published serially from 1868 to 1869), Lavrov joined the Paris section of the First International in 1870, and, although never formally identified as a Marxist, he later supported Marx's opposition to Bakunin when the First International collapsed. From 1873 to 1876, Lavrov edited *Vperëd!* (Forward; Zurich, 1873–1874; London, 1874–1877), and co-edited *Vestnik Narodnoi Voli* (Messenger of the People's Will; Geneva, 1883–1886).

Leggatt, Ted (d. 1935) English anarchist. Leggatt was a carman in London's East End and an early member of the Socialist League; he was later associated with the *Torch* group centered around the Rossetti family. A tireless speaker, Leggatt addressed numerous propaganda meetings in the parks of London. In 1896 he was a delegate of the Carmen's Union to the socialist Second International Congress in London. A powerful advocate of anti-parliamentary direct action, Leggatt was arrested many times, and his activities were regularly covered in *The Firebrand*. He worked with both the Carmen's Union and Yiddish-speaking anarchists in Whitechapel at the beginning of the twentieth century. By 1935, Leggatt was said to have adopted a more mainstream perspective as a trade union leader in the Transport Union.

Lewis, Roman (1865–1918) New York Jewish anarchist and journalist. Lewis was a leading member of the Jewish anarchist group the Pioneers of Liberty, founded in 1886, and served on the editorial board of the world's first Yiddish-language anarchist periodical, the weekly *Varhayt*. In 1890 Lewis became the first editor of the *Freie Arbeiter Stimme*. After six months he left the post and began working for the cloakmakers' union. Modest Stein claimed in a letter to EG on 20 September 1929 (see *EGP*, reel 21) that Lewis could well have leaked the information to the police that alerted them to intercept Stein when he arrived in Pittsburgh to "finish off" Henry C. Frick after AB's attempts had failed. By the end of 1892 Lewis had become a social democrat and was later elected an assistant district attorney in Chicago as a Democrat. He committed suicide in 1918. His publications include *Der gezetslikher mord in Tshikago fun 11 November 1887: Der groyser proteses gegen di anarkhisten fun Tshikago* (The legal murder in Chicago on 11 November 1887: The great protest in support of the Chicago anarchists; New York: Pioneers of Liberty and Knights of Liberty, 1889).

Lingg, Louis (1864–1887) German-born American anarchist, carpenter, Haymarket defendant. Born in Schwetzingen, in Freiburg, Lingg joined the Lassallean Working Men's Educational Society before moving to Zurich in 1883, where he was drawn to anarchism, vehemently supporting propaganda by the deed. To escape military service, Lingg came to the United States in 1885, becoming an organizer for the International Carpenters and Joiners Union, and serving as delegate to the Chicago Central Labor Union. A member of the Chicago North Side Group of the IWPA, Lingg was one of five anarchists sentenced to hang after the bombing at Haymarket. He ignored much of his trial, spending his time reading instead. After he was sentenced, he declared to the court: "I despise your order, your laws, your force-propped authority. Hang me for it." Lingg took his own life the day before the execution by placing a dynamite cartridge, smuggled to him by fellow anarchist Dyer D. Lum, in his mouth. To EG he "was the sublime hero among the eight" Haymarket anarchists (*LML*, p. 42).

Luccheni, Luigi (1873–1910) Italian anarchist. Luccheni assassinated Empress Elizabeth of Austria in Geneva on 10 September 1898, stabbing her to death with a sharpened file. Luccheni supposedly had planned to assassinate the Duke of Orleans, who was to be visiting Geneva, but when he did not come Luccheni decided instead to assassinate the empress, who happened by coincidence to be in town. In a letter to the *New York World*, EG repudiated Luccheni's act, pointing out that because the empress was not a political enemy of anarchism, the violence was senseless and reflected badly on anarchists in general. Luccheni, who was sentenced to life in prison, hung himself in 1910.

Malatesta, Errico (1853–1932) Italian anarchist. Born in Santa Maria Capua Vetere (Caserta), Malatesta joined the IWMA in 1871, and met Michael Bakunin in Switzerland in 1872. Malatesta advocated insurrection as the primary strategy for the realization of anarchy; after taking part in several such actions he was forced into exile in 1878. Traveling widely, he met Peter Kropotkin and Élisée Reclus, and lived in London between 1881 and 1883 before returning to Italy. From 1888 to 1889 he edited *L'Associazione;* he later edited *L'Agitazione* from 1897 to 1898. Arrested in 1898, he escaped from his island prison in 1899 and traveled to the United States, where he edited (anonymously) *La Questione Sociale* in Paterson, New Jersey, from 1899 to 1900. During this period he was shot by a fellow anarchist during a heated debate over tactics. He refused to press any charges. He then moved to London where he worked as a mechanic. Malatesta had a considerable impact on American anarchist communist theory through his pamphlets *Anarchy* (London: C. M. Wilson, 1892) and *A Talk about Anarchist Communism between Two Workers* (San Francisco: Free Society, 1898). *See also vols. 2, 3.*

Manning, Henry Edward (1808–1892) English theologian. Manning joined the Roman Catholic Church in 1851, became Archbishop of Westminster in 1865, and a cardinal in 1875. Manning acted as intermediary in the London dock strike of 1889. In response to the Trafalgar Square "Bloody Sunday" deaths on 13 November 1887, he wrote: "Necessity has no law, and a starving man has a natural right to his neighbour's bread" ("Distress in London: A Note on Outdoor Relief," *Fortnightly Review* 49, 1 January–1 June 1888; London: Chapman and Hall, 1888; reprinted in *Miscellanies,* London: Burns and Oates, 1888). Anarchists, including Charles Mowbray and Voltairine de Cleyre, as well as EG in *Living My Life,* cite Manning as the inspiration for EG's words in the speeches she delivered during the 1893 unemployment demonstrations in New York City. Manning's works include *The English Church* (London: J. G. and F. Rivington, 1835), *The Rule of Faith* (London: J. G. and F. Rivington, 1838), *The Unity of the Church* (London: J. Murray, 1842), *The Grounds of Faith* (London: Burns and Lambert, 1852), *England and Christendom* (London: Longmans, Green, 1867).

Martin, James L. (b. 1851) Sheriff of Luzerne County, Pennsylvania. Martin, a former mine worker who was elected county sheriff in 1895, led the police forces that, on 10 September 1897, opened fire on a procession of 3,000 peaceful, flag-carrying, and unarmed miners, marching on an open highway toward Lattimer, Pennsylvania, where a strike was in progress. Martin's men killed 19 miners and seriously wounded up to 40 others. The incident caused an outrage in radical circles and led Samuel Gompers to write a caustic article about the incident, published in the *New York World,* criticizing the actions of the police force. Martin and his deputies were acquitted of murder and manslaughter charges on 9 March 1898 after a month-long trial in Wilkes-Barre.

Martine, Randolph B. (1844–1895) American judge. Martine was a graduate of Columbia University Law School and a prominent figure in Tammany Hall, the allegedly corrupt Democratic political machine in New York City. Martine was elected Democratic district attorney in 1884 and a judge of the Court of General Sessions in 1887, where he presided over EG's 1893 trial.

Marx, Karl Henrich (1818–1883) German philosopher of history, who developed the concepts of scientific socialism and international communism. Marx and his lifelong friend and political collaborator Friedrich Engels played an active role in the International Working Men's Association—the First International—from its inception on 28 September 1864. Principal works include *The Communist Manifesto* (1848, translated into English in 1888) and *Das Kapital,* published in three volumes, the first in 1867, the last two posthumously in 1885 and 1894 (the first volume was translated into English in 1886). From 1852 to 1861 Marx wrote hundreds of articles, published (in English) in mainstream papers as varied as the *New York Tribune* and the *National Workingmen's Advocate;* his articles written in German appeared in the *New England Zeitung* (Boston) and the *Turn-Zeitung* (New York), among others. Antagonistic toward anarchism, he and Michael Bakunin struggled for control of the International Working Men's Association, a tension replicated in the often discordant relationships between American socialists and anarchists.

Masur, Carl (dates unknown) German American anarchist editor and shoemaker, based in New York. Masur was a contributor to *Freiheit* and *Lucifer, the Lightbearer,* as well as a member of the Radikaler Arbeiter-Bund and editor of *Der Anarchist* (from 1891 to 1895).

McKinley, William (1843–1901) Republican president of the United States from 1897 to 1901. President McKinley was shot by Leon Czolgosz on 6 September 1901, in Buffalo, New York. Before serving as president, McKinley was a congressman from Ohio (1877–1891) and served two terms (1892–1896) as governor of Ohio. While governor, he formed a state board to regulate labor disputes and became friends with millionaire industrialist Mark Hanna, who managed his 1896 presidential campaign. McKinley is credited with being the first president to make the United States an imperial power, principally because, as a result of the Spanish-American War of 1898, the United States gained the territories of Puerto Rico, Guam, and the Philippines. While delivering a speech at the Pan American Exposition in Buffalo on 6 September 1901, McKinley was shot twice by Leon Czolgosz and died from complications of his wounds on 14 September 1901. Two collections of his speeches were published: *Speeches and Address of William McKinley from His Election to Congress to the Present Time* (New York: D. Appleton, 1893) and *Speeches and Address of William McKinley from March 1, 1897 to May 30, 1900* (New York: Doubleday and McClure, 1900).

Merlino, Francesco Saverio (1856–1930) Italian anarchist, lawyer, writer. Born in Naples, Merlino became a leading anarchist agitator and theoretician and a close associate of Errico Malatesta; both men were convicted of conspiracy in 1884 with six other anarchists, although Merlino fled the country the following year. He spent most of his exile in London, writing articles for Italian- and English-language periodicals, and scholarly works on anarchism and socialism; he was also active in the *Freedom* Group. In 1892 he lectured in the United States and founded two anarchist papers, *Il Grido degli Oppressi* and the English-language *Solidarity,* the latter with John H. Edelmann. Returning to Italy in 1893, Merlino was imprisoned for his 1884 conviction and released two years later. In 1897 Merlino repudiated the anarchist policy of abstentionism, calling for anarchists to participate in the electoral process and join a political front against the Crispi regime. The ensuing debate between Merlino and Malatesta was a major event in the Italian and international anarchist movement, the former arguing for a pragmatic alliance with parliamentarian socialists, the latter for the importance of doctrinal purity. Merlino then left the movement to join the socialists and eventually withdrew from party politics.

Metzkow, Max (1854–1945) Berlin-born socialist and later anarchist. A follower of Johann Most, with whom he was in correspondence from 1879 on, Metzkow was arrested in 1876 for distributing anti-militarist leaflets, and again in 1880 for high treason. Metzkow was sentenced to two years imprisonment, the first case under the Bismarck regime's anti-socialist laws in 1881. Upon his release in 1883, Metzkow left Germany for London where he was active in the Socialist League and the Autonomie Club. Metzkow emigrated to the United States in 1888 and worked as a compositor for Most's *Freiheit* and Dyer D. Lum's *Alarm*. Metzkow lived in Pittsburgh during the 1890s, where he was acquainted with Henry Bauer and Carl Nold and helped distribute the manifesto in support of the Homestead strikers with Bauer and Nold in 1892. Metzkow accompanied EG to Allegheny City in November 1892 when she made the first of two visits to AB in prison. Active in the International Typographical Union, Metzkow moved to Buffalo soon after the Homestead affair, where he worked on the *Buffaloer Arbeiter-Zeitung*. Metzkow was active in the anarchist movement until around 1900. *See also vol. 2.*

Michel, Louise (1830–1905) French anarchist, teacher, writer, Communard. After moving in 1856 to Paris, Michel combined teaching, literary work, and politics, becoming first a republican, then a socialist. A frontline fighter on the barricades during the Paris Commune, Michel was banished in 1873 to New Caledonia, where she taught, became a supporter of the colony's movement for independence from France, and was drawn to anarchism. Pardoned with her fellow Communards in 1880, Michel returned to France and joined the circle around the anarchist journal *La Révolution Sociale* (published in Paris between 1880 and 1881). In 1883 she was arrested with Émile Pouget after a Paris bread riot and imprisoned until January 1886. In January 1888 she was shot by an assailant while speaking in Le Havre, but refused to press charges. In 1890, to avoid another prison term, Michel fled to London, there founding and operating the libertarian International Sunday School. For the remainder of her life, Michel traveled frequently between England and France, propagandizing. In 1892, she joined Malatesta and Kropotkin, among others, in an informal group calling on anarchists to work more closely with trade unions. EG met Michel in London in 1895 and invited her to the United States, but the trip never materialized. During the Dreyfus Affair, Michel argued that anarchists should refrain from supporting Alfred Dreyfus, because he was a bourgeois career officer. A contributor to both *Les Temps Nouveaux* and, at its founding, to *Le Libertaire* (Paris, 1895–1956), as well as numerous other anarchist periodicals, Michel wrote essays, novels, poetry, history, her memoirs, and an opera. Revered for her legendary kindness as well as for her devotion to anarchism, she died while on a lecture tour in France in 1905.

Milner, Alfred (1854–1925) British colonial government official. From 1890 to 1892, Milner was the undersecretary of finance in Egypt. His book *England in Egypt* (1892) argued for greater British involvement in the country. From 1897 to 1905, Milner served as governor of Cape Colony, and also as British high commissioner of South Africa. Allegedly, his efforts to gain political rights for British settlers in Boer territories heightened growing tensions between the rival groups and precipitated the Anglo-Boer War, which began on 11 October 1899 when the Boer republics declared war on Britain. After the war, his career came under fire when local British settlers hostile to Chinese immigrants discovered he had imported indentured Chinese labor to work the South African gold mines. The British cabinet originally had agreed with his importation of Chinese labor, but Milner was censured by the House of Commons when it was discovered the Chinese were being flogged "like Africans." He resigned his post as governor in 1905.

Mollock, Frank (dates unknown) Austrian-born anarchist, baker. AB, EG, and Modest Stein met Mollock in Peukert's Autonomy Group and lived at the New York apartment he shared with

Josephine Mollock in the weeks preceding AB's attack on Frick. Mollock was arrested on 26 July 1892 in Long Branch, New Jersey, and taken to Pittsburgh on suspicion of being AB's accomplice. Years later, EG remembered in *Living My Life* her indignation when, a few days after Mollock's arrest, Josephine locked her out of the apartment under pressure from the landlord. The Pennsylvania police failed to prove Mollock had any role in AB's action.

Morris, J. H. (d. 1904) American anarchist, printer, and poet. Morris was co-founder and printer of the *Firebrand* in Portland, Oregon, in 1895; he also published its predecessor, *Freedom*, with Henry Addis and Mauritz Linden in Portland (1893–1894). After the paper's removal to San Francisco, Morris remained in Oregon but continued to contribute to its successor, *Free Society*.

Morris, William (1834–1896) English poet, writer, designer, and self-styled libertarian socialist. Morris joined the Democratic Federation (later the Social Democratic Federation) in January 1883 and was a leader in the anti-parliamentarian faction that split off in December 1884 to form the Socialist League. In addition to writing the League's manifesto, Morris edited its weekly organ, *The Commonweal*, from 1885 to 1890. He also wrote a number of popular pamphlets, including *Useful Work versus Useless Toil* (London: Socialist League Office, 1885), *The Tables Turned; or Nupkins Awakened* (London: Office of The Commonweal, 1887), *True and False Society* (London: Socialist League Office, 1888), and *Monopoly, or, How Labour Is Robbed* (London: Office of The Commonweal, 1890). His utopian novel, *News from Nowhere; or, an Epoch of Rest* (Boston: Roberts Brothers, 1890), a response to Edward Bellamy's state socialist utopian novel, *Looking Backward* (1888), was first serialized in *The Commonweal* between January and July 1890. Morris withdrew from the League in 1890 in response to what he considered some anarchists' irresponsible support of violence.

Morton, Eric B. (d. ca.1930) Norwegian-born American anarchist. Morton was nicknamed "Eric the Red," after the hero of an Icelandic saga, and also "Ibsen," after the Norwegian playwright, in AB's *Prison Memoirs*. At EG's request, Morton attempted to dig AB's escape tunnel during 1899 and 1900. Morton fled to join EG in Paris after the plot was discovered and after poisonous fumes in the tunnel infected his blood and caused him to contract a skin disease. *See also vols. 2, 3.*

Morton, James F., Jr. (1870–1941) New York lawyer, Harvard graduate, freethinker, free-love supporter, and anarchist. Morton first met EG in the late 1890s. Morton embarked on a cross-country anarchist speaking tour (1899–1900), ending in San Francisco where he briefly edited *Free Society* (1900). He moved in 1901 to the Home Colony, near Tacoma, Washington, where he taught school and edited *Discontent* (1898–1902) until it ceased publication in the wake of the McKinley assassination and the persistent and mounting persecution by the postal agencies. Morton's essay, first published in *Free Society*, "Another Blow to Royalty" about Bresci, was reprinted as a leaflet in 1900. Morton also wrote *Is It All a Dream?* (San Francisco: A. Isaak, 1900), which was published as a dual edition with Errico Malatesta's *Anarchy*, and contributed to *Free Society, Lucifer, the Lightbearer, Our New Humanity* (1895–1897), and *The Truth Seeker. See also vol. 2.*

Most, Johann (1846–1906) Bavarian-born orator, editor, actor; social democrat, then anarchist, and at this time a fierce advocate of propaganda by the deed. Most joined the labor movement in 1867 in Jura, then two years later, at a workers' demonstration in Vienna, he was sentenced to a month in prison for delivering a speech criticizing the German republic. In July 1870 Most was sentenced to five years imprisonment (although he was released after only a few months) for high treason for his role in organizing a march in front of the House of Parliament demanding "manhood suffrage." Granted amnesty in February 1871, Most was expelled from Austria and left for Germany, where he edited the socialist paper *Chemnitzer Freie Presse* between 1871 and 1873 and initiated the first satirical paper of German social democracy, *Der Nußknacker* (1871–1872), a supplement to the *Chemnitzer Freie Presse*, for which he was subject to several arrests. In his first year as editor of *Chemnitzer Freie Presse*, Most was summoned to court forty-three times. In February of 1873 he began a prison sentence in Zwickaue under charges of *lèse-majesté* and insulting the army. Severe and continued police harassment prompted him to leave for Mainz, where he edited *Süddeutschen Volksstimme* (1873–1874). Despite his criticism of parliamentary politics, in January 1874 Most was elected into the Reichstag, but in Berlin three months later while delivering a speech on the Paris Commune Most was arrested and sentenced to two years in prison. He was re-elected to the Reichstag in January 1878, but the relentless harassment and the passing of the anti-socialist laws prompted Most to leave Germany in December 1878 and never return. Most moved to London and became publisher of *Freiheit*, the organ of the German Communistic Workingmen's Club, in January 1879. *Freiheit*'s political stance had gradually evolved from social democratic to social revolutionary, and, by the time Most was publishing the paper in London, anarchist. Most was eventually sentenced (March 1881), in a trial that virtually ended freedom of the press in England, to eighteen months imprisonment (April 1881 to October 1882) for writing and publishing an article endorsing the assassination of Russian tsar Alexander II. Upon his release Most left for New York at the invitation of Justus Schwab, arriving on 18 December 1882 and resuming the publication of *Freiheit*. In 1883 Most took the lead in the writing of the Pittsburgh Manifesto, the first clearly defined statement of the anarchist movement in the United States, adopted by the newly founded International Working People's Association. Most's *Revolutionäre Kriegswissenschaft* (Revolutionary War Science), published in 1885, was essentially a manual for the *attentater*. On 12 November 1887, the day after the Haymarket anarchists were hung, Most delivered an incendiary speech in New York for which he was tried and condemned to a year in prison. He unsuccessfully appealed the conviction but served his sentence from June 1891 to April 1892. Most became embroiled in a bitter controversy with Benjamin Tucker, who accused him of complicity with the violent and criminal methods of some of Most's followers. Tucker, in his parody of Most's "Beast of Property," called "The Beast of Communism" and published in the 27 March 1886 issue of *Liberty*, accused Most's followers of committing arson motivated by greed as part of an insurance fraud scheme. Each man attempted to excommunicate the other from the anarchist movement. Most forbid his adherents to subscribe to *Liberty*, and Justus Schwab broke away from Most over the incident. In 1887, a split, which had been brewing for some time, between Most's anarchist collectivists and another wing of the German anarchist movement led by Joseph Peukert and proponents of Kropotkin's anarchist communism, solidified with the arrest of Johann Neve, who was a close comrade of Most's and well liked throughout the movement. Peukert was implicated in Neve's arrest because of his friendship with Karl Theodor Reuss, later revealed to be a member of the Berlin Political Police, and identified as "suspicious" at the time by Victor Dave, an anarchist and Most supporter. Influential among the Jewish anarchists, Most contributed to the *Varhayt* (1889) in New York, and was a popular actor and songwriter. Initially a close acquaintance of both EG and AB (he was for a time EG's lover, mentor, and organizer of her first lecture tour, when at the same time AB worked on the press of *Freiheit*), their move away from *Freiheit* and anarchist collectivism toward Peukert and anarchist communism in the early 1890s distanced them from Most. Most was critical of Berkman's attempted *attentat* on Henry Clay Frick in 1892; his criticism cemented their feud, which was never resolved.

In 1901, after President McKinley's assassination, Most was imprisoned for printing "Murder against Murder" in *Freiheit,* an article advocating political assassinations. During his time in the United States, Most's ideas on anarchism developed, first as a collectivist, then as a communist, then by the late 1890s back to the syndicalist ideas he had espoused in the 1870s. Most's varied political journey contributed to his growing ideological tolerance, although he remained a highly emotional and irascible man. Several of Most's works were translated into English during this period, including *The Beast of Property* (New Haven, Conn.: International Working Men's Association, 1890), *The Social Monster; a Paper on Communism and Anarchism* (New York: Bernhard and Schenck, 1890), and *The Free Society. Tract on Communism and Anarchy* (New York: J. Müller, 1891). *See also vol. 2.*

Mowbray, Charles Wilfred (1855–1910) English anarchist, lecturer, tailor, advocate of propaganda by the deed, onetime soldier. Mowbray was a member of the London branch of the Socialist League. His arrest on 20 September 1885 for obstructing a public thoroughfare marked the beginning of a long free-speech fight, involving unemployment demonstrations and Haymarket protests among other issues. After Mowbray was arrested following a meeting in Norwich marketplace, the authorities alleged that a bank and several shops were damaged by the crowd; Mowbray was sentenced to nine months imprisonment. He was excluded from the Zurich congress of the socialist Second International along with Gustav Landauer and other anarchists, who proceeded to hold their own "counter-convention." Arrested again during the Walsall case in April 1892 and, based on an article written by David Nicoll entitled "Are These Men Fit to Live?" (published in *The Commonweal,* of which Mowbray was the publisher), Mowbray was charged with inciting to murder, tried, and acquitted. When Mowbray was released, he resumed his agitation for the Socialist League, taking part in annual Paris Commune and Haymarket commemorations, along with Peter Kropotkin, Errico Malatesta, Louise Michel, and Saul Yanovsky. After the Socialist League disbanded and *The Commonweal* ceased publication, Mowbray traveled to the United States on a speaking tour. He spoke at the 19 August 1894 meeting at New York City's Thalia Theatre, celebrating EG's release from prison, the first of many times that they shared a platform. In Philadelphia, Mowbray sparked a free speech fight after his 28 December 1894 arrest for inciting to riot and sedition against the Commonwealth of Pennsylvania. Mowbray settled in Boston in 1895; his friends in America included the rivals Johann Most and Joseph Peukert. Harry Kelly credited his own attraction to anarchism to a speech by Mowbray. Kelly and Mowbray served as secretaries to the Union Cooperative Society of Printers and to the Union Cooperative Society of Journeymen Tailors, organizations associated with the Central Labor Union of Boston. Together with others, they founded *The Rebel* (an anarchist communist monthly) on 20 September 1895 and in 1896 published two issues of an anarchist paper called *The Match.* A few years later Mowbray opened a saloon in Hoboken, New Jersey. Returning to London in the 1900s, Mowbray was active in the Industrial Union of Direct Actionists, a federation of anarchist and syndicalist groups.

Neebe, Oscar W. (1850–1916) American anarchist, Haymarket defendant. Born in New York City, educated in Germany, Neebe worked in Chicago from 1866 to 1886, with short stints in New York and Philadelphia. Neebe was a manager of the Socialistic Publishing Society, publisher of the *Chicagoer Arbeiter-Zeitung, Der Verbote,* and *Die Fackel,* and an organizer for the Central Labor Union. One of the eight anarchists tried and convicted after the Haymarket riot of 1886, Neebe was sentenced to fifteen years but pardoned by Illinois governor John P. Altgeld in 1893.

Nettlau, Max (1865–1944) Austrian-born anarchist writer and historian. Nettlau became a socialist and then an anarchist communist as a student (1878–1880). Nettlau studied philology in Berlin and in 1885 traveled to London, where he worked on his dissertation on Celtic languages in the British Library. In London he was active in the Socialist League (1885–1890) and wrote articles for its paper, *The Commonweal*. Between May and August 1890 Nettlau edited and financed four issues of the *Anarchist Labour Leaf*, which consisted of articles he and Henry Davis had written. In the 1890s Nettlau contributed to Johann Most's *Freiheit*, joined the *Freedom* Group, and became a regular contributor to *Freedom*. From 1893 to 1894 he was a member of the *Commonweal* Group and anonymously wrote their declaration, "Why We Are Anarchists" first published as a series in *The Commonweal* in 1893, and in 1894, as a pamphlet. Independently wealthy until the post–World War I economic collapse, Nettlau devoted himself to studying, writing, and collecting anarchist material. EG met Nettlau for the first time during her 1900 visit to London. Through his travels, Nettlau met all the leading figures in the anarchist movement, including Peter Kropotkin, Errico Malatesta, Rudolf Rocker, Victor Dave, and Élisée Reclus, at whose invitation he compiled the first bibliography on anarchism, *Bibliographie de l'anarchie* (Paris: Bibliothèque des Temps Nouveaux, 1897). But it was Michael Bakunin who absorbed much of Nettlau's energy. Between 1896 and 1900 Nettlau wrote and published fifty multigraphed copies of a massive, three-volume biography of Bakunin and in his later years completed the last volumes of the biography. Other works include *Michael Bakunin, Ouvres* (Paris: P.-V. Stock, 1895–1913), *Responsibility and Solidarity in the Labor Struggle* (London: Freedom, 1900), which was first delivered as a lecture before the *Freedom* Discussion Group on 5 December 1899, and *Michael Bakunin; eine biographische skizze* (Berlin: P. Pawlowitsch, 1901). Other works followed, including a biography of Malatesta and a history of anarchism, although many remained unpublished. *See also vols. 2, 3.*

Neve, Johann (1844–1896) German socialist and later, anarchist. Born in Schleswig (then Denmark), Neve apprenticed to his father as a joiner. In 1866 Neve moved to Paris and in 1868 to the United States, where he lived until 1874. Neve then returned to Europe, first to Paris and finally to London, where he became for a decade one of the anarchist movement's most respected and active members, admired for his bravery in the smuggling of revolutionary publications and materials into Germany, and for his personal magnanimousness. Neve was arrested in Belgium in February 1887 and sentenced to fifteen years imprisonment. Neve's arrest—and the resulting accusations of police spies posing as anarchists aiding in his capture—deepened the split between the collectivist (Most) and communist (Peukert) wings of the German anarchist movement. Neve died in Moabit prison on 8 December 1896.

Nicoll, David (1859–1919) English anarchist, Socialist League member, co-editor with Frank Kitz of *The Commonweal* from 1889. Nicoll was at the forefront of the defense of the Walsall anarchists in 1892, and accused Auguste Coulon of being an agent provocateur. Nicoll was arrested after the guilty verdict and imprisoned for his condemnation of the proceedings, which were printed in *The Commonweal* and repeated at a rally in Hyde Park. After serving eighteen months, Nicoll wrote numerous pamphlets about the case and his sentence, including *The Walsall Anarchists* (Sheffield, n.d.) and *Anarchy at the Bar* (London, 1895).

Nieuwenhuis, Ferdinand Domela (1846–1919) Dutch freethinker and socialist, then anarchist. After a career as a Lutheran pastor, Nieuwenhuis left the church and in 1879 founded the socialist and pacifist journal *Recht voor Allen* (Justice for All; Amsterdam, 1879–1900), which was followed by *De Vrije Socialist* (The Free Socialist, 1898–1919). In 1881 Nieuwenhuis helped found a Dutch Socialist League and was a founder of the Dutch Social Democratic Party, and by 1888 he was the first socialist member of the Dutch parliament (1888–1891). Nieuwenhuis was attracted to anarchism after his disillusionment with parliamentary politics. He probably met EG in Paris during the suppressed 1900 International Revolutionary Congress of the Working People. Nieuwenhuis published numerous pamphlets, including *Het Internationaal Kongres te Londen in 1896* (1897), *Socialism in Danger* (London: J. Tochatti, Liberty Press, 1896?), and *The Pyramid of Tyranny* (London: Freedom Office, 1901). *See also vols. 2, 3.*

Nold, Carl (1869–1934) German-born anarchist. Born in Weinsberg, Nold immigrated to the United States in 1883. Nold was an associate and supporter of Johann Most. AB stayed with Nold and Henry Bauer in Pittsburgh before his attempted assassination of Henry Clay Frick. With Bauer, Nold was sentenced to five years, and served four, in prison on two charges: incitement to riot (stemming from their distribution of a handbill addressed to striking Homestead workers on 8 July), and conspiracy (with AB) to commit murder. Although Nold had not known AB before July 1892, in prison they grew very close (exclusively through notes smuggled between them and through their prisoners' journal *Prison Blossoms*). Upon his release from prison in May 1897, Nold worked for the reduction of AB's sentence and was active in the Berkman Defense Association. After a failed attempt to establish a cooperative farm, Nold lived in St. Louis, moving to Detroit in the early 1900s, where he remained politically active. Nold contributed to various anarchist publications including the *Firebrand*, *Free Society*, and *Discontent*. *See also vol. 2.*

Oerter, Friedrich Joseph "Sepp" (1870–1928) German anarchist, bookbinder, and onetime lover of EG. Oerter became an anarchist in 1890 and in 1892 edited *Der Anarchist* in New York, leaving in October for London, Holland, and ultimately Germany where he was arrested with his brother Joseph Friedrich "Fritz" Oerter (1869–1935) in December. Convicted in October 1893 for smuggling and distributing illegal literature and explosives, Oerter was sentenced to eight years at forced labor in the Münster penitentiary. His brother served eighteen months, sparking a decade of declining health. While his brother Fritz remained an anarchist all his life, Sepp became after 1912 a Social Democrat, during which time he was elected prime minister of Braunschweig (1920–1921); ultimately Oerter became a National Socialist.

Owen, William C. (1854–1929) English anarchist, journalist. Owen was a graduate of Oxford and an early socialist. He came to New York in 1882 and in 1884 moved to San Francisco, where he became an associate of California socialist Burnette C. Haskell, serving in 1885 as secretary of the central committee of Haskell's International Workmen's Association. In 1887, while living in Portland, Owen represented that city at the American Socialist Federation. Owen's early influences included Michael Bakunin, Herbert Spencer, and Henry George. In San Francisco Owen became acquainted with H. G. Wilshire, the son of a manufacturer, who had became a socialist and started *Wilshire's Magazine;* shortly after, Owen's wife left him for Wilshire. In 1890 Owen visited New York, where he denounced his early association with socialism and Burnette Haskell, calling Haskell and his Kaweah Commonwealth an autocracy. In 1891 Owen was an active lecturer in the Socialist Labor Party in New York. After leaving the SLP, Owen helped found the anarchist-leaning American Socialist League with John Edelmann and John Kenworthy. In 1893 he returned briefly to England, where he lectured and met Kropotkin, with whom he corresponded for many years. Though Owen admired Kropotkin, by 1895 he moved toward individualism, influenced by Benjamin Tucker's *Instead of a Book* (1893); he was also a regular subscriber to *Liberty*. Owen was a frequent contributor to a number of socialist and anarchist papers, including Haskell's *The Truth*, and became editor of the *Nationalist*, published first in Los Angeles and then in San Francisco. He contributed to the *Labor Enquirer* (1886–1887), *Solidarity, Firebrand, Freedom, Free Society*, and translated Kropotkin's "Words of a Rebel" for various labor papers, especially *Avant Courier* of Portland, Oregon. Owen was also the author of *William Morris* (New York: Humboldt Publishing, 1891) and *The Economics of Herbert Spencer* (New York: Humboldt Publishing, 1891). *See also vol. 3.*

Paine, Thomas (1737–1809) English writer, freethinker, and humanitarian. Paine was influential in shaping public opinion during the American Revolution and an active participant in the French Revolution. His major writings include *Common Sense* (1776), *The Rights of Man* (1791–1792), and *Age of Reason* (1794, 1796). Many anarchists and freethinkers, including Leonard Abbott, James F. Morton, Jr., and individualist anarchist E. C. Walker, joined the Thomas Paine National Historical Association. EG and other anarchists identified with both Paine's hostility to established religion and his attempt to keep government as small as possible.

Pallás, Paulino (1862–1893) Spanish socialist, then anarchist, typesetter. Pallás moved in his youth to Argentina, where he became an anarchist communist. In 1891 Pallás was involved with the revolutionary movement in Brazil, where he threw a bomb into the Alcantara Theatre in Rio De Janeiro in May 1892. Returning to Spain in October 1892, Pallás threw two bombs at Arsenio Martínez de Campos, the captain general of Catalonia, on 24 September 1893, in revenge for the Spanish officer's role in the violent repression of the Jerez uprising of January 1892 and the subsequent execution of four Jerez anarchists. Pallás missed his target and at least two bystanders died. Pallás was tried by a court martial and was executed by firing squad on 6 October.

Parsons, Albert (1848–1887) American anarchist and Haymarket defendant. Parsons, editor of the *Alarm*, was executed after the Haymarket affair. Parsons became a Confederate soldier when he was 13. After the war he settled in Waco, Texas, and became a Republican, publishing a weekly paper advocating the civil rights of African Americans. By 1872 he was married to Lucy E. Parsons, a woman of Mexican, Native American, and African American descent, and they moved to Chicago. Radicalized in part by the nationwide railway strike of 1877, Parsons founded the IWPA's American Group of Chicago in 1883, whose membership included Samuel Fielden, Adolph Fischer, Oscar Neebe, and August Spies. An accomplished orator and writer, Parsons began publishing the *Alarm* in 1884. He turned himself in to stand trial for the Haymarket bombing. Found guilty of murder, Parsons was executed on 11 November 1887. His works include *Anarchism: Its Philosophy and Scientific Basis as Defined by Some of Its Apostles* (Chicago: Lucy E. Parsons, 1887).

Parsons, Lucy E. (1853–1942) American anarchist, labor activist, speaker, writer, editor. Parsons was the widow of Haymarket anarchist Albert Parsons, whom she had met in Texas and married by 1872. After the Haymarket executions, Parsons traveled to England in 1888 where she was a guest of the Socialist League and met William Morris and Peter Kropotkin. Parsons applauded AB's attempt on Henry C. Frick, called AB a hero, and later spoke at a defense meeting for Carl Nold and Henry Bauer in February 1893. She met EG at the Chicago Trade Union and Reform Club convention in 1897. In the summer of 1897 Parsons and other prominent Chicago anarchists including Jay Fox joined Chicago Branch 2 of Debs's Social Democracy movement. Debs later expelled Branch 2 over the particularly incendiary resolutions it passed in response to the 10 September massacre of striking miners at Lattimer, Pennsylvania in 1898. In October 1897 Parsons participated in a defense meeting for the editors of *The Firebrand,* who were being prosecuted under the Comstock Act for publishing obscene material (including Walt Whitman's poem "A Woman Waits for Me"); the other speakers were EG and Moses Harman. At the meeting Parsons clarified her disapproval of the discussion of sex reform and free love within the pages of *The Firebrand* and expressed her intention to distance herself from any anarchist group associated with free love. In early 1898 she embarked on a speaking tour through the eastern states. She joined the Socialist Party of America in 1901. Parsons was the editor of *Freedom* (Chicago, 1890–1892) and a contributor to a number of papers, including *The Alarm, Labor Enquirer* (Denver), *The Rebel,* and *Free Society.* She wrote *The Life of Albert Parsons* (Chicago: Lucy E. Parsons, 1899), and published two of Albert Parsons's works, *Famous Speeches of the Eight Chicago Anarchists* (Chicago: Socialistic Publishing Socety, 1886) and *Anarchism: Its Philosophy and Scientific Basis as Defined by Some of Its Apostles* (Chicago: Lucy E. Parsons, 1897).

Pelloutier, Fernand Léonce Émile (1867–1901) French anarchist, syndicalist. Pelloutier was educated in religious schools and then Saint-Nazaire College. As a young journalist, Pelloutier moved from republicanism to socialism, and then, in 1894–1895, to anarchism. He joined Jules Guesde's Marxist Parti Ouvrier Français in 1892 but left after the party rejected the tactics of the general strike and union independence. Widely regarded as the father of anarcho-syndicalism, after 1895 Pelloutier was the general secretary of the Fédération Nationale des Bourse du Travail. Pelloutier, who focused on class struggle, envisaged the union as the primary proletarian organization to lead the fight against capitalism in the form of industrial direct action culminating in the general strike. He was an associate of Jean Grave, Augustin Hamon, and Émile Pouget and wrote numerous articles in *Les Temps Nouveaux* between 1895 and 1901. Pelloutier was author of *L'organisation corporative et l'anarchie* (Paris, 1896), and founder and editor of the periodical *L'ouvrier des deux Mondes* (Paris, 1898–1899). He met EG in Paris in 1900. Pelloutier's influential *Histoire des Bourses du Travail, origine, institutions, avenir* (Paris: Schleicher, 1902) was published posthumously in 1902.

Perovskaya, Sophia (1853–1881) Russian revolutionary, populist. A member of the Chaikovsky Circle, a propaganda group of which Peter Kropotkin was also a member, Perovskaya became a leader of Narodnaya Volya (People's Will), a clandestine socialist group that emerged out of a split in the populist Zemlya i Volya (Land and Liberty) and adopted assassination as a political strategy. Perovskaya was revered by her contemporaries for her selfless determination, and Peter Kropotkin wrote fondly in his memoirs of her "earnest courage, her bright intelligence, and her loving nature," praising her as "a fighter of the truest steel" (Kropotkin, *Memoirs of a Revolutionist,* pp. 318–19). On the first of March 1881, Perovskaya stationed her Narodnaya Volya co-conspirators along the route of Alexander II, signaling them when he was in range of their bombs, and thus facilitating the successful assassination of the tsar. Arrested on 22 March 1881, she was hanged on 15 April 1881. The first woman political prisoner in Russia to be executed, Perovskaya stood out among the revolutionary women of Russia from whom EG often drew inspiration.

Peukert, Joseph (1855–1910) Bohemian-born social democrat, then anarchist; beginning in 1884, an opponent of Johann Most and his associate Victor Dave. Peukert co-edited *Zukunft* (The Future; Vienna, 1879–1884) from December 1881 until its suppression in January 1884. Some months later, Peukert arrived in London and joined the group that published *Der Rebell*, which included Otto Rinke. In 1886 the two men founded the Gruppe Autonomie and began publishing the journal *Die Autonomie* (1886–1893). Their program and orientation was from the start anarchist communist, following the new theoretical ideas advanced by Peter Kropotkin, rather than those advocated by Most, who at that time still identified as an anarchist collectivist. The Autonomists promoted decentralized organization, emphasizing individuals and small groups, and the tactic of propaganda by the deed. Most and his supporters, including Victor Dave, exchanged accusations and insults with Peukert, Rinke, and the Autonomists. All possibilities of reconciliation between the two camps were lost when Most and Dave alleged that Peukert acted as an informant for the police in the arrest of the highly respected anarchist Johann Neve in Belgium on 21 February 1887, and, in turn, Peukert also accused Dave of being a police spy. In 1890 Peukert immigrated to the United States, joined the editorial group around *Der Anarchist,* and attempted to clear his name. He took a public stand in favor of AB's failed *attentat* on Henry C. Frick in *Der Anarchist* and shared the platform with Dyer D. Lum and EG at the 1 August 1892 meeting praising AB's act. Disillusioned with the internal feuds of the anarchist movement, Peukert disappeared from the anarchist movement in 1894 and became involved in labor organizing. *Der Anarchist* ceased publication in 1895. Peukert also attended the 1905 founding convention of the Industrial Workers of the World as a representative of the Chicago Debaters' Club, an organization of primarily anarchists and social democrats. Toward the end of his life Peukert wrote his memoirs, *Erinnerungen Eines Proletariers aus der Revolutionären Arbeiterbewegung* (Berlin: Verlag des Sozialistischen Bundes, 1913). He died in Chicago on 3 March 1910. Although EG was not drawn to Peukert as a person, she maintained an amiable friendship with him for many years, and was especially appreciative of his efforts to secure labor union support for her in Chicago, where he lived during the last years of his life.

Phillips, Wendell (1811–1884) American abolitionist, orator, lawyer, and women's rights and labor advocate. In 1837 Phillips gave up his legal practice to dedicate himself to the abolition movement. He worked closely with William Lloyd Garrison, writing for Garrison's *The Liberator.* Phillips was the critical cohesive force behind the Anti-Slavery Society until the 15th Amendment was passed. He then shifted focus to prohibition, woman suffrage, the abolition of capital punishment, currency reform, and labor rights. In 1870 Phillips ran for governor of Massachusetts representing the Prohibition and Labor Reform parties, and won almost 15 percent of the vote. EG, as an anarchist, looked to him as among those who represented what she perceived as an anti-statist American tradition.

Pope, Abner J. (b. 1824) American anarchist, editor, and publisher of *The Firebrand.* Of Quaker background, Pope devoted much of his $30,000 inheritance to *The Firebrand* (based in Portland, Oreg.) and to the anarchist movement. He was arrested in September 1897 and tried in January 1898, along with fellow editors Abe Isaak and Henry Addis under the Comstock Act for sending obscene materials through the mails. As the primary owner of the printing press, he initially faced a $2,000 bail. Though the amount was reduced to $200, Pope on principle refused to sign a bond to the government and remained in jail, refusing counsel as well. After the editors were each found guilty on one of four counts, Addis and Isaak successfully appealed the verdict while Pope, holding to his belief that the United States had no right to govern him, declined to appeal. On 1 March 1898, he received a four-month sentence and a $1 fine. With *The Firebrand* banned from the mails, Pope was destroyed financially.

Pouget, Jean Joseph (Émile) (1860–1931) French anarchist, syndicalist and editor. Pouget launched his first newspaper, *Le Lycéen républicain,* when he was fifteen; later he became editor of *Le Père Peinard* (in 1889) and *La Sociale* (in 1895). Pouget was an active union organizer by the time he became an anarchist in 1880. On 8 March 1883 with Louise Michel, Pouget led a series of attacks on three bakeries, literally "taking bread," during a demonstration of the Parisian unemployed (an incident widely recognized as the first time the black flag appeared as an anarchist symbol). Sentenced to eight years in prison, Pouget served only three. Again the target of government harassment, Pouget fled to England in 1894 (where he continued to publish *Le Père Peinard*), returning after a general amnesty in May 1895. Active in the Dreyfus Affair, Pouget demanded justice for anarchists serving time on Devil's Island in his pamphlet *Les Lois scélérates de 1893–94* (Paris, 1899). A leading theorist of French syndicalism, in 1879 Pouget was an organizer of the textile employees union and in 1895, became a leading member of the Confédération Générale du Travail (CGT). In 1900 Pouget founded CGT's publishing organ, *La Voix du Peuple,* with Fernand Pelloutier. *See also vols. 2, 3.*

Quinn, T. Putnam (dates unknown) Irish American, New York and then Chicago anarchist. Quinn was an early member of the Knights of Labor in New York during the Haymarket affair. He became a member of Chicago Branch 2 of the Social Democracy of America in 1897, and was also a member of the Chicago Philosophical Society from 1901 to 1902. Quinn was a contributor to *Free Society* and wrote a laudatory obituary of John Altgeld in the 30 March 1902 *Free Society,* commending his pardon of the Haymarket anarchists.

Ravachol (pseudonym of François-Claudius Koenigstein) (1859–1892) French anarchist. Ravachol bombed the homes of the judge and prosecuting attorneys in the trial of the anarchists arrested at an 1891 May Day parade outside Paris. For his 1891 murder of a rich elderly man, he was executed on 11 July 1892. Ravachol—who claimed that bourgeois society was immoral, not he—idealized his crimes and for his audacity was elevated to the stature of a hero by many anarchists, artists, and intellectuals.

Reclus, Jean-Jacques (Élisée) (1830–1905) French anarchist communist and geographer. Born into the family of a dissident Protestant pastor, Reclus was a leading theorist of anarchist communism, distinguished by his unusual tolerance and generosity to other anarchist tendencies. Originally a follower of Proudhon, Reclus became closely involved with Bakunin in the 1860s and also Jean Grave. Reclus was imprisoned after the Paris Commune (1871) and sentenced to ten years banishment, which he spent in Switzerland writing his monumental *Nouvelle géographie universelle* (published as *The Earth and its Inhabitants;* London: J. S. Virtue, 1876–1894). Reclus placed particular emphasis on the free associative action of individuals and was an advocate of propaganda by the deed in the pages of *Le Révolté.* However, he was dismayed by the infighting and "verbal violence" rife in the anarchist circles of Paris and Lyon. Reclus wrote numerous works on anarchism, including the widely translated and reprinted pamphlets *An Anarchist on Anarchy* (Boston:

B. R. Tucker, 1884) and *Evolution and Revolution* (London: W. Reeves, 1884). From 1894 on Reclus lived in Belgium, teaching at a university founded in his honor.

Reitzel, Robert (1849–1898) German-born American anarchist poet, critic, translator. Founder and editor of *Der arme Teufel* (1884–1898), Reitzel came to the United States in 1870, and in 1871 was appointed minister of the German Reform Church in Washington. Reitzel traveled through the United States, lecturing on literary and social topics, and finally settling in Detroit. As an editor, Reitzel celebrated Germany's literary masters, especially the Romantics, and helped introduce German Americans to classic English-language literature of the United States and Europe, including the works of Emerson, Whitman, and Shakespeare. A champion of free speech, Reitzel assumed a prominent role in the campaign to save the Haymarket anarchists; in 1887 he and Dyer D. Lum planned, but never carried out, a strategy to free them. He spoke at the funeral of the Haymarket anarchists on 13 November 1887. Reitzel wrote in support of AB's attempted *attentat* and, in late 1892, he befriended EG, who visited him shortly before his death. His posthumous publications include *Das Reitzel-Buch einem Vielgeliebten zum Gedachtniss*, ed. Martin Drescher (The Reitzel-book: In memory of a loved-one; Detroit, 1900), *Abenteuer eines Grunen* (Adventures of a greenhorn: An autobiographical novel; Chicago: Mees, Deuss, 1902), and *Des armen Teufel*, ed. Max Baginski (Collected writings from *The Poor Devil*; Detroit: Reitzel Klub, 1913). *See also vols. 2, 3.*

Rémy, Léon (1870–1910) French anarchist; after 1905, socialist and militant syndicalist. Fluent in German, Russian, and English, Rémy participated in the 1896 London congress of the socialist Second International and was the secretary of the suppressed 1900 International Revolutionary Congress of the Working People in Paris. Rémy edited the reports of the 1900 congress, which were published in *Les Temps Nouveaux*.

Rhodes, Cecil (1853–1902) British diamond magnate, leading colonialist in Africa. Rhodes owned the De Beers Consolidated diamond mine, which by 1891 owned 91 percent of the world's diamond mines. Rhodes's accumulated wealth won him political power, and in 1890 he was granted the position of prime minister of Cape Colony by the British High Commissioner. Rhodes wanted to bring all of Africa under British control, and also recover American colonies for the British empire. In 1901, at the end of his life, Rhodes supported the decision of Alfred Milner to suspend the constitution of Cape Colony until the Anglo-Boer War, which broke out in October 1899, was over.

Rockefeller, John D. (1839–1937) American industrialist and primary founder of the Standard Oil Company. In 1863, twelve years after the first successful oil drilling took place in 1851, Rockefeller was inspired to establish his own refinery. In response to the steep and chaotic drops and rises in barrel prices, Rockefeller and his business partners consolidated their resources to form the Standard Oil Company in 1870. Through the then-legal railroad rebates and predatory pricing, the company grew to control 90 percent of the American oil industry by 1880; by 1882 Standard Oil had become one of the first and largest American trusts, and the target of political reformers as a symbol of greed. Always active in the Baptist church, Rockefeller increased his philanthropic activity as his wealth grew. By 1897 Rockefeller, largely retired from Standard Oil, spent most of his time giving away his earnings. In 1889 he gave $600,000 to help establish the University of Chicago.

Roda, Maria (b. ca. 1878) Italian anarchist. Roda was a schoolmate of Sante Caserio and member of an anarchist group to which Caserio also belonged. Roda and several of her Italian anarchist comrades were briefly imprisoned in Italy after Caserio assassinated French president Sadi Carnot in June 1894, in retaliation for the death of Vaillant. Immediately after her release from prison, Roda emigrated to the United States. Her speech on the occasion of EG's release from Blackwell's Island greatly impressed EG, who described the sixteen-year-old Italian as "the most exquisite creature I had ever seen." Afterward, at a gathering at Justus Schwab's saloon, Roda met Spanish anarchist Pedro Esteve, whom she later married and with whom she had eight children.

Rousseau, Jean-Jacques (1712–1778) French-Swiss political philosopher and writer. Rousseau was a strong critic of modern society, arguing that man is naturally good and is made unhappy and corrupted by his experiences in society. To Rousseau, the natural human state of being is self-sufficiency and self-governance, while social human beings become dependant and restricted. Natural human beings, he argued, are born neither good nor bad, and in a self-governing, strictly egalitarian community they would strive to be good. One of the first modern writers to seriously attack the institution of private property, Rousseau's most famous works—*Discourse on Inequality Among Men* (1761), *The Social Contract* (1762), and *Emile* (1762)—all explore in some way the relationship of the individual to society; these works influenced the development of European anarchist theory.

Ruedebusch, Emil F. (dates unknown) German-born sex reformer based in Wisconsin. Ruedebusch was the author of *The Old and New Ideal*, published first in German and then in English (Mayville, Wis., 1895, 1896); the treatise, in defense of sexual varietism, sold two thousand copies before it was banned in 1898. Ruedebusch was fined $1,200 by a federal court in Wisconsin for the distribution of his book. In 1906 *Mother Earth* reported that Ruedebusch was president of the Mayville, Wisconsin, Transvaluation Society (a term used by Nietzsche to reassess the worth of things in terms of their "value for life"). The society was dedicated to the transvaluation of all values pertaining to the relation of the sexes. Ruedebusch was a contributor to *Freiheit* and *Lucifer, the Lightbearer;* he also published *Die Eigenen: Ein Tendenzroman für Freie Geister* (One's own things: A tendentious novel for free spirits; Berlin: Johannes Räde, n.d.), *Frei Menschen in der Liebe und Ehe: Ein Versuch, die Menschen glücklicher und besser zu machen* (Free people in love and marriage: An attempt to make people happier and better; Mayville, Wis., 1895), and, with Helmar Lerski, *Lebt die Liebe! Aphorismen* (Love lives! Aphorisms; Schmargendor-Berlin: O. Lehman, 1905).

Schilling, Emil (dates unknown) Cleveland anarchist and subscription agent for *Free Society*. James F. Morton, Jr. stayed with Schilling during his 1900 cross-country lecture tour. Schilling came into contact with Leon Czolgosz in Cleveland in 1901 and after several meetings suspected Czolgosz of being an agent provocateur. Schilling's suspicions led to Abe Isaak's warning in the 1 September 1901 issue of *Free Society* that Czolgosz may be a spy.

Schuettler, Hermann (dates unknown) Chicago detective. Known for his dramatic arrest of Haymarket anarchist Louis Lingg, Schuettler was later promoted to assistant chief of police. *See also vol. 2.*

Schwab, Justus H. (1847–1900) German-born anarchist. Schwab immigrated to the United States in 1868; his Lower East Side saloon at 50 East First Street was a popular gathering place for radicals and writers including Ambrose Bierce, Sadakichi Hartmann, and James Huneker. EG used it as her return address for many years; it was also the address of the periodical *Sturmvogel*. Arrested for unfurling a red flag during the 13 January 1874 Tompkins Square riot, a demonstration of the unemployed dispersed by the police, Schwab evoked the Paris Commune and sang the "Marseillaise" as he was dragged away. Initially a socialist (Schwab was expelled from the Socialist Labor Party for his opposition to the Greenback alliance in the 1880 election), by the early 1880s Schwab embraced anarchism and became a founder of the New York Social Revolutionary Club. He played a leading role in the October 1881 Chicago congress of social revolutionaries as the representative of the Social Revolutionary Club of New York. The congress, which was attended by anarchists and others, denounced wage slavery and private property, and endorsed the resolutions of the earlier July 1881 London International Social Revolutionary Congress, including propaganda by the deed and other methods of armed insurrection. Schwab was instrumental in bringing Johann Most, through the Social Revolutionary Club, to New York in December 1882, when he formally introduced Most at his first appearance before an American audience. Schwab was a member of the International Working People's Association from its inception in 1883; he corresponded with Albert Parsons in Cook County Jail. A onetime business manager of *Freiheit*, Schwab was for many years an agent of Benjamin Tucker's *Liberty*. As reported in *Liberty*, Schwab broke away from Most in 1886, in a scandal that allegedly involved some anarchist communists setting house fires as part of an insurance fraud scheme. Though not directly involved in the fires, Most refused to condemn those who set them, after which Schwab distanced himself personally, but not publicly, from Most and *Freiheit*. In response, *Freiheit* issued a warning against Schwab to all anarchists; Most, however, still delivered a glowing eulogy for Schwab at his funeral. Schwab was also a leader of the German anarchist singing group Internationale Arbeiter Liedertafel, which no doubt enlivened his saloon. Schwab was a close friend and supporter of EG, who described him as having a "surprising capacity for friendship, a veritable genius for responding generously and beautifully" (*LML*, p. 320).

Schwab, Michael (1853–1898) German-born American anarchist and Haymarket defendant. Trained as a bookbinder, Michael Schwab joined the newly formed Bookbinders Union in 1872. Shortly afterward he joined the Social Democratic Party. Schwab immigrated to the United States in 1879, moving immediately to Chicago. He worked at various trades and traveled regularly, joining the Socialist Labor Party and, from there, gravitated toward anarchism. In 1881 Schwab became a reporter for the *Chicagoer Arbeiter-Zeitung* and then its associate editor. Together with others, including Oscar Neebe, Schwab was a founding member of the Chicago North Side Group of the IWPA, ran its library, and was a member of its general committee. He also acted as a distributor for *Freiheit*. In early 1886 Schwab spoke regularly at meetings and demonstrations in favor of the eighthour day and to the locked-out workers at the McCormick Harvester plant. Schwab was seen by the autonomist faction as a moderate, although he had spoken out in favor of dynamite. Arrested on 5 May, the day after the Haymarket explosion, Schwab was sentenced to death. He continued to contribute to the *Chicagoer Arbeiter-Zeitung*, smuggling articles out of the prison. Schwab appealed for clemency in November 1887, and his sentence was commuted to life imprisonment. Michael Schwab was pardoned by Illinois governor John Altgeld on 26 June 1893, moving back to his old job. He resigned from the *Chicagoer Arbeiter-Zeitung* in 1895, opening a shoe store which failed. Schwab contracted tuberculosis and was dying when EG visited him in spring 1898. She wrote, "I felt with a feeling of awe for the man whose staunch and proud spirit the cruel powers had failed to break" (*LML*, p. 221). He was buried at Waldheim Cemetery.

Seymour, Henry (1860–1938) English individualist anarchist, editor, and printer. Seymour was an early member of the National Secular Society. He published a pamphlet on Bakunin, *Michael Bakounine: A Biographical Sketch* (London: H. Seymour, 1888), and translated Élisée Reclus's *Evolution et revolution* (London: International Publishing, 1885). From 1885 to 1888, Seymour edited the *Anarchist,* a paper with a Proudhonist tone but still open to publishing articles from various perspectives of anarchist thought. In 1889 Seymour edited the *Revolutionary Review* and in 1892, as part of the free currency campaign, *Free Exchange* and *Free Trade*. From 1897 to 1899 Seymour edited the *Adult,* and in 1898 was honorary secretary of the Free Speech Defense Committee, working on the defense campaign of the Legitimation League's secretary George Bedborough, who was prosecuted for publishing *Sexual Inversion* by Havelock Ellis. Later he became honorary secretary of the Bacon Society and a pioneer of the gramophone record, editing the journals *Talking Machine* and *Sound Wave.* Seymour's pamphlets include *The Fallacy of Marx's Theory of Surplus Value* (London, 1897), *The Physiology of Love: A Study in Stirpiculture* (London, 1898), *The Anarchy of Love: or, The Science of the Sexes* (London, 1888), *An Examination of the Malthusian Theory* (1889), and *The Monomaniacs: A Fable in Finance* (London, 1895). Seymour was also the author of *The Reproduction of Sound* (London, 1918).

Solotaroff, Hillel (1865–1921) Russian-born physician and anarchist lecturer and writer. Solotaroff was an important figure in the Yiddish-speaking anarchist movement from the mid-1880s, when he was a principal activist in Pionire der Frayhayt (Pioneers of Liberty), the first Jewish anarchist group in the United States. EG heard Solotaroff lecture in New Haven in 1886, and sought him out when she arrived in New York City the following year. It was Solotaroff who introduced her to Alexander Berkman. Along with other members of Pioneers of Liberty, Solotaroff contributed to the 15 March 1889 Paris Commune anniversary edition of *Varhayt,* the first U.S. Yiddish-language anarchist periodical. Solotaroff was a speaker at the Proletarian Club in New York City in December 1890. He was also a main speaker at the 1891 New York City Yom Kippur ball. These annual balls served as an anti-religious expression for mainly Jewish anarchists who, while retaining a devotion to the secular aspects of being Jewish, aggressively rejected religion as an instrument of privilege and superstition in favor of science and reason. Solotaroff, along with Moshe Katz, briefly edited *Freie Arbeiter Stimme* after David Edelstadt's death in 1892. He contributed to various other Yiddish papers, including *Tfileh Zakeh* (Pure Prayer; New York, 1889–1893), an anti-religious journal issued annually on Yom Kippur by the Pioneers of Liberty. In 1897 Solotaroff hosted a gathering for Peter Kropotkin during Kropotkin's first visit to America, and later joined the executive committee of the Kropotkin Literary Society, founded in 1912. *See also vol. 2.*

Spencer, Herbert (1820–1903) English philosopher, sociologist. Spencer advocated the importance of the individual over society, and of science over religion. He argued for the application of complete laissez-faire in economic and social matters. Spencer was a strong proponent of the theory of evolution as applied to human society, characterizing social evolution as a process of increasing individualization. In 1882 Spencer traveled to the United States, where his works were popular and where he was well respected, visiting such notable Americans as John Fiske and Oliver Wendell Holmes. His only American speech, at his farewell banquet in New York, however, was openly critical of the American way of life. His works, influential among individualist anarchists, included *Social Statics* (whose chapter on "The Right to Ignore the State" he deleted, although it was later reprinted as a pamphlet by Benjamin Tucker in 1907, and Freedom Press in 1913) and *Synthetic Philosophy: First Principles* (1862). EG would write about the influence of Spencer's notion of liberty in *What I Believe* (1908). *See also vol. 2.*

Spies, August Vincent Theodore (1855–1887) German-born American anarchist, editor, Haymarket defendant. Spies came to New York City from Germany in late 1872 where he learned the upholstery trade. The following year he moved to Chicago, opening his own shop in 1876. Spies's interest in socialism dated from his attendance at a Working-Men's Party meeting in 1875, but his radical activity increased dramatically after the nationwide railroad strike of 1877. By 1880 Spies, a skilled orator, had been expelled from the Socialist Labor Party for his anarchist ideas. That same year he began working as manager of the anarchist *Chicagoer Arbeiter-Zeitung*, and in 1884 became the newspaper's editor. Along with Albert Parsons, Samuel Fielden, Adolph Fischer, and Oscar Neebe, Spies was a member of the IWPA's American Group of Chicago, founded in 1883 by Parsons. Arrested following the Haymarket affair, Spies was found guilty of murder and died on the scaffold on 11 November 1887. His last words, "The day will come when our silence will be more powerful than the voices you are throttling today," were inscribed on the monument dedicated to the Haymarket anarchists in Waldheim Cemetery in 1893.

Stein, Modest (born Modest Aronstam, nickname Fedya) (1871–1958) AB's cousin and schoolmate in Russia. Stein changed his name sometime after 1900. An artist who later became a successful illustrator, Stein immigrated to the United States in 1888 and joined AB in the anarchist movement in New York. Stein lived and worked with AB and EG from 1889 to July 1892 and was briefly EG's lover in a loose ménage à trois. As EG recalled in *Living My Life*, "Could I love two persons at the same time? I loved Sasha. At that very moment my resentment at his harshness gave way to yearning for my strong, arduous lover. Yet I felt Sasha had left something untouched in me, something Fedya could perhaps waken to life. Yes, it must be possible to love more than one! All I had felt for the boy artist must have been love without my being aware of it till now I decided" (*LML*, p. 45). Together the three were co-conspirators in AB's attempt on the life of Henry C. Frick (though to shield his reputation, Stein's role was intentionally omitted from the accounts in *Prison Memoirs* and *Living My Life*). When AB failed to kill Frick, Stein traveled to Pittsburgh intending to dynamite Frick's house, but when news of his presence was leaked to the local authorities he abandoned the plan. He later met EG in Rochester where she gave him money to return to New York. From there he traveled to Detroit, staying first with Robert Reitzel, and settled into a job at an engraving firm. Despite Stein's eventual interest in communism and his rejection of anarchism, he remained a close friend and financial supporter of EG and AB throughout their years in exile.

Stirner, Max (born Johann Caspar Schmidt) (1806–1856) German individualist. Stirner had a powerful influence on individualist anarchism both in the United States and internationally through his *Der Einzige und Sein Eigentum*, translated as *The Ego and His Own* (trans. Steven T. Byington; New York: Benjamin Tucker, 1907). Stirner's contention that enlightened self-interest was the only motivating force in human conduct (the philosophy known as "egoism") was adopted by Benjamin Tucker around 1891. The book itself was reviewed equivocally in the May 1907 *Mother Earth* by Max Baginski. Both EG and AB, at various times, called themselves egoists, and Stirner's influence on EG would grow during her next decade.

Swinton, John (1829–1901) Scottish-born journalist and labor activist. Swinton came to the United States in 1850 after a brief visit in Canada. He worked as a printer, became an abolitionist (joining John Brown's raid at Osawatomie, Kansas in 1857), and fought in the Civil War. Swinton developed a national reputation for his work as an editor and writer for the *New York Times* (from 1860 to 1870) and the *New York Sun* (from 1870 to 1883 and 1887 to 1897), as well as for founding his own highly regarded pro–labor union publication, *John Swinton's Paper* (1883–1887), a reliable source reporting on various strikes. Also devoted to free speech, the paper published an article by the National Defense Association's treasurer E. W. Chamberlain. Devoted to labor activism after the Tompkins Square riot of 1874, Swinton ran unsuccessfully that year for mayor of New York on the SLP ticket and for state senator under the Progressive Labor Party in 1887. He was also active in attempts to save the Haymarket anarchists. Swinton led efforts against the Chinese exclusion movement and tirelessly fought for Russian freedom. Swinton (who went blind in 1889) and his wife, Orsena (a daughter of the phrenologist Orson Squire Fowler), visited EG at Blackwell's Island in 1894. EG was fond of Swinton, whom she first met at Justus Schwab's saloon (Swinton, along with Johann Most, delivered the eulogies at Schwab's funeral). She credited Swinton with giving her a new outlook on her adopted country shortly after her release from prison in 1894, as well as her decision to devote herself to propagandizing in English to a wider, native-born audience. Swinton presided over Kropotkin's 1897 New York meeting at Chickering Hall. Swinton, who corresponded with Karl Marx, also wrote for European papers and published numerous pamphlets and longer works, including *A Model Factory in a Model City: A Social Study* (New York: Press of Brown, Green and Adams, 1887) and *Striking for Life* (Philadelphia: Keller, 1894).

Timmermann, Claus (1866–1941) German-born anarchist and editor. Timmermann immigrated to the United States around 1883. In St. Louis he edited and published *Der Anarchist* from 1889 to 1891. In the summer of 1891 Timmermann ceased publishing the paper and moved to New York. The following year, according to EG, she and AB confided in Timmermann about their Homestead plan, and he helped them write the manifesto to the striking steelworkers, "Labor Awakens." Timmermann was tried on 1 September 1893, and sentenced to six months on the charge of inciting to riot for his speech at the 21 August rally in Union Square, the political gathering that, for the same charges, prompted EG's arrest, trial, and imprisonment. In New York, Timmermann edited the anarchist papers *Die Brandfackel* (from 1893 to 1894) and *Sturmvogel* (from 1897 to 1899).

Tochatti, James (born Moncure Douglas) (1852–1928) Scottish-born anarchist activist and editor. A tailor by trade, Tochatti was a close friend of William Morris and active in the Hammersmith branch of the Socialist League. He founded the anarchist monthly *Liberty* in January 1894, a forum for libertarians of all hues, which clarified Tochatti's opposition to the anarchist strategy of bombings so prevalent in Europe. Financial difficulties and illness forced him to suspend publication in December 1896. Tochatti was never again as active in the anarchist movement, although his Hammersmith bookshop was used for political meetings. Later in 1912 Tochatti joined the campaign against Errico Malatesta's deportation from England.

Tolstoy, Leo (Count Lev Nikolayevich) (1828–1910) Russian novelist, philosopher, pacifist, and mystic. Tolstoy was best known for his literary works, including *War and Peace* (1869), *Anna Karenina* (1877), and *The Death of Ivan Illyich* (1884); his later philosophical essays, including *Confession* (1884), *What Then Must We Do?* (1886), *The Kingdom of God Is Within You* (1894), and *The Slavery of Our Times* (1900); and for his attempt to combine both in his more polemic fiction, including *Master and Man* (1895). His *Kreutzer Sonata* (1891?), banned by the tsar, was initially distributed in Russia by manuscript and lithograph form. Benjamin Tucker translated and distributed *Kreutzer Sonata* in the United States, only to have it banned from the mails under the Comstock Act; Tucker also published the first volumes of Tolstoy's *Church and State* (1891), a collection of essays on social problems. A portion of the profits from his last novel, *Resurrection* (1899–1900), was donated to Jane Addams's Hull House. Though Tolstoy himself resisted the title "anarchist," anarchists admired his compassion for the poor and his anti-feudal sentiments, recognizing that he was a pacifist and anti-militarist who condemned all acts of revolutionary violence. Anarchists also celebrated Tolstoy's rejection of institutionalized religion despite his advocacy of Christian love as the primary vehicle for improving society. EG respected Tolstoy as a great Russian literary talent, and appreciated the sentiments that propelled his work. Although the American anarchist individualist press wrote about Tolstoy and promoted and published his works, American anarchist communist papers of this period barely mentioned him. Tolstoy's ideas were also popularized in the United States by Ernest Crosby.

Tucker, Benjamin R. (1854–1939) American individualist anarchist. Tucker was the founder, editor, and publisher of *Liberty* (Boston, 1881–1892; New York, 1892–1908); he translated and published European literature in addition to works on anarchist individualism. In 1872 Ezra Heywood introduced Tucker to the New England Labor Reform League, whose membership included Josiah Warren, Lysander Spooner, Stephen Pearl Andrews, and William B. Greene (who became Tucker's mentor). In 1873, Tucker, Greene, and anarchist Ezra Heywood unsuccessfully petitioned the Massachusetts legislature for a mutual banking law. Tucker and the radical feminist Victoria Woodhull became lovers, traveling together, along with her sister Tennessee Claflin, in 1873 to France, where Tucker steeped himself in the writings of Bakunin and Proudhon. After Greene's death in 1878, Tucker emerged as the leading exponent of individualist anarchism. In 1876 Tucker translated Proudhon's "What Is Property?" and, the following year, part one of Proudhon's "The System of Economical Contradictions" in his journal *The Radical Review* (1870–1878). Tucker's translation of Proudhon's essay "The Malthusians" appeared in the freethought journal *The Boston Index* and his translation of Proudhon's debate with the French economist Frederic Bastiat was published in the New York *Irish World* in 1879. During this time Tucker also periodically worked as a reporter for the *Boston Daily Globe*. In August 1881 Tucker launched *Liberty*, the leading publication identified with anarchist individualism, and still the longest-running English-language anarchist paper in the United States. Tucker was a prolific translator and publisher of books and pamphlets on anarchism and related subjects; his magazine printed works by George Bernard Shaw, Émile Zola, Octave Mirabeau, Felix Pyat, Claude Tillier, and Sophie Kropotkin, among others. He translated and published the writings of Michael Bakunin, Victor Hugo, N. G. Chernyshevsky, Max Stirner, Herbert Spencer, and Leo Tolstoy in both book and pamphlet form. Tucker also published *The Transatlantic*, a biweekly literary magazine (1889–1890). Within the pages of *Liberty* Tucker was a devoted advocate of anarchist individualism and often argued heatedly with anarchist communists, maintaining that all forms of communism were authoritarian and antithetical to the principles of anarchism. By 1891 he had converted to the idea of egoism as outlined in Stirner's *The Ego and Its Own*. Following AB's *attentat* on Henry C. Frick, Tucker wrote an editorial on the inefficacy of violence, asserting that while he admired AB and considered Frick a thief, an anarchist revolution would never be realized through violence; Tucker summed up his argument as "No Pity for Frick, No Praise for Berkman." Tucker left a voluminous translation and publishing legacy, and only one book of his own, a collection of writings from *Liberty* entitled *Instead of a Book: By a Man Too Busy to Write One* (New York, 1893). *See also vol. 2.*

Turner, John (1864–1934) British anarchist, lecturer, journalist, and founder of the Shop Assistants' Union. Turner became an anarchist in response to the execution of the Haymarket anarchists; he joined William Morris's Socialist League. During the 1890s Turner was associated with the *Freedom* Group and from 1894 to 1906 was the official publisher of *Freedom*. In March 1896 at Harry Kelly's suggestion, he embarked on a seven-month lecture tour of the United States, with EG and other New York anarchists assisting with local arrangements and introductions. EG had previously met Turner during her 1895 trip to London. Through Turner's lecture tour EG was exposed to a wider native-born and English-speaking audience. In 1898, back in England, Turner was the national organizer for the National Amalgamated Union and in 1900 for the International Federation of Commercial Employees. His sister Lizzie, also an anarchist, was the companion of Thomas H. Bell, a Scottish-born associate of EG. *See also vol. 2.*

Vaillant, Auguste (1861–1894) French anarchist. Vaillant threw a bomb from the public gallery into France's Chamber of Deputies on 9 December 1893, injuring about eighty people. He was executed on 6 February 1894. At his trial Vaillant declared "the deputies are responsible for all society's afflictions." After his death Vaillant's daughter Sidonie—"the crown princess of anarchy"—was entrusted to Sébastien Faure. Vaillant's action led to the passage of the anti-anarchist *lois scélérates* and triggered Sante Caserio's assassination of Sadi Carnot. A pamphlet of Vaillant's speech to the court was widely circulated; the speech was reprinted by Benjamin Tucker in *Liberty* (24 February 1894), and Zola featured Vaillant in his novel *Paris* (1898) as the anarchist character Salvat.

Vaughan, Ernest (1841–1929) French socialist. Vaughan was a member of the First International and an associate of Élisée Reclus and Louise Michel. An enthusiastic admirer of Proudhon, he joined the International in 1867. After attending a meeting in support of the Paris Commune in 1871, Vaughan spent several weeks in prison, then took refuge in Brussels. There Vaughan founded a section of the International and collaborated on various newspapers including *Le Moniteur industriel*, *La Gazette de Hollande* (Paris, 1867), and *Le Mot pour rire*. Vaughan returned to France in 1880 and wrote articles for a newspaper in Lyon, *L'Émancipation* (1880). The following year Vaughan became manager of Henri Rochefort's paper *L'Intransigeant*, and in 1897 he founded *L'Aurore* (Paris). On 13 January 1898, *L'Aurore* printed "J'Accuse," Émile Zola's condemnation of the French government's conduct in the Dreyfus Affair. Vaughan's literary works include two volumes of humorous tales under the pseudonym "Frère Jean" (1866 and 1875), a collection of portraits of the politicians of the day entitled *Le Pilori de L'Intransigeant* (1885), and *Souvenirs sans regrets* (1902). Vaughan also wrote the postscript, "A Sketch of the Criminal Record of the Author," to Élisée Reclus's *An Anarchist on Anarchy* (Boston: B. Tucker, 1884).

Waldeck-Rousseau, Rene (1846–1904) French statesman and lawyer. Waldeck-Rousseau served twice as minister of the interior (in 1881–1882 and 1883–1885) and as premier (1899–1902). A member of the republican left, he supported the workers' right to strike, legalizing trade unions with the passage of the 1884 Waldeck-Rousseau law. In 1893, he defended A. Gustave Eiffel against charges of corruption in the Panama Canal trial; he was also instrumental in securing a pardon for Alfred Dreyfus in the Dreyfus Affair of 1899. In 1899, Waldeck-Rousseau was appointed premier, serving until 1902, when he resigned due to failing health. He was responsible for the Associations Law of 1901, which harshly limited the right of free association between religious orders. That year he also signed the extradition order expelling EG from France. His writings included *Associations et Congregations* (Paris: E. Fasquelle, 1901) and *Politique Française et Etrangere* (Paris: Bibliothèque Charpentier, 1903).

Weismann, Henry (1863–1935) Bavarian-born anarchist, editor, and trade unionist. Weismann immigrated to the United States in his teens, settling in San Francisco. A member of the anarchist International Working People's Association, Weismann helped publish Burnette Haskell's paper *Truth*. Weismann was active in the anti-Chinese exclusion efforts and the labor movement, organizing bakers, brewery workers, and coastal seamen. He joined the Knights of Labor in 1884 and helped found the Representative Council of the Federated Trades and Labor Organization. Weismann was arrested and imprisoned for several months on charges of possessing explosives while serving as president of the Anti-Coolie League. Weismann moved to New York in 1890 and the following year assumed the editorship of the *Bakers' Journal*, the official publication of the Journeymen Bakers' and Confectioners' International Union, of which he also became international secretary in 1895. Also in 1891 Weismann helped organize the New York City Federation of Labor as an alternative to the Central Labor Union. In June 1892 Weismann spoke at the anarchist communist International Club on the topic of "Revolution versus the Ballot." At the annual convention of the American Federation of Labor in 1896, Weismann successfully proposed a resolution calling for a reduction of the sentence imposed on AB for his attempt on Frick's life. In 1897 Weismann resigned from the AFL, left the labor movement, and later became a lawyer.

Westley, John (dates unknown) English anarchist, saddlebar filer. Westley was one of the Walsall anarchists arrested in January 1892 and charged with possessing explosives. He was found not guilty in April 1892.

Withington, Lothrop (1856–1915) American individualist anarchist. Withington was the son of one of the leading families of Newburyport, Massachusetts, whose interest in genealogy as a youth first took him to England. Beginning in the early 1880s Withington spent an increasing amount of time in London, where he was a member of the Manhood Suffrage League, a reformist and republican organization, and a close associate of Henry Seymour, whose paper, the *Anarchist*, published Withington's articles. A powerful speaker, Withington shared the platform with figures as prominent as Peter Kropotkin and William Morris. Withington's speech at the Communist Club on 7 October 1887, a London meeting protesting the impending execution of the Haymarket anarchists, was later published as *Constructive Murder* (London: International Publishing, 1887). In 1889 Withington published three issues of the paper *Democratic Review*. He wrote a classic work of genealogy, *Virginia Gleanings in England* (Baltimore: Genealogical Publishing, 1880), authored the pamphlet *Free*

Currency (London, 1889), and edited *Caleb Haskell's Diary. May 5, 1775–May 30, 1776* (Newbury-port, Mass.: W. H. Huse, 1881). Withington died on the *Lusitania* when it was torpedoed and sunk by German submarines in May 1915.

Yanovsky, Saul Josef (1864–1939) Polish-born Jewish anarchist. Born in Pinsk, Yanovsky immigrated to America in 1885, where he was an early member of Pionire der Frayhaty (Pioneers of Liberty). Arriving in London in March 1890, his experience as a capmaker in London's slums led to his involvement in radical labor affairs. Yanovsky authored *What Do the Anarchists Want?* (1890), one of the first Yiddish-language treatises on anarchism. Under his editorship, *Arbeter Fraint* (1891–1894) developed a cohesive anarchist program. Yanovsky returned to the United States in January 1895, where his organizational skills put *Freie Arbeiter Stimme* (1895–1919) on sound financial footing. He was perceived by EG as "despotic" and by AB as "rigid and dictatorial." Yanovsky criticized EG's essay "The Tragedy at Buffalo" as contradictory and called her lack of clarity a danger to anarchism. *See also vols. 2, 3.*

Zola, Émile (1840–1902) French novelist, naturalist, and social critic. In *Germinal* (1885), Zola's character Souvarine epitomizes the nihilist and *attentater*. In *Paris* (1898), the anarchist character Salvat is closely based on Auguste Vaillant. Zola was also a vigorous defender of Alfred Dreyfus.

The Adult London: vol. 1, no. 1 (June 1897), subtitled *A Journal for the Advancement of Freedom in Sexual Relationships*; vol. 1, no. 2 (September 1897), subtitled *A Crusade Against Sex-enslavement*; vol. 1, no. 3 (October 1897), subtitled *A Journal for the Free Discussion of Tabooed Subjects*; vol. 1, no. 4– (monthly); vol. 2, no. 1– (February 1898), subtitled *A Journal of Sex*; vol. 3, no. 1 (January 1899)–vol. 3, no. 3 (March 1899), subtitled *An Unconventional Journal*. The journal of the Legitimation League, organized for the purpose of ensuring the rights of children born out of wedlock. Edited by George Bedborough, it published articles on a variety of subjects, but particularly on sexual questions, including the nature of sexual attraction, "varietism," monogamy, and polygamy. The Legitimation League was closely connected with the *Lucifer* Group, beginning correspondence with *Lucifer* in 1893; the League named its headquarters Harman Villa, and in 1897, Lillian Harman was elected its president. Editorial responsibilities passed to Henry Seymour for the July 1898 issue, following the arrest of Bedborough for distributing Havelock Ellis's *Sexual Inversion*. Contributors included Oswald Dawson, Lillian Harman, Moses Harman, Emil F. Ruedebusch, E. C. Walker, and Lothrop Withington. The journal printed the work of James F. Morton, Jr., and a report of a lecture by Voltairine de Cleyre.

The Alarm Chicago: vol. 1, no. 1 (4 October 1884)–vol. 3, no. 3 (24 April 1886), weekly, then biweekly; n.s. vol. 1, no. 1 (5 November 1887)–; New York: (16 June 1888)–no. 47 (2 February 1889), weekly. Founded as a "socialist weekly" and the English-language organ of the International Working People's Association. Edited by Albert Parsons and Lucy Parsons from 1884 to 1886, and Dyer D. Lum, with Lizzie Holmes as assistant editor, from 1887 to 1888. Suppressed following the Haymarket incident. Contributors included William Holmes, C. L. James, Gertrude B. Kelly, and John F. Kelly.

Der Anarchist (The Anarchist) St. Louis: vol. 1, no. 1 (1 August 1889)–[irregular?]; vol. 3, no. 1 [?], biweekly. New York: (19 September 1891)–vol. 2, no. 24 (26 December 1891); vol. 4, no. 1 (9 January 1892)–vol. 4, no. 51 (31 December 1892), weekly; vol. 5, no. 1 (January 1893)–vol. 7, no. 9 (22 June 1895), biweekly. Anarchist communist newspaper, autonomist in viewpoint, which defined itself as the successor to George Engel and Adolf Fischer's *Der Anarchist* (Chicago). First edited by Claus Timmermann in St. Louis; then published in New York by Die Autonomen Gruppen Amerikas and edited by the Radikaler Arbeiter-Bund (Radical Workers League), whose members included Carl Masur, Otto Rinke, Joseph Peukert, and Sepp Oerter. Published an endorsement of

AB's attempt on Frick. EG was among its original contributors, but by the time of her imprisonment in 1893–1894, she was critical of the people working on the paper.

The Anarchist London: no. 1 (March 1885)–no. 40 (1 August 1888), monthly, various subtitles. Anarchist paper edited by Henry Seymour. Although from April 1886 to March 1887 it was associated with the anarchist communist Peter Kropotkin and the *Freedom* Group, before and afterwards it was an anarchist individualist publication. Predominantly a source of news, reprints, and articles by Seymour, it also printed works by Élisée Reclus and Lothrop Withington.

Der arme Teufel (The Poor Devil) Detroit: vol. 1, no. 1 (6 December 1884)–no. 822 (22 September 1900). German radical and literary weekly, edited by Robert Reitzel; continued in 1898, after Reitzel's death, by Martin Drescher. Perhaps the most successful German literary publication in the United States, with subscriptions peaking at over 7,000. Printed translations of the works of many literary figures, including Leo Tolstoy and Mark Twain. It published supportive editorials and articles about AB's *attentat* on Frick and was the only radical or labor journal that AB was permitted to read in prison. He recalled that "the arrival of the *Teufel* is a great event" (*Prison Memoirs of an Anarchist*, p. 166).

Die Autonomie (Autonomy) London: vol. 1, no. 1 (6 November 1886)–no. 211 (22 April 1893), weekly, subtitled *Anarchistisch-communistisches Organ* (Anarchist-Communist Organ). Anarchist communist paper, printed and published by R. Gunderson, edited by Joseph Peukert and others. Autonomist and uncompromising, the paper was central in the conflict between Johann Most and Peukert. Published early German-language translations of parts of Peter Kropotkin's *Conquest of Bread,* his article "The Spirit of Revolt," and excerpts of Élisée Reclus's *Evolution and Revolution.* Both EG and AB were strongly influenced by the ideas expressed in its articles. Of it EG wrote, "While not comparable with the *Freiheit* in force and picturesqueness of language, it nevertheless seemed to me to express anarchism in a clearer and more convincing manner" (*LML*, p. 74).

Die Brandfackel (The Torch of War) New York: vol. 1, no. 1 (July 1893)–vol. 3, no. 1 (January 1895), monthly, subtitled *Anarchistische Monatsschrift* (Anarchist Monthly). Anarchist communist paper edited by Claus Timmermann; published several of EG's earliest articles. Claus Niedermann edited the paper while Timmermann was imprisoned on Blackwell's Island in 1893. The first issue contained an eighteen-page spread supporting AB's *attentat.*

Chicagoer Arbeiter-Zeitung (Chicago Labor News) Chicago: 1 June 1876–13 October 1919. Began as the triweekly *Volks-Zeitung,* published by the Socialistic Publishing Society; became the daily *Arbeiter-Zeitung* in 1879. Initiated by socialists, it gradually transformed into an anarchist publication, with new editors August Spies and Michael Schwab from 1884 to 1886 and Max Baginski from 1894 to [1907?]. A popular paper, it published local news and articles in its four pages, and its circulation in 1886 was over 5,000. In 1910 it reverted to its original socialist editorial perspective.

The Commonweal London: vol. 1, no. 1 (February 1885)–[?] (December 1890), weekly, subtitled *The Official Journal of the Socialist League;* [?]–vol. 7 (whole no. 329) (September 1892), monthly, subtitled *A Journal of Revolutionary Socialism;* n.s. vol. 1, no. 1 (1 May 1893)–vol. 2, no. 32 (6 October 1894), weekly, subtitled *A Revolutionary Journal of Anarchist-Communism.* Libertarian socialist, then anarchist communist organ of the Socialist League; the paper reflected the League's changing politics. It was edited by William Morris from 1885 until his resignation in 1889, at which point David

Nicoll, appointed assistant editor in 1889, presided until his arrest in April 1892. George Cores acted as temporary editor for a month, followed by Henry B. Samuels from May 1892 to 1894, and finally John Turner and Ernest Young from August 1894 to October 1894. Regularly reported on EG's activities. Serially published Morris's *News from Nowhere*. David Nicoll published a number of later periodicals using the same name, *The Commonweal*.

Discontent Home [Colony] and Lakebay, Wash.: vol. 1, no. 1 (11 May 1898)–vol. 4, no. 31 (30 April 1902), weekly, subtitled *Mother of Progress*. Anarchist communist newspaper founded by O. A. Verity, Charles H. Govan, and others and published by James F. Morton, Jr. Contributors included Henry Addis, Kate Austin, Moses Harman, Lizzie Holmes, William Holmes, C. L. James, Francis B. Livesey, and Ross Winn. Joseph Labadie's "Cranky Notions" column was reprinted periodically. On 18 December 1901, it was discovered that a number of issues of the paper had been held up at the Tacoma post office, by order of the postal inspector in Spokane. James E. Larkin, Charles L. Govan, and James W. Adams were charged with using the mails to distribute articles on sexuality deemed obscene under the Comstock laws. On 11 March 1902, charges were dismissed, but on the 30th the entire Home Colony post office was shut down. Publication of *Discontent* continued by assuming a new name, *The Demonstrator*.

The Firebrand Portland, Oreg.: vol. 1, no. 1 (27 January 1895)–vol. 3, no. 32 (whole no. 136) (12 September 1897), weekly, subtitled *For the Burning Away of the Cobwebs of Superstition and Ignorance*. The newspaper was an important forum for the propagation and discussion of anarchist communism among American-born, English-speaking anarchists. Contributors included Kate Austin, Steven T. Byington, EG, William Holmes, W. C. Owen, and Ross Winn. In September 1897 editors Abe Isaak, Henry Addis, and Abner J. Pope were prosecuted—and the paper banned from the mails—for publishing obscene material, including Walt Whitman's poem "A Woman Waits for Me." In June 1898 charges were dismissed. Isaak resumed the publication as *Free Society* when he relocated to San Francisco later that year.

Forverts (also labeled in English, *Forward*) New York: 22 April 1897–28 January 1983, daily; 4 February 1983–, weekly. Yiddish-language socialist paper, for many years the largest and most successful Yiddish-language publication in the world, edited by Abraham Cahan from 1902 until his death in 1951. Serially published a Yiddish translation of selections from EG's *Living My Life* from 30 May to 31 October 1931.

Freedom London: October 1886–December 1927, monthly. Principal English-language publishing organ for the theoretical development of anarchist communism; founded by Peter Kropotkin and Charlotte Wilson, among others. Editors included Wilson, James Blackwell, Joseph Pressburg, Alfred Marsh, John Turner, and Thomas Keell. Reported news of EG's activities and lectures. Continued publication under various titles after 1930, including *Spain and the World* and *War Commentary*.

Free Society San Francisco: 14 November 1897–December 1901, weekly, 4 pages; Chicago: February 1901–1904, 8 pages; New York: 27 March 1904–20 November 1904. Succeeded *The Firebrand* (see above). Anarchist communist newspaper edited by Abe Isaak. *Free Society* was the principal English-language forum for anarchist ideas in the United States at the beginning of the twentieth century. Contributors included Kate Austin, Voltairine de Cleyre, Michael Cohn, Jay Fox, EG, Lizzie

Holmes, William Holmes, C. L. James, Harry Kelly, James F. Morton, Jr., and Ross Winn. In its 28 April 1901 issue, published the first English translation of Peter Kropotkin's article "The Black Invasion."

Freie Arbeiter Stimme (German transliteration, which appeared on masthead, for *Fraye Arbeter Shtime*, Free Voice of Labor) New York: July 1890–May 1892, May 1893–1894 and 1899–1977, weekly. Yiddish-language anarchist paper, edited by Roman Lewis, J. A. Maryson, David Edelstadt, Hillel Solotaroff, and Moishe Katz, consecutively; then by Saul Yanovsky, who edited the paper after its revival in 1899 until 1919. Its masthead included Haymarket anarchist Albert Parsons's words "Let the voice of the people be heard." During the 1890s it regularly covered EG's activities and advertised her talks and lectures, although it published an editorial criticizing EG's article "The Tragedy at Buffalo." Among the paper's contributors were Peter Kropotkin, Johann Most, Max Nettlau, Rudolf Rocker, and poet Morris Winchevsky. It was the longest-running Yiddish-language anarchist paper in the world.

Freiheit (Freedom) Principally London and Paris; also Dielsdorf, Switzerland; Buffalo, N.Y.; and New York City: 4 January 1879–13 August 1910, weekly. German-language social democratic, then anarchist paper, edited primarily by Johann Most. The most powerful and popular German-language anarchist paper in its time. Justus Schwab was co-editor during the paper's first year in the United States. From September 1897 to July 1898, it was published as the weekly supplement to the *Buffaloer Arbeiter-Zeitung*, of which Most was then editor. Max Baginski and Henry Bauer edited *Freiheit* after Most's death. Published works of Hippolyte Havel, Robert Reitzel, Rudolf Rocker, and many others. From 1892 onward, the paper took a stand in bitter opposition to EG, although it published appeals from the Berkman Defense Association. Between August and December 1889, EG worked at the *Freiheit* office, and, for some time, AB also worked as a compositor on the paper.

L'Humanité nouvelle (New Humanity) Paris and Brussels: May 1897–1903, subtitled *Revue internationale* (International Review). Anarchist and cultural journal founded by Augustin Hamon, with editorial assistance from Victor Émile Michelet and Louis Dumon-Wilder. A journal of social thought and literature, it published works by Peter Kropotkin, Havelock Ellis, George Bernard Shaw, Domela Nieuwenhuis, Victor Dave, Russian playwright Leonid Andreyev, Leo Tolstoy, and Maksim Gorky. EG apparently submitted articles, but none were published. The journal would be the role model for *Mother Earth*.

Internationale Bibliothek (International Library) New York: no. 1 (April 1887)–no. 13 (June 1888); no. 15 (May 1890)–no. 18 (August 1891). Published by John Müller, the journal was primarily devoted to the writings of Johann Most, including "Die Gottespest" (The god pestilence, June 1887) and "Die Gesellschaft" (The free society; August 1887). The magazine also published Peter Kropotkin's "Appeal to the Young" (October 1887) and Max Nettlau's "Historical Development of Anarchism" (June 1890). Influential in the development of EG's political and theoretical ideas.

Le Libertaire (The Libertarian) Paris: 1895–1 August 1914, weekly. Anarchist communist newspaper, founded by Sébastien Faure and Louise Michel, edited by Faure. An influential French anarchist paper, published in 1899 as the daily *Le Journal du Peuple*, and reappeared in 1919 under its original title.

Liberty London: vol. 1, no. 1 (January 1894)–, monthly, 8 pages; vol. 3, no. 1 (January 1896)–, 12 pages; vol. 3, no. 11 (November 1896)–vol. 3, no. 12 (December 1896), 8 pages. Anarchist communist journal, founded and edited by James Tochatti. Published articles expounding a wide variety of anarchist ideas, including articles by Augustin Hamon, J. C. Kenworthy, Peter Kropotkin, David Nicoll, Louise Michel, W. C. Owen, and Henry Seymour; also carried reports on EG's activities during her 1895 European tour.

Liberty: Not the Daughter but the Mother of Order Boston: vol. 1, no. 1 (6 August 1881)–, biweekly, 4 pages; vol. 2, no. 16 (17 May 1884)–; vol. 7, no. 3 (7 June 1890)–, associate editor Victor Yarros; vol. 8, no. 7 (25 July 1891)–vol. 8, no. 36 (13 February 1892), weekly; New York: vol. 8, no. 37 (30 April 1892)–, without Yarros; vol. 9, no. 45 (August 1893)–, monthly; vol. 9, no. 47 (24 February 1894)–, biweekly; vol. 10, no. 10 (22 September 1894)–vol. 17, no. 1 (April 1908), varied frequency. Anarchist individualist paper with an international reach, founded and edited by Benjamin R. Tucker. It was instrumental in introducing the works of Friedrich Nietzsche, Pierre-Joseph Proudhon, George Bernard Shaw, Max Stirner, and Leo Tolstoy to America. Contributors included E. H. Fulton, Joshua K. Ingalls, Joseph Labadie, Dyer D. Lum, John Beverly Robinson, and Victor Yarros (also for a time its associate editor). Although highly critical of EG and anarchist communists in general, the paper usually extended its support to them when arrested, but, following AB's attempt on Henry Clay Frick, it offered "neither sympathy for Frick nor support for AB."

Lucifer, the Lightbearer Valley Falls, Kans.: 1883–1896; Chicago: 8 May 1896–6 June 1907; various subtitles, including *A Journal of Investigating and Reform* and *Devoted to the Emancipation of Women from Sex Slavery*. Mostly a weekly newspaper, founded and edited by Moses Harman; co-editors included Lillian Harman and Edwin C. Walker. Published articles on anarchism, atheism, and free speech, but became especially well known for open discussions of sexuality, marriage, and feminism. EG spoke at various *Lucifer* circles, and the paper regularly featured her talks and interviews. Supported efforts to release AB. Contributors included Kate Austin, Voltairine de Cleyre, Edward Bliss Foote, Jr., Edward Bond Foote, C. L. James, Abe Isaak, James F. Morton, Jr., and Emil Ruedebusch. Was dated "E.M." (for Era of Man) from the death of Giordano Bruno in 1600, rather than the birth of Christ.

Le Père Peinard (Cool Daddy) Paris: 24 February 1889–16 March 1902. Anarchist communist and syndicalist newspaper, founded and edited by Émile Pouget. Written in a working-class vernacular style, it was one of the most popular French labor papers of its time. Replaced briefly in 1895–1896 by *La Sociale* (see below). Commented favorably on EG's activities.

Prison Blossoms (also *Zuchthausblüthen*) Western Penitentiary, Allegheny City, Penn.: no. 1 [1892?]–no. 48 [1904?]. German- and English-language publication, handwritten mostly on 3-by-5-inch cards and circulated by Henry Bauer, AB, Carl Nold, and unknown other prisoners. It included poetry, essays, and stories of prison life. Essays by AB included "A Few Words as to My Deed" and a series titled "Prisons and Crime," which included an essay on homosexuality. A number of issues rescued and preserved were consulted by AB while he was working on his *Prison Memoirs of an Anarchist*.

The Rebel Boston: vol. 1, no. 1 (September 1895)–vol. 1, no. 4 (January 1896), monthly, first issue 8 pages, then 12 pages, subtitled *A Monthly Journal Devoted to the Exposition of Anarchism Communism*; vol. 1, no. 5 (February 1896)–vol. 1, no. 6 (March/April 1896), under new subtitle, *An Anarchist Communist Journal Devoted to the Solution of the Labor Question*. Anarchist communist journal, founded and edited jointly by Charles Mowbray, Harry Kelly, James Robb, and N. H. Berman. Contributors included Voltairine de Cleyre, John Edelmann, Pietro Gori, William Holmes, William C. Owen, Lucy Parsons, and Ross Winn; also reprinted various articles by Peter Kropotkin.

Le Révolté (The Rebel) Geneva: February 1879–14 March 1885, weekly; Paris: April 1885–September 1887. Anarchist communist paper, founded by Peter Kropotkin, Varlaam N. Cherkesov, and others. It became the leading anarchist communist paper of its time. Edited from 1879 to 1883 by Kropotkin, and from then on by Jean Grave. In September 1887 the name was changed to *La Révolte* (see below).

La Révolte (Rebellion) Paris: September 1887–March 1894, weekly. Succeeded *Le Révolté* (see above). Suppressed in March 1894 after editor Jean Grave's arrest and imprisonment under French anti-anarchist laws. After his release, Grave continued editing, founding *Les Temps Nouveaux* in May 1895 (see below).

La Sociale (Social Affairs) Paris: 12 May 1895–18 October 1896. See *Le Père Peinard* above.

Solidarity New York: no. 1 (18 June 1892)–no. 23 (26 August 1893), mostly biweekly; n.s. vol. 1, no. 1 (1 January 1895)–vol. 1, no. 8 (15 April 1895); vol. 1, no. 9 (15 March 1898)–vol. 1, no. 16 (15 July 1898), subtitled *A Fortnightly Review of the Relations between Different Sections of the Working Community of the United States and an Exponent of Anarchist-Socialism*. The first English-language anarchist communist paper in New York, it was founded by Italian anarchist Saverio Merlino and John H. Edelmann. Of AB's attempt on Henry Clay Frick's life it said, "A cause which may enlist such men is sure to win." When Merlino left for London at the beginning of 1893, Edelmann assumed primary editorial responsibilities and sustained the journal through August when it suspended publication. He revived it in January 1895, an effort thwarted by lack of funds that forced it to close later in the year. When Peter Kropotkin donated the proceeds from his 1897 U.S. lecture tour, Edelmann revived the paper once more in 1898, with the additional assistance of William C. Owen and Charles B. Cooper. *Solidarity* Groups were formed in Brooklyn, Philadelphia, and Boston. Contributing authors included Lizzie M. Holmes, William Holmes, Marie Louise David, Dyer D. Lum, C. W. Mowbray, John Turner, and Lothrop Withington; also published were letters from EG and Harry Kelly. EG often helped the paper financially.

Die Sturmglocke (The Alarm Bell) Chicago: no. 1 (28 March)–no. 4 (18 April 1896), weekly. Anarchist paper edited by Max Baginski and supported by *Freiheit*.

Sturmvogel (Storm Bird) New York: 1 November 1897–[16 May 1899?], semi-monthly. German-language anarchist communist paper, edited by Claus Timmermann; its motto was "Lewwer duad ues Slaav" (Better dead than a slave). Printed news and agitational reports, including EG's accounts of her tours; also printed works by Peter Kropotkin and Carl Nold.

Les Temps Nouveaux (New Times) Paris: May 1895–August 1914, weekly. Anarchist communist paper, founded and edited by Jean Grave following his release from prison. With a circulation of around five thousand after 1902, it was a leading French anarchist newspaper. Frequently included *Supplément Littéraire*, which printed literature, social commentary, and lithographs. Published the report of the International Revolutionary Congress of the Working People in Paris in 1900. Contributors included Peter Kropotkin, Élisée Reclus, Fernand Pelloutier, Paul Delesalle, André Girard, and V. N. Cherkesov.

The Torch London: 1891–1893, subtitled *A Journal of International Socialism;* n. s. no. 1 (June[?] 1894)–, monthly, subtitled *A Revolutionary Journal of Anarchist-Communism;* vol. 2, no 5 (18 October 1895)–vol. 2, no. 12 (1 June 1896), monthly, titled *The Torch of Anarchy: A Monthly Revolutionary Journal.* Founded by the children of Pre-Raphaelite author William Rossetti, Olivia (later Olivia Agresti), Arthur, and Helen (later Helen Angeli). The first series was handwritten, duplicated using a hectograph, and sold in Hyde Park on weekends by the Rossetti family. Covered EG's tour of Britain in 1895. Contributors included EG, Frank Kitz, Errico Malatesta, Louise Michel, Octave Mirbeau, and Saul Yanovsky. With its last issue in June 1896, the Rossettis left the paper. Max Nettlau and Bernhard Kampffmeyer then purchased the printing plant and assumed the lease on the *Torch* office for the *Freedom* Group.

Der Verbote (The Harbinger) Chicago: 14 February 1873–30 April 1924, weekly. From around 1879 until 1919, *Der Verbote* was the weekly edition of the daily *Chicagoer Arbeiter-Zeitung.* Intended for a national audience, it contained national and international political and labor news. Editors included August Spies and Michael Schwab from 1882[?] to 1886, and Max Baginski from 1894 [to 1907?]. Was suppressed, along with *Chicagoer Arbeiter-Zeitung,* following the Haymarket affair but resumed publication when German-born revolutionary and philosopher Joseph Dietzgen became the new editor.

Vorwärts See *Forverts* above.

Berkman Defense Association Several organizations raised funds to assist efforts to free Alexander Berkman from prison. Immediately after AB's arrest in 1892, Harry Gordon and Max Metzkow organized the Committee for Berkman in Pittsburgh and Allegheny City, Pennsylvania. Over time, a core group of Berkman supporters formed different organizations, each with a variant on the original name. In 1895 EG appealed to the readers of *Firebrand* to send funds directly to Charles Schneider in Allegheny City to secure the commutation of AB's sentence. In 1896 Gordon reported that EG's lectures in Pittsburgh had raised approximately $30 for the Berkman Rescue Fund. In 1897, Harry Gordon assumed the role as treasurer of a group known simply as The Berkman Fund. The most prominent of the various defense groups appears to have been the Berkman Defense Association, whose organizers included Bauer, Gordon, Nold, EG, Edward Brady, Peter Heiber, and Justus H. Schwab, and whose mission, in 1896, included petitioning the state for a reduction of AB's sentence.

In 1897, the association sent a delegation (Harry Kelly and Edward Brady) to the Central Labor Union, which endorsed its resolution calling for an application to the Pennsylvania Board of Pardons for AB. In 1898 the association employed attorney John Marron to apply for a pardon on AB's behalf. The Pennsylvania Board of Pardons announced that it would base its decision largely on the wishes of Andrew Carnegie, owner of the Homestead steel plant. The defense association proceeded to recruit Benjamin Tucker to lobby Andrew Carnegie. Tucker drafted a letter to Carnegie calling Berkman and his supporters "penitent sinners" and AB's attempt a "foolish act of barbarism." The association vehemently disagreed with Tucker's views and withdrew its request. They then approached Ernest Crosby but ultimately decided not to appeal to Carnegie at all. Ironically in any case, the calendar of the state pardon board would not have accepted AB's appeal at the time intended. Saul Yanovsky, Michael Cohn, and Hillel Solotaroff, through a committee formed in 1899 at the convention of *Free Society* and *Freie Arbeiter Stimme* readers and supporters, began in 1900 to collect money for *Freie Arbeiter Stimme*'s Berkman fund. Within a short time the fund totaled over one thousand dollars. While the purported function of this fund was to pay for further appeals in Berkman's defense, the money was actually used to rent a house near the Western Penitentiary and dig the tunnel for AB's planned escape from prison. The attempt failed. Also in 1900 the United Mine Workers of America passed a resolution of solidarity with Berkman and petitioned for his release. In 1901 EG organized the Berkman Relief Association, again employing John Marron, who in November 1901 appealed for AB's pardon to the Pennsylvania State Superior Court without success and without AB's permission. After 1901 legal and extralegal attempts to free AB were for the most part abandoned. A new law automatically commuted AB's sentence to just five more years, after which he chose to stop petitioning a system that had given him no mercy in the past.

Central Labor Union (CLU) The Central Labor Union of New York, founded at a conference held on 11 February 1882 and attended by delegates from fourteen unions, was a local council composed of various trade unions in New York City. Initially influenced by a predominance of Socialist Labor Party (SLP) members, the CLU was socialist in spirit, and its actions were based on the group's assumption that both union and electoral political activity were necessary for working-class advancement. CLU membership grew rapidly and by 1886 it represented about 150,000 members from 207 different unions. The CLU sponsored lectures, mass meetings, parades and festivals, and is also credited with the founding of Labor Day on the first Monday in September. After supporting Henry George's unsuccessful "Single Tax" New York City mayoral campaign in 1886, the CLU shed the electoral aspect of its SLP roots, abandoned all political affiliations, claiming to have switched its focus exclusively to trade unionism.

By late 1888 the CLU had become affiliated with the American Federation of Labor (AFL), but charges of graft and corruption within the CLU prompted the remaining socialists to break away and form a separate organization—the Central Labor Federation (CLF). The Central Labor Federation then applied for affiliation with the AFL, which Samuel Gompers and the executive council of the AFL granted. In December 1889 the Central Labor Federation reunited with the Central Labor Union, but split again in June 1890, after a quarrel erupted between the two, only to merge back together after Gompers helped facilitate a reconciliation. However, by the time the Central Labor Federation applied for its charter from the AFL, among the organizations the CLF represented was the Socialist Labor Party (SLP). Gompers rejected the application on the grounds that the AFL was a trade union confederation and could not represent a political party. This decision led to a bitter dispute between the SLP and the AFL with Daniel De Leon calling for socialists to leave the AFL.

In addition to the New York City CLU, there were other analogous local organizations, independent of each other but with the same central labor union name, established in various cities such as Philadelphia, Buffalo, and Cleveland. Their organizing constitutions were often quite similar and their overarching goal was to unite the various trade and labor unions in their vicinity. In Chicago the Central Labor Union was closely linked with the anarchist-dominated International Working People's Association (IWPA), and in Boston there was a strong anarchist presence in the CLU, especially influenced by Charles Mowbray and Harry Kelly, who was the Boston CLU's financial secretary. The Detroit CLU (to which EG lectured in German in November 1897) published the paper *Der Herold*, edited first by the socialist Jacob Fuchs and then by Martin Drescher (a contributor to *Der arme Teufel* and *Freiheit*, and after Reitzel's death, the editor of *Der arme Teufel*). John H. Cook was for many years secretary of the Providence CLU. The Central Labor Unions provided a forum where anarchists were able to obtain trade union support for anarchists and their causes.

International Working People's Association (IWPA) The International Working People's Association, also known as the Black International, was the expansive organizational name adopted in 1883 at the Pittsburgh congress for the purpose of creating a unified radical socialist and anarchist movement. The leading delegates of the congress, notably Johann Most, Albert Parsons, and August Spies, drafted the Pittsburgh Manifesto detailing the organization's objectives, which included the destruction of existing class rule and equal rights for all regardless of class, race, and sex. The Black

International was a loose-knit federation of autonomous groups whose primary function was propaganda. It published numerous pamphlets and papers, of which *The Alarm* and the German-language *Chicagoer Arbeiter-Zeitung* were the most important. The IWPA grew in size steadily, reaching a zenith of about 5,000 members; most were immigrants, with Germans comprising the largest segment. Chicago, with a large immigrant population and poor living conditions for the working class, was the center and stronghold of the movement. The Chicago IWPA claimed the largest number of members and most active press and additionally, faced the country's most violent and repressive police force. In the United States, the IWPA competed with the International Working Men's Association (IWMA; also referred to as the Red International), established by Burnette G. Haskell and others in San Francisco on 15 July 1881. Although on several occasions proposals were made to unite the two organizations, no such affiliation ever took place. At the end of the 1880s Haskell's IWMA went out of existence, at which time the name IWPA was gradually replaced by IWMA; as an international organization, however, it had little practical influence or membership. Following the Haymarket affair in 1886, there was strong popular backlash against labor militancy and the IWPA declined in strength and ultimately faded away. IWPA meetings had often been the venue for EG's earliest talks. At an anarchist congress in Amsterdam in 1907, an attempt was made to revive the structure of the organization, but its most successful reincarnation would not take place until December 1921 with the re-constituting of the IWMA in Berlin, a conference attended by AB.

Liberal Clubs The Liberal movement adhered to freethought principles and focused especially on protesting the role of organized religion in state affairs. The national movement came together at the first Centennial Congress of Liberals, which met in Philadelphia on 4 July 1876, where members created a constitution promoting the adoption of a religious freedom amendment to the federal constitution. Its platform also included advocacy of public control of railroads, cessation of the sale or granting of public land, and legislation championing the right of workers to organize. Attempts to form a national party, however, were short lived, with internal disagreement about the proposed platform and overall doubts about the venture. The constitution called for the formation of "local auxiliary chapters of the National Liberal League," which led to the creation of many smaller organizations, including the Liberal Alliance, the Women's National Liberal Union, and many local Liberal leagues, joined together by a common adherence to the principles outlined in the group's national constitution and the concept and identification with the term "liberal." In 1884, the National Liberal League split into two factions, divided on the question of further involvement in social and political initiatives or limiting itself strictly to fighting for the secularization of the state. Following this split, one faction of the Liberal League was renamed the American Secular Union, with its own constitution and organizational structure, leaving those who favored more varied social reform activities to work in the regional and local manifestations of Liberal clubs.

The New York Liberal Club, also known as the Manhattan Liberal Club, had been founded in 1869 as an open forum for political discussion on all issues. The club sold radical publications including *Lucifer* and later, *Mother Earth*. Founding members include the Rev. Stickney Grant, socialist Charles Edward Russell, and muckraking journalist Lincoln Steffens. The New York group published *The Manhattan Liberal Club: Its Methods, Objects and Philosophy* by E. B. Foote, Jr. and Thaddeus Wakeman, an organizational history first commissioned by *The Truth Seeker,* a leading freethought paper and supporter of the Manhattan Liberal Club, for its twenty-fifth anniversary celebration in 1894. In her autobiography, EG recalls that she had attended weekly meetings of the

Manhattan Liberal Club from 1894 and that, despite her having become the subject of controversy within the club following the September 1901 McKinley assassination, she was invited to speak there on 8 October 1901.

Liberal clubs often provided EG and other radicals with a place to lecture. In Philadelphia, the Ladies' Liberal League and the Friendship Liberal League included anarchist members. The Friendship Liberal League was a freethought organization that sponsored lectures primarily on secularism, though Voltairine de Cleyre, James B. Elliott, and other members successfully influenced the group to broaden the range of its topics and include a discussion of anarchism. Charles Mowbray lectured before the club in 1894, as did John Turner in 1896. EG addressed the Friendship Liberal League in 1898 and again in 1901. The Ladies' Liberal League was an 1892 offshoot of the Friendship Liberal League of Philadelphia. Under the guidance of Voltairine de Cleyre and Natasha Notkin, it quickly outgrew its origins as a women's auxiliary and sponsored lectures on a wide variety of subjects, becoming an important forum for radical and feminist activity in Philadelphia. Prior to EG's visit, lecturers included Charles Mowbray, arrested after addressing the League in 1894, and Harry Kelly, who spoke before the group in 1896.

In New York there were a number of active Liberal organizations, including the Harlem Liberal Alliance, where both EG and Voltairine de Cleyre lectured.

National Defense Association Formed on 12 June 1878 by the physician and birth-control advocate E. B. Foote, Jr. and eight others, including Thaddeus Wakeman, a member of the Manhattan Liberal Club; Edward Chamberlain, a lawyer and free-speech advocate; Benjamin Tucker; and A. L. Rawson, a theological writer and artist, who was elected the association's first president. The National Defense Association proposed to investigate all questionable cases prosecuted under the Comstock laws, and defend those unjustly charged. The association often worked to defend its own members, many of whom were frequently targeted by Anthony Comstock for their publishing or distributing material considered obscene, providing both defense counsel and funds for bail. In 1878, the association worked vigorously to appeal the two-year imprisonment of Ezra Heywood, free-love anarchist and publisher of *The Word,* who was prosecuted under the Comstock laws for publishing *Cupid's Yokes,* a pamphlet that argued for the abolition of marriage. The association organized meetings and petitions to protest Heywood's imprisonment, which led to the decision by President Rutherford B. Hayes to pardon Heywood in December 1878. The association defended Heywood again in 1890 when he was sentenced to two years at hard labor for obscenity charges, with Chamberlain serving as his lawyer. Later, the association published *U.S. vs. Heywood: Why the Defendant Should Be Released* (New York: National Defense Association, 1891). The association also defended others targeted under the Comstock laws. In July 1882 it had defended an attack on Walt Whitman's *Leaves of Grass,* and in 1885 it defended Seward Mitchell, who was arrested by members of the Young Men's Christian Association for circulating a poem deemed obscene. In 1880, the association published Thaddeus Wakeman's *The Unanswered Argument against the Constitutionality of the So-called Comstock Postal Laws, and for the Inviolability and Free and Equal Use of the United States Mail* (New York: National Defense Association, 1880) and in 1881, the association published E. B. Foote's *Fable of the Spider and the Bees, Verified by Facts and Press and Pulpit Comments, Which Should Command The Serious Attention of Every American Citizen* (New York: National Defense Association, 1881), advertised as "Words of Warning to those who aid and abet in the suppression of Free Speech and Free Press." In 1886, the association argued for the repeal of a New York censorship statute, and published it later as a *Brief for Argument for the Repeal of Section 3893, Title XLVI, United States*

Revised Statutes (New York: National Defense Association, 1886). *Dr. Footes Health Monthly* also carried regular news and information about the National Defense Association and its work. Many of the members of the National Defense Association would help found the Free Speech League in 1902, including Edward Chamberlain, E. B. Foote, Jr., and Benjamin Tucker.

Pionire der Frayhayt (Pioneers of Liberty) The first Jewish anarchist group in the United States, the Pioneers of Liberty was founded on 9 October 1886—the day the sentences of the Haymarket anarchists were announced—by rank-and-file militants, soon joined by accomplished writers and speakers, including Saul Yanovsky, Roman Lewis, Hillel Solotaroff, Moishe Katz, J. A. Maryson, and David Edelstadt. The first activity of the Pioneers was the defense of their jailed comrades in Chicago, which corresponded with agitation and propaganda work among the Lower East Side's Jewish immigrants. The Pioneers were affiliated with the International Working People's Association. In February 1889, the Pioneers began publishing *Varhayt*, the first Yiddish-language anarchist paper in the United States, edited by Joseph Jaffa; it lasted only a few months, until June 1889. A significant feature of the Pioneers group was its secular and antireligious nature. While maintaining their Jewish identity, the Pioneers of Liberty rejected traditional religious practices and, beginning in 1889, held annual Yom Kippur balls which featured elaborate spreads of food, dancing, and singing that mocked the somber fasting of the holy day. Through these balls and other social events like lectures, picnics, and concerts, the Pioneers helped establish a revolutionary counterculture in New York similar to that which the IWPA provided in Chicago. Several workers' educational clubs were formed in the wake of the Pioneers, the most important of which was the anarchist Knights of Liberty of Philadelphia. The Pioneers in conjunction with the Knights of Liberty founded the Yiddish-language *Freie Arbeiter Stimme* in July 1890, whose first editor was Roman Lewis. Between 1889 and 1893, the Pioneers also published annually, on Yom Kippur, the paper *Tfileh Zakeh* (Pure Prayer). The Pioneers of Liberty became the model for similar clubs in other major eastern cities. AB was a member from 1888, but EG had no formal affiliation with the group.

Single Tax The single-tax philosophy is based on the idea that private land ownership is the fundamental source of social and economic injustice because landlords sap the wealth of workers and decrease capitalist investment. Single-taxers advocate eliminating the existing system of taxation in favor of a "single tax" on land intended to end land speculation, create common landownership, and abolish private property. Lifting the weight of taxation on productive industry would also increase wages. The movement achieved limited legislative success, though the theory remained popular for decades.

The single-tax movement emerged under the leadership of Henry George and Father McGlynn (who was expelled from the Catholic church for his support of single tax). Single-tax theory had taken root before George, but he specifically proposed single tax as a solution to the land question and popularized the theory with two books, *Our Land and Land Policy, National and State* (San Francisco: White and Bauer, 1871) and his landmark *Progress and Poverty* (San Francisco: W. M. Hilton, 1879). Bolton Hall, G. Frank Stephens, A. C. Pleydell, George Seldes, and others linked the theories underlying the single tax to those of anarchism. Supporters were most often middle-class intellectuals but also included Populists and wealthy individuals.

Among the first single-tax organizations were the San Francisco Single Tax Club—whose members included George and James G. Maguire—and the Free Soil Society, founded in New York in 1883, to which George also belonged. Single-tax organizations proved most successful on the local level; despite efforts, there were few national organizations, and single-taxers often preferred to work through organizations not solely focused on single-tax issues. Some influential national organizations were the Single Tax League of the United States (founded 1890) and later the American Single Tax League (1907). Among the local groups were George's Land Reform League of California (1878), the Free Soil Society (1883), various Land and Labor clubs and Henry George clubs (1880s), Anti-Poverty societies (late 1880s), and the Henry George Lecture Association (1899). The number of single-tax clubs increased exponentially nationwide between 1888 and 1889, beginning with the Manhattan Single Tax Club founded by Bolton Hall, Thomas Shearman, and Lawson Purdy; and the Chicago Single Tax Club founded by journalist Warren Worth Bailey. Among the 131 single-tax clubs formed by 1889, strongholds were in New York, Ohio, Pennsylvania, New Jersey, Indiana, California, Colorado, Illinois, Texas, and Iowa. Many of these, notably those in Philadelphia, Detroit, and Houston, arranged formal meetings with EG.

The first and largest American single-tax colony, in Fairhope, Alabama, was inhabited by colonists during 1894 and 1895; it was incorporated as a municipality in 1908, and lasted until 1954. Fairhope residents attempted gradually to shift state and local taxes from labor and capital to land, but were unable to fully implement the single-tax doctrine. A second colony, in Arden, Delaware, was founded in 1900 by the sculptor G. Frank Stephens and the architect Will Price. Among its residents were the novelist Upton Sinclair and the anarchists George Brown and Mary Hansen.

Single-tax newspapers included the *Single Tax Review*, the *Courier* (Fairhope, Ala.), *Justice* (Philadelphia), and George's *Standard* and *Economy*.

Henry George ran unsuccessfully both in the New York City mayoral campaigns in 1886 (aided by the CLU) and 1897 and in the 1888 presidential primary campaign. During his bid for the presidency, George wrote an editorial for the *Standard* in which he retracted his support for the Haymarket anarchists and affirmed the court's decision to execute them. Critics suspected that the shift was politically motivated and many, including EG and Benjamin Tucker, denounced George as a traitor.

Single-tax organizations formed in Europe in this period as well, including the Land Restoration Society in Scotland, the Land Values League in England, and the Land Reform League in Germany.

Social Democracy of America (SDA) The Social Democracy of America was organized at the final convention of the American Railway Union (ARU) on 15 June 1897. The group brought together members of the Brotherhood of the Cooperative Commonwealth (for which Eugene V. Debs had recently become an organizer), the Ruskin Colony, the Chicago Labor Union Exchange, and a number of more scientific socialists from Milwaukee, most notably Victor Berger, Jesse Cox, Seymore Stedman, Charles Martin, and Frederic Heath. The Social Democracy of America (with Debs as its unifying figurehead) was formed as a national organization of socialists that merged two strategies for achieving socialism—converting America into a cooperative commonwealth and electing their own candidates to public office. Many of its members believed that they could settle in a colony in a sparsely populated state in the West and ultimately vote in a socialist government, then repeat the process in other states. A strong tension existed between the utopian colonizers and the electoral political actionists, led by Victor Berger, who believed that socialism would be achieved through gradual, systematic reform. In an uneasy compromise, the SDA became a vehicle for socialist electoral activity, while maintaining its colonization efforts. Past leaders of the ARU were nominated to the new executive board of the SDA, including Debs, James Hogan, Sylvester Keliher, R. M. Goodwin, and William E. Burns. Each local branch of the SDA was both politically and ideologically autonomous. The SDA agreed to postpone its involvement in all elections during its first year; however, special dispensation was given to the Milwaukee SDA, which in February 1898 fielded a political ticket, netting over 2,500 votes. A special convention of Jewish activists in the Socialist Labor Party was held in New York at the end of July 1897 at which over 80 percent of the attendees voted to align themselves with the SDA, and broke with the SLP. In general, most of the SDA's energies were spent raising money for the purchase of land for its colony, an effort that was ultimately futile. The SDA, however, also maintained a policy of strong support for labor and following the United Mine Workers' strike of 1897, took an active part in an August 1897 labor conference on behalf of the miners.

The SDA included a number of anarchists among its active members. According to Frederic Heath, Johann Most in *Freiheit* advised readers to join the SDA, and other anarchist papers including *Free Society* were initially receptive to the organization. However, following the murder of nineteen striking miners in Lattimer, Pennsylvania, on 10 September 1897, Branch 2 of the Social Democracy in Chicago, led by T. Putnam Quinn, Lucy E. Parsons, and Eric B. Morton, passed a series of resolutions calling for the murder of "millionaires" in retaliation. Shortly thereafter, Branch 2 had its charter suspended by Debs and the executive council of the SDA. (Other charges against Chicago branches of the SDA included a suspicion that an excessive number of branches were formed in the city as a strategy for dominating the national convention with anarchist and colonization sympathizers.) On a national scale, the differences between the colonizers and the political actionists could not be reconciled. At the June 1898 national convention, a vote taken in favor of colonization and against electoral political action passed 53 to 37. Present at the 7 June 1898 convention in Chicago were EG, Lucy E. Parsons, T. P. Quinn, and other anarchists among the 70 delegates, representing 94 branches of the SDA. Following the vote, the socialists who favored an electoral strategy left the convention. The following day Berger, Debs (who by this time had abandoned his belief in colonization), and other political actionists formed their own Social Democratic Party. The SDA continued their convention, electing to the national committee James Hogan, W. P. Borland, R. M. Goodwin, John F. Lloyd, L. L. Hopkins, I. Frank, C. F. Willard, R. J. Hinton, and G. C. Clemens. Later that year, the SDA founded a colony on Henderson Bay in Washington state with approximately a hundred members and published the paper *The Co-operator*, but as a national organization, the SDA quickly dissoved. EG, who attended the 1898 convention, wrote in *Solidarity* shortly thereafter that she had no faith in the SDA: "I know that nothing short of the propaganda against political control and against economic dependence will satisfy." In 1901, Debs and the SDA, along with the Morris Hillquit faction of the Socialist Labor Party, would form the Socialist Party of America.

Besides their official newspaper *Social Democrat* (1897–1898), the SDA published Robert Blatchford's *Merrie England* (Chicago: SDA, 1897). In 1900 Frederic Heath's *Social Democracy Red Book: A Brief History of Socialism in America* (Terre Haute, Ind.: Debs Publishing Co., 1900) recorded the contemporary history of the movement.

Social Science "Social Science," a generic term used to describe any study of social issues, was often used by anarchists to describe the study of social issues from an anarchist perspective. Many early Social Science clubs had strong anarchist ties and influences without strictly defining themselves as anarchist clubs, and all seemed dedicated to open and free discussion. From 1898, the Social Science Club in New York offered free weekly lectures and discussions, involving many American-born anarchists. Also in 1898 a weekly Social Science Club was started in San Francisco for "free discussion on all questions." Advertisements for both clubs' meetings were placed in *Free Society*. In 1900, *Free Society* advertised another weekly Social Science Club in Chicago. An anarchist reading group called the Social Science Club was formed in Philadelphia in 1901 by Voltairine de Cleyre, modeled after a reading and study group that she and Dyer D. Lum had belonged to in the early 1890s. In an announcement in *Free Society* in 1900 she wrote: "Let us take up the work as quiet students, not as disputatious wranglers . . . let us saturate ourselves with the facts concerning anarchistic tendencies in society; then we may hope to convert others" (*Free Society*, 30 September 1900). Its first members included George Brown, Mary Hansen, Pearle McLeod, and Natasha Notkin, and met every Sunday evening. The club sponsored lectures and published Mary Hansen's *A Catechism of Anarchy* (1902). Hansen suggested in *Free Society* that although she had written the first draft, the essay was in fact a group effort of the Social Science Club; she explained that the club was not named as author because its members were not uniformly self-identified anarchists. The Philadelphia club also published de Cleyre's *Crime and Punishment* (1903) as well as the first English edition of Peter Kropotkin's *Modern Science and Anarchism* (1903), which was translated by David A. Modell, a Philadelphia physician, anarchist, and member of the city's Social Science club.

In December 1901, the revitalized New York Social Science Club sponsored a series of lectures, including "Anarchism and Communism" by Rudolf Grossman, "Discipline" by Elizabeth Ferm, and "Anarchists and Anarchism: Their Principles and their Tactics" by Alex Horr. The Boston Social Science Club lecturers included Adeline Champney, whose "The Woman Question" was later published as a pamphlet (New York: Comrade Co-Operative Press, 1903).

The many local Social Science clubs linked the phrase "social science" and anarchism, broadening the definitions for a more inclusive agenda. By 1906 the masthead created by EG for *Mother Earth* would read "Monthly Magazine devoted to Social Science and Literature," and the masthead of *Revolt* (1915–1916), a Chicago Swedish-language anarchist paper edited by Theodore Johnson, read "A Monthly Swedish Journal Devoted to Social Science and Revolutionary Thought."

Socialist Labor Party (SLP) The Socialist Labor Party, founded as the Working Men's Party of the United States in 1876 before being renamed the SLP in 1877, was the first major Marxist socialist party in the United States. It was, initially at least, almost exclusively a foreign-born and non-English-speaking organization with German-born male workers comprising the vast majority of its members and Jewish immigrants accounting for most of the rest (though native-born membership began to increase in the late 1890s). Partly as a result of this cultural and especially linguistic isolation from the rest of the country, the SLP appeared to achieve only limited political success. It was most effective in assisting various union organizing efforts, including the Central Labor Union and the United Hebrew Trades in New York City.

The party struggled in its early years. In 1880 the SLP officially supported the Greenback Labor Party, a party based on currency reform, and took an active part in drafting their national platform. Though the relationship between the two organizations was short lived, many radicals within the SLP left because of their opposition to the alliance, claiming that the Greenbacks were not socialists, while some SLP members with anarchist leanings left to form their own more revolutionary clubs. Albert Parsons and August Spies led the formation, in October 1881, of the Revolutionary

Socialistic Party (RSP), which was anarchist in spirit. But by October 1883 the RSP had essentially disappeared and many of its members reconstituted as they helped form the International Working People's Association in Pittsburgh. Fearful that the IWPA was stealing away its members and influence, prominent individuals within the SLP promptly proposed a consolidation with the IWPA—a plan rejected by the IWPA. Jewish anarchists and socialists proposed a conciliation in the form of a bipartisan paper in 1889, but after heated debate at a convention, the two camps split with few prospects for future cooperation. The SLP began to regain strength in the later half of the decade. In 1890 Daniel De Leon joined the party and soon after became its leader and editor of its paper, *The Daily People*.

The SLP focused its efforts on running candidates for public office in New York, where the bulk of its membership resided, though in the elections of 1898 the SLP received an unprecedented (for a socialist party) number of votes for its candidates nationwide. Many members of the party, however, were alienated by the growing rigidity of its Marxist orientation, especially under the perceived authoritarian style of De Leon's leadership. Others were opposed to the Socialist Trade and Labor Alliance (a trade union established by the SLP to organize unskilled workers) because many SLP members favored working within the already established American Federation of Labor. This tension resulted in a major split within the party in July 1899 when Morris Hillquit led a group that broke with De Leon and formed a Rochester faction of the SLP, which would ultimately be incorporated into the Socialist Party of America in 1901, soon eclipsing the influence of De Leon's SLP. The SLP's first English-language paper was *The Socialist* (1876), based in New York; it soon changed its name to the *Labor Standard* (1876–1877). Albert Parsons helped edit a Chicago SLP paper, also called *The Socialist* (1878–1879). The *Bulletin of the Social Labor Movement* (1879–1883) served as the party's official organ until it was replaced by the *Workmen's Advocate* (1882–1891), which was initially published in New Haven before moving to New York. In turn, it was replaced by the *Daily People* (1891–1900) and then the *Weekly People* (1900–1979). The SLP's first two German-language papers were *Arbeiterstimme* (1878) in New York and *Der Verbote* (1873–1924) in Chicago. In 1878 SLP members established the German-language daily *New Yorker Volkszeitung* (1878–1932), which became affiliated with the newly formed Socialist Party of America in 1901. In 1892 the weekly *Vorwaerts* (1892–1899) was established, and it too was considered an official party organ until the split in 1899.

Socialist League An early British anti-parliamentary socialist group, the Socialist League was formed in 1884 by departing members of the Social Democratic Federation (SDF), including William Morris, Eleanor Marx, Ernest Belfort Bax, and Edward Aveling. The founding followed a dispute with SDF leader H. H. Hyndman, who refused to resign from his leadership position following a no-confidence vote at a SDF executive meeting held on 27 December 1884. Their main grievances with Hyndman included the "nationalist and dictatorial methods he used to run the party" and complaints about his control over the party's journal, *Justice*.

Following their departure from the SDF, the League published two documents, *To Socialists* and *Manifesto of the Socialist League*. *To Socialists* was largely an exposition of the difficulties of working with Hyndman; and the manifesto, which was written by Morris and Bax, advocated "revolutionary international socialism" and explained their anti-parliamentary position. The League also published its own journal, *The Commonweal* (1885–1894). During this period, anarchist influence in the League grew. From 1890 *The Commonweal* was edited and published by David Nicoll and Charles Mowbray.

Despite the initial slow growth of the organization, by 1895 the Socialist League included over 10,700 members, after which its numbers declined; the organization disbanded in 1901 with less than 6,000 members.

In 1892 John C. Kenworthy (an English Tolstoyan and pacifist), William C. Owen, and John H. Edelmann (editor of *Solidarity*) among others founded a short-lived branch of the Socialist League in New York, which organized regular weekly meetings. Its members initially consisted of those "who were expelled from the Socialist Labor Party" (*Solidarity*, 13 August 1892, p. 4). Speakers at the meetings of the Socialist League of New York included Edelmann, Owen, Moses Oppenheimer (who also helped form the Free Speech League in 1902), Marie Louise David, and Saverio Merlino.

Socialist Party of America (SPA) At an Indianapolis convention on 29 July 1901 delegates from the Social Democratic Party and Hillquit's breakaway section of the Socialist Labor Party united to form the Socialist Party of America, led by Eugene V. Debs and Victor Berger. The party was committed to electoral politics and parliamentary socialism, and was structured in a loose party federation. Following the assassination of President William McKinley in September 1901, the SPA as well as other left-leaning groups attempted to distance themselves from anarchists and the political violence with which they were associated. However, attorney Morris Hillquit, an active leader of the SPA, defended Johann Most as an issue of free speech in the case against him for publishing the article "Murder Against Murder" in *Freiheit* on the day before McKinley was shot. Though the SPA often attacked anarchists, the two camps did communicate at times and work together, organizing formal debates, including Algie M. Simons's with Abe Isaak on "Socialism vs. Anarchism" in Chicago on 5 December 1901. Despite ideological and regional factions within it, the party grew impressively in its first years, with membership doubling by 1904. During the same time the SLP declined in strength dramatically, and the SPA became the country's foremost socialist party.

SELECTED BIBLIOGRAPHY

The Accused, the Accusers: The Famous Speeches of the Eight Chicago Anarchists in Court When Asked If They Had Anything to Say Why Sentence Should Not Be Passed upon Them. On October 7th, 8th and 9th, 1886, Chicago, Illinois. Chicago: Socialistic Publishing Society, [1886?].

Anderson, Carlotta R. *All-American Anarchist: Joseph A. Labadie and the Labor Movement.* Detroit: Wayne State University Press, 1998.

Andreucci, Franco, and Tommaso Detti. *Il movimento operaio italiano: dizionario biografico 1853–1943.* 6 vols. Rome: Editori Riuniti, 1975–1979.

Ascher, Abraham. *The Revolution of 1905: Russia in Disarray.* Stanford: Stanford University Press, 1988.

Ashbaugh, Carolyn. *Lucy Parsons, American Revolutionary.* Chicago: Charles M. Kerr Publishing, 1976.

Avrich, Paul. *The Russian Anarchists.* Princeton: Princeton University Press, 1967. Reprint, New York: W. W. Norton, 1978.

———. *An American Anarchist: The Life of Voltairine de Cleyre.* Princeton: Princeton University Press, 1978.

———. *The Modern School Movement: Anarchism and Education in the United States.* Princeton: Princeton University Press, 1980.

———. *The Haymarket Tragedy.* Princeton: Princeton University Press, 1984.

———. *Anarchist Portraits.* Princeton: Princeton University Press, 1988.

———. *Sacco and Vanzetti: The Anarchist Background.* Princeton: Princeton University Press, 1991.

———. *Anarchist Voices: An Oral History of Anarchism in America.* Princeton: Princeton University Press, 1995.

Bakunin, Michael. *God and the State.* With an introduction by Paul Avrich. New York: Dover, 1970.

———. *Statism and Anarchy.* Ed. and trans. Marshall S. Shatz. Cambridge: Cambridge University Press, 1990.

Barker, Charles Albro. *Henry George.* New York: Oxford University Press, 1955.

Becker, Heiner. "Freedom and the Freedom Press, 1886–1986." *The Raven* (London: Freedom Press), no. 1 (May 1987): 4–24.

———. "Johann Neve (1844–1896)." *The Raven* (London: Freedom Press), no. 2 (August 1987): 99–114.

———. "Johann Most." *The Raven* (London: Freedom Press), no. 4 (March 1988): 291–321.

———. "Hippolyte Havel." *itinéraire* 8 (1990): 37–38.

———. "Max Baginski." *itinéraire* 8 (1990): 28–29.

Bekken, Jon. "The First Anarchist Daily Newspaper: The *Chicagoer Arbeiter-Zeitung*." *Anarchist Studies* 3 (spring 1995): 3–23.

Bellamy, Joyce M., and John Saville. *Dictionary of Labour Biography*. 9 vols. London: Macmillan, 1972–1993.

Berkman, Alexander. *Prison Memoirs of an Anarchist*. 1912; New York: Schocken Books, 1970.

———, ed. *Letters from Russian Prisons*. New York: Albert and Charles Boni, 1925.

Bettini, Leonardo. *Bibliografia dell'anarchismo*. Vol. 1: *Periodici e numeri unici anarchici in lingua italiana*. 2 parts. Florence: CP Editrice, 1972–1976.

Beyon, John. "'Intermediate' Imperialism and the Test of Empire: Milner's 'Excentric' High Commission in South Africa." In *The South African War Reappraised*, edited by Donal Lowry. Manchester: Manchester University Press, 2000.

Bianco, René. *Un siècle de presse anarchiste d'expression française 1880–1983*. Vols. 1–3 (of 7). Marseille: CIRA, 1987.

Blackwell, Alice Stone, ed. *The Little Grandmother of the Russian Revolution: Reminiscences and Letters of Catherine Breshkovsky*. Boston: Little, Brown, 1917.

Blatt, Martin Henry. *Free Love and Anarchism: The Biography of Ezra Heywood*. Urbana: University of Illinois Press, 1989.

Bled, Jean-Paul. *Franz Joseph*. Trans. Teresa Bridgeman. Oxford: Blackwell, 1992.

Boos, Florence, ed. *William Morris's Socialist Diary*. London and New York: The Journeyman Press, 1985.

Boris, Eileen, and Nupur Chaudhuri, eds. *Voices of Women Historians: The Personal, the Political, the Professional*. Bloomington: Indiana University Press, 1999.

Briggs, L. Vernon, M.D. *The Manner of Man That Kills*. Boston: Gorham Press, 1921.

Brown, Marshall G., and Gordon Stein. *Freethought in the United States: A Descriptive Bibliography*. Westport, Conn.: Greenwood Press, 1978.

Buenker, John D., and Edward R. Kantowicz, eds. *Historical Dictionary of the Progressive Era, 1890–1920*. New York: Greenwood Press, 1988.

Buhle, Mari Jo. *Women and American Socialism, 1870–1920*. Urbana: University of Illinois Press, 1981.

Buhle, Mari Jo, Paul Buhle, and Dan Georgakas, eds. *Encyclopedia of the American Left*. New York: Cambridge University Press, 1989.

Buhle, Paul. "Anarchism and American Labor." *International Labor and Working Class History* 23 (spring 1983): 21–34.

Cahm, Caroline. *Kropotkin and the Rise of Revolutionary Anarchism 1872–1886*. New York: Cambridge University Press, 1989.

Carey, George W. "The Vessel, the Deed, and the Idea: Anarchists in Paterson, 1895–1908." *Antipode* 10 (1979): 46–58.

Carlson, Andrew R. *Anarchism in Germany, Volume I: The Early Years*. Metuchen, N.J.: The Scarecrow Press, 1972.

Carr, E. H. *Michael Bakunin*. London: Macmillan, 1937.

Chernyshevsky, Nikolai. *What Is to Be Done?* Trans. Michael R. Katz. Annotated by William G. Wagner. Ithaca, N.Y.: Cornell University Press, 1989.

Cohen, Joseph. "The Yiddish Anarchist Movement in America." Trans. Esther Dolgoff. Unpublished ms., Kate Sharpley Library.

Cole, G. D. H. *Socialist Thought: Marxism and Anarchism, 1850–1890*. Vol. 2 of *A History of Socialist Thought*. London: Macmillan, 1954.

Commons, John R., et al. *History of Labor in the United States*. 4 vols. New York: Macmillan, 1921–1935.

Confino, Michael, ed. *Anarchistes en exil: Correspondance inédite de Pierre Kropotkine à Marie Goldsmith, 1897–1917*. Paris: Institut d'études slaves, 1995.

Cooper, John Milton. *Pivotal Decades: The United States, 1900–1920*. New York: W. W. Norton, 1990.

Creagh, Ronald. *Histoire De L'Anarchisme Aux Etats-Unis D'Amerique: Les Origines: 1826–1880*. Grenoble: La Pensee Sauvage Editions, 1981.

Crosby, Ernest. H. *Tolstoy and His Message*. New York: Funk and Wagnalls, 1904.

Crotty, William J., ed. *Assassinations and the Political Order*. New York: Harper and Row, 1971.

Daniels, Doris Groshen. *Always a Sister: The Feminism of Lillian D. Wald*. New York: The Feminist Press, 1989.

David, Henry. *The History of the Haymarket Affair*. New York: Farrar and Rinehart, 1936.

de Cleyre, Voltairine. *In Defense of Emma Goldmann and the Right of Expropriation*. Philadelphia: by the author, 1894.

———. *Selected Works of Voltairine de Cleyre*. Ed. Alexander Berkman. New York: Mother Earth Publishing, 1914.

———. *The First Mayday: The Haymarket Speeches, 1895–1910*. New York: Libertarian Book Club, 1980.

De Leon, David. *The American as Anarchist*. Baltimore: Johns Hopkins University Press, 1978.

Debs, Eugene V. *Letters of Eugene V. Debs, Volume I: 1874–1912*. Ed. J. Robert Constantine. Urbana: University of Illinois Press, 1990.

Demarest, David P., Jr. *"The River Ran Red": Homestead 1892*. Pittsburgh: University of Pittsburgh Press, 1992.

Dolgoff, Sam, ed. and trans. *Bakunin on Anarchism*. Montreal: Black Rose Books, 1980.

Dombrowski, James. *The Early Days of Christian Socialism in America*. New York: Columbia University Press, 1936.

Donner, Frank J. *The Age of Surveillance: The Aims and Methods of America's Political Intelligence System*. New York: Knopf, 1980.

Drinnon, Richard. *Rebel in Paradise: A Biography of Emma Goldman*. Chicago: University of Chicago Press, 1961.

Egbert, Donald Drew. *Social Radicalism and the Arts: Western Europe*. New York: Knopf, 1970.

Egbert, Donald Drew, Stow Persons et al. *Socialism and American Life*. 2 vols. Princeton: Princeton University Press, 1952.

Eltzbacher, Paul. *Anarchism: Exponents of the Anarchist Philosophy*. Trans. Steven Byington. Ed. James J. Martin. New York: Libertarian Book Club, 1960.

Epstein, Melech. *Profiles of Eleven*. Detroit: Wayne State University Press, 1965.

Esenwein, George R. *Anarchist Ideology and the Working-Class Movement in Spain, 1868–1898*. Berkeley: University of California Press, 1989.

Falk, Candace. *Love, Anarchy, and Emma Goldman*. New York: Holt, Rinehart and Winston, 1984; rev. ed., New Brunswick, N.J.: Rutgers University Press, 1990.

———. *Emma Goldman: A Guide to Her Life and Documentary Sources*. Ed. Candace Falk, Stephen Cole, and Sally Thomas. Alexandria, Va.: Chadwyck-Healey, 1995.

Fellner, Gene, ed. *Life of an Anarchist: The Alexander Berkman Reader*. New York: Four Walls Eight Windows, 1992.

Fine, Sidney. "Anarchism and the Assassination of McKinley." *American Historical Review* 60 (July 1955): 777–99.

Fink, Gary M., ed. *Biographical Dictionary of American Labor*. Westport, Conn.: Greenwood Press, 1984.

Fishman, William J. *Jewish Radicals: From Czarist Stetl to London Ghetto*. New York: Pantheon Books, 1974.

Fleming, Marie. *The Anarchist Way in Socialism*. London and Totowa, N.J.: Croom Helm and Rowman and Littlefield, 1979.

Foner, Philip S. *History of the Labor Movement in the United States*. 9 vols. New York: International Publishers, 1947–1991.

———. *The Spanish-Cuban-American War and the Birth of American Imperialism, 1895–1902*. New York: Monthly Review Press, 1972.

Foner, Philip, ed. *The Autobiographies of the Haymarket Martyrs*. New York: Humanities Press, 1969.

Fox, Richard Wightman, and James T. Kloppenberg, eds. *A Companion to American Thought*. Cambridge, Mass.: Blackwell, 1995.

Freedom Centenary Edition: A Hundred Years: October 1886 to October 1986. London: Freedom Press, 1986.

Ginger, Ray. *The Bending Cross: A Biography of Eugene Victor Debs*. New York: Russell and Russell, 1949.

Girard, Frank, and Ben Perry. *The Socialist Labor Party, 1876–1991: A Short History*. Philadelphia: Livra Books, 1991.

Goldman, Emma. *Anarchism and Other Essays*. New York: Mother Earth Publishing, 1910. Reprint, New York: Dover Publications, 1969.

———. *Living My Life*. 2 vols. New York: Knopf, 1931. Reprint, New York: Dover Publications, 1970.

———. *Voltairine de Cleyre*. Berkeley Heights, N.J.: Oriole Press, 1932.

———. *Emma Goldman Papers: A Microfilm Edition*. Ed. Candace Falk, Ronald J. Zboray et al. 69 reels. Alexandria, Va.: Chadwyck-Healey, 1991–1993.

Goldstein, Robert Justin. *Political Repression in Modern America—From 1870 to the Present*. Cambridge: Schenkman Publishing, 1978.

Gompers, Samuel. *The Samuel Gompers Papers*. Ed. Stuart B. Kaufman, Peter J. Albert, Grace Palladino et al. 8 vols. to date. Urbana: University of Illinois Press, 1986–.

Good, Jane E., and David R. Jones. *Babushka: The Life of the Russian Revolutionary Ekaterina K. Breshko-Breshkovshaia (1844–1934)*. Newtonville, Mass.: Oriental Research Partners, 1991.

Hapgood, Hutchins. *The Spirit of the Ghetto*. New York: Funk and Wagnalls, 1902.

———. *A Victorian in the Modern World*. New York: Harcourt, Brace, 1939.

Harrison, Royden, Gillian Woolven, and Robert Duncan. *The Warwick Guide to British Labour Periodicals 1790–1970*. Atlantic Highlands, N.J., and Hassocks, Sussex, England: Humanities Press and Harvester Press, 1977.

Heath, Fred. *Social Democracy Red Book: A Brief History of Socialism in America*. Terre Haute, Ind.: Eugene V. Debs, 1900.

Heider, Ulrike. *Der arme Teufel: Robert Reitzel—Vom Vormärz zum Haymarket*. Bühl-Moos: Elster Verlag, 1986.

Higham, John. *Strangers in the Land: Patterns of American Nativism, 1860–1925*. New York: Atheneum, 1967.

Hillquit, Morris. *History of Socialism in the United States*. New York: Funk and Wagnalls, 1903.

———. *Loose Leaves from a Busy Life*. New York: Macmillan, 1934.

Hoerder, Dirk, ed. *Plutokraten und Sozialisten: Berichte deutscher Diplomaten und Agenten über die amerikanische Arbeiterbewegung 1878–1917*. München: K. G. Saur, 1981.

Hug, Heinz. *Peter Kropotkin (1842–1921): Bibliographie*. Grafenau: Edition Anares im Trotzdem-Verlag, 1994.

Hulse, James W. *Revolutionists in London: A Study of Five Unorthodox Socialists*. Oxford: Clarendon Press, 1970.

James, Edward T., Janet Wilson James, and Paul S. Boyer, eds. *Notable American Women 1607–1950: A Biographical Dictionary*. 3 vols. Cambridge: The Belknap Press of Harvard University Press, 1971.

Jensen, Richard Bach. *Liberty and Order: The Theory and Practice of Italian Public Security Policy, 1848 to the Crisis of the 1890's*. New York: Garland, 1991.

Johnpoll, Bernard K., and Harvey Klehr, eds. *Biographical Dictionary of the American Left*. New York: Greenwood Press, 1986.

Johnson, Allen, Dumas Malone, et al., eds. *Dictionary of American Biography*. 20 vols. 10 supplements. New York: Charles Scribner's Sons, 1928–.

Jones, Jacqueline. *A Social History of the Laboring Classes. From Colonial Times to the Present*. Malden, Mass.: Blackwell, 1999.

Josephson, Harold, et al., eds. *Biographical Dictionary of Modern Peace Leaders*. Westport, Conn.: Greenwood Press, 1985.

Kelly, Harry. "Roll Back the Years: Odyssey of a Libertarian." Ed. John Nicholas Beffel. Unpublished autobiography, Tamiment Institute Library.

Keil, Hartmut, ed. *German Workers' Culture in the United States 1850–1920*. Washington, D.C.: Smithsonian Institution Press, 1988.

Keil, Hartmut, and John B. Jentz, eds. *German Workers in Industrial Chicago, 1850–1910: A Comparative Perspective*. DeKalb: Northern Illinois University Press, 1983.

Kipnis, Ira. *The American Socialist Movement, 1897–1912*. New York: Columbia University Press, 1952.

Kohn, Stephen M. *American Political Prisoners: Prosecutions Under the Espionage and Sedition Acts*. Westport, Conn.: Praeger, 1994.

Krause, Paul. *The Battle for Homestead, 1880–1892: Politics, Culture, and Steel*. Pittsburgh: University of Pittsburgh Press, 1992.

Kroeger, Brooke. *Nellie Bly*. New York: Times Books, 1994.

Kropotkin, Peter. *Kropotkin's Revolutionary Pamphlets*. Ed. Roger Baldwin. Reprint, New York: Dover Publications, 1970.

———. *Memoirs of a Revolutionist*. New York: Dover Publications, 1971.

———. *Peter Kropotkin: Fugitive Writings*. Ed. George Woodcock. Montreal: Black Rose Books, 1993.

———. *The Conquest of Bread*. Cambridge: Cambridge University Press, 1995.

Levin, Nora. *While Messiah Tarried: Jewish Socialist Movements, 1871–1917*. New York: Schocken Books, 1977.

LeWarne, Charles Pierce. *Utopias on Puget Sound, 1885–1915*. Seattle: University of Washington Press, 1975.

Linderman, Gerald. *The Mirror of War: American Society and the Spanish-American War.* Ann Arbor: University of Michigan Press, 1974.

Linse, Ulrich. *Organisierter Anarchismus im deutschen Kaiserreich von 1871.* Berlin: Duncker and Humblot, 1969.

Macdonald, George E. *Fifty Years of Freethought: Story of The Truth Seeker From 1875.* 2 vols. New York: The Truth Seeker Company, 1931.

Mainiero, Lina, ed. *American Women Writers: A Critical Reference Guide from Colonial Times to the Present.* 5 vols. New York: Frederick Ungar, 1979–1994.

Maitron, Jean, ed. *Dictionnaire biographique du mouvement ouvrier français.* 3éme partie, vols. 10–15: 1871–1914. Paris: Les Editions Ouvrières, 1973–1977.

———. *Le mouvement anarchiste en France.* 2 vols. Paris: François Maspero, 1975.

Marsh, Margaret S. "The Anarchist-Feminist Response to the 'Woman Question' in Late Nineteenth-Century America." *American Quarterly* 30 (Autumn 1978): 533–47.

———. *Anarchist Women, 1870–1920.* Philadelphia: Temple University Press, 1981.

Martin, James J. *Men Against the State.* DeKalb, Ill.: Adrian Allen Associates, 1953.

Masini, Pier Carlo. *Storia degli anarchici italiani nell'epoca degli attentati.* Milan: Rizzoli Editore, 1981.

McKerns, Joseph P., ed. *Biographical Dictionary of American Journalism.* New York: Greenwood Press, 1989.

McKinley, Blaine. "'The Quagmires of Necessity': American Anarchists and Dilemmas of Vocation." *American Quarterly* 34 (winter 1982): 503–23.

Miller, Martin A. *Kropotkin.* Chicago: University of Chicago Press, 1976.

Morn, Frank. *"The Eye That Never Sleeps": A History of the Pinkerton National Detective Agency.* Bloomington: Indiana University Press, 1982.

Morton, Marian J. *Emma Goldman and the American Left: "Nowhere at Home."* New York: Twayne Publishers, 1992.

Most, Johann. *Marxereien, Eseleien und dersanfte Heinrich: Artikel aus der "Freiheit."* Ed. Heiner M. Becker. Wetzlar: Büchse der Pandora, 1985.

———. *Revolutionäre Kreigswissenschaft.* New York: Verlag der Internetionalen Zeitungs-Verein, 1885.

Mott, Frank Luther. *American Journalism: A History of Newspapers in the United States Through 250 Years, 1690 to 1940.* New York: Macmillan, 1941.

Nelson, Bruce C. *Beyond the Martyrs: A Social History of Chicago's Anarchists, 1870–1900.* New Brunswick, N.J.: Rutgers University Press, 1988.

Nettlau, Max. *Bibliographie de l'anarchie.* Brussels and Paris: Les Temps Nouveaux, 1897.

———. *Errico Malatesta: la vida de un anarquista.* Trans. Diego Abad de Santillán. Buenos Aires: Editorial La Protesta, 1923.

———. *Eliseo Reclus: La vida de un sabio justo y rebelde.* 2 vols. Barcelona: Publicaciones de la Revista Blanca, n.d. [1929–1930].

———. *Erinnerungen und Eindrücke.* Manuscript, 1940–1944. Vol. 8. Amsterdam: International Institute of Social History, Nettlau Archive.

———. "Biographical Sketch of Bakunin." In *The Political Philosophy of Bakunin: Scientific Anarchism,* edited by Gregori Maximov. Glencoe: The Free Press, 1953.

———. *Der Vorfrühling der Anarchie. Ihre historische Entwicklung von den Anfängen bis zum Jahre 1864.* (1925) Münster: Bibliothek Thélème, 1993.

———. *Der Anarchismus von Proudhon zu Kropotkin. Seine historische Entwicklung in den Jahren 1859–1880.* (1927) Münster: Bibliothek Thélème, 1993.

———. *Anarchisten und Sozialrevolutionäre. Die historische Entwicklung des Anarchismus in den Jahren 1880–1886.* (1931) Münster: Bibliothek Thélème, 1996.

———. *A Short History of Anarchism.* Ed. Heiner M. Becker. Trans. Ida Pilat Isca. London: Freedom Press, 1996.

———. *Die erste Blütezeit der Anarchie: 1886–1894.* (1981) Münster: Bibliothek Thélème, 1999.

———. *Anarchisten und Syndikalisten: Part 1.* (1984) Münster: Bibliothek Thélème, 1999.

Novak, Michael. *The Guns of Lattimer: The True Story of a Massacre and a Trial, August 1897–March 1898.* New York: Basic Books, 1978.

Oliver, Hermia. *The International Anarchist Movement in Late Victorian London.* London: Croom Helm, 1983.

Pakenham, Thomas. *The Boer War.* London: Weidenfeld and Nicolson, 1979.

Paperno, Irina. *Chernyshevsky and the Age of Realism: A Study in the Semantics of Behavior.* Stanford: Stanford University Press, 1988.

Parsons, Lucy. *Life of Albert Parsons.* 2nd ed. Chicago: Lucy E. Parsons, 1903.

Pataud, Émile, and Émile Pouget. *How We Shall Bring About the Revolution: Syndicalism and the Cooperative Commonwealth.* With an introduction by G. Brown. London: Pluto Press, 1990.

Patsouras, Louis. *Jean Grave and the Anarchist Tradition in France.* Middletown, N.J.: Caslon, 1995.

Pernicone, Nunzio. *Italian Anarchism, 1864–1892.* Princeton: Princeton University Press, 1993.

Peukert, Josef. *Erinnerungen eines Proletariers aus der revolutionären Arbeiterbewegung.* Ed. Gustav Landauer. Berlin: Verlag des Sozialistischen Bundes, 1913.

Pomper, Philip. *Peter Lavrov and the Russian Revolutionary Movement.* Chicago: University of Chicago Press, 1972.

Poore, Carol J. *German-American Socialist Literature, 1865–1900.* Berne: Peter Lang Publishers, 1982.

Post, Louis F. *What Is Single Tax?* New York: Vanguard Press, 1926.

Pozzetta, George E., ed. *Immigrant Radicals: The View from the Left.* New York: Garland Publishing, 1991.

Pratt, Norma Fain. *Morris Hillquit: A Political History of an American Jewish Socialist.* Westport, Conn.: Greenwood Press, 1979.

Quail, John. *The Slow Burning Fuse: The Lost History of the British Anarchists.* London: Granada Publishing, 1978.

Rabban, David M. *Free Speech in Its Forgotten Years.* New York: Cambridge University Press, 1997.

Reichert, William O. *Partisans of Freedom: A Study in American Anarchism.* Bowling Green, Ohio: Bowling Green University Popular Press, 1976.

Rich, Norman. *The Age of Nationalism and Reform, 1850–1890.* 2nd ed. New York: W. W. Norton, 1970.

Richards, Vernon, ed. *Malatesta.* London: Freedom Press, 1965.

Rischin, Moses. *The Promised City: New York's Jews, 1870–1914.* Cambridge: Harvard University Press, 1962.

Roberts, Nancy L. *American Peace Writers, Editors, and Periodicals: A Dictionary.* New York: Greenwood Press, 1991.

Rocker, Rudolf. *Pioneers of American Freedom.* Los Angeles: Rocker Publications Committee, 1949.

———. *The London Years.* Trans. Joseph Leftwich. London: Robert Anscombe, 1956.

———. *Anarcho-Syndicalism.* London: Pluto Press, 1989.

————. *Johann Most. Das Leben eines Rebellen*. 1924–1925. Reprint, Berlin/Köln: Libertad Verlag, 1994.

Roediger, David, and Franklin Rosemont, eds. *Haymarket Scrapbook*. Chicago: Charles H. Kerr Publishing, 1986.

Salvatore, Nick. *Eugene V. Debs: Citizen and Socialist*. Urbana: University of Illinois Press, 1982.

Sanders, Ronald. *The Downtown Jews: Portraits of an Immigrant Generation*. 1969. Reprint, New York: Dover, Publications, 1987.

Schneider, Dorothee. *Trade Unions and Community: The German Working Class in New York City, 1870–1900*. Urbana: University of Illinois Press, 1994.

Schuster, Eunice Minette. *Native American Anarchism: A Study of Left-Wing American Individualism*. Smith College Studies in History, vol. 17. New York: AMS Press, 1970.

Schwab, Arnold T. *James Gibbons Huneker: Critic of the Seven Arts*. Stanford: Stanford University Press, 1963.

Scranton, Philip B., ed. *Silk City: Studies on the Paterson Silk Industry, 1860–1940*. Newark: New Jersey Historical Society, 1985.

Sears, Hal D. *The Sex Radicals: Free Love in High Victorian America*. Lawrence: Regents Press of Kansas, 1977.

Shannon, David A. *The Socialist Party of America: A History*. New York: Macmillan, 1955.

Shipley, Stan. *Club Life and Socialism in Mid-Victorian London*. History Workshop Pamphlet 5, Ruskin College, Oxford University, 1972.

Shore, Elliott, Ken Fones-Wolf, and James P. Danky, eds. *The German-American Radical Press: The Shaping of a Left Political Culture, 1850–1940*. Urbana: University of Illinois Press, 1992.

Shpayer, Haia. "British Anarchism 1881–1914: Reality and Appearance." Ph.D. diss., University of London, 1981.

Sicherman, Barbara, and Carol Hurd Green, eds. *Notable American Women: The Modern Period*. Cambridge: The Belknap Press of Harvard University Press, 1980.

Smith, Iain R. "A Century of Controversy over Origins." In *The South African War Reappraised*, edited by Donal Lowry. Manchester: Manchester University Press, 2000.

Sonn, Richard D. *Anarchism and Cultural Politics in Fin de Siècle France*. Lincoln: University of Nebraska Press, 1989.

Sorge, Friedrich A. *Friedrich A. Sorge's Labor Movement in the United States: A History of the American Working Class from 1890 to 1896*. Trans. Kai Schoenhals. New York: Greenwood Press, 1987.

Stepniak [Boris Kravchinskii]. *Underground Russia*. New York: John W. Lovell, 1883.

Stern, Madeleine B. *Heads and Headlines: The Phrenological Fowlers*. Norman: University of Oklahoma Press, 1971.

Tárrida del Marmol, Fernando. *Les Inquisiteurs d'Espagne: Montjuich, Cuba, Philippines*. Paris: Stock, 1897.

Tcherikower, Elias, ed. *The Early Jewish Labor Movement in the United States*. Trans. and rev. Aaron Antonovsky. New York: Yivo Institute for Jewish Research, 1961.

Thompson, Arthur. "The Reception of Russian Revolutionary Leaders in America, 1904–1906." *American Quarterly*, vol. 18, no. 3 (autumn 1966), 452–76.

Trachtenberg, Alan. *The Incorporation of America: Culture and Society in the Gilded Age*. New York: Hill and Wang, 1982.

Trask, David F. *The War with Spain in 1898*. New York: Macmillan, 1981.

Trautmann, Frederic. *The Voice of Terror: A Biography of Johann Most*. Westport, Conn.: Greenwood Press, 1980.

Travis, Frederick F. *George Kennan and the American-Russian Relationship, 1865–1924*. Athens: Ohio University Press, 1990.

Van der Linden, Marcel, and Wayne Thorpe, eds. *Revolutionary Syndicalism*. Aldershot: Scholar Press, 1990.

Varias, Alexander. *Paris and the Anarchists: Aesthetes and Subversives During the Fin de Siècle*. New York: St. Martin's Press, 1996.

Venturi, Franco. *Roots of Revolution: A History of the Populist and Socialist Movements in Nineteenth Century Russia*. Trans. Francis Haskell. New York: Universal Library, 1966.

Warren, Sidney. *American Freethought, 1860–1914*. New York: Columbia University Press, 1943.

Wexler, Alice. *Emma Goldman: An Intimate Life*. New York: Pantheon Books, 1984.

Whitman, Alden, ed. *American Reformers: An H. W. Wilson Biographical Dictionary*. New York: H. W. Wilson, 1985.

Wieczynski, Joseph L., ed. *The Modern Encyclopedia of Russian and Soviet History*. Gulf Breeze, Fla.: Academic International Press, 1976–1996.

Wilson, Nelly. *Bernard-Lazare: Antisemitism and the Problem of Jewish Identity in Late Nineteenth-century France*. New York: Cambridge University Press, 1978.

Woodcock, George. *Anarchism: A History of Libertarian Ideas and Movements*. Cleveland: Meridian Books, 1962.

———. *Anarchism and Anarchists*. Kingston, Ontario: Quarry Press, 1992.

Woodcock, George, and Ivan Avakumovi. *The Anarchist Prince: A Biographical Study of Peter Kropotkin*. London: T. V. Boardman, 1950.

Zucker, Adolf Eduard. *Robert Reitzel*. Philadelphia: Americana Germanica Press, 1917.

EMMA'S LIST

The Emma Goldman Papers Project thanks our sustaining sponsors (see p. vii) and the following additional donors, who have led Emma's List, for their vote of confidence and material support over the years.

IN REMEMBRANCE

LYDIA AND GEORGE ARONOWITZ, loved for their wit and passion. May their goodness and sparkle—like Emma's—live on. Remembered by Merrill, Andrew, Todd, and Adam Stone, and by Candace Falk.

LEONARD BASKIN is remembered by Lisa Baskin.

THOMAS H. BEADLING is remembered by Patricia A. Thomas.

SARAH BELLUSH, who loved and taught him to admire Emma Goldman, is remembered by her son, Bernard Bellush.

WARREN K. BILLINGS, dignified friend and colleague of Alexander Berkman, sentenced to life imprisonment in association with the 1916 Preparedness Day bombing, is remembered by his niece, Marguerite Joseph.

BEN AND IDA CAPES, Emma's dear friends and comrades, are remembered by David and Judith Capes, their grandchildren; by Bonnie Capes Tabatznik, their daughter; and by Susan Chasson and Albert Chasson, their niece and nephew.

ALICE CHECKOVITZ MAHONEY is remembered by her niece, Susan Wladaver-Morgan.

STEFANIE CHECKOVITZ WLADAVER (1920–2001) is remembered by her daughter, Susan Wladaver-Morgan.

MARLENE CAROL CLEMENS is remembered by her parents, Mary and the late Alan Dietch.

SARAH T. CROME, who helped found the Emma Goldman Papers, is remembered by Andrea Sohn, her niece; Esther and the late Eugene Revitch, her sister and brother-in-law; and by her friends Victoria Brady, Dale Freeman, Ken Kann, Stephanie Pass, Lyn Reese, and Judy Shattuck, and by her ever grateful colleague and friend Candace Falk.

SOPHIE AND JOE DESSER, Emma's dear friends and comrades, are remembered by their daughter, Mildred Desser Grobstein.

CHANELE (ANNA) SCHILHAUS DIAMOND, Emma Goldman's seamstress, is remembered by her son, David Diamond.

THE FERRER COLONY AND MODERN SCHOOL OF STELTON, NEW JERSEY, are remembered by Sally Brown.

EMMA GOLDMAN was remembered by the late Art Bortolotti with gratitude for fighting "her last battle with the authorities, a battle that lasted until her last breath," on his behalf.

EMMA GOLDMAN is also remembered by David Diamond with gratitude for encouraging him in his youth to pursue his love of music and the violin and "Kling in de ganze Velt" (Play for the entire world).

ESTHER LADDON, who gave Emma a home in Canada during her exile, is remembered by her daughter, Ora Laddon Robbins.

SARAH LAZAR is remembered by Shirley Van Bourg.

AUNT FAYE LEVY—a great lady!—is remembered by Merrill Stone, by her nephew Neil Solomon and family, and by her niece Candace Falk, whom she counseled over the years to "let Emma Goldman rest in peace, already."

RELLA LOSSY, who captured Emma's spirit in her plays, is remembered by Frank T. Lossy.

HENRY MAYER, friend and fellow biographer, is remembered by Candace Falk.

JANE MAVERICK WELSH is remembered by Beá Welsh Weicker.

JESSICA MITFORD AND BOB TREUHAFT are remembered by Peter Stansky.

CURTIS W. REESE, who delivered Emma's last eulogy at her gravesite, is remembered by his son, Curtis W. Reese, Jr.

BEN REITMAN, Emma's road manager and lover, is remembered by his daughter, Mecca Reitman Carpenter.

ZILITH ROSEN TURITZ is remembered by her niece, Nancy Chodorow.

ARTHUR LEONARD ROSS, Emma's lawyer and friend, is remembered by his sons, Ralph and Edgar Ross.

IRMA SHERMAN, aunt, soul-mate, and respected member of Emma's List, is remembered by her daughter, Valerie Broad, and by her niece Candace Falk.

JENNY SIDNEY, comrade and mother, is remembered by Barry and Paul Pateman.

JULIE VAN BOURG is remembered by her mother, Shirley Van Bourg.

KATE WOLFSON is remembered by her daughter, Irene Schneiderman.

IN HONOR OF THOSE WHO CONTINUE TO KEEP EMMA'S SPIRIT ALIVE

LOIS BLUM FEINBLATT is honored by the Malino family.

JANE M. BOUVIER is honored by her daughter, Virginia Bouvier.

DAVID CAPLAN is honored by his father, Michael Caplan.

ELEANOR ENGSTRAND AND MARGE FRANTZ are honored by Carol Jean and Edward F. Newman.

JANE FALK is honored by Neil Goteiner and N. Joseph, by Merrill, Andy, Todd, and Adam Stone, and by her sister, Candace, who all wish her continued good health and happiness.

JOSEPH FRIEDMAN is honored by his son, Larry Friedman.

DOROTHY R. HEALEY is honored by Carol Jean and Edward F. Newman.

CAROL LASSER is honored by Cathy Kornblith.

ANTONIA, who embodies Emma's spirit, is honored by her father, David Madson.

KIERSTEN AMANDA ROESEMANN is honored by her father and mother, Douglas N. Roesemann and Marla Erbin-Roesemann.

EMMA SAMELSON JONES'S graduation is honored by Renee Samelson.

VERA WEISS is honored by Barbara Bloch.

JEAN WILKINSON is honored by her friend Lyn Reese.

ARI WOHLFEILER is honored by Dan Wohlfeiler.

EMMA WOLF is honored by her parents, Louis Wolf and Dolores Newman.

JOSEPH ZELNICK is honored by Carl N. Degler.

INSTITUTIONAL DONORS

American Council for Learned Societies
The William Bingham Foundation
California Council for the Humanities
Chadwyck-Healey, Inc.
The Commonwealth Fund
The Ford Foundation
George Gund Foundation
Hunt Alternatives Fund
Lucius W. Littauer Foundation
The Los Angeles Educational Partnership
Milken Family Foundation
The Rockefeller Foundation
L. J. Skaggs and Mary C. Skaggs Foundation
The Streisand Foundation
Sun Microsystems
The Vanguard Foundation

Earl Warren Chapter of the American Civil
   Liberties Union
H. W. Wilson Foundation

INDIVIDUAL DONORS

Martha Ackelsberg
Janet Adelman
Harriet Alonso
Lisa D. Alvarez and Andrew Tonkovich
Ron Anastasia and Kim Anway-Anastasia
Elizabeth Anderson and the late Henry Mayer
Joyce Appleby

Bailey Coy Books
Jonathan Becker
Marlou Belyea
Richard Berger
Estelle and Howard Bern
Anne Bernstein and Conn Hallinan
Elizabeth Berry
Marsha and Stephen Berzon
Barbara and Arthur Bloch
Lynn A. Bonfield
Paul Bluestone and Susan Sanvidge
Anne Borchardt
Danice Bordett and William Schechner
Eileen Boris
Susan and Jeffrey Brand
Marion Brenner and Robert Shimshak
Ramsay Breslin
Sunny and Philip Brodsky
Robert Browning and Linda Maio
June and the late Abe Brumer
Paul Bundy
Julianne Burton-Carvajal

Michael Caplan
Mortimer Caplin
Candace M. Carroll
Clayborne and Susan Carson
JoAnn Castagna
Joseph and Susan Cerny
Yvette Chalom and Paul Fogel
Robert Cherny
Leah and Marvin Chodorow
Nancy Chodorow
Noam Chomsky
Harry Chotiner
Joy Christenberry
Pat Cody
Natalie Cohen

Elizabeth Colton
Margaret Corrigan and Larry Gibbs
Maureen Corrigan and Richard J. Yeselson
Nancy Cott
Carole M. Counihan
Victoria Crane and Matthew Engle
Matthew, Linda, and Ellen Creager

Carol DeBoer-Langworthy
Carl N. Degler
Anna DeLeon
Michael Denneny, Andrew Miller, Robert Weil
   (St. Martin's Press)
Cleo Deras and Carlos Hernandez
John P. Diggens
Jill and Martin Dodd
Martin Duberman
Robert Dunn

Samuel and Hope Efron
Diane Ehrensaft and Jim Hawley
Robin Einhorn
Laurel and Eugene Eisner
Robert Elias and Jennifer Turpin
Roz Elms and Donald Sutherland
Matthew and Victoria Engle
Shelly Errington

Jane Fajans and Terry Turner
Jane Falk
Elaine Feingold and Randall M. Shaw
Laura Fenster and Jon Rosenberg
Emily Filloy and David Weintraub
Barbara and Robert Fishman
Bruce Fodiman
Nancy Fox
B. Franklin and the late Joan F. Kahn
Marge Frantz and Eleanor Engstrand
Estelle Freedman
Mark Friedman and Marjorie Solomon
   Friedman
William Lee Frost
Lisa Fruchtman and Norman Postone

Judith Gardiner
Donald Gibson
Christina and John Gillis
Susan Glenn and James Gregory
Neil Goldberg and Hagit Cohen
Sam and Maria Goldberger
Rick Goldsmith and Susanna Tadlock
Nancy Gordon (Koret Gallery, Palo Alto, Calif.)
Nancy Gordon and Ken Kirsch

Richard Gordon and Meredith Miller
Joanne Grant and Victor Rabinowitz
Edward de Grazia
Marty Nesselbush Green
Janet Greenberg
Denyse Gross and Kenneth Morrison
Susan Groves and Eric Anderson
Mary Gutzi
Roland Guyotte

Alice Hall and Michael Smith
Robert Hamburger
Larry Hannant
Nina Hartley
Stuart Hellman
Frederick Hertz and Randolph Langenbach
Ronald Hill
Robert Hillman and Olivia Crawford
Sally Hindman
Adrienne Hirt and Jeff Rodman
Barbara Hoffer
Patricia Holland
Lorraine and Victor Honig

Elizabeth Jameson
Susan Jarratt
Thomas E. Jeffrey
Erica Jong and Ken Burrows

Jane Kahn
Kathy Kahn
Peggy Kahn
Roy Kahn
Susan Kaplan
Michael Katz
Bruce Kayton
Frances Richardson Keller
Loretta Kensinger
Richard E. and Linda K. Kerber
John Kessell
Alice Kessler-Harris
Kristina Kiehl and Bob Friedman
Kathleen King
Barbara Kingsolver and Stephen Hopp
Heather and Scott Kleiner
Cathy Kornblith (The People's Eye)
Julia Kraut
Jay Kugelman

Arthur Charles Leahy and Mary Kathryn Leahy
Eleanore Lee and Ronald Elson
Jesse Lemisch and Naomi Weisstein
Gerda Lerner

Cornelia and Lawrence Levine
Lynda and Carl Levinson (Max and Anna Levinson Foundation)
Rita Lewis and family
Rae and William Lisker
Kristin Luker

Nancy MacKay
Maeva Marcus
Mary Ann Mason
Antje Mattheus and David Kairys
Mary Lynn McCree Bryan
Maggie McFadden
Jennifer Mei and Han Min Liu
Diane Middlebrook and Carl Gerassi
Sally Miller and Peg Keranen
Sigrid Miller and Robert Pollin
the late Jessica Mitford and the late Robert Treuhaft
Dominic Montagu

Victor Navasky
Marty Nesselbush Green
the late Morris Novik

Kaoru Ohara

Nell Painter
Keith Park
Pamela Parker
Thomas Peabody
John Peck
Agnes F. Peterson
Janice Plotkin
Linda Post and Eugene Rosow
Carl Prince and family
Coby Prins
the late Adele Proom

Rabbi Ferenc Raj and Paula Wolk
Harold Ramis
Alan Ramo
Joan, Robert, and Heather Reese
Victor Roberge
Renée Robin and Scott McCreary
David Roediger and Jean Allman
Shelly and Coleman Romalis
Joanna Rose
Peter Rose and Daniel Burton Rose
Ruth Rosen
Carolyn Cavalier Rosenberg
Erica Rosenfeld and James Wilson
Florence Rosenstock and James Van Luik

Roy Rosenzweig
Matthew Ross and Gloria Lawrence
Sheila Rowbotham
Lillian and Hank Rubin
Lucio and Marcia Ruotolo

Prentice and Paul Sack
Harriet Sage
Samuel Salkin and Frankie Whitman
Renee Samelson
Ethel Sanjines
Susan Sarandon and Tim Robbins
Camille Saviola
Virginia Scardigli
Lois Schiffer
Danny Scher
Lillian Schlissel
Ann and Richard Schmidt, Jr.
Irene Schneiderman
Herb Schreier
Donna Schulman
Marilyn and Harvey Schwartz
Jules and the late Helen Seitz
Martin Selig
Mary Selkirk
Juliet Shaffer
Susan Shaw and Thomas W. Crane
Richard Sheldon
Julius and the late Irma Sherman
Hannah Shostack
Alix Kates Shulman
Barbara Sicherman
Harriet F. and John Simon
Kitty Sklar and Thomas Dublin
Arlene and Jerome Skolnick
Andrea Sohn
Mark Solomon
Naomi Solomon
Nancy Caldwell Sorel and Ed Sorel
Claire Sotnick
Daniel Soyer
Judith Stacey
Christine Stansell
Peter Stansky
Randolph and Frances Starn
Gloria Steinem
Pessl Beckler Semel Stern
Philip M. Stern
Jean Stone
Susan Strasser

Evelyn and Norman Tabachnick
Susanna Tadlock and Rick Goldsmith

G. Thomas Tanselle
Reesa Tansey
Patricia Anne Thomas
Sally Thomas
Irene Tinker
Barbara Tischler
William M. Tuttle, Jr.
Elaine Tyler and Lary May

Laurel and Gael Ulrich
Carol Unger

Patricia Valva
Katrina Van Heuvel
Jill and Rudolph Vecoli

Nora Wagner
Judith and Daniel Walkowitz
Deborah and Dan Waterman
Brenda Webster and Ira Lapidus
Bonnie Lynn Weimer
Lila Weinberg
Lynn Weiner and Thomas Moher
Susan Wengraf
Marcia Whitebook
Blanche Wiesen Cook
the late Norma Wikler
John Alexander Williams
Beth Wilson
Vickie Wilson (Alfred A. Knopf)
Barbara Winslow
S. I. Wisenberg
Ann Wrixon
the late Wu Ke Kang

Laura X

Susumu Yamaizumi

Fay Zadeh
Rhonda Zangwill
Naomi Zauderer
Martin Zelig
Margaret Zierdt
Roslyn and Howard Zinn
Joan Zoloth
Carol Zullman and Eric Taub

And special thanks to our many donors who chose to remain anonymous, and the literally thousands of others whose contributions, whether large or small, have been absolutely critical to the survival of the Emma Goldman Papers Project.

We at the Emma Goldman Papers honor the memory of Michael Rogin, member of our advisory board, whose appreciation dated back to his great aunt Rosie Rogin, who in 1906 was arrested with Emma Goldman; Alice Hamburg, a founder of Women for Peace; Helen Seitz, the lifelong activist who grew up in anarchist colonies and remembered sitting on Emma's lap as a child; Bob Treuhaft, labor lawyer and friend; Marcus Cohn, attorney and educator devoted to Emma and to the concept of freedom; Norma Wikler, who longed for the guidance of an Emma; and several sweet family members of the Goldman Papers staff, including Abe Brumer, Lydia Aronowitz, Faye Levy, Irma Sherman, and Ruth and Merlin Bowen, all of whom supported our work in their own quiet way; and we honor especially the memory of Ian Ballantine, Emma's nephew, editor, and co-literary heir.

ACKNOWLEDGMENTS

Collaboration is the core component of the Emma Goldman Papers Project. For over twenty years, many hands have created what has become a secular cathedral to the remembrance of things past and almost forgotten. Every effort, large and small, built the structure, added complexity and nuance to the work, and confirmed the importance of situating the advocates of free expression into the historical record as a lasting tribute to courageous spirits.

Emma Goldman's amazing foresight and daring, her insistence that both political and personal freedom are realizable—no matter how difficult the struggle or intangible the outcome along the way—remains an inspiration. The work of preserving and publishing the written artifacts of Goldman's active life has elicited an almost unmatched outpouring of generosity and enthusiasm from those whose determination and vision resonate with Goldman's essential daring.

Perhaps it is not surprising that the controversial side of Goldman—the anarchist deported from the United States, the woman feared for her challenge to organized government—also provoked storm clouds around the historical research for this documentary edition. We have weathered lapses in financial support and editorial continuity. Yet, always an individual or institution has risen to the occasion, made an extraordinary effort on our behalf, and the project, like Emma Goldman herself, has survived. That her papers and these volumes, so full of scholarship and insight into a world whose tracings are rare and whose importance has often been obscured by political prejudice, are now an indelible part of the historical record is the shared accomplishment of literally hundreds of people over the years.

Many of our extended family of friends and colleagues can assert with great authority and confidence that their individual efforts helped bring the project to publication and made all the difference. Every bit of research over the last twenty-two years added to the subtlety of our work—small details gradually linked to present a complex picture of Goldman's world. Others supported us by creating a foundation for our efforts, a frame for public history and meticulous research, providing archival sources and funding resources, cushioning us with kindness. In the mountain of words and ideas that comprise our work, none can express fully the depth of our appreciation for the devotion and selflessness showered upon us, sanctioning our perseverance, in spite of all odds, to preserve the written legacy of Emma Goldman.

It would be impossible to name all those associated with the Emma Goldman Papers Project over the years, whose remarkable solidarity and support have sustained us. And I, who have facilitated the Emma Goldman Papers Project from the beginning, have been privileged to spend so much of my life poring through Emma Goldman's papers in the company of those, past and present, drawn to the many facets of her exalted and complex vision.

It is a great pleasure to thank the extraordinary people and institutions without which publication of the selected edition of the Emma Goldman's papers would have been impossible.

First and foremost, a great tribute is due to the Project's editorial staff, whose tireless and creative work gave life to a time and a movement otherwise hidden from history. Barry Pateman, a scholar and archivist of anarchist sources, in his three years with the Project has transformed the raw coal of the almost twenty years of archival research into diamonds of scholarship. His association with the Emma Goldman Papers, which began in the Project's early years of searching through archives and private collections in England, came full circle with his arrival in California in 1999—when he became "the fastest study in the West." As a colleague—every step of the way from daily administrative tasks to intellectual engagement in the writing of the introductory essays—and as an enthusiastic mentor to students and aficionado of anarchist history, Barry Pateman's efforts are unmatched. It is largely to his herculean efforts that we owe the timely and accurate recording and contextualization of Goldman's American years.

The editorial group that has shepherded to completion the volumes covering Goldman's American years also stands out in the history of the Emma Goldman Papers Project as the very best. Jessica Moran came to the Project when she was a student at the University of California, Berkeley, and over time has assumed a critical role in coordinating, maintaining, and researching many crucial components of the volumes—including the biographical and organizational directories—and managing a plethora of incredible detail with amazing grace. In the process of her work at the Goldman Papers she found her passion for the archival world, which will, no doubt, benefit from her energy and insight.

As the work of the Emma Goldman Papers Project evolved, from the earliest days of searching for Goldman's correspondence, writings, newspaper reportage, legal and government surveillance reports, and photographic images for the comprehensive microfilm edition to the production of these volumes documenting Goldman's American years, every aspect of the public history outreach generated by the Project bears the mark of historian Robert Cohen and illustrations editor Susan Wengraf.

Robert Cohen began his association with the Project when he was a graduate student studying the history of student movements, especially of the 1930s. With his constant focus on free expression and education, he has followed the thread of his interests from the early years of the twentieth century with Emma Goldman on to the old left of the 1930s and to the new left of the free speech movement of the 1960s on the University of California, Berkeley, campus. An enormously generous and insightful colleague and friend, he collaborated on the selection of the documents for the volumes and critiqued the introductory essays, encouraging me to take a longer view on Goldman, to face her limitations even as I celebrated her grand achievements. And when, midstream in the Project's work, I faced a life-threatening illness, Robby Cohen was among the most devoted to the work, and his unwavering kindness to me during that harrowing time created a shield of support.

Susan Wengraf's impeccable visual sensibility and fascination with Goldman and her time graced the Project with an ever-increasing photographic archive that allowed us to attend to the edition's artistic form as well as historical content. Wengraf created a parallel narrative comprised of facsimiles of original documents from newspapers, magazines, government documents, and personal correspondence gathered from a wide variety of sources—complementing and distilling the volumes' daunting abundance of historical texts. Barry Pateman, in his other role as curator of the Kate Sharpley Library, generously added his original visual material. In the final hours, Wengraf was assisted by John Blaustein and Andrea Sohn, who generously gave of their time and technical expertise. Wengraf began the search for Goldman-related images almost twenty years ago—building our visual archive and helping to create a "family album" that evolved into a wonderful traveling exhibition. She continues to assist me, as I prepare to speak on Goldman at campuses around the nation, by creating the Project's slide show and streamlining it for local color and historical context.

The University of California Press, a place where scholarship and public interest meet, has been the perfect publisher for the Goldman volumes, from the day Stan Holwitz solicited the manuscript almost twenty years ago, to the wonderful experience of working with Director Lynne Withey, a woman whose flexibility, compassion, and intelligent guiding hand is largely responsible for the publication of these volumes. Every step of the way, the Project enjoyed the privilege of the remarkably skilled editors at the press. Most spectacular of all is Kathleen MacDougall, who has been immersed in all details of production as well as line-editing and questioning facts—elements of the publication that when done well make a book appear invisibly seamless and clear. We are grateful for her persistence and remarkable editorial sensibility and talent, and also for her belief in the social and political value of publishing this selected edition of Goldman's papers, which made our professional tie a wondrous collegial and comradely fit. Our A-team included the designer Nicole Hayward and acquisitions editor Mary Francis.

Indeed, the Emma Goldman Papers has been fortunate to have had the benefit of publishers who never wavered in their commitment to the work—from the gracious and intelligent publisher of the 1991–1993 microfilm edition and the 1995 analytic guide, Sir Charles Chadwyck-Healey and his associates, especially Mark Hamilton and Doug Roesemann, to the stellar editors at the University of California Press. We thank them all for their part in inscribing Emma Goldman's life and times indelibly into the historical record.

Among the historians devoted to the history of dissent and to recording the violent underside of the nation's response to issues of race and labor unrest is the revered Leon Litwack, indefatigable and captivating Morrison Professor of American History at the University of California, Berkeley, and chair of the very generous Faculty Advisory Board of the Emma Goldman Papers Project. Our designated "principal investigator"—his P.I. acronym could easily signify "prince of integrity"—stood by the Emma Goldman Papers tirelessly and, with compassion and enthusiasm, gave us his astute advice over the past decade of the Emma Goldman Papers Project. To have the camaraderie and respect of one who embodies the challenging spirit of Emma Goldman has been an honor. We thank him for his generosity and his willingness to go the extra mile even with his overflowing schedule, without which the Emma Goldman Papers Project could never have come this far—and for all that he has done for so many, with his characteristic combination of modesty and force. He held us together when we were drifting—as did members of our faculty advisory board.

A pattern of resilience, determination, and never turning back was set with the aid of two significant research companions—the magnificent and practical political visionary the late Sarah Crome and the multi-talented public historian Sally Thomas. Crome joined me upon her retirement from teaching and, although she initially cringed at the impracticality of Emma's politics, developed a fascination for the history of the anarchists, eventually becoming known among younger anarchist and anti-nuclear activists as "cosmic Sarah." Thomas worked with the Project in many different roles over a fourteen-year period and helped set a tone and direction that has remained our hallmark. Flanked by our muses the three Women for Peace—June Brumer, Rae Lisker, and

Beth Wilson—the "volunteers" whose weekly dedication for fifteen years to absolutely anything that needed to be done, added radiance and ingenuity to our work and contributed to the Project's ability to weather occasional storms of uncertainty.

The Emma Goldman Papers Project was conceived in an era of resurgence of interest in women's history. The initiator of the Emma Goldman Papers Project was the National Historical Publications and Records Commission of the National Archives. The NHPRC was mandated by Congress in 1934 to sponsor documentary editing projects to collect, organize, and publish the papers of the Founding Fathers. By the 1970s there was a groundswell of interest among historians in expanding the definition of the nation's finest leaders to include women, labor, and civil rights activists. The Emma Goldman Papers, sometimes labeled in jest as one of the "Destroying Mother" projects, began quietly in 1980, only to be silenced briefly by budget cuts during President Reagan's administration. The NHPRC has been the Emma Goldman Papers Project's most consistent supporter—setting an unparalleled standard of excellence and respect for documentary editing and laying the foundation for the abundance of high-quality historical editions in American history published in the twentieth century. The irony of a federal agency becoming the deported Emma Goldman's primary source of support was not lost on the NHPRC's long-time officer, Roger Bruns, who often mused that perhaps Goldman was mistakenly identified on the commission's list of mandated subjects for projects. Bruns jested that they might have presumed they were funding a great "archivist," rather than a feared "anarchist." Piercing through such speculation was the NHPRC's genuine belief in free expression as a crucial element of the identity of America, which propelled the commission and its remarkably kind and engaged staff to value Goldman's contribution to American history and sustain the long scholarly quest to document her life and work. In addition to the compassionate, modest, and erudite Roger Bruns, who not only guided the Emma Goldman Papers through the years but also provided critical feedback as I wrote the introductory essays, the Project was fortunate to have the support and clever counsel of Ann Newhall. On the commission staff, Tim Connelly impressively tended to the myriad of detail, proving that the best administrative work is done with kindness and intellectual engagement in the task at hand. A host of NHPRC associates shepherded us through our work over the years, including the empathetic Mary Giunta, who saw us through many of our hardest times, and the remarkable late Sara Jackson, a kindred spirit, who took pride in her contact with the Goldman Papers, declassifying government documents for the collection and even entrusting us with records of racial lynching to place in the hands of scholars who shared our belief that historians can make a difference by exposing and correcting the documentary record. Over time, the NHPRC staff became our most consistently involved colleagues—we especially thank Richard Sheldon, Nancy Sahli, J. Dane Hartgrove, Mike Meier, and Suzanne Meyers, as well as the many others who extended themselves over and over again on our behalf.

My appreciation extends to those who played an integral part in the history of the Emma Goldman Papers Project over the last twenty years—from staff members, volunteers, archivists, librarians, scholars in the United States and across the globe, students, grant administrators, and the many university and community facilitators of our work. While the editors who brought these volumes to completion in the last three years, checking and re-checking facts, writing and re-writing annotations, framing and re-framing the texts, and pushing themselves to the max with great equanimity and kindness to meet incredibly stringent deadlines, clearly deserve the lion's share of appreciation, others before them worked very hard to help lay the foundation for what is now the documentary history of Goldman's American years. Various configurations of the edition, ranging from one to three, and ultimately to four, volumes for the American years, have left tracings of different editorial styles—some of which were eventually abandoned and some absorbed. The volumes have benefited from the talents of each editorial group as they improved on the fine efforts of the one before it.

The Project also benefited greatly from consultation with Heiner Becker, German anarchist historian, biographer, and collector of anarchist archives affiliated with the International Institute for Social History in Amsterdam. Becker's remarkable archives and his breadth of knowledge provided a timely corrective to the sparse material from the 1890s in our 20,000-document microfilm collection. We especially appreciate his sharing of letters and anarchist journals in Goldman's native German language, most notably her earliest articles in *Der Brandfackel*. In part, because of Becker's contribution of copies of rare Goldman and Berkman documents written during the time of Goldman's political initiation, the first volume of the series, *Made for America, 1890–1901* (a title also conceived during his visit), includes scholarly sources and annotations that are both authentic and new—especially to an American readership.

During 1998 and 1999, a small group of graduate students in history at the University of California, Berkeley, valiantly attempted to bring the early configuration of this documentary history to completion. Carl Prince, professor of history at New York University and longtime documentary editor, generously took a "busman's vacation" during his frequent junkets from New York to California and spent months editing annotations and working with the graduate student research associates. Robert Avila coordinated the work of Monica Rico, Daniel Rolde, and Jason Smith, and worked with various undergraduate and graduate student researchers; together they created a format for the books, researched and wrote preliminary annotations, refined the editorial principles, and gave of themselves, taking valuable time from their own dissertation work to forward the work of the Emma Goldman Papers Project. Many of the Project's graduate student editors over the years had been trained in the field of documentary editing by Stephen Cole, who coordinated the early research of Jennifer Beeson, Chad Bryant, Robert Geraci, Sarah Kim, Brigitte Koenig, and Louise Nelson, among many others. Cole worked as an associate editor—first on the guide and index to the microfilm collection, for which he wrote the bibliographical essay, then on the Project's public history outreach material including two high school curricula, followed by the writing of grants for the formative stages of the American years edition. He was especially attuned to editorial principles and practices, and although the Project has since changed course, we are grateful for Cole's founding efforts on the volumes. Crossing over during this time was Sally Thomas, the longest-standing member of the Emma Goldman Papers Project, who worked first as an administrative assistant and public programs specialist and then as an editor, carefully transcribing the prison letters. Among the many ways in which she helped shape the Project's mission, her vision of broad Web access has become reality.

For a fuller account of the hundreds of people who worked with us over the years, especially as we collected material for the microfilm and guide, please see *Emma Goldman: A Guide to Her Life and Documentary Sources* (Alexandria, Va.: Chadwyck-Healey, 1995) for the lists of editors, administrative and program staff (especially the army of graduate students), research associates, production editors, editorial assistants, international search coordinators, international researchers, research assistants and translators, the hundreds of contributing library institutions, and donors. Among those who worked at the Project and helped set the path, we thank especially Ronald J. Zboray, the microfilm editor for the first six years; Daniel Cornford for his short but important year as associate editor; Thomas Peabody, who extended his research interests to serve as a key writer of the narrative notes for the microfilm edition; Alice Hall, who coordinated the government document series; Kurt Thompson, coordinator of the early computerization of our work; Dennis McEnnerney and Vivian Kleiman, who assisted in the very early domestic and international search; and the late Brenda Butler, our European and Asian search coordinator. Rebecca Hyman, Barbara Loomis, and Robert Cohen very wisely built our newspaper collection, always cognizant that the public perception of Goldman was a critical complement and counterpoint to our collection of her personal letters. To all those from near and far who came to work with us, even briefly, we extend our thanks. We hope that you can see the imprint of your work in this documentary edition and recognize the many facts that you tracked down years ago, now integrated into the historical fabric of these volumes.

For a more extensive collection of the sources from which much of the documents in this edition were selected, researchers may consult *Emma Goldman: A Comprehensive Microfilm Collection* (Alexandria, Va.: Chadwyck-Healey, 1991–1993). Though a remarkable number of new documents were found in the process of working on the annotations for the American years' edition, the material already in the Emma Goldman Papers Project microfilm collection, brought together from over a thousand archives and private collections, sets a broader documentary context (in raw form without the scholarly apparatus of annotations). The search for documents and their organization, identification, and publication in the microfilm archive laid the foundation for the book edition and took almost fifteen years. I thank the many people who worked with the Emma Goldman Papers in its early years, when its mission seemed more ephemeral, its tasks somewhat more mundane— and for the result, an archive that is a quiet gift to scholars and political activists.

A very spirited and talented group of undergraduate research assistants helped us pull the final details together, provided a fact-checking safety net, and shared our enthusiasm for expanding the scope of our documentary history to include a history of the anarchist activity in America and Europe that motivated and informed Goldman's work. This task required remarkable detective work and tenacity. Guided by Barry Pateman and Jessica Moran, the office has been buzzing with the excitement of discovery, the thrill of working with primary sources, and the sense that the time has come to fill this gap in the historical record—a mission the Emma Goldman Papers Project has been primed for and working toward for more than twenty years. Among the many students who helped with background research for the annotations and appendices and performed critical fact checking for the volumes, we thank especially Katherine Allen, Rajeev Ananda, Jennifer Beeson, Ryan Boehm, Esther Byum, Theresa Chen, Rebecca Cohen, Evan Daniel, John Elrod, Karen Rodriguez G', Jennifer Guth, Karen Hannah, Erik Hetzner, Lisa Hsia, Mary (Mollie) Hudgens, Alexandra Kemp, Jenny Lah, Hillary Lazar, Tamara Martinez, Dennis Marzan, Shani McElroy, Sanaz Mozafarian, Jenny Mundy, Sara Newland, Emma Pollin, Heather Reese, Mariyan Solimon, Sara Smith, Emily Spangler, Sayuri Stabrowski, Kristin Stankiewicz, Rachel Starr, Sarah Stone, Andrea Valverde, Ehssan Vandaei, Billy Vega, Nicole Waugh, Angeline Young, Nicole Zillmer, and Kenyon Zimmer, among others. Gabriella Karl transcribed documents, performed background research for the annotations and directories, and helped coordinate the work of the students, with a clear commitment to the Project that extended even to administrative tasks. The administrative coordination of such a research project is enormous—and we thank especially the generous-spirited Joanna Sterricker, Georgia Moseley, and Delcianna Windners for keeping the plethora of forms and budgets and grants and paychecks moving, allowing the book edition to move forward as well. And in this age of rapidly aging computers and dwindling finances, we thank

Michael Katz for his years and years of frugal technical problem solving and Jason Jedd for coming to our rescue so effectively over this past year of all-too-frequent computer crashes.

The Project was also graced with the generous talents of translators Paul Sharkey (for French, Italian, and Spanish), Eli Katz (for Yiddish and German), and Reginald Zelnik and Lisa Little (for Russian). We thank you all for your steady availability, linguistic and political intuition, and enthusiasm for our work. We are grateful for the many outside researchers who took an interest in our work and led us to new documents—among whom, we especially thank Nicholson Baker for his gift of the *New York World* collection and Robert Helms for the kind sharing of his extensive knowledge of Philadelphia anarchists, and the many archivists who pored over their holdings on our behalf, answering our queries and sending us their discoveries.

Every writer and historian needs a sounding board, constructive criticism, and people on the outside of the work willing to jump in and pretend to be the average reader, especially in the final hours when clarity is of the essence. I thank my many friends who functioned as outside editors and personal advisors—spending hours reading through drafts and re-drafts of the various configurations of this edition as well as the proposals, letters, and ancillary public history material. First and foremost among those who gave so generously of themselves and their talents are Lorraine Kahn, filmmaker, humorist, and cultural theorist; Julianne Burton-Carvajal, artful editor, professor of Latin American literature and film, local historian of Monterey, California, and biographer; my godson Daniel Burton Rose, offbeat political and cultural consultant; Joan K. Peters, professor of English and author of dazzling books on women and work—all of these friends have showered me with love and meticulous attention to the detail of the work, and deserve much credit for the good within it. I also thank my fellow-biographers, especially Ramsey Breslin, art critic, whose careful reading of the introduction to the first volume made all the difference, along with colleagues in the psychobiography study group, particularly Marilyn Fabe, film critic, Stephen Walrod, psychotherapist and art collector, and Alan Elms and William McKinley Runyan, leaders in the field of psychobiography, who together added depth to my understanding of the interaction between the historical and psychological conditions that shape individual experience. Remi Omodele, dear friend, neighbor, and scholar of the theater, not only brightened my daily life, wrapping family and work seamlessly together, but imparted her tremendous insight into the political history of the theater and Goldman's relationship to it. Harriet Sage, staunch friend and appreciator of books and of people, shared her keen psychological insights into the inner Goldman, and also coached me through sickness and health with wisdom and generosity.

Librarians and archivists are at the core of almost every dimension of our work. The foundation of all documentary editions are the primary sources and the books that provide an accurate historical context. A documentary editing project would be nowhere without the assistance of archivists and librarians, whose quiet, persistent, meticulous dedication makes all research possible. We thank you all. Fine anarchist collections are especially rare, and the Emma Goldman Papers Project has been fortunate to work on an almost daily basis with Julie Herrada, who succeeded Ed Webber and Katherine Beam as curator of the Labadie Collection at the University of Michigan; Herrada shared her material and her expertise with utmost generosity. The International Institute for Social History in Amsterdam, where Goldman placed both her own collection and Berkman's after his death, allowed much of their extensive Goldman archive to be integrated into our comprehensive microfilm collection and has continued to assist the Emma Goldman Papers Project, graciously filling in for previous omissions from her early political years, including rare Berkman items, and offering access to the many difficult-to-find journals and photographs preserved in their archive. We thank especially those who worked at IISH when the Project began—including Rudolf de Jong, Thea Djuiker, Kees Rodenburg, Mieke Ijzermans, and then-director Erik Fisher—and the current director, Jaap Kloosterman, for his ongoing assistance. We also honor the memory of Deborah Bernhardt, director of New York University's Tamiment Institute and Robert F. Wagner collections, who graced our project with archival sources and true friendship and camaraderie, and we thank those who followed her great example.

Fortunately for the Emma Goldman Papers, associate editor Barry Pateman is also the curator of the Kate Sharpley Library, the largest collection of English-language anarchist material in the U.K. Especially for the material on Goldman's early years and for full-run copies of rare anarchist journals, his collection cannot be matched. It has been remarkable to have access to a breadth of material, literally at our fingertips, deepening the Project's understanding of the anarchist movement and refining the historical research for the books.

The Project is also privileged to be part of the University of California, Berkeley, an institution with one of the most extensive research libraries in the nation. With over a thousand books circulating from their stacks to our office, a steady stream of interlibrary loan requests, almost constant use of the newspaper microfilm reading room, and frequent trips to the Bancroft Library's archival collection—we are deeply indebted to all who have facilitated our work, graciously approving the multitude of proxy cards in my name, patiently taking our orders, respecting our work, and even restoring rare manuscripts given to the Project. We thank Beth Sibley for expanding the collection on our behalf, Gillian Boal for her careful restoration, the staff at the circulation desk, especially Joyce Ford, a long-time colleague from afar, all the staff at the Interlibrary Loan Service, and all the staff in the Microfilm Reading Room, especially Vicki Jourdan. We thank also former director of the library Peter Lyman for his generosity to the Emma Goldman Papers, and we honor the current University Librarian Tom Leonard, and the director of the Bancroft Library, Charles Faulhaber, who has been especially kind to the Project, and his staff. In the process of working on these first volumes of the documentary edition, we have had the help of many talented archivists and librarians across the nation. As kindred book people, we salute your work, and thank you for your assistance over the years—we literally could not have completed our volumes without you.

We would like particularly to acknowledge the pioneering work of Richard Drinnon, who in 1961 (twenty-one years after her death) published *Rebel in Paradise,* the first biography of Emma Goldman. His book presaged the free speech movement on the Berkeley campus and the women's movement. The publication of Drinnon's work may have fanned the flames of protest as organizers welcomed in the discovery of a resonant historical spirit. The Drinnons helped me years ago, when I was pregnant with child and also with great hopes as I embarked on the writing of the biography *Love, Anarchy, and Emma Goldman.* Although we came to the Berkeley campus at very different times, it seems that Richard Drinnon carved the space for Goldman there, and led the way for "Emmasaries" everywhere.

There are no books at the Project's office as worn as those written by Paul Avrich, the renowned scholar of multiple books on the history of anarchism, who has personally and generously helped us with innumerable questions over the years. For his careful reading of our texts, and his camaraderie, we send him our profound respect and appreciation. His dignity and fine work continue to be an inspiration and our guide.

THE STORY OF THOSE WHO HELPED sustain the work of the Emma Goldman Papers deserves a book in itself. Like all good projects without a secure financial base—including Goldman's magazine *Mother Earth*—we have relied on the generosity of our friends and our kindred spirits to pull us through. Over time, our "Emma's List" (the counterpart to "Emily's List," a fund focused on electing women into public office) has evolved into a strong community bound together by a desire to preserve the courage of those who, like Emma Goldman, dared to challenge hypocrisy and to affirm what she considered everybody's right to a world of economic and social liberty. Our staunch Emma's List supporters at all levels have surrounded us with kindness, affirming the significance of our work and replenishing our resilience and perseverance. We thank you all, from the bottom of our hearts.

Like Goldman's own circle of political theorists, writers, journalists, and creative thinkers on the burning issues of her time, the wide array of professional and personal paths represented on Emma's List is a tribute to the all-encompassing hope and inspiration the story of her life continues to evoke. It is important to note, however, that Emma's List contributors by no means all agree on every aspect of Goldman's political trajectory. The unifying principle of their support is the belief that the history of the early battles for free expression and the story of courage of individuals like Emma Goldman deserve a permanent place in the nation's documentary record.

Among the most compassionate and generous of our sustaining contributors is Lois Blum Feinblatt, whose modest dignity and concern for every aspect of the Project's well-being has grounded us in love. Her commitment to the promotion of mentoring in the schools and her own work as a psychotherapist combined to bestow upon us all the wisdom, tolerance, and open-mindedness that characterizes Emma's List. The matriarch of a remarkably generous and politically impressive family, all of whom have contributed to the Emma Goldman Papers, Lois Blum Feinblatt has been the sweet soul who at various times underwrote the cost of our office space and whose constancy and faith in the value of long-term research allowed us to push on. Her daughter, Carolyn Patty Blum, a dear friend and colleague, is a lawyer who has championed human rights and protected political exiles and whose work—in the spirit of Emma—puts fear into the heart of torturers everywhere. She not only contributed to our material well-being but also was a brilliant reader for the introductory essays, especially on issues of human rights so integral to Goldman's work. Lois's daughter-in-law, Judith Smith, an insightful historian of gender and race, sent the Emma Goldman Papers Project the royalties from her book on urban history to promote our work; and her sister, Sarah Malino, also a women's historian, added her contribution as well. Lois's cousin, Sunny Jo Brodsky, quilted beautiful wall hangings with photographic images of Emma to adorn the halls of our Project and also designed a pot-holder containing Goldman's recipe for blintzes.

Cora Weiss, an Emma Goldman in her own right, proclaimed that "You don't have to be an anarchist to want Emma Goldman resources readily available. Women need role models on how to be effective advocates, and how to make a perfect blintz." Weiss is one of the most consistent, persevering nongovernmental advocates for world peace and the rights of women and girls in the twentieth century—her accomplishments and force of character have had a remarkable impact on the movement against war and for global harmony and freedom. With her leadership, the Samuel Rubin Foundation, committed to the promotion of work for peace and justice, graciously stretched their guidelines for many years to honor the importance of the documentation of the lives and activities of those in our past whose courage and vision laid the groundwork for the well-being of present and future generations across the world. One can only hope that the Rubin Foundation, and Cora Weiss too, will consider documenting their own impressive history as an example of how individuals can, in fact, make an enormous difference. We have been honored to have their support.

The most remarkable recent rescue of the Emma Goldman Papers Project came from Stephen Silberstein, a librarian and developer of computer systems who advanced the field of digitized access and catalogue information retrieval and was a supporter of the University of California, Berkeley's free speech movement. Working with others, Silberstein ensured that the history of that dramatic time in the 1960s would be a point of pride on the Berkeley campus. His contribution to the Emma Goldman Papers Project followed the path blazed by his generous establishment of the Free Speech Movement Cafe in Moffitt Library and an archive at the Bancroft Library that is also part of the California Digital Library, available via the Internet to students of all ages all over the world. We thank him for his support of the documentation of Emma Goldman's early battles for free speech, thus anchoring our work as part of the legacy of those who fought to uphold the right of free expression on college campuses across the nation.

The J. M. Kaplan Fund, through its project "Furthermore," has also contributed generously to our work, helping us get closer to publication and sharing our commitment to the documentary history of the long and arduous struggle for freedom as well as an appreciation for the feisty and courageous Emma Goldman.

A large proportion of our supporters, though by no means all, are people I've known for a very long time who generously extended their friendship to the Emma Goldman Papers Project. The constant thread that ties this extended family of friends is our belief in the possibility of change—the on-going quest for social and economic ethics, the blossoming of individual creativity, and the readiness to question authority in the name of social justice. Kernels of such values are evident in the myriad of activities and life choices of many on Emma's List.

The generous contributions of Judith Taylor, elegant poet and loyal friend, includes her finely honed literary sensibilities—and the willingness to make the judgment call at midnight for a sentence fix, to reign in excess, and to extend to the Project her compassion for the arduous process of years of small victories and minor setbacks. For her belief in the value of work outside conventional norms and her acceptance and tolerance for both "the good *and* bad Emma"—icon and complex political figure—we thank her.

Hannah Kranzberg, a soulful spirit and friend, who has helped give voice to the progressive Jewish community, to a vision of peace and justice, and to the arts, gave graciously of herself in my moments of despair—like Emma herself, Hannah is grounded in her culture and reaches beyond it, in the name of freedom.

Extraordinary documentary filmmakers and friends Bill Jersey and Shirley Kessler contributed generously to the Emma Goldman Papers Project over the years as kindred spirits in the challenging quest to make the history of the struggle for freedom accessible, piercing, and visually inviting. Their talents for celebrating the rituals of life have deepened my own understanding of the link between private and public history.

Among those friends whose contributions to the Project extended into the actual writing and research, are the magnificent Marge Frantz, radical historian, and Eleanor Engstrand, veteran librarian, both women for peace and pillars of the community, who saw me through the very beginnings of the Emma Goldman Papers Project, spent endless hours discussing nuances of history and musing about whether or not the world had in fact moved forward. They, along with the silver-tongued biographer of William Lloyd Garrison, the late Henry Mayer; the insightful historian of the "comrades and chicken farmers" of the Petaluma area, Ken Kann; and the modest Emma Goldman-like Sarah Crome, my closest early associate at the Project, invited me to join the Chamakome ranch, a cooperative retreat named after an earlier Native American village on the same ridge along the north coast of California. Surrounded by beauty and rare quiet, the Chamakome ranch has become for me a sacred space for finding the focus so vital to the writing and editing of the Goldman volumes. (I often wonder whether Goldman's ability to put her thoughts in writing could have been attributed in part to those who gave her "the farm," her country retreat up the Hudson River in Ossining, New York, and later, "Bon Esprit" in St. Tropez, France, where she wrote her autobiography.) For the privilege of solitude and the solace of community, I thank my Chamakome-mates, many of whom have also generously extended the ranch spirit of mutual aid to Emma's List.

I especially thank the John Simon Guggenheim Foundation for granting me the time for my own writing, the honor of being in the elevated company of its very impressive history of "fellows," and for the encouragement to develop aspects of my work that diverge slightly from the path of the Goldman Papers to include personal and political reflections upon these many years of editorial engagement with Emma.

One of the most gratifying aspects of Emma's List support has been the great privilege of receiving contributions in memory of those who lived in Emma's spirit and in honor of those who continue keep her legacy alive. Most touching of all are the contributions from the families of Goldman's nearest and dearest friends—a gesture of continuity that has grounded our historical research across time, across generations. The first of such contributions came years before the volumes had even begun. Art Bortollotti, the Italian anarchist jailed in Canada under the repressive laws of the pre-World War II era, won his freedom largely due to what was Goldman's last political battle—arousing public opinion on his behalf. In homage and appreciation to his dear friend and comrade, Bortollotti sent his generous contribution of funds for the preservation of Goldman's papers and the documentation of her political work with a note written on the Goldman stationery that he had saved for over forty years.

Mecca Reitman Carpenter, the daughter of Goldman's wayward lover and road manager, Ben Reitman, embraced the Project with great ideas especially for our public outreach and funding, as her father had done for Emma for over a decade. Giving generously of her own resources, she weathered our struggles and celebrated our victories. Years ago when I wrote the very graphic, erotic story of Goldman's complex and passionate relationship with Mecca's father in *Love, Anarchy, and Emma Goldman,* I feared the censure of members of the Reitman family who might take offense at the sexual themes of the book. Instead, I found the compassionate Mecca, who had worked through her own relationship to her father in the unusually accepting biography of his many loves, *No Regrets: Dr. Ben Reitman and the Women Who Loved Him,* never shunning the raw complexity of the clash of love and anarchy between her father and Emma. Even when her own health failed her, Mecca Reitman Carpenter did not falter in her support of the Emma Goldman Papers.

The same devotion that propelled Goldman's dear friends Ida and Ben Capes to move close to her Missouri prison, thus minimizing her isolation with the comfort of visitors during those bleak eighteen months from 1917 to 1919, also propelled the Capes children, grandchildren, nephews, and nieces to support the Emma Goldman Papers—one of the most moving outpourings of friendship across generations and across the continents. In a similar extension of camaraderie, we have received contributions from the sons of Goldman's witty lawyer, Arthur Leonard Ross; the daughter of Goldman's Canadian friends, Sophie and Joe Desser, who in her youth had also assisted Goldman with her secretarial work; the son of Curtis Reese, who delivered an oration at Goldman's funeral; the daughter of Esther Laddon, who provided Goldman a home base in Canada; and the daughter of Goldman's friend Kate Wolfson. David Diamond, composer and violinist, and son of Goldman's Rochester, New York, seamstress, Chanele (Anna) Schilhaus, sent his contribution with a remembrance of Goldman standing on a footstool with pins in her skirt as she cheered on his musical career as a violinist—"Kling in de ganze Velt" (Play for the entire world)—as the smell of her rosewater perfume suffused the air. Warren Billings, a friend of Alexander Berkman, who was jailed in connection with the 1916 Preparedness Day bombing in San Francisco, was remembered by his niece, who also contributed many of Billings's books by Goldman to the Project. The Ferrer Colony in Stelton, New Jersey, was remembered by many of the children of its members, including the late Helen Seitz, who as a child sat on Emma's lap when she visited the colony (Helen remembered being scared and repelled by the sweaty embrace of this anarchist celebrity); she told us that her parents met at a soiree in New York City given in Goldman's honor. Another dear friend of the Project is Amy Olay Kaplan, whose grandfather Maximiliano Olay was one of Emma Goldman's Spanish translators; together we uncovered her grandparents' hidden past. Others who joined Emma's List grew up in anarchist circles in Chicago, Toronto, New York, and London. The late Wu Ke Kang (Woo Yang Hao), a member of the Chinese anarchist circle living in Paris and translator of Goldman's works, was one among many who sent his support and recollections of Goldman's influence on China's early revolution—especially on the revered author, Ba Jin. The late Arthur Weinberg, who attended Goldman's funeral services in Chicago, kindly corrected the reminiscences of others interviewed by the Project about the event. One contributor found a chance notation in his mother's diary chronicling her attempt with a baby buggy to mount the stairs of a crowded hall in San Francisco, anxious to hear Goldman lecture. These and other stories add life and texture to our work, and the sweetness of human contact.

Contributors with personal contact to Goldman in her lifetime added their recollections to the Project's reminiscence file, which contains interviews with Goldman associates now deceased, ranging from Roger Baldwin, the co-founder of the American Civil Liberties Union, to Mollie Ackerman, one among many of Goldman's young secretaries and friends. Ahrne Thorne, editor of *Fraye Arbeter Stimme,* spent hours sharing his ideas and commiserating about the mammoth task I had taken on. Albert Meltzer, the London anarchist whom Goldman referred to as "a young hooligan," opened his heart to the Emma Goldman Papers Project, sharing his ideas and his books, widening his circle to include us and our work. Federico Arcos and his late wife, Pura, inspired by Goldman in their youth in Spain, opened their home in Canada and displayed their collection of Goldman's books and suitcases.

Most significant to the publication of Goldman's works has been the generosity and friendship bestowed upon us by Goldman's nephews and literary heirs—David and the late Ian Ballantine. I remember Ian Ballantine, the publisher of Bantam (and Ballantine) Books, sitting at his desk in a very tall office building in New York and proclaiming, "Aunt Emma never believed in restrictions of any kind, so why should I?" Over the years, David Ballantine, an author and collector of antique guns, shared with the Project various items his aunt had secreted away, including the ledger documenting those who contributed to her work, her legal fees, and the cost of incidentals for her magazine and lecture tours. Without their sanction, the written legacy of Emma Goldman could never have been as extensively preserved.

Parents, children, and friends—all have been honored on Emma's List. The group as a whole is a remarkable blend—joining together political thinkers Howard Zinn and Noam Chomsky; pioneers of the women's movement, most notably Gloria Steinem, and of women's research, such as Mariam Chamberlain, Gerda Lerner, and Naomi Weisstein, among many others; and stellar literary figures including E. L. Doctorow, Barbara Kingsolver, Marilyn French, Erica Jong, Ken Burrows, Dianne Middlebrook, Peter Glassgold, Brenda Webster, and the late and witty muckraking author Jessica Mitford, who was completely in thrall to issues raised by Emma's life but thought it "deadly boring" to brave organizing anybody's papers, no matter how great they were.

Among the more theatrical figures on Emma's List drawn to Goldman's life are Susan Sarandon and Tim Robbins, Harold Ramis, and documentary filmmakers Vivian Kleiman, Rick Goldsmith, Coleman Romalis (whose film on Emma Goldman in Canada includes an interview with the Emma Goldman Papers Project as well). Others include Pacifica Radio commentator and filmmaker Alan Snitow and Deborah Kauffman, who founded with Janice Plotkin the San Francisco Jewish Film Festival. The late Rella Lossy wrote a wonderful and playful theater piece on Ben and Emma. We have worked with several actresses who played Emma in the theatrical adaptation of E. L. Doctorow's book *Ragtime*, especially Camille Saviola and Mary Gutzi. Years ago, the actress Adele Proom impersonated Emma, pretending to break into what was an inspired benefit performance by the spirited singer and songwriter Michelle Shocked—a gathering of remarkable community and university activists who also read from the Goldman letters and speeches that most matched their own work. The political satirist and illustrator Ed Sorel once identified Emma in a cartoon as one of the "messy" characters with which a certain kind of political activist feels at home— a sentiment to which we all concur. Also among Emma's List supporters is Nina Hartley, feminist and pornographic-film actress, proudly carrying on the legacy of Goldman's celebration of sexuality and campaign against Puritanism.

Among the contributors to Emma's List are many who have devoted their lives to the documentation of the struggle for freedom. Most generous and enthusiastic among women's historians is Nancy Hewitt, who believes that much of what has shaped America is "wisdom from the margins." In her article published in *Voices of Women Historians* (1999; edited by Eileen Boris and Nupur Chaudhuri), Hewitt has claimed us all as the keepers of "Emma's Thread" of commutarian values and global visions. In a touching gesture of solidarity, over the years Hewitt has made contributions to the Project in honor of many of her students; when they earn their doctorates, they receive an archival photograph of Emma Goldman writing at a desk adorned with lilies, printed by Richard Gordon—the Project's donor gift to keep the inspiration flowing! We are honored by the financial support and intellectual vote of confidence from historians across the nation—Martha Ackelsberg, Harriet Alonso, Eric Anderson, Elizabeth Berry, Virginia Bouvier, Robert Cherny, Harry Chotiner, Blanche Weisen Cook, Nancy Cott, Carol DeBoer-Langworthy, Carl N. Degler, Martin Duberman, Tom Dublin, Bob Dunn, Robert Elias, Estelle Freedman, Susan Glenn, Jim Gregory, Susan Groves, Louis Harlan, Linda Kerber, Alice Kessler-Harris, Ira Lapidus, Jesse Lemisch, Lawrence and Cornelia Levine, Sally Miller, Nell Painter, Carl Prince, David Roediger, Ruth Rosen, Carol Rosenberg, Roy Rosenzweig, Sheila Rowbotham, Alix Shulman, Barbara Sicherman, Kitty Sklar, Daniel Soyer, Peter Stansky, Randolph Starn, William Tuttle, Laurel Ulrich, Susan Vladmir-Morgan, Daniel and Judith Walkowitz, Bonnie Lynn Weiner, and Susumu Yamazumi, among others—and from our colleagues among scholarly documentary editors, especially Rudolph Vecoli of the Immigration History Project, Maeva Marcus of the First Federal Congress

Papers, John and Harriet Simon of the Ulysses S. Grant and of the John Dewey Papers, respectively, and my dear friends Clayborne and Susan Carson of the Martin Luther King, Jr. Papers—all of whose historical work resonates with Goldman's and makes a difference—today. We are especially grateful for the research assistance and camaraderie of the Consortium for Women's History—most notably Esther Katz and Cathy Moran Hajo of the Margaret Sanger Papers, Ann Gordon and Patricia Holland of the Elizabeth Cady Stanton and Susan B. Anthony Papers, and the soulful pioneer of women in documentary editions, Mary Lynn McCree Bryan of the Jane Addams Papers. Members of Emma Goldman Papers faculty advisory board answered our queries and validated our work among colleagues across scholarly disciplines. Led by Leon Litwack, they include, among others, Lawrence Levine, Reginald Zelnik, Susan Schweik, and the late Michael Rogin, whose appreciation was familial and dated back to 1906, when his great aunt Rosie Rogin was arrested with Emma Goldman.

Emma's List has elicited an unusual gathering of supporters for whom Goldman's story taps into both their desire to promote the social good and their own streak of rebelliousness and daring. These desires are expressed in the way they live their lives and in the manner in which they choose and perform their work—and are the common denominator of this outstanding group. It has been an honor to be in their midst, and to have their support. Members of Emma's List come from a wide range of occupations—from workers in methadone clinics, psychotherapists, and doctors, to retired women who send $18 each year to signify "chai" or "life" in Hebrew. Many are archivists and anarchists, students, teachers, librarians, social scientists, university administrators and community activists, labor leaders, publishers, editors, journalists, newscasters, radio personalities, economics analysts, philanthropists, foundation officials, professors from an amazing array of scholarly disciplines, anthropologists, secretaries, flight attendants, architects, designers, photographers, public health advocates, environmental activists and arborists, scientists, statisticians, tennis and soccer moms and dads, Pulitzer prize winners, progressive religious leaders, gourmet cooks, computer whizzes and mathematicians, artists, progressive business executives, and a large contingent of progressive attorneys.

Among those who welcome our calls for help is photographer and friend Marion Brenner, who continues to grace us with her time and talent. The excellent and creative work of photographer Richard Gordon and graphic designers Andrea Sohn (the niece of the Project's co-founder Sarah Crome) and Lisa Roth on our outreach public-history materials has maintained the level of excellence in the Project.

San Diego consumer advocacy attorney Eric Isaacson, who found us through the Emma Goldman Papers website, single-handedly determined that he would change the bad reputation of his city in which Goldman's lover and manager Ben Reitman was driven into the desert—tarred, sagebrushed, and sexually attacked by a band of high-level city officials acting as vigilantes—as part of the incredibly brutal San Diego free speech fight of 1912. Recently, Eric Isaacson organized support for the Emma Goldman Papers Project, rallying his partners and friends to come to our aid in a moment of deep financial crisis. There is a kind of ironic justice underlying this outpouring of support for the Emma Goldman Papers from advocates for consumer and stockholders' rights who have chosen to share a portion of the proceeds of their victories with those who are documenting the papers of one of the great foremothers of the battle against corporate greed.

Our research base has always been the University of California, Berkeley. By far the most compassionate and forward-thinking members of the university's administrative team have been

Joseph Cerny, the former vice chancellor for research, and his core staff, associate vice chancellor Linda Fabbri, and director of budget and personnel Susan Hirano—all of whom recognized the value of the kind of research that didn't fit neatly into the established categories of the university. These volumes are a tribute to their belief and support, and to the quiet but critical efforts of others who add courage and vision to the mix of administrative duties. We also extend our thanks to Beth Burnside, the current vice chancellor for research, and her staff.

Seconded by the support of Chancellor Robert M. Berdahl, a champion of maintaining the university as a sacred space for interchange and inquiry for even the most challenging ideas, the Emma Goldman Papers Project has enjoyed a long period of relative security that allowed the work to move forward—and without which, these volumes could never have been published in such a timely and careful manner.

We are grateful for the year-long combined outright and matching grant from the National Endowment for the Humanities. More than ten years ago, NEH support solidified the Project's work with a three-year grant that coincided with parallel support from both the Ford and the Rockefeller Foundations. Those early grants helped create the base from which these volumes on Goldman's American years were written, and are greatly appreciated. We thank especially Sheila Biddle, formerly of the Ford Foundation.

There are anarchist archives across the globe in which all the work of processing the material is voluntary and completely run as a cooperative. Their staffs, unlike ours, all share the same anarchist political perspective. The idea of applying for government grants and constantly jumping through administrative hoops, or even accepting corporate funds, would be abhorrent to them. We revere their tenacity, devotion, and ability to merge the form and content of their work. We have benefited from their sources, and from their wisdom, and hope that they too value our efforts, recognize the validity of our struggles, and will reap the benefits of the Emma Goldman Papers' remarkable depth of research—now available to all.

To all our supporters, material and spiritual, the ever-generous members of Emma's List— many of whom are unlisted small donors with large spirits, and all of whom have carried us through our sparsest times—we wish to convey our sincere appreciation and respect and hope that you will take pride in contributing to a work intended for posterity. The most important grants are intangible—the gestures of support from friends, family, and community that affirm that this very long process is worth the effort.

To all those institutions, foundations, and individuals who have lent their names and generous spirit and talent to the Emma Goldman Papers, we thank you. Your contribution has laid the foundation for the comprehensive reach of the volumes. We appreciate your support but relieve you of responsibility for factual mistakes or errors of omission on our part. We are deeply grateful to our extended family of friends and colleagues, unnamed here but not forgotten, without whom this work would never have come this far.

EMMA GOLDMAN and the Emma Goldman Papers Project have been fixed constellations in my immediate family, looming over and around us with a constancy that has been both reassuring and disconcerting at times—a long-term relationship that has deepened with time. It has been more than twenty-five years since the day my husband-to-be and I browsed in a guitar store in Chicago's Hyde Park with my dog "Emma"—a rambunctious Irish setter–Golden retriever who burst into the shop after us. From the moment my friend, John Bowen, who worked at the shop, asked her name, my personal history was transformed forever. Scratching his head as he stroked the dog, Bowen remembered that he had seen back in the storeroom a box of letters that bore the large scrawl "E. Goldman" on the envelopes' return addresses. Within minutes, a boot box of old, yellowed letters appeared, and we were overtaken with the torrent of passion and torment between Emma Goldman, the great heroine of personal and political freedom, and the wayward and promiscuous Ben Reitman, her talented road manager and lover. It was not long before I embarked on the first of many challenging attempts to draw together and interpret the complexities of Goldman's all-encompassing spirit. For me, a young student in my twenties and very much a part of the women's movement and counterculture "love" generation, reading letters Goldman had written when she was thirty-eight years old seemed like prying into the surprising vulnerabilities of a very old woman. Many people helped me muster the confidence to write a respectful biography of her struggle to balance intimate life with her public proclamations. After more than twenty-five years of living with the papers of Emma Goldman, the perspective of age has became an important overlay and my concerns have shifted and broadened. All through my intense engagement with the issues in and around Goldman's life, the love and constancy of my family and friends kept me from losing myself to the past, from losing track of my own trajectory and parallel entitlement to a full life. For this, and more, I especially thank my husband, Lowell Finley, there from the very first discovery of Emma's letters, master of titles, editorial sounding board, advocate of free speech and political justice, shield of caring and love; my daughter Mara, an eloquent young woman, and son, Jesse, a creative young man with a vision—who have all allowed Emma to be a positive presence in their lives and have respected the preemptive demands of work on the Emma Goldman Papers Project with remarkable patience and affection.

When I was pulled by illness all too abruptly into a treacherous and tenuous realm of life and death, my family, friends, colleagues, and talented healers rallied to my support. I am forever grateful to have survived that harrowing time. That my children's lives were cradled in kindness and the momentum of the work of the Emma Goldman Papers hardly faltered, is a tribute to an extraordinary community for whom the desire to repair the world extends to caring for each other. Among the many who were at my side at that time, I thank especially Norma Blight, mother-in-law extraordinaire; Cornelia Sherman, cousin and soul-mate; and my dear friends Nancy Bardecke, Yvette Chalom and Paul Fogel, Ruth Butler and Arie Arnon, Joan K. Peters and Peter Passell, Remi Omodele and Ric Lucien, Meredith Miller and Richard Gordon, Cleo Deras and Carlos Hernandez, Deborah Hirtz Waterman, and from afar, my sister, Jane Falk, and my aunts, uncles, cousins, various in-laws, and adopted family across the country—all of whom never faltered in their caring and love. And where else but in the Bay Area can one find such remarkably forward-thinking restorers of health? I am profoundly grateful to my doctors Debu Tripathy and Laura Esserman, who combine amazing compassion with cutting-edge research, and to Michael Broffman (and his compassionate assistant Louise Estupian), doctor of acupuncture and complementary medicine, whose creativity and willingness to step away from the dominant paradigm is in the spirit of Emma herself. I thank also Adele Schwarz, Eileen Poole, Donna La Flamme, and Neil Kostick, whose intuitions about the intersection of the mind and the body gave me hope in my darkest hours, and to doctors Philip O'Keefe and Charles Jenkins and Risa Kagan, whose caring attention to detail literally saved my life, and to my sweet soulful support group—the "bosom buddies" Denyse Gross, Barbara Hoffer, Anja Hübener, and the late Jeannie McGregor.

Ultimately, the Emma Goldman Papers Project too could not have survived without a community of support—scholars, donors, political activists, and ordinary people whose imaginations were sparked by Goldman's daring. The unique and intrepid City of Berkeley has honored Emma Goldman "as a major figure in the history of American radicalism and feminism . . . early advocate of free speech, birth control, women's equality and independence, union organization" and commended the Project for its "perseverance" and for inspiring the "collaboration of scholars, archivists, activists, students, and volunteers, both in Berkeley and around the world." In 1998, the city council proclaimed May 14—the day of Emma Goldman's death—as Emma Goldman Papers Project Day. With the publication of these volumes, we hope to mark a rebirth of interest in Goldman as "a voice crying out against injustice and oppression, wherever it has existed"—and we honor all those who helped make our work possible.

WITH APPRECIATION AND RESPECT,

CANDACE FALK

INDEX

Page numbers in italics indicate illustrations; page numbers immediately followed by the abbreviation Ger. indicate documents in the German language; other abbreviations used include EG (Emma Goldman) and AB (Alexander Berkman).

American Federation of Labor (AFL) *(continued)* tion on AB's sentence by, 25n5, 561; speakers for, 99n14; support for, 535, 578; trade unions in, 98n11, 571

Americanization: argument for, 48; EG's European travels and, 62–63; pattern of EG's, 21

American Journal of Eugenics, 533

"American Justice" (EG): text of, 183–85Ger., 186–89

American Labor Union, 37, 499

American Railway Union (ARU): Altgeld's support for, 516; defense of, 526; officers of, 28n9, 344n3, 497, 527; SDA's formation and, 501, 575. *See also* Pullman strike

American Revolution: Kropotkin on, 538; mentioned, 145–46n6, 164, 179–80

American Secular Union, 528, 530, 572

American Single Tax League, 575

American Socialist Federation, 548

Am Olam (Eternal People) colonization movement, 104n9

anarchism: class's intersection with, 72–73, 357–59; colors symbolic of, 144–45n3, 208n7, 275, 449; EG's definitions of, 20–21, 77, 100–101, 173, 402; EG's influences on, 8–9, 39; EG as spokesperson for, 42, 57–59, 79–80; EG's trial as test of, 207–8; and historians, 2; liberty as central to, 355–56; misinformation about, 481–82; as philosophy of life, 426–27, 431, 434–35, 477, 479; single tax linked to, 574–75; social science linked to, 576–77; terrorism equated with, 79–80; themes and goals of, 153n6, 181–82, 225–26, 360, 394, 453; theory vs. practice of, 437; U.S. receptiveness to, 236–37, 357–59, 428, 429, 441; women's freedom as precursor to, 273; women's role in, 42–45, 289–92. *See also* anarchist collectivism; anarchist communism; anarchist movement; anarchists

Der Anarchist (St. Louis and New York): AB's prison letters in, 124Ger., 125–26; appeal for AB in (EG), 122Ger., 123, 496; demise

of, 27, 48, 140, 234, 500; description of, 563–64; editors of, 106n11, 529, 530, 542, 548, 558; EG's opinion of, 192–93; founding of, 493; letters to (EG), 116–18Ger., 119–21; location of, 495; masthead of, *117*; publisher of, 520

The Anarchist (London), 556, 561, 564

Anarchist American Group of New York, 237n5

anarchist collectivism: anarchist communist strand vs., 17, 101–2n3. *See also* Bakunin, Michael; Most, Johann

anarchist communism: anarchist collectivism vs., 17, 101–2n3; definition of, 490–91; evaluation of progress in U.S. of, 64; focus of, 8–9; interest increased in, 393; newspaper for, 551; possible representative of, 399; tensions in, 16. *See also* Kropotkin, Peter; Peukert, Joseph

Anarchist Labour Leaf, 547

"Anarchist Laws" (EG): text of, 209–10Ger., 211–13

anarchist movement: appeal of (EG), 8, 20, 70; conferences of, 368n3; culture of, 18–19, 62–63, 357–61, 397; debates in, 40–41; development of, 392–94; divisions in, 17–18, 25–27, 40–41, 53, 76–77; first national association in U.S., 491; lethargy in, 264; need for English speaking, 258; in relation to socialists, 54–55; solidarity lacking in, 397–98; traditions of, 2; in western states, 338. *See also* international anarchist movement; Pittsburgh Manifesto (1883); press, anarchist

anarchists: appearance of, 283–84; characters of, 13–14, 336; definition of, 57–58, 402–3, 431; EG on being, 29; EG's communication with, 32–33; ethics of, 400–403; European influences, 13–14; influential, 396; Italians as, 348; immigrants as, 13–14; on sexual issues, 12–13; socialists' break with, 39–40, 397, 501; socialists compared to, 41, 453; socialists' conflict with, 54–55, 96–99. *See also* Haymarket anarchists; political prisoners; Walsall anarchists (England) anarcho-syndicalism, 550. *See also* syndicalism

Andrews, Stephen Pearl, 559

Andreyev, Leonid, 566

Angiolillo, Michele: assassination of Cánovas by, 55, 274n1, 284n4, 341–42, 347, 501–2, 521; biographical summary on, 517; mentioned, 396, 456

Anglo-Boer War (1899–1902): Chamberlain and, 522; EG on, 60–61, 384–88, 509; opposition to, 382, 394, 395; outbreak of, 508, 543, 553; stakes in, 383n7

Anthony, Susan B., 186n1

Anthropological Society, 511

anti-anarchist laws: in France *(lois scélérates)*, 66, 418–19, 498, 522, 532, 534, 560; in Germany, 212; proposed in U.S., 80, 212–13, 471–72n4, 513

Anti-Authoritarian International: beginning of, 489; division leading to, 65, 398n12; final congress of, 490; participants in, 526

Anti-Coolie League, 561

anti-foreign labor campaigns, 229–30n1

Anti-Imperialism League (New York), 525

antimilitarism: EG's support for, 60–61, 384–88. *See also specific wars*

Anti-Poverty societies, 529, 575

anti-Semitism: Dreyfus case and, 324n2, 499; persistence of, 243–44; question about, 372n6; aversion to, 62

Anti-Slavery Society, 551

anti-statist tradition in U.S.: influences on, 145–46n6; mentioned, 248n4, 332, 426n8; representatives of, 536, 549, 551

appearance and clothing (EG): in Chicago arrest, 466; height of, 155n2; interest in, 158; newspapers on, 22, 35–36, 58, 111–12, 155, 243, 247, 283, 289, 290, 318, 331, 362, 423, 441; phrenological view of, 35, 214–16, 526; in prison, 197; on release from prison, 201

Appel, Theodore, 503

Arbeter Fraint, 367, 562

Arbeiterstimme, 578

Arbeiter Zeitung, 534, 564

Arden (Del.): single-tax colony in, 575

Der arme Teufel (The Poor Devil, Detroit): demise of, 509; description of, 564; founding of, 492, 553; as influence, 315; mentioned, 261; subscribers of, 305–6, 307, 308

Armour (company), 385n3

Aronstam, Elias A., 106

Aronstam, Modest. *See* Stein, Modest (Fedya)

Arrango, Alfredo, 277

art: authority in, 355; preference for modern (EG), 413, 415. *See also* beauty

ARU. *See* American Railway Union

Asch, Sholem, 46

Ashbridge, Samuel Howell, 440n2, 442, 446n1, 447–48

Ashorn, J. B., 344

assassinations: as acts of individuals, 427–28; anti-anarchist hysteria as response to, 471–72n4, 485; attitudes toward, 14–16, 103; denunciation of, 346–48; fears of, 63–64, 75; history of, 79; influences on, 68–69; motivations for, 132–33n3, 223–25, 246, 249, 341, 427–28, 463, 476; natural phenomena compared to, 475; responses to, 55–56, 66, 274–75, 342. *See also* propaganda by the deed *(attentats); specific people*

Associated Labor Press, 535

Associations Law (1901), 561

L'Associazione, 541

AT. *See Der arme Teufel*

Atlantic Monthly, 539

attentats. See assassinations; propaganda by the deed

L'Aube, 239

L'Aurora (Spring Valley, Ill.), 60, 77, 80, 478n

L'Aurore (Paris): founding of, 560; Paris congress and, 421; Zola on Dreyfus case in, 324n2, 421n18, 503, 528

Austin, Kate: biographical summary on, 517; Czolgosz defended by, 77, 475n6, 478n; EG's praise for, 71; ethics debate and, 402n6; location of, 314n39; mentioned, 46, 340n1, 428; report of, 509; speeches arranged by, 503, 508; written contributions of, 565, 567; works: "The Question of the Sexes," 13

Austin, Sam, 314n39, 503, 508

Austria: anarchism in, 238; EG's visit to, 500; minorities in, 407n6

Austro-Prussian War (1866), 530

authority: EG's definition of, 57, 353

"Authority vs. Liberty" (EG): delivery of, 505, 506, 507, 509; excerpt from, 353–56; popularity of, 57

Die Autonomie (Autonomy, London): contributors to, 127–28Ger., 129, 539; description of, 564; focus of, 9; founding of, 551; support for, 17, 519, 543; violent rhetoric in, 15, 101

autonomists: use of term, 101; mentioned, 103, 111, 119n1, 317, 551, 555, 530, 563, 564

Autonomy Group (American), 192n2, 494, 543–44. *See also* Gruppe Autonomie

Avant Courier, 549

Aveling, Edward, 578

Bacon Society, 556

Baginski, Max: biographical summary on, 517; editorship of, 564, 566, 568, 569; EG's meetings with, 359n8, 505, 513; mentioned, 257n3, 312n33, 497, 507; speeches of, 499, 503; on Stirner's egoism theory, 558; as suspicious of Czolgosz, 512

Baginski, Richard, 251n1, 26n5, 262, 517

Bailey, David G., 146n7

Bailey, Warren Worth, 575

Bakers' and Confectioners' Unions, 505, 561

Bakers' Journal, 97, 561

Bakunin, Michael: associates of, 526, 538, 541; on authority, 57, 355n5; biographical summary on, 518; economic collectivism of, 16; First International and, 398n12, 489, 540; on god, state, and religion, 273n7; as influence on EG, 8, 13, 212n1, 273n7; as influence on others, 548, 552, 559; influence of Marx on, 518; Marx's opposition to, 542; mentioned, 42–43, 50, 68, 483, 490, 559; Nettlau's biography of, 412, 414, 547; on propaganda by the deed, 15; written contributions of, 566; works: *God and the State,* 57, 273n7, 355n5

Ballantine, Stella (Cominsky) Comyn, 160n10

Baltimore Critic, 95

Baltimore (Md.): EG's speeches in, 95, 494, 496, 499, 501

Balzac, Honoré de, 419n16

Barondess, Joseph: arrest of, 168n12; biographical summary on, 518; testimony of, 168; union of, 425n7, 493; warrant for, 497

Barre (Vt.): EG's speeches in, 57, 353–56, 507; EG's visit to, 276n5

"The Basis of Morality" (EG): delivery of, 382n3, 505

Bastiat, Frederic, 559

Battola, Jean, 223, 495, 519

Bauer, Henry: AB's defense and, 369, 520, 570–71; arrest and imprisonment of, 26, 138–39, 258, 262, 501, 520; associates of, 543; attorney of, 125n1; biographical summary on, 519; code-name for, 254n2; defense of, 549; editorship of, 566; EG's reunion with, 307–9; EG's speeches and, 504; escape plan and, 502; Homestead strike and, 106–7n13, 495–96; mentioned, 188n3, 449; research material on, 265, 266; suspicions about, 113n4; visitors for, 255; written contributions of, 567

Bax, Ernest Belfort, 578

Beall, Edgar C., 214n1

Beaver Falls (Pa.): EG's speeches in, 504

Beccaris, Gen. Fiorenzo Bava, 505

Bedborough, George, 537, 556, 563

Bell, Thomas H., 62, 509, 560

Bellamy, Edward, 528, 544

Bemis, Edward W., 265–66

Benek, A., 382–83n4

Bennett, D. M., 151n1, 490

Berger, Victor: associates of, 518, 527; colonization project and, 339n2; leadership of, 501, 579; SDA convention and, 506; socialism of, 575; and Socialist Party, 512

Berkman, Alexander (Sasha): arrest, trial, and sentencing of, 23, 129, 217–18, 223, 249n7, 251n5, 496; associates of, 519, 527, 548; at-

tempted killing by, 16, 22–23, 25–27, 220,
318–19, 496; on *attentats*, 76, 78, 132–33n3,
434n3; biographical summary on, 519–20;
birth of, 489; and depression, 26; EG's loyalty to, 25–27; finances of, 109; and *Freiheit*,
18; on Homestead, 106–8; illustrations of,
101, 104; influences on, 7n14, 101, 156–57n4;
legal appeals of, 218n3; letters from (general), 26–27, 42; letters from (1892–1893),
124Ger., 125–26, 127–28Ger., 129, 132–39;
letters from (1896–1900), 254–56; letters
from (1901), 457–59, 484–88; living arrangements of, 21–22, 493, 494; memberships of, 574; mentioned, 57, 212, 389; motives of, 132–33n3, 223–25, 246, 249, 341;
names for, 106n12, 341n4, 471n3; newspaper articles on, 100–110; pardon denied for,
254–55; on personal transformation, 83–
84; on Peukert-Most conflict, 17; relationship with Anna Minken, 21, 24 (*See also*
Goldman-Berkman relationship); research
material on, 265, 267–68; suicidal thoughts
of, 136; support for, 37–38, 123, 125 (*See also*
Berkman Defense Association); suspicions
about (Most's), 113n4; on violence, 477n12;
works: *Prison Memoirs of an Anarchist*, 26–
27, 60, 414n1, 488n12. *See also* imprisonment (AB's)
Berkman, Joseph, 267
Berkman Defense Association: accusations
concerning, 40–41, 240–42; active people
in, 349–52, 369, 519, 520, 532, 548; appeals
of, 217–18, 237, 242n, 246, 251–53, 496,
500, 501, 506, 508; description of, 570–71;
efforts of, 56–57, 217–18; funds for, 40–41,
227n, 249, 250, 258, 260, 262, 312, 325, 535,
570; treasurers of, 241, 243n1
Berman, Nahum H., 401, 520, 537, 567
Bernhardt, Sarah, 331
Biedenkapp, Georg, 262, 262n3
Bienowitch, Yegor (EG's uncle), 424n5
Bierce, Ambrose, 555
Bimberg, Harry, 422
birth control: alleged obscene advertisement

for, 491; European pamphlets on, 66, 509;
Neo-Malthusian groups interested in, 64
Bismarck, Otto von, 212, 484, 543
black, as symbol of anarchism, 144–45n3,
208n7
Black International. *See* International Working
People's Association
Blacksmith Helpers Union, 511
Blackwell, James, 565
Blackwell's Island Penitentiary: daily activi-
ties in, 198–200; description of, 196–98;
horrors in, 200; mentioned, 95; Most's
sentences to, 275n2, 492–93, 494–95;
Women's Insane Asylum at, 520. *See also*
imprisonment (EG's)
Blatchford, Robert, 576
Blissert, Robert, 99
"Bloody Sunday" deaths (Trafalgar Square),
205n3, 541
Bly, Nellie: biographical summary on, 520; EG
interviewed by, 29–30, 155–60; illustration
of, *156*
Bodansky, Julius, 497
Boerne, Ludwig, 401
Boersma, Douwe, 510
bohemianism, 58, 63. *See also* anarchist move-
ment, culture of
Bonfield, Capt. John "Black Jack," 248
Bookbinders Union, 555
Borland, Wilfred P., 399, 520, 576
Boston (Mass.): EG's speeches in, 285–87,
305, 502, 504, 506, 510; social science club
in, 577. *See also Liberty: Not the Daughter but
the Mother of Order; The Rebel*
Boston Daily Globe, 559
The Boston Index, 559
Boston Investigator, 528
Boston Revolutionists, 491
Brady, Edward: AB's defense and, 520, 570;
appeal for AB's release and, 351n3, 352, 506;
biographical summary on, 520; businesses
of, 74, 467n11, 500, 504, 512; EG's relationship with, 24, 34, 63, 169n15, 194n1, 201,
496, 499, 500, 506, 510; EG supported by,

Brady, Edward *(continued)*
514; name of, 383, 408; testimony of, 30,
169–70

Die Brandfackel (The Torch of War, New York):
on anarchist laws (EG), 209–10Ger., 211–13;
cover of, *152*; demise of, 48, 234, 499; description of, 564; editor of, 558; founding
of, 497; on free speech (EG), 28–29, 149–
50Ger., 151–54; on judicial system (EG),
183–85Ger., 186–89; location of, 111–12n1;
on trial verdict (EG), 182n6, 183–85Ger.,
186–89

Brave, Barnet, 145

Brazil: bombings in, 549

bread as sacred right: anarchist/unemployed
demonstration for, 145–46; argument for,
151–52, 171–72, 205, 331; call to take, 174–
175; as central tenet of anarchism, 153n6;
mentioned, 27–28, 30; EG's testimony on,
174; Manning on, 205n3, 541; Paris demonstrations of, 543, 552; strikes and, 285; trial
testimony on, 162–64, 167, 168, 169–70

Bresci, Gaetano: assassination of Umberto by,
66, 422n5, 427–28, 463, 509; biographical
summary on, 520–21; death of, 455n1, 511;
EG's admiration for, 68–69; EG's eulogy
for, 74, 455–56; as influence on Czolgosz,
525; mentioned, 482; widow of, 514

Breshkovskaya, Catherine, 537

Brewers' and Malters' Union, 37, 505, 511

Briceville (Tenn.) strike, 231

Bricklayers' Union, 507

British Association for the Advancement of
Science, 69

Brocher, Gustave, 491

Brockway, Z. R., 200

Bronze Workers, 420

Brooklyn (N.Y.): EG's speeches in, 323n, 503,
504; strike in, 232

Brotherhood of Locomotive Fireman's Magazine,
520, 527

Brotherhood of Locomotive Firemen, 527

Brotherhood of the Cooperative Commonwealth, 339n2, 575

Brotherhood of the Kingdom, 525

Brothers War. *See* Bruderkrieg.

Brown, George: associates of, 528; living arrangements of, 575; in social science club,
577; speeches of, 446n4, 448n, 507

Brown, J. O., 250

Brown, John: associates of, 558; biographical
summary on, 521; as influence, 10; mentioned, 145, 166, 174, 456

Bruderkrieg (Brothers War), 16–18, 101–2n3,
382–83n4, 526

Bruno, Giordano, 247, 521, 567

Brutus: use of name, 341n4, 471

Bryan, William Jennings, 245, 249, 533

Buffalo (N.Y.): EG's speeches in, 316, 493,
503; EG's visit to, 466; McKinley's assassination in, 460n1, 461–62; Pan American Exposition in, 461–62, 512, 525, 542;
strike in, 231. *See also* "The Tragedy at Buffalo" (EG)

Buffalo Commercial, 471–72n4, 513

Buffaloer Arbeiter-Zeitung: editors of, 260n3,
261n5; founding of, 492; possible appeal
via, 251–53; publication of, 251n1, 543; supplement to, 566

Buffalo Herold, 260n3

*Bulletin International du Mouvement Syndical-
iste*, 524

Bulletin of the Social Labor Movement, 578

Bunker Hill and Sullivan Mining Company,
386n7, 476n11

Bureau of International Correspondence (or
International Federation), 66, 420, 433

Burmin. *See* Berman, Nahum H.

Burns, William E., 576

Byington, Steven T., 565

Cafiero, Carlo, 489, 523, 532

Cahan, Abraham, 565

Cailes, Victor, 223n6, 495, 521

Calhoun, WIlliam J., 279n10

Cánovas del Castillo, Antonio: assassination
of, 55, 274–78, 284n4, 347, 501–2, 517; biographical summary on, 521; French response

to assassination of, 281; motivation for assassination of, 341

Cantwell, Thomas Edward, 380, 396n4, 521

capitalists and capitalism: anarchism feared by, 195, 416; as basis of society, 364–65; commercial theft and, 29; development of industrial, 79; EG's opinion of, 157, 174–75, 181; as enemy, 333, 354–55, 474–76; exploitation by, 228–32, 283, 488; humanity of, 485; imperialism linked to, 384–88; justifications of, 316, 453; religion as ally of, 320; repression by, 244–46; role in Homestead, 223–25. *See also* police; private property; ruling class

Caplinger Mills (Mo.): Austins' farm near, 517; EG's speeches in, 314–15, 503, 508

Carlyle, Thomas, 60–61, 384, 387

Carmeaux glassworkers, 239

Carmen's Union, 540

Carnegie, Andrew: AB's appeal and, 349–52, 506, 570; biographical summary on, 521–22; mentioned, 56; partner of, 531; philanthropy of, 246n7; responsibility of, for Homestead strike, 224–25, 246, 318

Carnegie (Pa.): EG's speeches in, 504

Carnegie Steel Company, 521, 531. *See also* Homestead (Pa.) strike

Carnot, Marie François-Sadi: assassination of, 55, 206n5, 207n6, 275, 342n6, 427, 498, 554; biographical summary on, 522

Carpenter, Edward, 239n1, 466

Caserio, Sante: assassination by, 55, 206n5, 207n6, 275, 342, 427, 498; associates of, 554; biographical summary on, 522; execution of, 499; mentioned, 225–26, 238, 267, 396

Catholic Church, 53–54

"The Cause and Effect of Vice" (EG): delivery of, 451n2; description of, 453–54

Cavendish, Lord, 382–83n4

Cecil (Pa.): EG's speeches in, 511

censorship: opposition to, 573–74; in prison, 132n1; protest of, 505; symbol of, 271, 334. *See also* free speech, suppression of

Central Labor Federation (CLF), 98n7, 98n11, 571

Central Labor Union (CLU): alternative to, 561; anarchists vs. socialists in, 96–99; appeal for AB via, 251–53, 537, 570; delegates to, 540; description of, 571; EG's link to, 37; officers of, 280n7, 524; single-tax movement and, 531; SLP and, 577; speakers for, 236, 495, 503; unions affiliated to, 546

Century (magazine), 537

CGT. *See* Confédération Générale du Travail

Chaikovsky, Nikolai: biographical summary on, 522; EG's meeting with, 508; mentioned, 376, 395, 396, 509; Paris congress and, 394n11

Chaikovsky Circle of Russian revolutionaries, 18n37, 519, 522, 538, 550

Challeroi (Pa.): EG's speeches in, 504

Chamberlain, Edward, 490, 558, 573, 574

Chamberlain, Joseph, 387, 394, 395, 522

Champney, Adeline, 577

Charles, Fred, biographical summary on, 522; mentioned, 223, 394, 495, 521

Chartism, 530

cheirognomy, 216

Chemnitzer Freie Presse, 545

Cherkesov, Varlaam N.: biographical summary on, 522–23; journal founded by, 568; mentioned, 372n6, 395, 396, 509; Paris congress and, 393n10; speeches of, 62, 509; written contributions of, 568

Chernoe Znomia (The Black Banner), 144n3

Chernyshevsky, N. G.: influence on EG and AB, 13; mentioned, 559; works: *What Is to Be Done?*, 14, 21, 51, 138n3, 519

Chicago: EG arrested in, 464–70, 513, 514; EG's speeches in, 37, 288, 312–13, 502, 503, 505, 507, 510, 511; national labor convention in, 288n1, 310–12; Philosophical Society in, 552; Progressive Labor Organization of, 505; SDA convention in, 338–39, 344–45, 506, 576; Social Revolutionary congress in, 368n3, 491, 555; social science club in, 577. *See also The Alarm; Freedom; Free Soci-*

Comstock Acts (1873, 1876): arrests and prosecutions under, 42, 151n1, 312–13, 392–93n2, 490, 514, 533, 551–52, 565; Beall's book suppressed under, 214n1; challenges to, 9, 490, 505; free speech crushed by, 342; organization in opposition to, 573–74; passage of, 489, 523–24; political violence linked to, 55–56. *See also* censorship

Comstockery, 55

"The Conditions for the Workers of America" (EG): text of, 228–32

Confédération Générale du Travail (CGT), 552

Congress of La Chaux-de-Fonds, 491

Congress of Social Revolutionary Groups (1881), 368n3, 491

Conscription Act (1863), 164n9

Cook, John H.: biographical summary on, 524; as CLU leader, 571; meeting chaired by, 502, 504; speeches of, 282, 303n8, 501, 507

Cooper, Catherine. *See* Austin, Kate

Cooper, Charles B.: biographical summary on, 524; editorship of, 329nn1–2, 568; EG criticized by, 502; as possible delegate, 399

Cooperative College of Citizenship (group), 505

The Co-operator, 576

Cores, George, 565

Corna, Joseph, 369n9

Cornelissen, Christianus Gerardus, 433n7, 510, 524

Cornelissen, Lily, 510, 524

"The Corrupting Influence of Politics on Man" (EG): delivery of, 353n1

Coulon, Auguste, 223, 524, 527, 547

Courier (Fairhope, Ala.), 575

Cox, Jesse, 575

Coxey, J. S., 245n4

Cramer, Johanna Greie, 7, 156–57n4, 492

Crane, Walter, 222

crime and criminals: cause of, 453–54; elimination of, 158, 175, 182; ruling class's perpetration of, 244; society's responsibility for, 187, 197, 249, 341, 426–28, 434, 476. *See also* judicial system (U.S.)

Crispi, Francesco, 53, 335n4

Crocker, Richard, 422

Crosby, Ernest Howard: appeal for AB's release and, 352n5, 570; biographical summary on, 525; mentioned, 481–82; Tolstoy's popularity and, 559

Cuba: insurrection in, 245; Spain's repression of, 278–79n9; U.S. occupation of, 436; war's impact on, 385–87. *See also* Spanish-American War (1898)

Cuban Liberation Army, 385n2

Cultura Obrera, 529

Cupid's Yokes (Heywood), 151n1, 489, 490, 491, 573

Czolgosz, Leon: anarchists' defense of, 77, 475n6, 476–77, 478n, 479–80, 517; anarchists' denunciation of, 76, 78, 475n6, 482, 484–85, 487–88, 520; assassination of McKinley by, 74–75, 78–79, 460n1, 512–13, 542; biographical summary on, 525–26; citizenship of, 474–75; confession by, 460–63; EG linked to, 73–76, 452n1, 460–63, 464n1, 471–2 EG on interaction with, 466–68, 511; execution of, 477, 514; mentioned, 342n5; name for, 471; possible charges against EG and, 469–70; trial of, 514. *See also* "The Tragedy at Buffalo" (EG)

Daily People (SLP), 528, 578

Daily Record (Stockton, Calif.), 35

Darrow, Clarence Seward, 516, 526

Dave, Victor: anarchism of, 518; at anarchist congress, 491; associates of, 382–83n4, 547, 551; biographical summary on, 526; correspondence from, 482–83; EG defended by, 510; EG's visit with, 406; mentioned, 407; Most-Peukert split and, 101–2n3, 545; written contributions of, 566

David, Marie Louise: background of, 204n2; biographical summary on, 526; at gathering after EG's release from prison, 203, 204, 208; phrenological view of, 214; sketch of, 204; speeches of, 579; written contributions of, 568

Davies, Ann A.: biographical summary on,

Eddy, Mary Baker, 486

Edelmann, John H.: associates of, 526, 542, 548; biographical summary on, 529; death of, 399n14, 432; editorship of, 329nn1–2, 568; mentioned, 399; opposition to, 98; as Socialist League founder, 98–99n12, 537, 579; speeches of, 208, 237, 495, 496, 499, 500; written contributions of, 568

Edelstadt, David, 16, 556, 566, 574

Edelstadt, Sarah, 208n8, 499

education: anarchism's intersection with, 357–59; as class system, 59, 159; compulsory, 54, 340–41; free speech and, 31; possibilities in, 57–58, 443, 453; pursued in prison, 33; as responsible for vice, 453–54; university, 364, 374

Education and Defense Society (Lehr-und-Wehr Verein), 530

"The Effect of War on the Workers" (EG): delivery of, 382n1, 383n8, 509; description of, 60–61; transcript of, 384–88

egoism: EG on, 29; as rationale for being anarchist, 157; Stirner's definition of, 557–58, 560; as term for anarchist individualism, 125

egoist, 125n2

Ehrhart, F. J., 382–83n4

Eiffel, A. Gustave, 561

Eliot, George, 33

Elizabeth (empress of Austria): assassination of, 55, 346–48, 427n9, 506, 531, 540

Elizabeth (N.J.): EG's speech in, 494

Elkin, John P., 459nn2–3

Elliott, James B., 305n13, 329n3, 573

Ellis, Havelock, 556, 563, 566

Elmira Reformatory, 200n4

Ely, Robert Erskine, 438n1, 539

L'Émancipation, 560

Emerson, Ralph Waldo, 33, 145–46n6, 426, 553

emotions: expressed through deeds, 301; limitations of words to express, 45; maturity of, 486–87; power of, 485–86; reason juxtaposed to, 83; sorrow as, 485–86. See also happiness; love

empathy: documents as evidence of, 82. See also emotions

Engel, George: associates of, 530; on attentats, 15; biographical summary on, 529; execution of, 7, 492; as influence on American radicals, 156–57n4

Engels, Friedrich, 9, 43, 383, 529, 542

England: EG's reception in, 221–27, 237–38; EG's speeches in, 60–62, 358; free speech absent in, 395, 545; Haymarket remembrances in, 358; imperialism of, 230, 553; police in, 204, 223; potential for anarchist women in, 429; proposed importation of speaker from, 400; single-tax organizations in, 575; war protests as focus in, 394

English, Abraham Lincoln, 440n3, 446n1, 447–48

English language: EG's use of, 237n7, 325, 428, 504; German usage vs., 165, 168–69; necessity of using in U.S., 48, 317; need for propaganda in, 258, 429–30, 499, 558; newspapers in, 568; strikers' lack of, 287n2

Ensor, James, 413n2

equality: basis for, 364–65; false notion of, 474–75; gender, in Russia, 424–25; necessity of gender, 43–44, 322–23; racial, 52, 246

El Esclavo, 529

Esteve, Pedro: biographical summary on, 529–30; marriage of, 554; McKinley's assassination and, 463n5, 513; speeches of, 208, 422n1, 496, 499, 507, 510

ethics: debate on, 400–403

Europe: anarchist propaganda in (EG), 236–38; EG's medical training in, 38, 59, 63, 366–67; knowledge of American anarchism limited in, 398

European tours: departure for (EG), 370n1; description of, 59–67, 430n15; events of, 500, 508–10; illness during, 374; isolation felt in, 406–7, 413; motivations for, 38–39; plans for, 366–67; reflections on, 337–39, 392, 395; surveillance during, 389–91. See also London; Paris

Evening Bulletin (Providence, R.I.), 36

Exposition Universelle (Paris, 1900): architecture of, 413n2; art exhibits of, 413, 415; congress in conjunction with, 59, 65, 430; housing needed during, 370, 372n6, 379; size of, 397n8 role in, 71. *See also* "Authority vs. Liberty" (EG); free speech; free love; liberty

Freedom (Chicago), 528, 544, 550

Freedom (London): AB on *attentat* in, 521; on Brady, 24; compositor for, 521; contributors to, 519, 522, 523, 526, 527, 528, 534, 535, 537, 538, 539, 547, 549; description of, 565; founding of, 516, 538; funds for, 538; mentioned, 355n6, 380, 396; Nettlau's essay in, 375n9; publisher of, 560; on war and workers (EG), 384–88

Freedom Discussion Group (London), 509

freedom of the press, 442–43. *See also* free speech

Free Exchange, 556

free love: Austin's report on, 517; convention on, 489; EG's demand for, 43; opposition to, 12, 312–13, 507, 517, 550. *See also* sexual freedom

Free Press, 518

Free Press Defense Committee, 537

Free Religious Association, 489

Free Review, 533

Free Society (San Francisco, Chicago, and New York): on American anarchism (EG), 65; arrests of comrades associated with, 75–76; on authority vs. liberty (EG), 57; baptism story in, 369n9; on Bresci (EG), 74, 455–56; contributors to, 517, 519, 523, 524, 528, 535, 537, 544, 548, 550, 552; Czolgosz and, 468n14, 511–12, 514, 525; description of, 565–66; distribution of, 466n9, 519, 520, 524, 554; editor of, 544; EG's response to trial verdict in, 182n6; founding of, 503; on free speech (EG), 61, 353–56; funds for, 21, 538; on ideas and men (EG), 334–36; importance of, 392; on lecturing (EG letter), 67; letters to (EG's), 334–36, 344–45, 395–403, 434–37; location of, 392, 432–33, 510, 536; masthead of, *323*; on McKinley's assassination (EG), 471–78; mentioned, 329, 370, 380, 396; on New Woman (EG), 322–23; origins of, 516, 536, 565; on Paris congress (EG), 416–21; praise for, 48; on propaganda

(EG), 392–94; readers of, 535; on SDA, 576; on social science clubs, 577; success in western states, 338. *See also* "The Tragedy at Buffalo" (EG)

Free Soil Society (N.Y.), 574, 575

free speech: as basic human desire, 31; barring of radical journals and, 21; demand for, 29; defense of, 179–82; demand for, 29; early battles of, 30–32, 75; education and, 31; EG's essay on, 149–50Ger., 151–54; EG's trial testimony on, 176; EG's trial as test of, 194–95, 207; in England, 61, 395; in Paris, 413; suppression of, 61, 72–73, 225, 353–56, 395, 413, 416–19, 430, 440, 445, 446–47; suppression of workers' rights to and defense of, 151–54, 179–89, 194–95, 225; tensions over interpretation of, 40–41; threats to, 442–43; in U.S. vs. Europe, 318; in U.S. vs. Russia, 28–29, 285–87, 318, 440, 447–48; women's freedom linked to, 51

Free Speech Defense Committee, 556

Free Speech League, 574

"Free Speech Suppressed in Barre, Vt." (EG): text of, 353–56

Free Thinkers Magazine, 528

freethought principles, 572. *See also* Liberal Clubs

Free Trade, 556

Freie Arbeiter Stimme (Free Voice of Labor, New York): articles on EG, 97n6; contributors to, 518, 523, 528, 532; demise of, 495; description of, 566; editors of, 540, 556; escape plan and, 59; finances of, 562; founding of, 494, 574; Haymarket anarchists defended by, 16; police raid of, 80, 475n6, 514; predecessor of, 18

Freie Gesellschaft (Free Society): demise of, 509; founding of, 500; mentioned, 257; publication of, 257n2; readers of, 263

Freiheit (Freedom, London and Paris): AB and, 17, 102n4, 121, 519; on AB's *attentat*, 119–20n1, 496; compositor for, 543; contributors to, 517, 520, 539, 542, 547, 554; criticism of, 101–2n3; description of, 566; distribution

Freiheit (Freedom, London and Paris)
(continued)
of, 519, 555; editors of, 382–83n4, 538; on
EG's lecture tour, 335n3; EG's response to
trial verdict in, 182n6; founding of, 491;
manager of, 555; mentioned, 64, 257, 493;
on Paris congress, 393n5, 407n3; persistence of, 48; on SDA, 576; violent rhetoric in,
15, 16–17, 80, 513, 546, 579
Freiheitiener (freedomites): use of term, 260
French, Santiago Salvador, 498, 499
French government: communiqué of, 64, 389–
91; corruption of, 226–27; disappointed in
socialist, 417–19; extradition order of, 64,
439; intelligence report of, 408–9
French Interior Ministry, 64, 389–91
French language: newspapers in, 566, 567,
568; study of, 374–75
French Revolution: legacy of, 416–17; mentioned, 145, 164, 166; participants in, 549
Freud, Sigmund: as influence on EG, 11–12,
38, 77; EG attends lectures of, 500
Frick, Henry Clay: attempt on life of, 16, 22–
23, 25–27, 76, 109, 267–68, 496; biographical summary on, 531; Homestead strike
and, 106–7n13, 217, 521; motives for attack
on, 132–33n3, 223–25, 246, 249, 341
Friedman, Joseph, 125n1
Friendship Liberal League (Philadelphia): as
open venue, 573; speeches for, 305, 329, 502,
504, 507
Friends of Russian Freedom, 525
FS. See Free Society
Fuchs, Jacob, 260–61, 571
Fulton, Edward H., 264, 531, 567
funds and fund-raising: for AB's legal expenses, 40–41, 227n, 249, 250, 258, 260,
262, 312, 325, 535, 570; for anarchist press,
21, 27, 40, 257, 263, 376n10, 438n3, 538, 551;
for anarchist propaganda and meetings,
125–26, 237, 277; for EG's legal expenses,
187, 498; for medical training, 366–67n2;
newspaper on, 203; for Paris congress, 393–
94, 399; for publishing report on Paris con-

gress, 420; for speaking engagements, 68,
400–403, 444; for travels, 300, 302, 379,
407, 426

"Gaetano Bresci" (EG): text of, 455–56
Galleani, Luigi, 507
Gallifet, Gen. Gaston, 397, 417
Garfield, James, 79, 422n3
Garibaldi, Giuseppe, 523
Garland, Mahlon Morris, 280
Garment Dyers Union, 538
Garrison, William Lloyd, 525, 551
Garson, Leopold, 537
Gary, Joseph E., 516
La Gazette de Hollande, 560
Gelfman, Gesia, 427n10
gender: EG's incorporation of, 11–12, 43–44,
322–23; in Russia, 424–25; separatism and
essentialism and, 44. *See also* sexuality and
sexual desire, "The New Woman" (EG)
George, Henry: biographical summary on, 531;
as influence, 548, 574–75; support for, 528,
529, 571. *See also* Single Tax (movement)
Gephardt, Paul, 110
German Anarchist Society (Philadelphia), 504
German Communistic Workingmen's Club,
545. *See also Freiheit*
German government: communiqué from, 64,
389–91; official circulars of, 220; warning
about EG by, 38
German language: EG's use of, 32–33, 46, 86,
87, 243, 325, 415n5; English usage vs., 165,
168–69; newspapers in, 564, 566, 567, 568
German Painters Union, 511
German Social Democratic Party, 517
Germany: anarchist movement in, 101–2n3;
anti-socialist law in, 212; culture of, 46; possible housing in (Munich), 379, 380; potential for anarchist women in, 429; repression
in, 14, 401n5; single-tax organizations in,
575; student unrest in, 364. *See also* German
government
Gide, André, 239n1
Girard, André, 568

mentioned, 332, 476; resolutions in response to, 288n2, 550; SDA's response to,
576; EG's speeches on, 47, 285–87, 305,
327, 328

Hearst, William Randolph, 325n3

Heath, Frederic, 575, 576

Hegel, Georg W. F., 518

Heiber, Peter, 570

Heine, Heinrich, 401

Heinzen, Karl, "Murder against Murder," 513,
514, 546

Henderson Bay colony (Wash.), 576

Henry, Agnes, 240n1

Henry, Émile: biographical summary on, 534;
execution of, 498; mentioned, 193n4, 226,
238, 418n11

Henry George Lecture Association, 575

Der Herold (Detroit), 261n5, 571

Herschdorfer, F., 145

Herzen, Alexander, 483

Heywood, Angela, 42, 489, 494

Heywood, Ezra: arrests and imprisonment of,
151n1, 490, 491, 492, 493–94, 573; associates of, 559; at free-love convention, 489; on
sexual freedom, 42; works: *Cupid's Yokes*,
151n1, 489, 490, 491, 573

Hicks, Henry E., 99

Hill, David Bennett, 212, 534

Hillkowitz, M. *See* Hillquit, Morris

Hillquit, Morris: biographical summary on,
534–35; mentioned, 37; organizations and,
509, 527, 528, 576, 578, 579; speeches of,
147n8

Hinton, R. J., 576

Hochstein, David, 160n10, 535

Hochstein, Helena Goldman (EG's half-sister):
biographical summary on, 535; children of,
160n10; EG's stay with, 140n1, 493; immigration of, 4–5, 492; mentioned, 466

Hochstein, Hyman, 535

Hodel, Max, 15

Hoffmann, Julius, 120

Hogan, James, 576

Holmes, Lizzie: biographical summary on,
535; editorship of, 563; mentioned, 393n3;

speeches arranged by, 505; written contributions of, 509, 565, 568

Holmes, Oliver Wendell, 557

Holmes, William T.: biographical summary
on, 535; at convention, 498; on ethics,
401–2; friends of, 517, 530; mentioned, 393;
speeches arranged by, 505, 508; written contributions of, 482, 509, 563, 565–66, 568

Home Colony (Wash.), 508, 544

Homestead (Pa.) strike: AB on, 106–8; conditions evidenced by, 224; description of,
106–7n13, 495–96, 531; failure of, 265–66;
manifesto on, 543, 558; mentioned, 151n2,
217, 231, 337, 386

Hope Church (Pa.): EG's speeches in, 508

Hopkins, L. L., 576

Horr, Alex, 524, 577

hours. *See* wages and hours

Howells, William Dean, 245n5, 481–82, 481n2

Hugo, Victor, 559

L'Humanité nouvelle (New Humanity, Paris and
Brussels): contributors to, 263, 526; description of, 566; founding of, 533; readers of,
370, 372n6.

humanity: of capitalists, 485; division of, 487;
interdependence of, 59, 83–84, 365; purpose of, 362–63

Humbert. *See* Umberto (king of Italy)

Huneker, James, 555

Hungarian uprising (1848), 347n7

Hungary: independence of, 530; minorities in,
407n6

Hunter, Robert G., 459n5

Hus, Jan, 247

Huxley, T. H., 538

Hyndman, Henry Mayers, 382, 578

hypnotism, 361

Ibels, André, 239n1

Ibsen, Henrik, 239n1

Ibsen. *See* Morton, Eric B.

ice cream parlors, 22, 495, 500, 519

Idaho: strike in, 386, 476

"Ideas and Men" (EG): text of, 334–36

Il Grido degli Oppressi, 542

ILGWU (International Ladies Garment Workers' Union), 518

Illustrated American, 155n3

immigrants and immigration: as audience, 21, 46; culture of, 357–61; of EG, 492; isolation of, 48; laws on, 496, 526, 534, 558; violence against, 20; workers as, 229. *See also* Americanization

imprisonment (AB's): censorship in, 132n1; comrades in, 139, 258; conditions of, 132–35, 256; escape plan during, 59–60, 65–66, 138, 373n2, 414, 484, 485, 502, 508, 509, 520, 544, 570; injury during, 373; mentioned, 307; physical effects of, 138; raffles during, 258, 260, 262; sentence reduction in, 458–59, 511, 514–15, 571; solitary confinement in, 74, 77, 80, 373n2, 457, 484, 514; studies during, 486, 564; surveillance in, 255; visitors during, 130–31, 136–37, 459, 484, 496, 512, 532, 543. *See also* Pennsylvania Board of Pardons

imprisonment (EG's): descriptive account of, 34–36; effects of, 193, 200–202; EG's letters during, 33–34, 190–91Ger., 192–93; gathering to celebrate release from, 203–8, 499, 546, 554; as influence, 23–24; interview during, 155–60; length of, 160n12; occupations during, 430, 445, 498; reflections on, 194–201; release from, 34–35, 201–2, 499; studies during, 33; visitors during, 498, 499, 527, 558

incitement to riot: EG's testimony on, 172, 174; sentencing for, 177–79; trial testimony on, 162–64, 167, 169–70. *See also* People vs. Emma Goldman (trial, 1893)

Indians: slaughtering of, 230, 244

individualism: *attentat*'s cause and, 476; beliefs of, 402–3, 434; free associative action and, 552; as influence on EG, 10–11, 425–26, 453, 549; men and women's equality and, 323; responsibility of, 431; Spencer on, 556–57

Individualist, 526

individualist anarchism: egoism linked to, 125n2; ideas of, 10–11; influences on, 355n4,

557–58. *See also* individualism; Tucker, Benjamin R.

Industrial Union of Direct Actionists, 546

Industrial Workers of the World (IWW), 477n12, 551

Ingalls, Joshua K., 567

Ingersoll, Robert, 52n57, 315–16n40, 330, 343n

intelligentisia: appeal to, 71–72; revolutionary potential of (EG), 50–52. *See also* education; middle class

International Anarchist Convention (Chicago, 1893), 498

international anarchist movement: AB supported by, 38–39; communication channel in, 420; progress of, 236–38; solidarity lacking in, 397–98, 406–7, 413. *See also specific anarchists*

International Anti-Anarchist Conference (Italy, 1898), 506–7

International Association of Machinists, 281n8

International Carpenters and Joiners Union, 540

International Club Freiheit, 103n8

International Conference for the Defense of Society against the Anarchists, 346n2

International Conference of Neo-Malthusians, 64, 66, 509

International Criminal Police Organization (Interpol), 506

Internationale Arbeiter Liedertafel (International Workers' Song Circle): fund-raising and, 260n2, 262n1, 498; leader of, 555; Paris Commune remembered by, 262n2

Internationale Bibliothek (International Library, New York), 566

International Federation of Commercial Employees, 560

International Ladies Garment Workers' Union (ILGWU), 518

International Revolutionary Congress of the Working People (Paris, 1900): delegates to, 375n6, 391, 393, 523, 526, 527, 534, 548, 553; EG's participation in, 59, 62; EG's preparation for, 64–65, 66, 367–68, 396, 509;

Leibnitz, Gottfried Wilhelm, 486

Leishmann, John, 249n7

Lenin, V. I., 13n31

"Letters from a Tour" (EG, series in *Sturm-vogel*): description of, 43, 45–47; text of, 293–99Ger., 300–317

letters to the editor (EG's): on AB's sentence, 217–18; on assassinations, 346–48, 479–80; on funds for AB's defense, 240–42; on ideas and men, 334–36; on lecture tour, 337–39; on Most, 116–18Ger., 119–21; on payment for speakers, 400–403; on Pittsburgh anarchists, 329–30; on political violence, 55–56, 340–43; on propaganda by deed, 434–37; on speaking out, 344–45; on striking tailors, 219; Tucker/EG exchange as, 349–52

letter writing: importance to imprisoned AB, 134–35, 254, 458; promptness of EG's, 481

Levy, David, 145, 162n8

Levy, Ferdinand, 147n

Lewis, Jacob. *See* Kershner, Jacob A.

Lewis, Roman: biographical summary on, 540; editorship of, 566, 574; Haymarket anarchists defended by, 16; mentioned, 486; opposition to, 98; in Pioneers of Liberty, 574; speech of, 495

Liberal Alliance, 572

Liberal Clubs: description of, 572–73; focus of, 53–54; EG's speeches for, 305, 330, 479, 501, 505, 510

liberal democracy: pros/cons of, 42; seduction of reform in, 52–55

Liberal Progressive Society (Providence), 322–23

The Liberator, 551

Le Libertaire (The Libertarian, Paris), 421, 543, 566

Libertarian Lecture Society, 527

Libertas. *See* Davies, Ann A.

liberty: ideals of, 364–65; Paris as city of, 416–17; spirit of, 355–56. *See also* "Authority vs. Liberty" (EG); freedom

Liberty (London): contributors to, 523, 537; cover of, *222*; description of, 566–67; on EG's lecture, 221–27; founding of, 558

Liberty: Not the Daughter but the Mother of Order (Boston and New York): appeal for AB's pardon and, 349–52; contributors to, 526, 528; description of, 567; distribution of, 555; editor of, 10; founding of, 491, 559; as influence, 264n9; location of, 495; masthead of, 350; Most criticized in, 545; readers of, 549

Liberty Library Monthly, 531

Lieble, Otto H., 153n7

Liess, Emil, 337n1, 505, 506

Lincoln, Abraham, 79, 145, 164n9

Linden, Mauritz, 544

Lingg, Louis: arrest of, 464n4, 554; biographical summary on, 540; as influence on EG, 156–57n4; mentioned, 313–14; sentencing statement of, 31; suicide of, 7, 136, 492

literature: as authority, 355; celebration of German, 553; as effective propaganda, 412

Lithuania: EG's birth in, 489

Livesey, Francis Buck, 54, 340, 343n, 565

Living My Life (EG): on AB and *Freiheit*, 102n4; on article in *New York World*, 194n1; on Czolgosz's act and her subsequent arrest, 78, 464n2; on Debs, 312n32; on AB's escape plan, 60; on EG's 1893 illness, 140n1; on EG's extradition from Philadelphia, 153n8, 170n17; focus and context of, 3–5; on Havel, 534; identity of Yegor in, 445n11; on influence of Johanna Greie Cramer, 156–57n14; on loving two men, 557; on marriage, 537; on obtaining legal services, 161n6; on prison confrontation, 255n7; on Statue of Liberty, 5; on visit to AB in prison, 255n3; on wealthy sponsors, 366–67n2–

Lloyd, George K., 96–97, 109

Lloyd, Henry, 251n5

Lloyd, J. L., 344, 345

Lloyd, John F., 576

lois scélérates. *See* anti-anarchist laws: in France

Lôme, Enrique Depuy de, 325, 332

London: "Bloody Sunday" deaths in, 205n3, 541; EG's response to, 379; Russian exiles in, 395n2; EG's speeches in, 221–27, *371*, 374n5, *382*, *390*, *500*, *509*; surveillance of EG in, 389. *See also Die Autonomie; The Commonweal; Freedom; Freiheit;* International Social Revolutionary and Anarchist Congress; *Liberty;* Second International, London congress of

London, Jack, 505

Los Angeles (Calif.): EG's speeches in, 330n7, 506

Lo-Scalpellino (Barre, Vt.), 276n5

Louvre, 406, 413

love: EG's belief in power of, 12, 42–44; EG's definition of, 292; EG's, for two men, 557; labor of, 49; marriage's impact on, 29, 159; role in sexual freedom, 322; social class and, 43, 270–72. *See also* free love

Luccheni, Luigi: assassination by, 55, 427n9, 506; biographical summary on, 540–41; EG's denunciation of, 346–48; mentioned, 482

Lucifer Circle, 13, 502, 511

Lucifer, the Lightbearer (Valley Falls, Kans., and Chicago): alleged obscene material in, 151n1; contributors to, 517, 524, 528, 535, 542, 544, 554; dating of, 521; description of, 567; distribution of, 572; editor of, 42; founding of, 491; as influence on EG, 9; letters to (EG's), 479–80; location of, 500; on McKinley's assassination, 77; as model, 563; publication of, 533; readers of, 535

Ludwig, Gen. William, 386n7

Lum, Dyer D.: editorship of, 492, 535, 563; Haymarket anarchists and, 540, 553; mentioned, 577; speeches of, 496, 551; written contributions of, 567, 568

Lusitania, 562

Le Lycéen républicain, 552

lynching, 52, 61, 386

Lynn (Mass.): EG's speeches in, 506, 510

Madagascar: French occupation of, 226

Madison, James, 536

Maguire, George, 574

Maguire, James G., 574

Mainwaring, Sam, 382n1

Malatesta, Errico: associates of, 524, 529, 532, 536, 542, 543, 546, 547; biographical summary on, 541; as delegate, 234n2, 397n9, 491, 501, 523; deportation of, 558; EG's meeting with, 38, 500; First International and, 489; on heartaches, 44; as influence on EG, 9, 13; written contributions of, 569

Malthusian League, 66

Manhattan Liberal Club, 479, 510, 514, 572–73

Manhattan Single Tax Club, 237n5, 575

Manhood Suffrage League (London), 561

manifestos: on Homestead strike, 543; Michel and Kropotkin's, 153n6; of Socialist League, 578; on suppression of congress, 420, 421; on suppression of lecture, 355n6. *See also* Pittsburgh Manifesto (1883)

Mann, Tom, 62, 382n1, 509

Manning, Cardinal Henry Edward, 205, 331, 424, 541

Marcellus, Percy, 446

Marquette Club (N.Y.), 471–72n4

marriage: alternative to, 113, 158–59; EG's critique of, 29, 42–44, 309; as foundation of private property, 9, 43, 269; inequality in, 44, 269; pamphlet on abolition of, 151n1, 489, 490, 491, 573; EG's rejection of, 272–73, 289–90, 342

"Marriage" (EG): text of, 269–73

Marron, John, 570

Marsh, Alfred, 396n4, 536, 565

Martin, Charles, 575

Martin, James L.: acquittal of, 285n1; biographical summary on, 541; killings by, 287n2, 305, 321; mentioned, 332

Martine, Randolph B.: biographical summary on, 541; as judge in People vs. Emma Goldman, 161, 177–79, 182, 207

Martínez de Campos, Arsenio, 498, 549

Marx, Eleanor, 578

Marx, Karl Henrich: associates of, 529, 558; biographical summary on, 541–42; First International and, 398n12; as influence on

Marx, Karl Henrich *(continued)*
EG, 9; as influence on others, 382n2, 518; mentioned, 408; support for, 540

Maryson, J. A., 257n2, 566, 574

masses: appeal to (EG), 41, 320–21; fickleness of, 443–44; indifference of, 435; individuals vs., 431. *See also* public opinion

Masur, Carl, 106, 130, 192n2, 542, 563

The Match, 520, 537, 546

Matchett, Charles H., 496

May Day: celebrations of, 96–97, 99, 108–9, 120, 494; speakers for, 236, 495

Mayers, J., 99

McCormick Harvester (company), 492, 555

McCowan, Rev. H. S., 315–16n40, 330n5, 503

McDonald (Pa.): EG's speeches in, 508

McGlynn, Father, 574

McGuinness, Edwin, 284n3

McGuire, Peter James, 280, 303

McIntyre (detective in England), 223

McIntyre, John F., 161n3, 176n28, 207, 426

McKeesport (Pa.): EG's speeches in, 504

McKinley, William: AB on assassination of, 73–79, 484–85, 487–88; assassination of, 68–69, 73–79, 460n1, 461–62, 471n2, 512–13, 525; biographical summary on, 542; campaign of, 533; criticism of, 41; death of, 514; EG on assassination of, 68–69, 73–79, 467, 471–78, 479–80; EG's opinion of, 245, 249, 325, 332, 471, 476; gold standard and, 257; possible fears of, 274, 278, 422; public opinion of, 485; second inauguration of, 510; state troops used by, 245n4; treaty signed by, 506

McLeod, Pearl, 577

Mechanic, Julia, 464n2, 468n13, 485n4, 512–13

Melba, Nellie, 331

Merlino, Francesco Saverio: accusations against, 241; at anarchist congress, 491; associates of, 526; biographical summary on, 542; editorship of, 329n1, 568; on political participation, 53, 335–36; speeches of, 496, 579

Il Messaggero (Rome), 53

Metzkow, Max: biographical summary on, 542–43; escape plan and, 60; Homestead strike and, 106–7n13, 519; letters to (1892–1895), 130–31, 140; letters to (1896–1900), 251–53, 258–62, 373

Michel, Louise: associates of, 536, 546, 560; biographical summary on, 543; as delegate, 234n2, 397n9, 491, 501; in demonstrations, 144–45n3, 552; at EG's London speech, 221; EG's meeting with, 38, 500; exile of, 181n5; illustration of, *226;* manifesto of, 153n6; newspaper of, 566; school of, 240n1, 524, 543; speeches of, 30, 62, 226, 500, 509; written contributions of, 567, 569

Michelet, Victor Émile, 566

Michelson, Miriam: career of, 440n1; EG interviewed by, 72–73, 289–92, 440–45

middle class: EG's appeal to, 71–72; EG's hopes for, 72–73; revolutionary potential of, 50–52, 429, 443

Mikhailov, Alexander, 427n10, 491

Milch, Jac., 147

Mill, John Stuart, 33

Miller, Herman, 366–67n2

Millerand, Etienne-Alexandre, 397n10, 417n6, 418–19

Milner, Alfred, 387, 394, 395, 543, 553

Milwaukee (Wis.): EG's speeches in, 505; SDA's candidates in, 576

miners: conditions for, 338, 366, 368; national labor convention and, 310–11; as patriots, 327; Spanish-American War and, 61; strikes of, 386, 476. *See also* Hazleton (Pa.) massacre; Homestead (Pa.) strike; United Mine Workers

Minkin, Anna, 21, 24, 493, 494, 519

Minkin, Helen, 21, 114n6, 493, 494, 519

minorities: in Austro-Hungarian politics, 407n6; repression of, 229–30. *See also* immigrants and immigration; Native Americans

Mirbeau, Octave, 559, 569

Mitchell, Seward, 573

Modell, David A., 577

New York Times: on anarchist/unemployed demonstration, 144n1; on Cánovas's assassination, 276n6; contributors to, 558; on Czolgosz (EG), 466n6; on EG's speech, 422; on EG's trial, 173nn22–23; on gathering after EG's release from prison, 208n11

New York Tribune, 542

New York World: on anarchists, 36, 274–79; on attentats, 100–110, 496, 540–41; barred speech in (EG), 32; contributors to, 98n9, 520; on Czolgosz and EG, 471–72n4; on EG's speech at anarchist/unemployed demonstration, 96–99, 146n7; on EG's trial, 177–82; focus of, 85; on gathering after EG's release from prison, 34–35, 203–8; on Hazleton, 541; illustration of EG in, 480; interviews of EG in, 29–30, 111–15, 155–60, 172n21, 464–70; letters to (EG's), 219, 346–48; on prison conditions (EG), 34, 194–202, 499; on violence, 477n12

Nicholas I (tsar of Russia), 518

Nicoll, David: biographical summary on, 547; editorship of, 538, 564–65, 578; mentioned, 396n4, 524; on Walsall anarchists, 546; written contributions of, 567

Niedermann, Claus, 111–12n1, 564

Nietzsche, Friedrich: EG's reading of, 38–39, 500; as influence on EG, 10; as influence on Ruedebusch, 554; written contributions of, 567

Nieuwenhuis, Ferdinand Domela: associates of, 524; biographical summary on, 547–48; mentioned, 368; newspaper of, 510; Paris congress and, 417–18; written contributions of, 566

nihilists and nihilism: definition of, 100n1; deportation of, 245; as influence on EG and AB, 51, 267; AB's uncle's link to, 18n37, 424; Zola on, 562

The Nineteenth Century, 539

Nobiling, Carl Eduard, 15

Nold, Carl: on AB's attentat, 132–33n3; AB's defense and, 520, 570–71; arrest and imprisonment of, 26, 138–39, 258, 262, 501, 513,

520; associates of, 130–31, 496, 517, 519, 543; attorney of, 125n1; biographical summary on, 548; code-name for, 254n2; defense of, 549; EG's reunion with, 307–9; escape plan and, 502; Homestead strike and, 106–7n13; illustration of, 139; mentioned, 188n3, 373, 393, 401; EG's research material on, 265, 266–67; speeches of, 504; visitors for, 255; written contributions of, 567, 568

Norris, Charles Goldsmith, 464, 468, 470, 513

Notkin, Natasha: associates of, 527; EG's speech and, 510; as influence, 305n11, 573; mentioned, 428n13; in social science club, 577

Nowak, John, 462

Nowak, Walter, 462n3, 512

Der Nußknacker, 545

Oakland (Calif.): EG's speeches in, 58–59, 362–65, 508

Oakland Enquirer, 58–59, 362–65

obscenity: Comstock's definition of, 55–56; distaste for, 51, 73. See also Comstock Acts (1873, 1876); vulgarity

occupations (EG's): garment and dressmaking, 21, 27, 140n1, 158, 173, 425, 492, 493, 494; ice cream parlor, 22, 495, 500, 519; knitting and crocheting, 376, 379, 380; medical training, 38, 59, 63; nursing, 77, 291, 366–67, 430, 432, 444, 445, 482, 483, 500, 510; photography studio, 22, 495; in prison, 198–99, 430, 445; salesperson, 467, 504, 512; tutoring, 406

O'Connell, James A., 281

Oerter, Friedrich Joseph (Sepp), 192n2, 220, 389n4, 548, 563

Oerter, Joseph Friedrich (Fritz), 548

Office du Travail (Paris), 264

Ogarev, Nicholas, 483n14

Ohio: state troops used in strikes in, 245n4. See also Cincinnati; Cleveland

Ohio Liberal Club, 330, 505, 507

O'Mara (Pittsburgh police chief), 113–14

Platt Amendment (1902), 386n5, 436n6
Pleydell, Arthur, 305n12, 446, 448n, 574
police: AB investigated by, 100; anarchist/
unemployed demonstrations and, 144; anti-
anarchist hysteria of, 471–72n4, 485; attitudes toward, 248; authority of, 355, 360;
brutality and tyranny of, 153, 181, 223, 446–
48; as capitalist force, 162–64, 167, 171,
205–6; confrontations with, 46–47, 97;
EG beaten by, 80–81; EG's baiting of, 319–
20; EG's opinion of, 174, 452, 467; fear of,
422; free speech suppressed by, 440, 441,
442, 443, 447–48, 501, 502, 510; French
gatherings suppressed by, 419–20; at
gathering after EG's release, 203–4; statue
commemorating, 313n35. *See also* National
Guard; Pinkerton National Detective
Agency; surveillance
police records: affadavit, 148; on EG's arrest,
28, *165*; intake report, *473*; mug shot, *472*
political participation: debate on, 52–54, 334–
36, 542; Debs's focus on, 312; EG on limits
of, 52; organizations supporting, 575–76,
578, 579; as prostitution, 398
political prisoners: anarchists as, 187–89;
books on, 263–64; coining of term, 26; in
Russia/Siberia, 139, 181, 424, 522, 550;
woman as, 186
political violence: acceptance of (EG), 70–71,
432; appeal for AB's release and, 350–52;
discourse on, 14, 29, 83, 340, 341; EG's testimony on, 175; Hazleton (Pa.) massacre and,
288; individual acts of, 341–42; EG on inevitability of, 55–56, 81; as means to social
revolution, 226–27; predicted demise of,
76–77; refusal to advocate, 426–28; and retaliation concept, 55; against workingmen,
181. *See also* assassinations; propaganda by
the deed *(attentats)*
politics: EG's early years in, 5–6; of electoral
reform, 47–49; hypocrisy in, 52–54, 283;
impossibility of justice via, 221–27, 321,
500; personal issues and, 12–13; rejection of, 244–45, 249–50. *See also* liberal
democracy

Pope, Abner J.: arrest and imprisonment
of, 312n33, 392–93n2, 502, 565; associates
of, 516, 536; biographical summary on,
551–52
Populist Party (People's Party), 98n9, 99n13
Portland (Oreg.): EG's speeches in, 330n7, 506,
508. *See also The Firebrand*
Pouget, Jean Joseph (Émile): arrest of, 543; associates of, 524, 550; biographical summary
on, 552; as delegate, 234n2; in demonstrations, 144–45n3; editorship of, 567; mentioned, 368; Paris congress and, 417. *See also
Le Père Peinard*
poverty: extent of, 231; increased activism in
response to, 231–32; miseries of, 151–52,
171–72, 174, 224; EG speaking on causes of,
27–29. *See also* working class
Prescott, William Blair, 280
press, anarchist: attacks on, 80; EG's correc-
tions in, 70–71; EG's first writing in, 116–
18Ger., 119–21; EG's role in, 40–41, 48–
49; EG's tone in, 33; European circulation
of, 238; funds for, 21, 27, 40, 257, 263,
376n10, 438n3, 538, 551; influence on western states, 338; limits of, 398; role in anarchist movement development, 392–93. *See
also specific periodicals*
press, mainstream: anti-anarchist hysteria in,
471–72n4, 485, 575; biases of, 28, 47; credibility of, 434, 436, 467; criticism of, 58–59,
281; EG's appeal to, 31, 44–45; limitations
of, 364. *See also specific periodicals*
Pressburg, Joseph, 565
Press Writers Association, 340n1
Price, George M., 251n1
Price, William L., 446n4, 575
Prison Blossoms: contributors to, 434n3, 519,
520, 548; description of, 567; creation of,
26; on motives for AB's *attentat*, 132–33n3;
production of, 254n2
prisons: conditions in, 33–34, 194–202; food
in, 304–5; free speech advocates in, 151; patriotism in, 485; and self-education, 33; sentence reduction in, 458; U.S. vs. other countries', 196–97, 256. *See also* Blackwell's

Island Penitentiary; imprisonment (AB's); imprisonment (EG's); Tombs; Western Penitentiary

private property: criticism of, 171–72, 354–55, 554; marriage as foundation of, 9, 43, 269; opposition to, 181, 196. *See also* Single Tax

El Productor, 529

Progressive Labor Organization of Chicago, 505

progressive reform, 52

Proletarian Club (N.Y.), 556

Proletarier aus dem Eulengebirge, 517

propaganda: appeals for AB as, 26, 38, 40, 258; Czolgosz's act as, 475n6; development of (anarchist), 236–38; EG's arrest as, 304; EG's lecture on, 392–94; EG's role in, 318; funds for, 125–26, 237, 277; importance of, 260; need for English language, 48, 258, 317, 429–30, 499, 558; need for women speakers in, 428–30; question of force for, 340, 341; role of women speakers in, 5; speeches' effectiveness as, 412; suppression of speech as, 416, 443–44; in western states, 338

"The Propaganda and the Congress" (EG): transcript of, 392–94

propaganda by the deed *(attentats)*: AB on meaning of, 76, 78, 132–33n3, 434n3; concept of, 9, 14–16; consequences of, 132–33; defense of, 19, 129, 452–54, 549, 551, 552, 553; description of AB's, 16, 22–23, 25–27, 267–68; efficacy of, 119–21, 265–66, 341–42; EG's clarification of position on, 434–37, 453; EG's endorsement of, 225–26; by European anarchists, 38, 274–79; in individualist anarchism, 10–11; interview on, 160; justification for, 274–79; manual for, 545; motivations for, 132–33n3, 223–25, 246, 249, 341, 427–28, 463, 476; prediction of, 422; EG's refusal to judge, 70–71, 434–37; selflessness of, 245–46; use of term, 15; valorization of, 73–74, 422, 455–56. *See also* assassinations, political violence

prostitutes and prostitution: ethics and, 402; married women as, 272; political participation as, 398

La Protesta Humana, 517

Proudhon, Pierre-Joseph: as influence, 518, 530, 552, 556, 559, 560; translations of, 539; written contributions of, 567

Proust, Marcel, 419n16

Providence (R.I.): Cook's role in, 524; EG's arrest in, 303–5; EG's speeches in, 282–84, 302–3, 322–23, 501, 502, 504; mentioned, 36; threats against EG in, 284n3

psychology: EG's interest in, 479. *See also* Freud, Sigmund

"The Psychology of Political Violence" (EG): influences on, 478n

public opinion: EG in Philadelphia and, 440n2; fickleness of, 49; free speech suppressed by, 395; McKinley assassination's impact on, 79–81; in U.S. about Russia, 447–48. *See also* masses

Pullman strike (Chicago): arrest and imprisonment after, 500; defeat of, 232n3, 523; events of, 498–99; leadership of, 527; mentioned, 231; support for, 516, 526

Purdy, Lawson, 575

Pyat, Felix, 559

La Questione Sociale: editors of, 529, 541; founding of, 500; police search of, 463n5, 513; support for, 521

Quinn, T. Putnam, 288n2, 344, 552, 576

racial equality, 52, 246

racism: dispute about, 199n3; ignored in EG's speeches, 52, 61. *See also* anti-Semitism

The Radical Review, 559

Radikaler Arbeiter-Bund (Radical Workers' League), 102, 494, 507, 542, 563

Rahkmetov. *See* Berkman, Alexander

Rasnick, Martin, 464n2, 485n4, 513

Ratchford, Michael D., 280

Ravachol (pseud. of François-Claudius Koenig-stein): biographical summary on, 552; bombing by, 495; execution of, 496; mentioned, 238, 418n11, 482

Rawson, A. L., 490, 573

The Rebel (Boston): contributors to, 528, 550;

Rossetti, Arthur, 569

Rossetti, Helen, 569

Rossetti, Olivia, 569

Rossetti, William, 569

Rousseau, Jean-Jacques, 41, 248, 364n3, 419n16, 554

Royal Prussian Police: communiqué from, 64

Roz, Michael, 464n2, 513

RSP. *See* Revolutionary Socialistic Party

Ruedebusch, Emil F., 406n1, 407n8, 554, 563, 567

Ruedebusch, Julie, 406n1, 407, 408

Ruiz de Ugarrio y Salvador, Ricardo, 279

ruling class: condemnation of (EG), 71, 129, 151–54, 228–32, 474–76; education of, 57–58, 59; EG's testimony on, 174; fears of, 211–12, 248; judicial system in support of, 187–89, 197, 205, 207–8, 227, 320–21; love as out of fashion for, 270; oppression by, 171–72, 180–81. *See also* capitalists and capitalism; police; private property

Ruskin, John, 387–88

Ruskin Colony, 575

Russell, Charles Edward, 572

Russia: *attentat*'s effects in, 488; EG's birth in (Lithuania), 489; nostalgia about, 69–70; pogroms in, 491; political prisoners in, 139, 181, 550; prison conditions in (*See* Siberia); repression in, 14, 121, 495; revolutionary traditions of, 13–14, 424–25; student unrest in, 364; tsarism in, 14, 518; U.S. compared to, 41, 95, 187–88; U.S. extradition treaty with, 245n5, 523

Russian language, 414, 432

Rysakov, Ivanovich, 491

Sablin, Nikolai, 427n10

Saint-Imier International. *See* Anti-Authoritarian International

St. Louis (Mo.): EG's speeches in, 289n1, 315, 320–21, 503, 505, 507, 510; EG's visit to, 512; labor convention in, 310. *See also* Der Anarchist

St. Louis Post Dispatch, 44

Salvochea, Fermín, 495

Samuels, Henry B., 565

Sand, George, 33

San Diego (Calif.): vigilantes in, 477n12

San Diego and Arizona Railroad, 402n7

San Francisco: social science club in, 577; EG's speeches in, 330n7, 505–6, 508. *See also* Free Society

San Francisco Call: on Goldman's success, 51, 52; interview of EG in, 331–33

San Francisco Chronicle: on EG's speeches, 460–63; on McKinley's assassination, 75, 471–72n4

San Francisco Evening Post, 531

San Francisco Examiner, 471–72n4

San Francisco Single Tax Club, 574

San Francisco Tageblatt, 337n1

Sanial, Lucien, 303, 303n6

San Jose (Calif.): EG's speeches in, 506, 508

Scandinavian Painters Union, 37, 511

Schauwecker, Charles L., 166–67, 169

Schiller, Johann Christoph Friedrich von, 172

Schilling, Emil: biographical summary on, 554; Czolgosz's visits to, 511; as suspicious of Czolgosz, 460n1, 468n14, 512, 525

Schmidt, Johann Caspar. *See* Stirner, Max

Schmidt, Sarah, 208

Schneider, Alfred, 464n2, 485n4, 512

Schneider, Charles, 218, 241, 570

Schreiner, Olive, 270

Schroyer, Russell, 457

Schuettler, Hermann, 464, 466, 468, 469, 554

Schulder, Fred, 503

Schumm, Emilie (Millie), 517

Schurz, Carl, 121, 121n6, 307

Schwab, Justus H.: AB's defense and, 349n2, 351n3, 352, 506, 570; biographical summary on, 555; books loaned to EG by, 33; death of, 431; as editor, 260n1, 566; EG's release from prison and, 203; EG's sentencing and, 179; Most's immigration and, 545; raffle tickets and, 262n1; saloon of, 237n8, 423, 431, 558; sketch of, *204*; speeches of, 499

Schwab, Michael: biographical summary on,

Social Democrat, 576

Social Democratic Federation (SDF, England), 382n2, 544, 578

Social Democratic Herald, 518

Social Democratic Party (SDP): formation of, 339n2, 506, 509, 527, 576; members of, 518, 555; merger of, 512

Social Democratic Workingmen's Party, 280n7

Social Democratic Working-Men's Party of North America (Lassallean, SDWMPNA), 489

La Sociale (Social Affairs, Paris), 238. See also Le Père Peinard

Social Gospel, 525

The Socialist, 578

Socialist Labor Party (SLP): candidates of, 496, 558; description of, 577–78; as influence, 571; members of, 528, 529, 534–35, 536, 555; merger of, 527; newspaper of, 168n14; opposition to, 98n11, 518, 576; origins of, 490; representatives of, 491; speakers for, 237n5, 303, 529, 548; Spies expelled from, 557

Socialist League (Dutch), 548

Socialist League of England: description of, 578–79; founding of, 382n2, 544; members of, 521, 522, 538, 540, 543, 546, 547, 558, 560; as model, 98–99n12, 529; speakers for, 549. See also The Commonweal

Socialist League of New York: founding of, 98, 495, 529, 537, 579; speakers for, 526

Socialist Party (England), 533

Socialist Party of America (SPA): description of, 579; EG's criticism of, 54; formation of, 512, 527, 535, 576, 578; members of, 550; political support for, 69

Socialistic Publishing Society, 546, 564

socialists and socialism: analogy to, 246; anarchism compared to (EG), 41, 453; anarchists' break with, 39–40, 54–55, 397, 501; anarchists' conflict with, 25, 96–99; EG disavowed by, 501; hopes disappointed in French, 417–19; as reform, 360–61. See also Central Labor Union; Social Democracy

of America; Socialist Labor Party; Socialist Party of America

Socialist Trade and Labor Alliance, 99n16, 528, 535, 578

Socialist Unity Convention (Indianapolis), 489, 512

social order and society: capitalism as basis of, 364–65; crime fostered by, 187, 197, 249, 341, 426–28, 434, 476; political maintenance of, 249; Rousseau's critique of, 554; State distinguished from, 354; vision of, 1. See also capitalists and capitalism; class

Social Democratic Working-Men's Party of North America, 489

Social Political Workingmen's Society of Cincinnati, 489

Social Reform Club of New York, 525

social revolution: call for, 145–46, 171–72; force as means to, 341; individual efficacy in, 314; inevitability of, 181–82, 196, 201, 342n5, 486–87; precursors to, 226–27, 278–79; as sole solution, 328; trial testimony on, 167

Social Revolutionary Club of New York, 491, 555

Social Science Club (Boston), 577

Social Science Club (Brooklyn), 323n, 503

Social Science Club (Chicago), 577

Social Science Club (New York): activities of, 577; EG's speeches for, 510, 515; founding of, 80, 483; members of, 432n4

Social Science Club (Philadelphia), 432n4, 445n12, 510, 511, 528, 577

social science clubs: description of, 576–77; EG's speeches for, 323n, 445n12, 503, 510, 511, 515

Social Science Club (San Francisco), 577

Social Study Group (Paris), 532

Society for the Suppression of Vice, 523

Society of Ethical Research (Philadelphia), 504

solidarity: among political prisoners, 139; needed in movement, 397–98, 406–7, 413

Solidarity (New York): contributors to, 520, 524, 527, 535, 549; demise of, 497; description of, 568; difficulties of, 175n26; editor of,

Solidarity (New York) *(continued)*
529; on EG's travels, 48; founding of, 495,
542; funds for, 499, 538, 568; letters to
(EG's), 329–30, 337–39; mentioned, 396;
praise for, 48; reestablishment of, 254,
329n1; on SDA (EG), 576
Solotaroff, Hillel: biographical summary on,
556; editorship of, 566; escape plan and,
570; Haymarket anarchists defended by, 16;
mentioned, 257n2, 493, 494; in Pioneers of
Liberty, 574; speeches of, 432n4
Sotheran, Charles, 98
South Africa. *See* Anglo-Boer War (1899–1902)
Southern Railway scandal (France), 226
Southworth, Victor E., 401
Sovereign, James R., 280
Der Sozialist, 376n10, 407, 539
Sozialistische Monatshefte, 383
SPA. *See* Socialist Party of America
Spain: anarchist newspaper in, 529; anarchists
executed in, 256n9, 274n1; Barcelona bombing in, 498, 501; Corpus Christi Day bomb-
ing in, 256n9, 274n1, 341n3, 347, 501, 521;
Cuba's insurrection against, 245n6; Jerez
uprising in, 495, 497–98, 549; May Day celebrations in, 494; New York meeting about
anarchist activities in, 274–79
Spanish-American War (1898): criticism of,
49, 61; declaration of, 324n1, 505; imperialism of, 542; incidents preceding, 279n10;
opposition to, 324–25, 328, 332–33; patriotism in, 383; tainted beef in, 385; treaty to
end, 506, 507; workers affected by, 384–85
Spanish Civil War: anarchist colors symbolic
in, 144–45n3
speaking engagements (EG's): at anarchist/
unemployed demonstration (incitement to
riot), 145–47; Czolgosz's attendance at, 73–
74; disruption of, 39; effectiveness of, 5–6,
412; at gathering after release from prison,
34–35, 206–8; handbills and posters an-
nouncing, *358, 363, 367*; importance of, 21;
motivations for, 301–2; observations about,
67; payment for, 67–68, 400–403, 444;

preparation for, 170, 173; as priority over
studies, 63, 374–75; programs for, *371, 390;*
shift to English language in, 48; style of, 41,
47, 67–68, 331–32, 443, 452; venues for, 52.
See also lecture tours; *specific locations and
organizations*
Speed the Plough (Thomas Morton), 271n4,
334n2
speech. *See* free speech
Spencer, Herbert: biographical summary on,
556–57; challenges to, 538; EG's reading of,
33; as influence, 486, 548; mentioned, 355,
559
Spies, August: associates of, 549; biographical
summary on, 557; editorship of, 564, 569;
execution of, 7, 492; as influence on EG,
156–57n4, 247n3, 342n5, 475n7; mentioned,
41, 456; Pittsburgh Manifesto and, 491, 571;
on revolution, 342n5, 475n7; RSP and, 577–
78; at Social Revolutionary congress, 491;
speeches of, 145–46n6, 247n3, 248–49
Spooner, Lysander, 559
Spreckles, Claus, 402
Springfield (Mass.): EG's move to, 495
Spring Valley (Ill.): anarchists attacked in,
80; baptism story about, 60, 368–69; EG's
speeches in, 508, 510; EG's visit to, 507; Italian anarchism in, 60, 478
Squire, Mary, 536
The Standard, 531, 575
Standard Oil Company, 553. *See also* Rockefeller, John D.
State: as absolutist, 180–81; anarchism
feared by, 195, 416; as authority, 353–55,
360; Brown's challenge to, 521; crime sanc-
tioned by, 448; opposition to, 181, 196, 333;
oppression by, 171–72; violence of, 386–87,
477. *See also* anti-statist tradition; police; surveillance; wars
Statue of Liberty, 5
Stedman, Seymore, 575
Steffens, Lincoln, 572
Stein, Modest (Fedya): AB's *attentat* and, 22–
23; biographical summary on, 557; EG's rela-

tionship with, 24; immigration of, 104, 106; living arrangements of, 21–22, 493, 494, 519; mentioned, 254, 486; names for, 132n2; on Roman Lewis, 540; work in photography studio, 22, 495

Stephens, G. Frank, 305n12, 446n4, 574, 575

Stepniak, 538

Steunenberg, Frank, 386n7

Stevenson, A., 305n12

Stirner, Max: biographical summary on, 557–58; egoism and, 125n2; as influence, 10, 434–35n4; mentioned, 559; written contributions of, 567

Stockton (Calif.): EG's speeches in, 508

Stone, Carl, 366–67n2

Strasser, Adolph, 489

Straus, Oscar, 245n5

strikes: of cloakmakers, 168n12, 425n7, 518; in Coeur d'Alene, 386, 476; as context, 19–21, 36–37; in Cuba, 386; for eight-hour day, 492; EG's motives for, 285; in France, 418n10; of glassworkers, 239n4; outbreak of, 22, 231–32; series of railway, 490, 557; of tailors, 219; of textile workers, 506; in Virden (Ill.), 476. *See also* Hazleton (Pa.) massacre; Homestead (Pa.) strike; Pullman strike

Strindberg, August, 239n1

Strunsky, Anna, 505

Die Sturmglocken (The Alarm Bell, Chicago), 234, 257, 500, 517, 568

Sturmvogel (Storm Bird, New York): address of, 555; demise of, 48, 507; description of, 568; editor of, 558; founding of, 503; lecture topics listed in, 503–4; masthead of, *301*; travel reports in (EG), 43, 45–47, 293–99Ger., 300–317

Süddeutschen Volksstimme, 545

suffrage movement: criticism of (EG's), 71, 429; participants in, 527

suicide: EG on Paita's, 449–50; EG's eulogy and, 511

Sullivan, John L., 115n8, 194

Sullivan, Louis, 529

Sully-Prudhomme, M., 419–20

surveillance: of AB in prison, 42, 255; after EG's sentencing, 182; in Cleveland, 73–74, 452, 454; conference on, 506; in Europe, 38, 63–64; by French government, 64, 408–9, 419–20, 430, 509, 510; of gatherings, 227, 275, 278; by German government, 64, 220n1, 389–91, 500; international cooperation in, 346n2; EG's jokes about, 44; in London, 389; misinformation in, 389n2; in New York City, 422n2; in Pittsburgh, 326; in Providence, 302–3; in St. Louis, 289n1, 503. *See also* police

Swank, Lizzie May. *See* Holmes, Lizzie

Swinton, John, 199n3, 202, 499, 558

Swinton, Orsena, 499, 558

Switzerland: possible studies in, 59, 366–67n2, 375n7, 407

syndicalism: as influence on EG, 9, 538; leader in, 524, 552; Most's return to, 546. *See also* anarcho-syndicalism

Tacoma (Wash.): EG's speeches in, 507

Tarentum (Pa.): EG's speeches in, 504

Tárrida del Mármol, Fernando, 62, 256n9, 509, 510

taxation, 385. *See also* Single Tax (movement)

Teamsters Union, 530

Teed, Cyrus Read, 486n9

temperance movement: EG's disdain for, 43

Les Temps Nouveaux (New Times, Paris): on *attentats*, 14; circulation of, 238; clandestine proceedings of Paris congress in, 66; contributors to, 523, 524, 538, 543, 550; description of, 568; editor of, 407n7, 532; Hamon's essay in, 239n3; reports for Paris congress in, 420–21, 482n10, 517, 535, 553, 568

Tennyson, Alfred, Lord, 194

Tfileh Zakeh (Pure Prayer), 556, 574

theory. *See* anarchism; communism; egoism; individualism; nihilists and nihilism; socialists and socialism; syndicalism

theosophy, 486

Thiers, Adolphe, 417

Thimme, Edward John, 168–69, 170, 175

third sex: use of term, 374, 379

Thomas Paine National Historical Association, 549

Thoreau, Henry David, 10, 33, 426

Thorndale, Stella, 470

Tillier, Claude, 559

Tilton, Flora, 490

Timmermann, Claus: arrest, trial, and imprisonment of, 111–12n1, 145n4, 161–62n7, 167, 188, 196, 497, 498; biographical summary on, 558; business of, 500; editorship of, 106n11, 302n2, 563, 564, 568; EG's testimony on, 173; injury of, 192n1; letters to (1894), 190–91Ger., 192–93; mentioned, 383; pamphlet of, 262; speeches of (incitement to riot), 145–46; testimony of, 30. *See also Die Brandfackel; Sturmvogel*

Tochatti, James: biographical summary on, 558; editorship of, 566; EG's meeting with, 38; speeches of, 221, 223, 500. *See also Liberty*

Tolstoy, Leo: biographical summary on, 559; as influence, 525; mentioned, 456, 537; translations of, 564; written contributions of, 566, 567

Tombs (jail): description of, 177n1; EG in, 182, 196; Most in, 514

The Torch (London), 540, 569

Torch of Anarchy, 228–32

Toulouse-Lautrec, Henri de, 239n1

trade unions (general): corruption of, 219, 315; EG's criticism of, 71; Gompers's focus on, 311n30; McKinley assassination condemned by, 79; possible appeal via, 251–53, 258; socialists vs. anarchists in, 96–99. *See also* labor organizing; *specific unions*; strikes

"The Tragedy at Buffalo" (EG): AB on, 487; criticism of, 562, 566; description of, 16; hyperbole in, 78–79; mentioned, 479, 482; publication of, 514; text of, 471–78

Trall, R. T., 490

Der Tramp, 262n3

tramps: definition of, 208

The Transatlantic, 559

Transport Union, 540

Transvaluation Society, 554

Travaglio, Enrico, 464n2, 485n4, 512

Treaty of Paris, 436n6

Trumball, M. M., 265

Trunk, Johann Sebastian, 382

The Truth, 549, 561

The Truth Seeker, 151n1, 490, 544, 572

Tucker, Benjamin R.: associates of, 538; biographical summary on, 559–60; at free-love convention, 489; on Henry George, 531, 575; illustration of, 351; as influence on EG, 10, 264n9, 549; influences on, 558; as intermediary for AB, 56, 349–52, 506, 570; memberships of, 490; Most criticized by, 545; organization founded by, 573, 574; publishing by, 518; Tolstoy translations by, 559. *See also Liberty: Not the Daughter but the Mother of Order*

Turgenev, Ivan, 100n1

Turner, John: associates of, 528, 536; biographical summary on, 560; editorship of, 565; EG's essay on, 236–38; illustration of, 237; mentioned, 254, 316; proposed tour of, 400; speeches of, 237, 305n13, 501; U.S. tour of, 39, 67, 96–97n3, 234, 236n3, 500, 573; written contributions of, 568

Turner, Lizzie, 560

Turner societies (*Turnvereine*, gymnastic clubs), 309–10, 312, 502, 505

Turn-Zeitung, 542

Tweed, William Mercy "Boss," 532

Twentieth Century Magazine, 523, 524, 526

Typographical Union, 530

Uhly, G. C., 382–83n4

Umberto (king of Italy): assassination of, 66, 68, 74, 422, 427n12, 455n1, 463, 509, 521; Fatti di Maggio and, 505; mentioned, 346

UMW. *See* United Mine Workers

Unealt, Edith, 470

unemployment: capitalists' response to, 231; demonstrations due to, 27–28; 141–43Ger., 144–47, 151–52n3, 497; EG's essay on, 149–50Ger., 151–54; miseries of, 151–52, 171–72, 174, 224, 314, 338, 474–75. *See also* People vs. Emma Goldman (trial, 1893)

Union Cooperative Socety of Printers, 546

Union Cooperative Society of Journeymen Tailors, 546

Union Square (New York), 96, 97n4, 108, 120n4, 144, 146n7, 148n3, 153n7, 161n7, 162, 166, 168, 170, 180, 205n4, 558

United Brotherhood of Carpenters and Joiners of America, 280n7

United Brotherhood of Tailors, 219n1, 219n3

United German Trades (Vereinigten Deutschen Gewerkschaften), 251n1

United Hebrew Trade Organization: EG's link to, 37, 494; leaders of, 518, 534–35; SLP and, 577

United Labor League, 37, 445n12, 511

United Mine Workers (UMW): convention of, 288n1; EG's speeches for, 37, 47; officers of, 280n5; petition for AB's release and, 570; strikes of, 47, 310, 311, 576

United States: anarchy's future in, 357–59, 428, 441; *attentats*' effects in, 488; imperialism of, 384–88, 542; potential for anarchist women in, 429; Russia compared to, 41, 72–73, 95, 187–88. *See also* Americanization, free speech

U.S.-Russia extradition treaty, 245n5, 523

United States Steel Corporation, 521

U.S. tours: in 1890, 493; in 1897, 502–3; in 1898, 504–6; in 1899, 507–8. *See also* specific cities

universities, 364, 374

University of Berne, 374, 375

University of Chicago, 553

Universology of Koreshanity, 486

unlawful assembly indictment. *See* People vs. Emma Goldman (trial, 1893)

Ury, Adolph, 144n1, 497

USS *Maine* explosion, 324–25, 504

Vaillant, Auguste: biographical summary on, 560; execution of, 275n4, 342n6, 498, 522, 534; mentioned, 226, 238, 418n11, 554, 562

Vaillant, Sidonie, 560

Vanderbilt, Cornelius, 402

Vanderbilt, William Henry, 453

Varhayt (Truth), 18, 540, 545, 556, 574

Vaughan, Ernest, 560

Der Verbote (The Harbinger, Chicago), 517, 546, 569, 578

Verein Eintracht, 362, 362n1

Vereinigten Deutschen Gewerkschaften (United German Trades), 251n1

Verity, O. A., 565

Verlaine, Paul, 431

Verral, Percival, 470

Vestnik Narodnoi Voli (Messenger of the People's Will), 540

vice: cause of, 453–54. *See also* crime and criminals

Victims of Morality and the Failure of Christianity, Two Lectures (EG): contents of, 53n59

Victoria (queen of England), 213

Vienna (Austria): EG's visit to, 500

violence: as product of oppression, 435; EG's rejection of, 29, 359, 360, 477; society's responsibility for, 187, 197, 249, 341, 426–28, 434, 476. *See also* assassinations; political violence; propaganda by the deed *(attentats)*; repression

Virden (Ill.) miners strike, 476

Voice of Labor, 538

La Voix du Peuple, 552

Volks-Zeitung, 564

Volkszeitung (New York), 168, 169

Voltaire, 33

Vorwaerts, 578

Vorwärts. See Forverts

Vorwärts der Pacific Küste, 337n1

Vose, Donald, 508

Vose, Gertie, 508

Vperëd! (Forward), 540

De Vrije Socialist (The Free Socialist, Dutch), 368n4, 510, 548

Vuillard, Edouard, 239n1

vulgarity: distaste for (EG), 51, 73, 441. *See also* Comstock Acts (1873, 1876); obscenity

wages and hours: average in 1895, 231; of miners, 338; Russia vs. U.S., 95; shortcomings

8; conditions for, 38, 228–32; EG's appeal
to, 496; EG's opinion of, 436–37; oppression of, 180–81; as slaves, 152–53, 172, 228,
283, 332; U.S. vs. Russian, 360; Anglo-Boer
War's effect on, 60–61, 384–88. *See also*
cloakmakers; labor unions; miners; strikes;
wages and hours
working class: Adam and Eve as analogy to,
211–12; EG's embrace of, 36–38; exploitation of, 228–32, 333n8; marriage in, 270–
72; miseries of, 151–52, 171–72, 174, 224,
314, 338, 474–75; obstacles for women in,
428–29; plentiful goods within reach of,
249–50; Anglo-Boer War and, 60–61; starvation as limit on activism of, 50, 338, 444
Workingmen's Cooperative Association (Philadelphia), 510
Workingmen's Defense Association, 520
Workingmen's Educational Society (Baltimore),
95, 494
Working Men's Party of Illinois, 489, 557
Working Men's Party of the United States, 489,
490, 577. *See also* Socialist Labor Party (SLP)
Workingmen's Rifle Club, 492
Working Women's Society of the United He-
brew Trade Organization, 37, 494
Workmen's Advocate, 578
World War I: EG's criticism of, 49
World War II: French Resistance in, 533
Wright, E. S., 459
writing: lecturing vs., 68; by women anarchists,
428. *See also* letter writing

Yanovsky, Saul Josef: associates of, 539, 546;
biographical summary on, 562; Czolgosz

denounced by, 475n6; editorship of, 566; es-
cape plan and, 59, 508, 570; Haymarket an-
archists defended by, 16; mentioned, 257n2;
in Pioneers of Liberty, 574; speeches of, 507;
written contributions of, 569
Yarros, Victor, 567
Yiddish anarchist congress (1890), 368n3,
494
Yiddish language: attitude toward, 46; EG's
use of, *367*; newspapers in, 565, 566; trea-
tises in, 562. *See also Varhayt; Freie Arbeiter
Stimme*
Yogic wisdom, 486
Yom Kippur "balls," 102n7, 556, 574
Young, Charles R., 148
Young, Ernest, 565
Young Men's Christian Association, 573
Young Men's Liberal League (Philadelphia),
501
Youth (Jungen, group), 539

Zemlya i Volya (Land and Freedom), 18,
427n10, 519, 550
Zhelyabov, Andrei Ivanovich, 427n10, 491
Zibelin, Albert, 510
Ziegenhein (mayor of St. Louis), 289n1
Zionism, 413
Zola, Émile, 419, 559, 560, 562; on Dreyfus
case, 324n2, 421n18, 503, 528
Zuchthausblüthen, 254n2. *See also Prison
Blossoms*
Zukunft (The Future), 551
Zum Großen Michel (saloon), 111–12n1,
169n16, 496

Designer	Nicole Hayward
Compositor	G & S Typesetters, Inc.
Text	Scala
Display	Univers Condensed
Printer and Binder	Sheridan Books, Inc.
Indexer	Towery Indexing Services